Praise for Paper Tigers

'Coleridge writes like a dream. They're none of them very nice, these proprietors, even the nice ones. But they have a profound and lasting influence on the way we look at the world, and Nicholas Coleridge has done a magnificent job in showing them in all their gawdy and tawdry splendour'
Robin Lustig, *Observer*

'After all the previous cod literature on this subject, this is valuable and first-rate. You can hear the crashing of egos'
Roy Greenslade, *Vogue*

'The virtue of Mr Coleridge's admirable account is that it demythologises the proprietor'
The Economist

'A fascinating study of power and corruption'
Marie Claire

'It is a spanking good read . . . sharply written'
Godfrey Hodgson, *Independent*

'A gripping portrait of the ultimate movers and shakers. The art of their deals make for a riveting read, but it is the personal foibles, weaknesses, obsessions and super-egos of these world class power-brokers that bring vivid life and colour to the pages. *Paper Tigers* charts their rise and occasional demise with considerable wit and insight'
Kathryn Flett, *Arena*

'As newspaper ownership has been concentrated among fewer and fewer proprietors in recent years, the character and biases of these owners has become increasingly magnified through their influence over the news. *Paper Tigers* is the best and most intimate examination of their personalities, prejudices and foibles'
Clay Felker

'A book that resembles the work of the best travel writers – Jan Morris, Paul Theroux. Instead of China or Bali, he guides us intriguingly through the even lusher landscape of international press ownership. He is a vivid writer with a marvellous ear for the absurd. By perseverance and cunning, he persuaded two dozen of the world's most elusive men and women to share time and confidences with him. When they read his penetrating book, some will clearly wish that they had kept their distance'
Michael Leapman, *Country Life*

'Bright, inquisitive and assiduous. Coleridge parades his moguls entertainingly, with a spice of mischief'
Woodrow Wyatt, *The Times*

'It is a good read. Outstanding on Conrad Black and Vere Rothermere'
Paul Johnson, *Sunday Telegraph*

'Outrageously successful'
The Times

'Fascinating. A highly enjoyable book, sometimes a really funny one. His eyewitness descriptions are completely hilarious'
Charles Wintour, *Evening Standard*

'Engrossing. *Paper Tigers* will become the definitive account of the contrasting styles of newspaper barons'
Sunday Express

'This is a very important book. I jest that I may not weep at the hubris, rapacity and crassness of the proprietors Mr Coleridge parades before us'
Tim Pat Coogan, *Irish Times*

'Compelling and compulsive reading for anyone interested in the people who control much of the world's news. This is Coleridge's best book yet'
Graydon Carter, *Vanity Fair*

Paper Tigers

Nicholas Coleridge has written for
the *Daily Telegraph*, *Sunday
Telegraph*, *Sunday Times*, *Evening
Standard*, *Spectator*, *Vanity Fair*,
Tatler, *GQ* and *Harpers & Queen*
which he edited for three years. He
is Managing Director of Condé
Nast in London, and is married
with two children.

NICHOLAS COLERIDGE

Paper Tigers

The latest, greatest newspaper tycoons
and how they won the world

Mandarin

To Alexander and Freddie

A Mandarin Paperback
PAPER TIGERS

First published in Great Britain 1993
by William Heinemann Ltd
This edition published 1994
by Mandarin Paperbacks
an imprint of Reed Consumer Books Ltd
Michelin House, 81 Fulham Road, London SW3 6RB
and Auckland, Melbourne, Singapore and Toronto

Reprinted 1994

Copyright © Nicholas Coleridge 1993
The author has asserted his moral rights

A CIP catalogue record for this title
is available from the British Library
ISBN 0 7493 0727 7

Printed and bound in Great Britain
by Cox & Wyman Ltd, Reading, Berks

Contents

List of Illustrations

1. Mr and Mrs Arthur Ochs Sulzberger Snr
2. Arthur Ochs Sulzberger Jnr
3. Mr and Mrs Donald Graham and their daughter Laura
4. Mrs Katharine Graham
5. Otis Chandler
6. Dean Singleton
7. Ralph Ingersoll
8. James C. Kennedy
9. Ann Cox Chambers
10. Warwick Fairfax
11. Ramnath Goenka
12. Aveek Sarkar
13. Samir Jain
14. Robert Maxwell
15. Mr and Mrs Robert Maxwell and their son Kevin
16. Lord and Lady Rothermere
17. Lord Rothermere and Miss Maiko Lee
18. Mr and Mrs Conrad Black
19. Lord and Lady Stevens
20. Robert Hersant
21. His Highness Karim Aga Khan and the Begum Aga Khan
22. Ma Sik-chun
23. Sally Aw Sian
24. Louis Cha
25. Kamphol Vacharaphol
26. Mr and Mrs Tony O'Reilly
27. Mr and Mrs Rupert Murdoch and their daughter Elisabeth

Principal Dramatis Personae
and their newspaper flagships

The Aga Khan
Daily Nation
Taifa Leo

Sally Aw Sian
Sing Tao
Hong Kong Standard

Conrad Black
The Daily Telegraph
Sydney Morning Herald

Louis Cha
Ming Pao Daily News

Otis Chandler
Los Angeles Times
Long Island Newsday

Warwick Fairfax
Sydney Morning Herald
Melbourne Age

Ramnath Goenka
Indian Express
Financial Express

Donald Graham
The Washington Post
International Herald Tribune

Katharine Graham
The Washington Post
International Herald Tribune

Robert Hersant
Le Figaro
France-Soir

Ralph Ingersoll
New Haven Register
St Louis Sun

Samir Jain
The Times of India
The Independent

Kamphol Vacharaphol
Thai Rath

Jim Kennedy
The Atlanta Constitution
The Atlanta Journal

Robert Maxwell
The Daily Mirror
New York Daily News

Rupert Murdoch
The Australian
The Times

Asil Nadir
Gunes
Günaydin

Tony O'Reilly
Irish Independent
Sunday Independent

Lord Rothermere
The Daily Mail
Evening Standard

Aveek Sarkar
Calcutta Telegraph
Ananda Bazar Patrika

Dean Singleton
Denver Post
Houston Post

Lord Stevens
The Daily Express
The Sunday Express

Arthur Ochs Sulzberger
The New York Times
International Herald Tribune

Arthur Ochs Sulzberger Jnr
The New York Times
International Herald Tribune

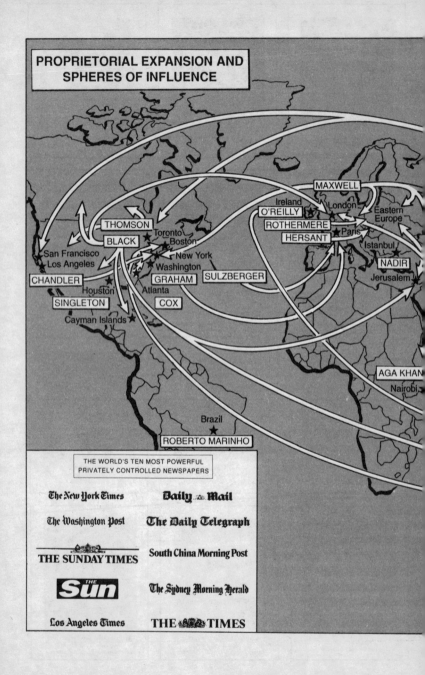

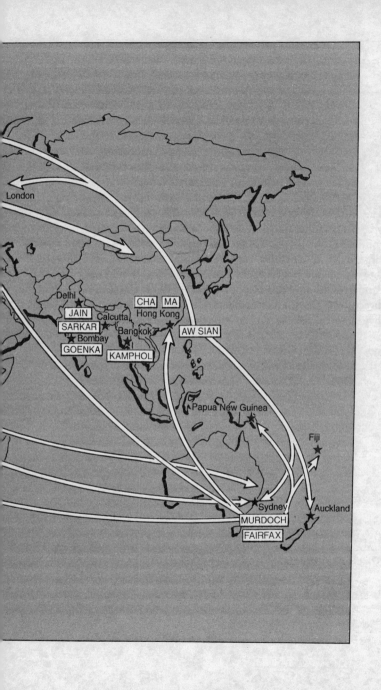

Author's Note

This book is about the world's greatest private newspaper proprietors, and the power and influence they wield across five continents. All either wholly own their empires or control such a large stake in them that their authority is unquestioned. Although the vast privately owned Newhouse newspaper chain in America is referred to on a number of occasions, I have not written about it directly for the simple reason that I work in another part of their diverse media behemoth, and there would be a conflict of interest.

1

The Proprietor as Predator

Some general observations on the nature of the beast

The first newspaper proprietor I ever met was Rupert Murdoch. I was 23 years old, and had only recently come to London. I had been invited to Sunday lunch by Prue Murdoch in the kitchen of her little house in Battersea. When I arrived, her father, who happened to be passing through town, was there too.

He struck me as a convivial if somewhat abrupt figure in ironed jeans and a navy blue blazer. He sat across the kitchen table, paging through an immense pile of Sunday newspapers.

'Have you read today's papers yet?' he asked me suddenly.

I replied that I had, though this was an exaggeration. I had actually skimmed through one newspaper in my morning bath.

'What were the three most interesting things in them, and the worst three, would you say?'

My mind went blank. The truth was, I had had a very late night and was hungover. I had difficulty recalling any three articles at all. I had barely glanced at the front page: for all I knew, the Prime Minister and half the Cabinet had resigned, or a jumbo jet crashed into Madison Square Garden causing hundreds of fatalities.

I thought it safest to single out certain regular features of the Sunday newspapers, and so avoid mentioning anything specific. Rupert Murdoch listened patiently to this exercise in obfuscation, occasionally nodding and raising one bushy eyebrow. Eventually he said, 'That's something that never ceases to surprise me about this country. You young people are more curious about what I'd term soft news than hard news. I've spoken to the editors about that before.'

Seizing the chance to turn the spotlight away from myself, I asked

Murdoch, 'What about you, have you read all your own Sunday newspapers?'

'That's not possible,' he replied. 'They're not all available. Our American papers will only shortly have finished printing – they're behind us timewise up to seven hours. Our Australian Sundays finished printing yesterday lunchtime – that's Saturday London time, early Sunday morning theirs – but they haven't caught up with me yet.'

The great myth about modern proprietors is that their power is less than it used to be. The fiefdoms of Beaverbrook, Northcliffe and Hearst, often invoked as the zenith of proprietorial omnipotence, were in fact smaller by every criteria than the enormous, geographically diffuse, multi-lingual empires of the latest newspaper tycoons. The profits and total circulations of the old-school proprietors were invariably lower, their papers thinner, the scope of their influence and news-gathering machines more local; none dominated so many world markets simultaneously as does Rupert Murdoch in Britain, the Far East and Australia, Robert Hersant in France and Eastern Europe, Conrad Black in Britain, Canada and Australia, and the Hong Kong proprietor Sally Aw Sian in every Chinese enclave on four continents. In terms of the circulation they collectively control, the two dozen leading proprietors are unprecedentedly powerful and becoming more so. Every week their newspapers sell 200 million copies. Half of the earth's surface is dominated by them.

As they have become more influential, however, so have they dwindled in number. As recently as 1970, there were 125 significant newspaper-owning families around the world, who between them controlled the great national and metropolitan titles of their countries. Now they have diminished to fewer than 30. The last two decades have seen newspapers concentrated in fewer and fewer hands. Some have been absorbed into amorphous chains owned by public companies; but most have been snapped up by a rapacious pack of paper tigers, who stalk the urban jungle for trophies to stay their hunger for newsprint and prestige.

Like big cats in the wild, every proprietor has his own jealously guarded territory. Los Angeles belongs to the Chandler family and their *Los Angeles Times*. The Grahams have Washington with the *Post*, the Sulzbergers' *New York Times* dominates Manhattan. The Cox Chamberses have Atlanta, Tony O'Reilly has Dublin, the Aga Khan has Nairobi, Samir Jain controls Delhi, Aveek Sarkar reigns in Calcutta, Roberto Marinho in Rio de Janeiro, while Kamphol Vacharaphol rules the roost in Bangkok.

When I first began following the fortunes of proprietors in 1985, there was a clear pecking order among the top 28 owners. During the next eight years this changed almost out of recognition. Empires rose and fell. The great Fairfax dynasty in Australia, which owned three of the most profitable franchises in the world, was bushwhacked in a family coup by the 26-year-old heir, Warwick Fairfax; the empire imploded, and eventually passed to Conrad Black. Robert Maxwell had only recently begun collecting newspapers when I embarked upon my research. Within seven years he had bought thirteen and was spoken of in the same breath as Murdoch (anyway by himself), before falling or jumping or being pushed overboard one November night in Grand Canary. Asil Nadir, the sleek Anglo-Turkish industrialist, had become a world-class tycoon selling lemons, cardboard cartons and microwave ovens before succumbing to the lure of newspaper ownership. He bought 27 papers in Turkey and Cyprus, looked set to devour more, but within two years was bankrupt. Ralph Ingersoll, a New England WASP and protégé of Michael Milken, the junk bond king of Drexel Burnham Lambert, went on a $1.5 billion shopping spree that secured him 240 newspapers in three years. By 1990, however, he had been obliged to let all but a handful of them go. Even Rupert Murdoch, outwardly the most successful and enduring self-made mogul, saw his empire falter and almost disintegrate in 1991 as its growing pains were diagnosed as cardiac arrest.

At the same time new proprietors began to roam the savannah. Conrad Black, who in 1985 scarcely merited a place on my roster, migrated west from Toronto, bringing down big game in London (the *Daily Telegraph*), Jerusalem (the *Post*) and Sydney (the *Morning Herald*). The young Texan publisher Dean Singleton, whom the rest of the pack sometimes scorn as a hyena, slunk about amidst the herds of North American papers, pouncing on anything that had become enfeebled and showed signs of drooping. From their vantage point in Taiwan, to which they had bolted following a heroin-smuggling scandal in Hong Kong, the mysterious Ma brothers nevertheless managed to rule their old newspaper jungle at arm's length, while prowling new paths around the Pacific Rim and in the Chinatowns of America.

3

Modern proprietors can be grouped into six overlapping categories, though it has to be said that none would feel remotely convinced or comfortable at being so bracketed. Newspaper owners remind me of fashion designers, interior decorators and university dons in their insistence that they operate in a class of their own, and that their contemporaries scarcely merit a sidelong glance. Had I excluded all the people I was advised to, my list would have contracted to none. Maxwell advised me to drop Murdoch ('He will be out of business before your book is published. You must trust me on this'), Conrad Black and Lord Rothermere both doubted I should include Lord Stevens of United Newspapers, Ramnath Goenka of the *Indian Express* recommended I exclude Samir Jain of *The Times of India*, Dean Singleton was sceptical that I'd admit Ralph Ingersoll, and vice versa, Maxwell entreated me to drop his newspaper rival in Kenya, the Aga Khan ('He is not significant in this context. You must believe me on this matter'). Two first division American owners insisted I reflect carefully before including the Sulzbergers 'because Punch is withdrawing himself from the scene, and the son – Pinch – has still to prove himself'. One of the same Americans declared that I'd be 'throwing the gates real wide' if I devoted much attention 'to Atlanta and the Cox Chambers papers down there'. Conrad Black doubted Tony O'Reilly had yet reached the threshold for inclusion. Sally Aw Sian baulked at the Ma brothers. And everybody, almost without exception, counselled against Robert Maxwell even before his fall.

Among newspaper owners, longevity means three or four generations. Barely five major newspaper-owning families have any history at all, and four of these are American: the Sulzbergers, Chandlers, Grahams and Cox Chamberses. Their stories all struck me as curiously alike: an exuberant great-grandfather, very often military and so known as 'The Colonel' or 'The General', who makes his fortune building railroads or steelworks, acquires a small newspaper in a town destined to explode in size, gradually buys out his competitors to achieve a monopoly. So emerges a mighty cash-cow that churns out first millions, then hundreds of millions of dollars in advertising revenues. These old families – the aristocracy of proprietorship – sit on prime franchises, virtually unchallenged, so complete is their stranglehold on the local community and economy. Their newspaper estates resemble the agricultural estates of European nobility; vast tracts of land are dominated by a Sulzberger paper, or a Chandler or a Cox Chambers. Among their rivals, they attract admiration and envy in almost equal measure. When I asked owners around the world which newspapers they'd most like to own, they invariably replied, 'the Sulzbergers' *New York Times*, the Grahams' *Washington Post* and the Chandler family's *Los Angeles Times* . . .' And yet the newer, entrepreneurial owners like Ralph Ingersoll and Dean Singleton, who have had to purchase their papers with borrowed money at high interest, could never resist telling me that these inheritors are only coasting, and their comfortable monopolies would be impossible to sabotage, however incompetently they were managed. In that, however, they are mistaken. The Warwick Fairfax episode in Australia demonstrated exactly how simple it is to destroy a fourth-generation family empire if you misread the future. The fall of the house of Fairfax leaves only one other *ancien* newspaper family in the First World: Lord Rothermere and the Harmsworths, owners of the *Daily Mail* in London, who themselves only narrowly managed to keep their hold on the greasy pole of proprietorship.

Jostling just behind the aristocrats are the group I came to think of as the Opportunists: the high-profile, first division players who inherited a tranche of capital or a modest newspaper that they've built up in their lifetimes into something much greater. It is no coincidence that most have expanded geographically, acquiring newspapers or launching editions wherever they've had the chance, in whichever city or country, since they didn't start off with a major power base like the Sulzbergers and Grahams. Rupert Murdoch, Conrad Black and Sally Aw Sian – the Tiger Balm heiress of Hong Kong – all fall into this group. So, to some degree, do Samir Jain and Aveek Sarkar. Although they inherited virtual monopolies in Delhi and Calcutta respectively, they have used them as bases from which to make inroads into the entire subcontinent.

The remaining owners fall into four categories, though they mostly qualify for more than one. These are political manipulators, number-crunchers, exhibitionists for whom ownership is only another means of attracting attention and proprietors so private that they are virtually reclusive. Louis Cha, the politically absorbed Chinese proprietor of *Ming Pao* in Hong Kong, Robert Hersant who has *Le Figaro* in Paris, and the Goenka family of the *Indian Express*, all own newspapers that act as vehicles for their political views (though Ramnath Goenka was so tightfisted that he qualified as a number-cruncher too). Ralph Ingersoll, Dean Singleton and Lord Stevens have embraced newspapers as businesses capable of generating ever greater profits if the corporate finance is correctly set. Tony O'Reilly, the chairman of Heinz who privately controls Independent Newspapers in Dublin, and the Canadian property whizz Mortimer Zuckerman, who bought the *New York Daily News* in October 1992, are both covert number-crunchers, but not insensible to the scope newspapers provide for prestige and exhibitionism. Robert Maxwell and Asil Nadir were both seduced by the singular glamour of proprietorship. The Aga Khan, Kamphol Vacharaphol (always known simply as Kamphol, pronounced Kampon) and the Ma brothers, despite owning big-deal newspapers themselves, go to extraordinary lengths to avoid the press. The Aga Khan lives in a high-security château outside Paris at Aiglemont; Kamphol and the Mas behind heavily fortified properties in Bangkok and Taipei.

In the end, the list was self-selecting. I simply included those owners whose names came up over and over again when I interviewed their competitors. When four proprietors shook their heads over Dean Singleton's high-risk expansion in Houston, I went to Houston. The more often it was suggested I blackball Tony O'Reilly (too marketing-led to have the authentic heart of a press baron), the keener I became to cross-question him in Glandore or Pittsburgh. My criterion for exclusion was lack of interest. In hundreds of hours of interviews, Lord (Kenneth) Thomson was barely mentioned, despite owning 130 papers in the United States, 55 in Britain and 50 more in Canada (including the influential Toronto *Globe and Mail* and the *Moose Jaw Times-Herald* of Saskatchewan, which narrowly steals the global award for the quaintest title from Conrad Black's *Dawson Creek Peace River Block News*). I have similarly excluded Christos Lambrakis of Athens, who owns half the Greek mass-market, Roberto Marinho, the octogenarian billionaire proprietor of *O Globo* in Rio de Janeiro, and the reclusive Mrs Axel Springer, widow of the founder of *Bild* in Hamburg, even though in his own time her husband was perhaps the most famous press proprietor in the world.

Although Thomson, Marinho, Lambrakis and Springer are all-powerful in their own spheres, they play virtually no part in the prehensile feuds of the paper tigers. They don't directly compete with the other proprietors, nor do their names appear in the lists of competing candidates to buy world-class papers. Above anything, they don't send shivers of fear down the spines of their rivals. They don't induce paranoia. They don't inspire stubborn jealousies of the kind that Robert Maxwell felt for Rupert Murdoch and which led him to compete far beyond the frontiers of prudence.

Ten of the owners in this book inherited their empires, fifteen started from scratch and built by acquisition. What is interesting is the almost arbitrary way that so many of the great newspapers have changed hands. Had his young brother-in-law, Orvil Dryfoos, not died of a heart attack, Punch Sulzberger would never have taken over the world's most sought-after paper, *The New York Times*. Had her husband, Philip Graham, not committed suicide one bleak afternoon at Glen Welby, their country house in Virginia, Katharine Graham would never have become the most influential liberal proprietor of the age. Had he not been persuaded by his wife over breakfast in Jamaica to fly back to England and prevent his father from selling the *Daily Mail*, Vere Rothermere would never have dominated the great middle-market of British newspapers. Had Sally Aw Sian's brother, Aw How, not been killed in a mysterious plane crash near Singapore, the great international Chinese newspaper empire would never have passed to her.

I was struck by how closely the paper tigers track each other's movements. They kept assuring me that they seldom meet, and yet if I mentioned that I'd seen Conrad Black the previous week, I'd be told, 'Yes, he was in London until the weekend. But now he's in Toronto.' Samir Jain was able to tell me, from his *Times of India* office in Bombay, precisely where his two competitors – Sarkar and Goenka – were that moment (New York and Chandigarh respectively) and exactly what he believed them to be up to. Otis Chandler in Los Angeles watches Dean Singleton in Houston. Arthur Ochs Sulzberger Jnr – the thrusting young publisher of *The New York Times*, generally known as 'Pinch' to distinguish him from his patrician father, Punch – watches his contemporary Donald Graham of the *Washington Post*. Sometimes I suspected my protagonists of believing that there are only 30 or 40 significant people in the entire world, all of them monitoring each other's schedules, second-guessing their decisions and flirtations, sceptical of their motives and prospects of success. They reminded me both of medieval warring kings and adolescent girls at a convent school.

To the outsider, and especially to left-leaning commentators, the notion that unsupervised private individuals can own newspapers is sinister and even repellent. Whether such-and-such an owner is a fit person to sift the news, and decide what we might or might not be permitted to read, lies at the heart of the debate about proprietorial ethics. The great new media empires spanning the world have subjugated more territory in a decade than Alexander the Great or Genghis Khan in a lifetime and funnelled responsibility for the dissemination of news into fewer and fewer hands. Rupert Murdoch needs to come up with political candidates on four continents for his newspapers to support. Almost every proprietor in this book has played some decisive part, through their newspapers, in the political or social history of their country: Katharine Graham's high-stakes stand-off with President Nixon over the Watergate tapes; Robert Hersant's remorseless advocacy of right-wing politics in France; Ramnath Goenka's decade-long feud with the Gandhis in which he toppled both Indira and her son Rajiv; Roberto Marinho's backing of the civilian regime of Tancredo de Almeida Neves against the military junta of General Joao Figueireda; Asil Nadir's self-serving championship in Turkey of President Turgut Ozal; Kamphol's public reticence over the dodgy Crown Prince of Thailand, which may have reprieved the last South East Asian monarchy; Rupert Murdoch's journalistic drag hunt of the British Royals which was largely responsible for the Queen's decision to pay tax, and accelerated the Prince and Princess of Wales's separation; Lord Rothermere and Rupert Murdoch's resolve, election after election, to get a Conservative government re-elected in Britain by respectively targeting (some would argue brainwashing) the middle and working classes.

The point has already been reached in which the traditional diversity of opinion in newspapers has been seriously eroded. News values are set, explicitly or implicitly, by the ever-smaller, ever-more powerful cabal of press tycoons. Their preferences and prejudices are disseminated down through their editors until they inform the entire corporate culture of their empire; until it becomes second-nature on a Murdoch paper that it will clip away at the foundations of the British Establishment – at its traditions, institutions and monarchy – and that virtually no article can find a place in the paper unless it conforms to that line.

And yet sometimes the proprietors are paper tigers in the Chinese meaning of the phrase: giving the appearance of being powerful, but secretly overborrowed or even broke. Ownership of the news allows proprietors more scope for bluff and bluster than anybody else. Until Maxwell went – literally – belly-up in November 1991, having diverted a billion pounds of other people's money into his private companies, barely a paragraph questioning his finances was published in any newspaper.

One of Asil Nadir's apparent motives in acquiring *Gunes* and *Günaydin*, two of Turkey's biggest dailies, was to deter them from poking their noses into his manufacturing and hotel projects on the turquoise coast. Newspaper moguls are practically unassailable. Their personal press is more indulgent than that of any other tycoon, and there is a reason for this. Proprietors themselves, perhaps feeling that there but for the grace of God go they, discourage serious criticism of their rivals. British newspapers owned by Murdoch, Black or Rothermere have scarcely ever published a rude profile of one another. In 30 years, nothing personally derogatory has been printed about the Sulzbergers, Chandlers or Grahams in a Sulzberger, Chandler or Graham newspaper. And there is another reason too. Newspaper editors don't wish to jeopardise future avenues of employment. They may take Black's shilling now, but who knows when they may need Rothermere's. The newspaper tycoon is, to all intents and purposes, inviolate.

Proprietors continually confided in me that such-and-such a competitor was going bust. 'You want to look at his debt ratio,' they advised me in London, Sydney, Texas and Bombay. But when I asked them why they didn't instruct their own business editor to do this, if it was such a great idea, they rolled their eyes and smiled like a Buddha.

People have strange expectations of newspaper moguls. They tell you that they despise the stereotype – the obese, conceited tycoon puffing on a cigar and manipulating the world through the editorial columns – but are disappointed when they don't get him. New York was entranced by Robert Maxwell when he bought the *Daily News* precisely because he fulfilled the cliché, with his yacht moored at the Water Club on the East River, the presidential suite at the Waldorf-Astoria and the stream of telephone calls (some stage-managed) from world leaders that punctuated every meeting. In Washington, Katharine Graham's presidential king-making and status as America's most powerful woman proprietor makes her the focus of boundless public curiosity. In Dublin, Tony O'Reilly's $75 million salary and bonus from Heinz, combined with his rather public penchant for the company of international statesmen, makes him more written about and speculated upon than anybody else in the country. In Hong Kong, the exact whereabouts of Sally Aw Sian's burgundy-coloured Rolls Royce is a source of perpetual fascination among the deal-makers of the colony. The comings and goings of Rupert Murdoch, as he races between Los Angeles, Sydney and London, are followed by his courtiers with the attention of China-watchers monitoring events across the frontier during the Cultural Revolution. Conrad Black's penchant for adding ever more world leaders and fellow tycoons to his boards of directors is discussed with cynical approval. People's attitude to newspaper owners reminds me of their attitude to the monarch; they criticise them for being too lofty, but are disappointed when they behave like ordinary people. The idealised proprietor looks like Lord Rothermere, portly but elegant, a baron with a hereditary peerage, but is mercurial and pugnacious like Robert Maxwell.

It is thin, nit-picking, gauche proprietors who are the objects of derision. Long before he had lost his family empire, Warwick Fairfax had lost the hearts and minds of his journalists. And he had lost them partly on appearance: gawky, unprepossessing, stoop-shouldered, myopic with wire-framed glasses and a strange deadness about the eyes, he struck his fellows in Sydney as a 'socially maladroit, greyday nerd'. I wondered how much longer he could have held on to the papers had he resembled the young Otis Chandler in the fifties – the handsome blue-eyed surfer with matinée idol looks – and raced energetically about the building like Rupert Murdoch, rather than isolating himself in his corner office on the 14th floor.

Samir Jain – the small, precise chief executive and owner of *The Times of India* – is similarly scorned for his Harvard Business School jargon and faith in algebraic symbols and Venn diagrams as the key to good newspapering. The epic board meetings at which he presides, explaining 'corporate systems' with the help of magic marker pens and laminated plastic screens, are a source of amusement in Bombay, as his competitors regale one another with his gnomic statements. One of my favourite stories is of a Calcutta editor who found himself sitting in an adjacent Indian Airways seat to Samir Jain on a flight between Bombay and Delhi. Asked how he controlled his newspaper empire, Jain proclaimed, 'I am chiefly interested in the *function* and *process* of management.'

'Samir, what exactly *is* "the process of management"?' enquired the editor.

'It is the details,' replied Jain. 'I like appraising my editors and deciding which one deserves which car, and which one deserves in-car air-conditioning.'

Pinch Sulzberger – the 40-year-old heir to *The New York Times*, with the obsession for change and state-of-the-art printing technology – induces similar scepticism from people who see his father's old, comfortable regime giving way to a new, more driven generation. In fact, the internal metamorphosis at the *Times* is a template for what is happening inside almost every newspaper in the world.

'The proprietors today are still pretty colourful aren't they?' said Lord Rothermere. 'Rupert's pretty colourful. Robert Maxwell was colourful and patriotic, you have to allow him that.'

In an industry in which the agenda is increasingly determined by corporate imperatives like profit and margins, it is remarkable how many flamboyant proprietors survive. Otis Chandler in Los Angeles, with his collection of muscle cars and rare stuffed animals, and miniature railway line snaking between the legs of his desk, is undeniably colourful. So is Louis Cha, the owner of *Ming Pao* and bestselling author of potboilers about mythological Chinese chivalry in which kung-fu warriors somersault backwards off horses. Tony O'Reilly is a former international rugby player, the highest-paid executive in North America and married to the richest woman in Britain, the Greek shipping heiress Chryss Goulandris. The Aga Khan is scarcely known as the owner of the largest-selling free-press in black Africa, because his proprietorship is eclipsed by his position as the religious leader of the Shia Ismaili Moslems and his reputation as a racehorse owner. Murdoch, who in the early days of the *Australian* used to escort an overnight planeload of copies across country dressed only in his pyjamas, is spiritually a puritan, but swashbuckling in business. Conrad Black, contentious, argumentative, is far and away the most colourful of the mid-generation of owners (though actually no less interested in profit and margins than his more monochrome competitors). Aveek Sarkar, the most influential proprietor between Bangalore and Singapore, reminds me of the classic Western tycoons between the wars: wilfully eccentric of mind and dress (unlike other

Indian tycoons, he wears traditional Indian dhotis and kurtas with diamond buttons at work), and holding incredibly strong opinions on every subject from the seismic to the trivial.

Proprietorship encourages self-satisfaction and vanity. Politicians, hoping that their careers or personal coverage might somehow be advanced, invite them to sumptuous dinners. 'Let us be completely frank,' Conrad Black was to tell me. 'The deferences and preferments that this culture bestows upon the owners of great newspapers is satisfying. I mean, I tend to think that they're slightly exaggerated at times, but as the beneficiary – a beneficiary – of that system it would certainly be hypocrisy for me to complain about it.'

Editors are alert to the slightest proprietorial prejudice, which they promptly reflect in their pages to curry favour. If the owner happens to mention that he doesn't care for *moules marinières*, a campaign against the danger of all shellfish is immediately launched. If he lets slip that he had a successful holiday in Spain, or a delayed flight, or believes that South American rain forests are an important issue, then travel writers, industrial editors and columnists are instantly assigned to follow up the story. Newspaper offices are echo chambers for proprietorial Chinese whispers. Suggestions from the owner become louder and louder as they reverberate down the chain of command. One morning the proprietor, passing his editor in the corridor, remarks, 'Do you know, as I was being driven into the office just now, I noticed that that delightful little print shop opposite the Connaught hotel has shut down. A great shame. Another victim of the difficult days no doubt.' The editor proceeds into conference, deep in thought, and tells his deputy, 'Marmaduke tells me that all the West End art galleries are closing down owing to the recession. Look into it, will you.' The deputy editor briefs the managing editor who primes the associate editor who memos the features editor, 'Lord Bucket is concerned about the demise of the London art market. Organise something for tomorrow's op-ed page.' By lunchtime the president of the Royal Academy is dictating 1200 words to copytakers for a fee of £2500, and the little print shop opposite the Connaught, closed for a fortnight's holiday, is being photographed by a man in an anorak from the picture desk (who has been expressly diverted for the purpose from the scene of a blazing fire).

The status of the owner is generally so far removed from everyday life, that for the huge majority of his employees he barely exists. A journalist joining a newspaper can at first see no higher than the editor. But as he reaches the foothills of power, another, much higher summit looms through the mist, dwarfing the peaks immediately ahead of him. The great north face of the proprietor, enveloped half the year in clouds and from that perspective unscalable.

I tried to pinpoint what makes proprietorial power so much more overwhelming than, say, owning a nationwide chain of supermarkets or department stores. Logically, the grocery and retail tyro should be afforded more respect than the tabloid tycoon, since a hypermarket is more substantial, tangible and enduring than a 48-page newspaper. And yet it is not so. Simply by owning a national newspaper, proprietors become *ex officio* experts on the economy, politics and the future of the world. They become the object of obsequious flattery, not just from their own staff but from a host of other sycophants – businessmen, senators, charity hostesses, potential employees – with something to gain. Mostly, as it happens, the flattery is misdirected. It is much easier for an editor to slip a good word or a puff into the paper than for the owner to do so. But most people don't realise this. So they ingratiate themselves with the proprietor, and hang on his every utterance.

Proprietorial kudos is largely kudos by association. The grocery tycoon, however essential his goods and however snazzily displayed, is ultimately selling only frozen food and cans of chickpeas. The department store billionaire is a shopkeeper with cosmetics on the ground floor and racks of slacks upstairs. The press baron's product is the intimate and scourge of presidents, popes and kings. The paper's logo and the Prime Minister's photograph are juxtaposed so, in the minds of the world, the owner of the paper and the players it writes about become fused.

And, with newspapers, it is impossible not to draw strong reactions. Readers develop prejudices that they associate with the proprietor. Whenever I was about to visit one, people said to me, 'Ask him why the hell he has x as his racing tipster' or 'Tell him to get his newspaper to support the president' or 'the Prince of Wales' or 'the Serbs' or 'breast scanning'. Anger at something a newspaper has written quickly converts into anger at the proprietor. People are always crediting Rupert Murdoch with being the sinister catalyst for some specific campaign in the *Boston Herald* or the *Sunday Times*. If you point out that he'd been in Sydney and California for three months, and is unlikely to have initiated an item on page four of the business section, they look either disbelieving or disappointed. Sometimes, of course, the proprietor is indeed the spectre at the feast. The *Sunday Times*'s increasingly savage republicanism certainly owes a lot to Murdoch. While the *Daily Telegraph*'s amnesty on Royal gossip is at the behest of Conrad Black.

What most immediately distinguishes the press baron from everyone else in the building is the reckless amount of space he allocates for himself. The Executive Floor. The Chairman's Floor. The Corporate Floor. The expression varies from newspaper to newspaper and country to country, but always there is a moment when the lift doors open on to the proprietor's specially woven carpet and the corridors double in width. After the mayhem of the packed editorial floors, reeking of cigarette smoke and take-away food, it is like stepping from Purgatory into Heaven. On the proprietor's floor, nobody speaks other than in hushed whispers. It is the silence of a doctor's waiting room in Harley Street, when the only sound is the ticking of a carriage clock and you are conscious that the furniture arranged against the walls – the davenports and escritoires – are there not because there is any expectation of letter-writing but rather to occupy the space. There are seventeenth-century globes on elaborate gilded bases. There are serpentine mahogany bureaux and marquetry *tables à écrire*. In Houston, on Dean Singleton's floor, there is a million-dollar Chippendale boardroom table which seats 24. The luxurious space is true even of the most number-crunching proprietors. Their own office suites would accommodate 50 accountants on a different floor, or 250 telesales girls in classified advertising.

Often these floors are referred to euphemistically by their numbers. The Fourteenth is the Sulzbergers' floor at *The New York Times*. The Fourteenth was Warwick Fairfax's at Fairfax. The Fifteenth Floor means Conrad Black. The Sixth is Rothermere. The Eighth is Kay Graham. An appointment on the Ninth Floor meant Robert Maxwell.

Notwithstanding their isolation, and the fact that they are chauffeured about in limousines with darkened windows and in private jets, owners kept assuring me that they have a special rapport with normal readers. None satisfactorily explained why this should be, but they felt strongly about it. Lord Rothermere told me that, on his periodic visits to London, he makes a point of taking a stroll along Kensington High Street, as a means of getting a feel for what is going on. Both Rothermere and Punch Sulzberger did a stint in the army serving in the ranks, and feel this had given them a special insight into the lives of ordinary people. Rothermere, who spent four years unpromoted as a private soldier, says now that he is grateful not to have been commissioned. 'I found it extremely helpful in understanding the true nature of society. I think it gave me quite an idea about what the real world is really like for the majority of people.'

Proprietors love to accentuate their street-cred. Ralph Ingersoll told me how as a youth he had sold circulation door to door. 'I got to know all the species of dogs in North America having to walk through the front yards and greet them bare-handed.' Donald Graham, discharged from the military draft in Vietnam, enrolled as a policeman in northeast Washington. Jim Kennedy covered City Hall as a reporter. Pinch Sulzberger covered Raleigh, North Carolina, with long hair and a leather jacket on a motorbike.

All this emphasis on being able to identify with real people is rather odd. Gianni Agnelli, in his capacity as owner of Fiat, doesn't keep saying that he hangs around garages in Turin. With newspaper owners, I came to detect an acute phobia about losing empathy with the readership, and how this might lead to a dramatic plunge in circulation and finally to the collapse of the empire. Newspaper franchises, for all their power, can appear vulnerable even to their owners. Their dependence on fickle readers, who might at any time switch papers, makes proprietors nervous. Virtually the only one who didn't claim a special relationship with the man in the street was Conrad Black.

The other great conundrum of proprietorship is that newspapers worth owning are in short supply. There are probably as few as twenty in the world that cut the mustard on all levels: newspapers that are prestigious and profitable, and situated in cities that invest the owner with a certain gravitas and curiosity value. These papers come up for sale very rarely. In all the time I was researching this book only eleven changed hands (and four of these were the same paper twice over). Each time, it was like a slab of raw meat being tossed into a pool of piranha fish: the predators darted from their respective corners, teeth bared, snapping at each other's tails as they circled the bait. When Murdoch bought the *South China Morning Post*, the pivotal English-language paper of the Far East, it enraged not only Maxwell but Sally Aw Sian who was galled at his audacity in trespassing on her turf.

When the *New York Daily News* came on the block, not once but twice in the space of eighteen months, it engendered two bloody cat fights, first between Robert Maxwell and Mortimer Zuckerman, subsequently between Zuckerman and Conrad Black. When Black beat Maxwell to the *Jerusalem Post*, he secured the only influential newspaper to change hands between Istanbul and Hong Kong. When he beat Tony O'Reilly to the Fairfax papers in Australia (conspicuously the *Sydney Morning Herald* and the *Melbourne Age*), O'Reilly resorted to his lawyers.

Ownership of blue-chip newspapers is sometimes compared with ownership of five-star hotels, which similarly engender fierce competition when they come up for sale. In the hotel world too, venerable names – the Ritz, Dorchester, Plaza – sell at huge premiums. In fact the analogy is not altogether apt. Newspapers are much rarer. An hotel chain can buy and market its way into a new town, because an important metropolis may support an astonishing number of large hotels, while a newspaper franchise is finite and hard to challenge. New newspapers mostly fail. Ralph Ingersoll's *St Louis Sun*, the most ambitious and expensive launch ever seen in an American metropolis, survived only 90 days before folding with losses of $120 million. Robert Maxwell's *London Daily News*, pitched directly against Lord Rothermere's *Evening Standard*, lasted three months and sustained losses, claimed Maxwell, of £50 million (this may, of course, have been an exaggeration. Once he had accepted his paper was a flop, he was keen to announce publicly the steepest possible losses for tax purposes). Rupert Murdoch's joint venture with Hubert Burda to launch a downmarket tabloid, *Super!Zeitung*, in the re-unified Eastern Germany, churned out a year's supply of topless models and envy editorials until it closed with undisclosed write-offs. The *Sunday Correspondent*, launched into an already vibrant Sunday market in London, expired in less than a year. The only successful launches have been Carlo de Benedetti's *La Repubblica* in Italy, *El Mundo* in Spain, Gannett's *USA Today* and, in Britain, the *Independent* and, arguably, *Today*.

How ought a proprietor fill his day? This single question exercised half the owners I visited. I was repeatedly asked how their rivals deployed their time. Proprietorship comes without a job description. There are no set office hours. Editors and managing directors can theoretically produce the papers for weeks on end while the owner suns himself in Palm Beach or the South of France. The balance between hands-on and hands-off is delicate. If they intervene too much and second-guess every decision, like Maxwell at the Mirror Group, it is difficult to retain good editors. If they intervene too little, and devolve all power, then newspapers can become rather soulless. When Katharine Graham first took over the *Washington Post* after the suicide of her husband, she sat alone in her big office, feeling superfluous. Decisions were being taken all over the building by competent executives, but she didn't know where or when and nobody informed her or encouraged her to join in. How, as the new proprietor, could she infiltrate her own newspaper? She learnt to call journalists into her office and invite them, politely and apologetically, to explain this or that nuance of foreign policy and inquire which candidate the *Post* was proposing to endorse in the election. Eventually her own voice joined – some say dominated – the decision-making process.

Geographical proximity has little to do with control. From his office on the Fox lot in Los Angeles, eight thousand miles from Wapping, Rupert Murdoch not only monitors what appears in his British tabloids but, through his thrice-weekly telephone calls to the editors, plays a decisive part in formulating policy. He told me that, despite his film and television distractions in Hollywood, he still manages to devote two hours a day to his newspapers. 'I guess half of that time is spent managing them and the other half reading them. But my reading of the newspapers these days is more like copy tasting, I go in and out of them.'

I asked him if it were frustrating when he didn't like what he found.

'It kills you. I tell you, it's terrible. You know they're getting it wrong over there and then you find they're persistently getting it wrong. Then it's time to start shaking the bushes a bit.'

Lord Rothermere, through some superior form of symbiotic intuition, manages to divine what is going on at Associated Newspapers from houses and apartments in Kyoto or New York.

'With Vere,' I was told by one of his executives, 'it really doesn't make much difference whether he's away in Japan or upstairs on the Sixth Floor. Both places are, in a sense, equally remote from the editorial floors which he almost never visits. I don't think he believes those floors are any of his business. So his editorial opinions are equally well informed wherever precisely in the world he happens to be.'

As far as news decisions are concerned, only five proprietors – Punch and Pinch Sulzberger, Katharine and Donald Graham and Otis Chandler – have ever regularly attended the daily editorial conference. For 20 years at five-minutes-to-five Punch Sulzberger has taken the elevator down from the Fourteenth to the editorial floor and pulled up a chair at the conference table alongside the dozen or so shirtsleeved senior staff. And yet, in two decades, he has almost never advanced an opinion of his own. His editors will discuss the City's politics, the future of the world, the onset of the next world war, but unless a direct question is put to him, he has neither the wish nor the presumption to chip in. In Sulzberger's view, the place of the proprietor is to pay the orchestra and collect the box office revenues, but not to wield the conductor's baton.

For proprietors, there are two principal means of control: philosophical and financial. Of the two, the financial is simplest to apply. Five of the owners in this book enforce the most stringent hands-on cost control. Dean Singleton and Ralph Ingersoll take an intellectual satisfaction in extracting maximum profits from marginal papers, 'like pumping high-pressure steam in a near played-out oilfield,' as Ingersoll puts it. Sally Aw Sian personally signs all expenses from every member of staff including messenger boys. At night, it is said, she takes sheaves of expense chits home to her ancestral Disneyland mansion in Tiger Balm gardens, where she and her mother scrutinise them in case a journalist has taken a cab across Kowloon where a tram would have done. Tony O'Reilly draws up precision business plans, in which every eventuality is anticipated and budgeted for. Lord Stevens tries to restrain his journalists by applying one of the most meticulous editorial budgeting systems in London. Robert Maxwell used to insist on signing every single cheque for more than 500 pounds, some of which he would tear in half, if he had arbitrarily decided they were unjustifiably high or unnecessary.

Pinch Sulzberger is hands-on, involving himself in everything from office chairs to the redesign of the Metro pages to the marketing of the colour supplement. Otis Chandler is officially semi-retired and hands-off, but rings the office several times a week with story ideas.

Ramnath Goenka was so totally hands-on that he was to all effects editor-in-chief. Conrad Black will give his editors the benefit of his opinions and set policy (pro-America, against royal gossip) but says that he has neither the aptitude nor the time to do the editors' job for them. Asil Nadir believed he was hands-on, insisting the front pages be faxed to him in Berkeley Square for approval every evening from Istanbul, but never in fact imposed any changes. Warwick Fairfax wasn't nearly hands-on enough for his own good, shutting himself away in his office on the Fourteenth Floor, seldom reading his own papers and unable to make conversation with his editors. 'I'd just like to be known as the owner,' he told Rupert Murdoch. So hands-off was he that eventually the papers slipped his grasp altogether.

The phrase they use most often is 'setting the agenda'. Owners were always telling me that 'setting the agenda' is what they really do. Katharine Graham, Otis Chandler, Tony O'Reilly and Rupert Murdoch all used it to describe their role. 'We have all these ships of the line, frigates and whatnot, sailing all over the place,' Lord Rothermere told me. 'The admiral doesn't tell any individual captain how to sail his ship, but he does tell him in which direction he should head.'

Many media owners have developed a taste for pandemic theorising. As they become further and further removed from the day-to-day running of their newspapers – dancing on the ceiling of the corporation – they must, for want of detail, depend upon overview. And what is the purpose of a proprietor if it isn't to supply a global perspective, perceive a pattern in the chaos of demography? And so they will talk about cultural shifts in the baby boom generation – 'the pig in the python', economic implications of the rise of the Pacific Rim, and environmental pressure groups in California and New Mexico.

When I asked Otis Chandler what is the greatest pleasure in owning a newspaper, he replied without a trace of self-consciousness, 'The opportunity it gives you to do important things to improve this planet Earth. Whether it be in science or helping to solve human issues or improve the environment or economic and educational opportunities for people. In other words, unlike any other business, a newspaper gets into every other business you can think of, and it just gives you that opportunity to try to improve and educate politicians and citizens of all types, to give them some guidelines as to how they can lead a better life and improve the *quality* of their life.' Asil Nadir, at the height of his short-lived newspaper empire, claimed to 'own my newspapers in order to benefit humanity and human culture'.

Generally their priorities are confused, their motives mixed. There is a pull of loyalties between making money and shoring up the reputation of the paper. If a large part of the motivation for buying an important newspaper is the prestige that accompanies ownership, there is little point in starving the thoroughbred until its ribcage shows through its flanks or fitting it up with a tacky bridle. This principle is more readily understood by the newspaper aristocracy – the landed monopolists – than by the heavily borrowed newcomers. The editorial budgets of *The New York Times*, the *Washington Post*, the *Los Angeles Times* and – to a slightly lesser extent in Britain – Lord Rothermere's newspapers, are enormous. Scores of journalists and columnists are deployed at political conventions, sporting events, wars and natural disasters, all of them billeted at the best hotels with expense accounts that are hardly queried. When the proprietor goes out to dinner at the height of the Bosnian civil war or the Somalian famine, he takes a vicarious pleasure in informing friends that 15 of his best reporters are at the heart of the turmoil, and that he has the inside story on what's going on over there.

But for the highly geared new American owners like Singleton and Ingersoll, the commitment to quality is ambivalent. Both assembled vast empires with record speed: Ralph Ingersoll's 240 newspapers took him less than five years to acquire, Dean Singleton's 71 in eleven states were snapped up in about eight years. The later part of the eighties saw the greatest scramble for newspaper assets ever known, with papers changing hands at unprecedented multiples. It made William Randolph Hearst seem, by comparison, cautious and vacillating.

The impetus for the feeding frenzy was very simple: the new proprietors believed that extraordinary financial returns could be derived from the fact that newspapers were America's last unregulated monopoly. Increasingly, in every city and township across the United States, there was only one paper, typically family-owned. Since there was no competition, pricing was in the hands of the proprietor. If they bought out the families, they could hike the advertising rates, hike the cover prices and turn a modestly profitable operation into a cash-cow. The arguments for owning newspapers were suddenly compelling.

Notwithstanding that – even before the recession – newspaper penetration was declining as a percentage of the American population, and newspapers' market share of the nation's advertising budget was waning, the new school of proprietors grasped that, publishing in a vacuum, they could control all the variables. If you owned the only paper, local businesses had no choice other than to advertise with you or cease newspaper advertising altogether. Prices could be doubled overnight. And readers, having no choice either, must either read your local paper or not at all. So quality could be reduced without any risk of defection to a competitor.

By the late eighties non-traditional buyers like Ingersoll and Singleton, fuelled by non-traditional sources of finance, were tearing from township to township in their Gulfstreams and Westwings, out-bidding and out-charming each other to procure monopoly papers from third- and fourth-generation families. Prices soared. Four times gross *revenues* – not profits – became commonplace; five times was not inconceivable. Scripps Howard, the quoted corporation, is believed to have paid nine times gross for the exceptionally dynamic market of Naples, Florida. As there were only about 430 independent daily newspapers left in the US (out of a total of 1000 dailies and 7000 weeklies), the supply and demand theory alone indicated that an ever increasing weight of money would chase an ever dwindling number of deals.

Ralph Ingersoll explained to me how he justified the multiples. 'I've always been more daring than the old family ownerships [who mostly sold him his newspapers] in exploiting the advantages of . . . what's the polite word? Monopoly is the impolite word, the *exclusive market position*. When we bought a new paper we felt we could charge rather more, both for circulation and advertising, than was part of it previously. We did away with the old boy advertising rates; rates that were kept low so as not to anger friends and neighbours. Some of the papers we bought had been operated on something other than the profit principle. They [the sellers] equate what we [then] did with being the sons of bitches they wouldn't be.

'The second thing we would do,' said Ingersoll, 'was rationalise the workforce to some degree. And then we'd fix the printing. Most of these newspapers we bought had already converted to cold type, but the conversions had been botched by the families [I acquired them from]. We'd fix them.'

'Botched how?'

'They weren't disciplined enough – they were too sentimental about the old staff relationships. And we simply *knew* how many productive hours per page it takes to produce a newspaper and we were willing to reduce the staff, buy out the positions. So it was not uncommon for us to be able to *treble* the profitability of a newspaper in two or three years. My concept of a good newspaper is the difference between a 10 per cent profit margin and a 30 per cent profit margin.'

Singleton, meanwhile, was refining what has been called his 'cut and slash' philosophy of newspaper management: the five steps from unprofitability or modest profitability to a business capable of repaying the interest on the corporate finance and posting decent profits for the proprietor.

1. Buy Newspaper
2. Cut Staff
3. Cut Quality
4. Cut Objectivity
5. Hike Advertising Rates

Buying newspapers is sometimes compared to betting at a casino at which the roulette table is in perpetual play, and where enormous wins alternate, almost arbitrarily, with huge losses. In fact, as the new proprietors realised, owning newspapers is like owning the bank. The odds can be reset constantly in the bank's favour, and the variables – editorial costs, advertising revenues, staff numbers, union agreements – manipulated even as the wheel is spinning.

One of the most curious relationships is that between the owner and his journalists. Every proprietor assured me that he valued his writers, but several sounded like they were only paying lip-service and were unable to name anyone in particular. Especially among new owners who made their first fortune doing something else, there is often both fear and contempt for journalists. Among the older proprietors I found ambivalence. They accepted that star writers embellished their papers, and helped sell them, but they seemed vaguely to resent their high salaries and were dubious of their loyalty and values. Partly this was the consequence of peer pressure. Owners are held personally responsible for the opinions of their journalists, over which they normally have little or no control. Punch Sulzberger says that his friends frequently chide him ('you and your goddamn scandal sheet') for some derogatory remark in *The New York Times* about themselves or their businesses. 'The tendency is for people to get pretty exercised when they're upset with a newspaper,' Jim Kennedy, the Cox heir to the *Atlanta Journal* and *Constitution*, told me. 'People [often] say something to me when we're out to dinner, if they don't like what's been written.' The more prominent the proprietor, the worse it becomes. If they move socially among politicians and industrial tycoons, every single fellow guest at a dinner party can take them to task over their treatment by the paper. When Otis Chandler's *Los Angeles Times* hired the radical cartoonist Paul Conrad, Chandler was rung several times a month at breakfast time by the Governor of the State of California, Ronald Reagan, or his wife, complaining about his portrayal in that day's issue. Finally Chandler gave instructions that calls from the Reagans should not be put through.

Few proprietors have journalists as close friends. Punch Sulzberger, Kay Graham and Aveek Sarkar have two or three each. Vere Rothermere has only two, Sir David English and Sir Patrick Sargeant, though he told me that, if he possessed a house in London, or dining room in his Paris flat, he 'probably would invite some of them to dinner'. Unlike his father, who believed that journalists are inter-changeable and could be bought like books by the yard, the present Lord Rothermere sees to it that their offices are the most capacious in the building. Rupert Murdoch and Conrad Black have both married journalists. Murdoch, in his early days in Australia and New York, used to drink and gamble with them, but now mostly just grabs a bite to eat (as he puts it) with an editor in the works canteen. More than any other owner, Murdoch arouses feelings of both intense loyalty and hatred among journalists. Black, notwithstanding his much quoted opinion of them ('ignorant, lazy, opinionated, intellectually dishonest and inadequately supervised'), enjoys their company because they are politically informed and don't mind staying up late with him. Pinch Sulzberger is trying to get to know the entire newsroom (about 1000 people) by inviting them home to supper in batches. Samir Jain and Lord Stevens both appear to regard them, to some degree, as the foe. David Stevens prefers the company of merchant bankers and fund managers, though he will periodically summon a journalist up to his office to put him right on some aspect of current events. Samir Jain views his editors and journalists as elements whose power needs constantly to be diffused ('those blue-blooded brahmins of the editorial floor!') and takes pleasure in giving the best offices to his managers instead.

Since most owners appear among their rank and file so seldom, these visitations assume an almost legendary dimension. There are journalists on the *Daily Mail* who still speak, 20 years later, of the evening Vere Rothermere accompanied them for a drink at the pub as though the episode took place only a few days ago. In Bangkok, Kamphol's periodic sightings in his trademark dark suit, dark glasses, topaz and diamond ring, white silk shirt and pointed white shoes are discussed for weeks on end. Rupert Murdoch's longtime henchman, John Evans, says that working for him you end up as a junkie: you need your daily fix of Mr Murdoch.

A media broker in Florida, who has sold papers to a third of the owners in this book, told me his secret for setting up a sale. Newspapers, he claimed, resemble their owners: not always physically but certainly in character. He said that over a ten-minute highball with a potential purchaser, he can divine whether they are temperamentally a tabloid or broadsheet proprietor, and the exact journalistic tone they would feel comfortable controlling. As a theory, it has merit. Rupert Murdoch – energetic, egalitarian, tough, right wing, suspicious of anything pretentious or fancy – fits the editorial formula of the *Sun*. *The New York Times* – discursive, civilised, comprehensive, somewhat schizophrenic in its attitudes to change – is an amalgam of Sulzberger Snr and Jnr. Maxwell's *Daily Mirror* was as inconsistent and bombastic as its owner. Tony O'Reilly's Irish papers are verbose and rather cultured. Conrad Black – Establishment but occasionally waspish – resembles the *Sunday Telegraph*. No adjective about *Le Figaro* – dry, literal, bourgeois, conservative – would not apply equally to Robert Hersant. Kamphol's *Thai Rath* is flashy, big league and sleazy. Rothermere's *Daily Mail* is family minded, instinctively conservative but Establishment only up to a point. Samir Jain is trying hard to make *The Times of India* more marketing-led like himself, but is confounded by the culture of Indian journalism. (The exceptions that explode the theory are Otis Chandler, lean and focused, while his *Los Angeles Times* is fat, sprawling and diffuse; and Ralph Ingersoll, well bred, elegant and patrician, proprietor of papers that are for the most part scrappy and downmarket.)

Physically they belie the stereotype. Most are disconcertingly fit, engaged in punishing programmes of exercise and sport. Murdoch jogs in the dark in Beverly Hills at 4.30 a.m. Punch Sulzberger works out in a gym every morning at 6 a.m. Otis Chandler surfs and goes on arduous hunting trips across Alaska and the Himalayas. Jim Kennedy, the fittest of them all, shoots duck and quail and bicycles 2900 miles across America from California to Georgia. Aveek Sarkar plays such a hard game of tennis that he has to change his shirt four times a set. The Aga Khan races powerboats. Tony O'Reilly still plays in charity rugby matches. Rothermere keeps stress free through Zen Buddhism. Warwick Fairfax liked to surf, though it never showed on his grey, indoor complexion.

I became interested, too, in the influence of the proprietors' wives. Because the content of newspapers is subjective, and is something on which everybody who can read holds an opinion, it is inevitable that the woman who shares her bed and breakfast with the owner is a pervasive and relentless critic. Many come to see themselves as Everywoman: briefing their husbands on what the women of the nation are really thinking. (There is no way of knowing whether this should hold true in reverse, since neither of the world's prominent female owners, Katharine Graham and Sally Aw Sian, are currently married.) Pat Rothermere told me that however late she returned home from a nightclub, she would always read all the next day's newspapers 'marking things to draw to Vere's attention. I don't ring all the editors direct because I don't want to cut Vere's balls off.' Lady Fairfax had no such qualms, and frequently rang the *Sydney Morning Herald* with late-breaking social news, until she was ordered to desist. Rupert Murdoch told me that his second wife Anna – who he met when she was a cadet reporter on his Sydney *Daily Mirror* – is 'the most critical of all our directors at board meetings. She'll speak up, you bet she does. She's got least to fear!' The glamour-puss political journalist Barbara Amiel – Mrs Conrad Black – occupies a pivotal position on the London scene, friend to journalists and conduit of news and opinion to her husband, she reinforces Black's right-leaning ideology. Chryss Goulandris – Mrs Tony O'Reilly – seems genetically programmed to be the wife of a world-class owner, and is a beady monitor of the press to boot.

There was great excitement in the 1990 annual report and accounts of virtually every media owner in this book. The corporate brochures produced for shareholders all featured, on their opening page, an identical photograph: East and West German students linking arms along the top of the Berlin Wall. Whenever I saw this picture I thought how much more fitting it would be if, instead of students, a motley row of newspaper proprietors were linking arms along the newly breached wall. Rupert Murdoch, Robert Maxwell, Vere Rothermere, Robert Hersant, Silvio Berlusconi, Mrs Axel Springer, Hubert Burda, Ralph Ingersoll. That year every owner who could raise the five-million-dollar floor price seemed to be scurrying through the hole to snap up Eastern Bloc media.

A Goldman Sachs vice president who choreographed the shopping spree likened it to dancing. 'Dancing partners are getting paired off quickly; the best dancers get snapped up first.' To me it seemed more like a game of media Monopoly, with the cash-rich owners of Park Lane and Mayfair blowing small change on cheap blue properties like the Angel Islington and the Euston Road.

It was a curious interlude: the year the owners became obsessed by Eastern Europe. In almost every case it was the proprietor himself who was moved to buy something there. 'I don't know that my management thought it a very bright idea,' Lord Rothermere told me. 'I said to them, "You're too cautious, you're not thinking enough about the long term." '

It seemed to me that there were three reasons proprietors went mad for the East. The first had to do with their life *outside* the media. In the spring of 1989, at the kind of dinner party where the other guests are arbitrageurs and top flight merchant bankers, the opportunities of Eastern Europe became the number one topic of conversation. Doing business amidst the rubble of communism acquired a sort of glamour. Entrepreneurs with a reputation for cleverness leant against the mantelpiece and said, 'I've just spent the last three days in Budapest and Prague,' and, 'Do you know, only four hours ago I was in Krakow.' They said there were factories employing tens of thousands of people that could be bought for a few hundred thousand pounds, and that the opening of the East meant a hundred million potential new consumers. Media owners, anxious to make similar observations, embarked upon adventurous fact-finding tours with their wives and girlfriends.

And there was a great advantage to shopping in the East; it was so close. Maxwell could reach Budapest in his G-4 in two-and-a-half hours, allowing him to finger two or three newspapers, terrorise the staff, shake hands with the president and still be back in Holborn in time to interfere with the next morning's *Daily Mirror* editorial. Rothermere could spend a week at the Budapest Hilton acquiring *Kisalfold* – his regional daily in Gyor-Sopron – and be only one hour ahead of London. Murdoch could inspect his Hungarian paper, *Mai Nap*, without anyone realising he'd left London. Hersant could fly from Paris to Warsaw in under two hours, choose *Rzeczpospolita* from the half dozen Polish dailies on the block, and return to his desk at Avenue de Général Mangin by late afternoon. When Ralph Ingersoll was looking to buy the *Leipziger Volkszeitung* in Eastern Germany, he had to lunch on cold cabbage and dumpling in Leipzig, but could begin and end his day in London at the Savoy. The proprietors who migrated east almost always shopped alone and negotiated their deals without the assistance of their corporate management. There was a frontier spirit about these trips: adventures into the grey unknown, giving management the slip. The Great Western Media Tycoon meets the New World Order.

One of the most seductive things about the Eastern Bloc papers was their size. The circulations were enormous. Some exceeded a million. In Prague, *Rude Pravo* – 'Red Right' (Prop: Czechoslovak Communist Party) sold 1,100,291. In Sofia, *Rabotnichesko Delo* – 'Worker's Cause' (Prop: Bulgarian Communist Party) sold 820,000. *Nepszabadsag* – 'People's Freedom' (Prop: Hungarian Socialist Workers' Party) sold 450,000.

And everything appeared to be for sale. The new regimes in Warsaw, Bucharest, Prague and Budapest were eager to dispose of their over-staffed, loss-making monopolies. To proprietors accustomed to big newspapers changing hands at the rate of one every three to five years, it was a feeding fest. More intriguing still was the fact that so little was known about these papers: their editorial reputations, printing plants, staff numbers. You could look up *Scinteia* – 'The Spark' – (Prop: Central Committee of the Romanian Communist Party) and read that it has a daily circulation of 1,410,000 but not have a clue whether, post-communism, it would continue to sell a single copy. So many government-owned papers owed their dizzy circulations to favourable newsprint allocations, or to a policy of dumping thousands of pro-party papers at factories and collective farms. And the journalists who staffed these papers were often not genuine journalists at all; they were secret policemen whose function had been to keep news *out* of the press.

'When I took a look at the Leipzig paper, we had Stasi in the newsroom,' said Ralph Ingersoll. 'It was a very complicated thing, whether they could ever make the transition to news *gatherers* from news *supressors*. You couldn't just get rid of these people: you had to make good the West German politicians' promises to force wages up and maintain staffing levels. It's very much a mixed and murky picture, knowing what to bid. In Leipzig we were underbidders to Springer Verlag. I honestly bid what I thought was the full price – 75 million marks – and lost. They were well over us. Nevertheless, at the time I was bidding, the profit margins were the highest in Europe. The average Eastern newspaper was running operating margins in the high 30s and the *Leipziger Volkszeitung* was running in the low 40s. It was very profitable. The problem in East Germany which was not foreseen is that by legislative fiat the companies operating there are being required by the Treuhandanstalt, the state agency, to bring their wages up to West German parity within a pretty damn short period of time. It's a forced march.

'That is part of the reason,' said Ingersoll, 'that quite a number of deals that were struck are coming unstuck; owners are reneging on them. It's proving to be a lot more difficult to make profits over there than we expected. The franchises are immature. I guess you'd be better off buying a 20,000 circulation monopoly paper in Nebraska than a 350,000 circulation paper in Bratislava.'

By the spring of 1992 the Eastern European boom was dead. The media owners had identified more convenient and richer trophies.

The two great landmasses where they don't yet have a toe-hold – China and the former Soviet Union – seem increasingly likely to acquiesce. The billionaire Hong Kong owners – Sally Aw Sian, Louis Cha and the Mas – are poised on the Chinese border to invade, and Rupert Murdoch's *South China Morning Post* is limbering up for Chinese-language editions. Media analysts predict that by the end of the millenium both Beijing's tedious mass-circulation dailies (*Gongren Ribao* – 'Worker's Daily', prop: All-China Federation of Trades

Unions, circulation 2,000,000 and *Renmin Ribao* – 'People's Daily', prop: Communist Party of the People's Republic of China, circulation 4,000,000) will be snapped up by a Murdoch, Hersant or the Hong Kong running dogs, and filled with massage parlour sex, headless corpses and spot-the-ball contests. Amidst the debris of the Soviet Union, *Pravda* (circulation 1,500,000, down from 20,000,000 in three years) looks even more vulnerable.

Prolonged exposure to newspaper empires affected my sense of geography. The great franchises became landmarks both more evocative and pervasive than museums and mausoleums. When I thought of New Delhi, it was no longer the Qutab Minar that flashed into my mind but *The Times of India*. Sydney meant first and foremost the *Morning Herald*. Paris meant *Le Figaro*. And when I thought of New York, it wasn't the Central Park skyline that personified Manhattan, but the great white whale: the Sulzbergers' *New York Times*.

All the Cash that's Fit to Print

The Sulzbergers and *The New York Times*

You turn the corner from Broadway on to West 43rd Street and suddenly it's upon you, towering above and stretching away from you, occupying a whole block of the city like a Soviet ministry or museum, the great brick offices of the world's largest newspaper, *The New York Times*.

Along the façade, a frieze of griffins bearing shields and four drooping pennants emblazoned in blue with the paper's logo. On either side of the entrance, bulbous glass lamps of the kind you associate with police headquarters, so coated with the grime of New York City that at night they emit only the feeble glow of a child's nightlight. To left and right, a score of blue garage doors and a notice 'TRAILERS ONLY IN THIS BAY'; but instead of trailers, executive cars: a fleet of Mercedes, Chryslers, a Lincoln parked tight along the vanways. Above the entrance, a Greek warrior brandishing a spear and a bare-breasted siren taking the weight of a vast globe, so positioned that the United States of America – New York in fact, probably West 43rd Street – stands at the epicentre of the map. There is the famous maxim 'ALL THE NEWS THAT'S FIT TO PRINT' and a bronze plaque to 'Adolph S. Ochs 1858–1934, who made *The New York Times* one of the world's great newspapers by setting standards of excellence and responsibility'.

He created too, though it doesn't say so, one of the most obese newspapers on the planet. The Sunday edition – that great tofu-coloured wodge of newsprint – is as thick as a paving slab, its outer section bulging at the fold to contain the hundreds of pages, the alphabet of sections, the reviews, magazines, travel, sport and business specials, real estate directories, department store promotions, second-hand car catalogues, product discount brochures, samplers, health and vegetarian food supplements, handbills, flyers for transcendental meditation centres and crackpot religious cults, vouchers entitling you to 99 cent rebates on franchised fast-food, book club membership inducements, proprietory drug offers; the vast, conscientious, authoritative, blubbery, barely signposted mass of Ontario woodpulp that is heaved, at who knows what cost to the sciatic nerves of an army of delivery-boys, to 1.7 million homes and has helped to make the Sulzbergers one of the four most influential newspaper dynasties in the world.

Although far from the largest newspaper organisation (revenues are $1.8 billion, ranking the New York Times Company 231st on the *Forbes* list for net income, well behind the Chandlers' Times Mirror with revenues of $3.6 billion, but ahead of the Grahams' Washington Post on $1.3 billion), the Sulzbergers have an arresting roster of media properties; in addition to the flagship *Times*, they have a half interest in the *International Herald Tribune* (though this is left largely to the co-shareholders, the Grahams of the *Washington Post*, to run), 27 daily and nine weeklies located mostly in the South East, 17 magazines, five TV stations, two radio stations and the expected (for families of this kind) assortment of paper and pulp mills. In late spring 1993 they bought the *Boston Globe* for $1.2 billion, pitching themselves against Murdoch, who has the *Boston Herald*, and effectively wrapping up the Eastern seaboard.

Like so many global newspaper dynasties, the Sulzbergers are in transition. Arthur Ochs Sulzberger Snr – Punch – for 30 years the great panjandrum, is relinquishing part of the empire to his son, Arthur Ochs Sulzberger Jnr – Pinch. Punch and Pinch. Punch likes his nickname, has embraced it all his life; the son hates his, says nobody much uses it except for media commentators, says it is inappropriate, a facile play on words. 'Put it this way,' he told me, 'if my father hadn't been known as Punch all his life, would anyone say I'm known as Pinch? I think not. It's just a lazy means of categorising me as different from my father.'

And no doubt he's right. The Pinch label exists only as an alliterative subsidiary of Punch. But, others argue, it also contains a kernel of truth. Punch and Pinch. The old, jocular, gladhanding regime gives way to the new generation number-cruncher. In fact the preoccupations of the son are not much different from the preoccupations of Donald Graham at the *Washington Post* or Samir Jain at *The Times of India*: tightening the operating costs, attending to market research, refocusing the product, pinching the paper's waistline. The internal metamorphosis of *The New York Times* is a template for what is happening inside almost every newspaper, everywhere.

The elevator doors opened five different times on the journey up to the 14th floor, to reveal successively: a black woman from somewhere like Flatbush – a cleaner with a tea-cosy on her head – bearing two metal buckets and a slimy mop and whistling deliriously; three fat men in overalls shifting a skewed metal table; a woman carrying a Styrofoam tray containing six Styrofoam cups and a heap of bagels – when the lift doors opened she made no move to step in, just stared dully at the shaft, but when they began to close she said 'motherfucker' while making no attempt to obstruct them; an old man wheeling an iron hospital bedstead covered by a sheet; three Italian security guards, or so they appeared, congregating in a sinister huddle around a fire hydrant. Each time the elevator doors parted, I felt I was being eyeballed by creatures of the Manhattan subway system, and that a lift ride through the New York Times was the vertical equivalent of travelling from the Cloisters to the World Trade Centre.

Small bevies of journalists, muffled up against the snow outside, rode to the editorial floors, but it was the vast supporting cast of maintenance men, security honchos, printers and electricians who seemed to dominate *The New York Times*, milling sullenly along the corridors like the inmates of some temporary hall of residence. The New York Times building did not seem like a newspaper office at all; it reminded me of an infirmary, an Indian government ministry, the United Nations building. Of the hundreds – thousands – of functionaries going about their business, barely one in ten had the gait of a newsman.

Eventually the elevator reached the 14th floor – the Chairman's floor – and the contrast could not have been greater if the doors had opened on to the Arizona desert. After the hubbub of the lower floors, a lunar expanse of beige carpet and an eerie, arid silence. Of all the executive floors I was to see while visiting newspaper owners, *The New York Times* is the largest. A man could lose his way in that great beige dustbowl; take one false turning and you could wander in circles for days. Every 250 yards, or so it seemed, there was some solitary landmark: a venerable old globe, a bookcase containing leather-bound copies of the newspaper, a writing desk where lost visitors to the 14th might scribble some valedictory message. Very occasionally there was a picture: a framed settlers' map of New England or a portrait of a gentleman in a wig scratching his ear with a quill pen. Those offices that I passed were deserted and so bare of possessions that it was doubtful they were occupied at all. Some great distance further on, across another barren expanse of beige carpet, was the private office of Arthur Ochs Sulzberger Snr, Chairman and Chief Executive Officer of the New York Times Company.

Punch Sulzberger was studying a list of names typed upon a sheet of writing paper. These were some benefactors expected that next evening at a small dinner party for the Metropolitan Museum of Art, of which he is also Chairman. He looked slightly bemused by the names on the list, as though it were a surprise to him that he was shortly to play host to these strangers. He shook his head wearily. 'I'm sure messed up in spades tomorrow night,' he said. His attitude was that of a benign British aristocrat resigned to the prospect of entertaining a group of church wardens.

He was wearing, as Conrad Black had predicted he would be, his Marine Corps emblem. His face, at the age of 65, was a little grey from a recent illness – an abscess of the jaw under a wisdom tooth – but his expression is amiable and self-deprecating. Unlike his son, whose eyes are rather hungry, Punch Sulzberger's eyes are miraculously relaxed; the Chairman and CEO of the New York Times Company acted like he was well into the third week of a vacation at Nantucket.

I said, 'Your office is remarkably quiet. This whole floor in fact.'

He nodded. 'There is a certain degree of privacy here impossible to obtain on the other floors.'

Then he added, 'But I leave my door open 99 per cent of the time.'

He gestured along the corridor towards the great beige savannah, to prove how easily his office, with its open door policy, might be breached.

'It's even quieter when I first get in,' he said. 'Then there really is *nobody* about. My wife's always screaming at me not to leave home so early, it disrupts the household, but I'm an early riser, always have been. I like to go to the gym at 6.30, that's the Cardio-Fitness Center in the McGraw-Hill building. David Rockefeller has the locker next to mine, it's an entertaining place. And then I come in here at about a quarter-to-eight and have a whole hour to myself. No secretary then, so I buy a doughnut in the cafeteria, make a cup of tea for myself – everything's left out ready for me – and I'm happy as a clam.'

'Is that when you read your newspaper?'

'That's exactly when. But never carefully enough it seems. People complain about what we've said about them, and I've seldom anticipated what it is they're not going to like. After nine o'clock I get insulated from the readers by my secretary, but early in the morning when the telephone rings I answer it myself. People are surprised by that, I think.'

'What do you say to them when they complain?'

'I don't get into a fight about it, that's the main thing. A bit hot under the collar sometimes, but not a fight. Public argument doesn't do any good I've discovered. So I try to blunt the critics. If they're serious I say, "I'll get back to you," and then I try and check out why we said this or that. And if they've been reasonable about it, I might very well ring them back too.'

'What about friends who complain?'

'Oh my friends are *always* complaining.' He chuckled. 'They say, "*Punch*, you and your goddamn sheet, you know what they said today?" The better you know them, the more inclined they are to give you a little jab. They pick you up on this and that. That's your friends for you.'

Then he said, 'You know the only time this friendship business is difficult is when one of your friends is running for office. Or, worse, if a *couple* of your friends are running for the *same* office – that does make it difficult. They ring up and ask you, "*Punch*, are you supporting me?" and then the other fellow, your other friend, rings up too asking the same question: it can be awkward. But I've supported friends against friends and, you know, at the end of it all, the real friends stay friends.'

'Do you turn to any particular page first in the *Times*?'

'The obituaries. The first thing I do after I've made my cup of tea is turn to the obituaries to see who's gone. Which reminds me, someone I used to know died recently, I read his obituary over the weekend and must write to his widow.

'By the way,' he asked me, 'do you read the *Times*? I don't mean the

London *Times* which of course you read, everyone in London reads *The Times*, I mean *my Times* – our *Times* – *The New York Times*.'

I replied that very occasionally I bought the Sunday edition which is the only edition imported by London newsagents. Punch Sulzberger looked enormously pleased, even grateful, that I bought his newspaper in England.

'It takes some getting used to,' he said. '*The New York Times* isn't an easy newspaper. You have to potter your way around it a bit, until you learn where to find what interests you.'

'Apart from the obituaries, what do you recommend?'

Punch Sulzberger thought for a bit through half-closed eyes, smiled, gazed up at the ceiling of his office with the airy concentration of a restaurant-goer choosing something especially nice from the menu for a friend.

'Now *what do* I recommend?' He continued thinking. 'I'll tell you what I always read myself,' he said at last, 'and that's the science section. Now that *does* interest me, especially the *unexpected* articles they put in, the latest inventions. And on Sundays I read the columnists depending on which ones they are.'

'Do you see much of your columnists and journalists?'

'I certainly like 'em,' said Punch Sulzberger. 'I take a great interest. Unlike some British proprietors I feel perfectly comfortable getting in there and poking about. I'm not like Astor who just stayed in his office and watched it all fall apart, or the Hartwells of the *Telegraph* who sat back and did not a goddamn thing. I like to go to the news conference every day at five o'clock to hear what's going on. Not that I take a particularly active role in it, I like to stand way at the back, get a feel for what they're thinking. And I go to the editorial type lunch every day when we invite outside guests in. I think the journalists are used to me being around now. They're quite comfortable with it. They know the final word on editorial opinion is mine. That's been tested. Not often, thank God. You feel you can say this now, but it's taken time to get to this point. And the editors know that neither I nor my son will interfere very often. That's not the way we like to do things.'

'If you don't like something in the paper, do you make that widely known?'

'I make my favourable views known considerably further down than my unfavourable ones. If I don't like how we've done something or other, I'll mention it to the editor of the editorial page or the executive editor or the managing editor and let them carry the burden. But you know,' he said, 'you have to be sensitive too about congratulating your journalists too freely in case you get it wrong. There was a marvellous story, years ago now, involving my father when he was publisher. In those days Turner Catledge was executive editor and on one occasion Catledge had to call a journalist into his office tell him he wasn't very happy with his work. The journalist looked surprised. "I don't know what you mean, Mr Catledge," he said, "I've had letters from Mr Sulzberger, drawers full of 'em." And it turned out that my father, who enjoyed this particular man's writing, was sending him little notes of congratulation, unaware that Catledge was dissatisfied with him. So I always check first with the editor before saying anything, to make sure it's OK.'

The decoration of Punch Sulzberger's office might best be described as masculine taste with a few surprising aberrations. His desk, his chair, the leather blotter and ink stand are all of the inoffensive, substantial kind you would expect to find in a neglected corner of the New York Yacht Club. But sitting up and begging behind him on a shelf are a pair of Chinese china pugs, and propped against his chair is a tapestry 'Love Me Love My Cigar' cushion: one of the few mottoes I don't recall seeing among Lady Rothermere's definitive collection of mottoed tapestry cushions in her London flat.

On Punch Sulzberger's coffee table sat a copy of the previous day's *Sydney Morning Herald* and it occurred to me that perhaps he was about to swell the ranks of bidders for the Fairfax newspapers, then still a few days away from being sold to Conrad Black.

'Are you buying Fairfax?' I asked.

'From Mary?' Punch Sulzberger looked distinctly apprehensive at the thought of Lady Fairfax. 'That indomitable lady! She's bought up half that hotel you know, the Pierre, where she intends living in the ballroom, so people say.'

'But would you buy her family newspapers?'

'I think we've pretty well decided that we don't buy overseas, we've scratched the foreign field. We looked at newspapers in Eastern Europe like Vere Rothermere and Rupert Murdoch – like Bob Maxwell! – but decided against because a) it's too far away b) there are no bargains in life and c) no control. Who could say what the managing editor or whoever would get up to over there, or what they'd really be thinking. They'd be there . . . and I'd be here . . .' He surveyed his office, his blotter, the Chinese pugs, '. . . and who would know the first thing that was really going on?'

'But you own at least one foreign publication, in London.'

Punch Sulzberger brightened up. It so happened that I had unwittingly mentioned one of his favourite publishing properties.

'Ah, *Golf World*,' he said lovingly. 'I can tell you our *Golf World* in London merits a lot of inspection!

'We have an apartment on Mount Street,' he explained, 'right up the road from the Connaught hotel. My wife and I were going to get a condominium in Florida and then we discovered that Carol wanted to be on the east coast of Florida and me on the west coast of Florida, so we compromised on Mount Street which was the smartest thing we ever did. That was a smart move! Each Thanksgiving Day we give a party at Claridges and then drive around all over the country in the car. And later I go visit *Golf World*.'

'Do you visit British newspaper owners while you're over?'

'Only Vere Rothermere. He'd be my closest friend of the other owners. I see him when he's here or vice versa; saw him recently in Paris for dinner with his Japanese girlfriend. And I've got to know Conrad Black. Conrad invited me down to lunch at his new place on the Isle of Dogs. *What a journey that was*!

'Of the owners over here, well, I see them you know at board meetings, annual conventions. Kay Graham – and Donald [Graham] – I run into them. It's generally cordial unless they've poached one of our people. Then I might say, "*You sonofabitch, waddaya doing*?" but I'd say it all in a friendly way. We've recently taken the military correspondent from the *Washington Post* actually and Kay didn't ring me up. I thought she might because I guess she's pretty pissed about it. With poaching at that level I knew what we were trying to do but didn't know we'd locked in until afterwards. They keep me informed. I'd know in advance about the things one's especially interested in like the theatre critics and the London, Paris and Washington bureau chiefs.

'Do you want to see the boardroom?' he asked suddenly, and ushered me to the very end of the beige corridor and into a vast baronial hall like the keep of a Scottish castle. There is a great stone fireplace with logs in the grate, and around the table which is hewn from a single piece of wood, high-backed winged chairs. The effect made one think of both Charles Foster Kane's Xanadu and a phoney medieval banqueting hall catering for tourists. We both appeared stunted and insubstantial beneath the vaulted ceiling. Clustered on every inch of tablespace, and along the beam above the fireplace, are autographed photographs of heads of state: Presidents Nixon, Reagan, Bush, Margaret Thatcher ('To Punch . . .'), Henry Kissinger, Chiang Kai-shek.

The pantheon of White House incumbents reminded me of a story, probably apocryphal, about Punch Sulzberger's mother, Iphigene Ochs Sulzberger, when her son was invited to the White House for lunch. Knowing her suspicion for anything to do with the Government, Punch didn't tell Iphigene about his private lunch with the President, Vice President and Chief of Staff until immediately afterwards when he rang her from his car.

'Guess what?' he said. 'I've just had lunch at the White House with the President.'

At the end of the line there was an ominous silence. Then Iphigene Ochs Sulzberger asked, in her most sceptical voice, 'And what did *he* want then?'

'There's a great one here, look, of President Ford reading *The New York Times*,' went on Punch Sulzberger. 'I couldn't resist it, and this is the Japanese Prime Minister. I went there shaking the tin for the Metropolitan Museum.'

I asked, 'Are these personal friends or work friends?'

'The statesmen? Work friends. I guess one could delude oneself and say personal friends, and many of them have become such, but it's not really me they want to be buddies with, it's the newspaper.'

'Do you mentally divide people into newspaper friends and home friends?'

'I get mighty confused at times. People tell me things at dinner parties or at the weekend and it's hard to know their real motive. I have to ask them, "Were you telling me this because you want me to know for the newspaper or as your friend?" It's a narrow line and sometimes the guy who tells you the thing doesn't know himself whether he wants me to pass it on. If he says it's OK, I'll relay it as an anonymous tip through the executive editor. I'll say, "Look, you don't know where this came from but you might like to take a look . . ." '

More than any other newspaper, the internal machinations of West 43rd Street are themselves newsworthy. A change of publisher, of editor, or columnist, a shuffle of personnel on the editorial page, the merest tinkering of typography and it merits attention, interpretation. The satirical magazine *Spy* runs a monthly page about the *Times*, with shrunken headshots of Punch and Pinch and the senior editors at the top, chronicling the feuds and power shifts. Does Punch Sulzberger read it?

'Yes.' His guffaw sounded like an explosion and echoed around the vaulted ceiling of the boardroom. But then he changed his mind and said, 'I haven't looked at it for months and months. I got bored – it is always attacking the same people, which means *us*. And even *I* can't understand what they're getting at half the time. And I work here! It's like *Private Eye* in England. You have to have a translator. Captain Bob – even I knew who he was [Maxwell]. But the rest, who knows? You need a *translator*!'

'But what about *Spy*'s premise that this is the most tense newspaper on the planet?'

'I think it's considerably less than it was.' And then he added, sounding uncannily like his friend Vere Rothermere, 'A bit of tension is good, isn't it? Creative tension: that's the expression they use. But I don't get any sense of any great turmoil any more. You get *individual* turmoil, that's inevitable when you have people. And I'm sure it's reduced. Partly because we've contained the size of the staff. I won't say we've reduced it, but contained it. So we don't have people sitting about any more with nothing to do, waiting for a railroad accident. These days they can express themselves through their writing. It used to be that the only place you could do that on *The New York Times* was the sports department. The sports reporters used to be the only fellows allowed to write in an interesting way. Now there's plenty of opportunity, pretty well all over the newspaper.'

'The clue to Punch Sulzberger,' I was told by one of his most senior editors, 'the thing that distinguishes him from every other newspaper publisher you've mentioned, is that you could meet him away from

New York and if you didn't happen to know he is the owner of *The New York Times*, he'd never mention it. That's away from New York. I guess you'd be hard pressed to find anyone in this city who didn't associate the name Sulzberger with the *Times*, but if you ran into him someplace in Europe or on one of his fishing trips, he'd never broadcast the fact he owns the greatest newspaper in the world. It's not that he's not proud of having the *Times*, or even that he's particularly self-effacing, he's just an exceptionally well-mannered and well-adjusted man. And he wouldn't see owning the *Times* as sufficient justification for commanding attention. He doesn't need that. He's been involved with the paper for most of his life and he doesn't need the big build up like most of the others.'

The modesty of Sulzberger is the first thing anyone mentions about him. The second is that, for all the gentlemanly charm and ability to appear disengaged from the internal tussles of his company, he is as closely identified with the destiny of his flagship newspaper as are the Grahams with the *Washington Post* and the Chandlers with the *Los Angeles Times*. The ascension of his son to the position of Publisher in January 1992, and his own partial abdication to the role of chairman and Chief Executive Officer of the New York Times Company, has done nothing to lessen this identification. Until the day he physically removes himself from the building, there will always be the two camps, two generations: the Old Guard and the New Guard, the Punch-bags and the Pinch-boys.

Arthur Ochs Sulzberger was born in New York City in the bitterly cold February of 1926, the only son of Arthur Hays Sulzberger, who would become owner and publisher of *The New York Times* nine years later, and the legendary Iphigene Ochs Sulzberger whose own father, Adolph S. Ochs, had been owner and publisher of the newspaper since 1896. Three daughters had already been born to Arthur and Iphigene: Marian, Ruth and Judith; all of them today substantial stockholders in the company, in their own right and through tortuous family trusts. His older sister Judith had already, as a baby, had her name abbreviated to Judy. To celebrate Arthur's arrival into the world two years after hers, Arthur Hays Sulzberger composed and made sketches for a little monograph, privately printed in Gothic script, in which he wrote that his son had 'come to play Punch to Judy's endless show'. The nickname stuck. The annual report to shareholders of the New York Times Company is signed Arthur Ochs Sulzberger (not that you can decipher it: his signature resembles a flattened coil of barbed wire), but the Chairman signs his interoffice memoranda and many of his letters 'Punch', and he is greeted as Punch and referred to as Punch by friends and colleagues beyond a certain level of intimacy, by his secretary (though when she spoke of him to me she called him Mr Sulzberger), by virtually everyone in fact apart from his wife who resolutely calls him Arthur.

The Sulzbergers were brought up partly in the City in a large brownstone at 5 East 80th Street, partly at the capacious family mansion at White Plains. George Plimpton, who was sent to the same New York prep school, St Bernard's, remembers Punch vividly at this period. 'A very pleasant little boy, left footed, he played football outside left. St Bernard's was an unusual place in many respects, unusual for New York, in that it was very, very British, started by a Mr Jenkins in the thirties. I think we were all aware, as children often are, that the Sulzbergers were a bit better off than most of the rest of our families. The great thing was to be invited to the enormous mansion at White Plains. I remember my first trip being collected in a huge limousine – I'm sure I've never seen a bigger one – and halfway up the Merritt Parkway the back wheel blew up. I remember we were required to stay in the back, not allowed out to help change the wheel, and I can still recall the great heave of the car as the chauffeurs (there were two) lifted it to fix the fresh tyre. That was the first time I realised other people were different from us.

'And then,' continued Plimpton, 'there was the house – just enormous, quite vast, with this ballroom with a model railroad on a track that you could ride round on. Punch loved to play hide and seek in that house because he knew all the corridors, all the backways. One time I was hunting for Punch and I had this pistol, a water pistol, ready to squirt when I found him. I opened a door at the end of a long corridor and found myself face to face with this very old lady propped up in bed on pillows with a nurse by her side. The sudden apparition of a young boy with a pistol must have frightened her very much because she died the next day. That was Mrs Adolph S Ochs, the old matriarch from the past.'

Punch Sulzberger's progress at St Bernard's was considered by his parents to be disappointing, and when dyslexia was diagnosed he was transferred to another fashionable school, the Browning. His performance did not improve and he grew despondent and belligerent. His mother, Iphigene, obtained him a summer job in the Department of Animal Behavior at the Museum of Natural History.

'It was sited in a penthouse on the roof,' Sulzberger later told the *New Yorker*. 'I was assigned the task of finding out whether or not turtles could hear. I constructed a great T-shaped box out on the roof, suspended two bells over it, and put some turtles in it. Then I rang a bell. If they turned in the direction of the bell, they would find that the food box was open. For a while, nothing happened. Maybe I never got the turtles hungry enough. One day – a Friday – they all turned the right way. I was so excited that I came in the next morning, when the department was officially closed, and repeated the experiment. This time, they all turned the wrong way. My experiment with the turtles ended inconclusively.'

His parents decided that he needed a break from New York so sent him as a boarder to the Loomis School in Windsor, Connecticut. Hardly had he arrived than he hit on the idea of going into the Marines. This initially struck the family as an eccentric notion, but he insisted and was eventually allowed to sign up.

'Before I entered the Marines, I was a lazy good-for-nothing,' he later told his mother. 'The Marines woke me up.'

The Marines episode lasted for 18 months where he served as a corporal (like his friend Lord Rothermere, he did his initial military service in the ranks), then completed a leisurely degree at Columbia University before being recalled by the Marines for the Korean War where he was bumped up to lieutenant. He has said, in his typically self-deprecating way, 'My family didn't worry about me for a minute. They knew that if I got shot in the head it wouldn't do any harm.'

Friends who knew him at this period say that Punch's success as a soldier startled them; he found the rhythm of military life, with its pleasingly surreal bureaucracy and long periods of structured in-activity, easy to adapt to, and his familiar Marines tie ('*That tie!*' – Conrad Black) is a memento of a happy period.

After the war he signed up as a reporter on the *Milwaukee Journal* where, he says, 'I was in charge of everybody who died. I wrote obits. I never got to meet my subjects.' Within 11 months, however, he had been subsumed into the family company; for a year he was appointed a roving foreign correspondent in France, Great Britain and Italy, a role that enabled him to rove most agreeably between hotel bar and smart party in whichever European capital city he chose, before returning to New York as assistant to the publisher.

Although Punch's father was the publisher in question at that time, he did not in fact return to West 43rd Street as the crown prince. It so happened that another man, his brother-in-law Orvil Dryfoos, was already being groomed to succeed. Dryfoos had been on the *Times* for 12 years, having joined it six months after his marriage to Punch's eldest sister Marian. Arthur Hays Sulzberger was a terrific fan of Dryfoos and had talked him into quitting Wall Street, where he had a seat on the Stock Exchange, and joining the newspaper with the prospect of eventually running it. Everyone who met the urbane, worldly Dryfoos was impressed by him. There are still portraits of him hanging all over the New York Times building: in one he is leaning against a desk like a handsome matinée idol with set jaw, resonating power and sophistication. When the 28-year-old Sulzberger appeared on the scene, Dryfoos, at 41, was indisputably heir apparent; what Sulzberger was heir to, if anything at all, was unclear.

The parallels of his predicament with that of the young Vere Rothermere at Associated Newspapers are really very striking. Like Rothermere, Punch Sulzberger had no clear role. 'Punch wasn't treated very well,' a colleague told the *New Yorker*. 'His family undersold him. He was kept away from the hub. His duties were ill-defined. He was a late developer. Some of us were asked to take care of him. He was never given an important job. He was briefly a copyreader on the foreign desk here. He was named assistant treasurer in 1957, but I doubt if he ever got into the treasurer's office. Punch was very fond of Orvil Dryfoos, and Orvil reciprocated this feeling, but the attitude of at least one of his superiors was "get that boy out of my way".'

Within five years, however, the course of the succession had altered utterly and dramatically. Arthur Hays Sulzberger suffered the first of a series of strokes that confined him to a wheelchair, and Orvil Dryfoos took over as publisher in 1961 while his father-in-law moved up to Chairman of the Board. Two years later, in the aftermath of the great printers' strike of 1963 when the *Times* failed to publish for 114 days, Dryfoos died of a heart attack. For 26 days of rumour and counter-rumour, the paper was without a publisher. It was said that on whichever floor the elevator doors opened, you would always find a little group of rumour-mongers congregated around a fire hydrant, each with his own privileged intelligence on what the Sulzberger family would or would not do. The only certainty was that the choice would be made by the voting trustees – Punch's father and mother – and they, when they'd gathered themselves from the family tragedy, chose their son. 'My son, Arthur Ochs Sulzberger, has more than proved himself over the many years he has been here,' was how Arthur Hays Sulzberger began his announcement in the *Times*. The appointment was additionally marked by an article in *Times Talk*, an in-house staff journal, entitled 'My Brother the Publisher' by his sister Ruth. This revealed:

'He never remembers anyone's name, but is impeccably skilful either in disguising the fact or making Old Nameless feel wanted. He is a strict housekeeper and compulsive neatener. He likes to catch planes and trains much too early, and is content to waste whole half hours just waiting for a departure to be announced. He thinks ahead about flat tyres' – and no wonder, after his schoolboy limo rides to White Plains with George Plimpton – 'and has a glove compartment in his car full of inflators, blinkers, patches and instant road-blockers.'

His enthusiasm for gadgetry of all kinds is immense. He has developed a golf machine at his country house in Stamford, Connecticut with a plunger and ball attached to a string that indicates the length, loft and angle of a drive. He likes to weed and dig in his garden wearing a special zip-in suit, of the kind Churchill wore during the War but with refinements of his own devising. He is an expert on electric light bulbs and barbecue equipment and is never happier than when puttering around in his workshop and instructing his grandchildren in carpentry and clay modelling. 'I think he must own every generation of every major household gadget that exists,' says the paper's executive editor Max Frankel. 'Corkscrews, knife sharpeners, a new type of tape recorder or alarm clock. I haven't been up to his country house in years but there are always new gadgets for planting, some barometer of a new type. And when you're discussing some problem with him in his office he'll say, "Well maybe they could make a plastic base for it and then this and that" and he'll start designing it all on his desk.'

Whether Punch Sulzberger is a decisive, canny businessman, or simply a charming putterer who found himself at the helm by lucky genes, lies at the heart of every estimation.

'The paper is the overriding concern of his life,' says his friend Sydney Gruson, 'and in the end *The New York Times* has been a huge success under him. He's the best publisher in America by far. You have to understand how well he's handled the organisation and kept it all together. If he didn't have a great aptitude for it, this wouldn't have happened.'

'Punch is kind of an opaque character,' says the veteran Manhattan editor Clay Felker who has worked for virtually every proprietor except Sulzberger. 'He gives the impression he's warm and friendly and jokey and informal but he's really rather cold blooded and even ruthless. It means nothing, surface jollity: he'll say, "Clay, my friend", but I don't reckon it goes very deep.'

'He's very unintrusive, very wise in a way that I think is frequently and mysteriously underestimated,' says *Times* managing editor Joseph Lelyveld. 'On major issues that affect news coverage and the news department I have the sense that we can rely absolutely on his support. When we talk about things, he asks very sensible, well-focused questions. He listens closely and very well and then when he takes his decision in a funny way you scarcely know it's been taken. No edict comes down, no big statement is made, no decree is issued, but the things move forward.'

'It's not an easy thing to talk about one's own boss objectively,' says executive editor Max Frankel, 'but to work for him is an enormous, enormous pleasure. He has an extraordinarily gentle hand, at least to those of us who are loyal to him. If you displease him, if you cross him, all you're likely to hear, if you listen carefully, is a question! "What made you do that?" or "What led us to do that?" That sort of thing. And if he feels like giving what would be called anywhere else a command he asks for your help. And this is not just a manner, this is the essence of the man. He asks wonderful questions – like his mother, indeed. They usually betray a very probing mind and a great respect for what he doesn't know. He's not ashamed to sound dumb in his questions which a lot of people in his position are incapable of doing, they'd rather not ask than betray a field of ignorance. In fact I've learned it from him. I was one of the people who went through much of his life worried that he would expose himself by asking dumb questions. Punch Sulzberger taught me that you can be respected and still ask dumb questions.'

Sydney Gruson, who worked closely with Sulzberger at the *Times* for a quarter of a century before becoming a senior advisor at Rothschild Inc, says of him, 'He was always my boss and he's a very easy man to work for. Some would say *too* easy, because he won't engage himself fully in the struggles that go on in an institution as large as *The New York Times*. He remains for many people above the fray. Which isn't always the best way since power has to reside somewhere and it tends to fall to other people. It's not so much that he's lazy, he's just *intellectually* lazy about it; he'll only involve himself where deadlock or a great impasse is concerned. Then he has an incredible sense of *what's right*. It isn't always *correct*. But when it's a case of what's *right* for the paper, it's almost a *fingerbitskerfould*, a feeling in the end of the fingers. Very few people ever get fired by Punch. They don't always get the jobs they want, but they don't get fired. You can't make everybody happy all the time, but he'll take a lot of trouble to make those that he cares for as happy as he can.'

'He's a gregarious, friendly guy, who likes the good fellowship of office parties,' another senior editor has said. 'He's a great conciliator. He likes everybody. He thinks that a trip together, a lunch together, a drink together will solve all problems.'

'He tries very hard, even when he has a small errand,' says Max Frankel, 'to make it a point of being seen and walking round the building. He'll call and say "I want to discuss something, have you got a few minutes?" and you say "I'll be right up" and he'll say "no, no, no, I'll be down".'

'In meetings,' says Gruson, 'he's mild. A very good listener but impatient of repetition. His critics would say he's got a short attention span, but I happen to like that sort of attention span for meetings. He runs a good meeting: gives everybody their say, doesn't believe in cutting them off. And when he makes up his mind he's damn near impossible to budge. Up to a certain point he's totally malleable, but no further. He doesn't like confrontation, he'll do anything to avoid it. He once said to my ex-wife, "I don't like being pushed into a corner, but if they do push me into a corner, they'd better watch out."

'As a friend,' Gruson went on, 'he's wonderful. Kind, considerate, a little intellectually lazy about friendship too! He's very *warm* to his friends, of whom he does not have very many close ones. I reckon he's hardly touched by the rest [of mankind]. His close friends are almost all journalists, Arthur Gelb and his wife, Jim Greenfield and his wife, the Grusons.'

'Is he a shy man?'

'Yes, I think sometimes he is,' says Joseph Lelyveld. 'In his various roles at the *Times* and as chairman of the Metropolitan Museum board he has sometimes to give a speech and I think he finds that a really wrenching experience.'

He also makes speeches at the Newspaper Publishers Association. Their tone is deadpan, jocular, sometimes sophomoric like the godfather of the bride making a speech at the wedding reception. When he gave the keynote address at the 1989 Chicago ANPA convention, he began: 'Thanks, Charlie, not only for those nice words, but, far more importantly, for your fine leadership in making this convention possible. With you at the helm, the Convention Arrangements Committee at the oars, and a strong breeze from the Windy City, we are bound for a memorable voyage!'

Later in the same address he broached the less familiar topic of free expression: 'Salman Rushdie, an author of Indian birth,' he proclaimed, 'published an almost incomprehensible novel called *The Satanic Verses*. The results were terrifying. A mad holy man reached across his country's borders and called for the author's death. Thousands riot, dozens are killed and normally brave defenders of free expression hunker down or bend with the wind. Undoubtedly, the book is offensive to many Muslims. But books are published, plays are written and movies produced throughout the year that are deemed offensive by some group or other. And civilised people have learned not to murder the librarian or bomb the theatre to express their distaste. In this case, the cruel, intolerant reach of the Ayatollah has touched us all. At times we have been afraid to cruise the Mediterranean or fly an American airline in Europe. Now we are afraid to go to the bookstore.'

'He moves about town a lot,' continued Lelyveld, 'knows a lot of people, sees a lot of people, but I think basically he's not really socially adventurous. He has an inner circle of friends he feels closest to and he goes to the same few restaurants.'

'After dealing with problems all day, he's very much a man to shuck off problems in the evening,' says Sydney Gruson, 'he hates sitting down to a hard intellectual discussion. Conversation at the *Times* tends to be pretty serious stuff and at the end of the day he likes to escape. What he likes to do is look at Western movies or read light biographies or go out to eat. He loves to choose steak. But this town is full of small, noisy Italian restaurants and that's where Punch likes to go too, he's a great frequenter of them. One of the worst things that can befall him is to be seated between two absolutely strange women at a dinner party. He'd be good, because he has a nice soft gentle quality, but he won't like it and he won't bestir himself to make himself fascinating to them. He doesn't really want to make new friends at this point in his life. He's very fond of his wife. Carol's not involved in the newspapers very directly, only in the sense that she's a very intelligent woman and knows the players quite well. She's not at all a me-too person, she has views of her own. She loves to go travelling with Punch. They recently got back from Eastern Europe – Berlin and Prague – and I guess that's par for the course. They don't go very much to the sun, Punch claims too much heat doesn't agree with him. He'd much rather go salmon fishing in Alaska or Canada. And when he plays golf he's happy as a sandboy. The last time we played golf together was over at Lyford Cay. We were on the very first hole: three good shots to the green, Punch bent over his cart to pick up a putter and *bingo*, his back went, seized up in spasms and he hasn't touched a golf club since as far as I know.

'What's remarkable about him,' Gruson said, 'is the way he's almost impervious to flattery. He is the object as you can imagine of a good deal of – I was going to say idolatry, but flattery will do.

'We were discussing someone on a particular occasion and I said, "He's an awful person".

'Punch replied, "Oh I don't know, he's always been very nice to *me*."

'I said to him, "Will you name me *anyone* who hasn't been very nice to you and your family? Everyone in this town is very nice to the Sulzbergers of *The New York Times*." '

In one respect Punch Sulzberger is unique among newspaper owners: he attends his newspaper's daily page-one news conference to discuss the headlines. Every afternoon at five minutes to five he takes the lift down from the 14th to the editorial floor and pulls up a chair at the conference table alongside the executive editor, managing editor, picture editor, foreign editor and the rest of the dozen or so senior staff. Apart from the Grahams in Washington and, in his heyday, Otis Chandler in Los Angeles, who will breeze into the conference when a major story breaks to plug into the adrenalin, no other proprietor in the world has either the time or the wish or indeed the presumption to sit in on conference. Would the others do so if they could? Some would probably like to. It is not hard to imagine Conrad Black wrapping his tongue around global news priorities, or Rupert Murdoch or Dean Singleton or Ralph Ingersoll or Samir Jain. But only Punch Sulzberger, and now increasingly his son Arthur, actually does so as a matter of routine.

'I'll tend to sit myself on the sidelines to listen and learn, it is a great way of picking up on the way our people are thinking,' Sulzberger told me, sounding curiously like Rosalynn Carter explaining her decision to sit in on her husband's White House cabinet meetings.

Arthur Hays Sulzberger never attended conference, and the story goes that, shortly after assuming control of the newspaper, Punch asked the then managing editor whether there was a 'Keep Out' sign on the door or would he be welcome to sit at the back. The managing editor replied as follows: 'My answer to you is the same as my answer to Marshal Field who asked a similar question when he owned the Chicago *Sun*: "For what you pay, you can sit in anywhere you want to".'

Sit in, but not contribute. That anyway is how Punch Sulzberger has always interpreted his position. The debate will rage around him, over him, across him, editors will argue, postulate and extrapolate, but Punch will keep quiet, interested and a trifle quizzical, like a parent at a school debating contest, the difference being, of course, that he is paying the whole school's fees. His editors will discuss the City's politics, candidates for President, ecology, the onset of the next world war, but unless a direct question is put to Punch Sulzberger he wouldn't dream of advancing an opinion of his own.

'I don't know what it would take to get Punch to chip in,' says one of his team. 'If we were debating whether or not his own apartment at ten-ten Fifth Avenue overlooking the Met should be demolished, he might say something. But there again he might not.'

In other forums, however, he can make his proprietorial preferences very clear.

'We have lunch with him fairly frequently and go over our various long-range reporting enterprises,' says Joseph Lelyveld. 'Not in the sense of him grilling us, just keeping him posted and if something goes badly off the tracks he's capable of being quite distressed.'

'Does he look distressed?'

'*Pained.* We got into a big flap over naming the victim of that rape case in Palm Beach with Kennedy's nephew. We didn't do it mindlessly, we'd been wrestling with this issue for several years. We'd had an ongoing debate about when you do this and when you don't do it, and it finally seemed to us that it had reached the point [to name her]. I think we were clearly wrong. Much of the staff felt we were clearly wrong. There was a lot of internal discussion. Punch, who was in London at the time, felt we were clearly wrong and I happened to go to London on another mission and we had lunch together – at Claridges – and we talked about the whole thing and he listened to how we got to the point we were at, and expressed his reservations about it all.'

'Was that an occasion when he looked pained?'

'Yeah. Very pained. But it was interesting because he was following all this from afar, he was talking to a lot of people about it, he knew about it but *he wasn't calling in and saying "What the hell are you guys doing?"* And when he was informed he wasn't timid about saying what he felt, but he said it characteristically in a very understated way. Asked a lot of good questions, for some of which I didn't have very good answers. He's more than courteous and sort of avuncular in a way and friendly, collegian. But it made me very aware of him as the ultimate custodian of the standards of the paper and that's a role he plays with enormous tact.

'At the same time,' says Lelyveld, 'he really supports the independence of the news department and on major issues – the Gulf War, the collapse of the Soviet system, one of these huge stories that just busts budgets – we don't need to ask anybody around here how far we can go. We know there is an unstated assumption that we can do everything we have to do on the great stories. So we'll go for it. As an editor I've never had any doubts about that. And nobody around here says, "Well, do we really need to send that many people?" '

'Is this simply because he's competitive for the paper?'

'Yeah sure. He assumes we are too. But he knows, he sure knows. He sees the other papers. He has a text terminal in his office and he roams around in our various directories and keeps informed. He likes to read summaries and stories. Who knows what he reads? He knows the system and he uses it.'

'Very few people have bothered to review the record of what Punch has accomplished,' said Max Frankel. 'Back in the seventies the great story is what he did in rescuing this paper from poverty. It was an excellent newspaper but it really had come upon hard times, along with New York. It had unions that wouldn't let it automate, and from there until about 1987 it was quite a miraculous turnaround. Many people wrote about its hard times but very few have written about that.'

Punch Sulzberger's accomplishments, or rather the accomplishments of his tenure which isn't exactly the same thing, are straightforward. This is what he's done:

1. Acquired separate streams of income by buying a stable of magazines (*Family Circle, McCall's*, numerous golf, sailing and tennis monthlies), television stations and new newspapers, particularly in the South. The point of these acquisitions wasn't simply for straight profit so much as for a steady flow of alternative income for a specific reason. It gave him leverage with the unions at *The New York Times*. As Max Frankel puts it, 'He could say to them "Now look here, the days when we regarded it as the end of the world to lose a day's publication are over. We're either going to have a war or we're going to talk about how we will both benefit from automation". And that was the beginning of a long and arduous and ultimately successful negotiation, and eventually, after many decades of battling, we were able to move into the twentieth century. Now, in a different sense, these negotiations are continuing into the second generation but that, I guess, will be Arthur Sulzberger Jnr's life's work not Punch's.'

2. Streamlined *The New York Times* management. 'We had always been journalistically excellent,' says Frankel, 'but we had never been the kind of place a business school would turn to to admire our management. But he saw to that. He prided himself on not necessarily his *own* management but on the management matter. And we finally began to budget properly and to sell advertising

and not just take it down over the phone and so on. I'm exaggerating of course, but he is aggressive about recruiting the right team.

3. Promoted, endorsed – some still insist invented – the special subject sections that first appeared in *The New York Times*, then became part of the infrastructure of every significant newspaper around the world: the special business sections, the food, lifestyle, science, sports sections that seem now so obvious, so inevitable but were considered a risk, a financial gamble, even a trivialisation when first mooted. 'And he was always careful,' says Frankel, 'not to do it at the expense of foreign coverage, national coverage and what other people would call harder and serious journalism, so no one had to be ashamed of working at the *Times* or accuse him of money grabbing or selling out to the reader. But none the less the paper, in his day, came to look very different from what it had been. Quite a remarkable achievement at a time when all other newspapers here were dying.'

Arthur Ochs Sulzberger Jnr – son and heir known as Pinch to outsiders, though not generally to insiders and never to his face – was waiting for me in his office, seated not behind his substantial teak desk but upon an oatmeal-coloured sofa in the video-viewing section of the room. Facing him was a giant grey-faced cybernetic screen, already turning toytown blue as a printing plant filled its great expanse.

'Before going into questions I'm going to show you a video,' said Pinch. 'Our new plant at Edison, New Jersey. Until you've seen what we're doing over there, it's futile asking questions.'

At the age of 40, Arthur Ochs Sulzberger Jnr might best be described as vehement. With his jacket looped over the back of his chair, tan-coloured braces defiantly exposed, a full head of wavy brown hair and a steely, no-bullshit gleam in his eye, he conveys the clear message that he is vigorous, driven and impatient to the point of exasperation.

The video rolled through the opening credits, and a mellifluous voice-over shepherded us towards the mighty new printing plant, recently completed but not yet operational.

'The company's newest and most expansive enterprise,' intoned the voice-over, sounding like the soundtrack to a Disney *Wonderful World of Nature* documentary, 'is the New York Times's automated one-million-square-foot colour printing and distribution facility at Edison . . .'

Pinch Sulzberger suppressed the volume for a moment. 'That's the size of 22 football fields,' he said.

On screen we saw the interior of an immense empty hall, as deep as several convention centres, its roof supported by bright blue and green girders, the floor covered by what appeared to be bright blue railroad tracks, scores of them laid in parallel lines along the whole length of the building.

The mellifluous voice was saying, 'The Muller Martini print roll storage system can hold more than a thousand 9.5-foot rolls of the *Times*'s Sunday sections for insertion into the paper. This automated storage system will help to reduce costs. Rolls will be loaded on to the tracks by robot carriers, "cousins" of the IDAP automatic guided vehicles used for other transport chores.'

Pinch Sulzberger broke in again. 'Other newspapers have *some* of this,' he said, 'but nobody, *nobody* at this size and scope. This is new . . . I don't think anyone does this. It actually puts the roll on to the press itself. It clocks it.'

The voice-over became increasingly awestruck. Sometimes it dipped to a deferential whisper, as though some rare caribou was grazing nearby in the Saskatchewan tundra and mustn't be disturbed.

'The climate in the Edison plant is entirely management controlled, allowing 65 per cent more air-conditioning than the Times's West 43rd Street capacity.

'The Muller Martini storage and retrieval system incorporates five miles of conveyors, and 1950 storage wheels.

'The black ink tanks at Edison each have a 12,000 gallon capacity.

'The Edison facility is located 31 miles from New York City on 86 acres of land just off the New Jersey Turnpike at the intersection of route 287. This location will provide excellent access for delivery to all points – east, west, north and south. A Conrail freight spur will deliver newsprint directly into the facility . . .'

The facts being relayed began to assume a surreal quality. The technical information overload was so great that it no longer seemed to have any connection with newspapers. This was technology at its most scary. It could have been a NASA space programme or an advanced munitions factory that was being described. No wonder the labour unions went into a blue funk when they realised exactly what was being constructed off the New Jersey Turnpike. Barely a single human being was visible during the entire film.

I asked Sulzberger, 'When do you expect to start printing on this?'

He shrugged. 'We're not going to open this plant until we've got agreements with *all* of our unions on levels of manning.'

'Won't that be difficult to achieve? It doesn't look like you need *any* manning.'

He shrugged again. 'We're working on it,' he said. 'It'll take time. You can't expect people to alter their working practices straight away. It takes negotiation. Lots of negotiation.'

He laughed. It was a laugh that, ostensibly at least, was a weary laugh, but it sounded a pretty determined laugh.

'The creation of Edison breaks the log jam here,' he said. 'And Edison also replaces Carlstadt, seven or eight miles that way' – he gestured through the window beyond the port of New York – 'where we do much of our printing now.'

When he spoke about Edison a strange, almost obsessive gleam came into his eyes. This printing press, he knows, is the key not only to the paper's financial future, but to his whole conception of its *content* under his stewardship.

'This Muller Martini system offers us staggering flexibility in the way we operate . . . in the way we create a newspaper,' he said, eyes rotating at the thought of it all. 'With Edison we could produce a 160-page paper in eight sections *every day if we so chose*. We can print 70,000 impressions an hour, as opposed to 48,000 at Carlstadt. We could print colour in every single section *if we so chose*, colour for arts and leisure, colour for sport, travel, real estate. You see it could truly change the *whole nature* of *The New York Times*.'

'Where did you teach yourself about printing plants?' I asked.

'Boston. We designed this with a firm up in Boston. Not in London,' he noted, looking hard and meaningfully at me. 'London is not the centre for newspapers it once was.' When he'd allowed time for this undermining piece of information to sink in, he added, 'The presses themselves are Swiss. In the end you're looking at a billion dollar investment.'

'How's your colour going to compare with the new presses being installed in Japan and Singapore?' I asked, keen to reassert London's primacy as an information centre if nothing else.

Sulzberger looked temporarily nonplussed. 'You gotta excuse me,' he replied at last. 'I don't know what's happening with colour in Japan or Singapore.' Then he made a quick, scribbled note on a little pad by his side. I expect it read: 'Memo to self. Investigate on-the-run color in Japan, Singapore.'

'The colour we're looking for,' he said, 'is very low-key, very sophisticated colour. It's not going to be the kind of colour Americans are used to seeing. Not *USA Today* colour.'

As so often in *The New York Times* there are two camps on colour. Half the company, including Punch Sulzberger it is said, would be perfectly happy to stagger on without any colour at all as they've done for 139 years; the other half, championed by Pinch, can hardly wait for the yellow, magenta and cyan inks to start flowing down the brightly coloured tubes installed and ready for that purpose.

'Are a lot of your colleagues still opposed to colour?'

'Undoubtedly. *Change* in the words of the philosopher *sucks*, alright?'

He stood up to adjust the hands of a brass carriage clock that had somehow gained or lost a minute over the last six months. On the shelves next to the clock was an array of books on psychology and a large collection of pipes, clay pipes, rustic pipes, gnarled pipes, pipes with intricately carved bowls and stems. Arthur Ochs Sulzberger Jnr has assembled two collections in his lifetime. His collection of pipes is displayed in his office; his collection of British and American walking sticks is kept at home.

'With colour,' he said, 'we've got to prove one thing only. And that's that colour won't change the nature of *The New York Times* any more than going from eight-column pages to six-column pages changed *The Times*, or the addition of photographs, or going from a one-section to a four-section newspaper changed it.'

'And what are you going to publish in your bigger coloured newspapers that you can't publish now?'

Sulzberger looked thoughtful. 'Whatever it is,' he replied, 'that our readers need but don't yet know they need.

'That's the interesting one,' he said, 'finding out what that thing is. Like when we created Science Times on Tuesday. It was the fifth special section we launched, and the advertising side were all pressing us for fashion – "we want fashion on Tuesdays". But the news department said, "No. We've already given you four days of supplements with obvious commercial implications. We want one day for us. And we want science." The ad department said, "*Science*? There are no ads in science. Not *one* ad in science." But we went ahead with the science section and then one day some guy invented the personal computer and then, boom, the ads flooded in. And readers love the science section best. You could have asked them in market research surveys and they would never have said science, but it filled a void. Now we need to ask: where's our *next* Science Times?'

'Are you working on it? Who comes up with new ideas for sections? You? The editors?'

'We have committees,' he replied. 'Small groups. Some long-serving staff members, consultants. It's highly informal. I have many friends who are journalists and we discuss things. And colleagues on other papers I keep up with, like Don Graham in Washington and Jay Smith in Atlanta. And friends too who *aren't* journalists. My best friends are lawyers, painters, business people, investment bankers, journalists; it's one of the joys of living in New York, you can mix it up like that. And through seeing these people, it helps you know focus on new ideas.'

'What about buying new newspapers abroad. I know your father has resisted it, but is there a paper you hanker after?'

'*Isvestia*. I'd like *Isvestia*. Think of the opportunity. The size of the market, the whole Soviet commonwealth, and more than that: the ability to take a name, a great name, and create great newspapering around that. Not just the news but the *business* too.'

The strange, obsessive gleam was flickering again. In his mind's eye he could perhaps already see the million-square-foot printing plant outside Moscow at Yegoryevsk, the storage and retrieval systems, the robots and freight spurs and ducts of magenta ink.

But then he laughed. 'One shouldn't think of it. I've got $450 million already invested here and another $450 million to come. And I need new production facilities in Boston, new facilities in Washington. I need new facilities in Denver, Kansas City, and hell, I can't even afford Edison any more. Some days I don't think I can even afford *that* right now.'

*

Notwithstanding his position as eldest child and only son of Arthur Ochs Sulzberger Snr, it was not a foregone conclusion that Arthur Ochs Sulzberger Jnr would eventually succeed his father. And, indeed, this far he has only partially done so; his appointment as publisher of the flagship *New York Times* does not guarantee him the senior job as chairman of the whole New York Times Company. The family is overrun with competent grandchildren of Arthur Hays and Iphigene, many of them working in the company. All the diligent ones are owed significant roles in the long run. And there is another reason that Pinch Sulzberger's birthright has never been inevitable: he is the child of Punch's first, brief, fractious marriage to Barbara Grant Sulzberger (as she generally styles herself despite being twice re-married), the still-beautiful New Yorker with a reputation for being highly strung. Arthur Jnr was brought up along with his younger sister Karen, by their mother in an apartment 20 blocks away from their father, who within a year of the divorce had remarried. This second – and present – wife, Carol, already had one child by a previous marriage, Cathy, then bore another, Cynthia; so there was a parallel family of Sulzbergers for Arthur Jnr to contend with. It would be possible, if one so wished, to devise a mawkish psychological profile of the young Sulzberger, the child of the rejected mother, anxious about his relationship with his father, contrasting the coherence and warmth of the second family with his own, but since he shared this predicament with half the children in New York, there would be little merit in it. Just such a portrait in *Manhattan Inc* suggested that 'Punch has enormous amounts of fine qualities, but he has trouble getting close to people and there was, at that time, a bit of distance between father and son' and that, when Arthur Jnr went round to his father's apartment 'he saw a stepsister and a baby half-sister who were accepted as part of the family, and [he couldn't] help feeling that [he was] missing out.' But this is all guesswork. Certainly at weekends when he was driven up the Merritt Parkway – in Punch's Chrysler stationwagon, not a stretch limo – to his grandmother's Hillandale estate in Connecticut, he was absorbed into the extended Sulzberger family with its numerous cousins from the Golden, Cohen and Dryfoos clans.

Surprisingly for the eldest son of an *ancien* Jewish family, Arthur

Jnr was brought up at his mother's behest as an Episcopalian and confirmed at that most definitive of Upper East Side churches, St James on Madison Avenue. In his book *The Search for God at Harvard*, Ari L. Goldman, a former religious correspondent for *The New York Times*, recalls a conversation with Arthur Sulzberger Jnr in which he had described his 'betwixt and between state' – a child of a prominent Jewish family raised as an Episcopalian who now subscribes to neither religion very seriously. 'Ninety-nine out of 100 people consider me Jewish,' he is reported to have said. 'How could a Sulzberger not be Jewish?'

He was sent to school at one of his father's alma maters, Browning, but with greater academic success. He was always bright. By the time he was 13, however, his relationship with his mother had encountered turbulence and a scheme to send him off to boarding school was gaining momentum. He announced to his mother that, love her as he did, he had decided to leave home and live permanently with his father. It was a resolution that seemed to imply more than a transient adolescent preference for one parent.

From his new, larger but somewhat baby-sister-dominated apartment, Pinch completed school, did four years at Tufts where he majored in political science, then a journalistic stint in North Carolina on the *Raleigh Times*. Photographs at this period show him pitching up for work on a Harley Davidson in a black leather jacket with sheepskin collar, denim shirt, jeans and a studded belt with Apache silver buckle. His John Lennon-style glasses, long, lank hair and vaguely petulant mouth give him a troubled air. As a reporter he was considered thorough and engaged: 'mixing it up with people on the scene. He did a lot that young Yankee reporters aren't necessarily good at,' Chris Sherman, now an editor at the *Orlando Sentinel*, told *Manhattan Inc.*

By this point his mother had divorced her second husband, the Wall Street banker David Christy, and moved with her third husband to Topeka, Kansas. During one of his visits, Arthur was introduced by his mother to the girl who literally lived next door, a rather pretty, on the ball brunette named Gail Gregg. Eighteen months later they were married in the backyard of the Greggs' home and Pinch's side of the family included, in addition to his own mother and father, one stepmother, two stepfathers, his sister, his half-sister, his stepsister, one half-brother and the numerous Golden, Cohen and Dryfoos cousins. Sulzberger and Gail Gregg (she generally retains her maiden name) moved to London, Arthur to work for the Associated Press Agency, Gail to take up a parallel job at UPI. Arthur Sulzberger described this to me as 'a great period for us both. We both worked on stories, sometimes even the same stories. Gail usually wrote them better. She beat me on stories. She was a fine journalist. But she's given that up now, partly I guess because of me. And with the kids around' [they have two young children that they both help look after] 'she took the decision to become an artist instead. She paints.'

Returning to the United States he joined *The New York Times* for the first time: initially deployed in the Washington bureau, later on the Metropolitan staff in New York. Contemporaries in Washington ('where I was a congressional correspondent, which meant some days great stories, some days – long days – with not so great stories' he told me) remember him as pliant, professional, eager to do whatever was asked of him. Like Donald Graham at the same age, he was curious about Washington at all levels, not only at the political. He was something of an idealist about good journalism, especially news. And, in an unobtrusive way, he was fiercely competitive. When the *Washington Post* covered a situation more sharply, more fully than *The New York Times* he minded. Back in New York on the Metro desk he would typically file a couple of stories a week. This was mostly brisk way-we-live-now journalism. A representative piece was a report on how a neglected brownstone in Park Slope was stripped by scavengers right down to the cast iron pipes of the bathtub, which were dismantled 'so the lead joints – worth pennies each – could be taken'. His writing style, one notices, often incorporates Anglophile vocabulary: here pennies each, not cents.

His route to the Publisher's job, though by no means uneventful, was at least more foreseen than that of his father. 'I'm a journalist who happened to get off at the wrong floor,' is what he says, and he makes a point of knowing as many journalists on the paper as possible. He arranges dinner parties at home for reporters and columnists and 'seems determined', says one colleague, 'to get to know all one thousand people in the newsroom'. Most guests seem to enjoy these evenings. 'They're informal, usually held in the kitchen,' says one. 'His wife is a nice lady and you can say whatever's on your mind about the *Times*. It's a pleasant, easy way to communicate with a Sulzberger.' Others are harshly – to my mind churlishly – critical. 'He'll invite a whole bunch over from the staff and expect them to be open about their opinions of the paper. Would *you* be open? Nobody fucking says *anything*.' Or else they suggest that there is something undermining, even disloyal, to the senior editors, about Sulzberger conducting a supper-meeting at which questions of office morale and editing policy must inevitably emerge. 'Can you imagine how Max Frankel feels with his staff socialising with *his* boss?' asked *New York* magazine.

How Max Frankel actually feels is sanguine, unless he is simply expert at appearing so. 'Arthur now knows almost everybody on the staff and makes it a point that, if we hire somebody, within a few months that person is likely to be invited to a small dinner with Arthur. He sees people too on an individual basis when we hire them. He *wants* to know people. And he's doing the same on the business side. He's deeply involved in getting to know not only the people but the problems and the things that are on their mind. He sees it as a great learning opportunity.'

The learning curve. That is an expression Pinch uses a lot. You sometimes feel when you talk to him that learning – learning about the business, learning more about himself – is part of a very conscious programme of self-improvement. At weekends he puts himself through endurance tests, rock climbing in upstate New York or in Utah. 'He's crazy on all those outward bound trips that all the young networkers like Michael Kramer go on,' I was told. 'The days in Utah, guys being guys, learning to depend on one another.'

The expression 'hands-on' could have been invented for Arthur Ochs Sulzberger Jnr. There is no area of *The New York Times* that does not absorb him. The same almost obsessional interest he has for printing presses extends to everything else: distribution, newsprint, warehousing, the make and height of chairs that journalists sit upon and whether they are orthopaedically beneficial, budgets, delivery-truck fleets, pension schemes, marketing, expenses, deployment of staff. Whether or not they consider all these matters the right and proper preserve of the Publisher and heir to the newspaper, funda-mentally colours people's opinion of Pinch Sulzberger.

'Pinch has joined the bean counters,' some colleagues say. 'He reads every report, everything he can suck into his office. He is a vacuum cleaner. He will second-guess every decision anyone's ever made. He sends notes to Frankel and Lelyveld all day long, suggesting they do this or that. And he's not always subtle about it. He can be unnecessarily tactless. He has none of Punch's diplomacy and common sense.'

The charges against Pinch, simply put, are these:

He is unprepared, as he assumes command of the paper, to allow everything to remain just as it was before. He is too publicly eager to shake things up, too intolerant of the loyal old retainers who have produced *The New York Times*, every day from before he was born. He sends directives to department heads inviting them to single out the dead wood and ship it out. He has made it clear that the paternalistic culture of the company does not extend to employing non-productive staff members until they choose to retire.

'When I first started at the paper, the *Times* had a place for people who had served it well and were burning out,' one former reporter has commented. 'Now you can't grow old gracefully at the *Times* any more.'

Pinch is abrupt. He sets targets for progress: 'By October we must achieve such and such'.

He is motivated by the bottom line and profit margins: 'He wants those margins of 17 and 18 per cent.' Like Samir Jain of *The Times of India* (who so admires Pinch's priorities, though they have never yet met) he reveres market research and is more inclined, say some, to put his faith in a dossier of research statistics than in the *fingerspitzgefühl* of his editors. Above anything, they complain, he has allowed the idealism of youth, his idealism as a journalist, to be extinguished by his responsibilities as a bean counter; that nothing matters to him quite so much as being applauded by one and all as a cool-headed, objective businessman.

The defence of Arthur Sulzberger Jnr is less emotive.

What on earth, you ask, would be the purpose of owning a newspaper if you were inhibited from expressing your own point of view. And many of the questions Pinch is asking, the changes he's imposing, are the same questions and changes that are churning every other newspaper in the world. 'Arthur Sulzberger,' Donald Graham told me, 'is the best-trained Publisher that newspaper – any newspaper – ever got. I think he's absolutely terrific: well prepared, smart, just what that paper needs.' Graham has also said, 'One of the great things about being the Publisher's son is that people's expectations are so low. But in the case of Arthur, I think it is an unbelievable piece of good fortune for the *Times* that he's as good as he is.'

And what else is Pinch Sulzberger expected to do other than take control? Should he sit in his office like Lord Copper, his head empty of thought, sketching upon his writing pad a little picture of a cow? It would be reckless to delegate entirely to others the great questions of distribution, newsprint, warehousing (though perhaps not ortho-paedic benefits of office furniture). And extravagant to preside without comment over the most highly staffed newspaper in the world, content to pay salaries to staff members who long ago lost sight of any connection between the profession of journalism and the publication of articles. Rash too to affect a vainglorious disdain for market research when *The New York Times* has one of the most complex readerships, demographically and ethnically, in the world.

Exactly who the 1.2 million daily readers of *The New York Times* are, and who might be inclined to read it in 20 years' time, is the toughest question for Pinch Sulzberger and his contentious cohorts of market researchers. If you circle the ten blocks around the *Times* building itself it is easy enough to find candidates who *aren't* reading it. The demographics of New York are changing so rapidly, argues Sulzberger, that every preconception about editorial content needs to be examined. According to the 1990 census, New York is now 43 per cent white, 28 per cent black, 24 per cent Latino and 7 per cent Asian. What is it that we publish, he might ask, of any possible interest to a second generation Chinese in Chinatown, to a Vietnamese, a Korean, a Pole, a Harlem black or a Puerto Rican in Crown Heights? 'We can't be local,' Punch Sulzberger has said, 'we're not New York's home-town paper. We're read on Park Avenue, but we don't do well in Chinatown or the East Bronx. We have to approach journalism differently than, say, the Sarasota *Herald Tribune* where you try to blanket the community.' Pinch, however, is concerned that the paper's preoccupation with international news has lessened its relevance to its powerbase. The *Times*'s penetration – the percentage of metropolitan households that buy the paper regularly – is lower than its peers across the country: the *Washington Post* has an average penetration of 62 per cent; the *Los Angeles Times* and *Chicago Tribune* around 24 to 25 per cent; *The New York Times* finds its way into only 10 per cent of homes. When Arthur Ochs Sulzberger looks out of his office window he sees a polyglottal society in which many groups – white as much as non-white – are finding his newspaper worryingly peripheral. So much of the coverage that had always seemed so appropriate for the *Times*'s readership – the wedding announcements, the Manhattan party photographs of the week, the recommended Sunday brunches and so on – succeed only, found the market research, in inducing estrangement in Chinatown, Grosse Pointe, Palo Alto. Sulzberger and his editors (and especially the editors) looked on with horror from behind a one-way mirror as focus groups of intelligent people said they had little interest in picking up a big fat copy of *The New York Times*. And the white middle-class readers, for whom the Sunday brunch listings had once been so serviceable, are moving further and further out of the City, to zip codes where Otis Chandler and the Los Angeles Times Company's *Newsday* is poised to seduce them.

Sulzberger's response is twofold. He is urging his editors to review the paper section by section, page by page, column inch by column inch, as though they were starting again from scratch. 'If we were starting anew, what would we do?' And he is championing a mindset that he calls 'a multiplicity of responses'.

'Pinch has a lot of grand thoughts about where this country is going and how the paper should respond,' says one *Times* man who has heard him on the subject. 'He believes that we're living in a society where traditional institutions are becoming less significant. He sees outside forces – whether foreign investment, Italian designs or Canadian fishing disputes – as playing a bigger role, making for a more diverse world in which we've got to operate.'

He talks of a future in which the *Times* will be comprised of three different papers, each with its own tone: a metropolitan edition for New York and its suburbs that will become more of a hometown paper – a paper to engross Chinatown and the East Bronx as much as the Upper East Side; a regional edition for the Eastern Seaboard, and an enlarged version of the national edition. Pinch's vision embraces satellite printing, plants all over the place like Gannett's *USA Today*, zoned home delivery, short press runs. And it embraces, too, a higher proportion of racial minorities working on his paper as journalists. This is a particular crusade of Sulzberger's. At a conference of the

National Association of Black Journalists in Kansas City, he spoke enthusiastically of creating more jobs and promotions for minorities in the newsroom, and entreated the association to 'keep pushing'. He gives as his reasons both the 'moral imperatives' of affirmative action and that 'diversity makes good business sense in these current tough economic times'; in other words, a raft of Chinese and black reporters might empathise more closely with, or at least interpret more lucidly, those sections of New York society beyond the ken of the main newsroom.

'We haven't set numerical targets,' says Joseph Lelyveld, 'but I think we've begun to achieve a critical mass of really talented and important [black] people at the *Times*. Not just a kind of statistical ratio but people who will matter. So when the key editors meet to take important decisions about the direction of the paper, they won't all be taken by a bunch of white males. I think this certainly feels right to Arthur Sulzberger, and that's probably the prime motivation. He's sensibly aware that if we don't have diversity in the newsroom our coverage is going to suffer. I don't think any of us believe that blacks cover black stories better than whites do or anything like that – it's not that mechanistic – but a mixture of backgrounds and sensibilities is crucial for pushing the paper forward in its broadest sense.'

Newspaper dynasties that have held on to their titles for more than 80 years are surprisingly scarce: there are none at all in the Far East, none on mainland Europe; one only in England – the Rothermeres; none in South America, Australia or the Middle East, one in Canada – the Thomsons, one in Asia – the Bilgins, owners of *Sabah* in Istanbul; and three, if you stretch the point, in the United States: the Chandlers, Grahams and Sulzbergers. One of Robert Maxwell's more self-deluding pronouncements was that the global communications empire he was forging would endure 'beyond the end of the next century' – beyond 2100 – but in fewer than six years it was broken up and sold off. During the early phase of the Sulzberger story, it seemed doubtful that their own communications empire would endure even that long.

Adolph Ochs – grandfather of Punch, great-grandfather of Pinch – who launched the New York Times dynasty, began his career aged 11 as a delivery boy for the local newspaper, the *Knoxville Chronicle* in a small town in Tennessee near the Great Smokey mountains. Leaving school the following year he worked first at a grocer's, then a drugstore, didn't enjoy either so obtained a job as tea boy and printer's devil at the *Chronicle*: his duties included polishing up brass lamps and refilling type cases. By the time he was 19 he had worked on a number of small papers in Tennessee, on the printing machines or selling advertising, including a stint on a new newspaper in Chattanooga that failed. It so happened that the rival paper in Chattanooga, the *Times* – the paper that somehow or other had beaten off the newcomer's challenge – itself ran into difficulties at this point. Ochs, aged 20, decided to buy a half-interest, borrowing $300 from the local bank. There were those who thought he had overpaid, since circulation had fallen below 250 copies and most subscribers and advertisers didn't bother to settle their bills. Somehow or other, with vintage frontiersman initiative, Ochs succeeded in turning the enterprise around, installed a new press in this dusty town with no sidewalks, weathered the Tennessee yellow fever epidemic that wiped out half his readers, all the while refusing to publish slander (then, as now, the normal way of enticing new readers) and being thoroughly public spirited. Within ten years he had become rather rich by Chattanooga standards, but unfortunately the run of luck was to end. It so happened, according to his daughter Iphigene in her memoirs of the same name, that Chattanooga became the focus of a hysterical land boom. People got it into their heads that this particular town, where many of the locals still carried pistols in holsters when they went to the shops, was poised to become the Pittsburgh of the South, a great railway hub, and real estate prices increased ten, 20 times in a year. Adolph Ochs, along with everyone else, bought heavily, and when the boom was declared a false alarm he lost, along with everyone else, virtually all his money. The printing plant was pledged as collateral against his debts and he set off to New York in search of further loans, travelling on foot from bank to bank to save on cab fares, in an attempt to hold on to the paper.

It was at this inauspicious low point of his career that *The New York Times* came up for sale. Ochs would say afterwards that as soon as he'd heard it was available (by telegram, sent by a friend on the staff) he knew he must get it. The loans he sought from the New York bankers, still visited on foot, became larger. Few of them thought that this pedestrian Tennessee debtor from Chattanooga was necessarily the man to take on *The New York Times*, particularly since the *Times* itself was on its knees. It was the number four newspaper in the City (two of its competitors were owned by Joseph Pulitzer and William Randolph Hearst) and circulation had fallen to 9000; an almost unattainably bad sale in a city the size of New York. Weekly losses, scaled up for inflation, were almost as severe as those of the *New York Daily News* when Robert Maxwell (whose own debts, scaled down for inflation, must have matched those of Adolph Ochs) acquired the city's number three paper with a circulation of 600,000.

The discouragement of the majority of the bankers was exceeded only by that of Ochs's family back home in Chattanooga. All too aware that they'd probably lose their local paper, they were aghast at the idea of buying another lame duck. But Adolph Ochs was convinced that only by expanding could he survive and the negotiations in New York continued. The bankers, impressed by Ochs's stamina, proposed a compromise; he was invited to run, rather than own, the paper for a salary of $50,000, about a million dollars a year today. He declined, holding out for ownership. Eventually the bankers, who included J P Morgan, agreed to a complicated deal involving deferred stock. Adolph Ochs and his family effectively owned and controlled *The New York Times*.

That they have succeeded in retaining control (if not absolute ownership) of the paper since 1896 only emphasises how well they have been advised. The stock, right from the start, was closely held. Until 1969, when the company was first traded on the American stock exchange, it was wholly private. Punch Sulzberger remembers as a child that 'our financial statement was a closely guarded secret. It was really studied by only three people – Dad, Godfrey Nelson [the financial director] and Julie Adler [a cousin]. It wasn't published. I understand that at the annual meeting it was passed around rather rapidly and then recaptured by Mr Nelson.' When Adoph Ochs died he left complex trusts that benefited his daughter Iphigene and his grandchildren. The trust for Iphigene Ochs Sulzberger held 83.7 per cent of the New York Times Company's Class B voting stock, which is not publicly traded and elects nine of the 14 board members. Class A stock, with limited voting rights, was held by about 15,000 individuals and institutions in 1990, and elects the remaining five board members. With the death of Mrs Sulzberger her strategic Class B shares passed to four new trusts benefiting her four children, 13 grandchildren and 24 great-grandchildren, and extends 21 years beyond the lifetime of her last surviving descendant alive on 5 August 1986. On the same day in 1986 an agreement was drawn up for the grandchildren and great-grandchildren that provides for no sale of Class B stock outside the family unless it is offered first to all the other family members, then to the newspaper company itself at the same price as Class A shares. And in the event of the company not wanting it (or not being able to afford it) the voting shares still have to be converted to sterile A shares before they can be sold. In other words the Sulzbergers have made it practically impossible for any voting stock to be passed to an outsider for about a hundred years. No Murdoch, no Maxwell, no Chandler or Singleton or Ingersoll, no media broker in 30 years' time can pick off the peripheral cousins one by one, buy out their shares and lever their own men on to the board of *The New York Times*.

One of Pinch's favourite stories recounts how Jesse Jackson came to lunch in the *Times*'s private dining room, where Arthur Sulzberger Jnr himself was the host.

As he left, the presidential aspirant noted that the Sulzbergers were free to endorse any candidate they chose.

'Aw no, Mr Jackson,' Pinch is said to have replied, 'we don't own this place. The stockholders own *The New York Times*.'

'Come on,' replied Jackson bluntly, acknowledging the impotency of the 15,000 public investors. 'It's *you* who control the voting stock.'

Arthur Sulzberger, say colleagues, tells this anecdote frequently, largely because it is exhilarating to him that it happens to be true.

Certainly the board of directors has a cosy, familial feel to it. The Class A directors, as they are clearly labelled in a gesture of corporate apartheid, are drawn from the same caste of professional executives as most large American companies, and include the Chairman of IBM, the Chairman of RJR Nabisco and the former US Ambassador to Great Britain, Charles Price II. Turn the page of the annual report to the Class B directors, and you're into the Sulzberger family photograph album: Punch and all three of his sisters, swaddled by faithful company retainers. Between the four children the Sulzbergers own, for themselves or beneficially or in options, 18,846,547 combined A and B stock. Their collective worth as a family stands at around one billion dollars.

Notwithstanding this reassuringly large fortune, one of the peculiar things people say about the Sulzbergers is that they're not that rich. What they mean is that there is no great second business to back up the media company: no airline or suitcase factories like the Aga Khan, no jute mills like Samir Jain, no short-time parking or car wash machines like Sally Aw Sian. Their profits derive solely from media and paper mills in Canada and Maine. 'When there's a downturn in lineage in the newspaper business,' people kept telling me in a hushed be-sympathetic-for-the-Sulzbergers voice, 'they feel it more than most families like that.'

Like other vastly rich dynasties they attract apocryphal stories about lucky windfalls. A good one involves Iphigene Ochs Sulzberger as a very old lady. Her doctor had recommended she take more exercise, and so every morning she would parade up and down Madison Avenue for an hour with her nurse. One morning she urgently needed to find a lavatory, so decided to slip into the Campbell Funeral Chapel at 1076 Madison Avenue to make use of their bathroom. Feeling that it wasn't seemly solely to use their facilities, she added her name to a list of mourners by the side of an open coffin. Six months later she received a cheque for $5000. The deceased had stipulated in her will that everyone who took the trouble to come and pay their respects in the funeral parlour would receive a cheque.

What nature of people are the Sulzbergers? Historically they are central Europeans, descendants of a Bavarian Palatinate family who emigrated to America in 1848, though they also derive from earlier Dutch and Spanish Sephardic settlers named Hays and Peixotto. Lines of ancestry are commemorated again and again in their middle names. Sulzbergers have Hays, Peixotto, Ochs or Adler as given names, and if descent through the female line means they don't automatically get Sulzberger as a surname it is frequently slipped into the mix somewhere else. Politically, they are liberals. 'From time to time,' Punch Sulzberger told me, 'strangers will come up to me and say, "Mr Sulzberger, can't you do something about those *communists* you employ on that darned sheet of yours?" ' But the journalism of *The New York Times* isn't leftist so much as politically correct: mildly anti-government, trend-obsessed, partial to stories about minorities, Third World countries, senators with unsuitable escorts. Socially, the Sulzbergers as a clan are strong on what might be termed responsible citizenship. They immerse themselves in charities, fund raising, the local community. They are unflashy. Punch's younger sister Judith Peixotto Sulzberger is a doctor in the allergy and clinical immunology department of the St Luke's-Roosevelt hospital; the eldest sister Marian Heiskell has chaired committees on the New York environment and sits on boards like Consolidated Edison and the Ford Motor Company; Ruth Homberg is publisher of the *Chattanooga Times* and sits on every board, big and small, in Chattanooga: universities, museum, symphonies.

Their charity work has an old-fashioned, pre-Reaganite quality to it. Apart from the New York Public Library and the Metropolitan Museum, few of the causes they support are fashionable. They would rather show up at a committee meeting at a hospice than a $500-a-plate gala benefit. And, with the exception of Punch's wife Carol who looks rather soignée when the occasion demands, it is rare to see a glitzy Sulzberger.

Most branches of the family have children in the company: Ruth Homberg's two sons, Michael and Stephen Golden, who began their careers on the *Chattanooga Times*, both joined the Times Company. Judith Sulzberger's son Daniel Cohen works on the advertising side of the paper, is close to Pinch and as a student motorcycled all over Europe and America with him. Each of their parents has the same voting rights; each will wish to see their children appropriately occupied. Such arrangements could imply tensions, but they can also provide a cohesion and stability difficult to attain in an entirely meritocratic corporation. The Sulzbergers are light on their feet.

If you flag the New York Times Company's 35 regional newspapers on a map of the United States, you observe that, with only three exceptions, they are clustered together in a handful of states: Georgia, Alabama, Florida, Louisiana, Mississippi and the Carolinas in the South; Kentucky and Tennessee in the mid north-east. The exceptions are a couple of papers in California, the *Santa Barbara News-Press* and the *Press Democrat* in Santa Rosa, and a third on George and Barbara Bush's doorstep at Kennebunk in Maine, the *York County Coast Star*. These concentrations of newspaper realty – on the map the flags flutter together like great military encampments – are a consequence of the

Sulzbergers' conservatism. The overnight newspaper empires of the mid-eighties, when the new proprietors, like Dean Singleton and Ralph Ingersoll in America and Robert Maxwell and Conrad Black in London, snapped up whatever was going, were inevitably geographically diffuse. When they found a paper for sale they took a view on the franchise and multiple, and bought. Where these properties were located wasn't a factor. The papers were conceived as self-contained profit centres, where disciplines of economy and scale could be imposed by fax, by telephone, by remote-control management from some distant headquarters. The new proprietors were like *nouveau riche* landowners who, in their hunger for acreage, were prepared to buy estates and farms in scores of different counties, hundreds of miles apart. The theory went that once you'd grasped the principle of newspaper proprietorship – the variables of staffing, printing, advertising yields – you could with the same ease successfully run an evening paper in Thermopolis, Wyoming as Thermopilai, Greece.

What this new breed of owner didn't concede (or rather *couldn't* concede, such was the speed and scope of their acquisitions) was the utility of a cohesive chain. The Sulzberger regional set-up, with its headquarters in the Cox-Chambers heartland of Atlanta, is a tightly run profit-orientated, low-falutin', local-news-first operation that supplements its championship of southern values with syndicated Big City columns from *The New York Times*. Frequently this *Times* connection has been used to great effect: the Sulzbergers' *Gwinnett Daily News*, acquired in the mid-eighties in a suburb of Atlanta, began to challenge Jim Kennedy's *Atlanta Constitution* and *Journal* with a flood of cheap, available *Times* material that the Cox chain had to generate for itself. Whether or not Manhattan journalism travelled well to the South was much debated. 'A lot of what they [the *Gwinnett Daily News*] publish is way over the heads of readers in Gwinnett County,' I was told by an indignant Cox-Chambers editor. 'If you live someplace off Highway 85, who gives a corncob for what Abe Rosenthal's columns say about anything?' At the same time, other Cox staffers emphasised the greater sophistication of the *Constitution* and *Journal* and how important it was to retain this margin of quality over the *Gwinnett Daily News*. Now they no longer need to worry. Four years after they began their turf fight with the Cox-Chamberses, the Sulzbergers admitted defeat and closed the *Daily News*.

The titles of the Sulzberger papers alert you to their mindset: the *Daily Corinthian* of Corinth, Mississippi; the *Lenoir News-Topic* of Lenoir, North Carolina; the grandly named *Daily World* of Opelousas, Louisiana, where little world news is actually derived from further afield than Opelousas itself. The *Tuscaloosa News* of Tuscaloosa, the lumber centre of Alabama, is a Sulzberger too, and the weekly *Banner-Independent* in Booneville, Mississippi: the free press of the Deep South 'of confederacy and alligators in the Mississippi delta' as they were described to me by a *New York Times* misanthrope on West 43rd Street. Nevertheless when the Ansbacher media brokerage company compiled a private inventory of all the Sulzberger papers in 1989 they put a value of $1.2 billion on the Sulzberger local press (against a high of $3.8 billion and a low of $3.3 billion on *The New York Times*). Some of their local circulations have been tiny, comparable with the Canadian papers of Conrad Black and Lord Thomson. Sales of the Sulzbergers' *Daily Enterprise* in the coal town of Harlan, Kentucky were so modest at 7000 a day that they divested themselves of it in 1990 to the American Publishing Company of Frankfort, Illinois, along with the weekly *Claiborne Progress* whose progress never much exceeded 6000 copies. One current Sulzberger paper in Florida, the *Florida News Sun* in Avon Park was still selling as few as 3500 a week in the late eighties, which would take the robots of *The New York Times* Edison plant in New Jersey less than three minutes to print.

What is the Sulzbergers' grand plan? There are three separate theories, not mutually exclusive, on how their media empire might look by the end of the century. It depends on succession and timing. Will Pinch eventually inherit the entire company from his father and determine policy for the alligator press too, or will that portfolio pass to one of the cousins? And if Pinch does get it all, how quickly will this happen? The three theories are:

1. *Punch as chairman for life*. Unlike Europeans, Americans seldom retire. That is the principal difference between the two cultures. As soon as Europeans reach the age of 50 they begin to plot their escape; Americans channel their energy into staying

on, retaining a toehold, an office, a secretary, a corporate title
(this is the land of a million non-executive chairmen emeriti,
unconsulted consultants, grand-old-men and former-presidents,
seemingly without hobbies or pastimes, who embark at 65 upon
a second full-time career above the fray, buttonholing their
successors with increasingly irrelevant stories about colleagues
long since dead). If Punch Sulzberger retains the Chairmanship
of the entire New York Times Company including its regional
papers and TV stations until he is 75 or 80, hardly unfeasible,
then Pinch will channel all his energy into expansion of the
flagship. *The New York Times* currently prints at ten different
sites: Tacoma, Washington; Torrance and Walnut Creek,
California; Austin, Texas; Sarasota, Florida; Atlanta; Chicago;
New York; Carlstadt and Warren, Ohio. Pinch will champion
the new technology, order new plants and, many believe,
attempt to establish *The New York Times* as a genuine national
newspaper, available in every single small town across the United
States. (At present you can buy the *Times* somewhere in all 50
states and in 66 foreign countries, but *buy somewhere* is not the
same as available. Drive north-south through Middle America
from Plentywood, Montana to El Paso, New Mexico and you
have as much hope of finding *The New York Times* as the *South
China Morning Post*.)

2. *Pinch as chairman by 1998*. There is a school of thought, denied
   by Pinch, that he hasn't much interest in his magazines or
   television stations. He is before anything a newspaper man.
   According to this theory he will sell the broadcasting group – the
   six stations with names like KFSM in Arkansas and WREG in
   Memphis, Tennessee – and the tennis and golf publications (he is
   not a golfer) and channel the capital back into buying more
   newspapers, especially newspapers with surplus print capacity
   that might produce part of the national run of *The New York
   Times*. Logically, he would be keen to pick up papers in the
   interior where he owns nothing, like Houston (Dean Singleton's
   Post would be an obvious target) and Kansas and St Louis. The
   obstacle, however, is that this theory makes no economic sense.
   The broadcasting division is profitable, the magazines highly so.
   And he would be unlikely to reverse the company's

diversification programme, shifting investment from a still-expanding medium (broadcasting) into an (at best) mature one (newspapers).

3. *Pinch as chairman in 2014.* This supposition depends, for full impact, on a dramatic shift in the world order of proprietorship. Pinch at 60 is the most experienced newspaper owner anywhere. *The New York Times*'s daily circulation has doubled to 2.4 million and the Sunday edition exceeds three million. The new printing plants (there are now 20) are the most efficient on the planet; so versatile that almost every state in the union has its own regional edition of the *Times*. Pinch is venerated for his technological vision by analysts in five countries (the stock is by now also quoted in London, on the Hong Kong Hang Seng index in communist China, the Nikkei in Tokyo, the DAX in Frankfurt) and seizes opportunities to expand the company abroad. He does not share Punch's discomfort about what overseas managing editors would really be up to, and acquires major newspapers in Hong Kong, Singapore, London and Brazil. This is the theory of Pinch the global newspaper baron.

'Think about it,' a former analyst at the Standard and Poor's Corporation bid me. 'What's to stop the *Times* making it globally? If the Sulzbergers put that newspaper on the block tomorrow they'd get three billion dollars for it. It must be the most valuable newspaper property anywhere. What's worth more? The *LA Times*? I doubt it. The *Sunday Times* in London? You'd be pressed to get half that, even in a good year. So if the son ever goes shopping – serious shopping – the leverage and prestige that newspaper gives him is enormous. If you knew that the New York Times Company was in the market to buy, would you offer your newspaper first anywhere else? You wouldn't, because those guys score in all three departments: they're class, they're posted and they're solvent.'

All the Proprietor's Men

The Grahams and the *Washington Post*

Americans have a fondness for lists, ranking things qualitatively one-to-ten. America's ten best automobiles, ten best holiday resorts, richest people, most generous benefactors, tallest buildings, fastest growing cities, most effective executives and serial killers. With newspapers, these rankings are almost impossible to construct, though this doesn't deter numerous media journals, generally affiliated to universities like the *Gannett Center Journal* at Columbia, from having a go. The charts they publish, like rock charts with last year's position in brackets, are the product of painstaking comparative research: how did a hundred contending newspapers respond to this breaking news story or that, how much space did they devote to this environmental convention, what depth of coverage – and what impartiality – was given to the presidential primaries?

Proprietors regularly asked me whether I'd read, and agreed with, these charts. The preferred reply, I deduced, had one elevating their own flagship newspaper a few places up the ranking.

'Which newspapers around the world strike you as most impressive?' asked Conrad Black at a pre-General Election dinner he gave in London in the Orangery at Claridges.

'The *Washington Post*,' I began, spieling off examples in no particular order. '*The New York Times*, in their own theatres *The Times of India* and the *South China Morning Post*, *Le Figaro*, *El Pais*, Roberto Marinho's *O Globo* . . .'

Black's attention began to wander.

'. . . the *Daily Telegraph*, the *Sydney Morning Herald* . . .' He brightened as I mentioned two of his own.

'But I'm surprised,' he growled, 'to hear you place Kay Graham's *liberal* and some would say *pernicious* newspaper so prominently on your list. I *like* Katharine Graham personally, but the amount of sloppy, ill-considered and certainly unmerited veneration for that newspaper – that *sacred cow* – of hers is frankly incredible. The way people adulate Kay Graham in Washington, you'd think she was St Francis *of Assisi* or *Margaret Thatcher.*'

Tony O'Reilly asked me in Glandore the same question about ranking, but before I could reply ventured that, without question, the *Washington Post* is the foremost newspaper in the world. 'This is not simply because I sit on its board of directors,' he said, 'but because in terms of its authority, of the depth of its coverage, of *intent*, the *Washington Post* is a world-class publication. When you pick it up you can be as certain as ever possible that you're reading journalism without bias. It's a truly *independent* newspaper. I think the Grahams have proved their independence often enough over the years.'

The *Washington Post* long ago achieved the status of legend. Probably only two other titles in the world are better known: *Pravda* and the *Daily Planet*, immortalised respectively by the frenzied counter-propaganda of the Cold War and by Superman. Neither have proprietors. And the history of the Grahams' ownership, since Katharine Graham took over after her husband Philip's suicide in 1963, has been enthralling: the grieving widow thrust on to the world stage, reluctant to sell the family flagship despite numerous offers, and instead transforming herself into a formidable power broker and apologist for inviolable journalism; the tall, engaging heir, Donald, for whom his mother had kept the paper going as his birthright; the stable of high-profile editors and journalists – Ben Bradlee, Bob Woodward, Carl Bernstein, Meg Greenfield – whose own careers have seldom been out of the news, and have consolidated the *Post*'s reputation as a newspaper with an influence far exceeding its 850,000 weekday circulation; the publication of the Pentagon papers and the hounding of Richard Nixon over the Watergate break-in which eventually led to the overthrow, for the first time, of an American President by a newspaper, and the *Washington Post*, covered with glory, taking its place among the angels.

When Conrad Hilton was asked by a journalist what the three crucial elements are in a successful hotel, and he replied, 'Location, location and location,' he could as easily have been talking about newspapers. It is the *Washington Post*'s stranglehold on the capital city of the richest democracy on Earth that gives it its clout. It is the paper the President reads first. It is the paper the First Lady reads first. It is the daily newspaper of the whole chowder of senators, diplomats, lobbyists, journalists, newsmongers, media academics, World Bank monitors, lucky chancers and kibitzers that caw around Capitol Hill, seeking a ride on the back of history.

And yet Washington struck me too as a precarious place from which to publish such a cerebral newspaper. When I retrieved it from the doorhandle of my polite hotel in Georgetown it seemed entirely coherent – the narrow columns of judicious, somewhat sanctimonious reporting – and yet when I picked up the same edition beyond the Beltway, it seemed nothing less than a miracle that this city of above- average poverty with its majority black population and every variety of urban deprivation, should so completely embrace the *Washington Post*. That it has been able to do so owes much to the complex, often generous, occasionally somewhat callous, liberal-minded, bottom-line-motivated leadership of Katharine Graham, who in the summer of 1993 officially announced her intention of standing down as Chairman of the *Post*.

The corporate offices of the Washington Post Company are located on the eighth floor of the Washington Post building at 1150 15th Street, North West Washington. Katharine Graham's visitors are invited to wait in a sealed glass box – a glass corridor between the elevators and Kay Graham's suite – with doors at both ends, like a deep-sea diver's decompression chamber. Here one may reflect for a few minutes on four well-spaced exhibits: the portraits of her father, Eugene Meyer, purchaser of the *Post* at a bankruptcy auction in 1933, and of Philip Graham, a large migraine-inducing canvas of orange, lime green and purple stripes entitled 'Cool Sling' (1964) by Gene Davis and an enfeebled pot plant whose life expectancy, you felt, was short in this airless glass transit bay.

Katharine Graham sat very upright in a chintz-covered chair. Her back was so straight and taut that I wondered whether she might be in convalescence from spinal surgery. Her appearance in a navy blue Oscar de la Renta dress with white pleats and big white buttons the size of coffee saucers was powerfully neat. On her feet, narrow black pumps. Her manner was quizzical. It was apparent that she could not remember exactly why she had consented to this conversation, having made a number of courteous attempts to avoid it. It had taken almost two years of lobbying to secure an audience in her office. She sent word that she never gave interviews, it was a firm rule of her life. And the experience of others only validated her protests. Magazine profiles about Katharine Graham invariably kick off with the writer's frustrated attempts to see her. 'I get kind of snarly about these things. There's nothing in it for me. I'm sure your life would be easier if we talked but mine wouldn't be,' is Mrs Graham's preferred line of defence.

'You've got to remember how shy she is,' people told me. 'She becomes quite anguished at the prospect of personal publicity.'

Others, however, became indignant if you suggested she might be shy. A New York magazine editor said, 'Oh God, you haven't swallowed *that line* have you? Kay Graham shy! She's probably the shrewdest and most calculating woman in Washington. She gives power dinner parties near enough *every week*. People like the President and the Chief of Staff and CEOs of multinational companies go to them. And let me tell you they don't have to be dragged kicking and screaming to her door either. People fly from any town in America to have dinner in Georgetown with Mrs Graham. You *will not* buy into this "shy" theory that's put out about her.'

On my first encounter with Conrad Black I was struck by the way his face divides horizontally – the amused smile, the graphite eyes. With Kay Graham the fold is vertical, the two halves separated by deep frown lines that run like a railroad track from a terminus above the bridge of her nose. In portrait photographs the right half (as you face her) is the soft side: a warm right eye, sympathetic tilt to the mouth. On the left side the eye is icy, controlling, and there is a determined downturn to the mouth. Physically she is an imposing woman, hair swept back in a steel-grey helmet, ear lobes clamped by pearl earrings as big as quail's eggs. In magazine articles about the top ten most influential American women her role as chairman of the board of the Washington Post Company gives her an automatic place in the top three. She professes to find this exasperating.

'I think it's sort of *nonsense* and it's also slightly *sexist* because they don't seem to refer to Punch Sulzberger as the most powerful *man*, I observe. And yet he's in exactly the same situation of controlling a very powerful paper. I think also that they misconceive what the power [of proprietorship] is. They believe I *literally conceive*, that I *run downstairs* and tell people to do something, which in fact never happens. The paper and the magazine and the stations – the whole company – can be influential and *is*, and the *Post* front page sets an agenda by what it plays up or doesn't. People here pick it up. There's a lot of press in Washington, obviously. So to that extent it's a power and indeed a responsibility.'

'On a day-to-day basis do you feel part of the unravelling of the news?'

'When I was Publisher – before Don took on that role – I was more directly connected with the editors and I was down there [on the fifth – the editorial – floor] almost every day in one way or another. I went to the editorial board meetings – the opinion pages I guess you could call them – when I had the time or when I *knew* something. The editor would ring me in my office and say, "Kay, you should be down here because we're going to discuss x".'

'Isn't it inhibiting for journalists having the owner sitting in? I would have thought that your voice carried more weight than ten others.'

'I hope not. We have a pretty good, healthy atmosphere around here. I enter discussions, I would say, as an *equal* voice and not a *tipping* voice. I describe it as a *continuous conversation*. So I don't think they feel, in most situations, that I'm the employer and they're the person working for me.'

Then she said, 'I guess too that by my pretty constant presence they get used to it and become less intimidated by the fact you're the Publisher. They know we have run this organisation with a great deal of autonomy and I've often said "Liberty not licence" – that doesn't mean they can do anything they want, but it means they can do anything they want *within the ambience or atmosphere of the place and the general mindset*. And that usually occurs because when you hire an editor you presumably hire somebody you think is in general agreement with your views and then you let them be the decider of the issues. You have to trust people and make them free to make their own decisions. I've never been hands-on in the way that Rupert Murdoch is hands-on. Rupert tears up front pages and really influences how those papers run.'

'How often do you see things in the *Post* that aren't done the way you want them to be done?'

Katharine Graham laughed. She has a sardonic don't-tempt-me laugh, sophisticated and smoky and droll.

'Well I criticise quite a lot – I still do that,' she replied, 'and bear complaints from other people who come to me. It may be someone that writes me, or calls up, somebody I sit next to at dinner or bump into in the street. Then I take it to the editor and discuss it with him, and he discusses it with the reporter and sometimes I'm persuaded that we're right and sometimes I'm persuaded that we're wrong. But it's *the editor* who finally decides.'

'But what happens on those occasions when *you* believe the *Washington Post* has got it wrong and the editor thinks they've got it right? What do you tell the somebody you sat next to at dinner? Aren't you responsible for what's in your own paper?'

'You have to be. You're the ultimate authority. So I guess that sometimes you just feel a little guilty because you don't feel you've done a wonderful job in this or that but mostly, whether you do or whether you don't – usually you do – you have to defend your people. I don't like it when I think we are at least half wrong, I hate defending us, but I do it.'

'Isn't the *Washington Post* the world's greatest visiting card: through owning it you can get to see whoever you like.'

'It's mostly true, yes. It's one of the very spoiling things about newspaper life. It gets you into wonderfully interesting situations or people whom you would not otherwise see and I think that's a great privilege.'

Katharine Graham surveyed her office. Ranged in front of the books along her shelves are 40 or 50 framed photographs, of herself with Nancy Reagan, of herself with Presidents Kennedy, Johnson, Bush, Gorbachev.

'I thought,' she said, 'when I went to work that the greatest pleasure would be the involvement with the news and people on the news and to a great extent that is a great pleasure. It's a very exciting and invigorating and intellectually a very satisfying thing. However I'd had no business experience and after I learned about business issues I became equally involved and satisfied with that part of it; I thought it was equally interesting and exciting and of course they're intertwined.

You can't do one well without doing the other well. They are *absolutely interconnected.'*

'So the famous letter you sent to your sister years ago was fundamentally misguided.'

'*That letter*!'

She had written it in 1937 as a 20-year-old student at the University of Chicago; a letter that was almost a manifesto of her ambitions, sent to an elder sister.

'What I am most interested in doing,' she wrote, 'is labor reporting, possibly working up to political reporting later. As you can see, that is no help to Dad. He wants and needs someone who is willing to go through the whole mill, from reporting, to circulation management, to editorial writing, and eventually to be his assistant.

'This presents the payoff in problems. I detest beyond description advertising and circulation, and that is what a newspaper executive spends most of his time worrying about . . . I [also] doubt my ability to carry a load like the *Washington Post*, and . . . I damn well think it would be a first-class dog's life.'

Katharine Graham as first-class dog and business tyro: in the photographic archive of the Associated Press they have five thick folders of pictures of her, maybe six hundred images. One hundred are of Mrs Graham the party-goer, the famous picture of her towering over Truman Capote on the dancefloor, at the ball he gave for her in New York in the white and gold ballroom of the Plaza hotel, and lots of her stepping out of a limousine on her way into a fundraiser dinner. But five hundred photographs are of Katharine Graham standing behind a lectern, reading-glasses on her nose, drinking glass and a carafe of water in front of her, addressing rooms full of stockholders and analysts at AGMs. When she took her company public in 1971 she propelled herself into a world of quantifiable margins and operating revenues, executive incentive schemes, stock price modules and cost cutting. Neither of her flagship publications, the *Washington Post* and *Newsweek*, would ever again enjoy quite the same freedom, the lack of accountability they had previously. And there are those who observe that the constraints of becoming a publicly traded stock was no burden to Katharine Graham: that the discipline of Wall Street gave her the leverage to reclaim the leadership of her company, from the printers, from the editorial barons with their disregard for budgets, from management. Katharine Graham, they say, relished it all because she learnt she has an aptitude as a businesswoman.

'One of the things people say about you, as you know, is that in recent years your love affair with advertising and circulation has eclipsed your love of journalism.'

'I think you evolve, you grow and you learn and you change. I mean I've gotten very interested in things I didn't used to be interested in.'

'Like?'

'Like business news.'

'The articles and books about you all imply that when you took over the *Post* you knew nothing: nothing about business, nothing about newspapers. You must surely have picked up quite a lot as the daughter and wife of *Post* publishers.'

'Well I knew things that weren't very helpful.'

'Like?'

'I'd been a reporter.'

'Why wasn't that helpful?'

'Well I guess it was *somewhat*. I had been very close to the issues in the sense that I was close to both my husband and my father and I'd always been involved with what was going on. But it's the difference between watching somebody swim and swimming. It really isn't very helpful to have watched. I didn't know anything about business, how to run a business and how to manage. I didn't know how to manage anything.'

Here lies the genesis of the shy Kay Graham theory. It is clear that it pleases her to accentuate her early, naive period. She told me, 'I was very ill at ease in certain situations like editorial lunches; it took me a long time to feel that I could ask a question. And quite often if I'd been in a meeting I'd sort of feel I'd really screwed up. I didn't ask that or I *did* ask that!'

And she has said of the first years of her proprietorship: 'It took me some while to cease thinking constantly of a certain scene from the old musical comedy *The Vagabond King*. You may recall the moment when the suddenly enthroned vagabond – for the first time dressed in royal robes – descends the great stairs, slowly and anxiously, tensely eyeing on either side the rows of archers with their drawn bows and inscrutable faces.'

I said to this imposing, determined, straight-backed woman, 'You don't seem at all shy now.' On the contrary, she struck me as supremely confident.

'I used to be. I think I've to a large extent overcome it because I've lived this life for such a long time. But it can return if I'm in a certain situation where I'm not at ease.'

Her private life was described to me as 'a mixture of semi-public engagements, the parties at home that she feels her position at the head of the company impels her to give, and more evenings spent alone than you'd imagine. On those evenings she tends to stay quite late in the office, then is driven home and does what any other 76-year-old widow on her own does in Washington, reads books, newspapers, watches television.'

'Is your copy of the *Washington Post* delivered to you the night before?'

'Yes. I do get it direct from the presses, at 11.15. About 30 of us get the first edition.'

'It's delivered to your house? On a bike? In a car?'

'Oh I guess in various ways over the years. I think it's a taxi that now seems to deliver it. I'm not waiting outdoors to see. Quite often I'm asleep or out. Sometimes I get it when I come in and yes, I try to read it or a lot of it. Most often, when I'm home, I go to bed early and then wake up at two and go get it off the mat and read it. Because I try to read the [Wall Street] *Journal* and the [New York] *Times* too and so if I've read most of the *Post* it does help.'

'What order do you read it in?'

'Well, oddly, front to back! I flip through it in that direction.'

'Why oddly?'

'Well it seems like an orderly, rather boring way to do it!'

'And do you read the sports?'

'No. I do *not* read the sports. I *look* at the sports. There's only one sport I know anything about and that's tennis and the others don't interest me but we have a couple of wonderful writers back there and so if I see a story by one of them – Boswell or Cornheiser or somebody like that – I'll pick that up. But on the whole I know that my son Don is a passionate sports fan and knows everything about it so I don't have to read it, *he* reads it.'

'Do you get a strong instant impression whether it's a good or a bad day's paper?'

'There are some days I think why isn't a story there or why is the one you think important hidden away on page 15.'

'Would you then, when you come in, ring the editors and ask?'

'I used to. I'm more temperate now but I'll do it if I see somebody or I'll collect three instances before I jump.'

'Do you like journalists?'

'Yes I love them.'

I said, 'That's quite rare in a proprietor. Quite a lot I've spoken to say they don't really.'

'That's appalling. Conrad [Black] gave a speech to that effect once. I jumped him. I wrote him and said I was *shocked*.'

'Did he reply?'

'I guess he did. We're friends again now. But I enjoy [journalists] more than anybody else. A great number are personal friends.'

'Do you get distressed when they leave to join somebody else's newspaper?'

'When somebody you greatly value leaves it does hurt your feelings terribly. When I was new I didn't expect it and I got very excited about losing. I got personal about it in a stupid way. It was unstylish. Because it's in the life.'

'Do you see many of the other owners?'

'A great many. Punch [Sulzberger] is a great friend and the *LA Times* people and Rupert Murdoch's a friend. I like him very much and admire him. Well I guess I don't particularly admire some of his newspapers but I think he's a wonderful, extraordinary manager and he's an interesting and brilliant person and he's *nice*. His wife Anna's charming and he is. They're interesting and fun. They're just great.'

'You've got the second swankiest board of directors in the world after Conrad Black. What role do they play?'

'A very major role and we use them very seriously and they feel free to speak their minds. A good director doesn't usually do it at a board meeting but they'll do it out of the board meeting. You can bring up issues but you don't really jump at management at a board meeting. If you think we're really wrong of course you can vote against us. I think that I'm sorry Warren Buffett [the Omaha financier] is off our board. He's off because when Cap Cities bought ABC he had to get off ours and on to theirs. But he's still a big owner and he's still very much involved and he is particularly useful. At first we didn't have a lot of people who'd run companies so we were very successful in getting Jim Burke [former chairman and CEO, Johnson & Johnson] and Don Keough [President and COO, Coca-Cola] and Tony O'Reilly and they are very helpful. Ralph Gomory is very helpful on technology, Bill Ruane is very helpful on financials.'

'How often would somebody like Donald Keough ring you up and discuss something to do with the *Washington Post*?'

'I'd ring *him* up maybe once or twice between board meetings.'

Then she said, 'It's very helpful for me having these people involved, because I have my own rules, that I sometimes violate, about *not* being involved myself. Not being involved with things outside the company I mean, half governmental things. I think that as papers got more dominant over here, most publishers backed away from either political involvement or indeed the board kind of involvement that they used to do. Since we're supposed to be critics of the government under our first amendment – or the whole Bill of Rights – you don't want to be connected with them. And you don't want other people to *conceive* of you as connected with the government; nobody here would, but people abroad tend to think of a paper like ours as a government spokesperson.'

'Have people ever said that to you?'

'Yes. Yes. Third Worlders think you are in league with the government. Arabs or Middle Eastern people quite often think that. I find it quite ironic, since we obviously lived through these spectaculars like the Pentagon papers and Watergate.'

'Were you fearful during those two episodes?'

'Yes, I was very nervous.'

'Were there moments when you wished they had never arisen?'

'Well there were moments when I was extremely anxious about how it was all going to turn out and could we survive the next administration. It never occurred to me during the first two years that what happened might happen, *it just never occurred to me*. And they [the Nixon administration] challenged our television station licence, so I was extremely concerned for the company and whether we could survive. They were very powerful and they were there and they could do us a lot of harm and they tried. So sure.'

'Was winning Watergate the watershed of your ownership?'

'That and my interview with Gorbachev. That was certainly great.'

'Had he read the *Washington Post* regularly before?'

'I'm sure not.' She gave a little laugh. 'But I think they do get it at the Kremlin, I know that. And they watch us. The White House and the Kremlin, sure, they both watch us.'

It was not always so. At the time that Katharine Graham's father, Eugene Meyer, acquired the *Washington Post* the paper had four competitors. Washingtonians could choose between the dominant *Evening Star*, the *Daily News*, the *Herald* and the *Times* (then both Hearst papers) and the struggling *Post* which ranked fifth in both circulation and advertising. It is customary in condensed newspaper histories to emphasise how appalling the old issues used to be, but actually the pre-War *Washington Post* wasn't without merit; merely sleepy and debt-ridden and thin and demoralised. Eugene Meyer in the thirties was not unlike Robert Maxwell in the seventies: he craved ownership of an important newspaper but was repeatedly frustrated. He had tried to buy the loss-making *Herald* but had been rebuffed. 'I always *buy* newspapers, never sell them,' William Randolph Hearst had declared. Four years later he had bid £5 million for the *Washington Post* from its mentally disturbed proprietor Edward McLean but had again been thwarted. By 1933, however, McLean was unable to pay a large newsprint bill to his supplier and the court ordered the newspaper to be sold at auction to satisfy creditors. As is normal when a paper is on the block, there was widespread public speculation. Many were the names, all mega-rich, from drugstore magnates to reactionary billionaires, tipped as the certain next owner. Many of them pitched up on the day of the sale including the mad McLean's estranged wife, Evalyn, who had the distinction of owning the legendary Hope diamond, a rock the size of a golf ball, which she wore somewhat ostentatiously pinned to her coat in the front row. Fortunately for Meyer she had no intention of trading her brooch for a decrepit printing plant and dropped out of the bidding at $600,000. Hearst, keen to kill the *Post* off, went up to $800,000. Meyer, who would have bid up to $2 million, raised Hearst another $25,000 and in the process initiated a newspaper dynasty.

There are really only two things that need be said about Eugene Meyer: that he was a vastly rich man and that he must have been the first newspaper owner ever to advance a spurious explanation for his purchase. 'I feel this is the best way I can make myself useful at a critical time,' he said, which may be translated as 'my licence to interfere'. 'Power,' he would later rather vacuously philosophise, 'means different things under different conditions and in different contexts . . . [Newspaper] power can be used as brute strength, or it can be used as the highest form of influence in connection with truth or eternal verities . . . Ideas, I think, have more power than anything. That's why I bought a newspaper – because it's a place where you can work in *the field of ideas*. If you study out the right ideas and translate them into language which others can understand, you exercise power very usefully and helpfully. *People like to be told what to think.*' Meyer added, 'If you give them the truth and back it up with clear explanations . . . you are exercising very great power in a very useful way.'

Others thought it more probable that he simply enjoyed having a power platform. He was a confident extrovert with a bald head and pince-nez who had made his fortune investing in oil, railroads, copper and chemicals. Like so many businessmen who have made big money in the finite world of industry, he had both an excessive respect for ideas in the abstract – for the drama of debate – and for the rightness of his own opinion on all topics. As a newspaper owner he was in his element. He was also well suited to it. His fondness for intervening in world affairs led the paper to appoint top class editorial-page columnists. He was sanguine about losing a million dollars a year supporting the enterprise through the Depression, confident everything would eventually come right, and he invested, too, much of his time and energy in building his paper's circulation and prestige, if not its profitability which remained as remote as ever. On one occasion at the pit of the Depression, he explained to the assembled staff why he could not award pay increases that year. Everyone, he suggested, should make sacrifices. 'You should realise,' he said, 'that I have made no addition to my collection of French Impressionists since I bought the *Post*.' When his daughter Katharine – the only one of his five children to be interested in newspapering – married Philip Graham, a clever young lawyer, Meyer invited his son-in-law to become Publisher, and in order to ensure he felt comfortable in this role Meyer made over to him the controlling shares.

The young Grahams were considered, even in the context of Washington, a sought-after couple. Of Philip Graham – who bears such a strong physical resemblance to his son Donald – no adjective is used quite so frequently as charismatic. He was quick-witted and free-thinking with an early ability to laugh and charm. As the Publisher of the *Washington Post* he enjoyed ex-officio status at the capital's top tables, but he had, beyond that, a gravitas that made him invariably the focus of any dinner party conversation. I am assured that people many years his senior in age and experience naturally deferred to him. He was exceptionally well connected politically, and friends felt – though he hardly said so himself – that every third call to Philip Graham's office came from the present or future President of the United States.

His influence on the *Post* – and nobody understood the potential influence of the *Washington Post* more than Philip Graham – was considerable. He was an instinctive businessman. People seldom saw him pore over figures and yet he grasped not only the broad picture but the fine detail. He wrote fluently and lucidly and inspired others to do likewise. The *Post* improved. When the rival *Times-Herald* came up for sale (the two titles having merged some years earlier) it was Graham who at once recognised the imperative of buying it and incorporating it into the *Post*. Their combined circulation made the *Washington Post* the dominant paper of the city. Financially – intellectually too – it was secure and poised to become a mighty money machine.

All this ought to have made Philip Graham fulfilled, but it did not. To his close friends it became increasingly obvious he was sick. His exuberance had a dark side; away from the glow of public attention, without an audience of politicians, hostesses and power brokers, he was troubled and self-denigrating. His wit, people told me, always laced with cynicism, grew bitter. He saw less and less value in the constant jockeying for position in Washington, and yet some part of him needed too to be at the apex of it all. He had the notion that his contemporaries thought less of his achievements at the *Washington Post* because he was the owner's son-in-law; that he had steered the paper to hitherto undreamed-of levels of profit and prestige was forever undermined by this one nagging doubt. It has been suggested that he was caught in a terrible dilemma, entirely of his own devising and recognised by nobody but himself: the greater his success at the

Post, the more exacting his stewardship, the greater the influence of the paper, the greater the profit, then the greater his link to the Meyer family, to his parents-in-law, and so the greater his discomfiture in his role as nepotistic son-in-law. There would always be someone, in another room, voicing the one reservation about him that became his haunting obsession: that had he not married Katharine Meyer he would not now be the publisher of the *Washington Post*.

His health deteriorated further and faster. Shielded by his staff, he began to skip meetings. He raged incoherently about his lot in life. He took to raving at his friend John Kennedy on the telephone, or crashing into the White House without an appointment, to harangue him in person about minor details of legislation. In a famous episode, while he was in seeing Kennedy, Graham grabbed the red phone – the military hotline – and shouted, 'scramble the planes.' The President had to wrest the receiver from his hands to countermand it: 'This is the President. Cancel that order . . .' The President finally told Kay Graham that she had to do something about it. But Katharine Graham was in no position to do anything. Her husband in his sickness had turned on her too, had embarked upon a barely concealed love affair with a young *Newsweek* journalist, was threatening to divorce Kay, marry his girlfriend and to take the company away from her too (which he was probably entitled to do since Eugene Meyer had given him, and not his daughter, the majority of the voting shares). The drama unfolded, chewed over and dissected in every Washington drawing room and by every employee of the company. Was their Publisher indeed mad, and on whose side – husband's or wife's – would they testify if it came to court? Philip Graham, alternately euphoric and suicidal, became brazen: he took his girlfriend everywhere, travelled abroad with her to inspect the *Newsweek* foreign bureaux, gave large dinners in London at the Connaught with her as his hostess, invited her to accompany him to newspaper conferences and watch him give hectoring, half insane speeches. Eventually, after a breakdown on a rostrum in Phoenix, he was admitted to a psychiatric hospital. His wife visited him daily with picnic lunches. He made progress or so it appeared, and in due course was permitted to spend weekends at Glen Welby, their country house in Virginia. One Sunday afternoon, while Katharine Graham was resting in another room, Philip Graham took his own life with a shotgun.

Thus it was that Katharine Graham at the age of 46, having devoted the previous 20 years of her life to raising her four children, came to be in absolute financial and editorial control at the *Washington Post* corporation.

Initially – for the first terrible 72 hours after the suicide – there was widespread doubt that she would even keep the papers. Otis Chandler expressed interest in buying them, as did the Newhouses. Her eldest daughter Elizabeth – Lally – was 20; Donald was 18 and set to go up to Harvard; William and Stephen were 15 and 11. People reckoned she would do well to sell out, be shot of the whole company, and make a new life wherever she chose, well away from the painful associations of Washington. In fact she did quite the opposite. Her mother, resilient old Agnes Meyer, reminded her that Eugene Meyer hadn't revived the *Post* at great personal effort and expense so that Kay could sell it off just as it had come good. And even in the earliest days there was the dynastic factor, that the *Post* should be retained until Donnie (as his mother will still sometimes refer to him) was ready to take over. And so on the eve of the funeral, Katharine Graham, with her deep aversion to public speaking, called a full meeting of the company's board of directors and department heads – the editors, lawyers, managers from the *Post*, *Newsweek* and the company's television stations – informing them only that she wished to make an important announcement. Still rehearsing the lines she had written about the future of the company, she was helped into the car by Lally, who in the confusion of the moment jumped in too for the ride with her mother, forgetting she was dressed only in her nightdress. In the boardroom on the seventh floor of the old *Post* building, Katharine Graham took her place, ashen faced, dressed in black, eyes downcast, and began to address the group. Her theme was continuity: despite rumours to the contrary, she said, this company will not be sold. 'This has been, this is, and this will continue to be a family operation. There is another generation coming along, and we intend to turn the paper over to them.'

The most frequently pedalled piece of misinformation about Katharine Graham is that she is the first woman proprietor in America. In fact she is only the latest in a long tradition. Cissy Patterson had vigorously directed the *Washington Times-Herald* in the fifties before the Grahams snapped it up; her cousin Alicia Patterson ruled *Newsday* on Long Island long before the Chandlers appeared on the scene.

Dorothy Schiff owned and edited the *New York Post* for 37 years before Rupert Murdoch talked her into selling it one day over lunch in her sixth-floor suite in her old newspaper building facing the East River; Oveta Culp Hobby was chairman of the board of the *Houston Post* until it passed via Otis Chandler to Dean Singleton along with her million-dollar Chippendale boardroom table. Nevertheless it is still principally her rare status as a woman in a world of men that engrosses commentators about Katharine Graham.

'The industry has always been highly confused about how she should be seen, indeed how she sees herself,' I was assured by a Boston media broker. 'I guess people just view newspapers as a particularly masculine preserve: the connotations with late-breaking news, the big story and men's room macho. And they imagined Kay Graham would drown in that great ocean of suits and the men wouldn't let her within spitting distance of a decision that counted. But it didn't work out that way. She made some tough choices. She let some people go. She hired her own teams and got things how she wanted them. So then the same people who said she was soft started saying she was a tough cookie. The turnover of senior executives has been higher, I reckon, at the Washington Post Company than in many other media companies, but I don't believe it would be an issue if Mrs Graham were not a woman.'

In her early days as owner she says she saw being female as a disadvantage; in the office she wanted to be considered as an honorary man. And she says that she found it hard to engage with office life: meetings took place all over the building – she never knew exactly when or where – at which decisions were taken by executives who seemed absolutely confident of their ability, and she had no way of contributing. It wasn't that they meant to exclude her, only that nobody imagined she wished to be involved at that level. She felt she might easily spend the rest of her life sitting aloof in her office, feeling superfluous. Her company was like a fairground carousel, spinning smoothly round and round under its own momentum, but at too great a speed for her to step aboard.

She was advised by a friend, the journalist Walter Lippmann, to ask questions, one at a time, starting with simple subjects and, when she felt she understood those fully, moving on to more difficult ones. So she took to calling executives and journalists into her office inviting them, meekly and apologetically, to explain this or that nuance of foreign policy or precisely how it was that the *Post* covered the political conventions: who exactly went along from the paper, what did they all do? And she stopped sitting behind her desk when they came to see her, directing them instead to her sofa which she realised was more conducive to revealing conversation. After a year of this she felt sufficiently bold to phase out the editor she inherited and replace him with the buccaneering Ben Bradlee – her own man – which in turn allowed her to feel that the *Washington Post* too was at last under her control.

As she grew in confidence, Katharine Graham altered in character too. She came to accept, and then to enjoy, the fact that as the owner of the *Washington Post* she would be lobbied and lauded by a constant succession of prominent businessmen and politicians. Some of these, she famously told a friend, would make sexual overtures to her, and then she would watch them, amused but untempted, thinking, 'You'd really like to fuck a tycoon, wouldn't you?' She became less diffident too about imposing her will on the paper. At meetings she can be terse and will cut short even her most senior people when they are midway through explaining some complicated problem if she finds it tedious. 'Yeah, yeah, we know all that.' She is pernickety over detail. 'This should not be confused with perfectionism, which is a trait we all recognise as laudable,' I was told by a former colleague. 'We are talking here *pernickety*.' She has a habit, at editorial board meetings, of beaming mentally in and out; one minute she is fully engaged – enthused, decisive – the next her attention appears temporarily to have evaporated, as though she is thinking about something quite different, or even about nothing. This can be annoying for the other participants. Some of the procession of top management who were courted, hired and arbitrarily dismissed by Katharine Graham say that she gives insufficient attention to the minutiae of everyday newspapering, but will later, upon a whim, become excessively exacting, asking why she hasn't been informed about this or that triviality.

On the other hand she retained Ben Bradlee as her editor for the whole of her reign, and their relationship has always been a warm one, perhaps because Bradlee never envisaged that it *wouldn't* work, never became obsequious, remained his own man, while accepting always that Mrs Graham was the boss and that her opinion on all matters was a factor that could not be taken for granted.

Something her detractors say about her, as a means of explaining her volatility, is that Katharine Graham doesn't really hold consistent opinions on anything. Her political and social convictions are in a perpetual state of flux. She is a convinced Republican, but an instinctive Democrat. She is a hawk who argues that every possible step should be taken to avoid war. She is a patriot who would never allow her patriotism to cloud her objectivity. She will explain with great eloquence the shortcomings of the American presidential system, but will defer to no one in Washington in her enthusiasm for entertaining presidents.

'When you ask her view on something topical,' says the ex-girlfriend of one of her sons, 'you find that she never actually has an opinion herself. But she'd always just had dinner the night before with the person in the best position to have an opinion.'

'If you think about it,' I was told by a Washington hostess, a longterm friend of Katharine Graham, 'it is probably quite an advantage to be a female if you happen to own a major newspaper. At dinners you are inevitably seated next to the most prominent male guest, who ninety-nine times out of a hundred is the most interesting person in the room. A *male* newspaper owner only ever gets seated next to somebody's *wife*, so has much less opportunity than Kay to cross-question the guest of honour. So in that respect certainly it has been a lucky break for her, being a woman.'

She is steely under fire. In a crisis she will defend her journalists and her newspaper more tenaciously than anybody. Her conduct during the Pentagon papers and Watergate episodes, when the *Post* persisted in publishing material in the face of concerted government opposition, was unwavering. It is worth speculating which other proprietors would have shown the same resolve under similar conditions. Lord Rothermere probably would, as would Punch Sulzberger and Otis Chandler. Rupert Murdoch and Conrad Black, perhaps.

Both episodes placed different pressures on her as owner. The Pentagon papers, the great leaked official history of the Vietnam conflict – thousands of pages long – that proved that the American government had consistently lied about their conduct of the war, including the cover-up of the My Lai massacre and the sustained bombing of Cambodia, required an instant reaction. *The New York Times* had broken the story first, published three lengthy extracts and been temporarily injuncted by the government, before the *Washington Post* managed to secure its own set of the papers. These arrived in two large boxes of photocopied documents, unindexed and unsorted, which Ben Bradlee and a task force of journalists worked on all day and all night at Bradlee's home. Simultaneously, in an adjoining room, a team of *Post* attorneys accumulated more and more good reasons why it would be madness for the paper to publish. Eventually, at the final hour before the presses had to roll if the Pentagon papers were to be printed, Katharine Graham was telephoned at home – she was hosting a party on her lawn – and briefed on the up and downside by first Bradlee, then the attorneys. The decision was hers alone. 'I say we print,' declared Katharine Graham at last. The following day Henry Kissinger, then President Nixon's national security advisor, telephoned his friend Mrs Graham at her office. 'Have you heard, Kay,' he asked, 'that Anatoly Dobrynin, the Russian ambassador, is saying that there is nothing more for him to do in Washington now that the *Post* has published all the country's secrets?' And yet, three days later, the *Post* was exonerated in court.

The Watergate imbroglio – the single episode that propelled the *Washington Post* into the firmament of world newspapers – was different: slow-burning, intermittent and infinitely more dangerous for the Grahams. So much has been written about the political espionage, wire-tapping and break-in at the offices of the Democratic National Committee, and the gradual revelation of the President's involvement by Bob Woodward and Carl Bernstein, that it is possible to underestimate the potential damage to the *Washington Post* had their investigation faltered. Katharine Graham is the first to admit that her nerve sometimes began to desert her as the risks escalated. It was like 'wading little by little into a stream . . . You were in up to your waist having gotten yourself in gradually. I couldn't say "This is getting too dangerous". Having put them [the editors] in you stuck with them.' And yet it bothered her that so few of the other significant papers followed her into the water, and as the disclosures of the celebrated source, Deep Throat, were eked out month after month she wondered sometimes whether they might be entirely mistaken, and that nothing of substance lay behind Watergate at all. At one point, the company's television licences in Miami and Jacksonville were challenged by several of Richard Nixon's supporters, a tactic that the

White House tapes later showed had been suggested by Nixon himself. ('The main thing is the *Post* is going to have damnable, damnable problems out of this one. They have a television station. Does that [federal broadcasting licence] come up too? . . . Well, the game has to be played awfully rough . . .') Later there was the warning off by Kissinger – a moment Katharine Graham described as 'blood-chilling', and the lewd threat from John Mitchell, the former attorney general. When Bernstein called to read him a story alleging that Mitchell had controlled a secret Republican fund to gather information on the Democrats, Mitchell exploded: 'Katie Graham is gonna get her tit caught in a big fat wringer if that's published.' Shortly after Nixon had resigned, and the *Washington Post* was triumphant, Bradlee, Woodward, Bernstein and several other Watergate heroes in the newsroom presented Kay Graham with an antique wooden clothes wringer as a memento of her support. In every subsequent profile of Katharine Graham one is assured that this wooden wringer sits in pride of place in her office, but by the time of my visit it had been replaced by a spray of white irises in a narrow glass vase.

The thing people tell you first about Donald Graham – the single fact upon which other newspaper proprietors latch, as though this were somehow the key to his whole personality – is that Donald E. Graham is *the best-prepared publisher in North America*. To be sure, there are rivals for the palm. Have not James Cox Kennedy, Pinch Sulzberger and long, long ago, Otis Chandler been singled out as the best prepared? And yet half the owners I visited – Tony O'Reilly, Ralph Ingersoll, Rupert Murdoch – named Don Graham as the best-tutored, clearest-thinking, *least confused* of the new generation of inheritors.

The publisher of the *Washington Post* and CEO of the Washington Post Company is an uncommonly tall, somewhat stooping character as though, over the course of his 47 years, he has become painfully accustomed to cracking his head against low beams. His arm span when he makes an expansive gesture – which he frequently does – is immense; it is easy to credit that he can reach the walls simultaneously at opposite ends of his office. His long face has a weatherbeaten look, his smile is lopsided and a touch goofy. When he's ready to talk he tilts his chair back, swings his feet on to the glass coffee table and says, 'Shoot'.

'*Shoot*': ask away, let the questions roll. You feel instinctively that he prefers action to waffle. A biro pen sits in the breast pocket of his white shirt. His watch he wears strapped upside-down, with its face underneath his wrist, as if protecting it against some sudden, violent activity. His socks, making a cameo appearance between pinstripe suit trousers and a pair of thick rubber-soled, almost orthopaedic, brogues are of blue and purple tartan.

'*Shoot*'. You can see why he made a good policeman when, discharged from the military draft after two years in Vietnam, he took the decision to enrol as a patrolman in northeast Washington.

'I'd always planned, when I got back from Vietnam, to get on to the paper,' he said. 'But two or three months before, there'd been a major riot in Washington triggered by the assassination of Martin Luther King. I had been in Vietnam reading about it. And I had grown up here but had been away for six years in college and in the army and I knew that I didn't know a lot about the town. I wanted to learn something about it. A journalist has a very good way to get an understanding, but I wanted to see it from some other point of view than as a journalist. The police, as it happened at the time, were desperate for people and I told them that I would like to come on. I told them that I would only stay about eighteen months and they said that would be above average. So I went through the academy which takes sixteen weeks and then I was a patrolman in the 9th precinct, walked a footbeat some and spent most of my time driving a scout car.'

It struck me that, as a preparation for newspaper ownership, the life of a patrolman is better training that any circulation department or newsroom. How often, parked against a sidewalk on a stake-out or routine break, does one see a scout car manned by police officers reading newspapers? And with what thoroughness, as the hours grind by, do they read every last story, paragraph and sentence from the first page to the last?

On the glass coffee table, already scrumpled by his orthopaedic rubber soles, was a modest sheaf of media: the *Washington Post*, the *Washington Herald* – the evening paper of Everett, Snohomish county – and *Newsweek*: the full portfolio of Graham newsprint. It was the smallest and most select roster I'd seen for months. I had grown accustomed, when calling upon proprietors, to being faced by a whole wall of mahogany shelves built to display their chains of hick weeklies.

These had begun to blur into a single unit which I thought of as the *Little Prairieland Cornet and Pennysaver*; the footsoldiers and pawns of proprietorial prestige whose principal function is to pad out the shelves and company report. Donald Graham's office, by contrast, is almost suspiciously free of newspapers.

'That's because I don't read *enough* newspapers,' he said. 'I read about three or four a day. People try to do those rankings the whole time – which is America's best paper? – but it's an absurd exercise unless you read far more newspapers than I can. Aside from the *Post*,' he said, 'I don't read any other papers on a consistent basis than the *Wall Street Journal* and *The New York Times*.'

'Do you think of those two papers as your peers? Are they the ones you measure your own performance against?'

'Sure. Though the *Post* is very different from the *Times* and the *Journal*. It's because we're decentralised, we rely more on the initiative of reporters than those two other papers do. The *Times* has a tradition of very strong, very capable desks which control their coverage. But if you see an unusual story on any given day in the *Washington Post* it's quite likely the idea originated with a reporter. That's expected here.

'The interesting thing about the *Post*,' he went on, 'is that it's both national and local. It's high-brow and low-brow; we run more comics, I think, than any other newspaper in America. We've always had a very high readership among relatively low-paid, relatively less-educated people in the Washington area as well as a high readership among PhDs.'

'Isn't that true of most American papers? It's equally the case, isn't it, in Los Angeles and Atlanta?'

'Yeah, it's standard for US papers.' The penetration, he said, can hit 80 per cent. 'Take a typical town. If you went up to Buffalo where our friend Warren Buffett owns the paper, they've got something like a sixty, sixty-five per cent penetration of the whole town. If you get smaller than that, if you go to an American city of population sixty or seventy thousand the paper might be expected to have 20,000 circulation and I would expect it to have 75 per cent readership or more. It's different to the English idea of a quality paper and then a mass paper.'

And nowhere is the idea of the mass-quality *local* newspaper more pronounced than in Washington. The *Post* may be the dominant paper of the capital city of the foremost democracy on the planet, but even to obtain a copy outside its immediate catchment area required ingenuity.

'We truck about 1500 copies to New York every day, grudgingly.'

'Why grudgingly?'

'It does us little or no good to circulate in New York. Correction, maybe it does us *some* good if some copies wind up in advertising agencies or whatnot but we have the economics of a local newspaper, we live on the advertisers, we expect our readers to be people who frequent their stores. We know we could sell a large number of newspapers around the US and possibly around the world but we have no interest whatever.'

I thought I detected, too, more than a touch of big city arrogance in this reply: if you want to read the *Washington Post* you'd better come to Washington. And if you *don't* live in Washington, if you play no part in the great power circus around the Senate and the White House, then maybe you have *no business* to read the *Washington Post*.

I said, 'Everyone tells me you're unusually well prepared for your role. You've done everyone else's job in the company on your way up.'

'I *had* spent a fairly long time poking around here at the *Post* before I became publisher,' he said. 'It was haphazard but fortunate. I started here as a city reporter; I worked as an editor on that desk. I worked as a clerk in the budget section of the accounting department; I sold ads for a while both in classified and display; I was a clerk in the promotion department; I was assistant home delivery manager in circulation for a good while and I spent the better part of two years in what was then the *Post's* biggest problem, the production department. I also had the better part of a year as a writer and intern on *Newsweek*. And then after *Newsweek* I came back here and had one glorious year as the sports editor, which I greatly enjoyed, and then I became something called assistant general manager and was in that job about five minutes and we had a strike, which you probably know all about.'

Somewhere in the story of every proprietor there is the episode of the Great Pressroom Strike. For Donald Graham the baptism of fire began at 4 a.m. on 1 October 1975 when he was awakened by a telephone call informing him that pandemonium had broken out in the *Post* pressroom. The prevailing contract between paper and printers had expired at midnight, but it had been understood that work would continue while negotiations were in progress. The printers, however, had a change of mind. And aware that for three years the *Post* had been sending its executives to courses in Oklahoma City to learn how to put out a paper during a prolonged strike, the pressmen resolved to smash their presses. A foreman was restrained with a screwdriver held to his throat, while a mob of printers ripped wires from their machines, vandalised the plates, stripped parts from the presses and then set them alight. Graham raced round to the plant in a taxi to be confronted by a vision of hell: fire trucks, police, arc lamps, a picket of belligerent printers and the foreman dripping with blood from a wound above his eye. It was the prelude to a long and tendentious strike – as vicious as the great *Los Angeles Times* union-bust of 1910 and Rupert Murdoch's 1986 lockout of his London printers at Wapping. The paper was produced by a skeleton staff, Katharine Graham supervising the postroom journalists who'd confronted the moral dilemma and crossed the picket (most did), substitute printers shipped in to replace the striking pressmen and Don Graham assuming overall responsibility for keeping the *Post* on the streets.

'The paper was being run by a most able general manager named Mark Meagher,' remembers Graham. 'Mark arbitrarily said, "Look Don, I have my hands full. I will make myself responsible for the labour negotiation itself and for public comment and marshalling resources and you just see to getting the paper out every day." We had done some preparation but we had *not* expected to be struck, so it was a somewhat jerry-rigged effort but we did it with some 125 people, getting the paper out for four and a half months until all the strikers returned.'

Throughout this period colleagues remember Graham as unflagging, regularly sleeping in the office rather than running the gauntlet to get home, rather serious, solemn even, hating the antagonism with the printers, feeling it should somehow have been avoided, and yet appalled by the violence to colleagues and printing plant alike. Never for a moment did he countenance a compromise on anything but the company's terms. 'Fundamentally,' I was assured, 'Don's one of the good guys. He expects all of us who work on the *Post* to give it the same loyalty he shows himself. He wants his people to be rewarded – rewarded financially – just a little bit better than on equivalent papers elsewhere. The key phrase here is *just a little bit better*. Nothing crazy, nothing out of line, just ahead of the industry norm. That's Don Graham: steady, fair, sound, dare I suggest predictable.'

And yet I was also told, 'He's wound up tighter than a spring. Donnie's always made a point of being nice to everyone, a regular guy, but *inside* there are layers of repression he'll never deal with; psychologically, there's a lot of rage there. To his credit, he's tried not to let his background do him in, but it is still there, just underneath the surface.'

'Before the strike,' Don Graham told me, 'our circulation must have been 300,000 less than it is now. We're, say, 850,000 daily and one-million-one something on Sunday. It's gone up a great deal. We crossed 400,000 daily in 1960, we crossed 500,000 in 1970, the *Star* went out of business in 1981 and that added 100 or 200,000 to the readership. There were three major East Coast afternoon papers: the *Star* the *Philadelphia Bulletin* and the *Cleveland Press* that went out about the same time. In each case the morning paper had about 50 per cent duplication. We kept it and we went on growing from there.'

'What exactly does the paper mean to you? When the *Washington Post* comes into your mind what does it stand for?'

'Well the publisher's priorities here are simple – on this there's no disagreement at all between my mother and me, although you could try it out. Ten times the most important thing the publisher does here is pick the editor, editors. There are two editors that report to me, have reported in the past to my mother when she was the publisher, and one of the first things I did when I became publisher was pick Meg Greenfield as the editorial page editor. Another thing over the last many years, as the succession very gradually evolved here, was to select Len Downey as Ben Bradlee's successor. So I've done, for the time being, the two big things that I gotta do.'

'If it hadn't always been clear to you that you would almost certainly inherit the *Post*, do you think you would have come into newspapers?'

'To begin with it was very carefully *not* made clear to me that I had some family destiny here. My father, who was running the paper when I grew up, never put an ounce of pressure on any of the four of us to think of ourselves as a future newspaper owner. I felt the same set of tugs that everybody in a family business feels: part to it and part away from it.'

'When you were growing up was it newspaper talk at home all the time?'

'Not exclusively. There was a good deal of it but my dad was also a lawyer – *it was all Washington talk* – and very, very interested in politics. My mother had grown up in a highly government-orientated family. My grandfather had been in government service from World War I through the Depression and only got into the newspaper afterwards, and indeed went back, so it was *Washington talk* all the time.'

'And is it unrelenting Washington talk in your own house?'

Don Graham laughed. His long arms shot out in a gesture of defence, as if to say, 'No way José, what a horrible idea'. Then he said, 'At home I like to read a lot. I spend most of my time when I'm not here with my family – my wife Mary and four kids who are aged . . .' he hummed and haaed for a bit '. . . who are aged ten through 19: everyone just changed birthdays so I have to recalculate. And I garden. I don't do *anything* extraordinary. Mediocre tennis.'

'People keep telling me you're much more low-key than your mother. Are they right?'

'I think that's a misreading of my mother, she's a very, very low-key person. The first thing to understand about her, of course, is how she came to the job and what she was when she came to it, very shy and very self-doubting. Any understanding of her has to start with that. It would amaze you if you could see a tape of her making a speech 25 years ago. She was very uncomfortable in any kind of public role and she's taught herself how to be on the public stage but I would say, to this day, she doesn't enjoy it a lot and it's always a considerable effort.'

'Is the Washington Post Company low-key too?'

'We've certainly been very *prudent*, and the greatest business executives never get credit for what they *don't* do. We've turned down any number of opportunities to buy newspapers, TV stations, whatnot. The prices just didn't make economic sense to us through the eighties. It was enormously frustrating. There's some very accurate published descriptions of Barry Bingham calling Kay and saying, "We'll sell the *Louisville Courier-Journal* to you if you'll just match Gannett's price." Yes it was frustrating. We checked out a great deal that we did not buy. But we kept a degree of financial discipline that in retrospect looks pretty good.'

'Does that give you a quiet satisfaction?'

'Not even quiet! A noisy satisfaction! We've got cash in the bank well in excess of our debt and we are ready and able to make an acquisition now if the price is right. The media market today in the US is sort of like the residential market. Most people would like to sell their house at the 1988 price and the same is true of the newspaper business. Everybody remembers what they thought their company was worth a few years ago and it is tough for sellers – it's easier for buyers than it is for sellers to say the world's changed. That's why there have not been many transactions lately. I don't, for example, think anyone's going to make a great deal of buying newspapers from Rupert Murdoch.'

'Why?'

'He's a shrewd man. When he sells he's going to sell for a premium price.'

The striking thing about the *Washington Post* is the number of rival proprietors who hanker after it.

When I took to asking which two or three newspapers they most craved if they became available, no three choices ever excluded the *Washington Post*. Dean Singleton and Ralph Ingersoll both put the *Post* first, no doubt seeing in it all the solidity and understated prestige that their own buccaneering adventures in the newspaper trade can never satisfactorily provide. Conrad Black and Rupert Murdoch both nominated it, partly mischievously, since the *Post*'s instinctive liberalism and political correctness would be hard for either to condone for long. The Aga Khan mentioned it approvingly, as one of the few newspapers on the planet that gives serious coverage to his Third World projects. Robert Maxwell applauded it while expressing the view that, properly managed by someone such as himself, it had the potential to be vastly more profitable and authoritative. He told me, 'There are countless opportunities, presently being missed, for the *Washington Post* to be proactive on the world stage at the highest levels of government.' In Bombay, Ramnath Goenka had cited the *Post* as a rare example of a major Western paper that had gone up against the government and won, and consequently had a natural synergy with his *Indian Express*. In New Delhi, Samir Jain admired its editorial policy of 'having two editors, one for news and one for opinion, which of course prevents either party from claiming excessive powers and so believing themselves to be the *owner* instead of salaried editor.' In Hong Kong, Sally Aw Sian ruefully noted that it was rare for a newspaper to have a virtual monopoly in a capital city, and that she had often calculated the potential for extra profits if the *Post*'s editorial operations were tighter.

Notwithstanding its scale of operations – perhaps even *owing* to its scale of operations – the *Washington Post* remains hugely profitable. Operating revenues for the Washington Post Company grew between 1981 and 1990 from $753 million to $1.4 billion, of which 48 per cent of revenues and 51 per cent of operating income derives from the newspaper division: effectively the *Post*. In the American media big league the Washington Post Company has consistently ranked seventh in operating revenues, behind Time-Warner, the Chandlers' Times-Mirror, Gannett, the Chicago Tribune group, Knight-Ridder and the Sulzbergers' New York Times Company. As a stand alone newspaper, however, the *Washington Post* generally ranks third or fourth. The stock price, after a sluggish patch immediately following the float, has been strong. The Grahams' policy of rather cautious expansion – a cellular telephone company, some cable TV, sports pay-television in places like New England and Philadelphia, the purchase of an extra 17 per cent of the *International Herald Tribune* – if not exactly blowing the analysts' minds on Wall Street has never crashed and blown out their computer terminals like the fall of Maxwell or Asil Nadir. By the mid-eighties Warren Buffett was able to write a letter to Katharine Graham which, given its congratulatory tone, unsurprisingly soon found a wider audience. Buffett wrote: 'Berkshire Hathaway [Buffett's investment vehicle] bought its shares in the Washington Post in the spring and summer of 1973. The cost of these shares was $10.6 million, and the present market value is about $140 million. If we had spent the same $10.6 million at the same time in the shares of other [media] companies, we would now have either $60 million worth of Dow Jones, $30 million worth of Gannett, $75 million worth of Harte-Hanks, $30 million worth of Knight-Ridder, $60 million worth of New York Times or $40 million of Times-Mirror.

'So – instead of thanks a million – make it thanks anywhere from $65 to 110 million.'

As a newspaper property the *Post* scores highly with all three criteria: reputation for strong journalism, consistent profits and the unquantifiable element of swank and consequence. There is a theory that the real reason the Grahams have expanded their empire more slowly than the competitors is that there's really nothing they want to own so much as what they own already. In business, runs this theory, the normal spur is trading up; you own the third best hotel in town, when the second best becomes available, you want it. And then when the best hotel comes up, you want to own that too. The Grahams reckon they *already own* the best property. What might excite them? Only a metropolitan or national paper in the same league. Neither *The New York Times* nor the *Los Angeles Times* are liable to come up for sale, and in any case Katharine Graham dislikes New York. She told me, 'I just wouldn't take one [a newspaper there] as a *gift* because that *atmosphere* in New York, I think it's just the hardest place in the world to run a newspaper and who needs it? I mean it's really union dominated and the city itself of course has such hideous problems now that I would not at all like to be there.'

They could assemble a chain of local papers but there would be a snag. If they bought the neighbourhood press in say Boise, Idaho or Bismarck, North Dakota, then *they'd have to go there*. There'd be sabbaticals from Washington, overnight stays in dull hotels, meetings with executives much less able than the ones at 15th Street. And the potential profits from small papers would make little impact on the company's bottom line, certainly not in proportion to the fag of administering them.

As a purchaser for a national newspaper abroad, however, the Grahams shouldn't be too readily discounted. If the London *Independent* were ever to become available, then the judicious, debt-free Grahams might want to take a close look at it. And if Rupert Murdoch ever chose to divest himself of the London *Times*, then the Grahams of the *Washington Post* might just think it justified the stopovers and botheration.

The Emperor's New off-the-peg Papers

Ralph Ingersoll's $1½ billion shopping spree

Ralph Ingersoll intrigued me for two reasons. More than any other owner his story was entwined with that of his peers. His name came up again and again. No matter which proprietor I visited, Ralph Ingersoll had been their rival or ally at one time or another. He had competed with Dean Singleton, Tony O'Reilly, Otis Chandler, Donald Newhouse and the Pulitzers. He had sold newspapers to Conrad Black and Ken Thomson and procured them for Punch Sulzberger. He had discussed joint ownership with Robert Hersant and Rupert Murdoch, had shuttled Warwick Fairfax and Kay Graham across America on his jet. He is a tall, 47-year-old New Englander with a high forehead, Roman-nosed, soft-spoken and fastidious: the only man I'd ever heard of who has his swimming trunks bespoke by his tailor.

His sallies and incursions are as global as the big boys. One of the first things he said to me was, 'You know there's no fundamental difference between newspapers from one continent to the next. It's of no consequence where you buy them.'

But I was struck more than anything by the enmity Ingersoll could engender in rival proprietors. It exceeded even that engendered by Lord Stevens.

'You're proposing to put *Ingersoll* into your book?' asked an aghast Conrad Black, as though his inclusion somehow devalued the integrity of the whole enterprise. Other American owners kept impressing upon me that he is a dead duck, down the tube, a busted flush.

The trajectory of his ownership seemed to tell one as much about the modern proprietor as the story of Rupert Murdoch or Punch Sulzberger.

When I first started following the newspaper owners in 1985 Ingersoll was a minnow and it did not cross my mind to include him. Three years later, championed by Michael Milken the junk bond king of Drexel Burnham Lambert, he had bought or launched 228 substantial newspapers, making him – in sheer quantity – the third-biggest proprietor on the American continent. Within four years he had lost almost the entire lot. And now he was ricocheting around Europe, intent upon forging a new newspaper empire from the ashes of his previous one.

And there was another reason that Ralph Ingersoll interested me. A mutual friend of ours had become embroiled in a religious cult in upstate New York run by an Indian mystic, the Guru Mayi. Our friend had been persuaded to buy a house on the ashram and had moved there with her children, but now she wanted to sell up and leave. The cult was resisting her departure. She knew she must escape but she lacked the means and the willpower.

When Ingersoll heard about her predicament, he leapt into action. He and his wife drove straight from Connecticut to the ashram, fought their way past the cult security, bundled our friend, the children, the luggage into his car and speeded out of the compound. Later he and his team of attorneys doggedly negotiated the return of her assets.

People described Ralph Ingersoll to me as an intellectual – cerebral – but also as an action man.

The great Ralph Ingersoll shopping spree, which lasted just under four years and bagged him his 228 new newspapers, was the biggest and fastest newspaper acquisition splurge ever known on the planet.

At its peak it engaged dozens of media brokers, scores of bankers, dozens of lawyers to search out, fund and complete on the myriad deals Ingersoll was cutting, day after day, in virtually every state of the Union. One newspaper broker who travelled with him during this period told me, 'We lived in his plane. Sometimes Ralph flew long distance twice, three times a day: Lakeville to Ohio to Philadelphia and back to Connecticut. And all the time we were airborne he was hitting the phone, closing on one deal, embarking on the next.'

He snapped up 41 newspapers in St Louis, 13 in Youngstown, 49 in Philadelphia and then he began spending seriously. In August 1986 he bought the Connecticut *New Haven Register* and its morning counterpart the *Journal-Courier* for $185 million. He bought the Morristown *Daily Record* in New Jersey for $155 million. He swooped into Anderson, Indiana and bought the little local *Herald* and *Daily Bulletin*. He touched down in Asheboro, North Carolina and picked off the *Courier-Tribune*. Then he bought six more. He flew to Long Island, acquired 76 weeklies and mounted a lateral challenge to Otis Chandler's *Newsday*. Then in August 1987, in his single biggest deal, he paid $400 million cash to the Horvitz family of Cleveland for four Ohio dailies and the Troy *Times Record* in New York state. This is believed to be over $50 million more than the underbidder who was, as so often, Dean Singleton.

And each time he needed more money he got it. In the mid-eighties, the pool of venture capital from Warburg, Pincus & Co and the endorsement of Michael Milken and Drexel Burnham ensured a bottomless supply. Newspapers were sold as a glamour industry and Drexel's July 1986 bond offering for Ingersoll was substantially oversubscribed. In less than two years he had raised more than $1 billion in new debt, half of it in junk bonds. His team of advisors was the hottest and most ferocious in North America: the lawyer Martin Lipton, the dealmaker John Vogelstein of Warburg, Pincus & Co and Milken himself. They were endlessly inventive. July 1987 found Ralph Ingersoll and Michael Milken together in Mexico City, visiting President Miguel de la Madrid to discuss Milken's proposals for securing Latin debt through newspaper investment.

I asked Ingersoll, 'What was the largest number of newspapers you owned?'

He furrowed his brow. He was sitting behind an expansive partner's desk in his London office, a Georgian townhouse in Buckingham Street. 'The largest number?' he mused. His eyes swept the office, resting for a moment on the Aubusson carpet, the rococo console table, the volumes of photographs of Italian palazzos, the red-flame gas fire flickering in the Georgian grate, before settling on an incongruous litre-bottle of Listerine mouthwash that sat on a pile of art books. 'The largest number?' he repeated. 'You want the precise number?'

He looked slightly bemused, like the owner of a vast Australian sheep station on being asked exactly how many rams and ewes he owns.

'I'm not sure that I can answer your question accurately,' he said at last. 'We bought a lot of chains, groups of papers. They weren't single transactions.'

But he was still pondering on the empire's size. 'In absolute titles we probably had about 200. No, *more* than 200. God, we had 180 weeklies and about 60 dailies.'

'Is that the largest shopping expedition for newspapers there's been?'

'Probably. Certainly.'

'It's more than one a week for four years.'

'Yup. But sometimes it was single papers, sometimes groups.'

'Did it matter where they were geographically?'

'No. My father's view had always been that he would only buy a paper if he could get to it in about two to three hours from New York. I stuck to that rule of thumb. I just used faster airplanes. I just got the fastest machine I could find, a Westwing jet, very long-legged; it could reach the West Coast non-stop against the winter winds which no other light to medium jet can do. Then I started ranging further afield, a lot further afield. Then it didn't matter where a newspaper was to buy it.'

'What did you spend altogether buying them?'

'On the whole lot? Well you could figure it out. It would have had to be at least a billion and a half.'

'How did you find enough papers to keep up the momentum?'

'I had a network. I knew – still do I suppose – everybody on the continent. I knew lots of people and I knew their families and I knew when opportunities would present themselves. For many years I'd been unable to do deals that were worth doing, because Gannett and Thomson were around and had the money. And finally with Warburg I had enough capital to take advantage of these situations. And Warburg was extremely enthusiastic. They wanted to build, quickly, a world-class company. You see we started with nothing. When Warburg and I started we had no papers. There were papers I owned privately in New Hampshire and Indiana, but before May 1984 when I did my first deal in St Louis with Warburg, we had *zero*. So we bought rapidly. It was a good deal with Warburg. I owned half of it and had voting control. They had the other half. My job was to find, acquire and run the papers, their job was to supply capital.'

A media broker who accompanied Ingersoll on part of the shopping spree told me, 'Ralph is one of the most *charming* people I have ever met. Of course, one can question his sincerity, but the point is that this sheer charm made him a formidable acquirer of newspapers. When Ralph was trying to wrest some paper from its longstanding owner, he was always brilliantly well-prepared. He would order a local history book covering "Nowheresville, Indiana" before going in to see the owner, which materially helped him charm the guy off his perch. Sinclair McCabe – key deal-doer for Thomson – had at least as much money and certainly had his own charm; but there simply wasn't anyone close to Ralph in the charm stakes.'

I asked Ingersoll, 'How did you manage to keep tabs on all these papers once you'd bought them?'

'We had a pretty basic formula for how we did it. The formula has always been to increase pricing. I've always been more daring than the old family ownerships in exploiting the advantages of . . . what's the polite word? Monopoly is the impolite word, the *exclusive market position*. When we bought a new paper we felt we could charge rather more, both for circulation and advertising, than was part of it previously. We did away with the old boy advertising rates. Rates that were kept low so as not to anger friends and neighbours. Some of the papers we bought had been operated on something other than the profit principle.'

'Didn't people complain when you jetted into town and hiked everything so dramatically?'

'They [the sellers] equate what we did with being the sons of bitches that they wouldn't be.' But he observed that they were always happy to accept the premium prices he offered when he cut the deal.

'The second thing we would do,' said Ralph Ingersoll, 'was rationalise the workforce to some degree. And then we'd fix the printing. Most of these newspapers we bought had already converted to cold type, but the conversions had been botched by the families. We'd fix them.'

'Botched how?'

'They weren't disciplined enough – they were too sentimental about the old staff relationships. And we simply *knew* how many productive hours per page it takes to produce a newspaper and we were willing to reduce the staff, buy out the positions.'

'How many production hours *does* it take to produce a page?'

'A broadsheet? One or two. Tabloid, effectively half of that. And productive means net hours of work that you're paid for. Typically in hot metal the best papers in North America were running at about ten productive hours per page. With the advent of photo-composition that had been cut in half to five, if they did a decent job. We cut it to 1.5, 1.2.'

The telephone rang. He took the call. I heard words like Bahamas, drug running, real estate. The call ended.

'Excuse me for that,' he said. 'I'm selling some properties on Cat Island. I bought a beach property some time back in the Bahamas, and after we moved in we discovered that our beach was being used as an entry-point for drugs. So I bought the other six houses along the bay to ensure they weren't utilised by these drug smugglers. The situation's better now, so I'm disposing of them.

'There was one other thing we did in newspapers,' he went on, 'and that was introducing new editions, particularly Sunday papers. I think I created more new Sunday papers than any other company on the continent. And we forced the circulations, we made the six-day base take the seventh-day delivery. So it was not uncommon for us to be able to *treble* the profitability of a newspaper in two or three years. Well you can imagine, doing that over and over and over again, Warburg and the banks became quite enthusiastic about the whole business, notwithstanding the fact that fundamentally it had become, post-1973, a liquidation business. Making money in North American newspapers today is akin to taking oil out of a West Texas oilfield, not exploring for new oil. It's like pumping high pressure steam in a near played-out oilfield. That's North America. In other parts of the world there are deeper reserves.'

In fact Ralph Ingersoll didn't restrict himself, in his hunger for potent newspapers, to continental America. His shopping sprees took him to England, Southern Ireland, mainland Europe, Australia. He bought the British *Birmingham Post* and *Mail* group including the highly profitable Coventry *Evening Telegraph* for £62.5 million. He bought 50 per cent of Irish Press Newspapers, owners of the *Irish Press*, *Evening Press* and *Sunday Press*, propelling himself into a full-blooded circulation war with Tony O'Reilly. He looked at joint ventures in Rome with Carlo Caracciolo, in Paris with Robert

Hersant. And in the earliest days of the Fairfax debacle Ingersoll made it his business to make himself agreeable to Warwick and Mary Fairfax.

Ralph Ingersoll's brief encounter with Warwick Fairfax, six months after he revealed his suicidal masterplan to buy out the entire company, is one of the strangest juxtapositions of modern proprietors: sleek, worldly Ingersoll and nerdy, know-nothing Fairfax flying together in a private jet over California to a secret audience with Michael Milken in Los Angeles. All three characters, one notes, were destined to lose their primary empires within a few years.

'I actually was trying to sort out Warwick's problems for him,' Ingersoll told me. 'He came to me and I *did* solve his problems. I got him all the money he wanted. But he fucked it up anyway. I mean he was impossible to do business with.'

'What did you make of him as a person?'

'Oh at least as bad as his press. He's a very, very weak character, that's charitable. Disorientated. He showed up in New York courtesy of Ansbacher at one point because he was looking for a partner, a large minority partner, in the *Melbourne Age*, which Robert Maxwell was trying to get his hands on at the time. I took him up to the Knickerbocker Club and we had a long chat one night, with him drinking Coca-Cola, which is probably the first time it's ever been served at the Knick. He's a very hard person to understand. I couldn't make hide nor hair of his thinking. I just couldn't understand what the hell he wanted so I asked him – I remember it as if yesterday – I said, "You've got to explain what you're trying to achieve," and he was incoherent, he just didn't know.

'So I said, "I think you have, basically, the following decision to make. Would you like to be a newspaper publisher or a banker?" He didn't understand. I said, "If you would like to be a banker I would take Robert Maxwell's offer," which as I remember was getting on to $800 million for the *Age*. "And then I'd ask him if he wouldn't like to buy the *Sydney Morning Herald* too and I'd sell the *Australian Financial Review* to the *Financial Times* and finish the liquidation of the whole thing and then you could be a banker, you could lend your money to other people and maybe that would be a fun thing to do," which was also perplexing to him. Not what Mummy had in mind. "On the other hand if you would like to be a publisher then you're going to have to find a way to refinance this at a fixed rate long-term debt. And given the pickle you're in and the amount of money you need there is factually in America only one source of that kind of money, which is Drexel, people who know that business very well and can deliver on a large scale." He'd heard of Drexel but he didn't know very much about them. And he needed to move pretty quickly. So we talked about that during the evening and the next morning at breakfast, and I said, "Look, if you really want to do this I'll take you out there." So I put him on my plane and we flew out to LA.'

I asked Ralph Ingersoll, 'What was Warwick Fairfax like to travel with on a small plane?'

'Squirrely. Odd, very brief attention span, insecure. Sometimes you meet people who just dart around and they're quite fun. He wasn't even fun, he wasn't charming. He's supposedly a born-again Christian. I went to Groton which is an Episcopalian school, and I'm quite interested in theology and would have been quite prepared to talk theology for four hours but he wasn't interested. But we were locked in and sat at very close quarters for quite a long time going west against the headwind. So I got to know him quite well. Very anxious about his mother, and had very strange domestic living arrangements. You'll find this hard to believe but it's a true story: I had suggested we wait a week or so to go out and meet Milken. It would give us time to put together a story. Because all I had in the Knick that night was what I could get on the back of a jotter card about sales and income, most of which turned out to be wrong. But he couldn't wait the week because he had to go back to Australia in two days. Now why did he have to go back to Australia? I couldn't offhand think of a single thing that was more important in the world than getting this money to save his newspaper empire. And the reason he had to get back to Australia – this is not a joke by the way – is that he lived in a flat with two other fellows and they had divided the chores. One of them cooked and one of them did the shopping and one of them did the housekeeping and they rotated. And next week Warwick was on cooking, his rotation was coming around. He had to be back to keep his end of the bargain. And I'm trying to visualise "Wocka" in a *chambre de bonne* on the sixth etage in Sydney with the other fellows, all born-again Christians, doing the cooking while an empire burns. It was quite odd.

'Anyway we arrived in LA and I introduced him personally to Ackerman and Milken and Kissek and the whole lot of them. And they were enchanted by the prospect. They didn't think a whole lot of Warwick, but they liked the idea of doing a big high-profile media deal in Australia. At that time the Australian currency was unstable so there were large swaps involved and there were a lot of things that they liked. And they sent a team down to Sydney, and it was a real media circus, you know TV cameras following them around constantly. At the end of the day, from Fairfax's point of view, it worked. I thought he'd get himself in trouble getting the deal done and what I hoped would happen was that I could get involved at least with a management contract to run it and fix it and that was what Drexel was hoping for. And then very rapidly it became apparent that the Fairfax company was bankrupt and that the balance sheet was going to have to be completely rebuilt. Warwick wasn't even on deck while this was going on. He just stuffed his head ostrich-like in the sand. His mother, in the meantime, I got quite involved with, we had a lot of conversations. Her qualifying questions were what sort of a Christian was I. You have to understand she's a Polish Jew who converted and she started asking me most complex theological questions about the tenets and beliefs of Episcopalians as opposed to Lutherans. She was putting me through my paces. She is cuckoo. She's entertaining though.'

Conrad Black would later tell me of the courtship. 'Mary Fairfax was impressing herself on Ralph Ingersoll as this devout Episcopalian, which is like Yitzhak Shamir passing himself off as the patriarch of the Greek Orthodox Church.'

Then Ralph Ingersoll said, 'Seriously, Fairfax is a deal I would love to have done. And should have done too, I was the obvious person. I talked to Rupert [Murdoch] about it, had lunch with him at the Knick to talk about it. I had a much better team than Conrad [Black] at the time. I had Martin Lipton, Drexel and Goldman Sachs, an absolutely world-class team. I still have a file on Fairfax – it must be a foot thick – and I could have done it but the timing was everything and Conrad Black was in the right place.'

'Where were *you*? The *wrong* place?'

'When the Fairfax business first blew up I was in St Louis.' He laughed hollowly. 'I was presiding over another project that, er, fell somewhat short of expectations.'

*

The adjective most often chosen to describe Ralph Ingersoll is 'patrician'. *Forbes* magazine encountered a 'lock jaw patrician clad in faultless tailoring and writing with a gold-tipped fountain pen'. The *Chicago Tribune* found a 'debonair patrician, a European kind of guy'. In due course, when the going got tough for Ingersoll after the failure of his *St Louis Sun*, the word patrician began to take on pejorative connotations in his press, as though owners might legitimately be tough, tyrannical or manipulative, but have no business being patrician.

Patrician is in fact a quality that applies to few proprietors. Lord Rothermere is patrician. Punch Sulzberger is patrician. Ralph Ingersoll II comes from an old Connecticut family – the Ingersolls were early settlers, arriving from Nottingham in England in 1629, and a forebear named Jared Ingersoll was a signatory to the Constitution – but their recent background had been professional and literary rather than grand. His grandfather was the Chief Engineer of the City of New York who built the Queensboro bridge, before retiring upstate in the late thirties where he said 'there are fewer people and more fish'. But the patrician side of Ralph Ingersoll's character – the attention to manners, the insistence on good restaurants and hand-made shoes – is just one aspect of this complicated, creative but thwarted strategist. And his childhood, for all the prosperous overlay of a large, comfortable house in Lakeville, Connecticut was altogether too anguished for a classic WASP upbringing.

'My mother died in 1948 when my younger brother was born and I was one and a half,' says Ingersoll. 'My father remarried a couple of times, from my point of view quite unsatisfactorily. He's not here to defend his views, but from my point of view he married not one but two women who were well beyond neurotic. One of them is still alive – and I can't boil her in oil so I guess she'll just go on until she doesn't go on. But my childhood was not a particularly happy one.'

In 1985, shortly after his father's death, Ingersoll and his brother Ian filed a suit against their father's estate. The court battle was partly intended, it appeared, to wreak revenge on their second stepmother, a woman who, Ralph Ingersoll is convinced, fed his father's spleen and encouraged his estrangement from his sons.

His real mother had been a Sears-Roebuck heiress who had scandalised her family by taking a job on *Life* magazine. Here she met and fell in love with Ralph McAllister Ingersoll I, the legendary managing editor of the *New Yorker* and publisher of *Fortune, Time* and *Life*, who would later run the chain of small-city newspapers that prompted an irreparable split with his eldest son.

'My father was very remote,' Ingersoll told me. 'Bear in mind he was 46 by the time I was born, so when I was a teenager he was well into his sixties and away travelling all the time, so I was cared for by governesses and nannies and shunted about. I saw my father only a few days every year.'

At the age of 14, no plans having been laid for his school holidays, Ingersoll took a job on one of his father's papers in Pawtucket, Rhode Island. 'I was not an unhappy conscript, *au contraire*. I was delighted to go by railroad to Pawtucket on my 14th birthday, move into the YMCA at $10 a week and to work for the *Pawtucket Evening Times* as a reporter. I was tall for my age – six foot at 14 – so I didn't seem too seriously an object of pity. I could certainly write well enough to fulfil the mandate, which was to write for New England millworkers with sixth grade educations. I didn't have a driver's licence so I reported anything I could walk to. Fortunately Pawtucket was the site of the first textile mill in America, the old Slater mill, and very densely built so one could walk to the police station, the fire station, the school board meetings.'

He was sent to Groton, the Episcopalian boarding school – 'one of America's Harrows' – but was booted out for bad attitude. This constituted his refusal to kneel in school prayers ('I cited the reference in the Old Testament to the effect that I needn't kneel before graven images') and his invention of a clever money-making scheme at Groton school dances. 'All fifth and sixth formers were entitled to invite a female, but I observed that not all fifth and sixth formers had girlfriends. I therefore bought their spare dancecards off them for $10 and charged $20 to fourth formers who required one for their own purposes. The balance I used for an entertainment fund, so to speak. Eventually one of these dances got a little out of hand and the scheme was blown. I wasn't sure whether they were charging me with importing alcoholic beverages or trading at a profit, the latter being the more serious charge.'

He went to work on a newspaper in Spartanburg, South Carolina, the *Herald* ('which is now owned by Punch Sulzberger and which in fact I helped him get'), where he covered black religious revival meetings in tents and profiled forest rangers who lived in lookout towers 18 storeys high, never came down for 30 years and had memorised the whole Bible. One of the many inconsistencies in the career of Ralph Ingersoll is that he loved this off-beat journalism, and yet the 200 high-margin newspapers he would later create made it almost a point of principle to devote no space to this kind of quirky writing.

Feeling that his son was perhaps too young to give up altogether on education, Ralph Ingersoll I sent him abroad to Switzerland, to the old League of Nations school, the Ecole Internationale de Geneve, and subsequently to Grenoble University. Thinking he might prefer to be a doctor than a newspaperman, he read chemistry. He got to know the society guru Krishna Murti and his homeopathic Greek physician and became involved in a dubious enterprise driving homeopathic drugs from London to the Dalmatian coast via Trieste and Athens. 'I couldn't risk getting caught going through an airport with all that loot,' he told me; then added, with typical Ingersoll insouciance, 'That's how I happened to come to know Yugoslavia so well.'

He returned to America and newspapers and took a job on his father's flagship in New Jersey, the Elizabeth *Daily Journal* ('A paper that Dean [Singleton] eventually got'). He was 22. The next six or seven years would be seminal for Ralph Ingersoll; years that would see him become fixated by the profit potential of newspapers, become enormously rich, a 'big picture' philosopher, convinced that only through ownership could he ever become wholly his own man. It was at this point that Ingersoll became close to the first of several great influences in his life. This was Charles Spooner, his father's chief executive. 'Bear in mind that my father is now divorcing stepmother one, courting stepmother two and I'm on my own. Chet Spooner, who had lost both his own children in accidents, took an unusual, not unnatural, but significant interest in me as a sort of surrogate father. We were very close. He taught me to fly, to be an acrobatic pilot, and to field-strip and reassemble complex typesetting machines. Spooner was as practical as my father was cerebral. His view of life was that it is terribly important that you never ever bluff about anything. If you're going to have views on production you ought to know how to operate all the machinery, and if you operate it you should be able to take it apart and put it together again. And he taught me too how blue-collar people think and why. In those heavy union days it was very important to make your alliance not with the white-collar workers – nor with the writers who I felt were my natural allies – but rather with the printers and typesetters and truckdrivers. And so what later became something of a speciality for me – the managements of labour relations during a very fractious period – really issued from a basic empathy, an understanding of the way people who work with their hands think.'

All the above – the stripping down of machinery and empathy with truckdrivers – can only, it must be said, take the student of Ralph Ingersoll by surprise. Although I would unquestioningly have credited him with numerous other accomplishments – the selection of a perfect Sancerre, for example, or forecasting of the yield to the nearest decimal point on a page of classified advertising.

'What *do* blue-collar workers think?' I asked him.

'Well they think a lot about a lot,' he replied airily, 'which is something other elements of society seem not to appreciate. Here in London your Eastender thinks about a lot more things than you might think he thinks about. And in any event in my world at the time those people were the centre of gravity. Newspapers – appearances not-withstanding – are manufacturing businesses, and always the majority of employees have been in manufacturing.'

Charles Spooner encouraged Ingersoll to quit journalism. 'He knew I could write well, but he wanted me to do difficult things which I didn't want to do such as sell advertising and sell circulation door-to-door. I got to know all the species of dogs in North America having to walk through the front yards and greet them bare-handed. And I learnt at an early age about America's addiction to soap operas. If you're selling newspaper subscriptions to housewives at two, three, four o'clock in the afternoon you bloody well don't interrupt, you talk to them in the commercial breaks.' He had been recalled to headquarters for four months to act as Spooner's assistant general manager when 'there was a really material turning point. Chet had a stroke. I was 27, we had about a dozen newspapers at the time, and I took over. My father had married the new stepmother and had effectively withdrawn himself from the scene. I ran the range – or flew the range as the case was. Chet was wheelchair-bound. The deal was Chet would remain as

Chief Executive, I became Chief Operating Officer and was sort of the ears, eyes and legs.'

The important thing to grasp about the 12 papers Ingersoll was running for his father was that they didn't actually belong to his father at all. Ralph Ingersoll I was proprietor in everything but fact. He was a minority shareholder who operated the papers for a large consortium of investors. 'They were people who made cement, had property, made TV shows, textile manufacturers, you name it,' says Ralph Ingersoll II. 'Basically all first generation entrepreneurs who wanted to diversify. And what they had in common was that they were all getting very much older and the ownership of the company was fairly unstable.'

Another thing they had in common was that they liked money, and greatly relished the idea of receiving a great big cash dividend. During the mid-seventies the asset value of newspapers began to rise steeply. Ingersoll's consortium was well aware of this; partly because Ingersoll, intent on keeping them sweet, kept telling them so. Eventually they hit on the idea of putting one of their papers on the market, to test whether the values really were as high as they were being told. They chose the flagship Elizabeth *Daily Journal*. Ralph Ingersoll II had valued it at $10 million. Lehman Brothers, independently for the shareholders, said it was worth only $6 million. The cement, property, TV and textile entrepreneurs were outraged at Ingersoll. 'If we were off by that order of magnitude then, you know, hell wouldn't have it,' he remembers. 'Everybody was extremely unhappy and I was directed to sell our flagship for as much as I could get. I sold it for $13.9. So then everyone was extremely happy except for me. I mean, I was 29 years old and had just sold for nearly 14 million a newspaper that had been valued by Lehman Brothers at six. But it had been sold – our flagship – despite my objections. It was a very important point in my life, because it demonstrated to me that not only had I not known who owned our biggest paper, but I'd never actually taken an interest. I was so distraught, I was ready to quit.'

But he didn't quit. 'Instead I negotiated a management contract, structured rather like a Marriott or Hyatt contract, in which I not only had part ownership of the asset but a super-preferred interest in that I got paid off the top. So for some time in the early eighties I was actually the highest-paid newspaper executive in North America. There was quite a period when I earned one million dollars a month net. So I was starting to generate quite a lot of money.' Ingersoll added to the chain, perfecting his fierce technique of cost-cutting. Most of the acquisitions were small, loosely operated family newspapers like the Terre Haute *Tribune-Star* in Indiana. As soon as he had cut the deal, his hound dogs were unleashed from Ingersoll headquarters in Lakeville, Connecticut and staff learnt just how lean and cost-conscious a newspaper operation can be. The publisher of one of his smaller papers in Connecticut, the *Milford Citizen*, explained the editorial formula: 'What our readers want is the school menu each week, local high school sports. We don't see our job as reporting on nuclear power plants except when they are virtually in our own backyard. [In return] we service [take advertising from] the local grocery store and cleaners.' He simultaneously converted all his newspapers from hot metal to cold type, in the process shedding 600 printers. His empathy with the blue-collar workers' thought process was never more greatly tested. Only one strike could not be averted. 'They blew a cop's foot off, there was a lot of shooting, but we published every day.' And all the while his profit margins grew. 'Thirty per cent, 40 per cent was normal. I hit 50 per cent with a newspaper once. That was in Fall River, Massachusetts.'

It is easy to understand Ralph Ingersoll's satisfaction during this period. As an intellectual exercise the asset-stripping of editorial quality, the distillation of a paper to its essential core, the eradication of every superfluous dollar and cent and the instantaneous impact on the profit and loss line must have been intoxicating. Newspaper as money machine. And the more he scythed the budgets, the more he became aware that it made no difference. The papers still sold. The grocery store and cleaners still sent him their advertisements (for where else could they place them in a monopoly market?). And one can see too why he found it irresistible to broadcast his triumphs, and why a host of less rigorous proprietors became increasingly irked at hearing so much about Ralph Ingersoll II's dizzy profit margins. These included Ralph Ingersoll I, still nominally at least the head of the company.

'My father's view,' says Ingersoll II, 'was that if anyone with talent used that talent to make money, it was somehow graceless and unseemly. He came to believe I had sold out because he thought I was devoting myself mindlessly to the making of money. As the dispute became more bitter, I just pleaded guilty as charged. My concept of a good newspaper is the difference between a 10 per cent profit margin and a 30 per cent profit margin.' Finally in 1981 Ralph Ingersoll forced his father out of the business and a year later eliminated his million-dollar-a-year share of partnership profits.

More than anything Ralph Ingersoll II became conscious that he must somehow buy out the whole company. 'Along the way I was becoming myself quite a significant source of capital, and I made it my business to go out and find some other sources to a) buy out our old shareholders and b) buy more newspapers. Now whether it was worth doing from an economic point of view was not something I'd ever considered during that period, I was just hell-bent to beat them [the shareholders]. So I shopped around and eventually I was introduced by a media broker to Warburg, Pincus – that's how I met them – and he said I might be better off with an institutional partner.' Ralph Ingersoll looked momentarily rueful. 'So Warburg, Pincus and I teamed up in 1984. And it was then that we began seriously to buy and launch a great number of newspapers during a four-year period of time.'

Ralph Ingersoll had a plan which every other proprietor in America considered reckless. But Ingersoll the strategist had rationalised the numbers and was convinced his scheme would work. What he proposed was the launch of a brand new metropolitan daily newspaper, the first to be launched in North America for 60 years, reversing the relentless tide of closures across the continent. And in another aspect too it would overturn conventional wisdom. Ralph Ingersoll's new newspaper would launch as the number two paper to a reasonably successful market leader.

Ingersoll chose St Louis, Missouri, as he was already familiar with the market through the 41 free newspapers he'd bought five years earlier. This suburban chain, which ringed the whole city like a circle around the sun, had a combined circulation (as he told advertisers) three times greater than that of the metropolitan paper, the *St Louis Post-Dispatch*. And he argued that his newspapers, being home delivered to almost a million targeted homes, were more credible than the pay-for *Post-Dispatch* that could be purchased by anyone from a tin vending machine on the sidewalk.

His bracelet of small papers had laid siege to St Louis. But now Ingersoll was raising his sights. Using Warburg, Pincus muscle and the print facilities of the suburban weeklies, he would launch a new pay-for daily. It would be called the *St Louis Sun*. 'We are about the business of *re-inventing newspapers*,' Ingersoll told *US News and World Report* at the time. His star as newspaper baron was never higher. The word 'visionary' was freely bandied about. 'In less than a decade after seizing control,' boggled the *Wall Street Journal*, 'he has parlayed his father's modest business into a billion-dollar empire.'

There was much speculation about his real motive. The one most often suggested was respect. His 228 newspapers were, with few exceptions, editorially mediocre. He possessed no flash flagship. And if you posed the question 'What has been Ralph Ingersoll II's great contribution to journalistic excellence?' answer came there none. Maybe he is bored, speculated commentators at the time, of being described as 'The new breed of press scion more attuned to balance sheets than broadsheets'. And the ghost of his father was predictably given a further work-out. Would the *St Louis Sun* be Ralph Ingersoll's vehicle for newspaper respectability?

Anyone who believed that didn't know Ingersoll. The newspaper he envisaged was never intended to be some journalistic showpiece. He wanted to own a successful newspaper: a success de facto. His intellectual pleasure lies not in a finely turned opera review but in the correct interpretation of the market. His fulfilment is found sitting upon a well-stuffed sofa in the most expensive hotel suite, sifting demographic data, getting a fix on the populace of Missouri. And the more he studied the data, the more confident he became.

'I guess I'd been partly inspired by Rupert Murdoch,' Ingersoll told me in the kitchen of his London home in West Eaton Place. 'It was the inspiration of Murdoch that led me to launch the *Sun* against the *Post-Dispatch*. I was struck by one of his annual reports in which he commentated, almost boasted, that he was proud that News Corporation competed actively and directly in every market in which it published and that it had no monopolies. I never heard a publisher boast about such a thing before. And it seemed to me that some share of the remarkable creativity and growth of News Corporation ventures might result from a state of mind that said it's better to be alive and vital and *competing* and fighting for an audience than to be the type of company which is just pumping oil out of a West Texas oilfield. And I admired the way that Murdoch conspicuously acquired newspapers only in competitive markets – San Antonio, New York, Chicago, Boston, London – and his capability to create new audiences. So I had been thinking that sooner or later we too would have to extend our capacity to create new audiences.

'And St Louis was a city where there had been historically, for more than 150 years in fact, two or more daily newspapers,' said Ingersoll. 'Since the war there had been two: the *Post-Dispatch* owned by Pulitzer and the *Globe-Democrat* which had been owned by Don Newhouse, and the Newhouse paper had declined in relative terms. So Newhouse had been involved in a joint operating agency agreement with Pulitzer and they tried to cease publication of the *Globe-Democrat* but the Justice Department interceded and prevented them, citing anti-trust laws, and forced them to offer it for sale. And so they sold the *Globe-Democrat* to an entrepreneur who was under-capitalised and Newhouse ended up owning half the Pulitzer newspaper.

'So when I first came to St Louis the two newspapers were competing and that meant that neither one of them had a particularly remarkable circulation – they were each around 250,000 which was a third less than they'd been 20 years earlier; they'd shrunk quite a lot despite the enormous population growth. And therefore the disparity between *our* aggregate circulations [of the 41 weeklies] of more than 800,000 and the circulation of either one of these papers was so large that it made it possible for us to have a very substantial business.

'However by 1988,' he went on, 'the *Globe-Democrat* was going through additional turmoil and eventually, after a couple of fits and starts, it was folded by its entrepreneur owner. And that left the Pulitzer-Newhouse daily alone in the market and it very rapidly increased its paid circulation. And therefore the competitive advantage of my suburban ring was seriously diminished. We felt, and were encouraged to feel by leaders from every quarter of the community, that if we launched a new newspaper in St Louis it would find a ready audience in former *Globe-Democrat* readers – which actually had

200,000 in paid circulation when it died – and it was a *terrible* newspaper the last couple of years. It had been once a terrific newspaper, but latterly it was an awful newspaper. And yet its readership was very stubborn. The Newhouse-Pulitzer paper that was run by the Pulitzers had a very liberal political orientation in a community that was very conservative. And the consequence was that we did a study and we recognised that if we launched a new newspaper and staffed it rationally we could break even on 125,000 paid circulation. And if they could get 200,000 on a really rubbishy paper that had been a shadow of its former self, we thought that if we did a first-class job we would be able to do a lot better.'

The fascinating thing about Ralph Ingersoll is that, even though I already knew the St Louis launch had been a spectacular failure, he was still capable of captivating me with its brilliance as a scheme. I could picture him spellbinding a room full of bankers. He has perfected the technique of logical progression, of unrolling his premise with such clinical conviction that you find yourself thinking yes, yes, just allow me a slice of the equity.

'In addition,' said Ingersoll, 'I was encouraged by the Toronto Sun Company of Canada. One of the most interesting newspaper entrepreneurs in our generation is Douglas Creighton, who was the chairman. Doug Creighton had created the *Toronto Sun* and in the space of a few years produced a dynamic alternative to the *Toronto Star* and the Thomsons' *Globe and Mail*. So here was Toronto, able to support three papers – the *Sun* had by then 300,000 circulation daily and 450,000 on Sunday – and while metropolitan Toronto is somewhat larger than metropolitan St Louis it wasn't *very* remarkably larger. If you scaled it down it would have sort of implied 225,000 daily to their 300,000 and I needed only 125,000 to break even. Creighton had gone on and done this twice more in western Canada, in Alberta and Edmonton, and in both cases had created successful, competitive daily newspapers in much smaller markets than St Louis. So I thought given the experience of Creighton and given the success of Gaspar Roca in Puerto Rico in launching the San Juan paper *El Vocero*, and given the success of Carlo Caracciolo in Rome with *La Repubblica* and of Jean-Luis Cebrian in Madrid with *El Pais* and then Andreas Whittam Smith here in London with the *Independent*, I could see that in recent years there *had* been a number of successful launches. But not in North America.'

And so, persuaded of the viability – the virtual infallibility – of his scheme, Ralph Ingersoll launched the *St Louis Sun*.

'And I have to say that there was no corner cut, we wanted for nothing to do this. We recruited a terrific editor, a former managing editor of the *Toronto Sun*. We recruited the general manager of the rival *Post-Dispatch* to be publisher. We recruited a significant staff, had very exotic colour printing equipment and we spent about eight months building a distribution system. We set up home delivery routes, had 5000 retail outlets, 5000 vending machines, everything you could want to launch a modern newspaper. I emphasise this because there can be no excuse that we were hurrying or we lacked funding. And I was substantially involved in the launch myself as the sort of editor-in-chief and chief public spokesperson. We bought a home in St Louis and moved there for a year. And then the launch promotion began. We launched with terrific fanfare: heavy promotion, television, we spent millions. I'm satisfied the promotion was so well done that no adult in the St Louis metropolitan area either failed to hear about the newspaper or see it. So we don't have any excuses in that department either. And the advertising support was very robust, it was just rising constantly.

'And yet,' said Ingersoll dolefully,' it *did not work*.'

'How quickly did you realise this?'

'Ninety days. Factually what happened is that after about 90 days the single copy sales, which in economic terms was more important, settled down to a number in the range of 17,000.'

'That low?'

'Yup. Even with heavy lottery promotions and wingos and bingos and all the tricks of the trade. At the same time on the home delivery front something even more troublesome happened. We had launched with 70,000 home delivery orders paid in advance, but in 90 days' time a lot of people failed to renew. What happened as we went forward is that it became necessary to increase the investment in marketing sales to find new home delivery subscribers. And by the time we'd been going four months the turnover, what's known as the turn rate in the business, on home delivery was running at an annual rate of 300 per cent. That means that to keep 50,000 paid circulation we had to sell 150,000 orders. It was breathtaking. Even in Southern California, a famously transient market, the highest turn rates ever seen were in the order of 150 per cent. And here we were double the highest rates ever measured. And of course what happens after you've called around all the telephones in a market with a million homes a certain number of times is that eventually it wears out, it's like you wear out a saddle and you just can't ride it any more. So you can certainly project at some point, no matter how much money you pay and with all the telemarketing techniques available in North America, the market was rejecting the product.'

'Did you close it then?'

'I had no choice. We found ourselves in the spring, after four or five months of this, faced with a circulation effectively one third of what we required and losing $2 million a month with absolutely no prospect of ameliorating the losses and we decided in the circumstances to stop it.'

'Did you decide that?'

'Yes, I had to. Singlehandedly.'

'And your conclusion is what? There was no market?'

'Precisely. We did an extensive post-mortem. I'd had Ruth Clark, who is the best newspaper research person in North America, in our corner day and night; there was no insight that research money could buy or focus group testing could produce which we had not expended. And the conclusion we came to in our post-mortem is that the middle-class household in St Louis is just inundated by information.'

Ralph Ingersoll pointed to the paisley tablecloth on his kitchen table, the design composed of hundreds of small serifs.

'Imagine,' he said, 'that each of the little flowers on this cloth is a source of information available to a household. Twenty years ago the frame was sort of like this' – he marked a shape about a foot square – 'with about ten flowers in it. Shining most brightly would have been a local newspaper, then three important TV networks – ABC, CBS, NBC – and then probably a shopper, a couple of radio stations and maybe two cable channels.

'Twenty years later,' he said, 'that frame has at least 200 points of light in it, 200 of these flowers. In St Louis each household has at least 35 cable channels, though the new cable systems offer 120 channels. It has direct mail pieces to the order of 50 to 60 per week coming into the home, often more in the better demographic zip codes. It receives 12 to 15 giveaway newspapers and magazines. There are at least 50 radio stations, 30 TV channels. And then in addition they're getting two or three telemarketing calls per night trying to sell them something.

'And in the midst of all this overload,' said Ingersoll, 'the homeowner is making some effort to sort out and consume what is useful. And what the market determined – it's absolutely clear to me – is that there was no demand in St Louis for another newspaper, no need for another such animal. And I decided at that point that something really fundamental had changed.'

The demise of the Ingersoll empire, when it happened, happened very quickly. Talking about it now, so soon after the event, he is insistent on the correct choice of words. 'Collapse' and 'fall' he will not allow. 'It didn't really fall apart, it was *dismantled* in a particular way, it was just taken apart in pieces.'

The trigger for the fall – the dismantlement – was Michael Milken and the junk bond market. America in 1989 was enthralled by Ivan Boesky's revelations of insider dealing at Drexel, and the scandal soon prompted questions about the whole ethic of the mid-eighties financial markets and its breezy financial instruments. Despite having no involvement in junk bond manipulation, as the debate escalated, Ralph Ingersoll came to personify the Milken client; the more so after he championed his mentor on television, rallying support from other Milken-backed entrepreneurs and signing an advertisement in the *Wall Street Journal* 'Mike Milken, We Believe in You'. At the precise moment that the *St Louis Sun* was folding after just 213 issues with losses of $25 million, Milken was facing 98 racketeering counts.

It was against this inauspicious backdrop that Ingersoll needed to reset the interest rate on one of his $125 million junk bonds.

'At the end of the day,' says Ingersoll of the event that felled his empire, 'what actually tripped the enterprise was something that none of us foresaw. We had issued after the market crash of '87 one of the most notorious tools – infamous maybe – the so-called reset note which has effectively a floating interest rate in which the rate in the future is determined by what the market place thinks it would have to be to cause the security to trade at par. And in the middle of all this the US government for political reasons smashed the market, they tried in earnest to smash the high-yield bond market. So what basically happened – I've never talked about this before – was that in the spring of 1990 it became apparent that resetting resets [on junk bonds] was technically impossible, mathematically impossible. You couldn't set the interest rate high enough to make the bond trade at par. I suppose if you set the rate at 50 per cent somebody would pay at par but then the company couldn't pay the interest, so what's the point? So the issue was if we can't reset the thing high enough we're going to have to buy it back. So I called up Michael Brown at Thomson and sold him a handful of our papers in Ohio and Indiana for $275 million and I used the money to pay off all our banks. So we're sitting there with our balance sheet with no senior debt, and then what we thought we would do is use this balance sheet, which then had plenty of credit, to buy the bonds back. Our role model was the Hall family of Hallmark cards in Kansas City which had employed Goldman Sachs to do exactly this in respect of a company called Univision which was a Spanish-language TV network which they owned and still own, and it had worked very well for them. But sometimes, on a second time around on a new invention, people catch on and ask for more. So we made a tender offer for the bonds – Warburg did – and it wasn't accepted. So it was restated. Anyway, after about three passes at this and with the bond needing to be reset, we had no choice but to retire them.'

The financial press had a feedingfest. The coverage was almost uniformly vindictive. That Michael Milken's most high-profile beneficiary was unable to reset a junk bond appeared to some commentators to be just punishment for his hubris.

'I don't know that we were unique in what we were doing,' says Ingersoll, 'but I think it's the old story: we did what we did on a large scale relatively quickly and that always unsettles people who have been plodding along at a different pace. I didn't think of it in personal terms. Perhaps others did.'

The hiccup over the single junk bond default focused the attention of the business press on the entire Ingersoll edifice and concluded it was precarious. 'Junk has smeared his dreams of an American publishing empire,' reported the Hartford *Business Journal*. 'Junk bonds are the equivalent of poison apples for many [of his] employees.'

Others blamed Ingersoll for failing to anticipate the advertising recession and for paying prices vastly above their market value to acquire newspapers. Others blamed him for launching the *St Louis Sun*. 'Everyone in the industry said the paper was ill-fated from the start,' said Kenneth Berents, a stock analyst with Alex Brown in Baltimore. 'Had he not gone out on a limb for the *Sun* he might not be having the problems he's having today. The *Sun* may have cost him his whole empire.' Still others found Ingersoll at fault for 'antagonising the bond holders by offering low-ball bids' and for 'believing his own marketing bullshit'.

Rather like the days immediately following the death of Robert Maxwell, there was hardly a person alive who did not have his own pet explanation for the unexpected turn of events.

Within two weeks Ralph Ingersoll had bowed to the inevitable. Days of tortuous meetings with Warburg, Pincus produced a compromise. Ingersoll would relinquish his 50 per cent stake in all 212 American newspapers and the debt would be assumed by Warburg. In return, Ingersoll got to keep his 16 European papers: the Birmingham Post and Mail group (which he also subsequently relinquished to a management buy-out for £125 million) and the three papers in Ireland.

'Warburg had come back to me,' says Ingersoll of the deal, 'and said "We're prepared to put in more capital, so are you prepared to either dilute yourself out of control or would you like us to divide the assets?" And I was *not* interested in losing control so I said I'd divide the assets. And the reason I did that had not a little to do with conclusions I had reached about what's happened to newspaper values and what's going on. It had become apparent to me by the late eighties that the American newspaper industry is in fundamental, structural decline.

'And bear in mind the timing of when we closed our transaction,' he went on. 'We had to get government approval because of the scale of it, and then we closed it actually on 2 August 1990 within two hours of the time Saddam Hussein slammed into Kuwait. Oh boy. That was when we and Warburgs formally separated. It was in London, it was at 6 a.m. We had been working all night. As you know, from that date the world has been in serious turmoil and what started out as a seemingly mild, cyclical recession turned into the worst recession since the Second World War. The US recession is unlike any they've seen before.'

Did he jump or was he pushed: once again it was a great Maxwellian conundrum that rang in Ralph Ingersoll's ears as he Concorded out of New York for the last time bound for his new, rather modest European empire.

In America, most parties assumed he was pushed, or at least didn't have much option to stay. To the Europeans he was simply another foreign multimillionaire media baron, full of North American know-how, come to teach us how to sell newspapers.

Two things I found unusual about Ralph Ingersoll. The first was his impetus. In my travels I'd encountered every species of proprietor and motivation: political influence, social clout, vanity, in Britain a Knighthood, duty (the inherited paper that must be perpetuated), a sense of responsibility (owners were always assuring me of their commitment to the local community). But none of them except Ingersoll would admit to a simple, artless love of money. In his conversation about newspapers the bottom line recurred like a heartbeat; it punctuated his every observation with the frequency of a comma. And yet he did not strike me as vulgar, in the way that so many other eighties entrepreneurs were vulgar. His taste is rather discriminating and well informed. Like Aveek Sarkar of Calcutta, he does not hesitate to tell you the only place to have a suit or cotton shirts made. If you need the name of the prettiest hotel to stay in Nassau, Mexico City or Lake Como, Ralph Ingersoll can recommend the nicest room and ablest concierge. In the dining room of the London Ritz he looked up from the menu to the waiter and asked, as though the future of the world hung on his reply, 'Tell me what you're *proudest* of today.' The newspaper broker Hylton Philipson told me, 'Ralph likes to think of himself as a Renaissance man and a true citizen of the world. He even sent one of his sons to university in Tokyo. He certainly thinks more globally than most other proprietors. Dean Singleton by contrast would be lost in Europe.'

He married young to a glamorous German named Ushi who wears Lacroix couture, smokes cigars and cuts her husband's hair herself. They have two sons and two daughters: Colin, Matheus, Tiffany and Alexandra. Their house in Lakeville, Connecticut was described to me as 'a Gatsby home, immensely comfortable, with beds turned down, suitcases unpacked for you'. In London, when he doesn't feel equal to the 15-minute journey from his office behind the Strand to West Eaton Place, Ralph Ingersoll puts up at the Savoy.

His friend Tessa Dahl says, 'He is phenomenally generous. He's a marvellous benefactor if you're in tough straits or if you need to borrow a yacht. He lives in about seven time zones. He disappears into his study after dinner and makes phone calls until three or four in the morning.'

He prides himself on his abstruse knowledge. People say he is fallible to name-dropping, but his field of expertise is wider than smart society. And the thing that interests him the most – the subject that really fascinates him – is the modus operandi of other newspaper owners.

On this topic he is without equal. No other proprietor I visited knew more than 15 of their peers. Ingersoll appeared to know or have examined the balance sheets of almost all. And his unprompted opinions on them are qualitative:

On Tony O'Reilly: 'I don't think Tony knows very much at all about newspaper publishing. Tony O'Reilly knows a lot about packaged goods marketing, which is what he's paid to know about. He's a very competitive individual and he bought those Irish newspapers for a song. Tony's one handicap is that his newspaper company's vehicle doesn't have any money. Independent isn't much of a company. And he only fell into the Australian provincials because he had an Australian wife, before he let her go. I don't think Tony thinks a lot about newspaper publishing. I like him as a competitor.'

On Rupert Murdoch: 'In our generation he stands a full head above the rest of the crowd. It's a funny thing, there aren't a lot of media owners besides Rupert who actually think *deeply* about the future of newspapers. The operation he's started in East Germany with Hubert Burda, *Super!Zeitung*, stands out as the most interesting new newspaper in Eastern Europe. A sort of German *Sun!*' [But perhaps this is just another example of Ingersoll's too impetuous, intellectual excitement over anything new. Within a month of our conversation Murdoch had folded *Super!Zeitung*.]

On Donald Graham: 'Don Graham has significant insights into circulation marketing. But I don't think Don has ever had an opportunity to work in a market that's remotely representative of the way the rest of the world lives. Washington's very special. If anything they own can give him insight it would probably be *Newsweek* which is clearly failing.'

On Vere Rothermere: 'In the UK scene I rate him very highly. He's a keen operator. I think he understands his market very, very well, probably as well as anybody. Vere stands out. And his London *Evening Standard* is the best afternoon newspaper in the world.'

On Conrad Black: 'Conrad was sort of a David Stevens in Canada, just a younger version. As a newspaper proprietor, I don't think he has any insights. He has a lively intellectual life but I don't think he thinks deeply about newspapers. Conrad doesn't have experience in sales and marketing phenomena. He is an opportunist – in no respect a pejorative.'

On public company publishers who think deeply: Jim Batten at Gannett is someone who has thought relatively deeply – he's been forced to because *USA Today* has virtually wrecked the Gannett Company. And the shrewdest publisher is David Laventhol at the LA Times Company. Of all the people who run public companies in North America, I rate him tops. He's really had a baptism of fire between Long Island and LA.'

I asked him, 'If you could own anybody else's newspaper which one would you choose?'

Ralph Ingersoll half closed his eyes in concentration. 'I would say at the top of my list would be the London *Financial Times*, which is my personal favourite newspaper. In Germany I'd most like *Handelsbladt*, published in Stuttgart, it's sort of the *FT* of Germany. The *South China Morning Post* probably not on balance, that's being squeezed pretty hard right now. *El Pais* would be an interesting one, it fills a singular position in Spanish society. The European papers are all fun papers to own. I would say just on principle that it would be fun to own *Le Figaro*.'

And then he added, 'In North America I would of course put *The New York Times* there. There's nothing else really left in America that's interesting, they're all a huge headache.'

It occurred to me that fate had dealt a cruel hand to Ralph Ingersoll in not presenting him with one world class flagship. He would enjoy it so much. Instead he was destined to begin over and over, trading up, like an art collector whose only ambition is to own one good Rembrandt but ends up with a house of small Chagalls on hire purchase.

I asked, 'Would you like to have inherited a major paper?'

'I'd have liked that. A major paper would have been a platform from which to work.'

Then he said, 'There's still a lot of money to be made in the newspaper business. It's just that the reserves aren't as deep as they once were. It's like an oil man looking at West Texas rather than the North Sea.' He is exploring himself, he said, in East Germany. 'We were the underbidders for Leipzig. The newsroom was almost entirely composed of ex-Stasi whose brief, of course, had been to keep news out of the paper rather than report it in an engaging manner.

'The market price of newspaper assets has fallen just as far and fast as property. But property has long-term value characteristics which newspapers don't.' And matters, he predicted, would become worse. 'The newsprint industry is in distress, there's the cyclical problem of over capacity.

'Newsprint prices are about to go up *a lot*. It's going to have a material adverse effect on serious metropolitan dailies, especially broadsheets like Conrad's *Telegraph* and Rupert's London *Times*. And the long-term effect of television and cable is only beginning now to become apparent. CNN is around the clock and in every major market there is an all-news radio station. So everywhere you can get all the news. Newspapers which previously enjoyed positions of security in the market – because they met a *need*, the need to know the news – are finding their audience is being shattered. I am not clairvoyant, but I've been immersed in this all my life. And everyone including Warren Buffett who owns the *Buffalo Evening News* is noticing it. Display advertising has in any case been decreasing since the mid-seventies, briefly masked by the classified bubble during the Reagan boom, but all the fundamentals have been eroding. The day will come soon when we will absolutely lose control of our advertising pricing and this has started to happen.'

One could not, of course, altogether dismiss the suspicion from one's mind that Ralph Ingersoll's pessimism was prompted by his own empire's evaporation. Had circumstances been different, would he not now be accentuating the inherent strengths of newspapers? I could imagine him explaining, in exactly the same empassioned way, the benefit to advertisers of targeted, rich, literate newspaper readers in the midst of an increasingly amorphous metropolitan chaos.

But Ingersoll says he is thinking deeply now about a seismic shift in Western media priorities, not just his own.

'One of the most interesting sets of statistics I've come by is from a man named Owen Landon of Landon Associates in New York which is a company that represents about 600 daily newspapers in respect of national advertising sales. He told me that in 1980 of the total advertising spent in North America 60 per cent went into traditional media – radio, TV, newspapers – and 40 per cent went into underwriting tennis matches, auto races, special outdoor advertising and so forth. By 1990, in only ten years – half a generation – that number had shifted from 60 per cent to 27 per cent. Now we're talking about 60 per cent and 27 per cent respectively of a *huge* number – I don't know how many tens of billions but it's enormous – so you wonder what the hell is going on. All general circulation media now get quarter of the pie and three quarters of the pie is going somewhere else. I've seen this upmarket, middle market and downmarket. A lot of the food advertising, the money that used to go automatically into newspapers, now goes into paying supermarkets to rent the shelves. It goes into price promotions, outdoor promotional projects. Miller beer threw a birthday party for a year for the entire state of Texas to promote Miller over Budweiser and ended up in number one position in Texas. It didn't involve a lot of conventional advertising.

'So when you put all that together,' said Ingersoll, 'one finds the newspaper publishing business in a terrific state of flux.'

I said, 'As someone embarking upon his third newspaper empire, doesn't that bother you?'

Ralph Ingersoll laughed. 'Growing up with a pair of psychotic stepmothers and kicked around the world in different schools,' he said, 'I'm quite accustomed to change – and turbulent change. I don't feel particularly threatened by it.'

Cut and Slash in the Lone Star State

Dean Singleton's Survival Journalism

When you fly into Houston Intercontinental airport from just about anywhere the aeroplane makes a lazy loop around the mirror-clad skyscrapers refracting at all angles into the sky, as if showing them off in an impromptu cyclorama of Texan swank. Philip Johnson and I M Pei's skyscrapers range along the highground like the teeth of a metal comb, and the blood-orange Houston sunset has an air of menace as though you are flying into the immediate aftermath of an atomic accident.

As the plane banks over the West Loop – Interstate 610 – the great circular freeway spawned by the sixties oil boom, you can just make out the roofs of both of Houston's competing newspapers: Hearst's *Houston Chronicle* on Texas Avenue, and way across town near the Galleria shopping mall, the squat concrete headquarters of the *Houston Post*, which also acts as corporate headquarters for America's youngest and most controversial self-made proprietor, William Dean Singleton.

I was curious to see Singleton because so many people were insistent that I shouldn't. Three American proprietors and one London-based one had already assured me he was superfluous for my purposes, and three had chosen the same adjective to describe him: *sleazeball*.

They had said, 'I wouldn't waste your time going down to Houston. Dean Singleton may not have those papers in a year's time.'

Or they asked, incredulous: 'Why Dean Singleton of all people?'

'Because Dean Singleton has 71 newspapers in 11 states and he's not yet 40 – and he didn't inherit them.'

And then I would shoot a line about Dean Singleton being the best example of a new kind of owner; a non-patrician number-cruncher who none the less understands newspapers and has persuaded two blue-chip investors and a legion of banks to lend him the capital to fund an instant empire.

This line of argument was always inflammatory.

'Well that may be so,' I was told. '*For now*. But he's still a Texan sleazeball.'

The offices and printing plant of the *Houston Post*, suspended in a near-impenetrable cat's cradle of overpasses and underpasses near the West Loop Freeway, resemble a great white concrete tomb: a sarcophagus in a parking lot. On the shadeless tarmac there are designated car spaces: RESERVED FOR SALESPERSON OF THE MONTH, TAMMY BUCHANAN and RESERVED FOR PUBLISHER, MR DEAN SINGLETON – a gold Porsche – and a prospect of six freeways, scrubland and somewhere on the horizon a looming rocket-shaped building, the Transco Tower.

Two sides of the plant are windowless, and the glare of the sun off the concrete walls and the bonnets of cars makes you skew your eyes as you approach the entrance. Above the lintel, a motto chiselled into concrete: LET FACTS BE SUBMITTED TO A CANDID WORLD – *The Declaration of Independence*. This struck me as intrinsically flawed. Surely it is the facts themselves that should be candid. It seems too great an expectation that the readers of the *Houston Post* be candid too.

In the lobby, the formalities that were by now routine: the black security guard was evidently new to the job, for he had never heard of Dean Singleton nor had any notion of how to make contact with his office (ignorance of the existence of the owner was almost a theme of my travels: Arthur Ochs Sulzberger Snr, Samir Jain in Bombay and Louis Cha in Hong Kong were similarly total strangers to their own security men); a plastic security badge clipped to my breast pocket; a lift door opening on to different floors during the ascent, offering vistas of computer screens, bundles of newspapers, unoccupied desks. On each successive floor the building fell more silent. It was disconcerting. A newspaper produces expectations of noise: the screech of tyres on tarmac as a reporter sets off in pursuit of the big lead, the rattle of printing presses, the intransigent hectoring of the news editor enforcing deadlines. The *Houston Post* is as silent as a space laboratory.

And finally, more hushed than all that went before, the corporate floor: half a furlong of dark blue polka-dot carpet, a corridor as wide as a road. To either side, panelled double-doors open on to rooms – chambers, salons – of indeterminate corporate function. Their decoration is breathtakingly ostentatious. I could see Biedermeier chairs, walls covered from picture rail to skirting by gold latex chainmail, Chinese cabinets painted with scenes of geishas bathing in pools by pagodas. Through another door I saw a 17th-century dining table capable of seating 24 people, evidently used in the boardroom.

'That's Chippendale – the table,' remarked Dean Singleton's matronly secretary, Pat Robinson, as we passed by.

'Genuine Chippendale?'

'Sure. When Mr Singleton bought the newspaper the Chippendale was valued at a million dollars in the inventory.'

'So it was here already?'

'Mrs Hobby, who owned the paper before us, chose most of the furniture herself for the corporate suites. It's French Riviera. She purchased it from the French Riviera itself.'

Dean Singleton's secretary – who, it soon emerged, is also his sister, ten years his senior – ushered me into a fresh suite of rooms. The doors here were even taller and more substantial than before, painted jet black to set off their ornate gold door-furniture. You felt that it would take several people to drag these heavy doors open and shut.

'This is Dean's outer office,' said Pat Robinson who, having revealed her parallel existence as sister, dropped the Mr Singleton bit. She indicated the jet-black bookcases, polished parquet floor and a low glass table, as big as a snooker table, with stunted gold legs like elephant's feet. The decorative effect reminded me of King Fahd of Saudi Arabia's state yacht, the *Abdul-Aziz*, or of a VIP set hastily assembled at a Gulf airport for Arab ministers needing to be photographed greeting one another.

One whole wall is given over to a display of the latest issues of Dean Singleton's 71 newspapers. I picked out the *Yakima Herald-Republic*. Superficially at least, its appearance reminded me of a thousand other North American newspapers: a strip of coloured photographs above the logo beckoning you inside – a baseball player, a blonde Hollywood starlet, a picture of Tipper Gore waving a flag – the colour printing very slightly out of register and causing all three to acquire a ghostlike aura; below the fold, a lurid photograph of a tragedy – an overturned Greyhound bus – and a cute local story involving children and a lucky coincidence.

'Which one is that paper you're lookin' at there?' asked Dean Singleton, appearing at my side. He has a languorous Texan drawl which, I noticed, would become increasingly emphatic when he talked about the South West.

'The *Yakima Herald-Republic*.'

Dean Singleton nodded, and seemed for a moment to be searching for some interesting remark to make about it, but then decided not to, or else was unable to, so just said, 'Yeah, that's one of ours, the *Herald-Republic*.'

You are struck first by his physical bulk. For several days everyone I had spoken to – his editors, managers – had made a point of telling me how fit Dean Singleton is. Charles Cooper, who edits the *Houston Post*, had said that Singleton works out every morning with a personal trainer at the Sweetwater Country Club before coming into work, and that this trainer has instructions to push him hard. And I'd been told that he skis up in Utah – is regarded as a brilliant skier – and had bought a chalet up in the mountains at Park City 'in Robert Redford Country'. What no one had mentioned is his youthful pudginess. At 39, he looked like the editor of a college newspaper, sustained by a diet of root beer and donuts. His clothes too had a sophomoric air about them: blue Oxford shirt monogrammed WDS, red flowery tie, thick grey socks – possibly football socks – concertinaed around his ankles.

He arranged himself on a Biedermeier chair, next to a spindly gilt table on which stood a miniature basket of pink flowers and trailing, plastic ivy.

'You seeing Ralph Ingersoll as part of all this?' asked Dean Singleton. A note in his voice, for all its Texan languor, somehow alerted me that the preferred answer was no.

'I've seen him, yes.'

'But not for your book. I think Ralph, for all practical purposes, will be out of the newspaper business.'

I pointed out that he still had his Irish newspapers, and was talking about buying papers in East Germany.

'Yeah?' said Singleton. 'Well, Ralph talks big. Ralph's a smart guy, a very smart guy, but I think he made the mistake of reading his own press. We all make that mistake occasionally but Ralph's press was pretty big.'

'Your own press has been big too.' This was true: his two-year ownership of the *Dallas Times Herald*, bought from Otis Chandler's Times Mirror Company for $100 million, and his spectacular purchase of the *Houston Post* and the *Denver Post* within a week of each other for a combined $245 million, has made Dean Singleton the most written-about proprietor in Texas and Colorado. Magazine profiles have flatteringly compared him with William Randolph Hearst and Frank Gannett, pointing out that, in less than five years, his newspaper chain has overtaken both in number of titles.

'I was rather stunned at the publicity that the purchase of Dallas and Houston and Denver brought.' Singleton's proprietorial shorthand made it sound like he'd bought up the whole town, not just the newspapers. 'It bothered me at the time, and it still bothers me. I would prefer to never have publicity. I don't like publicity. I don't like to read about myself. I would be just as happy to never read about myself ever again because I don't enjoy it, I don't enjoy the intrusion. What happens if you're high-profile,' he went on, '– and we've become high-profile – and you're a private company so you don't really want to talk about your finances – you have many people who just assume you've got the same problems an Ingersoll has. They begin speculating, and it's very damaging to have them speculate. I saw a story last week. Somebody wrote scandalising me about how I was a child of the junk bond era and have piled up mountains of junk bond debt. *I never did a junk bond in my life*.'

'How did you respond to that article? Did you protest? Did you sue them?'

'Nah, you just make it worse. If you write them and tell them you never did a junk bond in your life then they'll ask, "Well, what kind of financing *did* you do?" And you say, "We did bank financing and institutional financing." Then they'll ask you more questions about it and you're not going to tell them anyway, so you're better off just to leave it alone. It's irritating that people just try to dream up things to write about you and they don't have the facts.'

Then he said, 'I've known Ralph Ingersoll for many years you know. He's kind of a friend. When I was beginning buying newspapers and he was buying newspapers we kind of had a gentlemen's agreement; if he saw something he didn't want he'd call me and if I saw something I didn't want I'd call him. If we both wanted it, we had a bidding contest.'

'Who usually won?'

'Oh, Ralph did. He usually won because he was more aggressive on price than I was – as a matter of fact I don't recall *ever* winning a bidding contest against Ralph! He *always* won. And then we competed in '81, '82 – I was publisher of the *Trenton Times*, he owned the *Trentonian*. When we got there he had the upper hand and that no longer is the case and I think my three years there had a lot to do with it. We were in litigation against each other, he sued me and I sued him.'

'For what, falsifying circulation?'

'Yeah. We'd see each other for depositions in court and tear each other apart and then go away and have lunch together! It was never unfriendly. That was in Trenton. Newhouse owns that paper now. We bought it from the Washington Post Company. From Kay Graham. Now it's Newhouse.'

'Do you miss it?'

'Nah, I don't miss it.'

This surprised me. Most proprietors found it difficult to feel dispassionate about a newspaper in which they'd invested time and emotion. Like grand hotels or old girlfriends, newspapers seem to retain a special hold, more powerful than simple profit seeking.

'Don't you ever miss newspapers after you've sold them?'

'Sometimes you buy newspapers that don't fit as well as you thought they would fit, you buy newspapers that don't do as well as you thought they would. We have sold newspapers in the past and we'll sell others, I'm sure. As we find others we want to buy. Sometimes you have to sell some you have in order to afford the ones you want.'

'So where does the satisfaction lie for you?'

'It's a bit like owning a nice racehorse. I mean a racehorse that wins races. It's the same watching a newspaper that is average when you buy it become excellent. The pleasure is watching the awards come in. Take a paper that wasn't very good three or four years ago that's named the best in the state this year – there's a lot of pleasure in that.'

'And if it doesn't win, you sell it, like a racehorse owner?'

'If something comes along you like better.'

'Aren't you missing Dallas at all?' Singleton's acquisition in 1986 of the *Dallas Times Herald* had propelled him up into the second division of world proprietors. For two years he had grappled with the paper, changed the format, the philosophy, the editors, given interviews in his jet at 36,000 feet about how the turn-around was coming good; and then he had sold it.

'No,' he replied. 'I'm *glad* to be out of Dallas.'

'Do you regret going in?'

'If I had my life over again I wouldn't go into Dallas. The competition in Dallas was much stronger than I anticipated it to be; the competing newspaper had a much more solid franchise and they were doing a much better job of developing it than I thought. And the demographic difference in the two newspapers was much greater than I'd thought. But we got our money out of Dallas, we sold it for a profit. I sold it to one of our partners [John Buzetta, an East Coast Italian].'

'And is he making a success of it?'

Singleton shrugged. I sensed that he was working hard at non-chalance.

'Don't know,' he said. 'I don't know that much about what he's doing with it. I understand he's making a profit, but I don't know the competitive situation today.'

'When you go back to Dallas now, do you feel diminished by not owning a paper there any more?'

'I just don't go back into that town.'

'You just fly over it?'

'Yeah. Since I sold the paper I think I've been back only once.'

'Does it make you feel uneasy?'

'Sure it does. We only owned it for two years but it was a fun two years in a lot of respects. But we found we were working too hard to maintain what we had, and we didn't like where we were and we didn't like where we thought we could be, and so it felt good to get out. And especially it felt good to get out with our pants on.'

But only just. Six weeks after I visited Singleton, the *Times Herald* was shut down by Buzetta who sold its assets to the rival *Dallas Morning News* for a fire-sale $55 million. Where there had previously been 40 American markets with competitive newspapers, now there were only 39.

*

William Dean Singleton – he jettisoned the William for the racier Dean at school – was born in 1951, the fourth of five children of an oilfield pumper in Graham, Texas. At some point in the escalating Dean Singleton legend it got about that his father had been an oil baron of Oscar Wyatt proportions, but this is fanciful: Singleton is quick to emphasise his modest upbringing in Graham.

'My father in oil? Well that's being charitable; he was an oilfield construction worker, which in those days was a day-labourer.'

The newspaper they had delivered at home was the smalltown semi-weekly *Graham Leader* which Singleton snapped up – 'for sentimental reasons' according to his sister – in 1986. This kind of local-boy-done-well acquisition is a recurring feature: when he bought the *Dallas Times Herald* one of his first acts was to give an interview dwelling on how he'd been turned down as a teenager for a job as copy boy on the paper, and how he'd flown back into town in his corporate jet to buy the company that wouldn't hire him. He also took a two-page advertisement in the trade paper *Editor & Publisher*. Under the headline 'How I Got A Job On The Dallas Times Herald', Singleton wrote: 'I interviewed at the *Times Herald* in 1970. They told me I was too young and inexperienced to get hired. But they told me to come back in a few years. Well I guess you could say *I'm back*.'

There are plenty of prescient stories of Singleton the wheeler-dealer. When he was eight he decided to sell Christmas cards door-to-door. Finding himself under-capitalised, he wrote a letter to the card company in Scarsdale, New Jersey, requesting a line of credit. The company complied. Thirty years later, door-to-door home delivery of newspapers is his newspaper credo, though he insists to a sceptical world that under-capitalisation is no longer a problem.

He worked in summer vacations for the *Wichita Falls Record News* and, while going through junior college in Tyler, Texas, for the *Tyler Morning Telegraph*. After a year he transferred to the University of Texas at Arlington where he majored in business studies though, to his apparent pride, failed to receive a diploma. It pleases him now to call himself 'a college dropout'; like Robert Maxwell used to and Vere Rothermere still does. He often emphasises how little he learnt at school and, *inter alia*, how well he has managed without.

He worked while at Texas University on the *Dallas Morning News*

– competitor to the *Times Herald* – as a sub-editor but was joshed by his peers.

'We called him Teeny, Weeny, Deany or Stinky,' the journalist Bill McAda told *Business Month*. 'He was a plump-faced, plump-bellied little boy who wasn't even old enough to buy his own beer when we went out after the paper was put to bed. We had to buy it for him.'

In 1972, deciding he'd had it with Dallas and name-calling, he set out to buy himself a rural weekly. There was, however, a hitch. The money he'd saved was insufficient to acquire a newspaper. But he'd been asking around, and he heard about a man named Edwin Eakin, who along with his partner ran a weekly paper and a printing plant in the west Texas town of Quanah. Singleton rang Eakin and they set up a meeting in Jacksboro, about halfway between Graham and Paradise, at somewhere called the Green Frog Café on Highway 300. Despite this unprepossessing setting, Eakin was sufficiently impressed by Singleton to give him a break, and appointed him publisher of a new weekly they formed in Clarendon, Texas (population 2500). Eakin and a partner funded the venture, putting up not more than $10,000. Not long after he arrived in Clarendon, Singleton married Cynthia Lowe who worked as a part-time compositor in the printing room; her father, Bill Lowe, was a prominent attorney in the town who came from an old Texan ranching family. Although the marriage to Cynthia scarcely lasted three years, Singleton continued to cultivate his ex-father-in-law who later lent him money for newspaper investments. Critics of Dean Singleton are quick to carp at this aptitude for cultivating useful people; others call it standard entrepreneurship. All agree that, when he sets out to make himself agreeable, he is very agreeable indeed. 'Dean used to use the word *romance*,' Edwin Eakin has said. 'It meant that if you were trying to sell a guy an ad, or influence him, he'd always say, "Now you've got to *romance* 'em".'

Singleton romanced Eakin and his father-in-law into backing a second paper up the highway at Azle, just west of Fort Worth; he hired a career journalist named Ray Bell as editor and the paper prospered. By 1975 both his newspapers were making a decent, though very modest, profit and Dean Singleton was fidgety. The smallness of his operation at this time cannot be overstated. Clarendon and Azle were so parochial that in a matter of weeks you knew every single inhabitant by name; by the time the newspapers were published at the end of the week, most knew all the news already from the gossip in the local store. The turnover and staffing levels were such that, by comparison, many of Conrad Black's newspapers in upstate Vancouver seem like *The New York Times*. Dean Singleton, by now aged 24, was itching for a proper challenge. As chance would have it, a metropolitan daily called the *Fort Worth Press* became available, since its owners, the Scripps-Howard Corporation, wanted to pull out. For 54 years the paper had played second fiddle to the *Star-Telegram*, and a queue of prospective purchasers did not immediately form outside its premises. The other big chain publishers felt the *Fort Worth Press* was beyond redemption and the competition too well entrenched, but Singleton saw it as the ideal vehicle for his transition to a bigger league.

'The first thing he did,' Eakin has recalled, 'was to lease a Lincoln Continental. I told him, "You're making a big mistake. You ought to get an old beat-up pickup and go down there and make people feel sorry for you." But that was his way of creating the illusion of a big-time newspaperman.'

He pitched up at his new office in his big new proprietor's car, wearing a sharkskin suit and smoking a cigar and, some say, 'kicked ass unmercifully'. Like the new owner of many an unsuccessful enterprise, Singleton found it all too easy to dismiss, rather caustically, every achievement and attitude of the old regime. He established himself – rather in the manner of Robert Maxwell assuming the helm of the *New York Daily News* – as the sole arbiter of matters editorial and financial. Two weeks before a statewide election, the *Fort Worth Press*, at Singleton's behest, published a damning editorial opposing each of the eight propositions of a particular candidate; two days before the election, however, Singleton changed his mind and ordered up an editorial championing them. No mention was made of the earlier pieces.

His short tenure at the paper is remembered, too, for a startling internal memo circulated by the publisher to all reporters. This read: 'On Page 5 of today's *Press*, you will find an ad from Mitchell's Department Store. It is an ad full of coupons with various special buys on merchandise. Mitchell's is comparing our results with the morning *Star-Telegram*'s. They will count the NUMBER of coupons they get from the *Press* and the *Star-Telegram*. If we make a good showing we will have a regular schedule of advertising from Mitchell's. If they don't receive many coupons, we likely won't get their advertising. In a sense, YOUR JOBS DEPEND ON THE NUMBER OF COUPONS MITCHELL'S GETS FROM THIS ADVERTISEMENT. Please get your wives to look at this ad, decide what items you can use from this ad and TAKE THE COUPONS to a nearby Mitchell's store. Buy anything that you might need in the future. This is very important. Please, please have your wives shop at Mitchell's today and redeem as many coupons as possible. The COUPONS ARE VERY IMPORTANT. DON'T FORGET THEM. Your jobs depend on the results from these ads. I'll see you at Mitchell's today!!!'

It is not known exactly how many of his employees Singleton spotted in Mitchell's when he went discount-shopping for the future. Apparently not enough, because within 90 days of taking over the *Fort Worth Press*, his reign as publisher ended. One Wednesday afternoon the staff was gathered together in the grimy newsroom to be informed by Singleton that he was folding the newly revived paper. His farewell speech struck many of his staff as ungracious: he blamed them, and the editor – his old mentor Bill McAda – but not himself. When angry reporters began lobbing insults and beer cans at him, he and his sharkskin suit rapidly slunk off in the direction of the Lincoln Continental. It was in this state of disarray that Dean Singleton first quit the Lone Star State, not to be seen there again until his triumphant second coming almost a decade later.

Of the episode he says now, 'It's one of those chapters in my life I wish I could erase. And bear in mind,' he told me, 'that I was 24 years old at the time.'

At the very mention of the words 'Fort Worth', he had visibly flinched. I guessed that, like Dallas, it was a place he chose to fly over.

'You gotta understand,' he said, 'that I was very inexperienced then. At the time Scripps-Howard announced that they were going to close the *Fort Worth Press*, there was a group of local Fort Worth businessmen who were tied to a couple of very prominent state politicians who wanted to save it, and I ended up being the man to do it. And I didn't have the money to do it, didn't have anywhere *near* the money to do it, but these people pledged the financial support. So I went to New York and negotiated the deal with Scripps-Howard and put together the game plan. But before we got the plan off the ground they [the Fort Worth businessmen] left me hanging in the lurch. So we had the plan, the project but not the money, so I raised some money from people who were close to me at the time – knowing that we didn't have enough money to do it but thinking it would be a start. Ironically in the last days of the *Fort Worth Press* we transferred the stock of the company to another group who claimed they *did* have the money to keep it going, when in fact they didn't have it either. So actually when the *Fort Worth Press* went under we didn't own it. None the less we borrowed sizeable amounts of money from the banks that had been good to me in the past, and I felt an obligation to see that they got all their money. Over the next several years they *did* get it too because I worked for wages to pay it back. You can't really know what success is unless you've tasted defeat. I learned that I never wanted to taste it again.'

Singleton and his wife were divorced around the time of the paper's closure. He has subsequently claimed that his devotion to newspaper ownership strained the marriage: 'She didn't understand and I wasn't going to change.'

Single and jobless, Singleton headed northeast to Boston and found a job with a Boston outfit that repossessed failing newspapers. This meant waiting until a proprietor's debt to his creditors had exhausted their patience, then moving in on the bank's instructions and running the demoralised staff until a new owner was found. On one such assignment in Westfield, Massachusetts, Singleton met a gopher for Joe Allbritton, the high-profile Houston financier who had recently bought the *Washington Star* to compete against the Grahams' *Washington Post*. In due course Singleton got to meet Allbritton, who said that he was planning to buy the Westfield paper and would Singleton care to run it? Allbritton later extended the brief to identifying and buying a whole group of troubled dailies that Allbritton Communication could turn around. By his 27th birthday Dean Singleton was president of the newspaper division and president of each of the five daily papers that he had targeted. It was during these days as Joe Allbritton's protégé that he refined what has been called his 'cut and slash' philosophy of newspaper management: the far from unique five steps to profit employed by proprietors from Seattle to Sydney, ie:

1. Buy Newspaper

2. Cut Staff
3. Cut Quality
4. Cut Objectivity
5. Hike advertising rates

Whether or not this is a remotely fair dissertation on the Singleton philosophy rather depends on who is doing the talking.

The Dean-as-monster scenario went like this: Singleton was 'a flesh eater', according to a former reporter at the *Trenton Times* which he bought for Allbritton from Katharine Graham, 'with zero humanity', intent only on drubbing up advertisement pages with little regard for editorial integrity or independence; interesting (ie, boat-rocking) articles were suppressed, staff numbers slashed (on his first day at the *Trenton Times*, the editorial staff was contracted from 80 to 56), offices left undecorated (the atmosphere in the newsroom at Paterson, New Jersey, where he ran the *News* 'was akin to that of the bottom of a dirty ashtray, and by the day's end you were desperate for a shower'), unions discouraged.

Others (and other owners) say, with equal conviction, that Singleton in those early days was a pragmatist absorbed by resuscitating terminally ill newspapers. Philosophical questions like editorial independence were secondary; the prerogative of profitable operations but not unprofitable ones. Singleton coined the phrase 'survival journalism'. Investigative stories could wait until the papers were out of the casualty ward. 'What they [Singleton] wanted was short, good-news stories,' remembers a former staff member. 'The editor put up a big bulletin board in the newsroom urging us to *say something nice*.' When a reporter wrote a story about a crime wave in a local shopping mall, which somehow slipped into the paper, it was retracted the following day: *no crime problem in mall*. 'They didn't want to scare people off shopping in the mall [which might have hurt regular advertisers]. All this fancy-footwork achieved its purpose. By the time Dean Singleton felt ready to leave Allbritton and strike out on his own, the chain was profitable and secure. And his alliance with Allbritton also gave him an introduction to big numbers. In 1982 he negotiated on Allbritton's behalf a $354 million option to buy the *New York Daily News*, then the country's largest daily newspaper. Among the bidders Singleton outmanoeuvred was New York real estate mogul Donald

Trump. The option was eventually allowed to lapse allowing the paper, after many adventures, to pass first to Robert Maxwell, then to Mort Zuckerman.

Sir David English, Chairman of Lord Rothermere's British newspaper empire, recalls spending an evening with Singleton at this period. 'He had a Beatles haircut, pebble glasses and cowboy boots, and we had dinner in a steak restaurant in Worcester, Massachusetts. When the waiter took our drinks order, Dean said, "I'll have a grasshopper." I couldn't understand what he was asking for, he has quite a drawl, but he kept repeating, "I'll have a grasshopper." This turned out to be a creme de menthe cocktail – bright green with a head to it – and he continued drinking grasshoppers throughout the meal. None the less I was very impressed by him. He *is* impressive. Later I asked him to join Vere Rothermere and me for dinner in New York, in the Oak Room at the Plaza. Vere was very impressed by him too. In fact we tried to get him to come to London, we'd have liked him to become general manager of the *Daily Mail* or something. I remember Vere saying, "If we get him he won't stay long. I can tell that man wants to *own* newspapers himself." '

In 1983 Singleton left Allbritton for a partnership with Richard B. Scudder, a fourth-generation New Jersey newspaper publisher who had made a fortune twelve years earlier by selling his family's *Newark Evening News* and a newsprint-recycling company to Media General Corporation, the Richmond, Virginia-based conglomerate owned by the old money Bryan family. Equipped with $3 million of the 69-year-old Scudder's money (including $200,000 that Scudder lent Singleton for his stake in the company) the two men formed Gloucester County Times Inc, to buy the *Gloucester County Times*, a 30,000 circulation daily in Woodbury, New Jersey, from the Texas-based Harte-Hanks chain. In 1985, requiring more capital to feed their acquisitive appetite, they also formed Garden State Newspapers and took on Media General as a partner. A newspaper broker who acts for Singleton told me that 'it would be hard to imagine two backgrounds with less in common than Dean from Texas and the blue-blooded Bryans from Virginia, and yet they have an interesting and successful partnership.' Media General agreed to put up the cash for down-payments on newspapers in exchange for 40 per cent of ownership, according to *The New York Times* in a speculative piece about Singleton's secretive set-up. Singleton and Scudder also created MediaNews Group, the management company that operates all of the papers.

For the next three years – right through the middle eighties when newspaper multiples were at their highest – Singleton was on buying sprees. Only Ralph Ingersoll was gobbling up titles faster or more voraciously. In 1986 alone, Singleton purchased 35 new papers – one every ten days – including the *Dallas Times Herald*; to some observers he seemed to have become a newspaperoholic, only fully engaged when he had a pen in his signing hand, cocked over a contract.

Reviewing the group now, it is hard to see any pattern to their purchase, beyond Singleton's conviction that he can increase the franchise of any newspaper by managing it skilfully. Geographically they are dispersed. There are six papers in California including the *Alameda Times-Star*; 15 in New Jersey including the *South Bergenite* and *Suburban Trends* (a paper as unenthralling as its title); six in Connecticut, four in Pennsylvania, two in Michigan, two more in Virginia including the *Stafford Sun* and the *Quantico Sentry* of Charlottesville; a paper in Yakima, five in Texas, one in Denver – the *Post* – eight in Utah with names like the *Jordon Valley Sentinel* and the *Murray Eagle*, and the Fairbanks *Daily News-Miner* that he bought in Alaska in February 1992. Another media broker, who advised Dean Singleton on many of these acquisitions, describes flying with him in the company Hawker Siddeley from state to state, crunching the numbers at 30,000 feet, landing at some local airstrip, being met by a limousine, inspecting the premises and plant, negotiating, striking a deal, flying on to the next place while lawyers remained behind and completed the paperwork.

Hylton Philipson of Pall Mall Capital says, 'You have to give him due credit for boldness, particularly in terms of buying into competitive market where others may not dare to tread. York, Pennsylvania is a case in point. I sold Dean the *York Dispatch* which had been declining for years and was still owned by the Young family. It was in direct competition with the *York Daily Record*, owned by a professional group (The Buckner News Alliance), which had a strong Sunday paper whereas the *Dispatch* had none.

'Strangely, the newspaper company in nearby Lancaster also had a Sunday-only paper in York. The first thing that Dean did was to buy out this Sunday paper and fold it into the *Dispatch*. After approximately eighteen months, and a considerable amount of struggle and bluff on both sides, the *Daily Record* sued for peace and accepted a minority position in the resulting joint operating agreement. The net result was that having begun by buying a property that few others would have considered, within two years Dean ended up with a majority position in a consolidated market. In value terms, the return on investment was fantastic.'

I asked Dean Singleton what characterises a Dean Singleton paper.

'Editorially,' he said, 'the stamp of a Dean Singleton newspaper is heavy concentration on local news coverage, heavier than most newspapers because I've always believed readers read their local newspaper for local news and get their national news someplace else.'

'Like where? Television?'

'Yeah, television. Secondly, all our newspapers tend to be very colourful. Also, great sports coverage – I started out working covering sports.'

'What did you cover?'

'Baseball, basketball, football. Local news coverage, colourful design and sports coverage would probably be where we concentrate heavily. On the business side, I think all of our newspapers are extremely efficient from a production standpoint.'

'Are those the big four factors when you take over a new paper?'

'Well the most immediate is the cost structure. Because, normally, if we buy a newspaper we probably borrow a lot of the money to buy it, so the bottom line has to be in check. Secondly the news content: is it a *local* product?'

All this emphatic talk about local news left me unconvinced. Dean Singleton did not strike me as a man who, by nature, was motivated by serving up user-friendly neighbourhood chronicles. It was only when power-Donalds like Donald Trump, Donald Newhouse and Donald Graham were mentioned that Singleton sprang into life, and I sensed that he harbours ambitions (though he denies it) of eventually owning a paper with world-class news coverage and a presence on the world stage. Local news, I guessed, is his business philosophy not his personal one. And that he hankers after a paper that devotes dozens of column inches to global leaders, rather than the new chef at the River Oaks Grill and the Spring Creek real estate guide.

I asked him, 'Who makes editorial policy judgements around here?'

'I do.'

'And how do you monitor your papers? I estimate you're publishing 201 issues a week.'

'Is that right? Yeah, I guess so. I flew 308 hours on the plane last year. I'll probably fly 400 this year. I try to visit each division, so I see the papers regular. It depends on the size. If it's sizeable I like to visit it once a month. If it's Denver I go twice a month, or New Jersey I go twice a month. If it's York, Pennsylvania I go once a month.'

The editor of the *Houston Post*, Charles Cooper, says Singleton is a hands-on proprietor even at long distance.

'If he's not in Houston the papers are saved for him and he does go through them, both in terms of looking at the news content and worrying about new advertisers or comparing our advertisers to the competition at Hearst and that. He does make it a point, from front to back. I get evidence that he looks very closely at his newspapers by some things that he'll point out.'

'What things?'

'He discourages what we call "jumps", which is a continued story, especially from the front page of the front section but going on to the other sections as well. Every survey that's ever done, nobody likes jumps – readers especially – but we keep inflicting them on people.'

'And does he hand down clear policies about content?'

'There's quite a developed view he endorses . . . a formula, certainly a concept, that he's pounded into us along the way. If I can compare us with the *Chronicle*, I can pretty much pick the six stories they'll run on their front page tomorrow by six o'clock this evening. They've picked a very traditional editorship whereas we try to be somewhat more lively. Not unpredictable just for the sake of it, but we try to consider the mix for the range of readers in Houston, so that everything doesn't come out of Washington. That's what Dean calls the white, middle-class editor's mentality – if it comes out of Washington it must be important. I edit everything here through a filter – a Houston filter – whether it happens in Washington, in Europe or anywhere else. *What does this matter to Houston*? I'm not saying I'm not going to run an important story out of Beijing because it doesn't affect Houston – but I am going to at least *consider* what it means to people in Houston. We're much more directed in that way; Dean says worry about Houston, worry about Texas, worry about the South West and just do it that way.'

I said, 'What's Dean Singleton like to work for? Easy or difficult?'

Charles Cooper laughed. He has a lazy Texan laugh – he was brought up in Midland, where George Bush lived for a while – that seemed to say, 'Sure he can be difficult, but *I'm still here.*'

'He's dynamic,' he replied, 'in the sense that he always seems to have a purpose. He's very good at small talk but doesn't seem to be that *interested* in small talk. He can be very funny, very cutting. He sometimes removes all the niceties and really comes to the point about individuals.'

'Is he a showman?'

'He is forceful, but not flamboyant. Not that ostentatious when you consider his money. His house is a very comfortable place – right on the fairway of one of the better golf courses in Houston. Right on the fifteenth fairway.'

'Does he play golf?'

'No. It just doesn't appeal to him. Nor to Mrs Singleton.'

'This is the new Mrs Singleton?'

'Adrienne. She's very lively, very funny, from New Jersey. Brown-haired – I guess sometimes goes to auburn a little bit – but light brown, long, long hair. She tries to take part in as many of the charity functions that we tend to have to go to. She cares for the two children. And of course they're very religious.'

The religious side of Dean Singleton – he is an elder of the Houston Baptist Church – is in many respects as unforeseen as Vere Rothermere's predilection for Zen Buddhism or Rupert Murdoch's much exaggerated conversion to born-again Christianity: there is nothing improbable in the fact of faith itself, only in these particular media barons' adherence to it. I asked Dean Singleton whether religion meant a lot to him.

'Yes. Very much. I was brought up a Baptist.'

'Does this affect your view of newspapers?'

'It probably changes my priorities a bit. I mean there is a greater place out there someplace. And long after newspapers are meaningless and have no relationship to anything the greater place out there will still be there. So, clearly, one's spiritual well-being matters over all else.'

I asked him, 'Do you give ten per cent of your income to the church as Baptists should?'

Singleton shifted his position on the Biedermeier chair, tensed.

'Well,' he said, 'I do what the Bible says, and the Bible says to do that.' And then he added, 'Let me explain that to you. All of our newspapers are in corporations that have their own shareholders. My tithing is my *personal* money. It doesn't mean that ten per cent of all the newspapers' earnings go to it, but my *own* earnings. And since we're very frugal about dishing out earnings to the shareholders it's not as much as you might think.'

I found it hard to establish where Dean Singleton's priorities lie. As a newspaper owner he is paradoxical. Ask him which paper in the world he'd most like to own and he replies, '*The New York Times*.' Why? 'Because it's the best, just the best.' But ask him which competitor he most admires, and he says, 'Thomson. Ken Thomson. Otis Chandler and Times Mirror are my idols, but Thomson fits right up there with them, but on a different level. Thomson does a great job of running all those small papers.'

The philosophical gulf between the Sulzbergers' *Times* and the Thomsons is so vast that only Dean Singleton would attempt to compare them. And yet this dual enthusiasm reinforces Singleton's schizophrenia as a publisher. One part of him hankers after the big acquisition, the thousands-strong staff of *The New York Times*. The other – the cautious cheeseparing Dean Singleton – identifies with the Thomson set-up with its shell staffs and high-profit margins.

Few people who know him doubt Singleton's determination to become a first-rank proprietor. He wants his empire, in number of titles, to be expansive, and he has achieved this. But he also wants to own newspapers of significance, or failing that newspapers in cities of significance. The *Denver Post* and the *Houston Post* may only be the second-largest newspapers in their cities, but at least they're *there*. To own the *Las Cruces Sun-News* in New Mexico (which he does) is all very well when you happen to be in Las Cruces, but to own the *Houston Post* has a certain resonance wherever you happen to be in the country.

His willingness to buy number two papers is the single most eccentric thing about Dean Singleton. It runs counter to every scrap of conventional wisdom. It is hard to think of any newspaper market in the world where the winner – the brand leader – doesn't enjoy a vastly disproportionate profit over its nearest rival. It is true of New York, Bombay, London, Hong Kong and Sydney; it is true of virtually every metropolis in North America that still somehow supports more than one paper. But the Dean Singleton credo says that in a thriving economy the deft proprietor, if he really understands his business, can make a fortune. Denver, he points out, is the largest city in Colorado; Houston is the fourth-largest in America. It is only the complacency and lack of enterprise of the established proprietors that has made them fearful of competing in a head-to-head newspaper war.

Whether Singleton is right, it is too early to say. The *Houston Post* is about 100,000 behind Hearst's *Houston Chronicle* in daily circulation; 200,000 behind them on Sundays. And Hearst carries 60 per cent of the advertising to Dean Singleton's 40 per cent ('up from 38 per cent since we bought it,' he says). Both papers, to my eye, look much alike, 'which is OK in a head-to-head,' says Singleton, 'because everyone can choose which box they drop their nickel into.' His *Denver Post* sells about 100,000 a day fewer than the *Rocky Mountain News* but narrowly beats the competition on Sundays. In Denver, as a Texan, Singleton is viewed as a foreigner – an outsider from across the state border come to tell Colorado what to think; but in Houston, where he's a native, he plays the homeboy card against New York-based Hearst. On the day he bought the paper, Singleton had the motto '*Houston Owned, Texas Proud*' added to the masthead (conveniently ignoring the fact that Hearst's Chief Executive Frank Bennack is as Texan as he is).

It struck me that for Dean Singleton, more than almost any other proprietor, newspaper ownership was an end in itself. He has no subsidiary agenda. There is no political crusade to propagate through the papers, no industrial empire to promote, no pressing journalistic mission beyond the much proclaimed preference for local news. You can make a case that Singleton's involvement in newspapers is simply to make money; that he might just as easily have sold canned juice or automotive spares. But I do not believe that explanation of his motivation. He is not insensible to the hard-to-quantify prestige of newspaper ownership. There is a side to his character that, like Conrad Black, enjoys pronouncing on the future of the world as only newspaper owners and former presidents can. And, like Ralph

Ingersoll, he pronounces philosophically on the future of newspapers.

'If we as an industry are successful,' he told an Associated Press conference in Des Moines, 'the newspaper you sell on the West Coast will be completely different from the newspaper you sell on the East Coast, so much [different, that] you don't even know they are both newspapers.'

He takes pleasure too in playing the licensed screwball at these conferences. 'We as a newspaper industry are making *too much money*,' he assured a disbelieving audience of fellow owners. 'Our margins are too high and we're taking too much money out [of our newspapers] and we've got to put more money back in.'

I asked him in his Houston office what inspired this unlikely outburst from a man whose repayments to banks will ensure high margins for the foreseeable future.

'The fact is we have debt to pay,' he said. 'A company like Gannett has dividends to pay to stockholders. There's not much difference.'

There is, of course. If you decide to reduce the dividend to stockholders, or suspend it altogether, they cannot repossess your company. And if you need to pay them a bit less, you don't need to renegotiate with every stockholder individually, as you do with banks.

'It's the deal he relishes; it's the deal that gives him his rush.' Almost everybody told me that. The newspapers themselves, they implied, were just the inevitable consequence of the deal and that once Dean Singleton has taken them over, moved himself in and realigned the figures, his next rush comes only when he renegotiates the original deal. This, though he refutes it, has become a hallmark of Singleton as entrepreneur. When Times Mirror sold him the *Denver Post* the $70 million they left in the deal was to provoke years of speculation about stages of repayment; his purchase of the *Houston Post* from the Toronto Sun Publishing Corporation subsequently involved waves of refinancing that necessitated a major reorganisation of the entire Singleton media empire. In spring 1992 he sold the *Yakima Herald-Republic* – the paper that had reminded me of so many other American broadsheets – to the Seattle Times. With a circulation of 38,000 in a monopoly market, it was a classic Singleton cash-cow. Many people reckon it was his favourite property outside Houston and Denver, and that he never would have let it go unless he was under some pressure.

Much of the hostility to Dean Singleton from other owners struck me as unfair; it reminded me of the hostility to Lord Stevens in London, the natural suspicion of the bumptious new kid on the block. And, since Singleton has no source of income beyond newspapers – no first career as an investment tycoon – it seemed ungenerous to condemn him for attempting to create a chain. And I wondered, too, whether it was possible for any new proprietor to come from nowhere to owning 71 newspapers before the age of 40 and not draw flak. I thought it would be easier to be accepted if you'd been lined up for ownership from an early age, like Donald Graham.

'It's not the money,' Singleton once told *Texas Monthly* during a press conference on the company jet. 'It's not money that drives me. When my father turned 65, times were getting bad in the oil patch, and in September they told him that they were going to retire him in October. They told him on a Friday night.

'That Monday he had a heart attack. My mother rushed him to a hospital. He said he didn't want to be left in the hospital – that he wanted to work till he died. That afternoon he was dead.'

Singleton took a breath. 'In the casket later my father had a smile on his face. It was as though he were saying, "I showed those bastards. *I didn't retire*."

'Well,' Singleton said, '*I'm not going to retire either*.'

David Burgin, who edited the *Dallas Times Herald* during Singleton's proprietorship and now runs his Alameda newspaper group in California, says that Singleton's bad press is unwarranted.

'It's unfair. He has a passion for the newspaper business unlike anything I've ever seen. He's a modern newspaperman who's not in it just for the money. If in the early days he made a few mistakes, well, so do I and so did you.'

6

A Fistful of Dollars

Otis Chandler and the *Los Angeles Times*

Wherever I went in the world, it was the *Los Angeles Times* that other proprietors used as the point of reference for their own newspapers. In Hong Kong Sally Aw Sian explained her global editions as the 'same concept as the *LA Times* sections for San Diego and Orange County'. Ramnath Goenka compared his 13 inky regional editions of the *Indian Express* to 'the grand plan of the late Mr Otis Chandler of Los Angeles City'. (I have no idea why he imagined Otis Chandler was 'the late'. As it happened Goenka would himself die less than six months later in his big, bare Bombay penthouse while Chandler remains the highly active controlling shareholder of the $3.8 billion Times Mirror Corporation.) And the continental European proprietors – Robert Hersant, Carlo Caracciolo, Hubert Burda – all defer to the *LA Times* as the best example of a slick, state-of-the-industry broadsheet.

All this reverence left me bemused. I could not fathom why the *Los Angeles Times*, of all the papers on the planet, should merit so much applause. To the occasional reader it conjures exactly the same feelings of disorientation and despair as the city of Los Angeles itself. It is a vast, sprawling newspaper – the fattest paper in the world, with the highest metropolitan circulation in North America. On Sundays the different sections are so numerous and diffuse that even to page your way through them from beginning to end could take you three to four hours. There are fistfuls of the *LA Times* that, however long I lived in that city, I know I would never penetrate. The newspaper in this respect is a mirror of its franchise. The reader forges his way through the *Times* from safe haven to safe haven, following familiar paths, hurrying past ghettos of alien and faintly threatening newsprint. Every area of Los Angeles – rich and poor – has its own station in the newspaper, coexisting side by side in a singular multiplicity of newsvalues. One minute you are in Hollywood or Beverly Hills, being apprised of the fine print of a filmstar's three-picture movie contract, the next you have swung off the freeway at an unfamiliar exit and are plunged into the Latino or Indo-Chinese underworld of drug triads and arsonists.

The scale of the *Los Angeles Times* is, in California-speak, awesome. It marks the extreme west of a European world map, the last great newspaper before the big turquoise emptiness of the Pacific Ocean. Its catchment area extending from the Mexican border to Santa Barbara in the north is 46,000 square miles, the size of the state of Ohio. And its parent corporation, Times Mirror, has inched its way three thousand miles east across America all the way to Long Island to buy *Newsday* and a cluster of significant metropolitan papers en route.

People kept assuring me that the *Los Angeles Times* is the future of newspapers. They said 'The *Times* is well ahead of any of the other big papers in its zoned editions. Some suburbs of the city are now getting a *substantially different paper* to other parts. The *Times* is getting to be like a cable service or a chain of neighbourhood radio stations. Otis Chandler,' people said, 'has invented a new concept in newspapering.' The papers you buy from a vending box on Long Beach and the edition you get home delivery in Orange County speak to different audiences. Some of these edition changes are surreal. On the day I interviewed its proprietor, for example, the Orange County edition ran a box at the foot of page one proclaiming 'Large Tumor Taken from Pope's Colon'. In the same day's San Diego edition, I found in the same box 'Aid Runs Out for Federal Defendants'.

Six feet two inches tall, his face nut brown from the sun and lightly fissured like an old pirate treasure map, Otis Chandler loomed behind his office desk, tinkering with the electric control panel set before him. From a tunnel behind a sofa a miniature railway engine chugged into view and looped, on what seemed like a half mile of track, between the legs of his desk, around an armchair, around the plinth of a stuffed Bengal tiger, skirted the legs of a stuffed Abyssinian bushbuck and a Botswana lion, then slowed to a halt at a midget railway junction by Otis Chandler's feet. Chandler knelt down on the floor. His quiff of straw-coloured hair and languorous blue eyes make him, at the age of 64, resemble a benevolent farm scarecrow. He adjusted the points on the track, then put the engine into reverse and shunted it carefully into a siding.

'All my business is run out of this office now,' he said. 'The Times Mirror and all that stuff. I built this place part as my office, part as my museum.'

He gestured around the vast concrete warehouse he has had constructed on the edge of an industrial estate at Oxnard, two hours west of Los Angeles off Freeway 110. From outside it looks like a bonded lock-up, practically impregnable with cuneiform concrete walls. Inside it is the showplace for Chandler's two great collections, of high-performance muscle cars and of stuffed animal trophies he has hunted and shot.

There is something surreal in their juxtaposition. An apron of toughened glass divides the cars from the stuffed animals, so that from Otis Chandler's desk the view is of an Ethiopian warthog breaking cover before a Pontiac Judge and a New Mexican cougar stalking a bright yellow Cyclone Torino. In all there are 92 animal trophies – elk, polar bear, black rhino, Alaskan moose – rearing on their hind legs or rigidly embalmed in a perpetual state of stealth. Gleaming in their shadow are the muscle cars: more than a hundred of them parked in lines like a car showroom, monster-motor Chevelles, Dodge Hemi convertibles, Superbirds, Shelby Mustangs.

'We went after the rare stuff first,' said Otis Chandler, 'to get them before the prices went out of sight.'

'Is that the cars or the animals?'

'It's true of both in fact. The rarest animals here – in terms of physical difficulty to hunt – are the ones across the room there, the big-horned sheep. Marco Polo sheep. I have the world record specimen. You can see they're quite majestic with magnificent heads. I got mine in Afghanistan two years before the Russians went in, hunting in the Himalayas at 19,000 feet without oxygen. That's how I got that beautiful Marco Polo ram.'

Otis Chandler occupies a dyadic position in the proprietors' firmament. On the global scoreboard of one to ten, he scores only a six. In the *Los Angeles Times* he owns one world-class paper, in *New York Newsday* he has a hot property and there are a handful of big second-division titles in Connecticut and the *Baltimore Sun* in Maryland. But despite his considerable financial leverage, Chandler has never chosen to thrust Times Mirror on to the world stage. They have never bought foreign newspapers. When the Eastern European press flooded on to the market in the late eighties you heard every serious player touted as a possible purchaser *except* Chandler. When the *South China Morning Post* was acquired by Murdoch, it puzzled some media brokers that Chandler hadn't seen expansion west to Hong Kong as the next logical adventure.

But in North America the perception of Otis Chandler is vigorous and rather glamorous. He scores a nine or ten. In the sixties his filmstar good looks, Californian suntan, full head of sleek, fair hair and perpetual air of having spent the afternoon on a surfboard gave him a cachet that eclipsed even that of Kay Graham and Punch Sulzberger. And his much broadcast ambition to raise the profile of the *LA Times* until it matched the *Washington Post* and *The New York Times* cast Chandler as an enigmatic young pretender, championing an energetic New West against the complacent East.

He withdrew four years ago from full-time participation, but has become no more invisible in Times Mirror Square than did Rupert Murdoch when he stepped down as chairman of his London newspapers. Robert Erburu may now be chairman of the corporation, the shambling and brilliant David Laventhol may be publisher of the *Los Angeles Times*, but Chandler's 32.3 per cent slice of stock and symbiotic identification with his flagship gives him an abiding presence.

'I consider the *Times* like one of my children,' he told me. 'I can never leave it alone! It must be like when you're an alcoholic, once you're hooked you can never let go.'

I asked, 'Couldn't that be rather irritating for your successors, to have you on their back all the time?'

'Oh sure,' he said. 'I have to be careful that those who are given the responsibility now don't feel I undercut them. Actually I think what happens is that the reverse is true. I'm so identified by employees with the paper, that they would be disappointed if they didn't see me or hear I was in the building. Particularly now with the recession they're very *encouraged* to see me around the building. They're reassured that I'm carefully monitoring what's going on with the paper. You have to realise that even though we're a large corporation they consider us a family-owned business, and I'm the most identifiable one they've seen for the last 40 years. So even though they may be unhappy with some of the cutbacks, they're more accepting if they think I'm involved in it or know about it. If Otis thinks this is OK, it must be OK.'

'How often do you speak to your successors as chairman and publisher?'

'Oh, I would speak to Mr Erburu at least twice a week, probably every couple of weeks to Dave Laventhol.'

'Mostly financial conversations?'

'No, not so much. Story ideas, conceptual ideas. Things I think the paper needs to improve, comments on what we're doing. How we're covering a particular story and how I think we can do a better job. Or how are we planning to cover this year's presidential campaign. Creative ideas mainly.'

Then he said, 'As you may know I've remained chairman of the Executive Committee of the Times Mirror Company, and my family owns over 50 per cent of the voting shares so I'd say I'm still involved from both the *ownership* standpoint and as a senior member of the management. But as far as the *LA Times* is concerned, I don't get involved other than that the publisher is a man I helped to find and put in and since it's our largest unit he and I stay in touch. He does not report to me but, knowing how much I put into that paper in my long career, he enjoys brainstorming with me and picking my brains on things he's thinking of doing. *The big ideas*. Right now we're focusing on building the paper in the inland empire: San Gabriel, San Bernardino, Ontario, Pomona. *The inland empire*. That's the big area we're focusing on.

'And of course Dave Laventhol happens to be a muscle car buff too,' said Otis Chandler, 'so he likes to come up here.'

'You've chosen a bad time to be in Los Angeles,' said Chandler. He pronounces 'Angeles' with a hard g and a truncated finish – Anglis – *Los Anglis*.

He was right about my sense of timing. I had flown into a hurricane, the aircraft circling half a dozen times above the city plucking up courage to land, downtown a river of burst water mains, the freeways closed because of flooding and landfalls. My parenthetic journey to Oxnard had been so long and complicated that I had been able to read virtually every edition of the *Times*. And I had seen for myself the considerable variations from place to place. Each edition gave its own neighbourhood the credit for having the worst weather. 'TORRENT HITS VENTURA COUNTY', 'SAN FERNANDO VALLEY AREA RECEIVES WORST DRENCHER'. The beauty of multi-zoned editions is that they allow every hamlet its local pride in disaster.

I asked Chandler, 'Is the Ventura County edition of the *Times* your local one?'

'Yeah. It's the only section I see now. I don't see, as I used to, all the other sections. But the edition I get here at the office isn't quite the same as the edition I get in the morning at home. The Ventura edition is broken down into cities and I live in a city called Camario, and they have one or two special items about Camario. It was my idea to put this section in and it's been very successful. We've gained a lot of readership and advertising.'

The fragmentation of a great newspaper into more and more highly targeted sections both fascinated and disturbed me. These editions within editions, each progressively smaller like a nest of Russian dolls, has effectively turned the *Los Angeles Times* into a chain of local newssheets wrapped inside a national newspaper. Tracts of content are common to every edition – dispatches from Washington, Wall Street and world news – and then over the page there's a story about a cat rescued from a tree in your neighbour's backyard. The sophistication and precision of these sections changes exceeds anything that Rupert Murdoch has achieved with the *Australian* or Samir Jain with his rather cursory edition-changes at *The Times of India*.

And yet their kaleidoscope of sections, for all their ingenuity, make some people uneasy. They challenge conventional values in news-gathering. 'In a great city like LA,' an editor in New York told me, 'there has to be some overall criteria for deciding what gets into the paper. Someone has to ask, "Is this story of sufficient significance *in itself* to interest, divert, whatever a large number of fellow human beings across Los Angeles?" What the *Times* is doing is sidestepping that question. They don't ask themselves any longer, "Is this story of *significance*?" They ask, "Will it interest about ten thousand people in a residential enclave someplace off the freeway?" They ask, "Will this connect with some little enclave in Monterey Park or Brentwood or Pacific Palisades?" Well I think that's a dangerous route for a serious newspaper to take. You run the risk of turning into a puff paper or a glorified shopper.'

And yet the ethnic demographic of Los Angeles – the *ethnicity* as they call it – is changing so fast that it is hard to see what other route the *Times* could take except ever more precise targeting.

'You go back to the 1910s, 1920s, there was a huge migration into the eastern parts of the United States from Europe,' said Otis Chandler. 'Poles, Irish, Russians, Jews – a great migration into Boston, Washington and New York – and these have now been integrated over the generations into our basic population structure, the multi-ethnic society. Then in the seventies, eighties and now the nineties the same thing began happening to California, except that our migrations are from Central and South America and Mexico and the Japanese and the Chinese and Indo-Chinese and Thais and Vietnamese and Koreans and people from Formosa. It's a huge influx of different cultures into Southern California. Recently I read that in one year 250,000 Guatemalans came in. Probably another 300,000 from El Salvador, and Mexicans coming in by the millions. That's one mighty headache for a newspaper like the *Times*.'

Otis Chandler frowned.

'So we have the language problem,' he went on. 'We have that in *spades*. They have to be able to read English before we can even *hope* they might want to read a paper like the *LA Times*. We've studied a Spanish-language edition of the paper.'

'And reached what conclusion?'

'Oh, we've studied that forever! It just doesn't take you anywhere. Because we always come up against the fact that those people who cannot read English tend not to be readers of newspapers at all. They're low economic people who wouldn't read a Spanish-language edition either.'

'What do they read?'

'Nothing really. There's a Spanish newspaper here, *L'Opinion*, which we own about 30 per cent of, but it's really read by the middle-class bilingual Spanish. In LA now there are Chinese news-papers, Japanese papers, Formosan and Thai papers, there are Korean papers, and the question we have to ask is, "Are these new residents in Southern California *ever* going to want to read a paper like the *Times*?" I *think* they will, but it's only going to be those whose parents are interested in pushing their children into multi-lingual society.'

'You published a special edition of the *Times* slanted towards black Americans.'

'We had to drop it. The advertisers wouldn't pay for it. They said that these weren't really people that spent much money in their stores.'

'How greatly did it vary from the other editions?'

'It was a whole special section of downtown news. We called it the Central Edition. News about what was happening downtown that would affect their lives: police, fire, local news. Primarily of interest to blacks and Latinos who live in the central core of LA as opposed to suburbia.'

A few months after I visited Chandler, the race riots of late May and early June 1992, following the acquittal of the four LA policemen for beating up Rodney King, caused the *Times* to reconsider its decision to abandon the Central Edition. It was revived as a community gesture as the South Central Edition, edited for blacks and Hispanics. The advertising department are gritting their teeth.

'We're still a city that's moving outwards and further outwards,' said Otis Chandler.

'Is all this changing the kind of material you publish?'

'Sure. I like to discuss this with Shelby Coffey [the editor of the *Los Angeles Times*]. What's the paper of the future? How's it going to look? How's it going to read? Particularly when more readers can maybe get along with watching CNN and network news and reading the *LA Times* maybe on Sunday only. It's going to be a real challenge for Shelby and the whole crew to figure that one out. The newspaper business in the nineties and beyond is going to be a very different business.'

Placing the power of the Chandlers in its Californian context invariably involves comparing them, rather spuriously, to other powerful families halfway across the world. 'They have the political clout and the glamour of the Kennedys,' I was assured. Or, 'They're a combination of the Rothschilds and the [Washington] Grahams.' Or, yet more improbably, 'The Chandlers are Gianni Agnelli and Henry Kissinger rolled into one. They have the money, the media and the *de facto* role as *eminence grise* for the whole of Southern California.'

It would probably not be going too far to say that physically, socially and financially, modern Los Angeles owes more to the Chandler family than to any other dynasty. That Los Angeles is a lolling, low-rise city is entirely due to the fact that they bought half the land in the San Fernando Valley and deemed that expansion should be horizontal. That Los Angeles has water owes everything to their audacious theft in 1903 of the Ownes Valley water supply, 200 miles northeast of the city, which they diverted across their estates to ensure the perpetual growth of LA. That Los Angeles became the great metropolis of the West Coast in the first place is largely thanks to Otis Chandler's great-grandfather, General Harrison Gray Otis, who in 1888 persuaded the nascent city Chamber of Commerce to dispatch a roadshow all over the Midwest, from Iowa to Nebraska, to induce settlers to emigrate to LA, and coincidentally to swell his circulation of the *Times*. That Los Angeles has the fattest and most profitable major newspaper in North America is entirely thanks to the Chandlers' pathological dislike of labour unions, which they challenged, fought and eventually beat at the beginning of the century in one of the ugliest industrial disputes ever seen in newspaper relations; a dispute that culminated in the blowing-up of the *Times*'s plant by union saboteurs, killing 20 printers in an explosion of hot metal shrapnel, and in the process turning the *LA Times* into a union-free shop. This would enable the Chandlers to add more and more pages and sections to their paper as California boomed, and to pioneer the new technology, without any of the tortuous labour negotiations that trammelled – still trammel – the Sulzbergers and Grahams. It meant that by the late seventies the profit of the *Los Angeles Times* was three times that of the *Washington Post* and seven times higher than *The New York Times*.

That Los Angeles became in the late fifties, and remains today socially the most meritocratic large city in America, owes everything – so I was told half a dozen times – to Buff Chandler, Otis Chandler's mother, whose social striving to overturn the ingrained superiority of Pasadena Old Money at the California Club and the Los Angeles Country Club led her to use the *Times* to champion the new, thrusting society of West Los Angeles and Beverly Hills. That the *Los Angeles Times* has managed, in the space of 30 years, to transform itself from one of the two worst papers in America to one of the three best, owes almost everything to Otis Chandler: the thoughtful, industrious, mildly eccentric, some say rather lonesome, but above anything determined proprietor of the most powerful newspaper between the Mississippi and Tokyo.

Otis Chandler's name, combining as it does the surnames of both his most resourceful forebears, could either have been auspicious or driven him rapidly into psychoanalysis: General Otis, founder of the dynasty, irascible, bellicose zealot, lover of feuds, hero of the Spanish-American war, who continued to wear military uniform in peacetime and named his home 'The Bivouac', who managed to buy into the *Times* for a few hundred dollars in 1882 and proceeded to talk up the unpromising township of Los Angeles – with no port, no water and no railway – into a high-rolling boomtown; and Harry Chandler, the General's son-in-law, who migrated to California in his twenties for the sake of his lungs, fell into newspaper distribution, colluded with General Otis to kill off the *Times*'s main competitor by ensuring poor delivery, and then married his daughter. The *Times* Otis Chandler would eventually inherit was spiritually formed by these two men. The paper's purpose, as they would proudly admit, owed nothing to impartial journalism. The *Los Angeles Times* of General Otis and Harry Chandler, and subsequently of his heir Norman Chandler, was a power accessory, a daily bulletin to coerce the populace of Los Angeles. It hectored. It fulminated. It shamelessly championed the politicians it cared for – conservatives, Republicans – and variously savaged or omitted altogether their rivals. It understood its role – its virulent partisanship – with the same clarity as Rupert Murdoch's *Sun* on the morning of a British General Election: *Defend Capitalism*. General Otis, who sometimes took it upon himself to write editorials in which his preferred punctuation was the exclamation mark, addressed himself to the kind of people he welcomed to his town: 'Los Angeles wants no dudes, loafers or paupers; people who have no means and trust to luck, cheap politicians, failures, bummers, scrubs, impecunious clerks ... The market is overstocked already. We need workers! Hustlers! Men of brains, brawn and guts! Men who have a little capital and a good deal of energy – first-class men!' It was vigorous, preposterous journalism of this nature which remained, for 60 years, the hallmark of the *Los Angeles Times*. Long after General Otis was dead and buried, S. J. Perelman could write of travelling across the United States by train: 'I asked the porter to get me a newspaper and unfortunately the poor man, hard of hearing, brought me the *Los Angeles Times*.'

Otis Chandler is in many respects an improbable candidate to have resuscitated West Coast newspapering. As a young man he was a rangy prep-school track star. At Stanford he became interested in weights and built himself up to 220 pounds of packed muscle to become a world-class shot-putter, missing the 1952 Olympics only because he sprained the wrist of his shot-putting arm. Holidays he spent surfing and even now, in his mid-sixties, he surfs four or five days a week. His life in newspapers has always consisted of stints of intense work punctuated by equally intense interludes for sport and hunting. Long before every CEO in North America thought it essential to install a nautilus gymnasium on their executive floor, Otis Chandler had installed one among the heating ducts of the *Los Angeles Times*. Frequently he pumped weights while reading memoranda about circulation penetration in Orange County and San Bernardino. Sometimes he allowed himself to be photographed doing these two activities simultaneously. For a shy man – a man who still has to push himself to give speeches in public – he has never fought shy of exposure. From the first moment it fell to him to personify the *Los Angeles Times*, Otis Chandler and his first wife, Marilyn, submitted to the gaze of publicity. The Chandlers were projected as a golden family. Photo-news magazines pictured them training together on the family running track, loading up their camper van for 'a winter wilderness outing' and animatedly stacking the dishwasher. Their Christmas cards showed them with their four children on the beach, blond, fit, tanned and each holding a surfboard.

Contemporaries say that, more than any other man, Otis Chandler was driven to attain precise goals: to lose this much weight before joining the Air Force, to ride a wave of such and such a height for a particular distance, to bag a hunting trophy of an exact size in a high-altitude location. His three ambitions, he said, were to shoot all 20 species of North American game, all types of the world's wild sheep and to own the greatest newspaper on the continent.

'I'm a real oddball on vacations,' he says, 'I like to go up into the mountains with an 80-pound pack on my back and get off alone. I get some of my best thinking done there. Most of the ideas I get of any value for the paper come to me while I'm sitting on a surfboard waiting for a big wave or on a mountainside in a snowstorm.'

There are two celebrated stories that vividly show Otis Chandler's sporting tastes and priorities. When he was invited to Lyndon Johnson's ranch for the first time, it was suggested they go deer hunting. This, it turned out, involved motoring around the presidential ranch in an air-conditioned Lincoln, shooting the deer through the electric windows and leaving the dead carcasses to be gathered by Secret Service agents. Chandler made no secret of his contempt for this synthetic trip.

'I like best to hunt two kinds of animal,' he told me. '*Dangerous* animals and *intelligent* animals. For danger, it's a toss-up between the tiger, jaguar and leopard. I've got all of them, all the dangerous cats syndrome. But I'd say that sheep are my all-time favourite animals to hunt because they're the most intelligent. The satisfaction is greatest when you're hunting something intelligent.'

On another occasion, in the middle of an episodic budget review, Otis Chandler's secretary interrupted the meeting with an urgent message in an envelope. Chandler opened it, read it, screwed it up and apologised to his colleagues that he'd have to rush off. After he'd gone, someone smoothed out the scrumpled note to see what it said. It read: 'The surf is up at 12.30'.

'It was a very dull meeting,' remembers Chandler. 'Then my secretary brought in this message from one of my surfing buddies saying there was 15-foot surf coming where I have a beach house, down in Newport Beach. So I immediately ended the meeting.'

When he set about transforming the *Times*, he approached the task with single-minded determination. '*I want the best*' he always said. In the first six years after his father made him publisher, the staff, the design, the tone, the mission, everything about the *Los Angeles Times* was updated and upscaled. New bureaux were opened all over the country. Finding that the *Times*'s representation in Washington was derisory, he headhunted an entire new all-star staff. Then he started on the world. The newspaper that had possessed only one foreign correspondent, in Paris, a much put-upon figure whose very existence was considered an extravagance, soon opened bureaux in every significant capital around the globe. Salaries were doubled, tripled. New sections, new zoned editions – all made feasible by the absence of unions – proliferated. Week by week the paper grew more obese. Soon the Sunday edition was regularly breaking 600 pages and weighed seven pounds. The great doubled-over hassock of newsprint was bigger than any newspaper ever before produced, anywhere. Even today, its pagination slimmed by recession, the *Los Angeles Times* is as fat as Murdoch's *Australian*, Black's *Sunday Telegraph*, Murdoch's *South China Morning Post*, Black's *Sydney Morning Herald*, Jain's *Times of India* and Hersant's *Le Figaro* all stacked into one. The special sections, each as fat as regular newspapers elsewhere, are devoted to the oddest subjects: 'Circuit City' advertising Super Scope Cordless Game Guns and the 'Golf Course Communities' supplements puffing 'a new Spanish Hills championship golf community in Camarillo'.

Otis Chandler's father, Norman, had made one very shrewd decision 15 years earlier, and by the sixties the benefits from this had begun to accrue. He had decided that, during the wartime newsprint rationing, almost all of the space in his pencil-thin paper should be given over to news, not advertising. His rivals at the *Examiner*, owned by Hearst, took the opposite view. By the end of the war the *Los Angeles Times*, having become required reading for its comprehensive news coverage, was perceived as the authoritative daily paper and rewarded with the lion's share of advertising.

And as Los Angeles thrived, so these advertisements multiplied. Some days there were 80, 90, 100 solid pages of classified, and as many pages again of real estate advertisements for new developments, condominiums, apartments. More journalists had to be drafted just to fill the news holes between the lineage. No wonder Otis Chandler encouraged his national reporters to write long; their stories, embarking with great brio on page one, frequently jumped six or seven times to areas deep in the paper, known as gooney-bird sections, where tiny columns of newsprint trailed like streamers around display ads for car auctions. Riding high on this wave of revenue, Otis Chandler's expansion was unrestrained. And all the time his principal motivation, it seemed, was an almost obsessive competitiveness with the great East Coast newspapers. The *Los Angeles Times*, he felt, was given insufficient credit by the East, despite all the improvements he'd made and all the staff he'd imported at vast expense, certain people – people at dinner parties in

Washington, delegates he met at newspaper conferences – persisted in patronising the *Times*.

He remains alert to snubs. When I visited him in Oxnard, he asked, 'Who else are you seeing for this book? Which other publishers?'

I reeled off the long list. 'And in North America,' I said, 'the Sulzbergers and Grahams too of course.'

'Why "of course"?' asked Chandler.

'Because I couldn't not include the owners of *The New York Times* and the *Washington Post*.' Chandler looked quizzical, as though he were scrutinising my reply for some implied criticism of the *Los Angeles Times*.

'I like to hire the *very best* journalists and pay them extremely well,' he said. 'I think that is really the thing that turned the tide for the *LA Times*. So people in the East really realised that we have a great paper out here. All you have to do is pick it up. Just go back a couple of years and look at the *LA Times* and the *Washington Post* and *The New York Times* in covering the Gulf War and I think you'll see that we did the best job *by far* of the three papers.'

'*Hiring the best*,' he repeated, enunciating each word separately, as though in so doing he received some almost sensual pleasure. 'You have to seek them out. Pay is important, but you don't want to pay the wrong people; you have to seek them out, the good people, and that's what I tried to do.'

'Did you do it yourself? Fly over to New York and invite somebody you wanted out to lunch?'

'Sure. Sure I did. And once I got a nucleus of people then the word got around that Otis was after building a first-class newspaper and they wanted to get on board. We have the opportunity of hiring almost anybody we want now.'

'I've heard it said that you only really started improving the *Times* when the Sulzbergers began selling *The New York Times* in California.'

'That's not true,' said Chandler. 'That's never been true. We'd begun before that, building up the paper. When *The New York Times* opened up out here, we never felt it. *Never felt it*. A nice man who's no longer alive – a son-in-law of the Sulzbergers, Orvil Dryfoos – had a misconception, because he had never spent much time out here or lived out here, that people in the West, who had moved west from New

York City wanted to continue the reading habit of *The New York Times* because none of the papers out here could give them enough news. He just completely misjudged it. He thought there would be a landslide of sentiment towards this West Coast edition which just didn't turn out to be true. It only got up to 100,000 circulation over the whole period, it was a very costly venture and just never worked.'

'Do you still feel competitive with the Sulzbergers and Grahams? Does it give you pleasure to pinch their staff?'

'We're rivals but close friends, so I try and avoid that. It's *done*, but I would do everything I could to avoid it. Say if we were after a new science writer or something, we would look everywhere rather than go directly after the science writer of the *Washington Post*. It's kind of an unwritten law: let's not pass people around amongst us. Still, Kay Graham's cussed me out a few times. I once took her bureau chief from the Middle East and she rang me up *properly*, with her usual style and there were some strong four-letter words. She's a dear lady.'

Otis Chandler's *Times* and Otis Chandler's Times Mirror Company have been, above anything, institutions in giddy transition. The shameless Republican-or-bust newspaper of the fifties has been superseded by a cerebral *Los Angeles Times* that sees balanced political reporting as an end in itself. The newspaper that championed Richard Nixon all the way from California to the White House would play a significant, albeit overshadowed, role in bringing him back down again. Chandler has sanctioned the appointment of liberal columnists and cartoonists whose opinions, in earlier regimes, would themselves have been the subject of indignant editorials. Often this made life difficult for him. The cartoonist Paul Conrad, headhunted to the paper from the Denver *Post*, made a speciality of hucksterish pictures of the then Governor of the State of California, Ronald Reagan. Several times a month the telephone would ring during breakfast at the Chandlers', and it would be Reagan complaining to the owner of the *Los Angeles Times* about that morning's outrage. These calls became so regular that eventually Chandler declined to take them. At this point Nancy Reagan began telephoning instead, complaining how the latest unwarranted attack on her husband had ruined *their* breakfast. Finally Otis Chandler gave instructions that Mrs Reagan should not be put through either.

By the late seventies Chandler began stepping up his zoned editions, opening a major bureau in San Diego to produce a substantial San Diego section. Already he could see the demographics of Los Angeles shifting. It became plain that dominating the heart of the city was no longer enough; they needed to become the predominant newspaper for the whole of Southern California.

At the same time his craving for national recognition lost none of its urgency. Times Mirror had gone public in 1964 – the first family-owned newspaper company to do so – and Chandler became increasingly conscious of the leverage this allowed him to expand. Times Mirror would become a national newspaper company, impossible to overlook. Already, in 1969, they had acquired the *Dallas Times Herald* and a year later Long Island *Newsday*. Now, in 1979, Chandler bought the *Hartford Courant* in Connecticut, followed the next year by the *Denver Post* and then by two more Connecticut papers, the Stamford *Advocate* and Greenwich *Time* in Fairfield County. The Texas and Colorado papers were initially conspicuously successful under Chandler's ownership. Appointing a new editor to the *Dallas Times Herald* Chandler's simple instructions to him had been, 'We would like a newspaper of uncommon excellence in Texas.' Take any reasonable measures to attract the most outstanding journalists in the country, he said.

In the great oil slump, however, both Dallas and Denver began seriously to hurt Times Mirror, and there was a measure of relief when Dean Singleton, in characteristic bumptious fashion, sent this message: 'What I'd like to do most is buy the *Dallas Times Herald* from you guys and show you how to run it.'

'It looked like Dallas was really going to take off with the oil and all of that,' said Chandler, 'and then it just went sour.'

I asked him, 'Did you feel any loss of face pulling out of Texas?'

'It hurt at the time because we had put a lot of effort into it. Sure, you have to regret it when a situation like that doesn't work out. But if you stay with something for sentimental reasons, it'll drag you down. And we're not that dumb.

'We knew that if *we* couldn't make it,' Chandler went on, 'then how's *he* [Dean Singleton] going to make it? We knew he would cut it way down; we knew he would do great violence to the editorial products we'd built up – which he did. He cut the editorial staff down to nothing.'

'How long did that take him to do?'

'Almost overnight.'

'Was that hurtful to you?'

'Mhmm. Sure. I have a home in Colorado and we saw the way the paper was going downhill and, sure, you hate to see that. Something you worked hard to build up.'

'Will it all work for him in the end?'

'Well he's a very ambitious, smart young man. But I don't think he's going to succeed in anything he's done – he failed in Dallas, he's failing in Denver, he's going to fail in Houston. That's what I believe anyway. I think his day has come and gone. This is a very difficult time and companies are going out of business all the time. That's why I'm glad we got out of Dallas . . .'

Rival proprietors waltz the earth in a perpetual state of armed truce, but it is a fragile armistice. A single incident on the border, a single incursion, can escalate into total warfare. And the flashpoint is always territorial: when a media owner outgrows his home fiefdom and begins to look with predatory eyes upon another proprietor's domain.

I could find no example of such an invasion that wasn't rancorous. When Punch Sulzberger's brother-in-law, Orvil Dryfoos, drove *The New York Times* on to the Chandlers' pitch on the West Coast, it was received with a hostility that eventually left Punch Sulzberger with little option but to retreat. Rupert Murdoch's intrusion at the Chicago *Sun*, with his hordes of editorial Visigoths from Fleet Street, was as welcome to the rival *Chicago Tribune* as the arrival of Robert Maxwell at the *New York Daily News* was to Peter Kalikow at the *New York Post*. When you mention the Sulzbergers' infiltration of Atlanta to Jim Kennedy of the *Atlanta Journal* and *Constitution*, his brow becomes furrowed and his eyes introspective. Maxwell's migration across Europe with the *European* was received by the Grahams' and Sulzbergers' *International Herald Tribune* with the same marked lack of enthusiasm as Sally Aw Sian's for Rupert Murdoch when he pitched up on her back doorstep in Hong Kong at the *South China Morning Post*.

One of the most interesting invasions, because it has been achieved laterally and almost covertly, has been Chandler and Times Mirror's squeeze on the Sulzberger stronghold of Manhattan.

New York Newsday, despite everything that has followed, is still widely thought of as *Long Island Newsday*. The original *Newsday* – the pure Long Island version – was founded in 1940 to service the middle-class communities of Nassau and Suffolk Counties; communities which by 1970, when Chandler bought the paper, had among the highest household incomes in the United States. Three-quarters of Long Island's population is employed within New York City limits. In the morning and evening the trains are packed with commuters travelling back and forth from Manhattan, and at weekends the seaside towns and villages along the southern shore – Southampton, Quogue, Westhampton – teem with Upper Eastsiders fleeing the city. It was these franchises, tantalisingly close to Manhattan, that inspired Otis Chandler to acquire the paper from its arch-Republican owner Harry Guggenheim.

Newsday pre-Chandler was a respectable, somewhat folksy local newspaper. If you wished to read about a record fish caught off the beach at Fire Island, or some sporting event at a school in Greenport, then you turned to *Newsday*. That in 20 years it would be transformed into the second best-read newspaper in Central Manhattan owes everything to Chandler and his factotum David Laventhol.

David Laventhol's arrival at *Newsday* actually predates its acquisition by Chandler. Because Laventhol has subsequently become so closely identified with the Times Mirror Company, it is generally assumed that this intellectually sharp, physically pudgy, vaguely shambling strategist came on board with the assailants from Los Angeles. In fact he had joined the paper from the *Washington Post* a few months earlier in 1969 and was virtually the only member of the old regime who, on hearing that Guggenheim was selling out to Chandler, did not contemplate the future with misgivings. Rather he saw in Chandler, with his billion-dollar Californian warchest, an opportunity to propel *Newsday* into a bigger league; to expand coverage, launch a Sunday edition, install new presses in a new building, and above anything make the psychological leap that would enable the paper to compete not only on the periphery of New York but forge into the very heart of Manhattan.

'The first time I met Otis was in his suite at the Waldorf Towers,'

Laventhol told me from his capacious beige corner office in Los Angeles. 'We met to discuss what he wanted to do with the paper now that he owned it. He made a strong first impression: as a man of very definite views, extremely knowledgeable. He is a good coach, in the sense that he doesn't say "do this, do that". With Otis it is always an exchange of ideas.'

Laventhol was appointed editor, subsequently publisher. For six years he fortified the paper's powerbase on Long Island. Then, in 1977, *Newsday* began a tentative run at Queens. Edition changes (similar in scope to the edition changes Chandler was introducing for the *Times* in Los Angeles) allowed some token coverage of local Queens news. This, Laventhol concedes, was not enough. 'When you crossed the Queens county line, they were New Yorkers,' he told *Manhattan Inc.* 'There was one big school district as opposed to a lot of little ones. The New York mayor was their mayor. It was all very large and very urban. It became clear we needed to have a different perspective.' So by 1983 Laventhol was building a comprehensive New York staff and increasing city coverage. Two years later the paper was formally rechristened *New York Newsday* and made a dramatic, no-holds-barred assault on the toughest newspaper market in the country.

According to legend, when the idea of *New York Newsday* was first suggested to Otis Chandler, the prospect of newsstands selling one of his newspapers right across the sidewalk from the New York Times building gave him immediate gratification. He liked the idea that, every morning on his way into work, Punch Sulzberger would see the newspaper trespassing on his patch; it compensated for the years of East Coast snobbery. And in a roundabout way it promised revenge on the Sulzbergers for starting their presumptuous West Coast edition of *The New York Times* twenty years earlier.

When Chandler talks about *Newsday* now he says, 'When we bought that paper in 1970 it had 350,000 circulation and no Sunday paper. Now we're close to a million daily and well over a million on Sunday and it's the fourth-largest newspaper in circulation in the country.'

The New York edition, however, has achieved a circulation of only about a quarter of a million in five years, concentrated in Queens, Brooklyn and Manhattan. Most analysts agree that it continues to lose money. Laventhol insists that actual circulation growth more or less matches his initial predictions. 'We understood how long it would take. We knew it would be a costly enterprise with circulation [of the New York edition] growing incrementally by only 30,000 to 40,000 a year. The paper will be profitable before it reaches the 400,000 mark and will ultimately settle in at about 500,000.' Then he says, 'It will be a strong economic unit. Newspapers are going for $1000 a subscriber. With a half million in circulation that's $500 million, and that's far less than any investment on our part.' (Laventhol's valuations are not ambitious either. A 1990 Ansbacher media briefing on *Newsday* gave it a high value of $975 million, a low of $812.5 million.)

The niche Chandler and Laventhol have sought with *New York Newsday* is somewhere between *The New York Times* and the pre-Maxwell *New York Daily News*. When the blueprint for the new edition was being discussed, the tone of the paper was established with a scale, zero to ten. If the *Daily News* as a blue-collar tabloid was zero and the *Times* as a highbrow broadsheet was ten, where would *Newsday* fall? Laventhol envisioned it as a four. 'Over the years it has become a shorthand way to talk about our positioning. That needle point stays between 3.5 and 5.5.'

'We're about a million-two-fifty daily and a million-five-some on Sunday,' said Chandler. 'That still gives the *Los Angeles Times* a comfortable margin over the competition.'

He was referring here not to the Californian competition but to newspapers that aren't strictly speaking competition at all; papers in other cities two, three thousand miles away where the *LA Times* is barely distributed. Otis Chandler was referring to the big arena – the whole North American continent – where the metropolitan daily pecking order goes: first the *Los Angeles Times* (1,177,251), second *The New York Times* (1,110,562), third the *Washington Post* (791,289), fourth Long Island *Newsday* (762,639).

'Our circulations have never been higher,' he went on, 'even in spite of the recession and the price increases we've put in.'

Not for the first time I observed the almost physical satisfaction some proprietors take in robust circulations. It was as though the sheer volume of family newsprint coursing every day through

Southern California made Chandler's blood pump faster, his step lighter. It was as though the million-two-fifty people were somehow buying into a part of *him* every day, rather than a hummock of printed-over wood pulp to read over their breakfast in a waffle house.

'What's damaging right now,' he said, 'is the economy which is hurting our advertising so badly. And I don't personally think we'll ever again have the advertising base we've enjoyed all the time I've been in the business.'

'Why's that?'

'We've had so many mergers and acquisitions and major companies going out of business and there's no way to replace that advertising volume. Pan Am is out of business, TWA is out of business, department stores are in bankruptcy, food markets have merged. Those are millions of lines of advertising we used to have that won't return to the paper.

'The other huge change,' he said, 'is going to be in the classified advertising department owing to the so-called "Peace Dividend" at the end of the Cold War. The cutbacks in aerospace and defence that will affect Southern California and our major advertisers are going to be horrendous. They're talking about 200,000 to 300,000 jobs just this year being eliminated because we won't be building any new weapons systems. And those jobs are 60 per cent of our classified. And at the same time we're being hurt by the lack of real estate sales, hurt by the lack of automobile sales. We're hurting all over.' (Hurting is, of course, relative. Newspaper revenues across Times Mirror declined by five per cent between 1990 and 1991 to $1.97 billion, with classified accounting for most of this shortfall.)

'The central question we and all the other major papers around the country are going to have to figure out,' he said, 'is how do we continue to produce a quality newspaper with the completeness and uniqueness of a word-class newspaper but to a much reduced page volume because of advertising? The *LA Times* for 25 years has been the largest paper in the world and we've averaged during the eighties probably 120 pages during the week and probably five to six hundred pages on Sunday. What if we now, for example, averaged 90 pages or even 80 pages daily? You can't give your editor the same editorial news hole he had before, because that would loosen the pages up to such an extent that it would have a huge impact on our profits. We have to maintain a certain advertisement-to-news ratio. So how does the editor cover the world in all its aspects, plus California and LA and everything else, with a reduced space? How's it going to read? Are there going to be more short articles and more news briefs – not like *USA Today*, I'm not suggesting we're headed in that direction – or are we headed in the direction of the British press which tends to be very few pages and a lot of very short – compared to us – articles or the Japanese press which is the same way? And if we're charging more for the paper on the one hand and yet we're giving them *less* because of less advertising, how long are they going to stay with us? I don't think any of us has the answers.'

Like Conrad Black, like Tony O'Reilly, like Ralph Ingersoll, it is grappling with the Big Questions that most absorbs Otis Chandler. Newspapering as intellectual pursuit. And it struck me that Chandler's logic about the future of the *LA Times* was drawing him to some fairly unwelcome conclusions: a city in which an ever thinner and less profitable *Times* struggles to find readers among ever more illiterate and disenfranchised immigrants.

I asked him, 'Where then is the great pleasure in owning a newspaper?'

He answered unhesitatingly. 'It's the opportunity it gives you to do important things to improve this planet Earth.'

He betrayed no self-consciousness in making this grandiose claim for newspaper proprietorship. 'Whether it be in science or helping to solve human issues or improve the environment or economic and educational opportunities for people. In other words, unlike any other business, a newspaper gets into every other business you can think of, and it just gives you that opportunity to try to improve and educate politicians and citizens of all types, to give them some guidelines as to how they can lead a better life and improve the *quality* of their life.'

Then he said, 'All my life you know people wanted me to run for office.'

'So why haven't you?'

'It's so temporary. Four years as governor, eight years as governor, then six years as a senator and you're gone. A newspaper goes on and on and on. There's a lot of information in a good newspaper every day that helps people, helps their children, helps them understand their government and their environment. It's just an entire rainbow of activities that a newspaper covers every day. And to me that's the real excitement of running a newspaper if you take it seriously. That's why I don't like some of the British press. I don't like the populist – so-called populist – press that Mr Maxwell identified with and Mr Murdoch identifies with because I think that's *irresponsible*. Not responsible, it's irresponsible.'

'In what way?'

'In terms of running the fluff. T&A – tits and ass. Mr Maxwell and Mr Murdoch either ordered it or enjoy having bare-breasted women in some of their papers. Page Three or whatever they call it in Britain.'

'I've heard both Rupert Murdoch and Robert Maxwell claim with great sincerity that they're intent upon improving planet Earth exactly like you say you are. I'm sure Murdoch in particular would say he identified with all your sentiments about newspapers helping to solve human issues.'

'I don't know how he could. I saw what Murdoch did when he had the *New York Post* and when Maxwell had the *New York Daily News*. The emphasis that someone like Mr Maxwell gave to the seamy side of life – the sex, crime and violence and drugs and misery of life, and sensationalised murders and rapes and that kind of thing and naked women – that is the *exact opposite* of what one should do if one has the opportunity of owning a newspaper. The owner has to set the guidelines. He has to say this is the quality of the paper I want to have and this is the standard that we have. And I *don't* want much, if any, sensational news and I don't want pictures of bare-breasted women and I don't want to delve into the private life of our President. I don't know how the Queen of England and her family can tolerate some of the stories! In this country I think you'd be shot – you *should* be shot – if you're a publisher, the way they pick on the Royal Family.

'I like Mr Murdoch personally,' he went on, 'but I don't think he has contributed *anything* to American journalism. He was a failure in New York, and when he had that paper in San Antonio they had more murders and rapes and suicides than people in San Antonio ever knew about until he came along! It's just a different way of looking at journalism. I'm of the old, conservative school that one should do one's best to inform the people about what they need to know, and not to appeal to their baser instincts about nudity and explicit language. I hate to see good newspapers do that and fortunately I don't think that

Mr Maxwell and Mr Murdoch have influenced any of us in this country to lower our standards at all and to chase that kind of news. They haven't influenced the *LA Times* or the *Washington Post* or the *Chicago Tribune*. I do however think that we – the major papers in this country – have to be very careful not to let our own television stations have an influence on us. They're going through this evolution just now of "how-sensational-can-we-get". And some of our editors, because their friends say "Did you see that juicy-looking blonde or that tremendous divorce settlement on *Entertainment Tonight*?", think maybe we should cover that. I'm sure Mr Murdoch would say it's news and that people want to read about it. Well I think one has to exercise some judgement – *a lot of judgement* – as to what they print and don't print. And I think it is the duty of the owner to exercise that judgement *himself*.'

'Are you training up either of your sons to exercise that judgement eventually?'

'I have two sons that were on the *Los Angeles Times*. My youngest is in the production department now, he's a minor supervisor and I don't know where he's going to wind up. That's Michael. He's been married three times and has five children. My oldest son, Norman, is dying of a brain tumour. He's 39 years old and has four children. He's been out of the company for three years.' Otis Chandler looked grave. 'A very sad case.'

'Are you safe from raiders as a family? Could your 7000 or so non-family shareholders betray you to another media owner?'

'We reckon we're safe. We've created two classes of stock. Two years ago. We re-incorporated in Delaware and staggered voting and all the usual anti-shark measures.'

'Were any sharks circling?'

'We were the most undervalued company on the New York Stock Exchange at one time. If you looked at the assets we owned and put values on each of them I think our market value at the time was about three billion and the breakup value was about eight and a half or nine billion. So that's when we decided we'd better protect our ass!'

Little Empire on the Prairie

Jim Cox Kennedy's *Atlanta Constitution*

An aerial tour of the entire circulation area of a newspaper is disconcerting. The downtown metropolis, outlying counties and residential enclaves – where houses cluster around golf courses, lie half-hidden among fir trees or huddle amidst freeways which loop around them like tarmacadam ampersands – present a panorama of possibilities. For a moment you see, like Christ on the exceeding high mountain, all the readers of the world spread out before you, and you wonder, if you owned this particular newspaper, what exactly you would need to publish every day to hold the attention of the downtown subscribers as well as those living around the golf courses, fir trees, railroads and freeways. When you approach Atlanta from the coast, you overfly first a strip of bleak, hazy farmland – Liberty county – then several more bleak, hazy farming counties – Bulloch, Laurens, Baldwin – and then the plane banks around the nineteen counties of metropolitan Atlanta itself – Cobb, Fulton, Gwinnett – with their palette of swimming pools and mile-long streets running parallel to railroad tracks.

Atlanta could be any one of a dozen sprawling American cities. There is an airport freeway with grass verges cut so smooth and close they look like astroturf, the full roster of chain hotels, food franchises, department stores. The advertising pages of Atlanta's neighbourhood newspapers – the Cox Chambers' *Atlanta Journal* and *Constitution* – are carpeted with space from the local Macy's, Saks Fifth Avenue, Rich's shopping mall. Whole zones of the city are engaged in a frenzied international construction race; billboards on half-completed towers announce financing from Sumitomo Bank of Tokyo and the Tokai Bank of Nagoya. People say 'Atlanta is Houston 15 years ago'. They tell you 'Atlanta is America's fastest-growing city'. They tell you that the population is increasing in some parts of the metropolis at nine or ten per cent a year, that there is a compound annual growth in retail sales of eight per cent, that 74 per cent of the population is aged under 40. And when they tell you all this they do so with an almost neurotic optimism, as though behind all the demolishing and drilling and dazzling new shopping plazas there is some Utopian grand plan, that at some imminent moment the expansion is going to halt, the construction workers tidy up and leave town and the new, coherent Atlanta be unveiled. In spirit, however, Atlanta struck me not as an American city at all but a Far East or Gulf Arab boomtown. The Atlantans are boastful; anxious you shouldn't leave town without seeing the tallest, flashiest new buildings. ('Have y'seen Peachtree Tower? Have y'seen Ravinia Tower and the GLG Park Plaza?') To get the 1996 Olympic Games meant as much to the city as it did to Seoul in 1988. That the world headquarters of Coca-Cola is in Atlanta is a matter of widespread civic pride. That Ted Turner's CNN ('the world's fastest-growing international cable channel') is based there in breathtakingly hideous downtown headquarters around a central atrium, part of Ted Turner's shopping mall and Omni hotel, is another. When an Atlanta restaurant is voted one of the country's top 100 by a poll of 60,000 frequent flyer business executives, it is headline news on both CNN and the *Atlanta Journal* and *Constitution*.

And yet many Atlantans have a bewildered look about them, endemic in boomtowns. More than half the population are immigrants to the state. After only two years in town a cab driver will say to you, 'Can you believe how this city's changed? It's growing too fast.' A 30-year-old restaurant is a landmark: 'For three decades Georgians and visitors alike have enjoyed fine dining at Atlanta's premier restaurant. The legendary landmark "Coach & Six" offers Atlanta favourites like prime rib, lamb chops, Maine lobster.' Atlanta's role in the Civil War and the fighting around the Chattahoochee River is commemorated all over this historically Confederate, demographically amorphous city.

Such is the scale, the hype that surrounds everything in Atlanta, it does not remotely surprise one to learn that the *Atlanta Journal* and *Constitution* is the nation's fastest-growing major newspaper. (Combined daily circulation for what is strictly speaking two separate newspapers – the morning *Constitution* and afternoon *Journal* – but is effectively two editions of the same paper with a substantial proportion of identical stories, rose by 10 per cent in 1990 to 511,168; 686,885 on Sundays.) I could not drive from the downtown area with its glacier-white skyscrapers to the suburbs of Peachtree and Buckhead without reflecting on Ralph Ingersoll's gloomy prognostications on the future of newspaper readers: the cable channel-hopping society for whom a conventional paper becomes increasingly peripheral amidst the information overload of junk media. He had described a suburban American readership with a 12-second attention span, incapable of completing more than the first few paragraphs of any story, jumping from article to article like a baby with a TV zapper, fundamentally not interested in the greater part of the material.

And yet, against this trend, the Atlanta paper is growing. It was not easy to explain why. Open the *Atlanta Journal* and *Constitution* and you might be opening any one of a dozen similar metropolitan papers across America. Trailing down the left column of the front page, a coloured table of contents, blindingly garish: orange, sky blue, cochineal, pea green, each panel of colour abutting the next in a blur. The effect is like watching a cartoon film with the contrast knob turned to maximum. And the stories themselves are impeccably honed for a television-immersed readership. The headline that day was the story of a popular figure-skating champion who had some years before written a letter to the Oprah Winfrey show but received no reply. There was an item of local interest about the origins of the Ku Klux Klan, and another, tagged exclusive, about soldiers possibly being discharged from a local army camp due to the Cold War thaw. That item was five paragraphs long. There are numerous sections – travel, business, Dixie living, perspective, style, comics – and those were just the conspicuous ones. Tucked and folded inside each section are further sections, each with their own orange and pea green index, alerting you to additional sections concealed inside themselves. Some of these sections consist only of a single folded sheet. Others turn out to be a huge advertisement occupying nine-tenths of the page, with a ribbon of words, often an advice column, trained around it in an inverted 'L'. (Some of these began: 'I like to shave in the shower but the mirror keeps fogging up' – Despairing, Rockdale County.) Much of the design makes you think of a menu at a hamburger restaurant: islands of words, two or three lines long describing dressings and relishes, immured in brightly coloured boxes.

It was not always thus.

Cox Enterprises Inc, proprietors of the *Atlanta Journal* and *Constitution*, 15 smaller daily newspapers – including the *Palm Beach Post* and a cluster of corner-shop titles in Texas, Ohio, Colorado and Arizona – seven weekly newspapers, 23 cable systems in 17 states, seven television, 14 radio stations and 26 car auction businesses – is the largest private media company in the American southeast. It is 98 per cent owned by two rather glamorous sisters in their late sixties, Anne Cox Chambers and Barbara Cox Anthony. Whenever *Forbes* magazine pastes together its list of the nation's richest people, Mrs Chambers and Mrs Anthony's assets are compounded, and they jointly emerge on four billion dollars as 'the richest women in America'. Neither sister much enjoys this annual citation. They are both, as the saying goes, very private. Anne Cox Chambers, the older of the two, is a pin-thin socialite who has never allowed her allegiance to the Democrats and her long friendship with Jimmy Carter to overshadow her parallel passions for her villa in Provence, her Atlanta estate, Rosewood, her duplex on Sutton Place, her 12,000-acre plantation in South Carolina or the Gulfstream jet in which she flits between New York, Washington and Georgia. Aside from a spell as the United States' most discriminating ever ambassador to Belgium, she has largely devoted herself to good works and fund-raising for the Democratic presidential campaigns of Carter, Dukakis and Clinton (while her flagship Atlanta newspapers, with no apparent sense of irony, resolutely pledge their support to the Republicans).

Cox Anthony, meanwhile, lives in a villa in Honolulu and in Australia. Although both sisters hold honorary positions in the newspaper empire (Chambers is Chairman of Atlanta Newspapers, Anthony Chairman of the family's Dayton Newspapers in Ohio) these are empty titles, and neither plays any executive role. Their principal involvement, according to Cox's Chairman, is participation in a quarterly board of directors meeting 'and then certainly the telephone allows one to be in touch with them all the time, which I am in any case of course'. The present Chairman and CEO of Cox Enterprises is a tall, thoughtful, vigorous, Clark Kent lookalike,

James Cox Kennedy, the son of Barbara Cox Anthony. Since 1987 the mantle of the Cox empire has devolved entirely on to his shoulders.

The Cox chain has an interesting effect on other newspaper owners. Four of them specifically recommended I miss them out. This wasn't I guessed, for the usual reasons – competitiveness, jealousy – but because their inclusion seemed to them to undermine the discrimination of my book.

'Cox is a boring company,' I was assured. 'They make a barrel of money but there's nothing interesting about them. They don't have any first-class papers.'

Another (North American) proprietor said, 'They're a private company but they're not private. I mean, they don't *behave* like they're private.'

'How do you mean not *behave*?'

'Their responses are those of a public company. They could be Gannett or Knight-Ridder. The decisions they take: they're the same far-sighted pussyfooting decisions a corporation takes when it's answerable to shareholders. Cautious, long-term investment. An editorial philosophy that says, "It's not our business to *have* a corporate editorial philosophy. Whatever the reader wants, we let 'em have it." That's why the Cox company has no voice. It's a chameleon. In one place they'll say this, in another they'll say that. It's like a waffle house or ice-cream soda chain. If the reader wants syrup, give him syrup, as much syrup as he can pour down his throat. Where are their papers anyway? Texas? Ohio? Nobody cares. There's no overview at Cox. Maybe that's a strength, but sure as hell it's dull.'

But once you get beyond the proselytising proprietors, then the vote for Cox improves.

'They're a company that's making it its business to survive and adapt,' said a media analyst at Morgan Stanley. 'They're attentive to the numbers, know their business well, are responsive to readers. They're not going to let the world change on them. Everything that's happening in the communities they cover, they're aware of. I find that impressive. And it's a conscious corporate policy that comes right from the top, from Jim Kennedy. He's an intelligent guy. He reads. He listens. He isn't surrounded by cronies telling him to push this government policy or this senator. I guess he's saying, "Who gives a shit who owns these newspapers anyway? The readers don't." And

I'm not even convinced that journalists and managers mind all that much who owns them, providing the pay's OK and health benefits are in place. Anne Cox Chambers and her nephew realise this very well. Jim Kennedy's not into ego trips, which is why the Cox company is going to expand its businesses faster during this decade than any of the other private chains.'

Revenues of just over two billion dollars make it the biggest single company in Georgia, though rather less than a third of its 27,000 employees work in the state. After a spell as a public company (Cox Communications Inc, formerly Cox Broadcasting Corporation, was quoted on the New York Stock Exchange from 1964) the entire operation was taken private again in the mid-eighties as Cox Enterprises. The stock is closely held in a series of inter-dependent family trusts, the details of which are sealed from public view by court order at Fulton Superior Court. Aside from the sisters, who are both daughters of Cox founder James Cox (the governor of Ohio and presidential candidate who bought the *Atlanta Journal* in 1939), the main recipients of these shadowy trusts are presumed to be Jim Kennedy and his sister, Blair Parry-Okeden, and Anne Cox Chambers's three children Margaretta Johnson Taylor, Katharine Anne Johnson and the son by her second marriage, James Cox Chambers. One of the few known facts about the trusts is that in 1987 and again in 1990 a tranche of shares was sold by the grandchildren back to Cox Enterprises, further ensuring the security of the family holding. The buy-back of Cox Communications cost the family $1.26 billion, saddling Cox Enterprises with a total of $1.8 billion in debt requiring tax-deductible interest payments which, as commentators are quick to point out, eases the Cox family tax problem for a couple of decades to come. Whether or not going private was a smart move in the long term is much debated. Cox management point out that it saved them from the 'distractions' of public ownership, as well as from corporate raiders who, at their most predatory in 1986, might have viewed the conservative Cox portfolio as a tasty target. Others, however, saw the Cox deal as a cop-out for exactly this reason. Strong management shouldn't need the protection of going private. Going private, they argued, was a funk; a tacit admission of lack of confidence and direction and typical of the company's Southern insularity. All interested parties agree, however, that the price the Coxes paid was cheap. 'They stole the company,' the New York analyst Mario Gabelli told *Georgia Trend*. The company's true value, he reckoned, was $120 a share, not the $75 that the Coxes paid; and this doesn't include any premium for peace-of-mind that immunity from raiders allowed them.

'The thing about the Coxes,' a *Chicago Tribune* executive told me, 'is that they can't go do a Bingham [the Bingham family of Louisville who lost their newspaper empire, including the *Courier-Journal*, through family feuding]; statistically it's practically impossible. There's never going to be a re-run in Atlanta of the Louisville fiasco. They may not be splashy at business, but they sure are powerful. And it doesn't *matter* if they're conservative and dull. Now they're private again there are no more media analysts to goad them or penalise the stock price. So they can sit tight down there in the South, nice and easy, doing it their way, which I guess is exactly how they like it.'

World headquarters of Cox Enterprises Inc is a muted low-rise brick building in a residential Atlantan suburb, 50 minutes from the city centre, on Lake Hearn Drive. It may be that Cox takes the prize for the dullest corporate foyer of all newspaper empires. Displayed above the reception desk is a peerlessly ugly tapestry: a vast woolly rug of woolly green fields and hills with woolly pink clouds drifting by. Beneath this tapestry is a glass museum case displaying recent Cox newspapers, locked, perhaps to prevent anyone from filching a free copy. The papers to the fore are the *Waco Tribune-Herald* (Texas, circulation 48,384), the *Arizona Pennysaver* (Mesa, AZ, circulation 500,453) and the *Valley Foothill News* (Yuma, AZ, circulation 6175).

The office of James Cox Kennedy – he prefers to be known as James C. Kennedy to keep his middle name in proper proportion – occupies a corner position on the top floor of the building, a huge square room with an odd wedge-shaped glass extension in the corner, like a narrow slice of pizza jutting into space. I asked him, 'What do you use that bit for?'

'I don't,' he replied. 'I can't imagine what anyone would do with themselves along there, even supposing they could fit down it.'

James Cox Kennedy loomed above me. Athletic and broad-shouldered, he is extraordinarily fit. Every morning of his life he swims a mile and spends an hour and a half working out. Every evening he bicycles 20 miles. At weekends he bicycles a hundred miles. He canoes, he surfs, he windsurfs, he plays tennis, he shoots quail, he fishes for trout, he hunts puma and mountain bear, he competes in triathlons, he had recently bicycled 2900 miles across middle America from Irvine, California to Savannah, Georgia. He radiates good health. At 45, he looks at least ten years younger. He had played a significant role, I knew, in finally securing the Olympic Games for Atlanta.

'There's a saying,' he said, 'about a dog chasing cars and one day it'll catch one. That was like us in Atlanta with the Olympic Games. Heaven knows we chased enough cars before we caught it.'

Then he asked, 'You'd like a water?' He poured from a jug into two glasses engraved 'Cox Enterprises'. Then he started, his eye arrested by something on the surface of the water. 'I don't *believe* this,' he exclaimed. 'Look at that water! This is meant to be my *special water*. It's got *bits in it*.' He fished around with his thumb and retrieved a speck of black matter from the depths and swiped it on to a sheet of paper. 'That's better,' he laughed. 'Pure water.'

Dressed in a dark blue suit with light blue pinstrip, red geometric Hermès tie and tortoiseshell glasses, he looks less the Southern newspaper heir than the head of some WASPy Wall Street mergers and acquisitions desk. The sole slightly uncool detail was the plastic identity badge dangling from his lapel.

'Don't people round here know who you are?'

'Got to set an example. We ask all our people to wear one, so if I don't . . .' Then he added, looking suddenly troubled, 'Security's necessary here, unfortunately. People come by and snatch the secretaries' purses.'

Like Donald Graham and Pinch Sulzberger, Jim Kennedy underwent a comprehensive, experience-everything training programme. Down from the University of Denver he wasn't convinced he wished to make a career in the family newspapers, but embarked upon a fast-lane induction that took him from the pressroom to the newsroom to covering City Hall as a reporter and selling display advertising. He was regarded indulgently by his colleagues as a competent, rather intuitive executive with the kind of off-beat foibles almost mandatory in newspaper heirs (setting pigeon traps on the flat roof of the *Journal* building, for example, to train his gun dog). As time went by, his journalism too increasingly specialised in field sports. Atlantans were treated, in their mirror-clad skyscrapers, to articles by James Cox Kennedy about salmon flies, fishing rods and the migratory patterns of bob-white quail. Later he was dispatched to Grand Junction, Colorado, as publisher of the Cox paper there, the *Daily Sentinel*. It was here that he learnt to hunt deer, bear and puma as well as serving on the Colorado wildlife commission.

'As you probably know, I consider myself a conservationist,' he said, rushing into the hunt-to-conserve argument that every sportsman must now embrace whenever the subject comes up. 'I like doing things to help wild animals of all kinds: the huntable species as well as the non-game species, all the migratory birds that come through the area. It's basically trying to provide habitat in Colorado for wild animals, and developing the kind of hunting regulations that suit Man – people like me who enjoy that – and yet has the least negative impact on the resource itself.'

Then he said, 'You know, I guess my best times in newspapers were in Grand Junction, so it's impossible for me not to call the *Daily Sentinel* my favourite of our newspapers. My two children were born there. They're Coloradans! And I went to school in Colorado so I really had an affinity – still do – for the West.'

'Do you still pay special attention to that paper?'

'Absolutely. I read it much more carefully than the others, looking for names of friends. In fact I look at *all* the names, wondering who's reporting now on what, and who are the new reporters on the staff of 35 in the newsroom. And then I read what's happening in that town where my children were born, because I remember the people and places so well.'

'And what about your other 24 papers? Aren't they jealous?'

'With the other newspapers,' he replied, 'well, I *see* them every month. I look to see how they're organised, their use of colour, editorial positions.'

Then, perhaps thinking this all sounded a bit bloodless, he added, 'Actually I receive some of our papers at home because of interests I have in certain parts of the country. My wife's family has businesses in Florida [he married Sarah Kenan whose parents own the Breakers hotel] so we get the Palm Beach newspapers. The Shiny Sheet, our *Palm Beach Daily News* [that neighbourly newssheet for billionaires] comes every day. And of course I read the Atlanta papers very carefully because I live here. So I'll call Ron Martin, the editor, to say, "Boy, I really like what you've done here today" because I'm right here living it. And I'll send notes to the other publishers, or call them, but not too frequently because I worry that it might carry more weight than it deserved. Of course it's *impossible* for me not to be on the phone almost daily with Jay Smith [Publisher of the *Journal* and *Constitution*]. No, not every day. It's hard for me not to, but I try and refrain. But very often I'll call him and say "Jay, I saw this in the newspaper, what's behind the story?" that kind of thing, we know each other very well. And then I generally end up telling David Easterly [President of the newspaper division] what I've just talked to Jay about, so it doesn't look like I've been going around him, so I guess you could say we stay pretty much in touch.'

He explained, too, that they have developed a sophisticated system of monthly publishers' reports: 'Not just financial, not just "what we did compared to budget", but what's going on in the community. I always read those. "The GM plant opened" or "The GM plant closed", that sort of thing. Or maybe we've been doing a particularly interesting investigative piece on corruption in the police department or whatever. It allows us here to understand what's going on in the local communities.'

This was at least the twentieth time that James Cox Kennedy had invoked local communities. And the annual Cox report, too, brims with community-friendly coverage: a truck driver who fosters children with special needs, black students watching a Cox-installed cable system, a black nurse who cares for premature babies.

'At Cox,' he said, 'we view newspapers as a very intensely *local* business. We believe that if you run good newspapers for the communities they serve, then they will be profitable and also be *contributing forces for good* to those communities. That, in a thumbnail, is the way we operate. It's difficult when a large company owns more than one newspaper because you struggle with how to manage it and maximise the returns and yet allow it to be a local entity. It's difficult for someone in Atlanta to give an opinion on what's best for Yuma, Arizona for example. [This is a reference to his *Yuma Daily Sun*, circulation 20,895, which Jim Kennedy visits every four years, flying first to Phoenix, then chartering a tiny plane with propellers.

"You think about the use of my time, taking a day to get there, a day back. I just don't do that more often".]

'With small communities like that,' he went on, 'we don't send out edicts. We don't tell our people, "This'll be our candidate for the coming presidential primary series or the election itself." That's determined locally.'

'So what distinguishes a Cox newspaper? If I pick one up somewhere, how can I tell it's one of yours?'

Jim Kennedy ruminated. He appeared to have trouble searching for the common factor.

I went on, 'You don't usually even print that it's a Cox paper under the masthead.'

'That's elective, not mandatory. You see we don't operate by formula. Nothing's in the same typeface. We don't invariably put the weather map here or there, so I don't reckon that you *could* distinguish a Cox paper unless you knew.'

The only three things about James Cox Kennedy upon which everybody seems to agree are that he's handsome, family-minded and unpretentious.

'He's so modest,' one amazed Buckhead matron told me. 'Jim and Sarah, they're raising those three kids just right.

'And let me tell you,' she confided, 'they *don't* live in the most expensive house in Buckhead either. There are houses round here for three or four million dollars and theirs maybe cost two. And they moved house recently to the next-door road, and do you know why? Because Jim said there was too much slope outside the old house for the kids to bicycle! Now isn't that something!'

He is a conscientious father, anxious to pass on his enthusiasm for bicycling and bob-white quail shooting.

'In fact that's what I was doing this weekend,' he said. 'My ten-year-old son asked, "Dad, can I invite two of my friends and their fathers and us go quail hunting?" We have a farm in South Carolina, slightly rolling with a lot of pine trees. It was fun, just the three dads and their three sons. We ride horseback when we hunt quail and watch the bird dogs work and when they point we get off and walk in, and when the birds flash we shoot them. It's not competitive. But yesterday while everybody was eating lunch I went out and bicycled 26 miles. The kids and fathers ate lunch and searched for arrowheads and then I came back.'

'Arrowheads from what period?'

'We haven't really dated them and it's something I ought to try and get a better fix on. We actually have two farms in South Carolina and we've researched the Indians but this farm we can't figure out what tribe was there, so we haven't been able to date the arrowheads. But it's wonderful for these children. They find pieces of pottery too and very often the Indians have used their fingernail, like this' – he made vertical scratching motions on his desktop – 'to make a design. And to see those children actually put their finger into a fingerprint that a man or woman made hundreds of years ago, it's really neat and they love it. So that was our weekend.'

There was a worrying moment, about halfway into this tale of filial bonding and Indian deposits, when I thought James Cox Kennedy might succumb to the emotion of it all and burst into tears. His delivery had become increasingly folksy and sincere, like the voice-over on *The Wonder Years* or like Pa Ingalls from the Little House on the Prairie. But what had struck me most was the 26-mile bicycle ride, substituted for lunch in the middle of an arduous quail shoot.

'What do you do,' I asked, 'if it's too wet to bike?'

'Oh, when it's not good weather I have an old bicycle on a turbo trainer,' he replied. 'You take the front wheel off. And once the children go to bed I go down there to the den and listen to rock and roll music on the headphones and ride. It's got to be rock and roll to keep you motivated. You can't listen to classical and keep that pace on a turbo trainer. So I usually do that for about an hour in lieu of a proper ride outside.'

I asked him, 'What's the difference between running a diversified media operation and a soft-drinks company like the Coca-Cola company down the street?'

'There's a *very big* difference. In a soft-drinks company what you want is for everybody to really like your soft drink and think it's the best damn soft drink available. When you're running a newspaper you have to realise that every day a large percentage of people who read it will find something in it they don't like or that they disagree with and will hold *you* accountable. And you have to be able to look those people in the eye and if the story is correct back them [the journalists] up. That's the big difference.'

'Do you get a lot of letters of complaint?'

'Letters from crazy people. Written upside-down and all over the place.' He laughed. 'There are some crazy people out there.' He gestured out of the window towards a street of prim suburban houses with car ports and backyards, and beyond them to a thicket of skyscrapers against the grey-blue Atlanta horizon.

'And people will say something to me in the evening, when we're out to supper, if they don't like what's been written. The tendency is, as you know, for people to get pretty exercised when they're upset with a newspaper. A great example is a friend of mine Billy Payne, who along with Andrew Young was the person most responsible for getting us the Olympics. Billy is a North Atlanta lawyer, former American football player, intense and very competitive, and he either believes that "you're on my side or you're on the other person's side". And he doesn't understand why our newspaper keeps pushing this Olympic effort to be more open so the people of Atlanta know what's going on. He says, "Jim, *why* do your people try to get into my shorts all the time?" And then I try to explain to Billy that it's the newspaper's *job*. We're always having those kinds of conversations.'

'The inference being that as the owner you ought to control what's written in your papers.'

'Ought to and *should*.'

'And how do you explain your failure?'

'I just tell him the way it is. You hire people and ask them to do their job and then you have to *let them do their job* and that I don't have time to edit every single word that goes into every single newspaper before it does.'

Often it is Kennedy himself who is the community's critic. When he learnt that the best local Christian school wouldn't employ Jewish teachers, despite having a sizeable number of Jewish pupils, he initiated a vigorous campaign of lobbying. He is active, too, in persuading more Atlantan country clubs to open their doors to Jews and blacks. One Peachtree social leader described him to me as 'a strange combination, an enigma. He's involved in all the right charities and it's a great bonus to get him on to your function committee because he's the most powerful man in this town. But you know he hates to put on black tie, which is disappointing because he looks so distinguished in formal wear.'

One of his colleagues told me Kennedy simply feels overt formality is inappropriate in a city like Atlanta, and that, as the proprietor of a newspaper bought by as many black as white readers, he is reluctant to identify himself exclusively with a small, rich, white minority.

'Racial prejudice is a part of all of us,' he told me. 'That's something I learnt from a big black man, Dr King, who used to do seminars for all of our newspaper managers. And you'd go in there for several days and when you came out you *understood* prejudice. And I understood that I have some prejudice in me, no matter what. And Atlanta will always have prejudice, and racialism will always be here.'

I wondered whether James Cox Kennedy would prefer to live somewhere else. Atlanta – 'The City Too Busy To Hate' – struck me as an awkward place, too thrusting to be altogether at ease with itself, and yet already soured by poverty and racial tension. I could see him running a newspaper chain in Los Angeles and surfing off the beach after work. And I could imagine him working in New York, with a weekend house in Connecticut, rather than grappling with the fractious, quirky South. But sometimes newspaper empires are like British country estates. Your inheritance is a lottery. If your family settled in some remote corner of Shropshire, that's where you live. James Cox Kennedy's inheritance is the *Atlanta Journal* and *Constitution* (the paper that 'Covers Dixie Like The Dew').

But he was saying, 'Atlanta is a very good place to live. Like so many others, Atlanta *the city* has an awful lot of challenges: the homeless and education and the crime rate. And yet it's a city that can come together and make things happen. And we have [ex] President Carter who's a great resource for Atlanta, trying to bring together the entire community – black, white, rich, poor – and to find some solutions. One of the reasons Atlanta is more successful than other Southern cities is that it's been better able to deal with the racial situation – better than Birmingham, Alabama. We make people focus their attention on these issues in our papers and I think now having a black female as editorial page editor of the *Constitution* is very important. I certainly don't agree with everything she says, but she's going to be a great editorial page editor.'

I wondered, too, whether Kennedy felt marginalised in Atlanta. Its civic slogan in this city of slogans – 'The World's Next Great International City' – still has a premature ring to it; I thought it must be more difficult for him in Atlanta to keep abreast of developments in the newspaper industry than for, say, Donald Graham in Washington.

'There's the telephone,' he said. 'I can call my contemporaries if I need to. The Donald Grahams and the Robert Decherds [CEO of Dean Singleton's old adversary, the *Dallas Morning News*], who are my age and have family ties, those people are both my friends and we get along well. And Don Newhouse. We're both in cable television and newspapers and I respect Donald and talk to him quite frequently. I call him, or he calls me and says "What do you think about this legislation?" or "What do you think about this programming endeavour?" or whatever. And you can call Don Newhouse any time; he's there. He goes in the crack of dawn and he's available and he always calls back.

'We also have a department here,' he went on, 'that creates for me personally a great clippings service. That really helps keep track. It's wonderful. They make copies of everything I might be interested in. I travel a lot on aeroplanes and I carry that file with me, and I sit in my seat and go, "I read that, didn't read this, read that," and so forth. So I keep a close eye on the other media companies – their innovations – to make sure we're in line. I don't know if any other CEOs in our business use this clippings system, I haven't heard of any who do.'

(But I had: Vere Rothermere.)

I asked, 'Was it your clippings file that first alerted you that the Sulzbergers were invading your territory?'

'With the *Gwinnett Daily News* you mean?' James Cox Kennedy looked mildly nonplussed. The New York Sulzbergers had bought a newspaper on his own doorstep and it was proving to be a spirited competitor to the *Journal* and *Constitution*.

'I've never known how involved the Sulzbergers themselves were in the decision to buy that paper,' he said, frowning. Then he cheered up. 'But if you look at what they paid for it and ask when they'll ever get that out . . . it'll be an *awfully* long time, even if they have the patience.'

(They didn't. On 24 August 1992 the New York Times Company closed the *Gwinnett Daily News* and sold the circulation to Jim Kennedy.)

'I think it's hard,' he said, 'for anyone to come from the outside into Atlanta and make something new work, however good the idea. I guess in some respects we're still sceptical of outsiders. I remember when Robert Maxwell came to visit us, selling the notion of getting partners to do ventures with him in Eastern Bloc countries. Merrill Lynch were taking him around and I guess he made several calls here in Atlanta. I met him in the little conference room right down the hall there, and he covered the table with photographs of himself with Gorbachev and all these prominent Russians. We sat there and you'd ask a question and he'd sort of roll right over and keep going. So we had about an hour and a half meeting with him. But he didn't find any partners down here in the South.'

This had happened a dozen times before: flying into a strange city, taking a taxi downtown to the newspaper offices, standing on the sidewalk, across the way, and staring up at a wall of dingy windows. The offices of the *Journal* and *Constitution* – 20 miles across town from Jim Kennedy's headquarters building – are a classic of their kind; seven storeys of concrete at the junction of Marietta and Cone, a view of a railroad track and car lot, a rampart of concrete, a battery of fire hydrants, a side entrance part-tiled with vanilla-coloured ceramic panels sullied by diesel smudges. The prestige of newspaper ownership often struck me as misplaced. Proprietors like James Cox Kennedy are revered and deferred to. He is by common consent 'the most powerful man in this town' and yet the newspapers from which his power extends are editorially appropriate rather than distinguished. The newspaper offices too are perfectly functional, but eclipsed by any one of a hundred landmark towers all over Atlanta. And the franchise of newspapers in these mercurial American cities struck me as precarious. Families move into town for a year or two, maybe buy the paper, move on. The turnover – the churning – of readers is scary. The British press lords like Northcliffe and Beaverbrook could legitimately speak of *owning* readers. Their newspapers were delivered into the same households for decade after decade. Their editors had all the time in the world to mesmerise and manipulate, until they could boast with confidence of delivering this many readers to such-and-such a politician on polling day. American metropolitan papers are more like inflatable swimming pools in a perpetual state of slow puncture, with the proprietor huffing and puffing with a foot pump, enticing new purchasers with lotteries, wingo competitions and crude coloured digests, to keep the circulation figures firm.

The relative prestige of the Coxes' flagship has been the subject of controversy. Where does it rate on the American stage? Less highly, clearly, than the Grahams' *Washington Post*, the Sulzbergers' *New York Times* and the Chandlers' *Los Angeles Times*, but how does the *Journal* and *Constitution* stack up against the Tribune Company's *Chicago Tribune*, the Hearsts' *Houston Chronicle*, the Newhouses' *New Orleans Times Picayune*?

Something people tell you all the time is that Anne Cox Chambers wishes her newspapers were better. When she jets up to Washington to see her friend and fellow liberal, Kay Graham, she has no top rate paper to leave behind her on the restaurant table. 'She'd like to be able to present her friends with a more impressive calling card,' I was assured. 'She'd like to say to people, "Just in case you missed this morning's *Constitution* I've brought you up a copy. There are a couple of articles in it that might amuse."' And local wisdom holds that Mrs Chambers was inspired as Jimmy Carter's ambassador in Belgium to play a more high profile role on the international stage; a role that in turn required her flagship newspaper to aspire to a bigger league, to break out of its homeboy mode and win Pulitzer prizes. If Kay Graham's paper won Pulitzers, why not Anne Cox Chambers's? And as this ambition coincided with James Cox Kennedy's appointment to Chairman of the family firm, the promotion seemed to augur a spirited new era at Cox.

'My heart,' he announced to his editors and publishers on the day he took over, 'is in the newspaper division.' His goal was to make the *Constitution* one of the ten best newspapers in the country.

All these factors played a part in what has come to be known as 'the regrettable Kovach episode': the appointment and subsequent resignation in a blaze of publicity of a top flight editor brought in (he believed) to transform the Atlanta papers overnight. The dramas that attended his hiring and departure suggest not only a great deal about the Cox empire, but the suppositions of a dozen comparable private newspaper chains around the world.

Until he was approached by Cox, Bill Kovach was the long-serving and highly regarded Washington bureau chief of *The New York Times*. Passed over by the Sulzbergers for one of their paper's top jobs when Abe Rosenthal retired, Kovach seemed available at the age of 54 for a great new challenge, so when overtures began to be made from Atlanta he was susceptible to the move. Exactly what Cox thought it was getting in Kovach nobody to this day is able to explain. Physically a great bear of a man, intellectually liberal, socially somewhat abrupt, he was the son of an Albanian who had emigrated to the South and run a short-order grill in a bus station in Johnson City. Bill Kovach had made his journalistic name reporting the Nashville race riots in the mid-sixties, and like many young liberals had been relieved to escape from what he saw as the bigoted, nigger-baiting South for a career first in New York then, more liberal yet, in Washington. Now he was returning as editor of the South's most prominent newspaper with (he thought) a mandate to change everything for the better. This he proceeded to do with the utmost vigour. Within a month of Kovach's arrival the newspaper was transformed into a kind of Dixieland *Washington Post*. If Anne Cox Chambers wanted a big league production then Kovach sure was giving her his best shot. The brightly coloured daily digest of contents (often seen as the litmus test of a popular as opposed to a heavyweight newspaper) was ordered off the front page; colour photographs were banned from the front until they could be printed in focus; deadwood staff were felled faster than the Amazon rain forest; Atlanta's large gay community, hitherto ignored, was fulsomely covered; the news staff swarmed all over the big political stories, wherever they happened to be, without regard to the price of aeroplane tickets, just like the Sulzbergers', Grahams' and Chandlers' boys were allowed to do; local Atlantan shibboleths like Coca-Cola and Georgia Power were toughly scrutinised (which had never happened before); journalists were dispatched on special assignments all the way from Atlanta to the Horn of Africa to investigate the pro-Western Sudanese government's use of famine as a weapon in its war against communist guerrillas; the painfully unfunny 'Judge Parker' cartoon strip was ejected from the comics page. And within a year the *Atlanta Journal* and *Constitution*, for the first time in decades, was nominated for Pulitzer prizes, not just one Pulitzer but five, a record unsurpassed by any other newspaper, ever.

All this triumphalism did not, however, delight everybody. Although the circulation was unaffected, Cox executives were concerned that significant local groups were becoming unhappy about the newspaper. Georgia's business community, accustomed to having their deals applauded by local pressmen, did not welcome the new hard-nosed reporting. An Atlanta newspaper, as they saw it, should be 'on team': working alongside them to make the World's Next Great City get there even faster, not sneering on the sidelines, nit-picking. And the Cox executives were sceptical, too, whether Kovach's incessant coverage of distant events – the Horn of Africa famine story was just one of a sequence – were of much interest to readers in Fulton, Gwinnett and Cobb counties. They worried that the cerebral black and white front pages would eventually alienate Atlanta's semi-literate, video-watching population, whose peripheral involvement was essential to keep up the circulation. And it further aggravated them when Bill Kovach gave interviews, articulating his vision of 'world-class journalism' and thus inevitably implying that the whole paper pre-Kovach was a smalltime mom and pop operation.

There was, of course, some truth in this. For 20 years the newspaper had, by common consent, stagnated. James Cox Jnr, the son of the founder and the last family member before Jim Kennedy to head the company, had been something of an absentee landlord, preferring to sail his yacht, *Shadow-J*, around Miami and drive his fleet of cars bearing licence plates JC-1 through JC-5. Thereafter the Cox papers were run by a succession of managers and stop-gaps, 'too many caretakers and not enough visionaries' as Melvin Mencher, the Columbia University journalism professor put it. They nevertheless made vast quantities of money. And the local population by and large enjoyed reading them. And if the editorial was perhaps a tad bland and deferential, well maybe, reasoned Cox, that's how the readers like it. As early as the summer of 1987, within a few months of Kovach's arrival, Jim Kennedy was telling interviewers, 'Our papers have been characterised as being in much worse shape than they are. Bill Kovach is not riding in on a white horse to save the *Constitution*.' Then he added, 'We prefer to promote from within. But if you're a football team and you have a chance to hire Testaverde, you do it.'

Ultimately it was a petty turf-fight with Cox management over the direction of their Washington bureau that caused Kovach to quit. The pretext, by then, hardly seemed to matter. For six months there was a great furore. Journalists took sides (mostly Kovach's, there being more moral mileage in championing the courageous liberal underdog against Management) and a mock funeral for Kovach was held, New Orleans-style, outside the *Journal* and *Constitution* offices. An effigy of Anne Cox Chambers was carried through the streets. Pat Conroy, the novelist and a friend of Kovach's, vowed that if Mrs Chambers didn't reinstate Kovach 'it will be the death of her reputation in American journalism, and she will die a woman despised by some of the brightest people in this city, including me.'

The family, through all this brouhaha, said nothing. Anne Cox Chambers was on holiday in the South of France. Jim Kennedy was in Atlanta when Bill Kovach rang him at home to resign personally and, according to Kovach, said simply, 'I'm sorry about what happened, but I don't know the details.'

Asked about the Kovach episode today, Kennedy says, 'It was a classic case of poor communications. We're a communications company and whenever we have problems it's over communications, and that was a classic. When Bill Kovach came here we basically said, "We want to have a great newspaper," and Bill Kovach wanted to produce a great newspaper, but we didn't agree beforehand what a great newspaper was and we felt – and we still do – that a great newspaper meant what the people who read it – the people of Atlanta – consider a great newspaper to be. And I think Bill was also concerned about his peers and others. And I think he took the approach that readers really don't know *what*, so *he* would give it to them. But we think better of our readers, we think they *do* know what they want. Bill did a hell of a job trying to do what his vision was, but his vision and our vision were different. We want a newspaper that carries – as newspapers can do – a broad menu of stories, a broad menu of topics; certainly not diminishing any areas. We can't cover the smallest item in a local community in Atlanta, but we don't want at the same time to have too much news about Iraq. We want a person to be able to read the newspaper and learn about what's going on in all parts of the world, but especially to try and tie that into what it means to them here in Atlanta.'

Within days of Kovach leaving, the newspapers had regressed to familiar territory. The brightly coloured daily digest was back on the front; blurry colour photographs were reinstated; Coca-Cola and Georgia Power were once again honoured citizens in their own hometown; and the *Atlanta Journal* and *Constitution* was enjoying the bankable plaudit of being, if not one of the ten best newspapers in America, then indisputably the fastest growing.

The Great Newspaper Bazaar

India's type-caste proprietors

The covered arcades around Vinod Circus and Lakshmi Street are Bombay's newspaper distribution district. Fanned out on the concrete floors of the arcades, their edges weighted with stones to prevent them gusting away in the rush of traffic, are editions of virtually every newspaper in India: not just the big circulation demi-nationals like the *Indian Express* and *The Times of India*, but hundreds – thousands – of upcountry and regional titles; newspapers from Madras, already a day out of date, that have crossed the subcontinent by train bringing their speculative, peevish commentary on Tamil Nadu politics; newspapers from Calcutta printed in Bengali and from Trivandrum in Tamil; newspapers in Urdu, Marathi and Telugu that seem to be printed on ricepaper, or on newsprint so porous that the ink from the hot metal presses has perforated clean through the page. There are local newspapers from Cochin and Orissa, and from towns so small you wonder they can support a newspaper at all – that there's news enough to fill them – still less that it's worth the trouble of bussing a bundle to midtown Bombay.

Every newspaper-vendor in Vinod Circus is equipped with a bamboo brush, a faggot of soft shoots bound together with orange hemp. Every so often they sweep a film of dust and diesel from the newspapers, though by the time they've covered their full display, a fresh layer of exhaust has already settled over the headlines. At the junction with Lakshmi Street sits an amputee on a wooden sledge, whose speciality is newspapers from Hyderabad and surrounding districts. His immobility prevents him from sweeping his papers clean, so their titles are all but illegible. He sometimes has a small supply of *The Times of India*, and within an hour of delivery these too look like week-old editions. After a stroll through Vinod Circus you hardly know whether you are inspecting the most vibrant newspaper industry in the world, or one too fragmented to be feasible. The array of competing titles in so many different languages is disorientating and scary. Their variety emphasises the vastness of the country – its 700,000 villages – its cultural diffuseness. People say that the Indian newspaper market resembles the fragmented markets of America in the thirties or Britain in the twenties, when William Randolph Hearst and Lord Northcliffe were buying up their countries' press. The sheer number of newspapers – listed nowhere, but estimated to be 25,000 – in fact makes proprietorial monopoly a distant prospect. But three tycoons, each based in a different city and a different culture, are nevertheless far and away India's most powerful proprietors. Each owns a nearly national flagship with bureaux and regional editions serving huge tracts of the country and tens of millions of readers. Delhi is the headquarters of Samir Jain, who owns and controls *The Times of India*; Calcutta is the powerbase of Aveek Sarkar, whose family owns *Ananda Bazar Patrika* and the *Telegraph*; a Bombay penthouse on the 25th floor of their Indian Express building at Nariman Point is the headquarters of the Goenkas, the legendary proprietors of the *Indian Express*, credited with the creation and overthrow of successive political administrations including two Gandhi governments. It is the rivalry and territorial ambitions of these three families that gives the Indian press its focus, and much of its impetus.

Four times a year Samir Jain – the short, natty executive – flies down from his corporate headquarters in Delhi for a board meeting in Bombay. Since he assumed the role of Chief Executive of the family newspaper group four years ago, when he'd just turned 30, he has been credited with 'Americanising' *The Times of India*, and imposing Harvard Business School techniques that he picked up during a short internship at *The New York Times*.

'Perhaps you would like to sit in on our quarterly board meeting as a non-participating observer,' Samir Jain suggested, 'which will enable you to assess our deliberations.'

It was clear, however, that Samir Jain was in two minds about this suggestion: drawn between his strong desire for me to witness India's most self-consciously analytical publishing house in action, and a well-developed – some say over-developed – obsession with corporate secrecy.

The Bombay boardroom of *The Times of India*, on the third floor of the Times building in D N Road, resembles a vast Victorian schoolroom with teak-panelled walls, dominated by a teak boardroom table that can, at a squeeze, seat 30. At the quarterly board meeting there were eleven directors, each seated on a conference chair upholstered in bright orange towelling with contrasting black towelling antimacassars. Marshalled in front of each of them were two ballpoint pens and several sheets of memo paper in a clipboard. These clipboards were to receive a good deal of use as the meeting progressed. In the middle of the table, so arranged that they were tantalisingly out of reach wherever you happened to be sitting, were three plates of chocolate bourbon biscuits which nobody, in the course of the three-hour conference, ever quite had the courage to seize and circulate.

I was interested to see Samir Jain's board of directors. In my preceding days in Bombay no Indian journalist I had met had passed over the opportunity to belittle them. They were mocked for their lack of newspaper background, for their presumption in joining *The Times of India* from other professions and believing themselves capable of understanding the industry. 'Samir Jain has brought in ... "managers" from places like Unilever and the Taj hotel group marketing department,' Vinod Mehta, the veteran editor and columnist, said disdainfully. 'He probably went to *headhunters* to find them! He doesn't insist on a newspaper background, in fact he prefers his executives not to have one. If you've sold life insurance or hotel rooms, Samir thinks there's no reason why you shouldn't sell newspapers.'

Samir Jain stood at the head of the table holding two stubby marker pens, one red, one blue. Behind him on the wall was a white laminated plastic board. 'Good morning gentlemen,' he said and proceeded to cover the white plastic board with algebraic symbols: x's, y's and well-rounded Venn diagrams.

'Perhaps I may begin, gentlemen, by asking anyone to tell me what it is that I am constructing.'

The directors assumed a leaden silence; some staring intently down at their clipboards, some at the ceiling, some studying the equation on the board with superhuman intensity, as though its meaning might suddenly become apparent if they regarded it sternly enough.

'Nobody can tell me?' asked Samir Jain, scanning the room with sharp, clever eyes over the bridge of his gold-rimmed glasses.

'Then let me elucidate. This, gentlemen, is a very crisp matrix, showing our market share of units, revenue and – most important of all – market share of profits.'

Jain uncapped his red marker pen and wrote the salient words beneath the equation: Units. Revenue. PROFITS. The marker squeaked its way across the board, and around the room there was the click of eleven ballpoint pens being cocked as the directors prepared to copy them on to their own clipboards: Units. Revenue. PROFITS.

'In America, Japan, Britain,' he went on, writing the names of these three countries up on the board, 'there is no single publishing house that has the market share we have. If we take the *Los Angeles Times* group, they have only four or five per cent, and they are the largest. None comes near to our market share of 20 per cent.' A gleam of satisfaction came into Samir Jain's eyes at this happy statistic, and the board, taking their cue from the Chief Executive, smiled smugly at their corporate good fortune. But in a moment Samir Jain was grave again.

'Now it may be that we are not now 20 per cent, we are maybe 19 per cent, with all the extraneous activity in the Indian market, and this is cause for alarm, because it will make *this*' – he underscored the word PROFIT with a blue marker – 'dip. If we maintain 20 per cent market share, we should make 50 per cent of the total profits. But with only 19 per cent, it is not a foregone conclusion. In *The New York Times*,' said Samir Jain, developing his theme, 'they put on their company report a graph of their rising market share and profits. News Corporation's balance sheet – that is Rupert Murdoch – do likewise and it makes marvellous reading. In India, publishing is not yet seen in these marketing terms, and especially,' he added darkly, 'not by editors.'

Of all the newspaper owners in the world, I met no one so single-mindedly wedded to marketing as Samir Jain. It is a science of such fascination to him that he is scarcely capable of any statement without reference to it. He reminded me of those Maharajahs of an earlier period in India's history who visited the industrialised West and returned fired with innovations to impose on their sleepy subjects.

And like all marketing converts, nothing delights him so much as describing his newspapers in dispassionate, marketing language: *the product* or *offerings* as in 'whether the market accepts or rejects our offering [*The Times of India*] only the market itself can determine'. Or else he will compare his newspapers with other non-newspaper products: 'An unsold offering is like an unsold airline seat or an hotel bed,' he says, his lips pursing slightly beneath his trim little moustache. 'Neither can be sold the next day. The opportunity is missed forever.

'This discussion,' said Samir Jain, still uninterrupted after 35 minutes, 'will now develop to that of strategy and synergy . . .'

His directors recocked their ball points and made appropriate fresh headings.

'. . . synergy of innovation with our existing offerings, which is what corporate life is all about.' Jain allowed time for this insight to sink in, before proceeding with a provoking statement and a conundrum.

'It took the Ancient Egyptians 2000 years to develop the water clock into the sand clock. Who can tell me why?'

Once again the board was struck dumb; the silence in the room broken only by the marketing pitch of a newspaper seller somewhere in the street outside.

'Nobody can tell us?' asked Samir Jain. 'The reason is simple: *they had no marketing department*. No marketing, no co-ordination, no planning executive. But with proper co-ordination they could have done it in 200 years, or 20 years had the Ancient Egyptians been Japanese.'

The Jain family are Marwaris – often called the ascetic Jews of India – vegetarian, non-drinking, by tradition brilliant merchants and businessmen, with strong bonds of kinship. Like most Marwaris they came originally from Rajasthan, the desert state on the border of what is now Pakistan, though the Jains later moved to the east coast of India, to North Bihar, where they founded a business empire based on jute, oils, cement and tar. The family lived in Calcutta – increasingly comfortably but with no great prominence – and it was from Calcutta that Samir Jain's controversial great-grandfather, Ramakrishna Dalmia, bought Bennett, Coleman & Company, an old and distinguished British trading house with useful concessions in jute. It also happened, as part of its portfolio of assets, to own *The Times of India*.

When Ramakrishna Dalmia died, his vast wealth intact despite a spell in Tihar jail following a complex investigation into tax evasion, Bennett, Coleman passed to his son-in-law, Shanti Prasad Jain, and subsequently to Samir's father Ashok Jain. Neither took any great day-to-day interest in the newspaper group – which by now, as well as *The Times of India*, included a daily financial paper, the *Economic Times*, the Hindi *Navbharat Times* and the *Marathi Maharashtra Times* – preferring to appoint strong editors and managers and concentrate on their jute, cement and new paper manufacturing businesses. By the early eighties, however, the traditional Bihar industries like jute were faltering. Ashok Jain – the physical opposite of Samir, a big-boned man, seldom seen without a pair of semi-metallic sunglasses – decided to transfer the family home from Calcutta to Delhi to be closer to the publishing house, which had suddenly become their most profitable business. There was a second reason, too, for the move. Ashok Jain was 50, and Marwaris traditionally retire as near to that age as possible. Start work young, work hard, increase the family business, pass it on, retire at 50: that is the Marwari custom. So shortly after returning with the family from Calcutta, Samir Jain, hitherto deployed in the jute division, became Chief Executive of India's most respected – some said moribund – daily newspaper, shortly to celebrate its sesquincentenary, 150th year, as the Establishment paper of record.

People who knew Samir Jain as a child remember him as precocious. 'Our grandfathers were friends,' says the writer Naveen Patnaik, 'and we used to go on holidays to the same hotel in Kashmir. I would say that Samir was rather a pert boy, a chatterbox, a know-it-all. People were always ticking him off for talking too much.' Later he became an enthusiast for 'systems', especially if another favourite word – management – was juxtaposed with them: *management systems*. He became convinced that, if only proper management systems could be imposed on his newspaper empire, then its position as India's preeminent publishing house would be assured. He took himself off to America, toured *The New York Times* and the *Washington Post*, marvelled at their management systems, and flew home via *The Times* of London where the pre-Murdoch management systems underwhelmed him. There is a story, possibly apocryphal, about Samir Jain being given a week's conducted tour of *The Times*, taking in all departments from production to political and diplomatic, culminating in a meeting with the managing editor.

'Now that you've spent a week with us, Mr Jain, do you have any questions?' asked the managing editor.

'Only one,' replied Jain. 'How do you prevent your journalists from pilfering sheets of paper for their private use?'

Ashok Jain and his eccentric wife Induja have three children, all of whom play some part in the Bennett, Coleman empire: Samir's sophisticated sister Nandita, 31, is Executive President and his younger brother, Vineet, 23, a Swiss business school graduate, recently joined the corporate planning division in Bombay. Samir and his wife Meera – who had an arranged marriage in the Marwari manner when Samir was 20 – live in an old walled Delhi house close to the Maurya hotel on the airport road; Meera, widely held to have little interest in newspapers, is seldom seen, and looks after their six-year-old son who has been partially sighted since birth, and his little sister. The strongest character in the Jain family is the matriarch, Induja, whose urgent religious convictions have, over the years, developed into a wacky New Age obsession with inner peace. At a press federation lunch at a Calcutta hotel she startled the audience of international press barons' wives – including Lady Rothermere from London – by insisting on making an impromptu speech. Frantic intervention by her peers failed to stall her, and Induja rose to her feet. 'Never forget,' she proclaimed ethereally, 'that all that matters in life is love, truth and beauty ... Love is truth and truth beauty.' The remainder of her 20-minute speech covered similar ground in different permutations.

It is at his compound on the airport road that Samir Jain entertains his editors.

'I went myself to his house one evening,' remembers a Bombay editor, R. K. Karanjia, 'and Samir arrived one hour late. He had been proof reading *The Times of India* and found that no page had less than ten mistakes, some had 20, one had 34. He was very angry about this.'

'He can be genial, even gregarious,' says Vinod Mehta, 'but he doesn't serve drinks at home alas, so these evenings have a way of seeming rather long if you're used to drinking, which of course most

Indian journalists are. He loves gossiping, but strictly about newspapers. He has no other interests in life. None that I can think of. He is profoundly uninterested in politics, profoundly uninterested in meeting politicians.'

Once a month *The Times of India* holds a lunch, at which the top editors in the group are paraded before a different government minister. Samir Jain's lack of political interest at these lunches is all too evident. 'He will say hello and shake hands,' says one of his assistant editors, 'but he is making no attempt to cosy up with that minister. As soon as he is able to, he drifts away to the back of the room to talk shop with any editor he can corner.'

Ninety minutes into *The Times of India* board meeting, Samir Jain was still firmly entrenched in his introductory homily.

'Now I am going to kill two birds with one stone,' he was saying, 'by giving you the written report on thought processes presently attaining in this company . . .' A messenger, who had been perched throughout the meeting on a stool against the wall, nursing a sheaf of photocopied memoranda, now distributed them around the vast teak table.

'Before we study these,' said Samir Jain, 'I would like to share with you a problem: how do we prevent these strategy documents from falling into the hands of our competitors?'

No suggestions being forthcoming, Jain answered his own question.

'*We cannot prevent it*!' he announced emphatically. 'That is the simple truth. Logically it is impossible to ensure. Why? Because I cannot deprive my own staff from receiving information that is going to help them function, and once such a document has entered the public domain, however much we may be good corporate citizens, the balance of security is altered to our detriment.'

The directors looked somewhat perturbed that this document – the contents of which were still a mystery to them – would so surely pass into the clutches of the enemy, but Samir Jain, the master strategist, was sanguine.

'Do not forget,' he said craftily, 'that if a competitor gets his hands on it – never mind who, be it Mr Sarkar of *Ananda Bazar Patrika*, or Mr Goenka of the *Indian Express*, or Mr Birla at the *Hindustan Times*, or

Mr Ambani at the *Sunday Observer*, or Mr Kapoor at the *Sunday Mail* – if he somehow obtains our restricted-distribution document, he doesn't know if it's a duck, a blind or the truth. If it says that I am going to launch a Hindi-language edition of *The Times of India*, he doesn't know whether it's a duck or really is on the drawing board. And this terrorises him. Why? Because he doesn't know what to do! Should he adopt our strategies himself, or ignore them? And this terrorisation helps our market share of profits' – Samir Jain underlined the word PROFIT once again with his stubby blue marker pen – 'because the competition is confused.'

The contents of this particular restricted-distribution document would not, as it happens, have terrorised anyone overmuch. I will not divulge its precise contents, beyond saying that many of its secrets pertained to the disposal of an outdated printing plant and the division of responsibilities between the Chief Executive and his Senior Corporate Executives.

'As you can see from the written report,' said Samir Jain, 'our modernisation programme has left us in possession of a surplus gravure press in Patna. Can anybody tell me what we should do with it?'

By now the prospect of any of the eleven directors advancing any suggestion whatever was so remote, that there was an audible gasp around the table when one of them spoke up.

'We should sell it, Mr Jain.'

'You think we should sell it do you, Mr—?'

'Yes,' he replied, but this time there was a quaver of doubt in his voice.

'And bring some profit into our company from the sale? Is that what you are proposing?'

'Yes, Mr Jain,' nodded the director, brightening slightly at Samir Jain's acknowledgement of his logic.

'*Wrong*, Mr—,' replied Samir Jain. 'We will *not* sell the old plant. We will *destroy* it. We will hammer the machine. And why will we hammer it? Can no one tell me? The reason we will hammer it is to prevent some other publishing house from laying their hands on it. Otherwise they might access it to print their own offerings. And why should we help some other publisher to come into the market and reduce our market share? No, we will hammer it.'

To a non-participating observer like me, it was by now improbable that any responsibility at Bennett, Coleman & Company could be adequately shouldered by anyone other than the Chief Executive himself. But here I was mistaken, for the Chief Executive now delineated, in the greatest detail, exactly where his own responsibilities ended and those of the Corporate Director began.

'You must remember,' he said, allowing a slight softening in his tone since the next matter, relating as it did to himself, must necessarily be more personal than the fate of the gravure printing press, 'you must remember that a Chief Executive like any animal would like the balance of convenience to come to him directly, but the balance of *inconvenience* to be somehow cushioned from him. If there is trouble at some plant, for instance, they say, "The Chief Executive must come." But I say, "Let the Corporate Director go. Let *him* go there with his dancing girls to sort out this trouble." Let the Corporate Director go incognito like Queen Cleopatra in *Asterix* the comic. Let him assess the trouble, and act decisively, with or without consultation with the Chief Executive. This is the corporate system. In a modern publishing house the Corporate Director solves these problems, allowing the Chief Executive time to implement Higher Strategy.'

A peculiarity of travelling through India is that, once you quit the big cities, there is little evidence of a newspaper industry at all. In Bombay and Delhi every roundabout, every building site, every housing project on the airport road bristles with billboards for newspapers: *The Hindu, The Independent, The Patriot, The Times of India, The Statesman*, most of them, in slogans brazenly echoing campaigns for British and American newspapers, overtly competitive. But even 50 miles into the countryside their visibility evaporates. There are vast tracts of India – larger than the largest American states – where no important newspaper whatever is available. In America there are states in which the *Los Angeles Times* and the *Washington Post* are obtainable only by subscription. But there is a difference: in India fewer than one-and-a-half per cent of the population ever buys a newspaper at all; nine million out of a population of 600 million. And this cultural phenomenon, that propels even the casual newspaper skimmer into the highest intellectual caste, has affected the status of journalists and the press. Aside from the three or four good national titles – and the Hindi newssheets produced in the bazaar that barely qualify as newspapers at all – you are still left with more quality broadsheets than anywhere in the world. Mass-market middlebrow newspapers, as they are understood in the West, do not exist. There is no equivalent to the *Boston Globe* or the British *Daily Mail* with their preponderance of women's interest pages and leisure-related features. In India, if you are part of the elite that can read a newspaper at all, you read news: political news, diplomatic news, news from countries around the world that are scarcely likely ever to be visited by the tiniest fraction of the readership; and in addition to the news itself, the Indian reader is given more commentary, editorialising and leader writing – by blue-blooded brahmins of the kind Samir Jain likes to oust from their offices – than anywhere else with a free press.

The Indian press may be the most distinctive on the planet, accommodating the widest range of political opinions and often brilliantly written, but with a pungent Indian flavour all of its own. The vocabulary is idiosyncratic and colourful: ministers 'airdash' across the subcontinent to the scene of accidents; criminals are always 'hardened', suspects 'grilled', jail-breaks 'audacious', exchanges 'heated'. It is a world in which 'reckless dacoits' are the subject of 'manhunts by rattled cops', and ousted politicians are 'charge-sheeted for cronyism'.

India is one of the last great tracts of land where Rupert Murdoch, Conrad Black, the Dow Jones company, Pinch Sulzberger and so on have no stake whatever: not even a five per cent sliver of an afternoon paper in Madurai or a freesheet in Mahabalipuram. Consequently editors are not drafted in from elsewhere in their proprietors' global empires to take a particular title tabloid, or mass-market, or to turn it into a seven-days-a-week operation. Nor is there much syndicating of Western material from wire services.

The effect of all this is that the names – the by-lines – of Indian journalists are particularly well known to their readers. 'Have you read Mr R. K. Roy's very fine leader-page article in today's *Indian Express*?' people will ask, with an enthusiasm that I seldom hear expressed for leaders in the *Washington Post* or *Le Figaro*, or 'Have you yet by any happy chance read Mr M. V. Kamath in this morning's *Telegraph*?'

This, in turn, makes Indian columnists especially susceptible to poaching by rivals. It used not to be so. Journalists at *The Times of India* would labour for decades over humdrum copy before they were given stories worth writing, and rewarded with by-lines. But the proliferation of new titles has produced an Indian star system, and proprietors are becoming used to endorsing salaries – still modest by Western standards, but impressive for India – to retain writers or lure them from the opposition.

This headhunting is often extraordinarily protracted. Columnists will procrastinate for month after month. In the weeks that I researched the Indian press I met three important journalists who were considering a move; one of them from a prominent Bombay to a prominent Delhi daily.

'When will you make up your mind?' I asked.

'Oh I don't know,' he replied languidly, 'I might spend a long weekend in Delhi at the fag end of the year, and decide after that.'

A change of job often entails not only a new editor and a new proprietor, but a change of seaboard and culture. And what is curious about India's three great newspaper capitals is the extent to which both the physical and the living city mirror the personalities of their most prominent owners. New Delhi, like Samir Jain, is systematic, analytical, purpose-built, thought-through, a city in which the roles of its prominent citizens – I nearly wrote corporate citizens – ministers, diplomats and consultants are defined even by their houses and the areas in which they live. The Goenkas seem to embody something of the essence of Bombay: disorganised, money-minded, obstinate, crusading, evasive. And the city of Calcutta, like Aveek Sarkar, is intellectual, exuberant, elegant, with a strong cultural bias and sense of its own history. (The comparison ends here. Sarkar's empire, unlike Calcutta, is neither poverty-stricken nor decaying.)

Aveek Sarkar is India's most sophisticated newspaper proprietor. 'He is magnificently rich, drinks only *grand cru* claret, smokes only Davidoff cigars, accepts only Bolivian coffee, has his silk underwear made in Lahore, and insists on having his suits made there as well because the tailoring is so superior to Savile Row,' were the first six facts I was ever told about him.

From his power base in Calcutta, Sarkar's sphere of influence is the entire eastern seaboard of India. 'Aveek can deliver the East,' a Delhi-based political lobbyist assured me. Whether Aveek Sarkar would ever wish to do anything so tiresomely manipulative is another matter. His flagship Bengali paper, *Ananda Bazar Patrika*, which gives its title to the whole group, has a half million circulation, 600,000 on Sunday. His English-language paper, the *Telegraph*, is the most intelligent broadsheet between Bombay and Singapore. His Hindi-language publication remains a bit of a mystery to its proprietor, since Sarkar cannot read one word of the language.

At 46, he has dark Bengali skin, a thick head of almost-white hair and an almost-white, perfectly clipped beard. The effect of the white against dark gives him the appearance of a black and white negative. His nails are immaculately manicured. His eyes, women point out, are at once soft and unusually shiny: 'Large and liquid like someone who's just had a vision.' He makes a point of wearing bespoke suits when in Europe and America but, on almost every other occasion, traditional Indian clothes: dhotis, and kurtas with diamond buttons, and grey cashmere shawls.

The first time I met him was at a dinner party given by Malavika and Vir Sanghvi. Vir edits his weekly news magazine *Sunday*. Sarkar was wearing a particularly luxuriant shawl called a shahtoos which was admired by some of the other guests.

'See this,' he said, slipping a thin gold band from his index finger. 'The shawl can fit through a wedding ring.' And then he threaded one end of the wrap through the gold band and whipped it out in a single fluid flick of his wrist. 'It is so fine you know,' he said, 'because it is woven only from the fleece of unborn goats.'

He is fascinated both by restaurants and clothes: he chooses his wife's wardrobe and when in London selects all the children's clothes at Please Mum in Sloane Street. 'Aveek knows the strangest things,' I was told, 'like the price of children's shoes in Paris compared with New York.' In Switzerland, he once tipped an hotel concierge $100 to secure a table reservation in Lausanne. When he plays tennis, which he does every day, he changes his Ralph Lauren tennis shirt four times each set. He enjoys grand gestures. Editors of his newspapers will receive, without warning, a painting or pen-and-ink drawing by India's hottest contemporary artist Bikash Bhatterjee delivered to their house by Sarkar's driver, wrapped in a big green Harrods carrier bag. He presented Benazir Bhutto, as a wedding present, an oil painting of her father being hanged. It was by the revered Indian artist Hussain, and when Benazir Bhutto unwrapped it she wept, apparently with joy. Editors are also given, upon their appointment, the gift of a bespoke suit, providing it is made in Lahore, where Sarkar flies them for their fittings. Some of his editors have enquired whether they might instead order their suit from Hong Kong, Milan or London. 'Certainly not,' replied Sarkar. 'The quality there is no good.'

One steamy Calcutta afternoon I visited Aveek Sarkar at his headquarters in Prafulla Sarkar Street. The street is named after his father who ran the newspapers until 1976. It is now one of the most congested thoroughfares in Calcutta; lorries delivering newsprint are gridlocked between tonga carts, motor rickshaws and Ambassador cars, as wave upon wave of jaywalkers seethe across the road. At night, Prafulla Sarkar Street is one of the areas where the Stoneman of Calcutta has struck; the roaming psychotic who prises up slabs of pavement and uses them to crush homeless families sleeping in doorways. Prafulla Sarkar Street struck me as an almost insanely inconvenient place for a newspaper, and yet it was cheering to find one still operating in the heart of a major city, and not sited on some distant airport road.

In the lobby of the building was a great throng of people. There must have been sixty or seventy. Some of these were security guards, some were messengers, some drivers, some seemed to have no purpose whatever, beyond idling in the lobby on plastic stools, or squatting on their haunches smoking cigarettes. I was escorted to a lift by eight or nine security men who at the last moment, as the lift doors were closing, decided on a whim – or perhaps because I was going to visit the owner – to crowd in too for the ride. On an upper floor, when the doors opened, they remained inside the lift, pointing vaguely in the direction of a corridor where a man was swabbing the floor with a rag. Eventually I reached a newsroom, busy with journalists and sub-editors tapping into computers. Sarkar's office leads directly off a corner of the newsroom, closer to the action than any other owner I visited. There is a small antechamber to his office, hung with 19th-century Daniell prints from *Oriental Scenery*, and then the panelled office itself, a jumble of files on the desk, an electric fan, and a leather

213

sofa piled with Indian, American and European newspapers and magazines.

Aveek Sarkar was wearing a dhoti – a garment like a toga crossed with a nappy – and smoking a cigar.

I made some remark about the proximity of his office to the newsroom, and wondered whether he sometimes wished he was the editor rather than the owner.

'Even when one's done hands-on editing oneself, one is still not satisfied,' he replied. 'You feel dissatisfied and unhappy. There is always some dissatisfaction whatever your exact role.' He took a long, far from dissatisfied suck on his Davidoff cigar and peered through the antechamber into the newsroom. 'Our family you know takes great pride in all our newspapers. It is our aim to achieve excellence you know, like that American book *In Search of Excellence*. So there is always dissatisfaction when one falls short of that.'

I asked him whether Calcutta was not a difficult place in which to achieve excellence. For several days people had been telling me scare stories about the city: how the electricity supply goes down almost daily, due to unforeseen surges on the circuit or wildcat strikes, and then the printing presses and computers stop working; how the unions in Communist Calcutta are stronger and more belligerent than anywhere else in India, and how the great influxes of immigrants into Bengal from Bangladesh have made conditions in the city barely tolerable. Even communications with Calcutta, as I had already discovered, are fitful. Telephone lines, telexes, faxes: none are reliable. I later learnt that, in the newsrooms of Aveek Sarkar's papers, people are especially employed to dial the newspaper bureaux in Bombay and Delhi all day long, in the hope that they might eventually get through. And when you ring the office from overseas, the general switchboard incomprehension makes it fruitless to leave a message, even if you spell your name phonetically: COLE-RIDGE. C – chappatti. O – Orissa. L – Limca . . .

Was it really feasible to achieve excellence here?

'Don't forget,' replied Aveek Sarkar, 'that Bengal was the only part of India to be Anglicised. It makes a big difference to the culture of the place. The Punjab was never Anglicised, nor was Bombay. Bombay was *Westernised*, quite different. First Westernised, then Americanised, they're all disco queens in Bombay now. But Calcutta, you know, *was* Anglicised and I believe that has imposed a certain order you know, under the surface.

'And there are advantages for our newspapers in Calcutta also. You have a far more detached view of things from here, because you are less involved with the immediate politicking between the ministries in Delhi. And you know all that politicking is not the real world. How do they call it, not seeing between the wood and the tree, the tree and the forest? In any case, I think that for India this highly centralised view is a passing phase. And then – for our people – there are other compensations in Calcutta. It is possible to get a far more decent place to live than in Delhi or Bombay where you must be cooped up in flats. And in Calcutta there are wonderful clubs. And of course in Bombay you cannot play golf.'

In his instinct for journalism, Sarkar is the most discriminating Indian proprietor. Not only can he recognise a good front page or an interesting article but also explain to you why it works. He can write headlines to fit. Occasionally – and this is rare for an owner – he will contribute an article to one of his own papers, not a self-serving piece of polemic, but a gossipy description of Benazir Bhutto's wedding, or an interview with General Zia conducted on a golf course in Rawalpindi.

'That one was shortly before he died,' Sarkar told me, 'so I entitled it "His Last Putt". Quite amusing, you know.'

'Another advantage of owning papers in Calcutta, as opposed to almost any other metropolis, is that the unstoppable population growth promises ever higher circulation. Sarkar expects his flagship to reach a million by the end of the century.

'Already,' he said, 'we have the single largest circulation in India, a fact our competitors do their best to overlook. The *Indian Express* prints "Largest Circulation in India" on the masthead of their papers. I can't think why. They really have no such thing you know, not on a single edition. They can claim it only if they add all their editions together. But if you are number three in Bombay, number five in Bangalore or whatever, so what? You just have a collection of motley publications.'

I asked him about his Hindi newspaper and how, unable to read or speak a single word of it, he managed to appraise it editorially.

'It is a matter of great pride to me actually that I don't speak Hindi,' he replied. 'Really I have *no interest* in speaking Hindi you know. I once called on Mrs Gandhi because she wanted to tell me something about some new book, and she made some remark to me in Hindi – which you know she loved to speak – and I said, "I'm sorry Madam, *I don't speak a word of Hindi.*" She was not overamused. Actually, I revel in the fact that I don't know Hindi. Whenever a new edition of our Hindi paper comes out I glance at it, and turn through the pages, and simply ask my editor to keep me informed about anything sensational, so I know what's there.'

Of all the proprietors I encountered in Asia, Aveek Sarkar was the best informed about what was happening, editorially, in the rest of the world.

During the time I was in his office, two deliveries of foreign publications were brought to his desk – I saw *New York* magazine and *Vanity Fair* from the United States, and copies of the *Sunday Times* colour supplement and *Tatler*, the society magazine from Britain, as well as Japanese and Hong Kong publications. Much of this editorial impetus stems from the period before he inherited the newspapers from his father, when he worked on the family newspapers at home and then in England.

'My brother Arup and I both entered the business in 1963, first during the holidays, or when some exciting news happened and we came in to watch the editors at work. From the start Arup looked after the business side while I concentrated on the editorial side. I did page make-up in the hot metal days and proofreading. I can still write a headline or a 20-point caption across two columns to fit. I remember once when Illingworth – you know the great cricketer Illingworth – was touring India, and we had to fit his name into a headline. Very difficult. The popular press solved it by calling him ILLY but we weren't allowed to do that. You cannot write ILLY in a quality newspaper.

'Then I met Harry Evans in Manila. He had just become editor of the *Sunday Times*. We were both there to attend a conference, the Press Foundation of Asia, in some UNICEF or UN hall or some other new building. And of course I was very excited to meet such a famous editor as Harry Evans, and at the end of the conference he himself suggested that I come and work with him, and eventually I spent a year in Britain. But there was a special condition that Harry imposed:

before I could come to the *Sunday Times* I must first do a stint on both the provincial papers that he had worked on. Everything he did, I was to do. I went first to the *Northern Echo* at Darlington. I stayed with a landlady in a village, I forget the name of the place now, though Darlington itself was a village after Calcutta. And from there I went to work for the *Manchester Evening News* and eventually on to the *Sunday Times*. First the Saturday subbing, then working in the art department under Edwin Taylor, then book reviews, business section and finally a month or so in Harry Evans's own office. I didn't really have a role there, just observed how a great editor works, and I was told not to comment or even open my mouth when confidential matters were being discussed. Those were the days, in the late sixties, when Harry was at his pristine best, supreme lunacy you know, it was supreme lunacy. I remember the paper was about to serialise Harold Wilson's diaries, and a union man came to see Harry and said they couldn't print the paper because Harold Wilson wasn't a member of the union and so couldn't contribute to the *Sunday Times*. I remember thinking that even the unions in Calcutta wouldn't refuse to print an article by the Prime Minister.

'By the time I came home to Calcutta, I felt that I could hold my own. And it made a difference, you know, to my outlook. If you look at journalism at its best in England, it is essentially a way of looking at the world. There are of course the details which are important – man does not live by eccentricity alone – but there is essentially a *curiosity* about English journalism.

'And the *Sunday Times* was influential for me too on the subject of typefaces. Times Europa was being designed, and there was a great deal of discussion about serifs and so forth, and I was listening to all those discussions. Subsequently I read up Le Corbusier and learnt more about modules and that sort of thing. To that extent, the best education is to become aware. And when you return, you at least have something to compare yourself with, the very best, and I was able to introduce a more modular design to some of our newspapers. Now everyone does it. But I think I was among the first to be directly influenced by Harry Evans and Edwin Taylor.'

I asked him which four publications in the world he would buy if they happened to be available.

'You are speaking now of hard professional decisions or ego trips?'

'Ego trips.'

'Well the *New York Review of Books* certainly. *The Economist*.' Thinks, thinks, thinks. 'Other than those two I can't think of any other ego trips I really want. For hard professional decisions, I'd like to buy *The New York Times* and *Time* magazine. Once upon a time I'd have said the *Sunday Times*, not any more.'

'Do you really think *Time* is that good?' I added that generally I found it dull and superfluous.

'It's *brilliant* not good,' replied Sarkar. 'To produce for instance a 4000-word article on a new medicine with graphics etc, as they did this week, I don't think anyone else would do it.'

'And do you really think Murdoch has ruined the *Sunday Times* that much?'

'Beyond dispute. All the talents have left.'

'But it still has good things in it. You can't dismiss it.'

'Of course they will still do good things because they are so rich! But no credit due to the organisation or the editors or the paper. It is week after week of nothing.'

'How do you account for it?'

'Because two of the great virtues of the English character are going out – the English idiosyncrasies that people loved, and a certain seriousness of purpose. Take *The Economist*. If you ask anyone serious outside England, they all read *The Economist*. England is *known* by *The Economist*. But when at a conference I asked the editor of the *Independent*, the editor of the *Guardian* and the editor of the *Observer*, none of them read *The Economist*, not really read it, they might glance through it, but not read it. I repeated this whole conversation to Harry Evans in New York and he said that's what England is like now. Nobody any longer thinks globally. Their publications might be *owned* by people who think globally, or at least act globally, but they don't do so themselves.'

'Have you considered thinking – acting – globally yourself and buying newspapers abroad?'

'I would like to, and will *have* to.'

'Which direction will you look, east or west?'

'In most countries to the east of Calcutta the laws of ownership are closed you know. I have considered a paper in Singapore, but that is difficult. And Australia. I'd love a paper in Hong Kong. Outside

Calcutta, I'd love Hong Kong and London the best. But that does not mean I should buy a paper there. An ego trip can be a bad business decision. And it depends too on when the Indian economy develops, and we become even more part of the world. At the moment the idea of economic nationalism is still strong, which makes it virtually impossible for a foreign group to buy into our press or vice versa.'

'What about a British newspaper. If the *Observer* came up, say?'

Aveek Sarkar looked thoughtful, and then energised, as though the notion of owning the *Observer* appealed to him very much. Perhaps he was visualising himself ringing Harold Evans in New York and saying nonchalantly, 'Harry, it's Aveek. I've bought the *Observer*. Would it amuse you to edit it?' Aveek Sarkar shifted his position in his chair, crossing his ankles, one sandalled foot over the other, and I was struck by the extraordinary cleanness of his toenails.

The new lobby of *The Times of India* in Bombay is the smartest newspaper foyer in Asia, eclipsed only by the lobbies of the *Los Angeles Times* and the *New York Daily News* with their huge Art Deco globes. A sweep of marble stairs leads you to an airy mezzanine decorated with architectural fragments from Shekhawati, the abandoned desert region in Rajasthan: complete 12th-century windows carved out of sandstone have been transplanted, along with ornate fretted door frames and massive blocks of stone with delicate reliefs. The architect of this stunning edifice was Nandita Jain, though the simultaneous reallocation of the floorspace was masterminded by her brother Samir. That is why the magnificent lobby leads, not to the journalists' floor, but to the classified and display advertising desks, where banks of salespeople at computer terminals sell special integrated advertising packages – 'slams' and 'salad bars' – across the Bennett, Coleman newspapers.

Nobody disputes that Samir Jain has transformed the company. 'He is a 21st-century man, 21st-century,' one of his marketing aides told me enthusiastically. 'He is demanding intellectually,' says N. P. Sing, his recently appointed Director of Response who was headhunted from a career with Tata oil and Philip Morris cigarettes. 'Conceptually he takes leaps and bounds. It is not a smooth, gradual acceleration. For his age he has incredible insights, and his perception of people is uncanny; he anticipates people's reactions in any situation very acutely.'

'When he took over,' says Vinod Mehta, 'Bennett, Coleman was more like the civil service than a newspaper company, there was – still is actually – more bureaucracy there than in any Indian government office. If you wanted to move this' – Mehta indicated a fat, black leather armchair – 'you would need to fill in three forms and obtain three sanctions from three different people. The whole company was too settled, and Samir was aware of that. What he is trying to do is change the whole place and he is very determined.'

The evidence of change is everywhere. Samir Jain took me on a tour of the news floors and on every corridor gangs of workmen, amidst great swirls of dust, were hammering down walls.

'These were the offices of the blue-blooded brahmins of the edit page,' said Samir Jain with satisfaction. 'Now everything will be open-plan.'

We diverted into an advertising office where the Chief Executive was introduced to a new recruit.

'The newspapers you are selling into,' he said as the new recruit stood to attention, 'are not Establishment papers, but the readers are the Establishment. That is vital to know. We want our readers to be seen wearing those expensive American gold watches.'

Above all Jain has wrestled with the editorial and management structure. The Old Guard has been stripped of responsibilities, new departments established, new channels of reporting introduced. Whether such-and-such an executive is a Samir man or not is a vital litmus test, much speculated upon in the rival national press.

'More than anything,' says Vinod Mehta, 'he is influenced by the editorial structure of those American papers he saw, *The New York Times* et cetera, and the way that editorial power there isn't invested in one man. He will point at the print line in the *Washington Post* with its long, long list of names – three executive editors, the op-ed editor, the edit-page editor, three associate editors – and he'll say, "Let's introduce this system here." But what the fuck's the editor going to do all day, that's what everyone wants to know.'

Samir Jain's conception of the editor's role is widely discussed. 'He certainly believes they are first and foremost managers,' continued Mehta. 'There is nothing clandestine in this view, he says it all the time.

The reason of course that Samir wants a range of different editors is to ensure that the ultimate power is vested in him. It is a battle for editorial control and he wants control of his own papers. Not that he is actually very interested in what goes into them: but he wants the control.'

One of Aveek Sarkar's Calcutta editors found himself in the adjacent Indian Airways seat to Samir Jain on a flight between Bombay and Delhi. Jain quickly seized the opportunity to lecture him on management systems.

'I am chiefly interested in the *function* and *process* of management,' proclaimed Samir.

'Samir, what exactly *is* "the process of management?",' enquired the editor.

'It is the *details*,' replied Jain. 'I like appraising my editors and deciding which one deserves which car, and which one deserves in-car air-conditioning.'

'He seldom walks on the editorial floor himself,' I was told by a Delhi journalist, 'but calls in his editors for conferences – long and frequent. He likes to discuss abstract ideas: what is the philosophy of the paper, what is its role in the matrix of Indian journalism. And he can get quite angry if people don't pay attention. There is a lot of theorising about what he calls "the role model": what should the editor do in a given situation: should he do x or y? He is rather against editors getting involved in the nitty-gritty, he thinks someone else should be doing that – the *journalism*.'

'Does Samir Jain like journalists?'

'Let me put it this way: he thinks they are prima donnas, and I think he has a deep-seated desire to humiliate them and to promote his managers at their expense. For too long he believes the managers have been the poor cousins and all the glory has gone to the editor.'

'In the end,' said Vinod Mehta, 'I think his role model is Murdoch: Murdoch sets the policy and the policy is clear and the editors deliver it every day. And he loves the way editors travel around with Mr Murdoch in his private jet and have conferences in the air with him. Mr Jain would love to have conferences in the air. Five or six editors on swivel chairs in an aeroplane, having a conference. That would be Samir Jain's ultimate kick.'

*

Ballygunge is the most cerebral and discreet residential district of Calcutta, and it is here that Aveek Sarkar and his wife Rakhi live in a large white colonial mansion, behind a high wall. It is a deep two-storeyed thirties building, and only the Bengali security guards in a sentry box at the gate distinguish it from a *Gone With The Wind* film set. Inside it is decorated with 17th-century and contemporary Bengali art, including an important collection of Tagores. From the window in the drawing room you can see a long green lawn, as perfectly buffed and manicured as Mr Sarkar's toenails.

Rakhi Sarkar is the oldest of three sisters; her two younger sisters married Aveek's two younger brothers. 'All were love matches, not arranged,' she says. The sisters were brought up in Trinidad, where their father worked for the IMF and was a government minister, and Rakhi Sarkar is pivotal in Calcutta's smart charity set; but unobtrusively so, not in the splashy American manner. She raises money for drug addiction and cancer hospices, and the Rama Krishna mission for destitute women and orphans. Like her husband she is a passionate supporter of contemporary Indian artists and is in the process of designing a modern museum for them in Calcutta.

We ate a Bengali dinner cooked by Rakhi. 'They have plenty of servants of course,' I had been told, 'but Aveek is proud that his wife cooks Bengali food. Aveek says she is keeping the tradition going.' Twelve different dishes were arranged for each guest in twelve bronze bowls on a large bronze platter, which you ate clockwise: three or four kinds of fish, the same number of Bengali dahls, several sweet puddings made with reduced milk, and bowls of pickled chillis and pickled limes.

'One thing I will never do is *mix* foods,' declared Aveek pouring Château Latour 1976. 'Either we eat Bengali food or French food or English food, which I was partly brought up on you know, we ate bread pudding a lot with my mother-in-law which was made with almonds. I cannot bear *international* cooking, any more than I can stand the cultural imperialism of so much that is passed off as Indian food. For tandoori chicken and Punjabi food I feel nothing but contempt. Most Indians anyway prefer bad Chinese food to good Indian food.'

Like Lord Beaverbrook, Aveek Sarkar enjoys the proprietorial privilege of the contentious statement. At the head of his own table, there is almost no subject on which he does not have an emphatic, and you sometimes suspect spontaneous, opinion.

'Mrs Thatcher was the most marvellous thing that happened to Britain this century,' he will say. And then, two or three minutes later, 'The Pope you know is not altogether to be trusted. He is as dangerously fundamentalist in his way as the Ayatollah Khomeini was.' And then again, 'There are only two great fashion houses in the world now – Escada and The Gap.' And 'There is really only one restaurant worth eating at in Europe – the Taillevent in Paris.'

What is interesting is that Aveek Sarkar does not, according to his employees, bring these emphatic opinions to meetings. On the contrary, he is an exceptionally reasonable and pragmatic proprietor who attends carefully to arguments before taking any decision.

But at dinner he is provocative, dogmatic, teasing, a gossip.

'Aveek is actually one of the greatest gossips in Calcutta – no, India,' says one of his editors. 'Often the gossip he spreads around is lacking in substance when you investigate it, so you have to check things out carefully before printing it. He will come into your office and say, "This industrialist is having a love affair with this actress," and you say, "Really? Surely not!" and Aveek says, "Yes, certainly. I'm surprised you haven't heard. It's the talk of Bombay." But when you get someone to look into it, there is sometimes an element of wishful thinking and mischief making. But he's the only proprietor I can think of who relishes excellent gossip stories, and takes the trouble to pass them on to his newspapers.'

People who knew Aveek Sarkar before he took over the newspapers say that he went through a crazy T-shirt phase, but subsequently made the transition to sophisticate. On the evening of his Ballygunge dinner party he wore a gleaming handloomed white shirt faced with dozens of tiny concertina pleats, each one of them ironed with the nut-like shell of an Indian fruit called a gila.

'My father told me always to be properly dressed you know,' he said. 'Whatever style you choose, do it properly. If you are going to wear English clothes, always wear a proper suit and tie. If you're wearing Bengali clothes, wear a proper dhoti. And only ever wear pyjamas between your bedroom and bathroom. These days in India we see Prime Ministers wearing pyjama on official occasions as though it were the national dress. *Completely mad.*'

Seeing him at home, sitting square on his dun-coloured sofa with his square cheek-bones, made Aveek look not Bengali but strangely Slavic and I asked him whether his family originated in Calcutta.

'We come from the Soviet Union actually in BC-time,' he said. 'We conquered this area and imposed our religion on it. But you know we made one mistake, which was the same mistake the invaders made in South Africa. We didn't bump off the populace. In America and Australia the invaders bumped off the populace, but we instead introduced rules about who could marry who, to prevent the invaders and the vanquished from mixing. In India we call it the caste system. In South Africa it is apartheid. But it is the same.

'Actually,' he added, 'the Sarkars are rather an unusual family. Three Sarkar relations started Communist parties in different parts of the world: one in China, one in London and one here in Calcutta. But in Calcutta, you know, we moved on from communism to newspapers.

'There is one strange thing about London,' he suddenly mused, 'which is that *there is no good hotel guide*.'

'Surely there are dozens of hotel guides?'

'None that give qualitative and value judgements. I'd like to write a London hotel guide myself one day actually. It is an odd thing, but whenever you look up the Inn on the Park in a guide, *it isn't in it*. But the Inn on the Park is excellent for service. *It is the best hotel*. The Connaught has retained its traditions, the Savoy I find is not as good as it was, at Claridges there are sometimes problems with heads of state, and there's the Berkeley of course, but I stay now always at the Inn on the Park *which is given no mentions*.'

'Why do you suppose that is?'

'I have an explanation but I'm embarrassed to give it, because it smacks you know of snobbery and class consciousness. But this is it. In England, the sort of people who write about hotels wouldn't ordinarily stay in them, not paying for their own stay you know. The best journalists would never make a career out of writing hotel guides, and the normal guests at these hotels cannot write. So the guide writers never quite catch the nuances or the expectations of what the other side wants. Whenever they write about the food or the restaurants or the room service they invariably get it slightly wrong.

'By the way,' said Aveek Sarkar, 'while we are speaking of England, do they still publish the Billy Bunter stories?'

I said I wasn't sure.

'Perhaps you could find out for me,' said Sarkar. 'I am missing one or two from my set.'

Some months later we happened to have dinner with Aveek and Rakhi Sarkar at Harry's Bar in London. True to his strictures on correct dress, he was impeccably turned out in the European manner. His socks, he mentioned, were from Lanvin. The Sarkars were stopping over in England on their way home from Palm Springs, where they'd been inspecting the Betty Ford Clinic with a view to opening a heroin rehabilitation centre in Calcutta.

'I sat up all night on the aeroplane reading Julie Burchill's S&F novel, *Ambition*,' he said. 'I have a habit whenever I fly of reading S&F books. Somehow one can't read them on land, but in midair it is permissible.'

He said he was pleased to be back in London 'for one special reason you know. I can read Nigel Dempster's column hot off the presses.'

It surprised me that Aveek Sarkar knew enough about Dempster's cast of characters to make this *Daily Mail* column so electrifying for him, but he was extravagant in Dempster's praise.

'He is the best, the number one. He writes with a zip and a passion. You know he is very highly paid, the most highly paid journalist in England, paid much more than the political writers actually. In fact,' asserted Aveek, 'gossip-writing is the only part of English journalism that isn't finished now.'

I replied that, on the contrary, quality English journalism struck me as unusually good.

'No,' said Aveek, 'it is finished. The American newspapers have taken over. They are making the running now. There is a chasm between the New York and the English newspapers as wide as the chasm between . . . between a mediocre writer like Norman Mailer writing an op-ed page article, and the same piece by a really brilliant writer like Ian Jack.

'Business may be finished in England too,' he said. 'There are only two great British companies now.'

'Which are they?'

'Reuters and Reebock. They are the only two.'

Aveek laughed mischievously, and said that he was nevertheless keenly looking forward to the next morning, when Nigel Dempster's zippy, passionate column would be delivered to his suite at the Inn on the Park.

Then he addressed the table: 'I have something to ask you all. Who do you reckon are the four most important creative people of this century?'

But before anyone could reply, he answered his own question.

'Picasso, Yves Saint Laurent, Fellini and Gabriel Garcia Marquez. They are the four greatest. But which one is the greatest of them all? *Which is Number One*? That is one matter I have not yet resolved.'

Express Towers is the tallest building in Bombay. It stands at the apex of Nariman Point – Bombay's Manhattan – overlooking the bay and jumble of smaller skyscrapers in its shadow. When you look up at it from pavement level, the concrete walls flecked with splinters of black marble have a sinister aspect, like an old Eastern Bloc police headquarters. The concrete buttresses up the side of Express Towers make perfect perches for large black crows, and their constant caw-cawing and sudden, ragged swooping adds to this sense of the macabre. On the 25th floor – the penthouse floor – of this, his own building, lived Seth Ramnath Goenka, India's most powerful and manipulative press baron, whose long shadow hangs like a wraith over the empire he founded.

Often, for months on end, he never left the penthouse, or was seen by more than a handful of his closest aides. But in some symbiotic way his views, pro-Hindu prejudices and political foibles infused his entire newspaper group; and infuse it still, two years after his death, even now that the empire has passed to his young grandson, Vivek Goenka, who was adopted by the founder on his deathbed. Editors can still be summoned up to the penthouse at almost any hour, day or night, which is why some of them keep a bed in their offices and sleep there, in case the summons comes, and columnists and leader writers receive telephone calls from the proprietor setting the newspaper's line on a political question of the moment.

'Anyone who doubted the real power of old Mr Goenka,' said one of his assistant editors, 'let him remember that he has brought down not one but two political administrations: that of Mrs Indira Gandhi after the emergency, and that of her son Rajiv Gandhi. Both owed their downfall – and they would admit this – to Mr Ramnath Goenka.' The Goenka papers propose and depose governments with a single-mindedness that would have shocked even Beaverbrook and Hearst. Their political journalism is a species of terrorism.

As you enter Express Towers you pass by a fleet of black Ambassador cars, permanently in the process of being hosed down, each so battered and corroded that the jet of water from the hosepipe threatens to penetrate the bodywork. As well as being India's most powerful proprietorial family, the Goenkas have the reputation as its meanest. If a car, a desk, a typewriter can somehow last another day then it must do so. Ramnath's motto 'A piastre saved is two piastres earned' is well known not only to the staff of the *Indian Express*, but at the Tamil daily in Madras, the Marwari paper in Bombay and at the *Financial Express*, the Goenkas' business title. I cannot say whether it is economy or incompetence that keeps the elevators at Express Towers in a permanent state of breakdown. With only four lifts serving 24 floors, and two under semi-permanent maintenance, the average journey time to the penthouse is 20 minutes. Editors summoned upstairs from their offices on the second and third floors, to hear the owner's latest gripe at Congress, have been known to run up the 25 flights of stone stairs instead.

The lifts do not in any case extend quite so far as the penthouse itself. At the 24th floor the visitor must leave the elevator – where he is faced by a sign 'Entry to upstairs is STRICTLY PROHIBITED', this in red – and walk the final flight, at the top of which two armed security men in khaki fatigues guard the door to the proprietor's apartment.

To gain entry to the penthouse was, I felt, something of an achievement in itself. For three days I had been telephoning from my hotel to reconfirm my appointment with the dying Ramnath Goenka, and for three days had been met with diverse postponements.

'Mr Goenka, he is sleeping right now.'

'Mr Goenka, he is meditating.'

And once, 'Mr Goenka, he is in his toilet right now.'

Sometimes when I rang there were inexplicable clickings and echoes on the line, as though the telephone was tapped, which it often has been in the past; but it could just as easily have been cheerful eavesdropping by a security guard, or fumbling of the receiver by Mr

Goenka's number one nurse, Mrs Delores da Costa, who seldom left his bedside.

I had some reservations about visiting Ramnath Goenka at all. He sounded too old, too confused in his mind for my visit to be anything but a pilgrimage. And, besides, I correctly doubted that he would live long enough to see this book's publication. But his friends in Bombay changed my mind. 'The Sethji,' said one, using the peculiarly Indian half-formal, half-familiar diminutive, 'will be living for many years to come. You have heard, I am sure, that he has many, many litigations with the courts and the tax authorities, and these give him great energy. Each time one of these cases is coming up before the beak he lives another five years.'

Another aide said, 'He is afraid to die. That is why he fights against it so strongly, and why he is giving so many monies to build temples. All over India he is building temples for this one reason, to keep alive.'

The Goenkas' penthouse, in the received wisdom of Bombay society, is the largest apartment in the city. This is partly because almost all the space has been given over to a single barely furnished room, with floor to ceiling windows on three sides giving on to a spacious paved verandah. Such furniture that exists is lime green: four or five lime-green semi-circular sofas and three lime-green mattresses. Everything is so widely spaced that the impression of emptiness is extreme. The walls are white, and in a distant corner a black and white television was watched by nobody but flickered permanently throughout my visit. At the opposite end was a door leading to Mr Goenka's bedroom, the nurse's room, a bathroom and kitchen. If he owned any books or paintings then he must have kept them in his bedroom, for none were evident.

After I'd waited fifteen minutes in the lime-green drawing room, acknowledged by nobody since my arrival, and feeling that to venture into the bedroom would be too great a liberty, an immensely old man appeared at the door, regarded me for a moment, then shuffled away again. He wore a grey vest and, wrapped around his waist, a handtowel that barely covered his white, scrawny thighs.

For another ten or fifteen minutes there was no further evidence of human life, beyond a distant sluicing of water and muffled instructions of a nurse. And then Ramnath Goenka was led into the drawing room, painfully slowly, each footfall scarcely tolerable despite the support of

Mrs da Costa and a walking stick, until he reached a green sofa, and there he was lowered – levered – down on to the firm green cushions.

A moment later we were joined by the other very old man – the man in the towel – now wearing a suit, who sat down alongside Goenka on the green sofa. This was Mr S. Mulgaokar – if the S of his initial ever stood for anything, it is long forgotten – for many years editor of the *Indian Express*, still his former proprietor's friend and interpreter.

His presence was fortuitous. 'Goenka is lucid for two or three hours a day,' I had been told, 'and then he's sharper than ever. He takes every strategic decision on his newspapers.'

But this was not one of his lucid hours. As he lay back against the green cushions, only his gasping for air and the occasional clutching of his fingers at the sleeve of his homespun khadi – a garment he was first induced to wear by Mahatma Gandhi – were proof that Goenka was alive at all.

I broached my interview with a straightforward question about the division of power between editor and proprietor.

But Goenka merely stared at me, too tired or dispirited to reply; his huge domed forehead and elephantine earlobes hardly capable of being supported by his neck, and lolling forwards on to his chest.

Mr Mulgaokar repeated my question into Goenka's ear, and eventually Goenka's short, muttered reply was relayed on to me by Mulgaokar.

'His answer to your question is: "They divide it".'

'Divide equally?' I asked.

This time Mulgaokar did not refer the question to Goenka but replied to it himself.

'When you work for Mr Goenka,' he said, 'you usually end up agreeing with his views. And if you don't agree, you publish his views anyway.'

Mulgaokar laughed cryptically. Goenka's editors were famous for their short life-expectancy; summarily sacked or shifted without warning from editing his national paper in Bombay to a humiliating job in Cochin or Chandigarh.

'You see,' he would tell people, 'now that there are all these big, big editors, what role is there left for us poor owners? My *only joy* comes from transferring my editors.'

When editors were new and still the apple of his eye, Goenka referred to them as 'my racehorse' or even 'my saint'. When the relationship soured he was caustic.

'But you said he was a saint,' Goenka was once reminded as another editor was dispensed with.

'You think this is the Vatican?' he shouted. 'Saints should sit there. Not edit newspapers.'

'Could you ask Mr Goenka please,' I asked, 'what advice he would give to anybody thinking of owning a newspaper?'

Mulgaokar bellowed the question into Goenka's eardrum and then, failing to get through in English, repeated it in Hindi.

Goenka looked troubled, as though he was searching for the right words. But at last he replied, this time audibly and clearly enough to be understood.

'The same advice,' he said, 'as Mr Punch gave to those about to be married: DON'T.' Then he chuckled, choked and gasped for air until Mrs Delores da Costa adjusted the lime-green cushions so that his neck and windpipe were better supported.

Mr Mulgaokar and the number one nurse looked understandably concerned about this coughing fit, and there was a move to carry him back to his bedroom, but Goenka shook them off and began saying something else.

'I – never – interfere – with – my – journalists – or – editors,' he wheezed, tapping his hand for emphasis on his stick. 'I – don't – like – that – I *should* – interfere.'

'No,' said Mr Mulgaokar, soothing him after this long outburst. 'If there was ever any kind of conflict between us it was only on very broad issues.'

Goenka let his great cadaverous head roll forwards on to his chest and, as it did so, I swear I caught a glimmer of immense cunning in his eyes that no sooner took hold than it faded again.

I decided to question him on his religious convictions, and was again surprised by the intensity of his reply.

'*Religion* has *nothing to do* with *newspapers*,' he said. '*Nothing, nothing*. You can't put a, a . . .' he tapped his stick angrily as the word eluded him '. . . *spoke* into, into . . .' And then his speech faded away again in mid-sentence and his head slumped back on to the green cushions, and after a moment or two it was clear that the last of his energy was spent.

'I don't know that he is of the state of mind in which he can compose any further answer,' said Mr Mulgaokar, and Nurse da Costa hauled the old man to his feet, taking his full weight on to her own shoulders, and began easing him towards his bedroom. But Goenka bridled when he saw the direction they were taking, and muttered something in Hindi.

'Not outside today Mr Goenka,' she replied in a brisk and jolly voice. 'Surely you are not wanting an outside walk today.'

But he persisted, and soon one of the long doors on to the verandah was unbolted, and Nurse da Costa suggested, in the determined way that nurses do, that I accompany them on their lap of the penthouse.

'Every evening we go on a little circuit, don't we, Mr Goenka,' she said. 'We find it beneficial, don't we.'

Ramnath Goenka was concentrating so hard on each uncertain footstep, that you could not tell whether or not the nurse's patronising chatter irritated him.

'Oh yes,' she added brightly, this time for my benefit, 'we find so many interesting things to look at right up here. We really are very lucky with this view.' Lucky, yes certainly, that Ramnath Goenka ordered the building, and paid for it to be put up in 1965.

'Sometimes we like to look at the little houses and the little boats in the harbour,' said Mrs Da Costa as we inched through the twilight. 'But we don't like to go too close to the edge, do we Mr Goenka, because that's dangerous and frightening, and we are not liking that.'

There are many different versions of the origins of Seth Ramnath Goenka. The most widely held is that he was born in Madras, the son either of a minor thakkur – something like an English squire – or a holy man. Another version says he was an orphan from somewhere in Rajasthan, who worked in an uncle's shop in Bihar before moving to Madras where he became embroiled in political activism. In a way it is extraordinary that none of his circle – his editors, his lawyers – have any definitive story of where he came from; but Goenka was so old and enigmatic that he was either unable to remember where he was born, or else his senior staff never felt it their place to enquire. He was certainly by the mid-twenties a member of the Madras Legislative Council; an assembly of Indians established by the British that introduced some element of self-government. Later, according to his friend R.V. Pandit, the Bombay music publisher, Goenka had a good deal to do with the political weekly *Swaraj*, which was his principle contribution to the freedom movement.

It was during the thirties that the Goenka newspaper empire began to take shape. Newspaper publishing, outside the British-owned Anglo-Indian media, was still a mission rather than a business and generally lossmaking. Proprietors were often relieved, after a few years of ownership, to divest themselves of papers that showed no prospect of ever breaking even, and Goenka was quick to acquire them. Initially there was no pattern to these acquisitions. He bought the *Free Press Journal* in Bombay, the *Indian Express* in Madras and the Tamil daily *Dinamani* from a mysterious proprietor named Sadanand. Later he added the *Andhra Prabha*, a Telugu-language daily, the *National Standard* in Bombay, a Calcutta English-language daily which he later sold, and the *Indian News Chronicle* in Delhi which he eventually converted into the Delhi *Indian Express*. During the fifties almost all of these newspapers underwent enormous changes, in which they were converted either into satellite editions of Goenka's flagship *Indian Express*, or else refocused as politically alert regional publications in Tamil, Telugu, Gujarati, Marathi and Kannada. But there was never any doubt that it was the *Indian Express* that Goenka cared most about. As the number of printing centres grew – there are now fourteen, with editions in Ahmedabad, Bangalore, Baroda, Bombay, Cochin, Chandigarh, Delhi, Hyderabad, Madurai, Madras, Pune and Vijayawada – so did Goenka's reputation as political kingmaker.

'He liked to *make* ministers and prime ministers,' says Vinod Mehta. 'He'd certainly go so far as to say that he *created* the new prime minister, and that all these people are beholden to him.'

'It is generally acknowledged by both Gandhi governments that they were broken by the *Indian Express*,' says R. V. Pandit. 'It was a sustained campaign. Once he thought the person who was in power was acting not entirely in the interests of the people of India, he would destroy them. He'd go at it from various angles you know, each day in his newspapers from a different angle; first corruption, then something else, a ceaseless battle.'

The extent to which Goenka involved himself in these campaigns is remarkable. In most newspaper groups it is the editor who promotes a particular journalistic vendetta, and the proprietor who speaks for the Establishment in suggesting that it has gone on for long enough.

At the *Indian Express* it was the proprietor in his penthouse who suggested fresh twists for sustaining the campaign, and had the galley proofs and page make-up brought up to the 25th floor for approval. Editorial conferences during these campaigns were held in the penthouse, and it was Ramnath Goenka's delight at these meetings to add some disclosure, that he'd discovered through his own channels, to those of the journalists.

'He was a very stubborn and brave man, and a complex one also,' says Vinod Mehta. 'Complex in the way that he allowed his own reputation as a proprietor to sink so low, when many of the campaigns he promoted have been admirable and courageous. The way that he treated some of his staff and editors so badly counted against him. And he had a foul temper. He swore like a sergeant major. But not in English; all his swearing was done in the choicest Hindi. On the other hand you could not say that he ever became grand. There was still something austere about him; the stick in one hand, the lohta in the other. A rags-to-riches story, but he remained ascetic and religious.'

At some point in the late twenties Goenka married, but his wife died young having borne a son and a daughter, and in the succeeding 60 years Goenka claimed to have been celibate. He nevertheless enjoyed being surrounded by quick-witted girls, and until he became ill the penthouse was brim-full of pretty young publishing assistants and writers.

'There is something attractive about him actually,' one of them told me only days before his death. 'And he cooked great vegetarian food, which he prepared himself: we used to sit on mattresses on the floor in the most expensive building in Bombay, and he'd boast to everyone how he spends less than 2000 rupees [£45] a month on himself. We called him 'the antique groper' though he never made any passes. I was quite a Goenka-groupie for a bit you know.'

Two great questions dominate any appraisal of Ramnath Goenka: how precisely he made his money, and the inheritance of his empire. Until his son, Bhagwandas Goenka, died ten years before his father of a heart attack at the age of 50, he was seen as the natural heir, already running part of the business in Bombay. Like Ramnath himself, he had a reputation as a womaniser, though less passive in application. Ramnath Goenka set up a foundation in his memory – the B D Goenka Foundation – which funds awards for journalism. This left four contenders for the *Indian Express*: Goenka's daughter; his daughter-in-law who oversees the family property portfolio; his fat grandson, Vivek Khaithan, who was in his early thirties and worked in the treasury side of the empire; and S Gurumurthy, Goenka's ingenious young lawyer who has played a central role in his disputes with the government and was an almost daily visitor to the penthouse in the final days. Nothing was revealed about a designated heir, even whether Goenka had made a will. One theory ran that the newspapers would be left in trust, to be administered by Gurumurthy. Within hours of his death, however, it emerged that Ramnath Goenka had secretly made a will after all, and that his fat grandson Vivek was named heir on the condition that he changed his surname to Goenka and maintained the political stance of the paper.

Of Ramnath Goenka's inner cabinet it was Arun Shourie, a former World Bank economist, who was closest to the proprietor and the great political vendettas. Apart from a short, unhappy tenure working for the Jains at *The Times of India*, Shourie worked continuously at the *Indian Express* from the Emergency onwards, much of the time as editor. He is a lean, rather melancholy-looking man, with unusually thick eyebrows and long fingers, and a volatile intellect that makes him embark, almost absent-mindedly, into political theses of great complexity, run out of steam then erupt again into life and vigour. His descriptions of the hounding of the *Indian Express* by successive governments, and how Goenka reacted to them, read like a hymn of praise from editor to mercurial owner.

'By the end [of the 1988 anti-Goenka campaign by Rajiv Gandhi's government] over 230 prosecutions had been heaped upon the paper,' says Shourie, 'by the Company Law Department, by the Revenue Intelligence, the Income Tax authorities, the Customs Department, the Enforcement Directorate, the chief controller of Imports and Exports. Advertisements to the paper had been slashed [under government pressure]. Banks were just not lending up to the credit limits which they had themselves sanctioned, they had stopped even answering letters, phone calls, to say nothing of receiving us for personal discussions. An attempt had been made to appoint govern-ment directors on to the board of the paper.

'Our facsimile circuits had been turned off in Bangalore. The Delhi edition had been successfully prevented from being published for 47 days – the building cordoned off by hired 'goondas' [mobsters] as well as mounted police. Offices of the paper all over the country had been raided. Personnel had been beaten up – six by acid hurled at them. Mr Ramnath Goenka's passports had been impounded. His houses had been raided.

'By the end we were on the brink of collapse. But as had happened in the Emergency we were saved by the mistake of the rulers: like Mrs Gandhi in January 1977, Rajiv Gandhi called an election, and he lost. The paper survived with just months to spare.

'[We were] prepared to lose all in the fight; apart from his great astuteness, his immense resourcefulness, his enormous resilience, this willingness to lose everything he had built up over 70 years has been the unique strength of Mr Ramnath Goenka . . . he staked everything.

'Time and tide,' Shourie went on, 'do not wait because we had taken on the State. Mr Goenka, already 85, drove himself into a stroke. It disabled him. The fight had to be conducted in spite of illness, of traumas, of dislocations of various kinds. At times he had to be shielded from public view. The government had its emissaries who came ostensibly to wish him well but in fact to ascertain how able he was to carry on. As Mr Goenka fought back to reasonable health, we realised that the illness, though nearly fatal, had not been able to touch his indomitable spirit.'

Unhappily for Arun Shourie – 'my racehorse' as Goenka affectionately called him – even this loyalty was not enough to secure his job indefinitely and, after a falling out with the proprietor over the Prime Ministership of V.P. Singh, his name joined the roster of fired editors.

'I thought you said he was your racehorse,' Goenka was reminded shortly after Shourie's expulsion.

'But this racehorse will destroy my tonga [horsedrawn cart],' thundered Goenka.

I had a room overlooking the inner courtyard of the Taj hotel, and it was here that I was visited for breakfast by S. B. Kolpe. Almost everybody in Bombay had recommended I talk to S. B. Kolpe, because he would give me 'the other side' of the Goenkas.

In fact it is a third view of Ramnath Goenka that Kolpe has made his speciality: not the Gandhi Congress or Opposition Party, but a Far Left view of the proprietor that is critical of him, not for political subversion against the Establishment, but as an anti-union employer and, says Kolpe, manipulator of the system for his own ends. Where Goenka is concerned, he is a man obsessed.

I had some difficulty making contact with Kolpe. I had arranged to meet for a drink at the hotel, but he arrived at the wrong time in the wrong room on the wrong floor and went home. The following morning he ate his way through the entire breakfast menu – the European as well as the Indian – showering the table with mouthfuls of banana and biryani, and random, hard-to-substantiate conspiracy theories about Goenka.

He is a small, paunchy man in a crumpled suit with a heroic leftist career. He is the editor of *Clarity*, a weekly newspaper known for its exposés of industrialists and politicians, and was chairman of the Bombay Union of Journalists and president of the Maharashtra Union of Working Journalists. During the Quit India movement he was imprisoned for two years by the British, which only strengthened his regard for the old Eastern Bloc regimes. He remains president of the Indo-Polish and Indo-Cuban Friendship societies of Bombay, and accepts invitations to international journalists' conferences in Moscow, Havana and Ulan Bator.

S. B. Kolpe's feud with Goenka dates from Goenka's refusal, during one of the protracted union disputes of the early seventies, to accept a minimum wage for journalists in the *Indian Express* group. Since then Kolpe has passed over few opportunities to denigrate Goenka both in *Clarity* and in specially printed little booklets: for his tax disputes, wealth tax and Customs and Excise cases, the origins of his empire, property deals and numerous insider share dealing scams that Kolpe insists took place.

'The jiggery-pokery of Goenka cannot be overstated,' he exclaimed through a mouthful of plain yoghurt. 'It is a matter of *financial tricks galore*!'

Some of these, were they true, do not sound particularly dramatic: change of use of some floors of Express Towers, which received planning permission as a newspaper building but is now largely sub-let to International Data Management, Mitsubishi and something called The Garware Shipping and Nylons Ltd.

'With Goenka, you must be always alert for a butter-will-not-melt-in-the-mouth feint,' said Kolpe through a mouthful of scrambled egg. 'You need only examine the labyrinth of companies and partnerships in his empire. You can be sure, he always receives his bonanza in black. *And it is all documented.*'

'Where is it documented?'

'It is documented *here*,' replied Kolpe triumphantly. 'Here in my own pamphlets. *Goenka, An Investigative Report*. And here, in *Goenka Unmasked*.'

The Goenka family holdings, it is true, are more complex even than the late Robert Maxwell's and enable them, say detractors, to frustrate the Indian tax authorities almost indefinitely. These holdings include: The Indian Express Newspapers (Bombay) Private Limited; The Indian Express (Madurai) Private Limited; The Andhra Prabha Private Limited; The Express Newspapers Private Limited (1946); Nariman Point Building Services and Trading Private Ltd; Ace Investments Private Limited; Traders Private Limited; Colaba Properties Limited; Mathura Properties Limited; Mount Road Properties Limited; Airlines Hotels and Caterers (Madras) Private Limited and National Company Limited.

'And that is not all,' went on Kolpe excitably through a mouthful of grilled tomato. 'In his organisation he has not excluded lap dogs and close relatives. And the newspapers themselves were obtained by jiggery-pokery.'

Mr Kolpe then told a long story about a man called Rajah Mohan Prasad, a Marwari businessman from Hyderabad, to whom Goenka acted as secretary in the late 1920s. According to S. B. Kolpe, Goenka was able to start his newspaper empire with money borrowed, or not borrowed, from Prasad, and that his brothers and other dependents are laying claim to the entire chain and property on the grounds that the seed capital was held on trust.

I mentioned the case to Mulgaokar when I visited Ramnath Goenka in his penthouse, and Mulgaokar smiled, raised his eyes to the ceiling and said, '*Ah, Kolpe*,' as though I had referred to an exasperating and slightly dotty aunt upstairs in the attic. 'Ah, Kolpe. A man of great principles. And like so many people of great principle, given to wishful thinking sometimes.'

'There were several remarkable things about Goenka that were not often considered,' says R. V. Pandit. 'He had a photographic memory, which enabled him to remember every document he had ever seen. He was also a Sanskrit scholar and could recite religious texts. On good days he could recite the Gita, a very long volume, and in conversation, if the subject of religion came up, he'd quote in Sanskrit for a long, long time. I remember him as a younger man, with sparkling eyes and the great inner strength that religion gave him. Mr Goenka was highly religious.'

His competitors were sceptical. Shortly after the accession of the grandson, Aveek Sarkar told me of Ramnath Goenka, 'When he died a halo appeared around his head, but I think it will be short-lasting. His newspapers are mediocre. But he was an interesting person. And in publishing if you are an interesting person, the publications and the owner can become sort of combined you know.'

The grandson, by common consent less enigmatic than Ramnath, is attempting to rationalise his promise not to change the stance of the papers while steering them gently away from some of their traditional prejudices. He has drafted in the elegant Parsee multimillionaire industrialist, Nusli Wadia, to advise him on modernising the group (though not, to date, on modernising the lime-green penthouse).

'All Vivek will succeed in doing,' I was told, 'is alienate the shopkeepers who bought the *Express specifically for* the bias. But Vivek says he doesn't care; doesn't care about losing readers if he can get the ideology right for the nineties.'

'Inside Vivek Goenka's fat frame,' a Calcutta editor advised me, 'there is a thin man struggling to get out. The struggle is intellectual, you know, as well as corporeal.'

One hundred and fifty minutes into *The Times of India* board meeting and Samir Jain had arrived – as he always must – at the subject of advertising.

'This morning,' he was saying, 'I was turning through the pages of the *Economic Times* and was highly disappointed by the advertisement on the corporate dossier page. Why isn't there a prestige advertisement on that page today? Why no high-ambiance hotel advertisement? I have specifically asked for this. A high-ambiance colour advertisement will enhance that page, and I have requested it.

'Ambience is paramount,' he went on, 'because we are delivering a sophisticated Bombay and Delhi audience, and they are a growing segmentation all the time. The Goenkas' *Indian Express* I believe has more sales than us; I say *believe* advisedly, because I do not mind, because their readers are not important. Mr Sarkar's *Ananda Bazar Patrika* sells four lakh copies in Calcutta, the largest sales from a single edition in the country. And yet I do not believe it makes much profit, because it does not deliver our sophisticated readers. *These are snapshots that tell you stories.*'

Outside in the corridor, with a good deal of rattling, clanking and hushed instructions, a post-board meeting lunch was being prepared, and as the smell of curried cauliflower and potato massala began to drift under the door, the level of attention became markedly less rapt.

But the Chief Executive still had several global overviews to impart before the board meeting broke up.

'As Kenneth Galbraith said recently,' quoted Samir Jain, ' "It must be said in defence of Marx and Lenin that they did not anticipate that on the lowest rungs of society it would become the norm for a porter or coalminer's son to buy a designer dress for his wife, or a sports car. Their system was not created to cope with that." '

Jain's assumption, one was left to deduce, is that India too stands on the threshold of such a society: one in which the porters at Bombay's Victoria Station, who presently live in hardboard shacks by the railway sidings, will choose designer dresses from the high-ambiance advertisements in the *Economic Times*; and the coalminers of Madhya Praddesh will bomb about in Ferraris, assuming the Indian government ban on all imported cars is ever relaxed.

'As a very young child,' said Samir, 'I remember an advertisement poster I saw. It was for Chanel No 5, and the slogan said "If you can afford it, buy it". I was very impressed. Why? Because it speaks of quality.

'But quality alone is not sufficient. Publishing today is *overt duelling*. Irrespective of whether you are the market leader, you must be seen to be angrily competing in the duel. They – the advertising agencies, the world at large – want to see you lose an eye, lose an arm maybe, a display of war, lose an editor, gain a columnist, it is to be enjoyed. You may have the best product, but you must be seen in combat, which in publishing means you must raise your ad-rate enough. Why? Because you must take enough money out of the market. Every morning I read about our clients in the *Economic Times* and they are making big profits, and we must take enough of it away from them for ourselves. Otherwise those clients will say, "I will place my advertisements in *all* the newspapers," which gives profit to our competitors. *Money must not be available for the competitors.*

'In the old days at these newspapers,' said Jain, fixing the table with glistening eyes over the gold bridge of his glasses, 'we used to live like male lions in the desert near Jaiselmer. We used to eat but not to hunt. *Now we hunt.*'

9

The Prodigal Son

Part One: How Warwick Fairfax tried to kick sand

On Sunday afternoon, 30 August 1987, Warwick Fairfax, then aged 26, called on his half-brother James at his mansion on Darling Point.

'He came to see me at 5.15 in this very room,' James Fairfax told me in his drawing room hung with modern art, with its wide view across Sydney harbour. 'I didn't know what he was going to tell me, he just said he needed to see me at some point over the weekend.'

Warwick's announcement was terse and astonishing. He informed James, who at 52 had been chairman of the family newspaper business for eleven years, that he was launching a takeover of the company, and that this would become public knowledge at nine o'clock the next morning. He expected the exercise to cost $2.25 billion and that, when successful, the 150-year-old media empire that included the *Sydney Morning Herald*, the Melbourne *Age* and the *Australian Financial Review* would be his.

'It was certainly more than unexpected,' said James. 'Warwick wasn't an easy person to get close to or know well, though I'd tried to keep in touch with him when he was doing his course at Harvard. He'd been working in our marketing department for a few months, learning the ropes, and we'd recently invited him to join the board so he could get some idea of what went on in the company. We had no idea he had been secretly planning this coup. It was rather shocking.

'Later that evening, when I tried to talk him out of it, he refused to take my telephone calls. He had developed an obsession that the company was about to be taken over by Robert Holmes à Court – a virtually impossible scenario, then.'

Warwick had then driven straight from Darling Point to his cousin John's house, arriving at about 9.30 p.m. John Fairfax, another substantial family shareholder, described himself as 'shattered' by Warwick's news; he thought it was madness. After Warwick had left, John telephoned James to discuss the situation and they agreed that John would make one last attempt to talk Warwick out of it, or at least get him to postpone the bid for 24 hours. John telephoned Warwick in his flat in Neutral Bay early on Monday morning but Warwick was immovable. He told his cousin that he had made up his mind and nothing whatever could change it.

Australia's three most prestigious papers – so rich in advertising revenue that Rupert Murdoch described them as 'the rivers of gold' – were about to become the subject of a rapacious custody suit. That the protagonist should have been Warwick Geoffrey Oswald Fairfax was not simply startling; it left Australia confounded. Among media owners around the world it caused a sensation. Newspaper properties of this magnitude seldom change hands; this was the first large takeover since Conrad Black bought the London *Telegraph* group two years earlier. And the more that media owners heard about the details of the Fairfax deal, the more likely it seemed to them that it would come unstuck. Before Warwick Fairfax had even ratified his takeover, other proprietors – Robert Maxwell, Sally Aw Sian – were gathering in case some juicy spin-off became available. In Hong Kong, Sally Aw instructed her *Sing Tao* bureau chief in Sydney to fax her every scrap of intelligence about Fairfax that appeared in the Australian press; in Holborn, Maxwell thought that Warwick was likely to divest the Melbourne *Age* if the new, overborrowed company ran into difficulties, and set about constructing a bid price; in Manhattan, Rupert Murdoch kept himself informed of developments but knew that the Australian monopolies board was unlikely to let him buy the papers; while on the Isle of Dogs, Conrad Black, who had met Warwick through his mother, Lady Fairfax, and was astonished by the sheer impertinence of his bid, had no inkling that he would become heavily embroiled in the drama.

From the start, Warwick's appearance counted against him: gawky, unprepossessing, stoop-shouldered, myopic with wire-framed glasses and a strange inner deadness about the eyes. 'He looked the greyday nerd, socially maladroit and rather driven by some kind of internal vision,' Leo Schofield, the Sydney writer and social figure told me. 'I remember him arriving at black-tie parties carrying an odd little plastic carrier bag and with unpolished shoes. At Kerry Packer's daughter Gretel's 21st birthday party he looked like the Prince of Nerds – funny shoes, trousers at half-mast. You've got to remember that, like a lot of young Australians of good family, he spent quite a period out of the country being educated, in Warwick's case at Oxford – Balliol – and at Harvard and then working for a spell at the Chase Manhattan Bank. When someone returns here from that kind of trip you expect them to be poised. But the reality was quite different. No one here could quite reconcile the reality of the gawky person before us with what we'd been told, about this person who'd just swept out of Oxford, Harvard etc.'

Other facts, too, struck discordant notes. When the young Fairfax – known in Australia as 'Young Wocka' – moved back to Sydney to make his bid for power, he based himself not in a large suite at somewhere like the Regent hotel, or at Fairwater, the family mansion on the harbour, but shared a suburban rectory with a community of Christian flatmates in the Neutral Bay area of Sydney where he slept on a fold-down truckle bed. 'My son is interested in only two things – Jesus Christ and journalism,' his mother, the Sydney social hostess Lady Fairfax, once said of Warwick. His deeply held commitment to an evangelical Christian movement coloured his every decision. When he eventually appointed himself chairman of the newspaper empire, he paid himself only $15,000 a year, explaining it was all he needed, and he chose a Toyota, one of the cheapest makes of car available in Australia.

The takeover has its roots in an old family feud dating back nearly a quarter of a century. In March 1977, Warwick's father – old Sir Warwick Fairfax – had been unseated in a boardroom shoot-out by his son from an earlier marriage, James. Shy, educated and erudite, James Fairfax made an effective if rather aloof chairman of the company which operated as a multimedia empire, but was regarded in Australia as a venerable institution.

Founded in 1831 and nurtured by generation after generation of Fairfaxes, it owned not only newspapers but magazines, television and radio stations, newsprint mills and real estate. Fairfax publications had an unrivalled reputation for independence and journalistic excellence (some said unmerited), and exerted enormous influence on Australian life.

One person, however, would never forgive the family for the

overthrow of Sir Warwick, and that was his wife Mary. From the moment she became Sir Warwick's third wife in 1959, Mary was disliked by other members of the Fairfax family. She was not only Polish and a Jew, which they felt was bad enough, but strident, publicity-minded and ambitious – all qualities the Fairfax clan sought to avoid, particularly in their choice of wives. She has been described as 'a Bubbles Rothermere writ large', though Lady Rothermere (the deceased wife of the chairman of Associated Newspapers) was generally considered circumspect next to Mary Fairfax, with her Widow Twanky couture ballgowns and ring-encrusted fingers.

'Mary had been slighted,' says Ralph Ingersoll who later attempted to help Warwick save the empire. 'Over the years the Fairfaxes had become rather grand and Mary was perceived as the Fergie of their world – a bit vulgar or whatever – and they treated her by all accounts pretty roughly. So when her husband was no longer on earth to shield her from that, she decided, in the way I've seen other stepmothers do in our universe, that she would avenge all the wrongs, real or imagined. So at the height of the market she encouraged her son to launch a pre-emptive strike, ultimately self-destructive. She thought she was going to level the playing field. But she blew the place up in the attempt.'

Mary Fairfax has subsequently claimed to have played no part in the takeover – she told me that she had pleaded with Warwick to call it off.

Warwick himself seldom showed any signs of proprietorial gravitas. Only two weeks before the fateful raid was announced, the then Fairfax editor Valerie Lawson remembers attending a small lunch in the boardroom for the editors to meet Warwick. It seemed a joke even then that he might eventually become chairman of the company in perhaps 15 or 20 years' time.

'I remember it being very awkward,' Lawson told me. 'Warwick had no charm and no confidence, and we tried to search around for a topic of conversation. We'd start one and it fell, start another one and it fell. I kept trying to think of something that might interest him. It was embarrassing. Eventually I remembered that he'd studied marketing at Harvard, so I asked him whether he had any fresh ideas for the positioning of our Sunday paper which was not doing too well. His response, after some sustained silent thought, was: "Maybe people don't like to read newspapers on Sundays" – not a vastly encouraging view for a future newspaper proprietor to hold.

'Eventually David Hickie, who was editor of the *Sun Herald*, asked in desperation if Fairfax ever went to the beach, and at last he brightened up. He said he loved Bondi, loved the outdoors, loved bushwalking and surfing. It was hard to picture this odd, nervy boy doing any of those things. He was the picture of the six-stone weakling who secretly longed to kick sand in people's faces.'

The corporate sand-kicking had in fact begun six months earlier, in a series of secret strategy meetings at a restaurant in Bondi, called Pancakes on the Beach. Warwick subsequently assembled a war cabinet that met two or three times a week in a suite at the Regent hotel, at Fairwater (where Lady Fairfax bustled in and out, handing out drinks and demanding a seat on the proposed new board) or, occasionally, at Warwick's spartan Christian community in the suburbs. The war cabinet consisted, at this point, of a former Bell group executive, Bert Reuter; a former editor of the savvy Sydney *Daily Mirror*, Martin Dougherty; and Laurie Connell, the former chairman of collapsed merchant bank Rothwells whose nickname was 'Last Resort Laurie' since he was often seen as the last choice for individuals seeking to raise finance.

Unable to obtain support from any of the Sydney banks, Warwick had had little option other than to recruit the services of these colourful characters. Dougherty, a smooth-talking public relations consultant described as an 'Irish charmer', had in recent years become a friend and confidant of Sir Warwick and Lady Fairfax. 'Marty' was an unlikely companion for Sir Warwick, but it seems the two men fulfilled the old adage of opposites attracting.

Marty Dougherty was less popular with other members of the family. At Sir Warwick's funeral, Marty asked Warwick's cousin, John Fairfax, if he could help as an usher. 'No,' John replied coldly. 'You can go and sit down in the seat you have been allocated.'

Dougherty in turn brought in the second key player, Connell, the merchant banker from Perth. Connell was known for what is generally described as a robust business style. A Western Australian politician was memorably reported saying he would not like 'to stand between Laurie Connell and a bag of money'.

When Dougherty telephoned Connell in Perth and outlined the deal, Connell saw its potential 'in about 45 seconds' and agreed to join them, for a personal fee of unprecedented hugeness – A$100 million.

The deal agreed, the plan was on. Code names were used on working documents to minimise the risk of there being any leaks – the Fairfax company was referred to as 'the Dynasty Corporation', Warwick was 'the Heir'. The war cabinet's final meeting to put the finishing touches to the strategy was held in a private room at the Regent hotel on Saturday, 29 August 1987; the day before Warwick's courtesy call on his half-brother James. After the meeting, Warwick drove home to his evangelical community 'to pray, and commend my scheme up to Jesus'.

His faith had taken root four years earlier, and 26,000 miles away, at Oxford. Fairfax had already been confirmed at St Mark's, Darling Point; but in England his religious commitment developed rapidly under the influence of Canon Michael Green who was the rector of St Aldate's, Oxford.

Green was well known as a leader of evangelistic missions in Britain and as the author of several evangelical tracts with titles like *Choose Freedom* and *I Believe in Satan's Downfall*. He spoke at the Oxford Union, and St Aldate's was well attended by God-minded students. During the summer vacation it was Canon Green's custom to take parties of undergraduates to Lee Abbey in North Devon, and on one of these retreats during his second year at Oxford, Fairfax experienced if not a conversion then certainly a quickening of faith.

Like his father 58 years earlier, he took a second-class degree in Politics, Philosophy and Economics; virtually all of his spare time he devoted to God Squad activities and table tennis, of which he was college secretary. Of his Balliol contemporaries whom I have interviewed, none can remember him at all, despite the fact that very rich young men with surnames like Fairfax attract above-average interest at Oxford.

After graduating in 1982, he briefly worked at the J Walter Thompson advertising agency in New York and then for three years at Chase Manhattan Bank, in a division specialising in takeover financing for media and entertainment companies, where the clients included the New York Times and Time Inc. To one of his colleagues he seemed bright but inclined to keep his own counsel, indeed often tongue-tied.

While living in Manhattan, Fairfax attended a Baptist church to which he had been introduced by friends of his half-sister Annalise. Writing to her from New York, he said he had decided, as part of his

Christian commitment, to involve himself wholeheartedly, as his parents had always hoped he would, in family and company affairs. Previously he had not been certain about his future, but this was something ordained by God, he said, and in the spirit of the Parable of the Talents he was going to give it his best.

Part of that best, as he saw it, was to gain a postgraduate degree of sufficient worth to persuade others that he was more than merely his father's son. Sir Warwick tried to deter him from this; but in September 1985 he began the two-year Harvard Business School MBA course. During one of the summer vacations he worked as an intern at the *Los Angeles Times* in its marketing department; a job which apparently involved delivering newspapers over picket fences from a van.

Fairfax returned to Sydney and moved in with some friends of his own age and religious conviction to the house in the grounds of St Augustine's Church of England, Neutral Bay.

One evening Fairfax was asked to drive out to the airport to collect a young American girl from Chicago who was arriving to join the community. This was Gale Murphy and within a few months, chaperoned by Jesus, they became engaged.

Warwick and Gale were already associated with an international prayer movement – a non-denominational fellowship centred in Washington. In Sydney, Fairfax also attended a North Shore church of the Christian and Missionary Alliance, the Australian branch of a long-established evangelical community with headquarters in Nyack, New York. According to some of those who knew Fairfax, he was always 'a person of great integrity, never interested in flashy clothes and flashy cars', and 'a committed Christian in everything he undertook'.

When Warwick announced his takeover, it wasn't simply its scale – the largest and most expensive in Australian corporate history – that stunned the financial community. Nor was it merely his youth. The ultimate absurdity was that Warwick would have become chairman of the company anyway – all he had to do was wait his turn. The motive for borrowing $2.25 billion seemed to be simple impatience. And the fact that Warwick pursued his bid even after the 1987 stockmarket crash left them incredulous.

From the moment the takeover was declared, virtually everything that could go wrong did go wrong.

Warwick's $7.50-a-share bid, announced the day before, involved extensive restructuring aimed at locking the 'crown jewels' – the *Sydney Morning Herald* – and certain other key assets into a wholly owned private company. Shareholders were also initially offered shares in a public float of 55 per cent of David Syme, a subsidiary company which owned the *Age*, but this offer had to be withdrawn when it was belatedly realised that if all the non-family shareholders accepted, it could lead to the issue of more than twice as many shares as planned.

Worse was to follow. While Dougherty was swearing that the family was united and would stick together, it was evident that control of the company was in doubt and the predators moved in: both Holmes à Court and Kerry Packer increased their Fairfax holdings to 9 per cent and 4 per cent respectively.

The only way for Warwick to buy out the family was to dispose of assets, and during a three-week period of intensive manoeuvring 'Last Resort' Connell found himself negotiating simultaneously with James and John Fairfax, Holmes à Court and Packer. At one point he spent all day in Sydney haggling with Packer and then all night haggling with Holmes à Court on board his private Boeing 727 en route to Perth.

James and John Fairfax did not abandon hope that Warwick could be persuaded not to proceed, but he was as inaccessible to his own family as he was to the press. John, after numerous telephone calls, at last managed to pin young Warwick down to an emotional meeting in his office. He bluntly told his cousin: 'This is no longer a takeover, it's a fire sale. You're selling everything. What you are doing is tragic.'

'What's got to be has got to be,' Warwick replied enigmatically. 'I've done this now and I've got to face the consequences.'

Three weeks later, the stockmarket crashed and blew Warwick's masterplan to smithereens. Most analysts assumed that it would now either be abandoned or postponed, but it seemed that Warwick was unable or unwilling to extricate himself from the events he had set into motion. Every day the interest on the money that he'd borrowed from the banks accumulated and, after the crash, as each day passed the newspapers he had bought were worth less and less money; as well as generating increasingly lower advertising revenue.

By the end of February, rumours abounded that the *Age*, the newspaper that Dougherty had previously said would never be for sale, was to be sold to Robert Maxwell – who appeared to be the only interested bidder – at a price of about $800 million. Staff immediately began mobilising to try and prevent such a move: fundraising T-shirts went on sale bearing Warwick's image and the legend: 'Never send a boy to do a man's job'. Journalists on the *Age* invited their young proprietor to Melbourne to tell them exactly what was going on; Warwick declined, explaining that he did not like 'talking to large groups of people'.

As the debt grew incrementally, directors resigned in droves. Executives would leave, fresh ones would be appointed, move into their predecessors' offices, then they too – apparently overwhelmed by the scale of the crisis – would bail out. At the end of 1987, the group general manager Greg Gardiner; the chief editorial executive Max Suick; and general manager Fred Brenchey all resigned. Information about who was staying and who was going became harder to get. In time, the chain of command was so ill-defined and confused that it almost ceased to matter.

10

The Piper at the Gates of Knowledge

Part One: The Audacious Rise of Asil Nadir

Asil Nadir had been on an accelerating corporate shopping spree for three years, and decided to buy something for himself. He knew exactly what he wanted – a Big Newspaper. It didn't particularly matter where it was, providing it was prestigious and influential. So he put the word out to media brokers and bankers that next time a major league publication became available, he was interested.

The revolving rumour that the London *Observer* was for sale, which recurs every two or three years, came round again in 1987 and Nadir – the Cypriot-born chairman of clothing-into-electronics giant Polly Peck – was front runner. For one thing, he could afford it. His shares in Polly Peck were valued at £500 million; in ten years the price had risen by 120,000 per cent making Nadir the hottest ticket on the London stock market. He exported Japanese Daihatsu cars to the Egyptians, romper suits to the Arabs, pizza to the Turks, employed half the population of Northern Cyprus to harvest his lemons, and had recently bought the Del Monte canned fruit empire and Sansui, the Japanese electronics firm. Now the *Observer* seemed to be within his grasp.

If he got it, people said, heads would roll. The *Observer*'s City pages had for years been waging a guerrilla campaign against Nadir and his companies, accusing him of overstatement in the report and accounts. His impending ownership engendered the same panic at the *Observer* as Kerry Packer's bid for the *Sydney Morning Herald* would later cause Fairfax journalists in Australia.

At the height of the *Observer* rumour I saw Asil Nadir several times having lunch at Mark's Club in Charles Street, round the corner from his corporate headquarters in Berkeley Square. I noticed him first because of his on-off wife, Aysegül (they have married and divorced each other twice), a striking woman in a Valentino jacket who picked at her food while her husband chain-smoked Silk Cut and drank bellinis. Sometimes they were joined by Turkish and Lebanese businessmen. A thin man among fat ones, Nadir looked alert and nimble-minded.

But he knew almost nothing about big newspapers. For several years he had owned a little daily in Cyprus, *Kibris*, but its circulation was less than 10,000, and I asked him why he especially wanted a British national newspaper.

'For three reasons I want to play my part,' he replied in a voice as smooth as Marmaris honey. 'I believe it is important for newspapers to stay as close to the truth as possible. And they should correct certain mistakes, certain untruths. And, you know, through owning a publishing house you are closer to the people.'

The *Observer* turned out not to be for sale, so Nadir conceived a second plan. He would make an offer for *Hürriyet*, the Turkish daily (circulation 470,000) in partnership with Robert Maxwell. The two tycoons met three times to discuss strategy: at Maxwell's Holborn apartment, at Nadir's Eaton Square flat and at Nadir's wooden haveli on the Bosphorus. *Hürriyet* is owned by the multimillionaire Erol Simavi and is one of the few profitable papers in Turkey, with regional editions in Adana, Ankara, Erzurum and Izmir. Maxwell and Nadir believed they could buy it for $100 million and that the lustre of their joint ownership would instantly enhance its book value, even before they'd made a single publishing decision. In the dining room of the Istanbul Hilton, they shook hands on the principle of a deal: each would raise $50 million by the end of the month, and then they'd surprise Simavi with an impossible-to-refuse offer. If Nadir got *Hürriyet*, people said, heads would roll. Its gossip pages had always been less than reverential to him. Unease at the prospect of Nadir as proprietor seized the offices of *Hürriyet*; journalists on its daily rivals *Gunes* and *Günaydin*, owned by Erol Simavi's elder brother, Haldun, fanned their alarm. Maxwell meanwhile flew back to London where, instead of raising his share of the capital, he temporarily lost interest in the whole idea, eventually telling Nadir that he was too absorbed with planning the *European* to bother with Turkey. Without a partner, Asil Nadir withdrew.

But the episode had whetted Nadir's appetite to break into Turkish newspapering. For five years every new business he'd touched had prospered, and it seemed that his ownership would improve anything. In Nadir's judgement the Turkish press – *Babiali*, literally 'the gates of knowledge' – was in a terrible state. In particular Nadir could not believe what he read about himself and his family. *Günaydin*, for example, published as fact the (untrue) story that Aysegül Nadir had been a soft-porn actress, and *Gunes* continually insinuated that his friendship with Turkish Prime Minister Turgut Ozal was somehow corrupt. Asil Nadir's investment in Turkey was escalating, he was building hotels and canning factories along the south coast, and these stories disturbed him. Moreover he distrusted journalists instinctively. At the Polly Peck AGM in London, when he was obliged to answer questions from the press, he sweated so heavily he had to put on a fresh shirt after every meeting.

Asil Nadir knew there was only one sure way to stem the flow of bad publicity in Turkey. In the autumn of 1988 he paid $70 million to buy *Günaydin* and *Gunes*, along with two other nationals – *Tan* and the political daily *Aktuel* – and ten regional papers. At the age of 47, Nadir found himself the proprietor of the Turkish equivalents of the London *Independent*, *Daily Express*, the *Sun*, the *Spectator* and the *Financial Times*. His market share of 32 per cent gave him, overnight, the power of Rupert Murdoch in England or Robert Hersant in France.

In Britain too, with the Polly Peck share price at an all-time high, Nadir was spending freely. He bought the 3000-acre Baggrave Hall estate in Rutland for £3 million, and a year later Burley-on-the-Hill, a Repton house overlooking Rutland Water that he planned to convert into a country house hotel. Baggrave farm was rebuilt with high-tech, temperature-controlled barns to house his breeding herds of prize Aberdeen Angus and British Charolais. His rapidly assembled collection of Islamic firmans, rare Ottoman documents, was reckoned to be the best in private hands anywhere in the world. With Aysegül, he gave splashy parties attended by people like Princess Margaret, Aysha Jaipur – mother of the present Maharajah – Queen Ferida of Egypt and Princess Neslishah, an old Ottoman royal.

Meanwhile, Nadir the new press lord announced his strategy. *Gunes* would become a quality paper. Turkish newspapers are historically atrocious, their front pages plastered with colour photographs of coach smashes, rescuers cutting blood-smattered bodies from the wreckage, handcuffed scowling criminals, small boys in uniform on their way to be circumcised, dead dogs and more coach smashes. Nadir installed a new editor, Metin Munir, with a brief to kill the carnage and gossip. The front page should be faxed to him in London every evening for approval. He would spend more money on television advertising than had ever been seen before. The best staff should be lured from *Hürriyet* at whatever cost. Politically his papers must support the government, rubbish the Greeks and discourage fundamentalism along the Russian border. He would himself be spending more time in Istanbul to oversee the plan. Circulation, he decreed, would triple within two years.

For a little over a year the Nadir papers boomed. Their front pages were transformed. In place of crunched coaches were photographs of Turgut Ozal. Stimulated by a TL18-billion (£4.5 million) advertising spend, circulation soared and *Günaydin* briefly overtook *Hürriyet*. At least a dozen of *Hürriyet*'s senior staff changed sides.

At this point Erol Simavi reopened negotiations with Robert Maxwell whose appetite for Turkish newspapers had returned, and the fat tycoon sailed into the Sea of Marmara on his yacht, the *Lady Ghislaine*. He moored off Istanbul and for several days it seemed that the paper would change hands. But as Maxwell flipped through the racier Turkish papers that would become his rivals, he was indignant at how rude they were about him: his dyed hair was mocked by cartoonists, and the editorials greeted him as a charlatan. Other, more pressing, acquisitions soon distracted him and the *Lady Ghislaine* drew anchor.

One evening in March 1990 I visited Asil Nadir in Berkeley Square. He had promised to show me the proofs of *Günaydin* and *Gunes* arriving from Turkey by fax. His sombre rococo office seemed unreal, like a stage set, with a 17th-century French globe, a picture book of Stubbs horses open at a mahogany easel, a fluffed-up tapestry of the Golden Horn and a VDU flashing exchange rate information. Nadir wore a double-breasted navy blue suit, white shirt and grey embossed tie. His hair was flattened with a peculiarly spicy unguent that smelt like brown sugar and eau-de-cologne. His handshake was disquietingly soft, like brushing against one of the seven veils.

His secretary stuck her head round the door. 'Your proofs are coming through, Mr Nadir, shall I bring them in?'

Nadir nodded and the two front pages were displayed on his desk. The fax line must have been bad because they were hard to comprehend; the headlines blurred and the text illegible. Asil Nadir regarded the pages for a while and nodded his consent. He can only have been admiring their general appearance, because you couldn't unscramble any of the smaller type.

I asked, 'What exactly are you looking out for here?'

'The good mixture,' he replied. 'I am checking that the articles, you know, are not too much all alike.'

On the front of *Gunes* was a picture of a child looking happy.

'I love children,' said Nadir suddenly. 'My biggest pleasure in life is helping children and turtles.'

'Turtles?'

'Hammer-headed turtles. It is not irreconcilable you know, business and turtles. In this decade we are seeing already a great reconciliation of everything.'

On the front of *Günaydin* there was a photograph of an hotel, very ugly and modern, and in the corner the logo of the Turkish Pizza Hut.

'Both are mine,' said Nadir. 'The new Sheraton at Antalya. One day you will stay there. And I have the franchise for pizza.'

I asked him whether the turquoise coast really needed another concrete hotel, let alone Pizza Hut.

'Cement must be one of the very worst inventions ever,' he conceded with a worldly-wise shake of the head, 'but very necessary. And pizza can taste good with fresh ingredients.'

'Are you a pizza lover?'

'Me personally?' He laughed silkily. 'No, myself I eat very sparingly. For breakfast, some bread, some olives, a tomato if the quality is good.'

He continued to squint at the proofs, mostly it seemed for my benefit. Metin Munir had already told me that Nadir seldom made any response to them.

'What's the best thing about owning these papers?' I asked.

'It is safeguarding the truth,' he replied. 'Not long ago in Istanbul, I gave a speech at a dinner for the 20th anniversary of *Günaydin*. In my speech I gave my guests my answer to that same question which I am often asked. And my answer is: *I have my newspapers in order to benefit humanity and human culture*.'

11

Bob the Max Takes Manhattan

Did New York really deserve Robert Maxwell

Until he acquired the *New York Daily News* in March 1991, Robert Maxwell never walked anywhere. His preferred modes of transport were helicopter, Gulfstream jet, yacht and stretch limousine, and any expedition, however short, preferably incorporated all four. Had it been possible to shuttle by helicopter from the Mirror Group building in Holborn to the Maxwell Communication Corporation head-quarters fifty yards away, he would have done so.

In Manhattan he took up walking. When his limousine stopped at red traffic lights, he would throw open the passenger door, clasp pedestrians by the hand or envelop them in an unexpected embrace. Then he would congratulate them on their good taste in choosing to live in New York City, and extract their gratitude for saving what had until recently been the biggest-selling newspaper in America. Every morning for weeks, dressed in his trademark camel-hair coat, red bow tie and *Daily News* baseball cap, he lumbered from the Waldorf-Astoria on Park Avenue to the newspaper offices on 42nd Street, trailed by posses of television and radio journalists, rubbernecks, vagrants, hawkers, bagpeople and dog-walkers – the crowd could be anything up to three hundred – jostling and pushing and calling out questions until his daily progress along the sidewalk resembled a tickertape parade.

'Hey Bob,' they shouted, 'You staying here in New York?'

'So long as I can be of service, Bob the Max will do his duty.'

'Mr Maxwell! Whaddya going to do with the *News* when you get it?'

'My father always told me, "If you're selling a rabbit skin, never discuss it until you've caught the rabbit." '

'Bob! Howdya like New York?'

'I love New York. *I am a New Yorker*. I have already told your mayor and the governor this. I have given them an undertaking on this matter.'

'Are you going to run the paper yourself?' shouted a reporter. His sceptical tone suggested proprietorial interference would be highly unwelcome.

'You have my word on it. I am a hands-on publisher. For six months I will be there day and night. I shall put a bed there. You must not doubt me. I regard this newspaper as my pet.'

Outside the News building, a semi-permanent bivouac of television broadcasting units, satellite links and flatbed trucks had taken a position along the kerb. Union bosses and negotiators greeted one another triumphantly amidst a thicket of placards and banners: 'WELCOME BOB MAXWELL', 'NEW YORK SALUTES THE MAX', 'AMERICA WORKS BEST WHEN WE SAY UNION YES!'. The arrival of Maxwell himself on the sidewalk activated such a frenzy of flashbulbs and arc lights, that the temperature outside that chilly March morning seemed perceptibly to rise by a few degrees.

'It's amazing,' his daughter Ghislaine told me. 'Dad's never been received like this anywhere before. He's cheered on the streets. People come up to our table in restaurants and want to talk to him, and say how great he is.'

When he was taken to Fu's, the famous Cantonese restaurant on Second Avenue, by his investment banker at Rothschilds Inc, Robert Pirie, the customers at every table stood up and began clapping. Maxwell joined in the applause. He took an almost childlike delight in other people's approval. At Annual General Meetings he used to lead the applause after his own chairman's report. The events following his death have tended to obscure his bizarre, often magnetic charm. It could be enormously powerful. People who instinctively disliked everything they'd heard about him, and everything he stood for, ended up working for him, lending him money or selling him their companies. He was capable, in the short term, of mesmerising women, bankers and world leaders. In America, he set about charming a city and a continent.

'Robert Maxwell deserves New York, and New York deserves Bob Maxwell,' the new proprietor assured his journalists in his victory address. 'New Yorkers now have a publisher they can count on. I am sorry only that I have wasted so long before coming here and helping you.'

Maxwell paused to kiss a baby held out to him by its black mother. She had judged it worthwhile to travel all the way from Crown Heights with her infant, an hour's journey by subway, on the offchance of catching a glimpse of the tycoon. Then he advanced from the sidewalk into the *Daily News* lobby. It is the swankiest, most impressive newspaper lobby in the world: swankier even than the *Los Angeles Times*, the *Sydney Morning Herald* and the Bombay offices of *The Times of India*. An enormous globe is suspended at the centre of a soaring Art Deco atrium; the grey marble floor is engraved with the points of the compass and the precise distances in miles to a hundred cities: MOSCOW, 4665; JERUSALEM, 5696; ATLANTIC CITY, 102; SYDNEY, 9933; NORTH MAGNETIC POLE, 2410. No other newspaper lobby informs you so emphatically and triumphantly that it stands at the epicentre of the universe, that it is the great conduit of information and power, that its pronouncements on matters political and affairs of state are momentous and decisive. It was the *Daily News* that inspired the Metropolis lobby of Clark Kent's *Daily Planet*, and when a location was required for the *Superman* films, 42nd Street itself was appropriated. I've been assured several times that, but for the lobby, Robert Maxwell would have resisted buying the newspaper. Entrance halls are famously seductive. Estate agents claim that purchasing decisions are based, beyond any other single consideration, on the impression formed by the front entrance. Perhaps when Maxwell saw an opportunity to get the *New York Daily News*, he visualised himself bowling across the lobby – *his lobby* – in his camel-hair coat, preceded by courtiers walking backwards.

He progressed towards the elevators, preceded by newspaper executives, union convenors and security guards walking backwards, and flourished a copy of the *Daily News* for the cameramen. The photo-call over, he tossed the newspaper on to the floor, leaving it to be scooped up and smoothed and returned to the kiosk by one of his entourage. He took the elevator up to his new office, emptied already of his predecessor's possessions, the bookshelves filled instead with several hundred hardback copies of his official hagiography by Joe Haines.

There followed a maelstrom of activity that, since it was witnessed by a rota of journalists specifically invited to spectate, has achieved notoriety: Maxwell summoning the supervisor of the paper's 130-strong security staff and informing him that he was the first person to be laid off along with his entire team ('That including myself?' asked the stunned manager. 'The area managers and all the rest?' 'The lot,' replied Maxwell. 'Everybody is laid off.'); Maxwell summoning the telephone executives and bawling them out for their supposedly poor service ('Do you value your jobs, sirs? If so, how do you demonstrate that? I pay your salary and you just sit on your backsides doing nothing.'); Maxwell firing his new *Daily News* secretaries at the rate of two a week (saying of one, 'She is not a secretary, she is an experiment.'); Maxwell boasting to employees that he was 'treated like Madonna in this town'; Maxwell's photograph appearing forty different times in his own newspaper in the first three weeks of his ownership; Maxwell entertaining former Senator Howard Baker, investment banker Felix Rohatyn and CBS chairman Laurence Tisch on the *Lady Ghislaine* having insisted they all remove their shoes before coming aboard; Maxwell going to a fund-raising event at the Waldorf-Astoria in aid of *Daily News* workers out on strike for a year, shortly before agreeing a deal with the union bosses to divest several hundred more jobs.

Maxwell's decision to buy the *Daily News* always seemed foolhardy, with hindsight it was inexplicable. His sprawling, debt-ridden media empire was difficult enough to keep afloat without fresh diversions and drains on resources. At the time of its acquisition, the strike-bound *Daily News* was losing $1 million a week. His weekly newspaper the *European*, then barely a year old, was losing an estimated £500,000 a week and widely considered to be not much good. He had swallowed Macmillan and the Official Airline Guide at a combined cost of $3 billion, but had hardly begun to digest them. Over the previous 14 months, as perhaps he and he alone fully understood, he had diverted £1.7 billion from his public companies and their pension funds to cover losses, loans, acquisitions and share support schemes. If you had sat down in March 1991 and thought up the worst idea for Maxwell to get involved with, it would have been hard to beat the *New York Daily News* (except perhaps a rum plan to launch a newspaper for Russian immigrants to Israel, which he had announced only a month earlier in the ballroom of the King David hotel in Jerusalem). At the height of Maxwell's eight-week honeymoon as the toast of New York, Rupert Murdoch remarked, 'Bob doesn't know what he's taken on. He hasn't a clue what's going to hit him.' The ten *Daily News* unions were the most intransigent anywhere. Their contracts which expired in March 1990 included a clause for 36,000 hours of 'static overtime', which was code for doing nothing. 'Truck unloading' clauses required delivery trucks to leave the plant only half full, so that double as many trucks and drivers were needed. Unions required a special room to be allocated where 200 printers could play poker on full pay. Newsagents who sold the paper during the strike had their shops firebombed, and advertisers who persisted in advertising had bricks thrown through their windows. In a year there had been 1300 reported incidents including 80 injuries.

Aside from the public kick of its lobby, there were probably four separate reasons why Robert Maxwell bought the *Daily News*.

The first was simply to satiate his craving to own newspapers. In his 25 years on the acquisitions trail, there is no example of Maxwell willingly passing up a single opportunity. To be out-manoeuvred by other proprietors, as he had been with the *News of the World*, *The Times*, the *Sunday Times*, *Today* and the *Jerusalem Post*, or simply refused permission to buy, as was the case with the *Tokyo Times* and the *Melbourne Age*, made him more bitter than any other owner. He was supremely conscious of the scarcity of newspaper properties, particularly conspicuous ones in big cities. The *New York Daily News* might never change hands again in his lifetime. And he was aware that ownership carried with it an intangible bonus: public fascination. Whoever had that paper would be profiled, lionised and splashed across the front covers of news magazines, not only in New York but around the world. When Maxwell's predecessor, James Hoge of the Chicago Tribune Company, was appointed publisher, his languorous WASP good looks and determined jaw had ornamented the media for months, and he wasn't even the owner. (Indeed when the paper came back on to the market after Maxwell's death, the two potential buyers, Conrad Black and the real estate tyro Mortimer Zuckerman, were fêted and dissected like presidential candidates.) Buying the *Daily News* seemed to give Maxwell a rush like a drug addict's shot of heroin. After months of being warned by analysts that his empire was overextended, and that he'd have to divest, the publicity surrounding the acquisition invigorated and reassured him. He was Bob the Max. He had replaced Donald Trump as Manhattan's favourite tycoon. He was given standing ovations in restaurants. How could they tell him he was broke anyway, when he'd just bought the *Daily News* (he'd actually been paid $60 million by Charlie Brumback of the Chicago Tribune Company to take it off his hands – money which he promptly sucked out of the company and diverted into other enterprises) and was busy firing staff and giving celebrity interviews?

Newspapers held another great bonus, that made them more desirable than any other kind of company. They are open and alive with activity 24 hours a day. Maxwell was constantly restless, and in the small hours of the night could make an appearance at any of his papers and be certain something was going on. If you own a merchant bank or a book publishing company or a department store, the enterprise shuts down from dusk to dawn. A newspaper for Maxwell was a never-ending conduit for his insomnia and hyperactivity. In the early days of the *New York Daily News* he shuttled back and forth, often twice a night, between the Waldorf-Astoria and 42nd Street, summoning staff up to his office at 3 or 4 a.m. or else commanding them from their beds for impromptu conferences on his latest five-year-plan for circulation promotion. On the evening he bought the Mirror Group, he had himself driven straight from the midnight signing session at the Ritz to Holborn Circus, where he was asked by a security guard his business in the building. 'I've just bought it. I am the new proprietor,' he replied, as he lumbered towards the leather-lined executive lift, travelled up to the ninth floor and appropriated the chairman's office. Less than a month before he launched the *European*, he rang the paper's distinguished publisher, Robin MacKichan, one morning at 6.30 a.m. demanding he get straight into work. When MacKichan arrived he found maintenance men already dismantling his office, Maxwell having ordered them in the middle of the night to force the door with a crowbar and seized the room for himself. 'I am taking over,' he announced to the amazed night staff. 'I am a hands-on publisher and I am editor-in-chief.' At the *New York Daily News*, he perambulated along the executive corridor, turfing managers out of their offices apparently at random. 'This space,' he told them, 'is now required for an excutive dining room. You must not cross me on this. I am your publisher.'

Thirdly, newspapers afforded him instant gratification. Whilst their appearance and editorial content are questions demanding great technical skill, they are equally subjects on which anybody at all can hold a view. Maxwell believed that his proprietorial authority gave him the right to intervene in every editorial decision at whatever hour. At the *Daily Mirror*, he would call the night editor at hourly intervals to enquire what was going on around the world, and impose his own scholium on the unfolding news ('Look, mister,' he told his editor Roy Greenslade on being informed that the Russians had invaded Lithuania, 'Don't you realise that Gorbachev wouldn't do anything without ringing me first?'). He loved the physical expression of power and control that a newspaper affords: the editors' and proprietors' offices in the eye of a vortex. 'Who is the hero that came up with this?' he would ask with withering cynicism, as he snatched the proof of a news page or a headline from a sub-editor's desk. 'Which genius is responsible for this?' and then force them to change the page entirely.

Lastly, newspapers liberated him from the constraints of reason. Something about their frenzy and immediacy enabled him to suspend disbelief. It was as though, having personally intervened in the content and commanded the great presses to roll, he could not believe the public's enthusiasm might not equal his own. 'Before I bought it,' he said, 'the *Daily News* was selling just 350,000 copies a week [though it had actually been claiming a circulation of 600,000, a figure the Chicago Tribune Company still insists was correct]. But we'll get it all back,' Maxwell stormed. 'I'll be at 900,000 to one million in less than a year. And given the advertisers' responses, I'll be showing a profit in my first year. Yes. Yes.'

When I was escorted around the *Daily News* by Ghislaine Maxwell, and introduced to the paper's circulation director Donald Nizen, he shared Maxwell's optimism. 'This paper,' he told me, holding aloft that day's front page of a grisly Brooklyn murder, 'it's like cocaine. Read it once – just one time – and you're hooked for life. That's what Bob Maxwell's done for the *News*. I'm telling you, this paper, it's *addictive*.'

The hands-on publisher, dressed in a pair of light blue trousers, white shirt and a tie like a box of fireworks – yellow and blue crackles and starbursts against a tomato-red background – sat in the stateroom of the *Lady Ghislaine*. On the table in the front of him lay the remains of his breakfast: three half-empty cups of tea, a dish of pickled cucumbers, gherkins and hard-boiled eggs, two whole watermelons, a cut-glass bowl of caviar and a basket of bagels. There were three telephones and a computer printout of the *Daily News*'s top 100 advertisers. Between spoonfuls of egg and pickled cucumber, Maxwell worked his way down the list.

'Hello,' he boomed into the receiver. 'To whom am I speaking? Good . . . This is Bob the Max calling on behalf of the *News* . . . You have heard of me? Good . . . I thank you . . . I am pleased to be of service. You have heard my new slogan FORWARD WITH NEW YORK! That is Bob the Max's slogan. Let us go forwards together. We at the *News* live by our advertisers. May I count on you? . . . Good . . . You will say yes in principle to returning?'

As each conversation ended, the next was already holding on the other line. He moved from one receiver to the next without missing a beat, ignorant of which company he was speaking to until he was well into his spiel. 'May I count on you?' he asked. 'May I take it that the great . . .' he glanced stealthily at the printout, 'the great Macy's Department Store will return to the *Daily News*? Good . . . Good . . . You will not regret backing the Max.'

For four hours the sales calls to advertisers proceeded without a break. He had spoken to the presidents of 75 businesses. His pleasure seemed to derive mostly from the ease with which his calls were put through, an endorsement of his overnight New York celebrity. He had asked each advertiser whether they had heard of him, and they all had.

Fame for Maxwell was a corporeal necessity. His own newspapers could partly sate his hunger for favourable publicity, but the notoriety that comes with ownership also helped satisfy his craving to be the centre of attention, albeit hostile. At meetings, it pained him physically if anybody else held an opinion not merely different from his own, but held one at all. In restaurants if he disliked the way a table was set, he would sweep the plates and cutlery on to the floor. When checking out of an hotel, it angered him so greatly if anybody was ahead of him at the cashier's desk, he would simply elbow the other guests out of the way and refuse to budge until his bill was dealt with. When people came to Headington Hill Hall, Maxwell arranged that the best cuts of meat were reserved for himself. A young stockbroker recalls being invited to lunch there before an Oxford United football match, one of the clubs of which Maxwell was chairman. The main course was roast chicken and as a large platter was circulated by a maid for the dozen guests to help themselves, he happened to notice that there was only leg and wing, but no breast which was his favourite part of the bird. At that moment the kitchen door opened and a second maid appeared carrying the host's own lunch: a plate piled with the breasts of three whole chickens, skewered by a pickled gherkin on a cocktail stick.

Maxwell relished his notoriety – his larger-than-life personality, as he saw it – to a quite abnormal extent. Although quick to sue the authors of unflattering profiles of him, the stairwell and passages at Headington were hung with several hundred framed cartoons of the tycoon, all vituperative. Public figures frequently buy cartoons and caricatures of themselves, including mildly abrasive ones to show they can take a joke, but the Maxwell cartoons depicted him as a monster and an egomaniac: Maxwell as Rambo brandishing a Kalashnikov, Maxwell as the Devil with a forked tail, Maxwell inflicting himself on the Queen to her obvious displeasure, Maxwell gloating as he made Scottish printworkers and Pergamon Press employees redundant. You wondered, as you looked at them, what kind of man put these reproachful cartoons into frames rather than into the bin.

He relished his reputation as a remorseless businessman. 'I am firm but fair,' was one of his favourite maxims, though he did not necessarily expect to be believed. He once told Joe Haines that 'Everyone who works for me has total job security'. Haines, astonished by the scale of self-deception, pointed out that Maxwell was in fact always sacking people. 'Yes,' replied Maxwell, 'but they are ex-employees and as such have no security at all.' Another maxim was 'Remember, if you want instant injustice, call me.' As a negotiator, his technique altered as he grew older. In his prime he would strike a deal, shake hands on it, announce it publicly to the press and only then begin the genuine negotiation, chipping and chiselling every clause in the contract until the price had been reduced by twenty per cent. By the time he bought the *Daily News*, his technique had become a question of form over content. He loved assigning the different parties in a dispute – the managers, newspaper guilds, Allied Printing Trades

Council – to adjoining suites, and himself moving from one to another like a United Nations envoy, while keeping the nation abreast of progress through television sound bites from the hotel lobby or the deck of his yacht. For Maxwell, the thrill of the deal increasingly became an end in itself, just as his splashy pledges to charity seem to have been made solely so they could be reported: his $10-million much-publicised pledge to New York's Polytechnic University, the $50-million promise, apparently made on the spur of the moment at a state lunch to honour Soviet President Mikhail Gorbachev, to create a Gorbachev Maxwell Institute in Minneapolis to study communications and the global environment, the $1 million he committed to solve racial tension between black, Hispanic, Vietnamese and Puerto Rican families in Queens. None of these promises were honoured; nor, it would seem, were they ever seriously intended to be.

As it happened, Maxwell's publicly negotiated tough deal to save the *Daily News* was less exacting than he wished the world to believe. He won concessions from the ten unions that the Chicago Tribune Company never achieved (the workforce would be cut by more than a third to 1800, bringing savings of $73 million a year) but when Mortimer Zuckerman and Conrad Black opened their own negotiations a year later after Maxwell's death, Zuckerman demanded and got another six hundred men bumped off the payroll. Even then Black believed Zuckerman had been too soft. '[Mort] will be dealing with the absolute bottom of the barrel, the riffraff of the New York newspaper union movement,' he told the Toronto *Globe and Mail*. 'He will be on his knees every day before the head of the pressmen's union and drivers' union to get his paper printed and delivered.'

You can make a case that it was the *Daily News* that scuttled Maxwell; that, without the distraction, he might somehow have steadied the empire, met the next debt repayment and won through like Rupert Murdoch. As the New York tabloid haemorrhaged a million dollars a week, the sums Maxwell wired to the Chase Manhattan account of Maxwell Newspapers Inc, owners of the *Daily News*, became astronomical, and these were augmented by further huge sums to the *European* and his host of loss-making boutique newspapers in Kenya and Eastern Europe.

Small wonder, after six months indulgence in New York in the most expensive hobby in the world, Robert Maxwell felt ready for the cruise around Gran Canaria.

Dining with the Hyenas

Lord Rothermere and his great British Empire

'If things get dicey Vere becomes a compulsive eater and he really balloons in weight,' said Sir David English, Lord Rothermere's great editorial panjandrum. 'When the *Mail on Sunday* was clearly going to be a disaster, even before it had come out, I was summoned to go and see him in New York. We met for breakfast in the dining room of the Carlyle hotel. They have a sort of serve-yourself breakfast, so we started with melon or something and then we had eggs. Vere ate three cooked breakfasts and was still eating them when they brought coffee at eleven o'clock, and then at twelve o'clock we had drinks, and then we had lunch. And I never got out of that dining room all day long, because then we had some tea and moved straight on to dinner, and all the time Vere was agonising, "What should we *do* about this newspaper? What should we do?" In the end I was made quite ill by not being able to leave that room. He had appointed Bernard Shrimsley as editor, but like most proprietors he's quite clever at protecting his own position. Shrimsley had introduced him to the staff and after that Vere had definitely decided that the *Mail on Sunday* was going to be a disaster because they were all grey men and grey women like Shrimsley. He told me that I had to be editor-in-chief and that I should go back and fire Shrimsley, which I absolutely refused to do because there were only five weeks to go before the launch and it wouldn't look good and, secondly, what would be the point if Shrimsley's grey men and grey women were still there? I couldn't get rid of a hundred journalists and replace them all in just five weeks. Nowadays, of course, Vere can and does say, "I urged English to fire Shrimsley, I told him to in the Carlyle hotel, but he wouldn't do it. English went weak on me at the crucial moment." It's quite untrue, of course, but at least when the *Mail on Sunday* began to turn around he stopped eating his 20 meals a day.'

Stories about Vere Rothermere are invariably set in similar locations; either grand ones – hotels in Manhattan, Paris or Vienna – or else vaguely sybaritic, a yacht off the South of France, a villa in Jamaica, a hot tub in Kyoto. The crucial meeting, anticipating the failure of his new Sunday newspaper, takes place not in a boardroom, or even in an office, but at the Carlyle, the hotel closest to his Fifth Avenue apartment. It is characteristic of Rothermere too that he had previously arranged to meet the entire staff of his new venture, and intuitively detected, between pleasantries, a dearth of talent. And characteristic to ascribe so much importance to the editorial voice of the newspaper. Sensing a miss-launch, he agonises over a 16-hour marathon breakfast not with the board or the marketing department but with his most trusted editor.

He's the last of the proper English press lords: that is what people tell you first about Vere Rothermere. And then they invoke a whole list of names – some members of his family, some not, some not even English – as prototypes of proper English press barons: Northcliffe, Beaverbrook, Harmsworth, Astor. Murdoch, they remind you, is Australian-turned-American, Maxwell was Czech, Black is Canadian; only Vere Rothermere was brought up here, an Englishman, an Old Etonian, a baron with a hereditary peerage, raised to inherit proper English newspapers. If you point out that Rothermere was partly brought up in America, is the grandson of a man once urged to accept the Hungarian crown of St Stephen, spends much of the year in Paris and Kyoto in Japan and hasn't, for tax reasons, spent more than 90 days a year in Britain since the seventies, they reply, surprised and indignant, 'Well, I saw him here only the other day.' From the number of sightings of Lord Rothermere you would think he lived in Britain 365 days a year. People told me they had spotted him the previous afternoon, staring into shop windows in Kensington High Street, close to the Associated Newspapers headquarters. Or they had run into him in Scotland, or he was lunching at the Savoy Grill with his financial advisor Sir Patrick Sergeant, or they'd travelled four floors with him in the tubular glass office lift.

It was an illusion I'd noticed with other newspaper proprietors too: an erroneous illusion of omnipresence. Perhaps because their visits to their newspapers are so disproportionately anticipated, and afterwards so much discussed and chewed over, a three-day inspection feels like a fortnight, a casual conversation on the escalator a full-blown encounter.

The third Viscount Rothermere is outwardly the most conventional British press lord, but inwardly the most complex. He is probably the only one who devotes any time to introspection. For all his superbly tailored suits, Rothermere is an original thinker and amateur poet, interested in Zen Buddhism and the paranormal, a reader of runes who describes himself as 'a student of human nature' which seems to mean connoisseur of human foibles.

He is the grandest proprietor to look at; tall, nobly built, with sleek grey hair. At 69 he strangely resembles Babar the elephant, the King of Celesteville. He has the aristocrat's affectation of pretending, from time to time, to be hard of hearing, so compelling his visitors to repeat their remarks. He walks, as very many rich people do, in a slightly swaying way as though he has just stepped back on to dry land from a large yacht. He has elaborate and courteous good manners, especially at doorways and in lifts where he is pressingly insistent that others should make their way first. Once asked which social class he reckoned he belonged to, he answered unhesitatingly 'nobleman'. And yet he is often diffident, and his willingness to initiate long silences unnerves both friends and colleagues. Editors speak of being called up to his office and received with such awkwardness that whatever it was he wished to tell them is left unsaid. Or else he will ring them from the house in Japan and the silences between sentences are so long that they wonder whether they've been cut off.

The writer and hostess Sonia Sinclair, who is a godmother to Rothermere's son Jonathan Harmsworth, told me, 'I think Vere's quite shy still, a mixture of shyness and laziness – he wants to be entertained. He likes people who bubble away. He doesn't usually instigate conversation, and from that point of view he's lazy. But he's got a great curiosity about ideas and people. It just requires a bit of digging away.'

And yet, unusually for a proprietor, he loves parties. Most owners are too tired. Vere Rothermere has so arranged his life that he seldom appears worn out by work. 'He's very much a nightbird,' says Sonia Sinclair. 'He adores eating rather late and then going on somewhere.

He loves dancing. If there's a party going he'll be there, but late. He'll turn up at a cocktail party at nine o'clock, just when people are leaving, and say, "Where are we going on to now?" '

The languor is deceptive. Rothermere never neglects his newspapers. When he travels, he rings his office three or four times a day and is uncannily good at gauging the internal machinations by osmosis. He once justified – explained – his long holidays as the opportunity for long-term planning. He has an almost Japanese fondness for strategy, though his concept of strategy has more to do with cunning, and predicting what his competitors might do, than research-led analysis. He enjoys the idea of stalking a newspaper, in the way that he assiduously stalked the London *Evening Standard* before wholly acquiring it in 1987. When he talks about his newspapers now, he likes to emphasise strategy. To his editors – particularly Sir David English, now the Chairman of Associated Newspapers and group editor-in-chief – he will deflect all editorial credit. But credit for the grand plan he accepts for himself.

And he is clear in his own mind about his achievements as a proprietor.

'When you look back on it,' he said – and I felt that he looks back on it fairly often – 'in 1970 we had two ailing papers [the *Daily Mail* and the *Evening News*] and the *Express* had three successful ones [the *Daily Express, Sunday Express* and *Evening Standard*]. But by 1983 *we* had three successful papers and *they* had two unsuccessful ones.' Lord Rothermere dissolved into loud gusts of mirth. 'Such is Fleet Street!' he said amidst more gales of triumphant laughter. 'And so now we have what we *ought* to have which is *three.*'

'Is three the ideal number?'

'Yes, what you *need*,' he said, as though he were advising a novice on the kit for some new hobby, 'is a morning, an afternoon and a Sunday newspaper. This allows a degree of efficiency. Ours are all the market leaders now. So in a way we've even outdone Lord Beaverbrook, because the *Evening Standard* wasn't market leader when he was alive. *But it is now.*' And then he convulsed again with patrician glee.

In addition to his three national papers, Rothermere's provincial subsidiary, Northcliffe Newspapers, is dominant in 23 areas of Britain, geographically more disparate than Lord Stevens's papers and particularly strong in Gloucestershire, Kent, Cornwall, Lincolnshire and South Wales. The *Western Morning News* is a Rothermere, so is the *Torquay Herald Express*, the *Hull Daily Mail* and the *South Wales Evening Post*. If they have anything in common it is only their strong empathy, like the flagship *Daily Mail*, with an aspirational British middle class and an emphasis on family values. The value of the Rothermere family's newspaper interests is estimated at £280 million, though media analysts reckon the value of the papers if sold outright would exceed one billion.

Of his provincial papers he says, 'They are probably now the most efficient chain of provincial newspapers in this country . . . I might say the world but that would be rather, er, boastful.'

He has also joined the proprietorial goldrush into Eastern Europe by buying the sixth largest daily newspaper in Hungary (circulation 93,000) in Gyor-Sopron. This, he emphasises, is a strictly commercial venture and nothing to do with his latent family claim to the Hungarian crown which he is not pressing.

But it is his British national papers – the family silver – that Vere Rothermere minds about the most. Especially in his nascent years as proprietor, before the papers were secure and were haemorrhaging money and in imminent danger of extinction, he strove for them, fretting over the figures late into the night.

'There were very anxious days at the *Daily Mail*,' says English, 'and we were working extremely long hours – eight in the morning until one or two the next morning. You either slept in the office or went to the nearest hotel. This was in the early days after the *Daily Mail* went tabloid, and the circulation went down and down for two years – it was like a nose-dive – before we pulled it up. I used to go and talk to Vere in his office, for a cup of tea or something at about one in the morning. He'd often still be there, poring over figures, seeing where money could be found to promote the paper and so on. One evening Pat [the party-loving first Lady Rothermere, who died in August 1992] rang him up and there was a sort of exchange over the phone which was fairly sharp – why he wasn't home. And I will never forget it because the office was completely shaded, it was almost like a scene from a movie, and Vere had been working with one of those green-topped desk lamps; the lamp was shining down on to his papers, which obviously did not have good news in them, judging by the amount of red ink in the figures and the look on his face. He said wearily, "One of my problems is with Pat because of the long hours I'm working. She wants me to be home for dinner or to take her out to a nightclub or the theatre." So I said, "Yes, but that's the same for all of us, we all work long hours. Pat must put up with it the same as every newspaper wife because we're fighting for our existence." And Vere replied, "Ah yes, but there's an amazing difference you see. I don't *have* to do it, not financially. I have to do it for my family pride and for my enormous interest in the newspapers. I *want* to do it but I don't *have* to do it. *You* have to do it because you haven't got any money! And that makes a big difference with your wife because she knows you're doing it to be successful, to make money, to do things for your children, to advance yourselves. I don't have to advance myself. If I gave up tomorrow and went to live in Jamaica it wouldn't make the slightest difference to me financially and Pat can't understand why I have to do it. She thinks I've lost interest in her or have got a beautiful secretary, she doesn't understand that it's the biggest thing in my life to succeed."

'Now that was very revealing,' said English. 'And on another occasion, at a period of bleakness, he said, "It's going to be terrible if we fail. We'll all be down, we'll all feel awful with a newspaper dying under us, but you've proved that you're a good newspaper man, David, and you'll get another job and will go on to other things. But if I go down I will be the man who lost the Harmsworth touch, I'll have lost the inheritance, there'll be nothing for me to do but to lie on the beach. I can't go and get a job as a newspaper manager somewhere else. I shall *have* to go to Jamaica and live in the sun which is the last thing I want to do." '

Vere Rothermere's office, overlooking the soaring central atrium of the Associated Newspapers headquarters in Kensington, reminded me of the state cabin on a thirties ocean-going liner. Its location on the penthouse floor means the view from his window is practically featureless, just a hazy white shimmer from the atrium skylight that makes you think of the sea. And the furniture and paintings too – the mahogany desk, box of cigars, the modernist painting of a flight of geese by the Canadian artist Claude Simard – have a nautical aspect to them. One of Rothermere's favourite analogies for himself is as

Arthur Ochs Sulzberger Snr ('Punch'), Chairman of the New York Times Company, and his wife Carol at a New York benefit supporting the Blind Aids programme at the Plaza Hotel. Asked which newspaper in the world they'd most like to own, more rival proprietors named the *New York Times* than any other.

The Inheritors. Arthur Ochs Sulzberger Jnr ('Pinch'), the driven young Publisher of the *New York Times*, at a Leadership dinner with *Times* colleagues. When he succeeded his father, the old, jocular gladhanding regime seemed to give way to the new generation number-cruncher. Left, Donald Graham of the *Washington Post* – 'the best prepared publisher in North America' – with his wife Mary and daughter Laura.

Katharine Graham – Chairman of the Board of the *Washington Post* – with granddaughters at her 70th birthday party. Complex, frequently generous, occasionally somewhat callous, liberal-minded and bottom-line motivated, she has become the most famous female proprietor on the planet.

Otis Chandler of the *Los Angeles Times* with his ex-wife Bettina. Six foot two inches high, his face nut brown from the sun and slightly fissured like an old pirate treasure map, his quiff of straw-coloured hair and languorous blue eyes make him, at the age of 64, resemble a benevolent farm scarecrow.

Off-the-peg proprietors. Dean Singleton, the Lone Star predator of Houston, Texas, and some of his 71 newspapers. Right, Ralph Ingersoll, the New England tactician who snapped up 240 papers on a $1.5 billion shopping spree. Singleton and Ingersoll altered the rules of American proprietorship forever.

The little empire on the prairie. James Kennedy heads up Cox Enterprises in Atlanta – flagship the *Atlanta Journal* and *Constitution* – and dominates the corner-shop press of Ohio, Colorado and Arizona. His billionaire aunt Anne Cox Chambers, left, owns the empire with her sister, Barbara Cox Anthony.

The Prodigal Son. Warwick Fairfax, the 26-year-old who bushwhacked his family newspaper empire in an audacious $2 billion coup, pictured in his corner office during his brief tenure as Chairman. Within four years the rivers of gold – as the *Sydney Morning Herald* and *Melbourne Age* are known for their classified advertising revenue – had been diverted to Conrad Black.

The Great Newspaper Bazaar. Three Indian
dynasties dominate the largest developed newspaper
market in the Third World, with the prestige of
Hearst and Northcliffe in the Twenties and Thirties.
Ramnath Goenka, founder and proprietor of the
Indian Express, toppled the regimes of both Indira
Gandhi and her son Rajiv in the course of a two-
decade-long feud, conducted from his enormous
lime-green penthouse in Bombay. In his final years,
only his gasping for air and the occasional clutching
of his fingers at the sleeve of his homespun khadi
were proof that Goenka was alive at all.

Aveek Sarkar, photographed
at home in Calcutta, is the
most significant owner
between Bangalore and
Bangkok. His opinions on
restaurants, hotels,
international fashion,
tailoring and journalism are
highly idiosyncratic and
discriminating. Right, Samir
Jain of the *Times of India*
introduced American
corporate strategy to Delhi.
He believes that had the
ancient Egyptians established
a Japanese marketing
department they would have
developed the sand clock
more rapidly.

Bob the Max takes Manhattan. Robert Maxwell revels in his new proprietorship of the *New York Daily News* by selling copies at the lobby kiosk. For six glorious weeks he was applauded by strangers in the street, and given standing ovations in Chinese restaurants. Right, he arrives at a charity benefit with his wife Betty and son Kevin. Newspapers held a great bonus for a restless insomniac like Maxwell. In the small hours of the night he could make an appearance at any of his thirteen papers and be certain something was going on.

'The last of the proper English press lords, raised to inherit proper English newspapers'. Vere Rothermere, far left, arrives at Claridges with his first wife Patricia for a ball given by the Queen. Lady Rothermere, who urged him to claim his birthright, died at her villa on Cap d'Ail in 1992. Left, Lord Rothermere with his Korean fiancée Maiko Lee, to whom he became engaged in October 1993, and with whom he had for sixteen years shared his life in Paris and Kyoto.

'Let us be completely frank, the deferences and preferments that this culture bestows upon the owners of great newspapers is satisfying.' Conrad Black of the *Daily Telegraph* and his wife Barbara Amiel, the Murdoch columnist, photographed at a Booker Prize dinner. In eight years Black has muscled his way from the third division of owners into the second and finally up into the first.

'My rival publishers must wake up at night and ask "How does that chap Stevens make *six times* what I'm making out of my national newspapers?".' Lord Stevens of the *Daily Express* and his wife Meriza at the Grosvenor House Antiques Fair. He reminded me of some species of wild animal – an ibis amidst a herd of blackbuck – that is virtually indistinguishable as an interloper except to other members of the herd.

Robert Hersant of *Le Figaro* and 23 regional newspapers from Normandy to Lyons, has made a decisive impact on the mindset of bourgeois France. His newspaper group is so obsessively private that it is startling it can bring itself to anything so public as to publish newspapers.

'I'm a newspaper owner by accident really, aren't I?' That the Aga Khan, 49th Imam of the Shia Imami Ismaili Moslems, has a newspaper empire at all is very little known. His Kenyan papers competed with Robert Maxwell and are the largest-selling free-press in black Africa. He is photographed arriving at Claridges for dinner with the Queen with his wife, the Begum Aga Khan.

Hong Kong's media mandarins. Ma Sik-chun of the *Oriental Daily News*, the biggest circulation paper in the colony, arriving handcuffed at court after a drugs rap. Below left, the Tiger Balm heiress Sally Aw Sian publishes her Chinese daily, *Sing Tao*, in six countries. Below right, Louis Cha of *Ming Pao* is Sally Aw Sian's rival for the Chinese middle-market.

'What Kamphol wishes in Bangkok, happens'. Kamphol Vacharaphol, owner of *Thai Rath*, is the most powerful proprietor in South East Asia. His regular uniform consists of dark glasses, white silk shirt, pointed white shoes, gold medallion and a topaz and diamond ring. At the office he wears a crocodile skin belt with personalised buckle, the letter K encrusted with diamonds.

Tony O'Reilly, Chairman of H J Heinz and
newspaper tycoon, with his new wife Chryss
Goulandris, the shipping heiress. O'Reilly is the
highest paid executive in North America, and as a
sideline has assembled an aggressive second league
empire of 47 newspapers across two continents. He
controls most of the Irish press and the east coast
of Australia. But when he competed with Conrad
Black for Fairfax, he lost.

Rupert Murdoch with his wife Anna and younger daughter Elisabeth arriving for the wedding of Kerry Packer's daughter, Gretel. Murdoch operates newspapers across more continents than any other proprietor, and owns more world-class titles including *The Times* and *Sunday Times* in London, *The Australian* and the *South China Morning Post*. Conrad Black and Lord Thomson control more papers, but Murdoch's combined circulation of 60 million a week is far greater.

The shredding of paper tigers, who lost 36
newspapers between them in three years. Warwick
Fairfax, above, leaves the Fairfax building in Sydney
for the last time, pursued by some of his former
staff. One of his last acts was to apply for a vacancy
as a junior news reporter on the *Sydney Morning
Herald*. Asil Nadir, top right, after being released on
bail from Wormwood Scrubs prison. 'To build a
castle,' he had said, 'you need two towers: banks
and newspapers.' But he was unable to retain any of
his sixteen titles. Below right, Robert Maxwell
contemplating his choppy future on board the *Lady
Ghislaine*.

Rather like one's first sight of the Taj Mahal, there
is a slight feeling of disappointment on first seeing
Rupert Murdoch that he isn't bigger. At 61, his
height is just below average and the deep furrows
across his brow are as pronounced and regular as
the backbone of a large pike. His left eye narrows
darkly when he concentrates, like a gunslinger in an
early Fox western.

Admiral of the Fleet. 'We have all these ships of the line, frigates and whatnot, sailing all over the place,' he declared of his own relationship with his newspapers, 'and the Admiral doesn't tell any individual captain how to sail his ship, but he does tell him in which direction he should head.'

At close quarters one is acutely aware of his great height and build. In a grey chalk-stripe suit and brown suede shoes, he looked like an English duke setting off for Sunday church, except that the salt and pepper silk tie was a shade too prosperous for the English countryside. It was the classic tycoon tie: the kind worn by Lord Hanson and Lord Weinstock at their AGMs.

I asked him, 'What does it actually feel like to own a newspaper, since not very many people do?'

And Vere Rothermere laughed – guffawed – with heaving shoulders. 'I couldn't honestly tell you,' he replied, 'because I don't actually know what it feels like *not* to own a newspaper.'

I had seen this side of Rothermere – the benign patrician with a sense of the absurd – once before, at a birthday party for his daughter Geraldine shortly after one of his great newspaper victories. The circumstances were these. Robert Maxwell had launched a new London evening newspaper, the *London Daily News*, in competition with Rothermere's monopoly *Evening Standard*. 'We'll see who has the deepest pockets,' Maxwell had boasted.

On the day of Maxwell's launch, Rothermere did a very clever thing. He brought back from the dead his other old evening paper, the *Evening News*, which he'd folded a couple of years earlier, and turned the fight into a three-cornered one. The revived *Evening News* was very bad, thin and scrappy but he priced it cheap – half the price of the other two evening papers, forcing Maxwell to reduce the price of his paper too. And the presence of two new papers confused the public. They couldn't remember which was Maxwell's new paper – the one being heavily advertised on television – and many bought the *Evening News* by mistake. Most stuck with their familiar *Evening Standard*, and within a year Maxwell had dug into his pockets quite deeply enough (which meant £50 million lost).

Two days after Maxwell's defeat I came across Rothermere. He was sitting on top of a pile of coats on a spare room bed, while his daughter's party went on next door. Finding him alone, I'd thought I had better say something while I searched for my coat. So I congratulated him on his victory over the *London Daily News*.

Rothermere had rocked with laughter.

'I thought up my strategy in the bath,' he told this stranger looking through the coats. 'I was in a hot tub in Japan and it came to me. I rang the office from the bath and told them "We're bringing back the *Evening News*". I don't believe they thought much of the idea at first, but eventually you know they allowed me to have my way.'

When I interviewed him in his office I asked, 'When you next saw Robert Maxwell after the evening newspaper war, what was his reaction?'

'Well I didn't see him for some time.' Laughter. 'Then I bumped into him at the Chelsea Flower Show actually. He was full of jovial threats. Lots of jovial threats. I like his wife very much, she's a charming lady, and she rather enjoyed it all too.'

'Is it easy supervising circulation wars so far from the battlefield?'

'Well there are telephones, and faxes. I speak to the editors, not every day, about once or twice a week. I get the papers delivered of course every morning in Paris, though in America it's a little more difficult, they come over to the New York office and they send me a selection to my apartment. Otherwise I get them couriered out, and they get there eventually you know. I also have a digest of the papers sent to me every day by fax. I specify what I want. We have a chap here who does this every day. He knows what I want to know because I've briefed him, and he takes his own initiative sometimes, gets in things that are exceedingly interesting to me. In fact so good is it, that whereas the only person who had the digest originally was me, now all these people – this great list of managers – get it too.' Rothermere chortled wryly at the me-too keenness of his management. 'Because if you *don't* have it you don't know what the chairman is going to spring on you suddenly.'

'When your *Daily Mail* finally arrives, when you're in Kyoto for instance, which bit do you turn to first?'

'I read it as it comes, from the front page to the back page, cover to cover. I'm told that other people don't, they start at the back. That's what I've been told. But I choose to start at the beginning and work my way through to the end.'

'Right through to the sport?'

'I'm not a particularly sporting person, but I do look at it always.'

'And the puzzles?'

'Oh the puzzles I never understand!' Loud laughter.

Lord Rothermere was consistently in London during the historic month when the *Daily Mail*'s circulation finally overtook its lifelong rival the *Daily Express*.

'It was 1988, wasn't it, the end of '88? The breakthrough happened over several days, like this.' Vere Rothermere moved his hands up and down seismographically, his left hand – the *Mail* – remorselessly gaining on his right – the *Express*. 'For several days we overtook them, then fell back, and then it happened more and more frequently and then it happened all the time. We all had celebrations, several celebrations, some in the office and a private dinner party at the Ecu de France for our senior people. Yes that was a great achievement.'

'What is your method for choosing an editor?'

'Well you know I haven't really chosen all that many,' replied Rothermere. This is true: Lord Rothermere's editors, with the exception of the launch editor of the *Mail on Sunday*, have exceptionally long tenures.

'But it goes without saying that you're looking for talent, you really are looking for that. And you're looking for a man who combines a lot of different talents. First of all he has to know how to produce a newspaper, he has to understand typography, he has to be creative, he has to be able to write. Because editing goes along with the recruiting of writers, a good editor has be able to create his own writers. He has also to manage a department and give leadership to his staff – and charismatic editors do this – to get the best out of his people. And he has to combine not only enormous skills but also have a lot of art. And he has of course to be in tune, or be able to get himself in tune, with the readership he's addressing. Now these are very difficult things to get. Some of them you can ascertain beforehand, find out if he has any knowledge of type, but the other matters you really can't tell until the man has the responsibility. Because you see in this business people have a sort of literary persona, which is distinct from their everyday persona. It comes through not only in the articles they write themselves, but it comes through into the whole newspaper. This is very important because it's the charm, and you can't know whether somebody has this ability until they're actually doing the job.

Sometimes you'll find this able and intelligent and charming man, but what he produces is something that's entirely lacking in charm. So it's totally unknown, it's a guess, you have to wait and see.'

'And presumably if you choose the wrong person you've got to change them pretty quickly.'

'Oh yes. It's far too important a job to be sentimental over it.'

'I keep being told you are an eccentric owner, because you like journalists.'

'Like keeping a hyena as a pet you mean!' Much noisy, high-pitched, hyena-like laughter. But then he added in a no-seriously-now voice, 'No, I do quite like journalists you know, I actually don't think they're all hyenas by any means! Seriously, a cross-section of them can be very talented, clever and amusing people,' he added with great sincerity, as though half expecting to be contradicted.

'Do you ever invite them to dinner at your house, or only entertain them on neutral ground at the Savoy Grill?'

'I don't have a house in London now,' replied Rothermere. 'But if I did I probably *would* invite some of them to dinner. I have done in the past. When they come to New York I do invite them to come and have dinner. I haven't got a dining room at home in Paris at the moment, because I've only got a small flat.' More laughter, full of implicit relief that the smallness of his Paris flat excused him from having to dine with hyenas.

'Your papers have a reputation, you know, for office politics. The corporate culture seems to encourage in-fighting; several people being given more or less the same brief, to see who rises to the top of the pile.'

Vere Rothermere nodded sagely. He looked profoundly relaxed. Whatever creative tension was engendered on the editorial floor did not extend to the chairman's suite.

'I think that's the mark of a good editor you know,' he said, 'keeping people motivated and on their toes. Any highly successful newspaper needs that vital ingredient. And of course that was one of the features of Beaverbrook's old *Daily Express*.'

'Do you see yourself in the Beaverbrook mould?'

'An old style proprietor, you mean? Perhaps. But the proprietors today are still pretty colourful aren't they? Rupert's pretty colourful. Robert Maxwell was colourful and patriotic, you have to allow him that.'

'Do you regard yourself as colourful?'

'Oh no, very drab.' Loud laughter.

And then he went on, 'It's part of the excitement you know, this competitiveness, being the fellow who gets the story everyone wants to read. After all it's probably the greatest fun in the world being in newspapers, better than the film industry certainly.'

'Why the film industry particularly?'

'Have you ever taken part in a film?' asked Vere Rothermere. 'I found it *frightfully boring*, the way they do the same thing over and over again. I'm not saying it would be so boring if you were participants, if you happened to be the director, or the people who act in it, or the cameraman doing it again and again to get that extra bit – *that extra bit* – that's fun. But if you're sort of watching it, an assistant stage-hand or something, God it's unbelievable, the same thing over and over and over again. At a newspaper there's always *something new* happening and you don't have to do the same thing over and over again. I don't think many people do that in newspapers, the same old thing. Not that I'm aware of. Perhaps they have to go away and rewrite their stuff many times if the editor doesn't like it, but repetition isn't really part of it.'

'Does that happen often on newspapers?' he enquired suddenly. 'Journalists rewriting their stuff over and over again, I mean?'

I replied that it varied from place to place, depending on the quality of the journalists and whether the editor was a martinet.

'Does it indeed!' he exclaimed. 'But you'd find it's still better than the film industry.'

For several months members of his staff had assured me that Lord Rothermere had converted to Buddhism. And yet when you asked them how they knew, they shrugged, they had never questioned him about it. So much in the culture of Associated Newspapers – the emphasis on winning, the institutionalised anxiety – is so absolutely alien to the precepts of Buddhism that I rather hoped it was true.

'I wouldn't say I'm a *practising* Buddhist – not exactly,' he replied, 'but I do find it very attractive. I've read books about it, and looked into it, and there's actually a lot in it you know. I find the *principles* of Buddhism enormously attractive, soothing if you like, they have a lot of ideas, ways of looking at things that ring some kind of bell with me, are very satisfying. I don't know when I first became a Buddhist – interested in Buddhism. All my life I think.'

'Were you a Buddhist at Eton?'

'I believe so. Even before that I think. All my life. After all I only went to the East for the first time ten years ago, and I was interested in Buddhism long, long before that. I certainly wasn't a Christian at Eton. College Chapel did its best to put you off religion I'd say. Christianity winds you up inside yourself you know, into a frenzy, but Buddhism has the opposite effect. Christianity is obsessed with sex, it's a sort of fixation, but Buddhism by removing the puritanism, the agitation, means that you don't have that internal frenzy. Guilt for Christians is a sort of aphrodisiac, the more guilty they become the better they like it. Buddhism by contrast helps keep sex in its proper place, you know they really don't bother about it one way or the other, they don't get into a frenzy about passions of the flesh. A Buddhist monk of course is not allowed to eat meat, he only eats vegetables and fruit. He does not indulge in passions of the flesh. But nor does he get himself into a state of hellfire about it if he does. I'll probably now have half the Buddhists in Britain write to me, saying I've got it all wrong you know, but that's how I understand it anyway.'

'As a Buddhist, do you expect to come back in your next life as someone else, a printer say or a reporter on the sports desk?'

'Oh good lord,' chuckled Rothermere, 'who knows if one's reincarnated or not? I daresay if there is such a thing one won't have much say in the matter. Others will decide that for one, if there *is* someone to decide. Perhaps, who knows,' he added with the optimism of the habitually fortunate, 'one might come back in more or less the same kind of position the next time around.'

Rothermere was born in 1925, the youngest of three children, the only son and consequently heir. After his parents divorced rather acrimoniously when he was five, he was subjected to a good deal of to-ing and fro-ing between his mother's house in Dorset, his father's press-baronial London home, Warwick House, and a suite in Claridges. He retains an affection for this hotel, and often puts up there when he's in London.

At Eton, according to a contemporary who now works for him, 'Vere was rather an obscure Etonian, hardly anyone knew him.' Those that did, see little resemblance between the shadowy schoolboy and the press lord. 'I was at prep school with him, I was at Eton with him, I was almost in the army with him and he was the dimmest man I ever met,' claims a Scottish grandee contemporary. 'But when I run into him now, he seems like a different person altogether.'

'I was always hard pressed to pass my trials [end-of-term exams],' remembers Rothermere. 'Although after I went to America [he spent a year at Kent School, Connecticut] I found the work much easier. American education is vastly superior to Eton education, though that's a bit unfair since all the Eton beaks [masters] were away in the army during my time and the only people left behind to teach us were either old or unfit. When I was there the teaching was all very late 19th-century in style, around 1880 I'd say. So the American education I got was a revelation of what education could be, absolutely transformed my whole life.'

University being considered too high a goal, he did national service but failed his commission and like Punch Sulzberger joined the ranks. He spent four years, unpromoted, as a private soldier, some of it serving in the Middle East. He says now that he is grateful not to have been an officer, because it was useful market research. 'I found it extremely helpful in understanding the true nature of society,' he told me. 'I think it gave me quite an idea about what the real world is really like for the majority of people.'

Later he would introduce circulation-building promotions into his newspapers to 'Win a Pub', confident from his days in the ranks that pub ownership is the aspiration of every non-commissioned Englishman.

Home from the army, he sought a role. His predicament, it was generally agreed, was awkward. No suitable job suggested itself in the family newspaper empire. As the proprietor's son he could not be given a menial job, and yet he was insufficiently experienced to do anything useful. Instead he was sent away on a series of long holidays – to the Bahamas, Mexico, Costa Rica – or kicked his heels at Warwick House.

'It was sort of generally assumed that I would one day inherit the mantle,' he says, 'and there was always a good deal going on at home, politics and everything else you know, the house was always full of interesting people. But not much discussion of newspaper editorial or editors. A lot of talk about *management*, the problems of management. But I'm not sure that anyone really knew the answers. Do they *now*?' Loud, ironic laughter from Rothermere.

Things looked up when, aged 24, he was found a job for 18 months with the Anglo-Canadian Paper Mills in Quebec. This reinforced his passion for North America, and gave him a lot of incidental knowledge about turning lumber into newsprint and the rudiments of printing. He remains disproportionately proud of this practical expertise, and will shamelessly air it with colleagues when absolutely confident that they are ignorant on the subject. Some colleagues claim that he is now more proud of the no-smudge clean-hands printing presses he has installed than he is of his newspapers' content. Others, however, say that the image of Vere Rothermere as a printing genius is an absurd piece of folklore.

'The way people talk,' says *Daily Express* editor Sir Nicholas Lloyd, 'you half expect to find him in a pair of oily overalls holding a spanner and finding out what's wrong with the printing press. I don't doubt that he's *interested* in it all, but not much beyond that.'

Eventually Rothermere was allowed by his father to return to London from Quebec, to an ill-defined job created for him at the newspapers.

'They put him in a glass box,' Lady Rothermere told me, 'in the middle of the editorial floor, with no secretary and no memos sent to him. He had nothing whatever to do, except hang around all morning waiting for lunch and all afternoon waiting to go home, and he was so frustrated.'

He protested, and was allocated slightly more interesting tasks. Bert Irvine, who would eventually become general manager of the *Daily Mail*, took him on a tour of the seaside towns of North Devon to assess circulation trends.

'We met in the comfortable bar of the Clarence hotel in Exeter,' recalls Irvine, 'and I must say I found him to be a very likeable young man – he was about five or six years younger than me, I believe. He told me I should not be buying him a drink, but was reassured when I said that they would go down on my expenses and that his father would pay in the end! I remember he made a great impression on my wife when he came home to tea. Not only was he handsome, but polite. He rose to his feet every time she entered our small 12-by-10 sitting room, and made small talk with my five-year-old son and three-year-old daughter, even taking her on his knee.

'We spent a few days touring seaside and country towns checking availability of the paper, putting up posters outside newsagents' shops, and I introduced him to agents and wholesalers. One particular episode stays in my memory. In those days part of the job in the remote country areas was to collect the usual bad debts from newsagents. I took Vere into one of these agents in North Devon – a warm-hearted, garrulous old woman in a smelly, isolated cottage. I said, "Now I have brought someone to see you: May I introduce Lord Rothermere's son."

' "Good God," she said. "Things must be in a very bad way in Fleet Street, if he has to send his son to collect my money." '

Rothermere was redeployed and launched his legendary promotions: Win a Pub, Win a Pension for Life, Win a Holiday, Win a Wristwatch. If he couldn't secure a big prize he gave away a small one: the object of the exercise was the magnetic three-letter-word *Win*.

'I suppose we kind of vaguely understood he was the heir apparent,' says David English, 'but he was very modest. I won't say he was exactly one of the boys but he was certainly not a very clear heir apparent in his demeanour or anything, so he used to come out drinking with us and have lunch and talk these competitions through. If it was a business lunch we'd go to the Savoy, or we'd go to the pub if we were just buying our own drinks. There was the Mucky Duck – the White Swan – and a pub called The Feathers where we mostly used to go. And there were still these funny little drinking clubs around Knightsbridge and the West End and we'd drink together in those places.'

'Did you talk about newspapers in these drinking clubs?'

'Quite often. And he does seem to like journalists' company, he seems very relaxed with them. I think he's very shy until he really gets to know people, but with journalists he's extremely good company. He does quite like, even now, being with newspaper men, going out for drinks and joking with them.

'He once summed his job up by saying that it isn't too difficult to run a newspaper if you appreciate the creative side,' continued English. 'His great uncle Northcliffe had started the *Mail* by getting a fantastic team of journalists and indulging them and encouraging them and stroking them and rewarding them and driving them as well. They were the cream of the organisation and in the old Daily Mail building they had the best offices and incredible expenses and dined at the Savoy and went off first class around the world. Journalists work very well when they're treated like that; if you can also motivate their natural competitive spirits they'll work extremely hard. But they've got to be treated like stars. The business people in Northcliffe's day were all at the back of Northcliffe House, sitting on high stools adding up the money in very cramped offices. And they were naturally deeply resentful and jealous of the journalists and all the high-kicking gang around Northcliffe. So when Northcliffe died, Vere's grandfather pushed all the journalists into the back rooms and cut their salaries and inflated all the management, so that they became the ones who started arriving in expensive cars and suits and highly polished shoes and dining at the Savoy. And from that point on the sale of the *Daily Mail* went down and the sale of the *Daily Express* went up. And Vere said his father continued that tradition because he too believed that journalists were interchangeable, you just went out into Fleet Street and rounded up the nearest ten and you had ten journalists. They didn't understand it had to be the right ten or it wouldn't work. So all Vere did when he took over, he's told me, was to kick all the management back into the back rooms and let David English and his people have the best offices and the best expenses and the sale of the paper went up! That's all you have to do if you want to be a newspaper proprietor! Well that's a shortened version of what you have to do but there's a hell of a lot of truth in it.'

The gossip columnist Nigel Dempster, who used to work on the *Daily Express* before joining the relaunched *Daily Mail*, remembers the relative kudos of the two rival papers when Vere Rothermere was first appearing on the scene.

'We used to look down at Associated Newspapers as a joke. And of course the boss of Associated Newspapers in those days was the late Lord Rothermere, Esmond, a vastly patrician figure but clearly a useless newspaper proprietor. So while the *Daily Express* was selling almost 4.5 million a day the *Daily Mail* was dwindling and, in terms of competition, everyone at the *Daily Express* – which was on the sunny side of Fleet Street – used to jeer at the *Mail*. Whenever we went out on jobs and saw a *Mail* man we'd scream with laughter. And Max Aitken [then owner of the *Express*] used to belittle Vere Rothermere too. I remember at Cowes, where Max Aitken was the king – he had the yachts, the finest house there, he was a member of the Royal Yacht Squadron, he was Admiral of the *Royal London*, all that sort of thing – Vere used to arrive in a little boat and Max Aitken would demean him, I mean scream with laughter. "There's Vere in his dinghy!" Well it's extraordinary that in 20 years the Express empire has all but vanished and, singlehandedly, Vere has restored a faltering empire and is now king of the castle.'

With hindsight, the *Daily Mail*'s transition from a broadsheet to a tabloid – or 'compact' as Rothermere grandly calls it – seems the obvious and only step to have taken. But at the time it was a considerable gamble. Unlike in America, there was no British tradition of middle-market tabloid newspapers, and received wisdom said it was both a risky and vulgar idea. Rothermere, says English, always believed the smaller paper would have two great advantages.

'One evening we had a very, very late and a very, very long dinner at Boulestin. Vere said, "Look, David, you work for the Mail group and you've worked with the Express and you know that the *Express* hasn't just got double our circulation and a much smarter image – it's even more profound than that – they psychologically dominate us and all *Mail* journalists actually feel themselves intimidated and in their secret heart of hearts believe the *Express* is better. Somehow we've got to break those things and the only way I can think of to do that," said Vere, "is to do something enormously dramatic, an all or nothing throw, which is to turn the paper tabloid." And he said he'd made a study, he thought that the time was now for a middle-market tabloid and that it would no longer necessarily be perceived by the public as purely the bottom end of the market. And that a change in itself, if we could pull it off, would turn the cards on all those other things: the *Express* would look old-fashioned and our staff would be lifted by this *coup de main*. He'd thought it all through, because he's quite a deep psychologist in all matters, actually.'

Preparations for the relaunch took place in great secrecy, with the news typefaces and page make-up being designed on Saturday by a small team under the supervision of English. Each dummy page as it was completed was shown to Rothermere, a fastidious typographer, for approval.

'He used to come round and look at them about lunchtime,' says English, 'and one day Vere suddenly looked up and said, "My God, it's half-past-three, none of us have had any lunch! Quickly! We need sandwiches! Fetch ham sandwiches, cheese sandwiches, ham and cheese sandwiches, tomato sandwiches! Bring lots and lots of sandwiches!" And there was a young sub-editor there who offered, "I'll go and fetch them." At which Vere said, "No, not you, you're *creative*, you're a *journalist*, you can't fetch sandwiches." And then he turned to Bert Irvine who was general manager – general manager of the *Daily Mail*, for God's sake – and he said, "Bert, you're management, you go and see to the sandwiches!" I always thought that was rather symbolic of his view of journalists and management.'

In due course a prototype of the tabloid was printed, again with the utmost secrecy, and the first copy off the press was rushed round to Rothermere for his comments.

'David and his staff had been working all day,' says Bert Irvine, 'and he obviously did not fancy presenting the finished product to Vere directly. He asked me to be his messenger. I duly arrived at Eaton Square about tea-time, to be met by a surprised Pat [Lady Rothermere] clearly not expecting me, the children and a sleepy Vere. He grabbed the copies eagerly and sent Pat to fetch tea. When she returned he asked her for her opinion. Obviously the secret had been well kept. She could not believe that we were thinking of changing her beloved broadsheet the *Daily Mail*, and Vere allowed her to blame me.

'A few days later,' says Irvine, 'Vere told me he had dined with Lord Mountbatten the previous evening and that apparently he had put forward some interesting ideas about the change of shape. Considering the great deal of time and money we had spent on researching our market, I ventured to express the view that the new *Daily Mail* was not aimed at Admirals of the Fleet.'

One of Rothermere's daughters, Geraldine Ogilvy, remembers the deliberations about the relaunch that went on at home.

'When he changed the larger newspaper into the smaller one,' she says, 'Dad used to ask us all the time "What do you think?"'

'I asked, "Why are you doing this, Dad? It looked good bigger."'

'And he said, "The paper's losing money and this will save money. And people will like it more in the end."'

'He used to work so hard at the time we hardly saw him,' she says, 'which was sad, because he usually used to read to us a lot. He's a marvellous reader out loud. He can do the voices. There's quite a theatrical streak in him.'

Later her father compensated for this period of distraction by taking his children on expeditions. 'In the school holidays there was always this battle between my mother who wanted to be in Monte Carlo or Jamaica, and my father who wanted to take us all on a yacht to Yugoslavia or something, somewhere really fun for the children. Especially when my brother Jonathan was growing up, Dad became rather adventurous and used to take us on riding holidays in Montana and Arizona. He loves that kind of thing: breakfast in a longhouse, a squashed up peanut butter and jelly sandwich for lunch, and square dancing after supper. We always say that his closest friends are his children – his only friends to be frank. He's very affectionate with his children, he's always hugging us like a big bear. We're a very tactile family, not very English in that respect; we express ourselves quite openly, for good and for bad. Which is nice when it's nice, but not so nice at all when not nice.'

At other times Rothermere makes a point of being elusive and mysterious. Disliking being tied down, he will fly off somewhere without informing anyone beyond his private office. He enjoys telephoning an editor, whom he has spoken to only the day before from Paris, and announcing, 'I'm ringing you from the Goldener Hirsch hotel in Salzburg,' or 'I'm in Tokyo at the Imperial.'

Sonia Sinclair remembers sitting next to Rothermere at a party for Imelda Marcos at the Philippines Embassy in London. 'Vere turned to me towards the end of dinner and said, "I'm leaving this country tomorrow for good. It's absolutely essential, otherwise I'll be virtually ruined by taxation, and I feel terribly strongly about keeping the empire together." '

According to his daughter Geraldine, her father 'owns nothing now, no property at all. The flat in Eaton Square was my mother's, the houses in Jamaica and California and Sussex and the South of France belonged to my mother. His flat in Paris is rented and the apartment in New York is a company one, I think. The house in Kyoto belongs to Maiko [Vere Rothermere's long-standing Korean consort, Maiko Lee, who he had met in a New York nightclub when she was 28, and to whom he became engaged after Pat's death]. I think he rather likes the freedom of not owning anything. One of his hobbies is going to have a look at run-down châteaux in France, and he talks about buying one every so often. But then you never hear about that plan again.'

His elusiveness has invested Lord Rothermere with a greater mystique than any other London-based proprietor. And it also means that he invests the editors he trusts with an unusual degree of authority. His father, Esmond Rothermere, held his editors in much the same low esteem that he held his journalists, and fell into a routine of changing them regularly in the hope some good might come of it. He had never formulated a grand plan for his papers, so editors were vulnerable to Esmond's abrupt changes of direction: one month his newspapers would head upmarket, the next month downmarket; to survive, an editor needed to be a chameleon.

Vere Rothermere's 22-year championship of Sir David English is comparable to Katharine Graham's support of Ben Bradlee at the *Washington Post* and Ramnath Goenka's virtual obsession with Arun Shourie at the *Indian Express* (until he eventually fired him). English is the highest-paid British newspaper executive; perhaps, with a weak dollar, the highest-paid editor in the world. His salary is estimated to be £800,000 a year. Rothermere described him to me as 'the perfect *Daily Mail* reader', by which he explained he means aspirational, enterprising, family-minded and conservative. It pleases Rothermere to imply, when talking about English, that Associated Newspapers virtually belongs to English; that English is the leaseholder and that he, Rothermere, merely owns the freehold. So long as he keeps the property in good structural repair, English can do what he likes inside. In July 1992, in an extraordinary cabinet reshuffle over a marathon lunch at the Vaudeville restaurant in Paris, English was promoted to chairman of Associated Newspapers, and the editorship of the *Daily Mail* passed to Paul Dacre, who Murdoch had been attempting to poach to edit *The Times*. You feel that Vere Rothermere is genuinely grateful that he's found in English someone who can – and wishes to – identify completely with Rothermere's readers; something which Lord Rothermere himself, by dint of his background, can never entirely do. And you get the impression too that English remains slightly in awe of his landlord, and will go to great lengths not to displease him. What Lord Rothermere might think is always an unspoken consideration on the paper. There is a famous story about a five-day serial on massage that the *Daily Mail* was intending to print.

On the eve of publication a terrible panic gripped the senior executives. Lord Rothermere's Korean companion Maiko Lee had recently been described in *Private Eye* as 'a hand masseuse', and it occurred to them that the proprietor might interpret the massage articles as a personal insult to his girlfriend. Already too late to remove the series completely (which had in any case been advertised on television), a clever compromise was reached. The word massage was substituted throughout by the word 'pressure'; the word 'hand' by 'digits'. The doctoring left the series hard to follow for the readers, but at least nobody in Paris would be embarrassed.

On more general editorial matters, English will energetically defend his position. 'He can make bad judgements,' says English of Rothermere. 'We had an exclusive story – and this is a very good example of the kind of disagreement we can have – an exclusive story by Baz Bamigboye that Rock Hudson had died of AIDS. Now it just happened that Hudson was very much back in the public eye, because he'd got into *Dynasty* which, at that time, was the number one show on TV. So it was a big story. First of all it was an exclusive. Secondly AIDS was the biggest story of the time, and it was Rock Hudson, who was in *Dynasty*. We used a big picture of Hudson and the next day Vere rang me and said, "I think it's a terrible mistake, the *Mail*'s gone mad. Fancy putting a story of this ridiculous old film star on page one! Nobody's even heard of him since the 1950s and we want *young* people, not *old* people, and it's a boring story about someone dying and who gives a damn?" So I said, "I'm sorry Vere but you've just lost all your sense of news. It's the most brilliant story, and it's a great exclusive." So we did have a big, big row on the telephone in which I told him he was completely wrong. I said to him, "You should be congratulating Bamigboye because this is a great *Daily Mail* exclusive which will be on the front page of virtually every paper in the world tomorrow morning," which of course it was. And he then rang up and said, "I've seen the other papers," – this was 24 hours later – "I guess I'm out of touch. I hadn't realised how important the AIDS story was; I hadn't realised this man was in *Dynasty*, thank God I've got you and Bamigboye. If I was editing the paper I'd screw it up!" Now that's a very charming way of coming back, and one of the things about Vere is that you *can* have a heated discussion. You can treat him as a fellow professional and you don't have to take his say-so on things if you think you're right. And he encourages people to be independent and stand up to him.'

'Does Rothermere ever give you story suggestions himself?'

'Ideas rather than stories. For example, some years ago, it was, should we not get on to the environment. He kept saying, "This is going to be a *big issue*. Shouldn't we be looking at rain forests because this is something that attracts young people and it's going to get a political aspect to it?" Those kind of general strategies which you can accept or not accept, because like anybody in newspapers with ideas, some are very good and some are very obvious and some are very awful. He's got a most catholic mind. He's a well-read student of history, of many periods, and he's got an extremely good memory. And of course he's extremely interested in world religion. He once said that if he had not been anything else, he would have liked to be a great chief sub-editor or a night editor. And he would have been good at that because he's got this encyclopaedic memory – he'd be good on *Mastermind* with the general questions – and could say, "No, that's not right, it was in 1492 that Columbus arrived in America." '

His daughter Geraldine agrees that her father could have been a historian or academic. 'He's more creative than people realise, but he's never had the confidence to use it. Because he's always had the newspapers to do and things to organise there.'

'The great conundrum of Vere's life,' says a former kinsman, 'is knowing precisely where he stands in relation to the Establishment. It seems to me that he is never quite sure if he's in it or out of it, and this makes him constantly uneasy. He half enjoys being the maverick outsider – the great power who has never been sucked inside – and yet he's perpetually driven towards being part of it. He is thoroughly ambivalent about his own position in society and in relation to the *Daily Mail*. On one level, the *Mail* is a pretty accurate reflection of Vere's philosophy: you do well in the free world and you go to Heaven. On the other hand, he's a much more complex and intelligent man than that. He can see through the way that the *Mail* leads people towards a pot of gold that doesn't exist. He has never been sure what he thinks of the Establishment. He got a hard time at Eton. He believed his contemporaries looked down on him because his family owned newspapers. Maybe they did and maybe they didn't, but that's how he interpreted it. So he has a certain amount of vitriol towards the

Establishment, or what he thinks the Establishment stands for. And yet, at the same time of course, the *Mail* has gradually become associated with the resurgence of the middle classes, and Vere finds himself running and owning *the* paper of aspiration of the great bourgeoisie. So he's part of it, and he's not part of it, and he's not altogether sure what he is. It makes him feel rather manipulative, but that doesn't necessarily worry him, he enjoys the game. He is fond of power, he can't conceive of not being in charge of everything – his papers, his family, wherever he goes he is always the boss. He can be charming, but if he feels his hand is being forced you encounter a very different animal. He prefers to encounter other people as the boss, not as an equal.'

According to Sir David English, Rothermere is an adept motivator. 'He's got a deep understanding of human nature and all that drives us. I think he knows all that is good and bad in Man and can apply it to individuals, and therefore can work out first of all *why* they're doing something or secondly, if he wants them to do something, *how* he can get them to do that something. He definitely is – and I've heard him describe himself in this way a great many times – a student of human nature.'

As an acquisitor, he is cautious. His empire has expanded more slowly than his competitors', and he has at least five times walked away from major deals, or else been beaten by a swifter or more reckless rival. Rothermere will not be rushed. Like an art collector debating whether or not to buy some particularly expensive painting, he likes to make several visits to view, examine it from close up and from far away, sleep on it. The Texan newspaper tycoon Dean Singleton remembers advising Rothermere on the purchase of small North American papers in the late seventies, and after months of tortured prevarication Rothermere decided not to go ahead. David English describes a similar episode when Rothermere came close to buying the now-defunct New York *Herald Tribune*. 'He wanted to get it and got a team together and was going to do it and at the last minute didn't do it.' And he considered getting into American supermarket newspapers – shoppers – very early on but, says English, 'let himself be talked out of it, and he's always regretted it because that was a real money-making thing.' In 1976 he toyed with buying the *Observer* from the Astors, an ambition less eccentric than it was widely viewed at the time, since he would have recaptured one of his family's old Northcliffe papers (as well as out-manoeuvring the Astors who had out-manoeuvred the Harmsworths over *The Times* after Lord Northcliffe's death). As it happened this ambition was thwarted by a trio of factors: hostility from the *Observer*'s journalists who considered Rothermere politically too right-wing, rival competitors prepared to pay over the odds (including the Chinese proprietor Sally Aw Sian) and a certain lack of enthusiasm on Rothermere's part, compounded by the feeling that he should be launching a new Sunday paper of his own rather than buying a liberal paper that didn't relish his arrival. He says today, 'I am very relieved looking back on it that we didn't get the *Observer*. I think it was a lucky escape.' (Instead the *Observer* was bought by the American oil company Atlantic Richfield which not many years later sold it on to Tiny Rowland's Lonrho which, in turn, eventually divested it to the *Guardian* in June 1993.

And in October 1980 Rothermere was in the frame to buy *The Times* from Lord Thomson but was beaten by Rupert Murdoch partly, some say, because Murdoch was on the spot in London and did everything possible to win the deal, while Vere Rothermere pressed his case at arm's length from Paris, reluctant to lock horns directly with his competitor.

Rothermere, however, finally succeeded with a long campaign to control the lucrative market of London's evening newspapers. By 1977 both sets of rivals – Rothermere with his *Evening News* and Max Aitken, Beaverbrook's heir, with the *Evening Standard* – had become fed up with their respective losses. However much Rothermere trimmed the *Evening News*, profit remained remote. A retired *News* manager told me that by this stage nobody even seriously believed that it was possible. From time to time eager young executives were lured aboard, and for six months paced briskly about the corridors muttering, mantra-like 'There *must* be a way, there *must* be'. But in due course their step lost its spring, and they began, most discreetly, to investigate the prospect of a transfer across to the *Daily Mail*.

The situation at Beaverbrook's empire was worse. Alone of their newspapers the *Sunday Express* was showing a decent return, and even this was undermined by a sombre corporate premonition that things there would probably deteriorate. By March of 1977 it suited all parties to talk and a plan was devised whereby the *Standard* would be sold to

Rothermere for £7.5 million and the combined evening paper – the *News* – would be printed on Beaverbrook's superior presses. This happy deal was on the point of being signed when news of it leaked out. There was an immediate outcry which took all parties by surprise. The death of the *Evening Standard* was projected as a near national disaster; the survival of the *News* as little if any compensation. Expressions of public support for the Beaverbrook paper bordered almost on the hysterical. At dinner parties it was repeatedly explained to Lord Rothermere that he happened to own the less interesting of the two newspapers. Old friends whose opinions he respected told him that the columnists, the political coverage, the cartoonists were superior in the *Standard*. 'But of course Vere knew in his heart of hearts,' says an old friend, 'that if he wasn't in newspapers at all, if he was a banker or something, he'd probably have read the *Evening Standard* in preference to the *News*. And that didn't make it any easier.' Every day a deal seemed more certain. 'I certainly believed we had it at the time,' Lord Rothermere says now. His father flew into London from Florida for the historic acquisition and, like Hitler at the gates of Leningrad, when victory seemed so imminent, booked a hotel room for the celebration party. On the eve of the signing, however, Jocelyn Stevens who was acting for Aitken, announced that Sir James Goldsmith, who owned a block of shares in Beaverbrook, was considering buying the whole Beaverbrook empire. He had requested a six-week delay which Aitken had granted.

There were also rumours of a Goldsmith–Tiny Rowland pact; probably the only pact ever to strike more fear than the Conrad Black–Kerry Packer pact 14 years later to buy the Australian Fairfax company. Lady Rothermere, who began describing Goldsmith as 'that panther' at about this time, said that she has never seen her husband so irritated. And the final deal only heightened his frustration: the construction and shipping firm Trafalgar House, which owned the London Ritz and the *QEII* liner, bought out the Aitkens over the head of Rothermere (and Rupert Murdoch who had joined in the dog show in the final round) and preserved the Express group as an entity in full and enthusiastic possession of the *Evening Standard*. This move not only delayed Rothermere's victory for another three years but also – though no one could have guessed this at that time – paved David Stevens's path as a future press baron.

All talk of a merger began to dwindle and Rothermere was left, most people felt, in an awkward position, and he declared his intention of spending the remainder of the spring in the South of France. But no sooner had he made his way to Cap d'Ail than a huge political scandal erupted at the *Daily Mail*. This was the Ryder slush fund affair – now chiefly of interest for the light it throws upon Vere Rothermere, since the sensational but bogus 'Exclusive' story about the car firm British Leyland has weathered less well than the proprietor. The hoax was very simple. The *Mail* believed it had uncovered a widespread bribery scam that the nationalised car firm was operating throughout the world to help sell its vehicles. The story had been leaked to the *Mail* by a Leyland executive, and when Leyland's chairman Lord Ryder declined to return telephone calls, his elusiveness was interpreted as proof of his guilt. The *Daily Mail* published, and a storm of accusations and libel letters were exchanged for weeks, David English eventually accepting that a catastrophically embarrassing mistake had been made and offering his resignation. Vere Rothermere, who had flown back into London to lend moral support, refused to accept it and, according to an Associated Newspapers man who watched his reaction during this fraught period, 'was remarkably unruffled by the whole affair, when all around him, his editors and lawyers, were thin lipped and tearing out their hair. Vere sailed in and out looking like a man who'd mislaid his car-keys, mildly vexed but confident they'd turn up somewhere eventually. He used to take people out to lunch at the Savoy and talk about everything except Leyland. He'd tell you about villages in the South of France off the tourist route, that sort of thing. Supremely unfazed by it all.'

Rothermere's sang-froid snapped only once. The then Prime Minister James Callaghan had hitherto stayed silent on the Beaverbrook–Associated talks, but irritated by the Leyland brouhaha indicated that any proposed merger between the two groups would have to be referred to the Monopolies Commission. It was further unofficially indicated that such a merger would probably be refused. Rothermere was furious and responded by suggesting that Callaghan's intervention owed less to the Leyland affair ('This deplorable but honest mistake') than to a recent furore in the *Daily Mail* over the Prime Minister's appointment of his son-in-law Peter Jay as British Ambassador in Washington. Rothermere's remark provoked a whole new controversy. Columnists took sides: nepotism versus sour grapes. For the first time Vere Rothermere saw that ownership of newspapers is not always protection enough against public censure. His own papers hesitated publicly to defend their proprietor but many others leapt at the chance to mock and admonish him. Charles Wintour, then editor of the *Evening Standard*, speaking after a lunch at – of all places – the Automobile Associates, let rip:

'I had intended to say no more about the current situation in Fleet Street, but Vere Harmsworth's statement today calls for comment. Today Mr Harmsworth, in attempting to answer the Prime Minister's description of the *Daily Mail*'s conduct as contemptible and a display of political spite, drags up the appointment of Mr Peter Jay to Washington. In other words, he is smearing the charge of nepotism against the name of the Prime Minister.

'Why is Mr Vere Harmsworth chairman of Associated Newspapers? Why is he in a position to squander millions of his shareholders' money in an effort to force the *Evening Standard* out of business? Why has he been able to sell his evening paper at an uneconomic price, to offer cut rates to advertisers who switch from the *Evening Standard* to his own paper, all, I believe, with the aim of compelling his competitor to surrender?

'May I suggest that the only reason why Mr Vere Harmsworth is chairman of Associated Newspapers is that he is the son of the second Lord Rothermere. And the second Lord Rothermere had the job because he was the son of the first Lord Rothermere. And the first Lord Rothermere had the *Daily Mail* because he was the brother of a real newspaper genius, Lord Northcliffe. Mr Jay is acknowledged by all to be a most brilliant man who is earning large sums entirely as a result of his own talents. Mr Harmsworth, however, is in a position to endanger the jobs of 1700 people in Fleet Street purely through a mere accident of birth.'

It is a reflection of Vere Rothermere's normal insulation from such attacks that Wintour's speech is virtually the only public criticism levelled against him in 30 years.

Two years later, in the months leading up to the 1979 General Election, the *Daily Mail*'s support for the Conservative Party's new leader, Margaret Thatcher, was remorseless and effective. More than any other British editor, David English empathised with Thatcher's radical middle-class conservatism and Vere Rothermere, confident that

English had caught the public mood, was happy to let him get on with it. Like many hereditary tycoons, his own political convictions are maverick. He once asked Sonia Sinclair, 'Why should I help the Establishment, what has the Establishment ever done for me?' And he will remark airily, late at night, 'I suppose this generation of the Royal Family will be the last, don't you? One really can't seriously imagine them being allowed to carry on into the next century, can one?' Seditious fancies of this sort do not find their way into his newspapers however, and the *Daily Mail*'s championing of the new spirit of free enterprise was directly to benefit its proprietor. Under a Conservative government an evening newspaper merger seemed much less contro-versial, and Trafalgar House had by now owned the *Evening Standard* for long enough to recognise the benefit of a combined paper; so in 1980 Rothermere closed his *Evening News* (which was estimated to have lost £38 million by its final edition) and in return got 50 per cent of the shares in the new Evening Standard company, with the option to buy the other half if Trafalgar House ever wished to sell. This was a clause of immense importance, since it explicitly prevented Murdoch, Maxwell, Goldsmith or any other panther from prowling around the *Evening Standard*. Rothermere also correctly guessed that Trafalgar might not wish to retain their newspaper subsidiary for long.

'Certain people I could name,' Rothermere told me, 'have come into this business of newspaper publishing in the last ten years saying, "This is how we're going to do it, blah blah blah" and then fall flat on their faces! And the reason they fall flat on their faces is because they're *not newspaper men*. If you're not an experienced newspaper man then you can lose a lot of money very quickly indeed. And in fact even if you are an experienced newspaper man, that is no guarantee of making money all the time as Mr Murdoch well understands.'

I asked him, 'Do you still feel disappointed that Murdoch beat you to *The Times*?'

'To *The Times* itself, no. But I'm sorry we didn't get the *Sunday Times*. That would have been, er, well worth having. But we were not prepared to go as far as Murdoch. Murdoch borrowed, as we've now all seen, to such an extent that it imperiled his entire company, and I was never prepared to do that.* And so one has very mixed feelings

* Note: This is a slight misrepresentation on Lord Rothermere's part. Rupert Murdoch's borrowings to buy Times Newspapers never imperiled News Inter-national; it was other, subsequent actions that required huge debt.

about not getting them really; it might have been rather an *enjoyable feeling* to own them, and there again it might not.'

Something I wanted to discover about Vere Rothermere was the extent to which he feels accountable for his newspapers' gossip pages. Both the *Daily Mail* and the *Mail on Sunday* have as their gossip columnist the smooth and omnipresent Nigel Dempster. He writes six days a week, and over 20 years has become a public figure in Britain, frequently on television and mentioned in pantomimes ('Ooh, everyone who's anyone is going to be at the Prince's ball tonight, Cinderella,' says an Ugly Sister at the Southsea Christmas show, 'Pavarotti, Fergie, Nigel Dempster . . .'). The women Rothermere is seated next to at London parties invariably scan Nigel Dempster, even if they do so surreptitiously. Most of them have also appeared on his page. So he is cross-questioned about his famous gossip columnist out of all proportion (as Rothermere sees it) to Dempster's seniority on the paper.

'Do your friends sometimes berate you,' I asked him, 'about stories in Dempster's column, stories about rocky marriages, divorces, elopements, that kind of thing?'

'Well they used to a lot when I lived in England, but I don't live in England now, *so they can't!*' Then he guffawed. 'That's why I live in Paris!' Then he guffawed again. 'I suppose readers of the *Continental Daily Mail* might take something up with me, but continentals very rarely appear in the *Daily Mail*!' Then he guffawed again.

'He's never interfered with me in my life,' says Nigel Dempster. 'When I started to write the column in 1973 my very first story was that Annabel Birley was about to have a child and that Mark Birley [the owner of the nightclub Annabel's in Berkeley Square] was not the father – they were obviously still married then – and that in fact Jimmy Goldsmith was the father. I had rung up Jimmy and the telephone was answered by Nicholas Soames, his faithful ADC, and he put me through to Jimmy who laughed and said, "*Be very careful*, Dempster, be very careful. I can't deny this, but be very careful." So I broke the story – 8 October 1973 – and wrote that Goldsmith and Birley, who'd been at Eton together, blah blah blah, a great story.

'Anyway, that very evening Vere and Pat went into Annabel's to be met by an incandescent Mark Birley who, as fate will always have it in these terrible altercations, allowed Pat to stay in the club but threw out Vere. And I never heard about this the next day. It was many years later – four or five years – that someone said to me, "You realise that because of you your boss was thrown out of Annabel's." And I said, "No, I've got no idea about this." He said, "Well it's absolutely true. It was that story you wrote about Jimmy and Mark." The very fact that Vere didn't tell me, and remonstrate with me, just shows what an amazing man he is.

'A similar thing happened,' went on Dempster, 'when I wrote a piece about Prince Rainier. It was something to do with him spoiling the ecology of the Mediterranean around Monte Carlo; he'd been blasting into the sea and spreading Monaco by building out. The headline was "Clown Prince" which occupied the bottom part of the page, but obviously Rainier saw it. And two days later Vere and Pat, who were staying in their villa in Cap d'Ail, went over to Monaco to the palace to have tea with Grace. And in walks Rainier, gives Vere a piece of his mind and throws him out. Not welcome. And this too I didn't hear about until a long time later. There's no doubt that he takes a close interest, but there's similarly no doubt that he doesn't go around complaining when his life is interfered with because of what has happened in his newspapers. I know he appreciates that newspapers are his business and that you're going to get complaints – it's like if you sell a car that breaks down you're going to get complaints – and he's very urbane about it when it happens.'

The relationship between proprietor and gossip columnist is an interesting one, and more so for Lord Rothermere than any other proprietor. When one of his contemporaries from school runs off with another man's wife it is highly probable that the story will be published first in Lord Rothermere's newspaper. When one of his fellow members of Boodle's, the Beefsteak or the Brook in New York is cuckolded by a polo player, it is Lord Rothermere's paper that broadcasts his mortification. Vere Rothermere, of course, seldom has the remotest notion of what is about to be published and yet, just as the owner of an international hotel group is vicariously blamed for a broken bathroom faucet, Rothermere is ultimately responsible. And as controlling shareholder he cannot even hide behind his statutory duty to the shareholders, and justify gossip as a necessary evil for circulation.

'Never once has he demanded for any story to be taken out because a friend has rung him up,' says Dempster, 'though there was a classic case when I broke the story of the belly dancer Pat Kluge. I had discovered that Mrs Kluge had had a connection with *Knave* magazine, had worked as a belly dancer, and was shortly to be the hostess in Palm Beach at a gala at which the Prince and Princess of Wales were going to be guests of honour. It was a gala in aid of Atlantic Colleges, which was why Charles was going to be there, and the person behind it all was of course Dr Armand Hammer. Dr Armand, for some reason, had a friendship with John Kluge, and the Kluges got wind of what I was going to reveal and rang Dr Armand and Dr Armand rang Lord Rothermere. A mighty man, Dr Armand.

'Anyway I had got wind that this was going to happen – the call to Rothermere – so I sent one of my people down to Charing Cross Road where they sell second-hand copies of old magazines and I got all the old copies of *Knave* magazine with Pat Kluge in them, and I had all these semi-pornographic photographs of her copied. At half-past-eight I had gone home, and my whole page was devoted to the story of Pat Kluge and John Kluge and Charles and Diana and the cover of *Knave* magazine.

'At half-past-eight, quarter-to-nine, the back bench [sub-editors department] was informed that Lord Rothermere was without and would shortly be in their midst. And sure enough, some time before the first edition went away – say, ten o'clock – Lord Rothermere appears behind the back bench, clearly in unfamiliar territory. No one had ever seen him on the editorial floor of the *Daily Mail* in living memory. And demands to see the first edition. And he looks at it and there is everything that Dr Armand has warned him about – the filth, lies. Dr Armand had told him that he will bring down the *Daily Mail*, the libel action will be so punitive that Vere will have not a penny left, unless this page is pulled right there and then. So Rothermere suggests that the page *is* pulled. Now fortunately I was primed to the possibility of this, so I had left a folder of all these astonishing pictures of Pat Kluge, so the night editor says, "Before you make a decision, Lord Rothermere, I'd like to say that the lawyers have looked at everything, they've passed it all and if you are in any doubt about the past of Mrs Kluge perhaps you'd like to take a look at this folder." So Vere sits down and starts thumbing through. And everyone is sitting there like church mice and they suddenly hear from behind them "Very interesting. *Very*, very interesting. Didn't know people could do *that*." And then Rothermere handed back the folder and said, "Keep the page as it is." A wonderful evening in the history of free speech!

'Against this, I have to say,' said Nigel Dempster, 'was the time when Vere personally tried to sack me.'

'Why did he do that?'

'I've got no idea. It was an odd episode. I'd been on a swing from Paris to the United Arab Emirates, to the Philippines, where I was staying with Imelda and Ferdinand Marcos with, amongst others, Gunther Sachs, Sean Connery, Micky Suffolk – a big gang – and I came back and wrote three columns about it because I felt it was such an extraordinary insight into these people's worlds. And for some strange reason Vere took against it.

'Anyway, not long afterwards it was [the interior decorator] Nicky Haslam's 40th birthday, and Nicky was giving an enormous party at his house in the country at which the guests would include Cecil Beaton, Diana Cooper, Joan Collins and Vere Rothermere.

'And as I arrived Pat Rothermere came up to me and said, "I've just come down in the car with Vere and he's going to sack you, I want you to know this, I want you to be warned."

'I said, "Why? I've never worked harder in my life."

'And Pat Rothermere replied, "He just wants to sack you and that's the end of it. Keep away from him."

'So I go back to the party until six o'clock in the morning, then go straight to the office and file a whole column about it – great scoop, bizarre pictures of people never photographed this way before, Bindy Lambton as a harpoonist, all the rest of it. And on Monday morning I'm called in by David English who says, "I think I should tell you . . . and I said, "You don't have to tell me, I already know. Vere wants to sack me," and David said, "Yes."

'What I think had happened,' says Dempster today, 'is that not long before I had written a memo to David English asking for a big pay increase, because my column was now the best-known column in the world.'

'But would Rothermere have discussed your salary?'

'My salary would have been discussed at board meetings. I'm told that when board meetings become very boring they read out my expenses. Oh yes, Vere would have been apprised of it. Monday I was sacked.

'But then David calls me in the next day and says, I'm not firing you. It would be quite impossible because how could my journalists respect me as an editor if I was to follow the whim of a proprietor? I'm bigger than that, I'm not going to fire you."

' "That's the most terrible piece of news," I replied. "I *want* to be fired." I had a good contract, you see, it would have cost a fortune to sack me. So I said, "You want me to subsidise this great newspaper group? I've got news for you. It's now June and I'm *leaving* as of January 1st. End of story. I won't have a holiday before then but I'm leaving." And finally David English said, "All right, we'll do what you want. You can set your terms but you've got to come to Paris and apologise to Lord Rothermere." So we thrash out some deal and part of it is that I have to fly to Paris in the company of David English to have lunch with Lord Rothermere where, at some stage of that lunch, I shall apologise for having been fired – apologise for what I've got no idea. So I was taken off to the Plaza Athenee where we had lunch in the restaurant where the only other occupants were four hookers who kept on waving in our direction – three men lunching alone. And sometime during this lunch David said, "I think you've got something to say to Lord Rothermere," and I said, "Yes, I'm sorry that we've had a disagreement." So that was the end of that. But it was extraordinary power play – never alluded to again.'

'And now you're on good terms with your proprietor?'

'I like him enormously, but I don't think I'm exactly a great figure in his life. Living where he does, he's much more involved in the EEC and politics and getting rid of Delors.'

Six weeks before she died of a heart attack brought on by an accidental overdose of sleeping pills at her villa at Cap d'Ail, I visited Lady Rothermere at home in London. Spanning the width of two houses in Eaton Square, her apartment was a cosier version of what the Empress Eugenie might have conceived if she'd relocated to Palm Beach. The overwhelming impression was of gold: Louis XIV side tables resplendent with gilt, faux-chinoiserie mirrors incorporating Chinamen bearing gilded parasols, elaborate vases with gilded rams' head handles. From the drawing-room ceiling was suspended, in a cascade of crystal teardrops, an immense Venetian chandelier topped with a taffeta bow. The sofas were so generously ruched in pale green and yellow taffetas that you felt, as you perched upon them, that you were sitting in the lap of a flamboyantly dressed ballgoer.

On every flat surface were photographs and more photographs; photographs in silver frames, photographs in leather frames, photographs awaiting framing piled up on the Aubusson carpet. There were photographs of Lady Rothermere with heads of state, with the Queen, with Liza Minelli, touring printing presses with her husband and being greeted by works managers with apprehensive smiles. On the mantle-piece stood a teddy bear wearing skiing clothes, and about 300 engraved invitations, some rather old, some from the oddest people ('the Public Relations Manager of Mobil Oil requests the pleasure of the company of the Viscountess Rothermere at a reception to launch . . .'). Scattered everywhere were little tapestry cushions embroidered with mottoes. When Lady Rothermere eventually joined me in the drawing room – she had had a number of changes of mind about which evening dress to put on – she supported herself on the sofa with three of these mottoed cushions, each dispatching a different maxim in my direction.

'*Jealousy is the tribute of Mediocrity to Genius*' proclaimed the tapestry cushion beneath her left elbow.

'*If you are swinging through the jungle, don't let go of the vine*' cautioned the cushion supporting the small of Lady Rothermere's back.

'*If you haven't got anything good to say about anyone, come here and sit by me*' invited the third cushion.

Patricia Evelyn Beverley Rothermere was the most memorable proprietor's wife in the world. Betty Maxwell may be more intuitive, Chryss Goulandris O'Reilly may be richer, Anna Murdoch may have accomplished more in her own right, but none was nearly so startling as the late Lady Rothermere, the once-beautiful J. Arthur Rank film starlet who partied so hard, travelled constantly around the world in the pursuit of fun, hated her gossip column nickname "Bubbles", dressed in a bedizenment of flounces and furbelows, ruffles and bows from Zandra Rhodes and yet, for all this apparent froth, played such a crucial part in the resuscitation of her husband's newspaper empire.

'It's because I'm a Taurus,' she assured me in her clipped, thirties film star accent.

'If I hadn't been a Taurus I could never have saved Vere. Only a Taurus could have got him what was rightfully his.'

Then she leant – tumbled – towards me on the sofa in a ripple of chiffon and asked, 'What starsign are you? Let me guess.' She seemed to be estimating the distance between my eyes, or was perhaps regarding the iris itself for some telltale sign.

'Pisces!' she exclaimed finally. 'You're Pisces! Am I right?'

I nodded.

'I knew you were a Pisces. So's Gianni Agnelli and Johnny Bulgari.'

I asked her to explain how exactly she had got Vere Rothermere what was rightfully his.

'We were on holiday in Jamaica,' she said, 'and Vere's father, Esmond, was under a lot of pressure from the opposition to sell out to the Express. They had a plan for putting the papers together, merging them. The negotiations were quite well advanced, there had been several meetings with Max Aitken and Lord Goodman and Jocelyn [Stevens], and Esmond might easily have sold out if they'd made a good enough offer. So one morning we were having breakfast next to the swimming pool and I said, "Look, Vere, you can swim any day of your life, but decisions are being made that are going to affect you and my son. Why are you not at those meetings in London?"

'And Vere said, "I haven't been invited."

'I said, "Even if you aren't invited you should be there because it's your future, and my son's future, that's being decided." So I told him, "I'm booking a flight back to London tomorrow and either you're coming or you're not." The moment we arrived we were driven straight to Warwick House: just my father-in-law, his wife, my husband and myself met. Esmond said, "I'm being screwed. I either have to trust someone completely or sell." I told him, "Never sell." And he said, "I will go along with it, if you promise to stay with Vere." And I said I would. So the next morning he cancelled all negotiations with Goodman, Aitken, Stevens and the others, and made my husband chairman and went off himself to live in South Africa. Vere was so shocked, he retreated to my bed for a fortnight!'

The precise nature of the relationship between the Rothermeres was not well defined, probably even to themselves. It was certainly, in its looseness, highly civilised. Vere Rothermere spends much of his time in Paris with Maiko Lee, and travels with her for long periods to Japan. When he is in London he seldom stays at Eaton Square, preferring hotels like the Halcyon, but if he happened to be in Manhattan at the same time as his wife, or in Beverly Hills, Jamaica or Cap d'Ail, there was no awkwardness and he gave every indication of being genuinely delighted to see her. And if he was in England for a weekend he was happy to stay with Lady Rothermere at Stroods, their house in Sussex.

Sonia Sinclair remembers being lent the New York apartment by Lady Rothermere, and the insight it gave her to the Rothermere ménage.

'I was staying there for a few days with Edna O'Brien [the novelist],' says Sonia Sinclair. 'It is an absolutely sumptuous apartment all done up by John Fowler, chintzy and flowery with marvellous pictures and views. But after the first night Edna said, "Oh it's so noisy, I couldn't sleep with all that traffic," so after that Edna installed her bed in a little linen cupboard, like a monk's cell, to sleep better. Anyway the next day Pat turned up – no telephone call, nothing, she just arrived. It was slightly unexpected, but fun you know. Everything changed: trunks everywhere, champagne, constant telephone calls, parties, parties. Then, the next morning, without Pat knowing, Vere turned up. Nobody had any idea he was coming. He just let himself in. It was like a Marx Brothers movie. Vere was a charming host, quite unfazed by Edna in the linen cupboard – I think he *is* unfazed you know. He took us all out to breakfast at the Carlyle.'

'Even when he's in Japan he rings me every day and asks me to tell him what's happening,' Lady Rothermere said. 'And I'll tell him there's an awful article, a terrible article, at the bottom of page 11 of the *Daily Mail*, or that the *Daily Express* has published something our people have missed. He needs me to tell him these things, not that he can always do anything. But someone has to tell him, who's in touch with the street. However late I'm back from Annabel's I read all the newspapers every night – the next day's newspapers – marking things to draw to Vere's attention. I don't ring the editors direct because I don't want to cut Vere's balls off.

'Have you met Maiko?' she asked me suddenly. 'Vere met her at Xenon in New York you know, and she moved in with him the very next day. At the time she made me very sad, that geisha, but now I'm used to it. Vere goes to the Far East with her. He says it clears his head and releases him from the pressures. But he comes back with all sorts of airy ideas so I don't let him go for too long – I wheel him in like a big fish on the end of my telephone line. But I do fear one day when he retires he will go and live in Kyoto. I've told him he'd hate it, he should be in the country where his children are. But he's very indecisive about things like that,' she said, rather affectionately.

'But my husband has at least been clever in one thing,' she went on, 'because he's rearranged the company so nobody can get their hands on it very easily. No Jimmy Goldsmith can just come along. Jimmy's a friend of course, but he's a panther. I keep telling Vere that Jimmy's a panther, you'd better watch out. You see they all want to own newspapers those panthers because they think it's power. They don't realise that it's the editors who have the power, not the owners at all.'

'Does Sir David English really have more power than Lord Rothermere?'

'In small ways yes. Power over the small things. Not the big things. David English is a great editor, he's the best, even if he does take liberties sometimes. But they all do, editors.' Lady Rothermere shook her head in the resigned way of other women when they talk about their nannies: 'Sooner or later they all start taking liberties, those editors.'

I asked her whether it was tricky: the owner-editor relationship.

'Well normally Vere doesn't like to get too close to them socially because it's difficult,' she explained. 'If you've got to tell them something the next morning about the paper, you can't be too close to them as friends. But the editors come to the weddings of our children – we invite them to those. And we have the Christmas party every year at Claridges for the staff and their wives. We *love* the wives,' said Lady Rothermere, 'because they are back-up for the dynamos who are the talent of our business.'

She was born Patricia Matthews, the daughter of a Hertfordshire architect, and was unostentatiously brought up in the Church of Scotland. As a teenager she was often ill – she spent a year in hospital with rheumatic fever and later snapped her spine in a riding accident – but by the time she was 16 she was unusually beautiful. She was only 18 when she married for the first time; she had met Captain Christopher Brooks, late of the Coldstream Guards, at a motor-racing event at

Goodwood and they became almost immediately engaged. He was rather a handsome 25-year-old, an exact contemporary of Vere Rothermere's at Eton, where they had known each other slightly but not well, Brooks being in with a faster set. Within a year of her marriage, Pat Brooks had given birth to a baby girl, Sarah, and embarked on a promising acting career; spotted by a Rank talent scout, she was offered a seven-year contract, enrolled as a starlet at the Rank Charm School, took the stage name Beverley Brooks, and began to get small parts in films, most memorably as a frothy deb in *Reach for the Sky*. Friends who remember her from this period say she was rather good: 'like the young Joan Collins but with more conviction'.

Within five years, however, her marriage to Brooks had lost momentum – anyway from her point of view – and she had met Vere Rothermere, by then aged 32, at a party. Rothermere began to spend a lot of time round at the Brooks's. 'He was endlessly hanging around our house and wouldn't go away,' says Lady Rothermere. 'I remember my first husband saying to him, 'Take your Daimler and yourself away from my wife!' Evidently Rothermere decided to take all three.

Lady Rothermere says now that, after her marriage to Vere, Darryl Zanuck wanted her to go to Hollywood, but Rothermere implored her to stay and she agreed to abandon her film career to support and advise him in London. 'Nobody in the newspaper business knew who Vere was,' she says, 'and because he was unknown I decided to ask the entire newspaper world to a party in our new house. I said to Vere, "Your fortune is as much your heritage as your father's. After all, he didn't make it, he inherited it like you will do, and like our son." I didn't know what would be involved in the marriage, or about the power struggle for an empire I would be caught up in. I just couldn't understand him, suffering so many hang-ups with his parents. I went through a lot of hell. I levelled with my father-in-law. I said to him, "I don't know whether I can handle it, Vere is so withdrawn." I am very religious you see; we had been married in the Church of Scotland, but after three months I had had enough. Three times he ran away from me. He had a yacht. And each time I found him and said, "You don't run away when you're a winner. Only a loser runs away, and you can be a winner." Three times I brought him home, and back to the newspapers. Esmond, my father-in-law, said, "If you leave him now, you'll break him forever." So I said, "Alright, I'll stay. But if I do, I'm going to fight and fight hard to let him stand up for what is his." And Esmond said, "You're throwing down the gauntlet, I don't want Vere in this biz." '

Much of what Patricia Rothermere said may be regarded as fanciful. Her husband's pivotal newspaper decision – like the decision to take the *Daily Mail* tabloid – were taken by him and him alone, without the knowledge, much less the advice, of his wife. And her periodic claims made late at night over a tumbler of champagne on the rocks and a bowl of onion soup at Annabel's, directly to influence the content of the newspapers were largely wishful thinking.

'Pat hardly ever rang me,' says David English. 'Only when she wanted help getting theatre tickets or something.'

She was not, however, without insight, and it is easy to see how – like the Scarlet Pimpernel, too frivolous to be taken seriously and so able to pick up interesting information from unguarded tongues – Lady Rothermere kept her husband abreast of the news. She had a well-developed suspicion of rival proprietors – predators – and was never off her guard.

Of the Murdochs she said: 'I like him, I like *them*, the Murdochs. Rupert's only once tried to double-cross Vere. We were having lunch with him in his apartment in New York, just Vere and I and Rupert and David Frost. And Rupert asked nonchalantly during lunch, "Well Vere, are you going to bid for *The Times*?" And Vere said that he wasn't, and that *very evening* Rupert put in his bid, which he never would have done if Vere hadn't been so honest. Sometimes Vere's *too* honest. You have to keep your wits about you with those sort of people.'

You feel that, above anything, she was the guardian of the next generation of Rothermeres; but that, unlike Lady Mary Fairfax, whom she in some respect resembled, she would never have allowed her own son to take the same drastic step as Warwick Fairfax and lose the birthright through impetuousness. In any case, she had already fulfilled her matriarchal duty by bearing an heir, at great personal danger, at a critical time.

Ten years after the Rothermeres were married, Vere's father, Esmond, against all expectations, remarried and produced a son, also called Esmond – half-brother for Vere, forty-two years his junior. Pat, at this point, had only got Rothermere girls – Geraldine, born in 1957, and Camilla, born in 1964. 'The arrival of this new son for Esmond took everyone by surprise,' says Nigel Dempster. 'He had married Mary Murchison, whose previous husband was one of the great oil Merchesons of Texas, and they set up home at Daylesford which he later sold to Heini Thyssen. When this son arrived all the trusts were jiggled around, because Vere had no heir for the Viscountcy, and all the newspapers would eventually have reverted to this surprise half-brother.' Pat Rothermere had been very ill when Camilla was born. At his wife's memorial service at St Bride's Church in Fleet Street, Rothermere spoke movingly of her bravery in trying to bear him an heir. 'Both mother and baby received absolution on the operating table. Camilla was there baptised. Neither was expected to survive.' Lady Rothermere had been told by her doctor she would die if she had another child. But the arrival of this son to her 70-year-old father-in-law made her determined, and she put a good deal of effort, too, into studying the methods of a Dr August Von Borosini for influencing the sex of her baby. Eventually, in December 1967, she was rewarded with a son, Jonathan Harmsworth, and Vere had secured Associated Newspapers for the next generation.

'For that alone,' says Dempster, 'I know that Vere believes he owed Pat an eternal debt. And so whatever happened in her life I don't think that he would ever have done anything but care for her.'

Jonathan Harmsworth, a tall, upright-looking boy in his early twenties, was sent to Gordonstoun and then, at his mother's suggestion, to Duke University in North Carolina. 'He found the attitude there wonderfully positive after school in Britain,' said Lady Rothermere. 'Here everything's *neg* – that's the word they use today at the schools: *Neg, neg, neg*. Jonathan says friends used to come into his study and say, "Don't you think it's *neg*?" When they tried to teach them American history, the other pupils said, "Why should I learn *American* history – it's *neg*." So I said, "Not Oxford. If you go to Oxford, Jonathan, people will only come to your room and take drugs and get depressed. Go to an American University, with all that open air." And in America, too, the name Harmsworth means nothing, almost nothing. Whereas here, because of the newspapers . . .

'Was I sensible?' Lady Rothermere suddenly asked me. 'Was my advice sensible?' She sounded like she really minded.

I replied that it sounded perfectly sensible.

'I am sensible,' she said. 'It is Vere who likes me to appear frivolous.

He once asked me, "Let me never see you serious, I like you always to be fun-loving and happy, it relaxes me." So I try to be, to please Vere, you see.'

Then, as though with renewed determination to be fun-loving and happy and please her husband in another time zone, she said, 'You must forgive me, I must meet some people now. At Annabel's. I do enjoy Annabel's though Mark Birley really charges one too much. A bottle of Laurent Perrier pink champagne is £65 at Annabel's but it's only £22 at the André Simon off-licence. I asked Mark if I could bring my own champagne in with me, but he said he'd have to charge me £15 corkage just to open it up.'

In May 1992 Lord Rothermere threw a party to mark the 21st anniversary of the relaunched *Daily Mail*. It was a gala expressly devised to emphasise the *Mail*'s triumph over the opposition, and more than a thousand people, including the Prime Minister John Major, numerous Cabinet ministers, composers, television personalities and rock stars were invited to a dinner at the Grosvenor House Hotel. Rothermere, who elected to sit between the television presenter Selina Scott and his own sister, Esmee Cromer, looked supremely patrician with his full head of silver hair and immaculately cut dinner jacket. The first Lady Rothermere, who hosted a table adjacent to her husband's, had invited the David Frosts, Bill Wyman and Johnny Gold, the owner of the nightclub Tramp.

A towering 21st birthday cake was wheeled into the ballroom and Rothermere stood next to Sir David English in the centre of the dancefloor, hands clasped behind his back, like an owner in the paddock at Goodwood inspecting his prize yearling with his trainer. Later he made a speech in which he credited English with being 'The greatest and most creative editor seen in Fleet Street since the time of Northcliffe, who breathed heart and soul into my newspaper like Michelangelo's Jehovah breathing life into Adam.

'The politics of my newspapers, Prime Minister,' he declared to John Major, 'are what my editors believe the politics of their readers to be. For myself,' he went on, 'I left Thatcher's Britain for Mitterrand's France because it is in Europe that our future lies.'

Four months later I heard Lord Rothermere again speaking publicly at an event of a very different nature, the service of thanksgiving for the life of his wife who had died of a heart attack. His own car had recently spun off a wet autoroute in France, and his arm was in plaster. In a matter of months he had aged, and his hair turned snowy-white. He spoke of his deep love for Lady Rothermere, of his gratitude to her for bearing him a son 'and so ensuring the future of our family newspapers', and how she had been traduced by rival newspapers, for reasons of jealousy, by turning her into a figure of fun. He said that he had written a poem entitled 'I Love You' in her memory, which he had slipped inside her coffin, and which he now read out in trembling voice:

> I was never old nor wise enough for you
> My pen has not the depth nor scan
> My mind the reach nor season
> To compose the strange music of your heart
> Oh, lady with the Mahler soul
> Why have you me in thrall?
> I have wept deep tears tinged with the blood of my life
> As love's sweet and secret sea
> Far below the burning sands of living.

Sixteen months after the memorial service, Lord Rothermere became engaged to Maiko Lee. He argued that the death of Pat, and the terrible shock it had given him, had made him acutely conscious of his own mortality; a sense that was heightened by the crash of his Porsche in a rainstorm, which landed not just him, but Maiko too, in hospital. The loss of his wife, he said, 'was terrible after so many years together, like soldiers in the trenches, and made me conscious of my own death, as if it were breathing down my neck. Pat was tempestuous like a tropical storm that takes its energy from its surroundings.' Lord Rothermere told *The Sunday Telegraph* that, if anything happened to him, Maiko would be in a better position – from a status point of view – as his widow than single, as a spinster.

Maiko Lee explained the complexity of her new status upon her engagement: 'I shall be officially Viscountess, but in normal life Miss Lee. It would be too complicated to be Miss Lee at formal dinners when Miss Lee might be put next to the kitchen.'

The Colossus of Canary Wharf

Conrad Black, dreamer of deals

On 31 January 1991, Conrad Black ambled into the Grill Room of the Savoy. A burly man with the physique of a prizefighter and shoulders as broad as an Alberta buffalo, he surveyed the room in a single sweep, registering the significant lunchers at other tables: Lord Rothermere, a competitor of sorts, lunching with his newspapers' chairman Sir David English; Lord Deedes and Sir Peregrine Worsthorne, both entertaining Cabinet ministers on Conrad Black's ticket; Lord Carrington, the former Foreign Secretary, now a member of two of Black's heavy-hitting boards at the *Daily Telegraph* and at Hollinger, the newspaper's holding company in Toronto. Later as they passed by his table at the end of lunch, Black was buttonholed by the chairman of Cable and Wireless, Lord Young, and Margaret Thatcher's former media advisor Sir Tim Bell.

'What did you make of the Chancellor's speech yesterday, Conrad?' asked David Young, and both men stood in rapt attention throughout Black's long and discursive reply.

His enjoyment of the role of influential proprietor was highly evident. He relished the attention, and yet you got the impression that he was deriving at least equal pleasure from the ritual of the exchange; the presence of these two Thatcherite knights hanging around the *Telegraph* owner's table in the Savoy Grill, soliciting his political opinions. It endorsed, as decisively as anything can, the pre-eminence of newspaper proprietorship over other brands of power.

Later Black was to tell me: 'Let us be completely frank, the deferences and preferments that this culture bestows upon the owners of great newspapers are satisfying. I mean, I tend to think that they're slightly exaggerated at times, but as the beneficiary – a beneficiary – of that system it would certainly be hypocrisy for me to complain about it.'

His voice has a lugubrious undertow that manages, in a highly idiosyncratic way, to convey considerable determination. Words are emphasised and underscored as though his conversation is being simultaneously transcribed, and he is signalling the necessity of italics to a stenographer. Sometimes, in full flow, he sounds like a New York police siren blaring across town.

Of the 30 proprietors I interviewed, Black is the most erudite. He talks in complex, elaborate paragraphs; his pronouncements on almost any topic contain a legion of sub-clauses and tangents, and frequently include half a dozen or more reasons for any particular course of action, enumerated in order of importance: the six reasons that he acquired the *Jerusalem Post*, four British Cabinet ministers who are fundamentally sleazeballs, five sleazeball American senators, seven reasons why Canada must be one of the most inexpertly governed countries in the advanced world over the last 35 years, four reasons why he invited Henry Kissinger to join the advisory board of Hollinger.

At 46, Conrad Moffat Black is the youngest proprietor of consequence who didn't inherit his newspapers. In eight years he has muscled his way from the third division of owners into the second division and finally up into the first. His newspaper properties in London, Toronto, Jerusalem, Melbourne, Sydney and the Caribbean give him a geographical spread sheet that matches Murdoch. In sheer numbers, his empire of 240 papers, mostly small dailies and weeklies in Canada and North America, propel him into pole position. Although their total daily circulation of 4.5 million is small fry next to Murdoch, Conrad Black has emerged since 1985 as a rapacious acquisitor, controlling the fastest-growing newspaper empire in the world. With Maxwell dead, Murdoch movie-making in Los Angeles, the Sulzbergers, Grahams, Chandlers and Thomsons tending their existing estates, Rothermere reluctant to expand heavily outside Britain, O'Reilly temporarily thwarted, Hersant embroiled in Eastern Europe and the Hong Kong media millionaires agitated by the impending advent of the Chinese into the colony, Conrad Black commands the high ground in the acquisitions field. More than any other major league owner, he has the finance, the gusto and freedom of movement to bid for big city papers. When he conceded the *New York Daily News* to his fellow Canadian Mortimer Zuckerman, he did so only because he demanded New York on his own terms or not at all.

By the spring of 1993, Black's principal media holdings included the *Daily Telegraph* – Britain's largest-selling quality daily, the great broadsheet of Toryism – and its sister *Sunday Telegraph* in London, the *Sydney Morning Herald*, *Melbourne Age* and *Australian Financial Review* in Australia, the *Jerusalem Post* in Israel and the *Financial Post* and *Le Soleil* in Toronto. In the United States, his Illinois-based American Publishing Corporation owns more than a hundred small newspapers with evocative titles, mostly in middle America, including the *Fort Morgan Times*, the *Monmouth Review Atlas*, the *Eldorado Daily Journal*, the *Kane Republican*, the *Flora Clay County Advocate*, the *Rushville Republican* and the *Punxsutawny Spirit*; in Canada, his Vancouver-based Sterling Newspapers group includes the *Alaska Highway News*, the *Kimberley Bulletin*, the *Summerside Journal-Pioneer* and the *Dawson Creek Peace River Block News*; the *Waikiki Pennysaver*; in London, the *Spectator*; in the Caribbean, he has 40 per cent of the Cayman Free Press, owners of the *Caymanian Compass*.

When visiting his competitors, I was struck by the degree of their fascination for Black. Aside from the late Robert Maxwell, Conrad Black was the proprietor they most wished to discuss. This was partly for social reasons: his recent marriage to the glamour-puss political journalist Barbara Amiel had caught the amused eye of both Kay Graham and Punch Sulzberger (particularly the post-wedding dinner he gave at the nightclub Annabel's, at which Black had sat between Margaret Thatcher and the Duchess of York). The British election-night party he'd thrown at the Savoy for 500 opinion makers of all political shades drew oblique commentary from Lord Stevens, Ralph Ingersoll and Rupert Murdoch. 'Conrad is decisive, he's not frightened to make his point of view known or want to see it reflected in his newspapers,' Murdoch told me. 'I think he's there to lead from the front and he's courageous. He's also, it would seem, enjoying all the fun that goes with the publishing business.'

It was interesting to watch how fast Black's proprietorial stock rose, even during the four years that I was stalking newspaper owners. In 1988 he was a shadowy figure from the frozen north, of whom nothing much was known beyond his fondness for Napoleon, his Catholicism (he is a convert from Anglicanism) and his reputation as a right-wing ideologue. Several owners doubted that he merited a place in this book, and suggested I substitute him for somebody more important. Four years later, it would be difficult for them to compile a top ten without including Black. It has become almost a cliché to compare him with Lord Beaverbrook, most legendary of Canadian press moguls who fraternised with the great and good of England and ended up parodied as Lord Copper in Evelyn Waugh's *Scoop*.

If you imagine a horizontal line across Conrad Black's face, from earlobe to earlobe, you see that it divides into two unrelated sections. His eyes, and the primeval shape of his forehead, betoken vigour, cunning, strength of purpose and more than a scintilla of callousness. However the line of the mouth, and its tendency to curl up disdainfully when discussing ideologies contrary to his own, suggest fastidiousness, self-mockery, worldly-wise cynicism and a certain intellectual narcissism. At dinner parties, he does not shun the opportunity to dominate the table with his filibusters on politics, history or anything else. Some people believe that Conrad Black weaves his tendentious theories as he goes along, purely for the linguistic satisfaction of being able to do so. Each topic is launched in a trail of provocative adjectives, that clatter behind his targets like railway carriages coupled to a steam engine. Black on journalists: 'Some of them are temperamental, tiresome, nauseatingly eccentric and simply just obnoxious. A number are ignorant, lazy, opinionated, intellectually dishonest and inadequately supervised.' Black on staff cuts following his takeover of the *Jerusalem Post*: 'Israelis do *not* go quietly. They're obstreperous, certainly compared to people in this country, and *this* country's hard compared to the United States. My God, they squawk and carp and take you to court and stir it all up and get all the contracts in front of the media.' Black on a distinguished American executive who narrowly missed getting an important job: 'He would have bankrupted that company in a year. He'd have turned it into the most scented sinecure since Caligula's horse.'

'I think in some respects Conrad is very shy,' says Daniel Colson, the Stikeman Elliott lawyer who helped negotiate the *Telegraph*, *Jerusalem Post* and Fairfax acquisitions and is now deputy chairman of Hollinger. 'He doesn't come across that way at all – he comes across as rather blustery – but the fact is that he is shy. He can lay it [the bluster] on so thick that, if you don't know him, you'd sort of step back and wonder. But he doesn't take himself seriously at all and in a small group is extremely entertaining and very amusing. He's good value.

'I don't wish to sound in any way obsequious,' says Colson, 'because it's not the way I am, and we have a relationship which has stood the test of time and one of the reasons for that is that I have never hesitated to tell him what I think about anything. But I have to say that Conrad is quite impressive in terms of constantly dreaming up possible ways to expand. He is without a doubt one of the world's greatest dreamers of deals; he is always thinking of possible deals here, there and everywhere. Let's put it this way, in the 21 or so years I've been doing what I do I've probably worked with every major investment bank and merchant bank on both sides of the Atlantic as well as the main ones in Asia. I would say that I've rarely, if ever, met anybody who can be as analytical about structuring a transaction as Conrad can. He really is exceptionally talented at figuring out different ways to skin a cat. He is one of these people who, if you're in a meeting and people keep saying 'you can't do that', is very resourceful in terms of coming up with different ways of doing what at first glance seems to be difficult if not impossible. But he is expansive. He sort of enjoys the hunt as well as the kill, and I think also he enjoys letting people in the room know that he is in control of the situation and that he is as smart as he is. He recognises that there can be significant advantages to having people recognise that.'

Black divides his year between his mansion in Toronto, with its three-storey elliptical library and copper cupola modelled on the dome of St Peter's in Rome, a house in Palm Beach ('It isn't everyone's cup of tea. Some people are offended by the extreme opulence, but I find it sort of entertaining') and a double-sized stucco-fronted house in Kensington that he bought from Alan Bond. For a man with so many corporate balance sheets hitting his desk, he is remarkably unhurried. He ambles into meetings, perhaps secure in the knowledge that the other participants will wait for him. He will allow appointments to overrun indefinitely if he is engrossed by them (and will end them mid-agenda when his eyes glaze with boredom). He arrives tardily into the office in the morning, often not making an appearance before noon, is chronically unpunctual for meals, and his employees have learnt to make no afternoon appointments when lunching with him.

'One rather has to clear the rest of the day if lunching with Conrad,' says *Daily Telegraph* editor Max Hastings, 'in case he wants to talk on about military history or something, which of course is no hardship for me.'

Notwithstanding his fabled contempt for journalists, most journalists on the Conrad Black payroll rather like him. I found little of the anxiety and paranoia over what the proprietor might think, when discussing Black with his editors, that you encounter in the Murdoch stable, and to an even greater extent encountered with Maxwell. His harshest journalistic critics (as opposed to his business critics) say only that he can be a windbag. His supporters describe him as generally reliable, consistent, genuinely intelligent, loyal.

'I am 60 years old and have seldom come across a display of loyalty and support from an owner as that which I receive from Conrad Black,' David Bar-Illan, the political and opinion editor of the *Jerusalem Post*, told me. 'At the beginning, when I first took over this role, it meant a revolution in the direction of the paper. It had previously been politically very much to the left and my coming in meant a drastic change, which inevitably meant attacks from a number of former contributors to the paper, including the most senior Israeli politicians, unhappy their hobby horse had been taken from them. They sent their complaints to Conrad in London, who defended me with this display of loyalty that I could never have expected from anyone. He didn't just reply with the form letter of a businessman but with passionate involvement, defending me in such a manner that he might even have risked friendships. From the moment I first met Black I was overwhelmed by his eloquence and extraordinary command of our language. He is incredibly informed about Israel, *incredibly*. It belongs very much to his world political philosophy that Israel is part of the Good Guys; I'd say he is more interested in the country *per se* than in the newspaper. I certainly don't know too many people abroad who have the knowledge and passionate interest and concern that Conrad has.'

'Does this passionate interest and concern mean he interferes a lot in your editorials?'

'As a proprietor he's a halfway-house – to me very advantageously so – between the Roy Thomson school of non-intervention and the Beaverbrook school,' Max Hastings told me, feet on desk, jacket on chairback, cigar clamped firmly aloft towards Black's office directly above his own. 'He loves looking at the papers without ringing up all the time and wanting to change a headline. There are moments when his attention is very firmly focused on the *Telegraph*, but there are also long periods, especially in the summer, when he's not here, when he's away in Palm Beach or somewhere. He'll sometimes wander into my office when he's here, and I lunch or dine with him a certain amount, about once a month. He's quite keen on wine actually. Plainly we have a lot of traffic at the time of elections. I've always thought the notion of editorial independence rather absurd. I'd think it very odd indeed in a capitalist society if Conrad was unable to express an opinion on something as fundamental as who runs the country.'

'Shortly after I'd taken over at the *Spectator*,' said Dominic Lawson, who edits the political weekly acquired by Black in 1988, 'Conrad remarked to me at the end of a meeting, "You know I like to contribute leaders from time to time." I replied, "So long as you respect my right as editor to edit them." I think he was trying to see what my response would be, treating it as a tennis game. My experience since then is that he conforms pretty much to one's ideal of a proprietor. Before I published my interview with Nicholas Ridley [the late Secretary of State for Trade and Industry who felt compelled to resign from the Government over his anti-German sentiments reported by Lawson in the article] I rang Conrad at the Hollinger HQ in Toronto, because I felt I ought to warn him we were publishing something rather controversial, and that it was indeed already typeset. Conrad just said, "Fax it to me when it's printed." And although I found out from other sources that the article had caused him some embarrassment, he was robust about it, in fact he never ever mentioned it to me. I can actually think of only one occasion when Conrad's expressed any opinion and a desire that we hadn't published something. We'd had a piece by Nicholas von Hoffman on why the US economy is doomed, and he just rang and said, "I wish you hadn't printed that".'

'Any element of condescension about the United States creeps into the paper, he's on to it,' says Max Hastings. 'There's a tendency, he believes, on the part of the English to condescend about everything American, and I would certainly say that our approach to the United States is affected by having Conrad Black as proprietor. One of the few subjects on which we disagree intractably is that Conrad insists US television is better than British television. He can't accept we have only four channels, he's a great sweeper of channels all through the night. Conrad loves television and he's very teasable about it. He's really perfectly prepared to be teased, it's one of his admirable qualities, and he takes it in very good part. Not teased about the balance sheet, but anything else, his unpunctuality or his fascination with military history. We were having dinner one evening in some Italian restaurant in Ebury Street, I was rather tired actually, when at half-past-ten at night Conrad suddenly asked, "Who would you say are the six greatest military commanders of all time?" and I said, "Conrad, for *heaven's sake*." But there's no deflecting him, and we argued the toss about it for a considerable time.

'I first met Conrad at the end of 1985 when I was flown to Toronto to be inspected by him for the *Daily Telegraph* job. As I entered his office I noticed a picture on the wall and said, "Ah, HMS *Warspite* entering Narvik in April 1940," and I've always suspected that he was pleased one had correctly identified this great moment in British naval history, it got our conversation off on the right foot. Periodically he'll try to floor one. I sometimes tease him that a tremendous collection of data can possibly be confused with knowledge.

'One of the things I find endearing about him, compared to one or two of the other proprietors, is that Conrad simply *adores* being a tycoon, he seems to get tremendous pleasure out of it. Although he is very seriously dedicated to the business of making money, he'll also do things – like his ownership of the *Spectator* – with room for fun. However he's concious that it's the newspapers that give him the thrust and power and the access that enable him to be a major international player. And he does *play* unlike some of his peers. Look at Rupert Murdoch, rushing about on tight schedules. But Conrad does enjoy a three-hour lunch with a couple of editors.

'Essentially he's a genuinely civilised man when most proprietors are brutes. He doesn't camp it up, doesn't swagger into a room making a big performance out of owning the *Telegraph*. I don't think one could call Conrad unpretentious, but he's not a megalomaniac. I judge all tycoons and politicians on how far they retain an ability for self-mockery. Conrad has retained this ability. Maybe one's been lucky, maybe there are issues on which one could come into conflict that haven't arisen yet. I'm not fool enough to think things would be so relaxed if they weren't going so well commercially.

'The tribute one would most make to Conrad is that there's not much one's wanted to do in one's time here that he won't support. He's been prepared to pay for the costs of covering major international events like the Gulf War, and if one goes to Conrad and says, "At a price we can get such and such a person for the paper," he'll invariably say yes. Despite all those quotes about him being antagonistic to journalists, he's actually been very supportive of journalists, though if he'd been the proprietor ten years ago it would have driven him mad. It's probably fortunate for him that he arrived at the end of the Old Fleet Street . . . that awful pub with terrible scenes being played out. The last office drunks were sacked by me three or four years ago and you just don't see people reeling about any more. There's less scope for mavericks and eccentricity than there once was, people work hard for long hours. Actually I don't think many merchant bankers would see much difference in the atmosphere here and in their own offices. If Conrad had seen it before, God knows what he'd have thought. The only respect in which Conrad's strong views about journalists manifest themselves is in his dislike of the extreme left-wing ones. You only have to speak to him about John Pilger or Christopher Hitchens and Conrad's passions are very strongly aroused.'

'He's certainly the child of the Establishment, but he's a quirky fellow,' says John Fraser who edits *Saturday Night*, Black's Canadian political monthly in Toronto. 'The Establishment over here is normally completely faceless: don't make waves, keep quiet, make money. What Conrad's done is the very antithesis of that. You feel he often does things precisely because it bucks against contemporary thinking, group thinking. His biography of Maurice Duplessis [Premier of Quebec between 1936 and 1959; 743 pages long, published in 1977] was not untypical; at the time he wrote about him, Duplessis was one of the most reviled figures in Canadian history, and that book earned him the jealousy of the professional historians as well as the bitchiness of some. I remember having lunch with him one day in a restaurant in Toronto, some place downtown near his offices. It was before I came to work for him but even in those days – maybe it was his great wealth – I deferred to him. After lunch we wandered over to a magazine store and browsed through the racks and Conrad picked up a copy of *Encounter*.

'I said, "You'd better be careful with that, you know the CIA fund it."

'Conrad replied, "Yeah . . . but not enough." Seven or eight years later, of course, Conrad began funding it himself.'

'The first time I attended anything publicly he was involved with was a dinner he gave for Margaret Thatcher in about 1988 up in Toronto,' recalls Ralph Ingersoll. 'It was the most amazing dinner, the annual dinner of the Hollinger company. He'd asked me to bring up Katharine Graham and Henry Kissinger with me in my Westwing. Katharine's always featured herself as part of the proletariat so she won't have her own airplane and Henry was a neighbour of mine in Connecticut. Henry, it turned out, was a non-executive director on the Hollinger board because Conrad collects dressy directors, and neither of them had any idea what the hell they were going up to. We were all fascinated.

'So we all flew up and we changed and went into dinner. It was described as the 57th annual Hollinger dinner. It turned out that Hollinger is an old mining company that's been around for 57 years and is now Conrad's media vehicle. So in order to dress the occasion up a little bit he described it as the 57th annual dinner. They probably ate out around a camp fire in British Columbia at the first annual dinner.

'And it was a very impressive gathering of the Toronto Club – he had every Supreme Court judge, every Cabinet minister. And when Conrad got up to introduce Margaret Thatcher he spoke for about 40 minutes. He was so enthused at having her there as his guest that by the time he'd finished she was the finest Prime Minister not in a generation, not in this century, not since Oliver Cromwell but in a thousand years! And he took up so much time that when she got up to reply she made a big joke of it and spoke for five minutes and sat down. It was very funny. But Conrad was having a good time and it was harmless.'

One of his London editors told me, 'In a way he's a power-worshipper, to the extent that he automatically assumes that the people in political office are the people you should meet. But at heart he's a romantic, which explains why he started out very favourable to John Major, but quickly became bored with him and switched his interest back to Mrs Thatcher. He has dinner with Thatcher eight or ten times a year I would think. He expects politics to be colourful and fun, so when it's all dreary, as it is with Major, he gets fed up. Having said that, it wouldn't be true to say that the *Telegraphs* have become anti-Major because Black sent an order that they should.'

'He's intelligent and he's well-educated,' says Charles Moore, the editor of the *Sunday Telegraph* who previously worked for Black as editor of the *Spectator*, 'though there are all sorts of completely closed areas [in his knowledge] which in some ways is rather attractive since he doesn't pretend; he doesn't talk rubbish or pretend he's read things he hasn't read or is interested in things he isn't, like culture really, art, opera, poetry, fiction. What he cares about is history, Catholicism, military strategy, politics, money. He likes to talk about what he's reading, normally a great big biography, sometimes conventional political biographies or sometimes more learned stuff: Arab relations with the West in the twentieth century, that kind of thing. And he does it slightly in terms of his heroes: Napoleon, de Gaulle and Cardinal Newman.'

'Conrad can be called many things, but trendy ain't one of them,' a Toronto contemporary assured me. 'Not unless his acute addiction to making money twenty years before it became mandatory qualifies as trendy.'

'As a proprietor he's good,' says Moore, 'because he combines being very interested in and knowledgeable about politics, but doesn't try to run the paper. One thing he's very good about – if a negative thing can be very good – is that he won't intervene politically before the event. He won't say, "We must do something this way", or demand to see an article before it's published. If he does intervene, which is very rare, he'll do so after the event and say he doesn't agree with such and such a line. And he's open to argument too. He likes to have a set-to about it. I don't mean he'll ever change his mind but he'll enjoy the argument.

'I first met him at the Downing Street dinner that Mrs Thatcher gave for Bill Deedes, though I already knew him from a couple of letters he'd written to the *Spectator*. One of them was an attack on an article by Christopher Hitchens on "Living with a sick President" about Reagan's polyps in his colon. Conrad wrote a furious letter, this disgusting article etc. It was shortly afterwards that Andrew Knight [Black's chief executive, until he defected to Murdoch] came up to me at the Tory Conference and said, "If the Fairfaxes [who then owned the *Spectator*] are in trouble, do think of us." '

As the Fairfax trouble deepened, Moore did think of Black, though his acquisition of the *Spectator* did not stay Black's contributions to the correspondence columns. When in January 1990 Moore wrote a teasing critique of his proprietor's literary manner, concluding that his 'epistolary style' was 'full of sound and fury, not signifying all that much', Black sent this reply for publication:

> Almost any stylistic critique is fair comment, and there is probably some merit in this one, but must Mr Moore react . . . like a bantam rooster? He would do better to congratulate himself on having sought and found for the *Spectator* a proprietor who responds so equably to the minor irritations, such as this one, that the *Spectator* inflicts upon that person who ultimately, and more or less uncomplainingly, pays the *Spectator*'s losses and endures Mr Moore's occasional condescensions.

'He's certainly the most charming and interesting and intelligent of the proprietors,' says Moore. 'Quite different from Murdoch who really strikes me as rather an evil man, I mean you couldn't produce those papers, the *Sun* and the *News of the World* without being so. No ordinary decent man would want to.'

'He's someone who obviously listens,' says Dominic Lawson, 'and this can be disconcerting. He rather stares at you – a rather basilisk stare – and goes very quiet. He tends not to butt in and interrupt you, which has the effect of making you careful in what you say. He's also quick to detect irony. I once asked him, "And how is your campaign for the canonisation of Cardinal Newman coming on?" To which he replied, "I detect more than a trace of Rabbinical scepticism in that remark, Dominic," a reference to my Jewish background. Conrad's not someone who indulges in small talk. He tends to come in and *immediately* launch into the sanctification of Cardinal Newman.'

In Britain, to an even greater extent than in Toronto, Black is a figure of almost statesmanlike stature, endlessly discussed by his staff and competitors. But his proprietorial impact varies in intensity in different areas of his newspaper empire. In Jerusalem his proprietorial personality is ethereal and ill-defined and faintly sinister. In America, despite his widespread newspaper holdings, he remains largely unknown, and there are editors who have worked for him for ten years without meeting him or having more than the vaguest notion of his personality or politics. 'Conrad Black could walk through the front door of any of his papers in Ohio or Idaho and nobody would have the first idea who the hell he was,' said one of his Ohio managers. 'Nobody knows what the feller looks like.'

I asked Black whether he ever read any of his provincial papers, 'the *Kane Republican*, say?'

'I never laid eyes on that one. No, I shouldn't say never. Rarely. We own a lot of little newspapers in the United States and I'm ultimately the proprietor of them, but I never set foot in most of those towns and have never read most of them ever.'

I rang the editor of Black's *Caymanian Compass*, Ursula Gill, to solicit her opinion of him as a proprietor.

'Who's that guy you're talkin' about?' asked Mrs Gill, who said she had just been swimming from the beach.

'Conrad Black.'

'I don't remember ever meeting that guy. Who is he again?'

'He's the chairman of Hollinger, the company that owns quite a lot of your newspaper.'

'I've heard that name of Hollinger someplace,' said Mrs Gill. 'But I don't know nothin' about that guy Black you're speakin' of.'

I asked Conrad Black how much further he saw his empire expanding.

'In the first place it's not an empire,' he replied. 'I feel slightly uneasy with imperial metaphors. I agree with those who feel that military analogies are grossly overworked when applied to business situations, especially in the aftermath of the war in the Persian Gulf, when half the business people one meets fancy themselves as miniature Schwarzkopfs or something. But may I offer a metaphor arising from the great Liddell Hart, who propounded between the wars, as you probably know, a military theory based on co-ordinated action with mechanised units – armoured units – and airforces. And he had this notion – an *expanding torrent* he called it – and the illustration he gave was like pouring water on a hillock. You couldn't exactly predict what course it would follow as it went downhill, you just knew it would go downhill and get to the bottom. I've found, in our company, that the acquisition trails are like that. Ten years ago I couldn't have predicted any of these acquisitions; I certainly couldn't have predicted the *Daily Telegraph*, I couldn't have predicted the *Jerusalem Post* or the *Sydney Morning Herald* and if anyone had predicted them for me I would have thought them pretty impetuous in doing that. But, in Mr Micawber's phrase, something does turn up and things continue to turn up fairly regularly. So I feel that the best job I can do is keep in touch with as many people as I can and do whatever I can to be considered a *desirable buyer* by those who may wish to sell. And just take the opportunities as they come up and avoid overpaying for things or chasing things.

'You doubtless read the other day in the *Financial Times*,' he went on, 'that we were being derided for not having a strategy. It's all very well for the *FT* to say shouldn't we have a grand plan. Well we *do* have a grand plan: it is the one they derided as a *non-grand plan*. The grand plan is to make deals. Yes, it would be very nice in one sense to have a strategy based on our becoming owners over time, for argument's sake, of *Le Monde* in France, Signor Agnelli's newspapers in Italy, Dr Burda's papers in Germany, the Tribune company in the United States and various interests in the Far East. But the problem is none of those is for sale. And no strategy is worth anything unless you can make the deals to carry it out. So our strategy is to cast our fly upon the waters and look upon any prospect that seems to have the possibility of being useful for us. And I don't think it's a bad strategy or one that embarrasses me particularly. If we had devised a strategy that conformed to what the *Financial Times* might consider to be orthodox, not only would we have never been in Australia or Israel, but sitting with the kind of strategy they might have considered appropriate to a clapped-out mining company – which Hollinger was when I got hold of it – we never would have been here in the *Daily Telegraph* either. Everyone thought I was *mad* when I bought the *Daily Telegraph*, but the strategy is to look for the deal and follow it. The *New York Daily News* could have been a good deal until Zuckerman presented the more militant and powerful unions with the opportunity for continuing business as usual. Then it ceased to be of any interest to us. But was it a mistake to look at it? No, it wasn't a mistake to look at it. What did we lose?'

'Conrad likes to use this expression,' says Daniel Colson, 'which was attributed to a quarterback of an American football league many years ago – a guy who played for the Baltimore Colts – who once asked what his gameplan was replied, "to fill the air with footballs". And I've heard Conrad use that many times, his theory being that if you throw enough balls up in the air, if you have enough deals cooking at the same time, one or two of them are bound to happen.'

People kept assuring me that, in order to understand this proprietor or that, I should look to their father for clues. The key to Rupert Murdoch's ambition was his competitiveness with Sir Keith Murdoch. The key to young Warwick Fairfax is old Sir Warwick. The motivation for Roberto Marinho could be found in his increasingly frail father, who died 21 days after acquiring *O Globo*, and so bequeathed his son a Herculean birthright. 'To understand Conrad Black,' I was repeatedly told, 'you must examine his relationship with his father; the talents and disappointments of George Black have more to do with Conrad's motivation than any single other factor.' His last words to his son, before he crashed through the balustrade of a staircase and fell to his death, were 'Life is hell, most people are bastards and everything is bullshit.'

George Montagu Black Jr was president of Canadian Breweries, the enormous conglomerate that owned beer-making businesses not just throughout the provinces of Canada but the United States and Britain. He had a reputation as a shrewd labour controller in a period of incessant union agitation, and for quickness at mental calculation: at board meetings he could multiply two six-digit figures in his head and arrive, almost instantly, at the correct answer to within two decimal places. Eventually he fell out with the chairman of Canadian Breweries, Edward Taylor, and at the age of 47 found himself without a job and with a distinct feeling of injustice. Not wishing to take up a full-time job in another corporation, he worked from home in Toronto, turning his passion for searching out undervalued stocks and bonds into a highly profitable occupation. Conrad, then aged 14, spent most of his evenings at home with his mother, Jean, and his increasingly reclusive father, playing chess (often replaying gambits by Cuban and Russian grand masters) and being tutored in the tactics of corporate warfare and the Dow theory (named after the first editor of the *Wall Street Journal*, Charles Dow, which postulates that there are three basic movements in the stock market and develops complex sets of indices to interpret and exploit these fluctuations). Three other themes dominated these intense father and son discussions: the relevance of historical perspective (the adult Conrad Black seldom makes any statement longer than 300 words without citing some historical precedent), the corporate lore of Argus (the vast Canadian holding company) whose board George Black had joined, and which Conrad would later take over in 125 days of savage corporate in-fighting and the art of seeing through grown-ups' deceptions (a trait Black shares with the late Robert Maxwell, who also claimed to be able to detect deception intuitively).

George Black installed a slot machine in the family drawing room so that Conrad, and his elder brother Montagu, could learn that gambling provides a disappointing rate of return against playing the stock market. When he was barely eight, Conrad saved 60 dollars in pocket money to purchase one share in General Motors. 'When I bought that share,' he would later recall, 'it was for motives that were then widely held by my elders. The Korean war was on at the time; Stalin was still in power; it was the height of the Cold War. To buy stock in General Motors was a wise means of participating in the growth of capitalism, supporting a great institution and casting one's vote with the side of justice and freedom in a worldwide struggle with the red menace which was then generally assumed to be lurking behind every bush and under every bed.'

Successful men invariably have prescient stories ascribed to their youth, proving an early aptitude for whatever they become famous for later on. The Conrad Black myths all concern money and power: a family friend remembers blinking in disbelief as he watched, through the summer haze, an eight-year-old Conrad carefully washing dollar bills and hanging them out on a line to dry; another recalls him spending whole afternoons sitting in his bedroom reading through the Canadian *Who's Who*, studying tycoons' career paths; the historian Laurier LaPierre, who taught the adolescent Black history at Upper Canada College, remembers saying to him one day after school, 'It seems to me, Conrad, that you're waiting. What is it you're waiting for?' Black replied that he'd been waiting to become chairman of Argus since he was seven years old, and that he was still waiting for that. 'It will come, one day,' he prophesied.

'Conrad's entire sense of life revolved around the idea that, through a combination of circumstance, accidents and evolution, God is granting him this extraordinary power that he must guard well and pass on,' recalled LaPierre. 'He has always felt himself to be a genuine instrument of history.'

Black's first biographer Peter Newman quotes Ian Dowie, a Canadian Breweries executive, returning a borrowed biography of Napoleon to George Black and asking his opinion of the relationship between Bonaparte and his ambitious marshals. George Black gestured towards his ten-year-old son: 'Ask Conrad; he's the authority.' Conrad rose definitively to the challenge, reciting every last detail of Napoleon's reticulated intrigues.

'Although I might have had trouble articulating it at the age of ten,' said Black, 'I wasn't unduly convinced of the durability of the Anglo-Saxon world as we had come to know it in the postwar period, a world of latter-day materialism advancing around the globe on the wings of the English language and the American dollar. I had a sneaking suspicion that we were living in a bit of a fool's paradise and began to be much more interested in French culture, particularly Napoleon and de Gaulle.'

There is a theory that Conrad Black emerged from his evening discussions with his father mentally so revved-up that classroom teaching seemed commonplace by comparison, and this eventually led to his being expelled from two private schools and failing his law courses. Black showed no remorse, in fact each setback only seemed to fuel his admiration for awkward, free-thinking entrepreneurs over the compliant mass.

'Childhood was a prison for him,' recalls John Fraser, who was a contemporary at Upper Canada College's prep school. 'I remember Conrad as someone whose head was practically splitting because he was so impatient to get out into the real world and away from this nonsense of a boys' school. My earliest memory of him was in about Grade Six and how terribly, terribly conscious he was of wealth and power. We were walking around the school grounds one day and Conrad was raving on about the whole of the college and said, 'E.P. Taylor [the founder of Argus] could buy this silly place 50 times over. He'd subdivide and make some money off it.' He was constantly sketching scenarios for taking over the college.'

Black complained to John Fraser, 'Do you realise this is exactly the format of those death camps in the Third Reich? Here we are at compulsory games, compulsory changes of clothes, being herded like animals to the showers – and I hope to God it's water and not Cyclon-B that comes out. This place is a concentration camp, but most of the inmates are oblivious to the fact.'

'That's the way Conrad talked then,' says Fraser. 'That's the way he talked when he was ten.'

Early entrepreneurial skill was demonstrated at UCC's senior school with the famous theft and copy of examination papers, sold on a sliding scale according to means and desperation. Black was found out ('One of the people to whom we sold an examination was discovered, and he sang like a canary flying backward at three o'clock in the morning,' he recalls with a classic Black simile) and expelled, learning an important lesson: 'As I was walking out the gates a number of students who literally 24 hours before had been begging for assistance – one of them on his knees – were now shaking their fists and shouting words of moralistic execration after me. I've never forgotten how cowardly and greedy people can be.'

His admiration for Napoleon and de Gaulle, and by extension for all things French, influenced his decision to enrol at a French-speaking Canadian university. 'He's a quirky fellow with a great sense of Gallic grandeur,' John Fraser told me. 'He has his own views on Canada, on what should be done here, and he's been particularly interested in Quebec ever since he did that bizarre thing: go to Laval University. I can't emphasise enough what an unusual thing that was to do.'

It was at Laval that he first met Daniel Colson. 'He was, frankly, not significantly unlike what he is today,' Colson recalls. 'Extremely articulate, dry wit and very interested in politics and power. He was unique in the sense that he was just that much more sophisticated, I guess, than the rest of us. We were all 20, 21 years old, but Conrad was much older in terms of his maturity level. He had much more advanced interests than I did or any of our other classmates. Yet he always hung around with us and was one of the boys. Even then he was a serious fan of Napoleon and Maurice Duplessis, about whom he subsequently wrote – talk about an epic, that was a serious tome! Most of us lived in the student ghetto part of Quebec City; I guess in any other city in the world they would be called slums, in Quebec they're called historic sites. Conrad, however, lived in the other part of town on the top floor of a very modern, fantastic apartment building in St Foy, overlooking the St Laurence River. It had magnificent views and he always had these Jane's books on fighting ships and his binoculars at the ready for anything coming up the river. He also managed to be possibly the only student who owned and drove a Cadillac. He wasn't ostentatious, just obviously had more money than the rest of us and lived accordingly. These were the heady days of Canadian nationalism in the mid-sixties. Trudeau had just been elected Prime Minister and as a result there was this rather uncharacteristic amount of goodwill floating around between English and French-speaking Canadians, to the point where a fair number of what you would consider to be pretty WASPy Anglo-Canadians such as Conrad Black and myself made the conscious decision actually to go to the bastion of French Canada and immerse ourselves totally in the language and culture.'

By the time he eventually returned to Toronto, Black was bilingual (he had picked up the colloquial twang of Quebec *joual*) and had become enamoured by the notion that the aesthetic of French civilisation is based on the creative faculty of choice. According to this philosophy, options are exercised not only in response to the dynamic of competitiveness and market forces but for their appropriateness to an individual's taste and preference; what the French call *la mesure*, the proper proportion of things. Black's sense of *la mesure* colours his proprietorships: he drives the business hard, but restrains his managers from inappropriate revenue-grubbing schemes. According to Charles Moore of the *Sunday Telegraph*, 'He'd never say, as I suspect Maxwell would have said, "The way to save the *Telegraph* is to produce a special colour supplement for black 25-year-olds." '

By his mid-twenties, Black had travelled widely in Europe and told friends that he was considering becoming a psychoanalyst. At around the same time he began to feel drawn towards Roman Catholicism and took instruction from Cardinal Paul-Emile Léger, the ascetic and aristocratic archbishop of Quebec. When Léger went off to the Cameroons to found a leper colony, Black followed, but after a fortnight in the jungle debating original sin and Man's mission on earth, he returned to Canada.

As early as 1969 Black had begun purchasing small newspapers in one-bar, one-petrol-pump Canadian townships. A university con-temporary, Peter White, now one of Black's two principal partners in

Hollinger, had bought for one dollar an all but dead Quebec weekly called the *Knowlton Advertiser* and persuaded his friend Conrad to run it for a few months as a lark. They changed the paper's name to the *Eastern Townships Advertiser*, which widened the catchment by a few hundred houses, bought a French language weekly in neighbouring Cowansville and gradually began to turn a small profit. Black during this period lived on the shores of Brome Lake, near Knowlton, in a boathouse belonging to White's mother. Most evenings he spent alone in this creaky, snow-bound little hut, since no friends lived within driving distance.

'It was a little shed that you could lift small boats into,' Black recalls, 'but it had been adapted into a cabin. It did have heaters – they didn't work very well – but if you could actually *get* to it it wasn't horrendously uncomfortable in the winter and was actually quite pleasant in the summer.'

By day he sold all the advertising for the newspapers and wrote most of the copy too. A year later, with a third partner David Radler (now President and CEO of Black's Sterling Newspapers and the *Jerusalem Post*), they bought the *Sherbrooke Record* which was the first proper newspaper in their Sterling chain. Thereafter they rapidly snapped up 22 tiny papers. Some of the circulations were so puny it was possible to know every reader by name: the *Kimberley Bulletin* still sells only 2000 copies a day, the *Chetwynd Echo* 1500, the *Mackenzie Times* only 1350 of its once-a-week Wednesday edition. If newspaper ownership is a game of Monopoly, Black was buying up the brown properties, the Old Kent Roads and the Whitechapels. The profits were modest, but then so were the purchase prices, and margins could be enhanced by cost-cutting. David Radler shifted headquarters to Prince Rupert to manage the expansion, and between 1972 and 1982 there was hardly a newspaper in British Columbia that, when it became available, wasn't sold to Black, to the growing irritation of Lord Thomson who regarded the Canadian outback as the exclusive preserve of his own chain.

'Thomson's strange about Black,' Ralph Ingersoll told me. 'He won't deal with him. It's some inverted Toronto class thing. I will never understand how the club works – but Thomsons, who at one point had been very much on the outside were now inside the power structure, and Conrad was outside. So they wouldn't sell him any papers. Maybe they just didn't like him. So he said to hell with that and built his own group.'

Before he bought any newspaper Black and his partners would visit its office in the evening and count the desks, which told them how many people worked there (this was before they'd seen the official report and accounts). If they found 25 desks, they reckoned they could reduce staff numbers to 18; if they found 30, the enterprise could probably get by with 20, and so on. The smaller Sterling newspapers still employ only three or four full-time staff; in the early days, Black used to inspect them in his by now chauffeur-driven Cadillac. Although there are those on the *Daily Telegraph* in London who whinge at Black's cost consciousness, by Sterling standards they have been indulged. The *Telegraph* from the start of the Black era has enjoyed something of the status of a rich man's second wife: within reason, and providing she doesn't take it for granted, she can have anything she wants.

Black's concept of *la mesure* as a businessman however makes him alert to anything he perceives as wasteful. 'He's pretty ruthless about cost-cutting,' says another *Telegraph* executive. 'He doesn't do this himself, he gets other people to do it. It's relentless, ongoing, it happens all the time. Immediately any costs rise above expectations, everything gets cut and people are sacked. He might be a bit over-ruthless on the technical side too. If you say you need such and such a number of printing machines to produce the newspaper, he says can't you halve that number. He certainly doesn't share the Sulzbergers' almost abstract enthusiasm for state-of-the-art plants.'

David Radler has said that his own experience in smalltown North American newspapers has taught him 'how to do without. All I want to see is efficiency. If I can see that an operation can be run by two people, and we have six, I want it run by two.'

Unless a proprietor inherits his newspapers, or slowly establishes his first fortune by founding them himself, there is invariably one pivotal business coup – usually the takeover of a cash-generating enterprise – that is clearly the genesis of the new press lord. For Conrad Black, it came on 13 July 1978, the date on which he became the undisputed controlling force in the Argus Corporation: the holding company he had spent his schooldays lathering over. The financial manoeuvrings of this coup made his takeover of Lord

Hartwell's *Telegraph* seven years later seem effortless by comparison. Named after the hundred-eyed giant of Greek mythology, Argus had been formed by the tycoon E P Taylor in 1945 as an investment trust with a deceptively simple operating philosophy. It conserved its capital by acquiring stakes in companies in which a dominant, but not majority, holding was sufficient for control. Dividends from these satellite companies were then partly divided between the shareholders, partly channelled into broadcasting and supermarket operations, and Argus effectively controlled Dominion Stores, the giant Massey Ferguson tractor company and Hollinger Mines Ltd (which now, after a number of abrupt changes of purpose, serves as Black's media holding company). At the time of his assault, Argus was worth $4 billion; Black, then aged 33, took control for $18 million in a contest of will that he later compared to Napoleon's successful strategy at the Battle of Rivoli. Much of it was masterminded in the Toronto Club, the tactics involving rapid-fire lawyers pitted against befuddled, elderly financiers who didn't twig Black's master plan until it was hand-delivered to the toppled chairman by Black himself. Exhibiting what was described as 'the balls of a canal horse', Conrad Black later remarked, with the bathos of victory, 'Maybe St Francis of Assisi was the last living man who wouldn't have liked control of Argus'. He shrugged off criticism as evidence of what Peter Newman later called 'the most indigenous of Canadian fevers: the rush to humble any individual who dares push ahead of the herd'.

In numerous respects the Argus takeover provided the template for his subsequent newspaper acquisitions. It contained all the constituents of a classic Black assault: councils of war in smart restaurants, private jets soaring across continents to obtain vital signatures on pledged votes, detailed scrutiny of forgotten articles of association and, above anything, Conrad Black's absolute conviction that he alone was the only fit and appropriate man to run the company. This is an impression he has successfully given time and time again. For one thing Black *looks* convincing as the sort of man to be running a company: substantial, conservatively dressed, articulate, respectful of old people.

'Unlike most of his contemporaries,' opined 'Bud' McDougald, the earlier Argus chief who saw Black as his protégé, 'this boy has the ability to think in modern terms while still maintaining tradition.'

Black in turn almost always speaks well of the old: 'I always get on with old guys. I *am* a historian after all. You have to feel a basic respect for what they've done, and I don't mean just because they're old. Besides I don't think of myself as being young. David Radler, my partner, claims I have a psychological age of 80.'

In one other way, too, the Argus affair had Black's stamp on it: he will quite often start off as a minority shareholder and later, having assessed and made allies, make his move. At Argus he started with 22 per cent (inherited from his father, shared with his brother). At the Telegraph, Black's initial holding was 14 per cent, which was enough to open the door wide and let him in. At United Newspapers (Lord Stevens's fiefdom, which owns the *Daily Express*), even his 9 per cent was seen as a chilling calling-card until he cashed it in.

Having won Argus he proceeded, piece by piece, to sell it off. Some people claim this had always been his plan, but it is more likely that his interest in tractors and shopping malls diminished as his enthusiasm for newspapers increased. His commitment to industry might also have been tested by a series of public disputes over his takeover bid for the Cleveland-based Hanna Mining Company and an acrimonious tussle over a surplus in the Dominion Stores pension fund, which he removed and later agreed with its trades union to split; an incident that prompted a Canadian political antagonist to describe him as 'that most symbolic representative of bloated capitalism at its worst'.

'It has taken some considerable time and a number of libel suits for me to live down the reputation attached to me by a left-wing politician in Toronto of being, in effect, a brigand who helped himself to the pension entitlements of defenceless people,' says Black.

Still based in Toronto, Black's wheeling and dealing gathered pace as he pummelled his portfolios and restructured his companies, including an unhappy interlude when he attempted a hands-on resuscitation of Massey Ferguson, where he took over as chairman. When he realised its resurgence was going to take longer than he'd imagined, or wished to spend, he resigned, donating the Argus holding to Massey's pension fund and using it as a tax loss. 'In any significant career in the history of the world,' Black said later, 'except for maybe Alexander the Great, there are setbacks.' There was a further setback the following year when his attempt to buy the group controlling Canada's most prestigious paper, the Toronto *Globe and Mail*, provoked the dismayed journalists on the paper into attempting their own buyout. This failed, but flushed out another bidder, Lord Thomson, who galled Black by winning this round. The Thomsons had recently backed out of Fleet Street, exhausted by the print unions, and sold their flagship newspapers *The Times* and the *Sunday Times* to Rupert Murdoch. There is a theory that this fanned Black's enthusiasm to buy a major British newspaper to prove that he could succeed where the Toronto peer had failed. His big break came in 1985 in the guise of the London *Daily Telegraph*, still the distinguished voice of British upper-middle-class conservatism, but a paper that had fallen on hard times with a pooped-out management and a declining circulation. Psychologically, the *Telegraph* was exactly what Conrad Black was looking for: a world-class conservative broadsheet in a capital city a long way from Toronto.

'Getting the *Telegraph* was really a new beginning for him,' Tony O'Reilly told me in Ireland, 'though I don't suppose Conrad would like anyone to view his career as anything but a seamless tapestry. Before the Telegraph deal, people like Galen Weston [the Toronto-based industrialist] were becoming pretty contemptuous of him; the combination of the Massey Ferguson and the Dominion Stores adventures had left Conrad pretty battered, I'd say.'

'I remember vividly Conrad phoning me one day,' recalls Dan Colson, 'prefacing his remarks as he often does by saying something to the effect of, "You're going to think I'm totally out of my mind, but I'm seriously thinking of perhaps putting some money into the *Daily Telegraph*. What do you think of the idea?" I remember equally vividly telling him to lie down until the feeling passed. The thing was in a shambles financially and a lot of people – if not most people – must have thought he was positively mad in wanting to take this financial gamble. Wapping was in full swing and everyone parading around East London with caricatures of Murdoch, burning him in effigy and all the rest of it. But Conrad knew the *Telegraph*'s reputation well and he recognised it as a unique opportunity to become the controlling shareholder of one of the world's great newspapers.

'Andrew Knight had called him in Toronto – they knew each other vaguely through Bilderberg [the international summit group of heavy hitters that meets in somewhat primitive surroundings to debate portentous questions like East–West relations and the future of the world], I think. Andrew was then at *The Economist*, which was half-owned by Evelyn de Rothschild. Rothschild's, of course, were trying to raise money in the private placement for the *Telegraph*; the deal was falling on its face – it couldn't find sufficient investors to take up all its shares – and Evelyn asked Andrew Knight if he knew of anybody who might be interested. He phoned Conrad and suggested he might have a look-out and Conrad phoned me and that's how it all began to happen. I had a number of meetings with Rothschild's and looked at the deal and eventually negotiated it on the basis that we would be prepared to put money in and salvage the private placement in return for certain concessions including the right of first refusal on the rest of the Berry family shares. We always expected that some day we'd get an opportunity to buy some or all of the remaining shares but, frankly, neither Conrad nor I honestly believed that we'd get that opportunity within months rather than years. As it turned out, even with the private placement successfully concluded, the *Telegraph* pretty quickly ran out of money. They needed to do a rights issue, and that's ultimately how we acquired control.'

Black's momentous takeover from Lord Hartwell and the Berry family, who had owned the papers since 1927, showed Conrad Black playing a subtler game than during the Argus battle, and demonstrating considerable proprietorial capacity for positioning himself above the fray. In almost a year of activity between May 1985, when he was first approached to take a £10 million shareholding, until the moment when he achieved control and appointed new editors to both his papers, Black came to London only twice, and then for the briefest of visits. Instead he watched and waited from his library in Toronto; watched the valiant but increasingly desperate attempts of Michael Hartwell to stay the crisis in his newspapers; waited until, as it surely must, further refinancing meant further equity for Black and his eventual triumph.

'I'm full of admiration,' says Ralph Ingersoll. 'Conrad was very patient and shrewd and played out enough rope until those guys hung themselves.'

'I recall one visit during the Telegraph deal,' says Colson, 'when Conrad arrived here off the Concorde – it was about ten o'clock at night – and phoned me from the car to say he was in town and could he stop by for a drink on his way to the hotel, which was the Four

Seasons. We were then living in Chester Street and I remember that evening quite vividly because we digressed constantly, it was almost like being back in university days with Conrad demonstrating his knowledge of all the Popes, all the Kings and Queens of England, the presidents of the United States – he could name them in reverse order. In terms of the Popes I recall it was about five o'clock in the morning and we were down to about the 14th century, and I don't think he'd missed one date yet. By the time I dropped him back at the hotel, having run out of Calvados, it was about six and the sun was coming up. The biggest problem of having Conrad to dinner is always the one of how to send him home. He's such a nighthawk, he thinks nothing of staying up until two, three or four in the morning.'

Black allowed the final events of the Hartwell era to play themselves out on the other side of the Atlantic, while he was kept daily informed, by fax and telephone, by Andrew Knight – already Chief Executive elect of the *Telegraph* – and Colson. Each week some fresh catastrophe, some unforeseen piece of grave news, propelled the *Telegraph* further from Hartwell and closer to Black's clutches; with each month his ownership became less a question of if than when. The contrast between the two camps, Hartwell's and Black's, says something not only about the two men's attitude to – and aptitude for – business but about the century itself. Lord Hartwell: dignified, poorly advised, deferred-to, optimistic; bewildered to find himself flying to New York for the day on Concorde to meet the potential investor (about whom, astonishingly, he had discovered nothing whatever) in a brassy hotel suite in the Kennedy Hilton; bewildered to find Black's advisors – Knight and the banker Rupert Hambro – better informed about *Telegraph* prospects than were his own managers who reported to him directly in his oak-panelled office on the fifth floor of 135 Fleet Street; bewildered when the auditors brought in by Hartwell's latest special advisor, David Montagu, found his newspapers to be on the threshold of bankruptcy, a fact that had hitherto been kept from him; ultimately bewildered that the agreement he had made with Black in the Kennedy Hilton at JFK really did prevent him from selling his own newspapers (of which his family trust still owned almost 60 per cent) to the Fairfax family ('More *our* sort of people'), Lord Hanson or anybody else but Conrad Moffat Black.

The Black team: resourceful, worldly-wise, entirely comfortable with the complex financial square dance that must accompany a takeover of a newspaper as important as the *Telegraph*; comfortable, above anything, in their assessment that the *Telegraph*, for all its intractable problems and looming debt, was an immense prize that they might eventually be able to pick up for a fraction of its value. Rupert Hambro had already told Black that he reckoned the *Daily Telegraph* to be the greatest serious newspaper title in the world outside Japan. 'It was a gamble,' says Colson. 'The sex appeal of the deal was clearly the potential to control one of the world's greatest newspapers. On the other hand I don't think Conrad was prepared to make the investment if he genuinely believed, at the end of the day, that it wasn't going to turn out to be a good one.'

Rupert Murdoch would say later that he reckoned the *Telegraph* would cost £1 billion to buy. Black took control for an initial £10 million cheque to Hartwell. In total he spent £119 million building up an 83 per cent stake between May 1985 and July 1992, when he floated the newspapers, leaving Hollinger with a 68 per cent stake in a company valued at just under half a billion pounds.

'The *Telegraph* has been a triumph,' says Tony O'Reilly. 'He's pulled off the coup of the century, absolute coup of the century. Yup, no debate about that. He got it for nothing and benefited enormously by Murdoch and Maxwell [duffing up the unions]. The climate changed and he got the timing right.'

'Was it luck or skill?' I asked O'Reilly.

'A very substantial quotient of luck and also good nerve on his part, because it wasn't as clear then that it would work out so well. He wasn't exactly born in the poverty ward, so he had an ability to take risks, but he took a brave one and to the victor the spoils. I think what one would say about Conrad is that his sense of humour makes all else forgivable. I am always struck by his overwhelming humility. I once told him I thought he was an unfrocked Jesuit.'

'What did he say to that?'

'He seemed rather flattered by the notion.'

'Black is like Agnelli,' says Ralph Ingersoll, 'he had the advantage and he didn't lose it.'

A group photograph of the directors of the Telegraph, taken in the new boardroom on the Isle of Dogs in 1988, demonstrates better than anything Black's Agnelli-like seizure of the advantage and reluctance to lose it. The directors are formed up in two ranks, in the manner of a school photograph, the more senior pupils afforded the privilege of sitting down on chairs in the front row, while the lower boys stand behind them. Lord Hartwell, made to stand, has adopted a half-askew position, his torso and shoulders turned defensively towards the camera as though he were about to be charged by a rhinoceros and is bracing himself for the impact; his expression hints at resignation and a certain distaste for the ordeal of being photographed. Conrad Black, as headmaster and chairman of the school governors, sits majestically in the centre of the front row in a black leather armchair – the only chair with arms – splaying his hands wide on the squashy, padded armrests, looking powerfully fulfilled and substantial as he occupies more than twice the space of both the Lords Hartwell and Camrose behind him.

As the *Telegraph* advanced editorially and started posting impressive profits, Black rose by common consent from the third to the second division of proprietors. As major newspapers became available, his name was added to the list of suitors. In 1989 he bought the *Jerusalem Post* for $20 million, narrowly beating Robert Maxwell. The acquisition followed what was by now becoming standard company tactics: Black in London masterminding strategy, David Radler in Hollinger's Vancouver offices frisking the operating costs, Daniel Colson in the field negotiating the deal line by line.

'I had been down there for several weeks and we closed on a Monday night at some ungodly hour – about two or three o'clock in the morning,' says Colson. 'And I went back to my hotel, the Hilton in Tel Aviv, and got up the next morning to meet some guy from the *Jerusalem Post* who was coming to collect me at nine o'clock. So I go down in the lobby about five minutes before he was supposed to pick me up, and the place was crawling with journalists. I asked, "What's going on here?" and was told, "Oh, Robert Maxwell's in town. He's giving a press conference." So I wandered into the press conference, and Robert Maxwell stood up and announced that he had returned to Israel in order to buy the *Jerusalem Post*, because the negotiations between Hollinger and Koor Industries, who were the owners of the *Jerusalem Post*, had fallen apart in New York. It was absolute crap! a) the negotiations never took place in New York, they took place in Israel, and b) the deal was already a *done deal*! So here was this guy having a press conference, saying he'd been invited to save the

Jerusalem Post. The *gall* of this guy Maxwell! There were well over a hundred people there in the ballroom or conference room or whatever the hell it was of *my hotel*.'

'I realise that one should always give the presumption of innocence to people not in a position to defend themselves,' says Conrad Black, 'but the fact is, Maxwell was compulsively devious, he couldn't even lie straight in his bed at night.'

Black moved the *Post* politically to the right, switching its support from Labour to Likud, and slashed staff numbers by 60 per cent. It was a strategy that challenged received wisdom that newspapers cannot be yanked successfully from one market into another, and yet circulation has increased not decreased. Black claims the change in editorial stance has been exaggerated by hysterical adversaries. 'I have been accused of devising a form of Jewish fascism which is just outrageous.'

Suspicion of his motives followed him from Jerusalem to Sydney when he joined the fray to buy the Fairfax newspapers. Despite the fact that in Canada he is an all but invisible proprietor, and in London seldom interferes, his image in Australia combined the least attractive aspects of Robert Maxwell, Rupert Murdoch and William Randolph Hearst. Emotional editorials were published on his unsuitability, and Fairfax journalists demanded that he sign a charter of editorial independence (Black declined). At a dinner in London at Brooks's following a *Spectator* board meeting at the height of the Fairfax tournament, Black departed early in order to appear on a live broadcast on Australian breakfast television. 'I am proposing to pass myself off as a sheep in wolf's clothing,' he remarked as he set off down the club staircase, whistling the opening bars of 'Waltzing Matilda'.

'I have been mystified by some of the political infighting that has been going on, that has represented me as a fanatical, right-wing interferer,' he told the *Sydney Morning Herald* shortly after he became its new owner. 'The rap on me, that I am some kind of overbearing authority freak who intervenes in his newspapers all the time is just a load of horse feathers.'

The level of paranoia had risen further the previous day when a confidential fax candidly assessing the Fairfax management had been intercepted on its way to Black and gleefully published in full on the front page of Murdoch's *Australian*. Not the least interesting aspect of the document was its dim opinion of the editors of the *Sydney Morning Herald* and *Australian Financial Review*.

'The whole thing was an amazing series of coincidences,' says Daniel Colson. 'It was the second or third week of December last year – our bid had just been declared the winner – and Conrad came down to Sydney and we went out to dinner, just the two of us, to sort of catch up on where things were at. We went to a restaurants called Bilson's down on the harbour and had a fairly lengthy dinner to talk about the events of the last few weeks or months. We got back to the hotel around midnight – we were both staying at the Ritz-Carlton on Macquarie Street – and the combination of the adrenalin and the high that I was on, with this deal just having been won, and Conrad being in a different time zone and being a nighthawk to boot, there was no question of either of us going to bed. So we sat up in my hotel suite with a bottle or two of wine and we were sitting there – it was about one-thirty in the morning – when the phone rang and it was Max Hastings's secretary from the *Telegraph* in London to say that she was trying to send me a confidential fax into the fax machine in my hotel room but she wasn't having any luck in getting through. So, being the technical genius that I am, I went over to the fax machine, discovered there was no paper in the damn thing, had no paper to put in and wouldn't have known how to do it had there been any, so I told her not to worry about it and to send it to the hotel fax number downstairs. By this time it was two in the morning, and I would phone down and have them bring the fax right up to the room. And so that's what happened. About fifteen, twenty minutes later the night security guy arrived at the door and Conrad and I were sitting there and he handed us this envelope with this fax. Later there was total confusion about what the fax really was, so let me make it clear that it was a fax that Nigel Wade, who's the foreign editor of the *Telegraph* and an Australian originally, had received, on an unsolicited basis, from some journalist in Sydney giving his views of the various editors and some of the senior people at Fairfax. It was obviously not very complimentary. In fact it was quite vitriolic. Wade must have shown it to Hastings, and Hastings must have thought it might be helpful to us, because we were just starting to decide what we were going to do with the company. Anyhow it would seem that the guy who delivered the fax was on the payroll of the Murdoch organisation and before delivering it decided to photocopy it and then provided a copy to a journalist from the *Australian*, which is Murdoch's paper, and I got a call the next day to say that they were going to publish! Needless to say I was absolutely astounded that he'd obtained a copy of this thing. So we called the police in and they sacked this night security guy. He admitted he'd made a copy of it. The *Australian* – in typical News Corp fashion – published the fax on the front page in its entirety. And of course it raised the roof at Fairfax. Everybody went bananas. And accused Black and me and Hastings of all kinds of things which, frankly, were simply not true, because we had never ever asked anybody for their view on these people. It was unsolicited. Black and I had sat there and read it, but we didn't put much faith in it, because it seemed to be the work of some disgruntled former employee. We didn't pay much attention to it. But the next day, when the thing hit the front pages of the opposition paper, all hell broke loose and we certainly paid attention to it then!'

Making his first formal appearance as the new proprietor of Fairfax, Conrad Black was moved to announce, 'You can see I don't have cloven feet or wear horns. Contrary to wide-spread rumours, it is not a plan of Mr Colson's or myself to erect a guillotine at Broadway [Fairfax headquarters] and move journalists through it on a random basis.'

Conrad Black's proprietor-sized office on the 15th floor of Canary Wharf in the Isle of Dogs makes you think of one of the grander suites at Claridges co-opted for a military briefing. There is an expanse of yellow silk upholstery, a mahogany breakfront bookcase, a portrait of Napoleon after Waterloo and another of Lord Nelson, and a substantial bronze of Cardinal Newman that Black commissioned for himself from Lady Quinton. But most of the pictures are oils and photographs of 20th-century warships: from every wall you are borne down upon by flotillas of frigates, cruisers, dreadnoughts, gunboats.

'The great majority they're – almost exclusively – naval scenes,' said Conrad Black walking me down the ships of the line. 'That's Montague Dawson,' he said, pausing at one of those painstaking naval vignettes that remind you of old half-tones in the *Sunday Express*. 'You see that's a Canadian Corvette there, which was Canada's best-remembered contribution to the Second World War and the antisubmarine war. A Montague Dawson Corvette, a quite nice painting, I think. And that's Montague Dawson's picture of the *Queen Mary* there, in wartime, so I have another picture of the *Queen Mary* there,' Black indicated its pair across the room, 'in peacetime, just as a contrast. And – what else have I got? – there's the *Bismarck* being sighted by that Catalina there, and there you have King George VI taking the salute on the *Implacable*-class carrier with a *King George V*-class battleship in the background. You have the same class aircraft carrier and the same class battleship in that little picture over there. There's the old Royal Yacht, *Victoria and Albert*, and underneath it are three *Queen Elizabeth*-class battleships at Scapa Flow . . .'

At this moment his secretary, Rosemary Millar, tapped on the door and relayed a message, at which Black turned happily to me. 'I'm sorry, you're going to have to excuse me for one moment, I've got to take an urgent call from South Africa.' He laughed. 'All my life you know I've wanted to able to say that: *"an urgent call from South Africa"*. That's the first time it's actually happened.'

From his office windows in the tallest commercial building in Europe, you see below you the Docklands loop of the River Thames with its uneasy mélange of Victorian warehouses and aluminium and glass developments, and then beyond them half-built marinas, service roads, bonded warehouses and the rising steppes of outer London. The view reminded me of Steinberg's *New Yorker* cover of the foreshortened panorama of 9th Avenue extending across the Hudson River to Kansas City, Nebraska, Japan and infinity; I felt that, if you stared hard and long enough from Black's window, you would eventually make out the offices of the *Jerusalem Post*, the *Caymanian Compass* and the *Sydney Morning Herald*.

In front of the window stands a vast and rather macabre Gothic desk, with gargoyle faces carved up the legs.

'Formidable isn't it,' said Black, 'but not as old as it looks.'

'Was it Lord Hartwell's desk?' When Black bought the Telegraph group from Hartwell the deal included all fixtures and fittings.

Black guffawed. 'No, the provenance is not in newspapers, it's an executive desk; about 100 years old, found for me by a decorator.'

He had recently bowed out from the contest to buy the *New York Daily News*, proclaiming that he 'had no interest in coming to New York to clasp my lips around an exhaust pipe'.

The neatness of the metaphor was affording him some comfort in retreat.

'My other one,' said Black, 'which I thought was not bad for a *complete* improvisation, was "We have other things to do besides trying to kiss that comatose princess awake". I made that up as I went along and thought it was, if I may say so, a reasonably good epigram.'

When I pitched a general question about the role of the owner in a newspaper like the *Daily Telegraph*, I received a reply of such length, precision and complexity that it threatened to add several dozen extra pages to this book.

'In my opinion,' he began, 'it is very important for a significant newspaper like this one to have what I would call a *balanced operation*. Whatever the vocation of the newspaper is, whatever its chosen orientation may be, it is important in such a newspaper, as it is in most organisations, to have some sort of balance. The role of the proprietor is, in some measure, to ensure that balance, by which I mean to ensure that none of the constituent factions effectively operates the newspaper to the exclusion of all of the others. And I think that the proprietor must use his influence to recruit and maintain the strongest possible working press for the purposes that particular newspaper is trying to serve, support the journalists and the editors who are there – if unfairly and unreasonably attacked or harassed unreasonably by litigious people – but also provide when it is necessary – and sometimes it is necessary – some *restraint* in the tendency of elements of the working press to indulge in *peculiarities* or *eccentricities*. A newspaper that is run by the journalists tends, in my experience, to be *sanctimonious* and *tendentious*. Therefore there is, in my judgement, a role for the proprietor to ensure that the journalistic input in the newspaper is optimised – to use the jargon – that it is at its maximum level in the best way that it can express itself. And, of course, I don't mean to focus exclusively on the relations between the proprietor and the journalists. It is also the job of the proprietor to make sure that the business is well run, and in that matter there is no one else to do that job as efficiently as he can do it, since he is after all speaking of *his own money*. And there is in my opinion no contradiction between – or there need be no contradiction whatsoever between – a newspaper that is both a good newspaper and a good business. And I hope, *with no unbecoming lack of humility*, that this company is an illustration of that.

'I gave an address at the Media Society,' he went on, 'that essentially consisted in large part of a rather *self-serving discourse* on the virtues of proprietors. And I took sharp issue with *Mr Bevins* [the name Bevins – Anthony Bevins, a journalist at the *Independent* who has irritated Black in the past – was uttered with the same weary scorn that the names Andrew Knight and Christopher Hitchens were to receive later on] who contends that only the *Independent* and the *Guardian* are virtuous papers amongst the national dailies in this country because they are unaffected by the *baleful* influence of proprietors. In the first place, of course, Andreas Whittam Smith would qualify as a part-owner and is far from being removed from the scene, which is as it should be.'

'Do newspapers, then, prosper in proportion to the strength of their proprietor?'

'Strength, obviously, can be defined in different ways. I'm not going to try and whitewash the more baroque tendencies of the Northcliffes or the Hearsts, but in general I think so. They give a newspaper personality, they show leadership within the enterprise and, to the extent that they abuse their positions of power and influence, the franchise suffers for that. The institutions they are the owners of (or, some would have, the custodians) deteriorate as a result of capricious or unprofessional behaviour by their proprietors, so they are at least in a position of penalising themselves for their own misconceived activities in the circumstances. I don't think a case can easily be made that the *Daily Mail* hasn't profited from having Lord Rothermere as its owner, or even the *Daily Express* from having Lord Stevens, though he's not a proprietor, he's a very assertive chairman. I accept there could be some controversy over *The Times* but none at all over the *Sun* as to whether it has flourished under Mr Murdoch. It was a derelict title that the *Mirror* in effect paid him to relieve them of and now it's the largest circulation daily newspaper in the Western world. It's not my place to sit in judgement on all these people, but I cite those.'

'Isn't it rather frustrating being just the owner, rather than the editor? You must keep opening up your own newspapers and reading opinions that aren't yours at all.'

'I think it would be to some people, but not to me because I find the best way of avoiding that is to hire editors I'm in agreement with. I mean your alternatives really are either an absolutely hands-off approach to editorial like Roy Thomson adopted and Ken Thomson still adopts. I couldn't do that. I mean then I would encounter exactly the problem just described, I'd be having apoplexy every time I read one of our papers. Life is too short for me to shorten it further with that kind of thing. Alternatively, you can meticulously interfere with and supervise the editors, but, in the first place, if you're going to do the job of editor yourself you might as well dispense with the editor and take the title and, you know, I have neither the time nor the qualification to do that. And in the second place you won't, in my opinion, get the highest quality people to work on that basis. High quality people require a bit more autonomy than that. A third alternative is, in effect, the capricious and frequent change of editor. A number of the prominent London newspapers have been in that position in the last few years, I need not mention them. Sacking editors, like the decapitation of any organisation, is very destabilising. So the best course is to try and get editors who, apart from being talented themselves, are people with whom you are in general agreement so that the number of instances of the kind you mention are not frequent.'

'What then is the chief satisfaction of owning a newspaper – as opposed to just buying a copy at a kiosk and reading it? Or from owning other companies, like your Canadian mining set-up?'

Black laughed. 'We were mining the *economy of Canada* rather than the *subsoil*! But it clearly emerges in several ways: one is the physical product and what you think of it; another satisfaction, in the case of the *Daily Telegraph*, is to publish such distinguished writers as we do. The third is financial. It's a very profitable company. But I wouldn't give an arbitrary weighting to those three elements. They're all there. I feel a keen pleasure in reading even a good book review in one of our papers. It is, I'm sure, that same pleasure that anyone has in participating in the production of something that objectively good, whether you're baking cookies or refining oil.'

'Is the political influence of newspaper owners as great as it's cracked up to be?'

'It's greater in this country than in North America for the most part, but I think it's exaggerated. But on the other hand it's the old story: if you're *perceived* as having influence in a sense you *do* have it. There's no doubt that the political leaders *believe* that newspaper owners have a big influence, and in certain circumstances some newspapers do.'

'Do you get politicians vying for your ear and friendship?'

'I would be unfairly disparaging them as a community and taking vainglorious airs unto myself to say any such thing. What I do find is that the Government figures, the leading personalities in the governing party, tend to give a lot of time and attention to various *Telegraph* personalities, of whom I am only one. But, I must be fair, almost all of them are very subtle and correct in the way they do it and all they are ever really asking for is a fair hearing and to be sure an important speech they might be giving or something is clearly understood. I have a fairly extensive experience of dealing with politicians in one jurisdiction or another and I've found the ones here to be quite correct in their relations with the press. I remember at the dinner we gave – Mrs Thatcher kindly gave – at Downing Street for Bill Deedes when he retired as the editor. He quoted Ian McLeod in saying that the relations between the press and politicians must be abrasive, and there is no way of avoiding those abrasions.'

'What about business friends attempting to influence their coverage in the City pages? Or, indeed, their coverage in the *Jerusalem Post*, the *Spectator* or the *Financial Post* [of Toronto, in which Black has a 15 per cent interest]?'

'I do get a little bit from business people, though not on underwritings or anything like that. Not on matters directly monetisable. Nothing even touching financial corruption, but sometimes in coverage of controversial matters. It varies you know. At the *Financial Post* in Canada, we tend to get a lot more overtures.'

I wondered too whether the remarkably heavyweight boards of directors and advisory boards that Conrad Black has been assembling for his newspapers is a journalistic hindrance when an important, or sleazy, story broke over any of their members. The main board of Hollinger features 13 of Canada's heaviest-hitting tycoons, and the boards of the *Daily Telegraph*, the *Jerusalem Post*, the *Spectator* and Black's Canadian newspaper group Unimedia Inc are even more generously basted with big players. The roll call reads like delegates at a golf tournament for executives of international corporations, of the kind that American CEOs attend most weekends. Every time a financial journalist on a Hollinger paper in Quebec, Ottawa or Saskatchewan files a story about those companies, he must feel inhibited by, or at very least aware of, a conflict of expectation. And the *Spectator* has found it awkward when publishing negative profiles of Lord Carrington [the former British foreign secretary] and Paul Reichmann of Olympia & York, both on Black's boards.

'Conrad Black collects these people like foreign stamps, but instead of sticking them into an album he sticks them on his writing paper and Annual Report,' I was told by a rival proprietor. 'There is nothing clever or admirable about getting a lot of fat cats to accept 15,000 dollars a year, or whatever it is that he pays them, for turning up at a board meeting followed by lunch. They don't need much arm-twisting.' And yet I detected more than a note of envy in this remark. The Black boards are not only hilariously high profile for a media company (they make even the celebrity board of the Metropolitan Museum in New York, let alone the Sulzbergers' *New York Times* board, seem like a B-list) but the variety of players has a lunatic bravado about it.

The main board of Hollinger, which meets twice a year in Toronto to be lavishly entertained at gala dinners at which ex-President Nixon and ex-Prime Minister Margaret Thatcher are rolled out as guests of honour, includes Henry Kissinger and Lord Carrington; the American news commentator David Brinkley; former American National Security Advisor Dr Zbigniev Brzezinski; the editor-at-large of *National Review* magazine, William F Buckley Jr; the British industrialists and financiers Sir James Goldsmith (who came off the board in 1992), Lord Hanson and Lord Rothschild; former US Assistant Secretary of Defense, Richard N. Perle; former Chairman of the US Federal Reserve, Paul Volcker and the American public affairs columnist, George Will.

The subsidiary boards are no less heavily encrusted. The *Jerusalem Post* board has the publisher Lord Weidenfeld and Major-General Shlomo Gazit, the former Chief of Military Intelligence in Tel Aviv. Until he disappeared overboard, it also rather oddly had Robert Maxwell, though Black is quick to point out that he never made it to a board meeting. Black also invited the journalist Lally Weymouth to join, but her mother Katharine Graham apparently vetoed the invitation, to Black's indignation, since she claimed there might be a conflict of interest with the family's ownership of the *Washington Post*. The *Daily Telegraph* board, in addition to Carrington and Goldsmith, includes Rupert Hambro, Henry Keswick of Jardine

Matheson (and a former owner of the *Spectator*), British Airways's Life President Lord King, the former Attorney-General Lord Rawlinson, Sir Evelyn de Rothschild, Lord Hartwell, his cousin Viscount Camrose and Sir Martin Jacomb of Barclays de Zoete Wedd. The *Spectator* board has, if anything, even more chairmen per shilling of turnover than the *Telegraph*: oil tycoon Algy Cluff (another former *Spectator* proprietor; indeed the only former *Spectator* proprietor not to be on a Black board is Warwick Fairfax), BAT Chairman Sir Patrick Sheehy, former Conservative Party Chairman Lord Tebbit and the financial columnist Christopher Fildes. In May 1993, the *Spectator* board was further embellished by the addition of Lord King and Barbara Amiel.

'On our Quebec Unimedia board,' Black was later to tell me, 'we have the former President of Quebec Mr [Pierre-Marc] Johnson and His Eminence Cardinal Carter, the Archbishop Emeritus of Toronto . . . I don't know of a *cardinal* being a director of *any other company*, do you?'

I do not. And it was hard to imagine exactly what contribution an Archbishop Emeritus could make to a communications company owning 18 weekly and three daily newspapers, though in 1989 Unimedia launched a small religious publishing house called Novalis which no doubt draws on the Cardinal's expertise.

I asked Black, 'Do these swanky boards make any quantifiable contribution?'

'Very much,' he replied, 'much mocked as I am in some quarters for my association with prominent people.' And then he declaimed at high speed from memory, and virtually in the alphabetical order in which they're listed in the annual report, the full roster: 'Dwayne Andreas, David Brinkley, Peter Carrington, Zbigniev Brzezinski, Bill Buckley, Jimmy Goldsmith, Allan Gotlieb, James Hanson, Henry Kissinger, Richard Perle, Jacob Rothschild . . .' and so, without pausing for breath or interruption, he rattled on through his stable of stars: 'These *uniquely distinguished groups*,' as he described them.

Black's adversaries are swift to cite the directors as *prima facie* evidence of social climbing. They liken his pleasure to that of certain Manhattan hostesses, as he reviews the array of former foreign secretaries, world peacemakers, Cardinals Emeriti and executive jet-setters seated around his boardroom table. And yet his motivation did not strike me as entirely social. I don't imagine he'd care one way or the other for an invitation to this party or that, unless the host happened to possess the surname of a Peninsular War general. I felt rather that his satisfaction came from procuring a suitably distinguished audience who could appreciate his bravura in buying up bits of Canadian, British and Israeli newspaper heritage and making money out of them by superior strategy. Conrad Black's boards provide him with corporate audience participation. He once said, 'I guess I've met everyone in the world I'm interested by. You know, I own a *lot* of newspapers.'

I asked, 'Somebody like Henry Kissinger. Is he actually useful to have around at board meetings?'

'Sure. I don't want to be pretentious, when ours is not that large a company, but a feel for political trends and likely developments is terribly valuable. The final piece of the puzzle in my determining that we should sell our position in the oil business down, was when Henry Kissinger told me that some of the leading Saudi figures had told him in the presence of the King of Saudi Arabia that they thought the standard oil price would decline to $10 a barrel. That was back in the latter part of '85. Well I thought, in that event, it was time for us, if we were able, to make an exit. So Dr Kissinger's advice was highly helpful to us. He hasn't always been able to come to the meetings but, you know, that's really not the point. You want them [the special advisors] to be available, and they certainly *are* available, when you need them.'

'What about Robert Maxwell? What inspired you to put him on to the board of the *Jerusalem Post* when you thought him "compulsively devious"?'

Black laughed ruefully. 'He generously accepted my invitation because he was, as I was, rather tired of reading at the time that he and I had had some vile disagreement because nothing of the sort had occurred. The worst I can say about him in this context is that after we topped his bid for the paper he announced he was withdrawing his own bid so we could take it over. *Withdrawing* it!' Black snorted. 'We had already *topped* it! It's like Robert Holmes à Court phoning me as he did to say that he'd decided not to top our bid for the *Telegraph*. We'd already *bought* those newspapers. I *owned* them already.'

'What was it about the *Jerusalem Post* that made you want it?'

'One reason was that it was so *ludicrously overstaffed*. It had been owned by a labour union before, so we knew it could be run much better. The second was that it had not been run as a commercial enterprise, so we knew we could heighten that; it had been run as an extreme left newspaper so was losing the advertisers, and we could put *that* right quickly. And more than anything because it is highly influential. Most of our great Western newspapers reporting on the Middle East use simply rewrite stuff from the *Jerusalem Post. The New York Times, Washington Post, Chicago Tribune, LA Times* all rely on the *Jerusalem Post*. The fact is, in terms of influence, We are It and It is Us.

'We won't,' he went on, 'have any difficulty over time in justifying the controversially high price we paid. It's certainly an *improving* business, despite the recession in Israel. I think it is conceded to be a good paper, even by all the most rabid of the partisans who left us. The Israelis are, as you know, extremely tenacious people and they are not the easiest workforce to *shrink*, but we are getting it down. It's coming along well.'

'How does it compare with the Cayman Islands?'

'You know, that little newspaper of ours [the *Caymanian Compass*] made one million dollars last year – that's Cayman Island dollars at .85 to the US dollar – not bad for an island – what – eight miles by six or something. I see that paper quite often. It comes to the Toronto office and they have a special bathing-suit issue almost every week you know. And some of the financial news is actually quite interesting. For a little paper in an out-of-the-way place it does, as you would I guess expect, heavier coverage of international financial news than you get on any of the neighbouring Caribbean islands. It's quite a little profit centre and it's a little Switzerland down there.'

'Do you ever go and inspect it?'

'Luckily not. It's a funny little island. You wouldn't want to spend much time there, not if you had an IQ in double figures. Unless you have a monastic streak or are just a fanatical scuba diver you tend to find it quite a confining place. But as a newspaper property, *We are It*. We have the market. If you want to advertise for a cook you do so through the *Caymanian Compass*. If you want a chauffeur . . . though why you'd need a chauffeur in a place like Cayman, you'd get a golf car. Editorially it's a bit of a hodge-podge, and the circulation is only about 6000, but it works.'

'Do you read the *Telegraph* right through every day?'

'I peruse it pretty carefully.'

'In any particular order?'

'From the front page to the back. I don't usually read the sports that carefully, I don't know as much about British sports as I should. But I tend to read the main news pages and inside pages, leader page, and obit page and to a degree the City pages more assiduously than others, but I look fairly carefully at almost all parts of it.'

'Are you the kind of proprietor who, when you read something good, sends a postcard of congratulations to the writer?'

'Sure.' But he didn't sound all that sure.

'Is it an unusual occurrence?'

'Once a week, twice a week. I sent John Keegan a letter yesterday. A *handwritten* letter. But that was over many days of absolutely magnificent coverage, and of course with John Keegan you're not only dealing with a correspondent, you're dealing with – as I've so often said – a Liddell Hart of the nineties. He's clearly one of the world's outstanding military historians.'

'Have you altered the paper much during your proprietorship?'

'The *Daily Telegraph* was a much less comprehensive paper when I bought it than it is now, a much thinner paper and with much less features. The old Camrose formula was a good one: always a very good selection on page three of these salacious stories presented in a rigorously sober way; sadistically explicit extracts from court transcripts and things like that. Good sense of humour, a lot of funny little stories that you really didn't get in most other papers, and this relentless truculent monarchist sentiment, constant references to the Royal Family of an unvaryingly respectful nature.'

'You still have that.'

'We have elements of all that. And the obituaries – thanks to Jock Colville and Hugh Mongtomery-Massingberd, have gone in seven years from being really quite bland to one of the real strengths of the paper – fully competitive with *The Times*. I'm a little bit partial but I think that our obituaries tend to be more informative and feistier. I mean, frankly they are occasionally a bit destructive and snide and that's an unattractive thing, and most people, including me, feel that whatever one might have thought of somebody their obituary should try to put them in the best light. But I think, in fairness, that this is not a frequent occurrence, it wouldn't be more than a few times a year.

One of the notorious instances of that was when the wife of Lord Stevens [the chairman of United Newspapers] died. That was a most regrettable episode which John Junor saw fit to interpret in a very spurious way and credit all kinds of motives to myself, of which I was completely innocent. I knew nothing about that obituary and deeply regretted what happened, as I wrote to Lord Stevens and as I believe he has accepted.

'At the *Sunday Telegraph*,' he went on, 'we started out with a 40-page newspaper with a pull-out *Guardian* ladies' magazine inside, full of articles on how to spot the pink-breasted finch or something in the Orkneys in February. Now we have a 100-page paper most Sundays and Andrew Neil [the editor of Murdoch's *Sunday Times*] is quaking in his boots in Wapping or down in that club of his, the Tramps.'

'On the subject of Wapping, have you made up your rather public falling-out with Andrew Knight? Is he to any extent forgiven?' Andrew Knight's defection as Chief Executive and Editor-in-Chief of the Telegraph group to become Executive Chairman of Rupert Murdoch's News International (despite holding £14 million of Telegraph shares) caused a sensation, and an exchange of highly charged open letters of recrimination between Black and Knight.

'Is he *forgiven*?' said Black. 'That's an interesting question. I mean, it's of interest to me; I'm not sure if it's of interest to anyone else, including him. Let me put it this way, I do not unsay any of the fears I expressed in my well-publicised and indeed textually reprinted letters to him that he was *disingenuous*. He was lacking in, I think, the duty he owed this organisation and me as an individual in telling us what his intentions were. There is no doubt in my opinion, no conceivable doubt, that he was in *substantive negotiations* with Mr Murdoch for many months prior to his announcing that he was joining that company. And he consistently denied to me that any such thing was happening, even though the Murdoch entourage was regularly building up the rumours of Andrew's impending arrival to a crescendo. And whenever I said to him that I certainly had no problem with that, I admired Murdoch too and if he wanted to work for Murdoch there would be no difficulty, but it had to be handled the right way, he consistently denied that any such thing was going on. With that said, you have to appreciate the nature of the beast. I think he is quite sincere in thinking the course he followed was not dishonest and, knowing

Andrew as I do, I think in an odd way he didn't set out wilfully to do anything dishonest. So, in answer to your question of whether he's forgiven, I don't look upon his conduct as being any less *tawdry* than I thought it was at the time but I don't think he had what is called in the law *mens rea*: the basis of guilt as both an illegal act and a guilty intent. I don't think he had a *discreditable intention* but I think that the *objective result* of his conduct, as a man of his experience and in other respects punctiliousness should have realised, was a most unseemly and ethically dubious form of behaviour. But I see Andrew from time to time. I saw him last night and relations have improved.'

'Would you have dinner together now?'

'No. But in the normal course of events he and I are sort of on the same circuit.'

'Do you see much of journalists socially?'

'Well, I'm sort of in an odd position. Some of the frequenters of the old Worsthorne *Telegraph* faction, [the circle of the *Sunday Telegraph's* former editor, Sir Peregrine Worsthorne] I'm within reason relatively friendly with some of them: the Paul Johnsons and Roger Scrutons (though I find him too belligerent to see more than twice a year), that group I do find somewhat interesting and a useful antidote to the soft-left compassionates.'

'Not ignorant, lazy, opinionated, intellectually dishonest and inadequately supervised?'

'That assertion of mine,' said Black, 'is the most popular passage for resurrection from a submission I wrote 20 years ago to a Canadian senate committee on the mass media, which attracted little notice at the time. But, in the last ten or twelve years, it has been regularly excerpted in the most diverse places, usually without reference to the fact that it was written in 1969 about Quebec separatist journalists. The people I was writing about strove for, among other things, the abolition of the English language in Quebec, a cause which surely would have difficulty in rousing the support even of the *Guardian* in its most compassionate moments. The so-called profession of journalism is heavily cluttered with abrasive youngsters who substitute what they call 'commitment' for insight, and, to a lesser extent, with aged hacks toiling through a miasma of mounting decrepitude.'

Black developed his theory of journalists in an address to the Media Society in London in January 1991.

'Many journalists,' he said, 'and most of the more talented ones, are happy to chronicle the doings and sayings of others, but a significant number, including many of the most acidulous and misanthropic, are, in my experience, inexpressibly envious of many of the subjects of their attention. In this country, where professional crafts traditionally enjoy a higher status and journalists tend to be more literate than in North America, this condition is less aggravated than it is there, but it is still quite evident at times. Some of the current gratuitous comment about the Murdoch organisation's finances are obviously just spite and envy.

'Especially when there is a drought in real news, the practice is almost universal of compulsively, almost rhythmically, building up and tearing down reputations. This is particularly true where, as is unfortunately the case in the UK, the spirit of envy is strong. And it happens in every field: sports, the arts, business, politics, the media themselves. It is a time-honoured journalistic formula, especially when there isn't much real news to impart. The local tabloid press's relentless elevation and demotion of members of the Royal Family is an example of this sort of thing.

'It pleases the journalist, as it pleases most people, to think of himself as an underdog, a person with a cause, if not a mission. This condition is accentuated in this country by Britain's admirable, but sometimes perversely exaggerated love of underdogs. And it is further aggravated by the penchant of many journalists to masquerade as a learned profession while behaving like an industrial union.

'The *Daily Telegraph* furnished a rather picturesque illustration of this tendency in the autumn of 1989 when I brought my hobnailed jackboot down on the necks of our journalists by proposing the Dickensian *Bleak House* idea of a five-day work week. The *UK Press Gazette* instantly reverted to an NUJ toutsheet. Serious financial journalists, with whom it is usually possible to have a sensible conversation, became hysterical muckrakers, febrile with righteousness, as if they were exposing the most repulsive abuses of the Victorian sweatshop. On that occasion the widely retailed theory of my implacable antagonism to journalists was noisily revived. In fact, I *like* most journalists and always have.'

'You really mean that?' I asked.

'Yeah. They're an interesting and *picturesque* mixture, aren't they?'

*

Since becoming the fourth husband of Barbara Amiel, Black's appetite for tycoonery and discursive conversation has if anything increased. Tall and attractive, with a husky voice and neo-conservative principles that neatly dovetail those of her spouse, Amiel has been described by Lord Rothermere's *Evening Standard* as 'the most powerful woman in London' for her perceived influence on preferment on Black's broadsheets. 'I met Barbara first at the home of a mutual friend in Toronto,' Black told me. 'She was then a prominent columnist in Canada. And I was – what was I? – I was a sort of upper-middle-echelon businessman who was assumed to be going somewhere, I guess – at least by our host, or he wouldn't have invited me. And I sat next to her at dinner and she had actually read my book on Duplessis, which completely astonished me.'

They married in the summer of 1992, not long after Black's first marriage to Shirley Hishon (who changed her Christian names from Shirley Gail to Joanna Catherine Louise shortly after coming to London from Toronto, on the understandable grounds that she had already lived half her life with names she neither chose nor cared for) had run out of steam and she'd withdrawn to Canada to study theology.

Black has three children by Shirley including a nineteen-year-old son who worked one holidays at the *Telegraph* and impressed his colleagues by demonstrating how he could strike a match on the sole of his shoe in the lift. Of his children, Black says, 'I'm very laid back. I make up for my [ex] wife who is the disciplinarian. I let them go to bed when they want, do what they want; hell, I have no dynastic designs so long as they do whatever they have an aptitude for.'

Black and Amiel's London circle revolves around the British end of that wider, international network of merchant bankers, corporate hustlers and power brokers who attend the Bilderberg conferences and give black-tie dinners for a dozen couples with similar credit ratings to themselves. 'He's much more important in the UK socially than he was in Canada. I don't know why, because there aren't that many people that are interesting in Canada,' says Ralph Ingersoll. Some detect his new wife's influence in Black's periodic broadsides in his own newspapers on subjects other than world history. On New Year's Eve he commandered the *Daily Telegraph*'s fashion page to attack the new fashion for long skirts. 'Anyone visiting Annabel's, any of the more fashionable pre-Christmas parties, or the Pierre hotel or Mortimer's in New York, or simply watching the general procession of fashion-aware women in London, New York, Paris or almost anywhere except North Korea, Teheran or Algiers, can observe a variety of lengths,' he wrote. 'Long has its place, but for most women it is a banal, humdrum and reactionary style.'

At weekends the Blacks periodically accept invitations to large houses in the country, such as Easton Neston where they stay with the Heskeths.

'One of the things I tease Conrad about most often is that he's invited to stay in country houses but would be every bit as happy in Chiswick,' says Max Hastings. 'Reading and talking are his great pleasures. Not fishing, stalking or shooting. I tell him, "You're missing all these great pleasures of living in England".'

Because Black is quixotic as a proprietor, it is difficult to predict how his roster of papers will look in ten years. When I first met him, he told me two things: that he doubted he'd ever buy newspapers in Australia ('I don't know many people there. And out across the Pacific you know, they're very long trips') and that he wouldn't ever be interested in buying the *New York Daily News* ('I don't know much about that kind of tabloid journalism. I don't feel any great sense of how best to produce that kind of a paper'). Within two years he owned Australia's smartest newspaper group and only narrowly missed buying the *News*.

There are three principal theories in circulation on how the Black empire might develop.

The first has him buying only at the top end of the market: seeking to consolidate a reputation as the authority on quality broadsheets. Ownership of the Telegraph and Fairfax positions him as a plausible candidate to acquire any one of a dozen papers in Germany, Holland, Scandinavia or the Far East, as they become available.

The second has him resolving, at some future date, to get out of newspapers altogether, if he was offered a sufficiently handsome premium. This is the theory of Black the dealmaker: that even the newspapers wouldn't be sacrosanct at the right price. Lord Stevens told me that he believes Conrad Black once offered him the *Telegraph*

('He doesn't express himself all that clearly on what he wants, I find. I find one goes all over the countryside'). This scenario has always struck me as highly improbable, since so much of Black's kudos and pleasure depends upon his position as proprietor. I asked him how deep is his commitment to the *Telegraph*. He replied, 'Considerable'.

'Would you consider selling it under any circumstances?'

'Well, as the chairman of a quoted company I can never responsibly say never, but the idea of disposing of the *Telegraph* is certainly not something I am considering at the present time.'

The third route has Conrad Black and Barbara Amiel ricocheting around the world on an almost perpetual paperchase, recipients of the 'endless round of sumptuous lunches and dinners' that Black has stated he finds such an enjoyable feature of London living. Every time a major paper comes to the block, be it in Detroit or Mexico City, Black will loom on to the scene with an entourage of bankers, brokers and attorneys, adding properties to a lengthening list. He is psychologically disposed to buy if he likes the merchandise and the price is right. In February 1994 Black paid £121 million to buy Murdoch's old paper the Chicago *Sun-Times*.

'The reason I greatly enjoy dealing with Conrad,' says Hylton Philipson of Pall Mall, who has been involved in several of his North American acquisitions, 'is that he never lets you down. If he says he's going to bid 20 million on something, he does, he follows through. But there's more to Conrad than making money. I went to visit him once to brief him about what is happening in Tibet. He allowed me to talk for an hour and was very interested: he saw it as another cause of fighting for freedom against Communist oppression. At the end of our conversation he picked up the telephone to Charles Moore, who was then editor of the *Spectator* and said, "Charles there's someone here I think you ought to meet." A few weeks later, the *Spectator*'s main leader was entirely devoted to Tibet.'

Ralph Ingersoll has a theory that Black's masterplan involves buying more and more tiny papers across Canada and North America with a view eventually to floating them on Wall Street. The *New York Daily News*, once it had been pummelled into profit, would have provided a flagship to give the offering focus.

'I once asked Conrad over dinner what he was doing, buying smaller than small things, and he told me what his theory was,' says Ingersoll.

'He boasted to me about it, explaining that he had 100 of these small papers in one holding company. If he went public the market would classify it as newspaper publishing sector and while it might not be rated as highly on a PE basis as Gannett or Knight-Ridder, it would nevertheless be valued in that sector, where in 1986, 1987 the multiples were very high indeed. He thought that by buying the smallest papers he could pay multiples on turnover or cashflow that were probably half of what the rest of us were paying for bigger companies. But at the end of the day if knit together it would trade at a higher multiple; it was a stock market play, a sort of arbitrage. I asked Conrad, "What happens in these markets as they become marginal to non-viable?" He said, "Well we'll just take them from daily to Sunday, weekly to bi-weekly; we'll just do whatever we have to to cut them down." And I asked him how he was getting around and assessing what to buy and what not to buy. He said to me that, mercifully, he had never been to any of these markets and he hoped never to go. Which I thought was reasonable enough. At least he wasn't pretentious at all. He said that this was straight stock market play.'

'The thing about Conrad Black as proprietor,' says Charles Moore, 'is that journalists the world over think of him as a classic proprietor – ie, interfering, power hungry, a new Beaverbrook because he's a Canadian. But he isn't like that. He's in fact a classic *new style* proprietor who sees his newspapers as a business. He doesn't say, "Let's bring the government down." That's simply not how he operates. He doesn't think about journalism or newspapers at all in that way.'

The Accidental Chairman

Lord Stevens, the man who fell to Fleet Street

'You're not seeing David Stevens are you?' asked Vere Rothermere. 'He isn't actually a newspaper proprietor, you know that?'

'I'm sure Stevens isn't making an appearance on your list,' said Conrad Black, with whom Lord Stevens is equal partner in the *Daily Telegraph/Daily Express* printing plant, 'he's not the proprietor of anything, he's a hired chairman.'

And Tony O'Reilly, who has a joint venture with Stevens in the Irish *Daily Star*, said: 'David Stevens isn't really one of our number of course. One couldn't accurately describe him as a *proprietor*.'

Their assessment of Lord Stevens of Ludgate, Chairman of United Newspapers, parent company of the middle-market *Daily Express* and *Sunday Express* and the downmarket *Daily Star* as well as 121 regional British papers and 11 more in eastern Spain, made me think of the co-op board of a discriminating Park Avenue apartment block, or else – so blunt and hostile were some of their remarks – of a mob of bouncers outside a hot Los Angeles nightclub.

And yet, to the world at large, Lord Stevens *is* a proprietor. He acts like one, and is perceived by other members of the Establishment to be one. At dinner parties he is introduced as 'David Stevens who owns the *Daily Express*,' and when this happens he doesn't split hairs. He reminded me of some species of wild animal – an ibis amidst a herd of blackbuck – that is virtually indistinguishable as an interloper except to other members of the herd. He is a hybrid, a nearly-proprietor, like John Curley, chairman, president and CEO of Gannett Inc in Arlington, Virginia, and Jim Batten, chairman and CEO of Knight-Ridder in Miami.

Stevens is not, in the pure sense, a proprietor at all: he doesn't *own* his newspapers, has no controlling interest in their stock, hasn't rigged the articles of constitution to comprise A shares and B shares, voting and non-voting, and he didn't inherit his papers. He made his career as a fund manager and, almost by accident, found himself the chairman of United. His predicament was described to me by his rivals in terms that made him sound like the caretaker of a substantial country house belonging to the National Trust, whereas they were sole landlords of their estates, to do with as they pleased.

One proprietor confided to me that 'David Stevens probably gets a *salary cheque on his desk every month,*' as though this was the least sophisticated eventuality imaginable. But then he added, 'I'd be obliged if you didn't quote me on that. Many of our best people here only receive salary cheques every month, and in point of fact there's not anything wrong with it.'

I was struck, all the same, by the widespread view that Lord Stevens is not even cast from quite the same mould as his peers. And by their readiness to point out that he manages his papers so tightly, and with such attention to the bottom line, that he might as well be in some other business altogether. David Robert Stevens, they said, may be *in newspapers* but he is not a *newspaperman*.

Much of this needling struck me as unfair. United Newspapers has grown very big under Stevens; in total circulation his papers are bigger than Lord Thomson's, bigger than Conrad Black's, bigger than Lord Rothermere's. Vast tracts of Britain have Stevens as their neighbourhood proprietor. You can drive across Yorkshire from Northallerton to Sheffield and never leave Stevens's territory: the *Batley News*, the *Harrogate Advertiser*, the *Knaresborough Post* are all his, and 24 others besides. His newspaper estates in Lancashire, Cheshire and Greater Manchester are ducal in their dimension: the *Skelmersdale Advertiser* is a Stevens, so is the *Wigan Observer* and the *Lakeland Echo*. If he looked out from the church spire of St Patrick's in Hendon he would have the satisfaction of knowing that almost everything is his as far as the eye can see: the *Richmond and Twickenham Informer*, the *Barnet Advertiser*, the *Uxbridge Informer* and 16 more in Greater London, Surrey and Middlesex. His 62 free newspapers in towns like Blackpool, Prescot, Abergavenny and Northampton have distributions that swamp Tony O'Reilly's parallel operations in East London. And Stevens has some good newspapers too: the *Yorkshire Post*, the

South Wales Argus. As regional papers, they are as editorially impressive as any middle American paper: Hearst's *San Antonio Express-News* or Pulitzer's *Tucson Star* in Arizona.

And yet it has become part of the folklore that *Lord Stevens is not a newspaper man*.

Newspaper profiles make tendentious comparisons: 'He is not quite in the Murdoch or Rothermere class yet,' 'But Stevens is up against Rupert Murdoch ... [and may be out of his league].' And he is charged too with being colourless, a man in a suit, a number-cruncher. This also puzzled me, since many of his actions could not be described as colourless; they seemed consciously showy. His dark blue Rolls Royce has the registration number DRS 20. The effigy of Lord Beaverbrook, Lord Stevens's great predecessor, which for many years stood in the hall of Express Newspapers, was replaced at Stevens's suggestion by a bronze bust of himself. He has developed a taste for marrying gregarious Eastern European women; his second wife Melissa, Countess Andrassy, was a zesty Hungarian who painted most of the rooms in their Belgravia flat in gold and sunshine yellow, and wrote a theoretical primer on 'How to be an Ideal Woman', before tragically choking to death upon a peach stone; the present Lady Stevens, the former Meriza Giori, is a vivacious Russian photographer who relishes escorting her husband to charity galas.

All the proprietorial shrugging at Stevens had its genesis in two contradictory reservations. The first was Lord Stevens's presumption, as a fund manager, at being a press baron at all. There is something about a cool logistician running the old Beaverbrook empire that riles his competitors. *The head versus the heart*. Beaverbrook was passionate, obsessed, intuitive, possibly insane. Stevens is dispassionate, strategic, bottom-line orientated, numerically smug. They are characteristics that Lord Stevens almost consciously endorses, year after year, when he announces his results (1991 profits 85.1 million on a turnover of 812.6 million). 'My rival newspaper publishers must wake up at night and ask "How does that chap Stevens who's not a publisher make *six times* what I'm making out of my national newspapers?"'

There is a consensus, too, that he has allowed his national newspapers to wilt through neglect.

This isn't altogether true. The *Daily Express* and *Sunday Express* – the papers which once, above all others, engaged the patriotic, Bulldog heart of Middle England – which in the 1950s sold 28 million copies a week between them but now barely scrape eight million, had lost momentum long before Stevens took over. Nor has he ignored them. Lord Stevens's filing cabinets bulge with jazzy marketing plans for his papers' resuscitation. He sanctions expensive redundancies for editors who get it wrong, and makes expensive appointments of fresh editors – like Sir Nicholas Lloyd and his wife Eve Pollard, the high profile couple who edit the *Daily Express* and *Sunday Express* respectively – to begin all over again. Some of his appointments and volte-faces have been ill-advised, like the strange episode in 1987 when he invited the architects of the sleazy *Sunday Sport* – porn king David Sullivan and his editorial svengali Michael Gabbert – to take editorial control of the *Daily Star*, Stevens's downmarket rival to Murdoch's *Sun* and the late Robert Maxwell's *Daily Mirror*. The result: a newspaper bristling with naked women and mesmerised by the single word ' Bonking' (main feature, 'How to be a Star bonker'). Lord Stevens put up with it for a bit. 'The word "bonking",' he stated bravely at the time, 'is now in the Oxford dictionary, as I understand it' – but the smile on Lord Stevens's face became thinner and grimmer, until the bonkers bonked off.

'It was an inspired idea of David's to bring those people in,' one of his aides insists to this day. 'It could have been genius. They were producing the newspaper – the *Sport* – that everyone was talking about, and he got them in and hired them and said, "Make *my* tabloid talked about". That's how David works. He does his homework, finds out who's got the best reputation, who are the appropriate executives, then hires them. It should have worked. It's just a pity they went too far.'

'I have always read the *Sunday Express*. Best newspaper in the country,' Lord Stevens told me. His father read the *Express*, he said, so did his grandfather. And I felt sure that all three generations of Stevenses perused it before lunch in the same way, as readers rather than newspapermen. His responses are those of a City mandarin, not of an old Fleet Street baron. He is like the customer who has eaten happily for 30 years in the same restaurant, but ask him to describe how the dishes are cooked and he is stumped, because he is a customer not a chef.

'David and I very occasionally have lunch,' Lord Rothermere told me. 'One feels that it ought to be useful, you know, to hear what the other fellow's thinking, though to be honest with you I can't say that we exchange much information that's likely to be helpful to one another; I don't really feel that we know each other that well. And I think we have arrived at our various situations in life, you know, from different directions, which means that we think about things in slightly different ways. One always feels that David Stevens is awfully well organised whereas we tend to do things here more, well, if you like *by instinct*.'

Until he was eased out of his fund management role, Lord Stevens of Ludgate had two corporate offices: his newspaper office on the top floor of Ludgate House, the glass and steel headquarters of United Newspapers; and the City office in Devonshire Square of his vast investment and fund management companies, MIM Britannia and Invesco. He prefers the fund management office. It has been suggested that Stevens likes to keep geographical distance and perspective from the seductive hurly-burly of the papers. He preferred to analyse the bare management figures well away from their offices. He has seen how other proprietors have fallen so badly in love with their papers that it has affected their judgement. Soon they are encouraging their editors to hire extra journalists, increasing the size of the newspaper, matching everything done by the opposition at any price.

The lift doors of Devonshire Square opened on to a large expanse of beige: beige carpets, beige cornicing, pastel walls hung with wishy-washy watercolours of windswept beaches and Big Ben. The visitor waiting in Lord Stevens's beige reception is given a choice of financial pamphlets to read; one of them, illustrated with a watercolour of a yacht at anchor in some Caribbean cove, is called '*TAXHAV£N: Escape the taxman's plunder*'.

David Stevens's own office was also beige: beige curtains with beige braid at the windows, more beige carpet, some good boardroom furniture, an antique desk, brass carriage clock, library chairs with new leather. In this setting, Lord Stevens reminded me initially of a top Harley Street consultant, perhaps an ear, nose and throat specialist.

But when he began speaking I was struck by his sense of purpose and bustle. Lord Stevens is a short man, in horn-rimmed glasses, chubby cheeked and with a full head of grey hair. He hasn't got natural gravitas, but he conveys a strong sense of command.

I had been told he can be terse with his subordinates, and that he is bad at putting people at their ease, but I guessed that the unease many journalists feel in his presence is the result of Lord Stevens's other life in fund management and management consultancy (he is also chairman of the consultants Alexander Proudfoot). He has a deadpan, boardroom wit that can be read sharply. And he particularly resents being viewed by journalists as a johnny-come-lately proprietor arrived from nowhere.

So when you visit Lord Stevens he gives you first a little lecture about fund management. He tells you how hard fund managers work – much harder and longer than journalists – and he tells you how he built up a small fund management firm into an enormous one, the biggest in the world outside America. The point of the lecture, I surmised, is twofold. Fund management, he is implying, is bigger and just as exciting as newspaper publishing and he is one of the biggest wheels in it. So whatever he says about the media must be seen in that context. And however smart his rival newspaper proprietors think they are, none of them has built up anything nearly so fine as his City operations.

Lord Stevens's lecture, delivered in a dry monotone, was lengthy, so in order to divert him on to newspapers I asked, 'Is there a great difference, chairing newspaper and City companies?'

'Well if I were making an observation off the seat of my pants,' he replied, 'I'd say not. I don't think being chairman of one is that dissimilar to being chairman of the other.'

The drawback of owning or being the chairman of newspapers, he said, is readers complaining to him when they object to an article. He said he felt frequently exasperated, because it was impossible for his secretaries to distinguish between fund managers who left telephone messages (and should obviously have their calls returned, being fund managers) and members of the General Public who might simply be disagreeing with Cross Bencher's political spin in that week's *Sunday Express* or the report of a greyhound race in the *Daily Star*.

'These people ring me up,' said Lord Stevens, 'because they've obviously read somewhere in the national press that I control these newspapers, and they want to argue the toss about matters about which, as likely as not, I know nothing whatever.'

way. Now, I happen to like to be on site because I think if you're in charge you have to be seen, whether you like it or not. That's my opinion. You *ought* to be seen and you really ought to work longer hours than anybody else. Now, a lot of people disagree with that and it's their privilege to disagree with me. I mean, they probably say I'm mad and I probably am. I mean, in the whole of my working life, which is 32 years, I've only taken off three days for golf. I know it's three days because I keep a tab on it. I was a very keen golfer, and I still enjoy golf. On the other hand I don't want to be away from the office and what's going on.'

I asked whether he thought his constant presence improved his newspapers. It occurred to me that it might in fact have the opposite effect. Lord Rothermere's long absences in Paris and Kyoto seem to burnish rather than diminish his proprietorial gravitas. Editors summoned to a meeting at his Paris apartment have at least three hours' travelling time in which to get into an appropriate frame of mind, and the rarity of such encounters lend them purpose and weight.

And I felt too that Rothermere, Murdoch and Black's memoed or telephoned instructions from Kyoto, Los Angeles, Toronto or wherever, gave them an impressive emphasis. 'The editor has just been rung by Lord Rothermere from the South of France. He liked your piece on left-wing councils' sounds better than 'Lord Stevens is thumbing through the paper upstairs'.

Stevens, however, argued that his vigilance had forestalled misinformation.

'I have the first edition delivered to my home in Cheyne Gardens every evening, and if we're in I try to look at it straight away.'

'So what time does it arrive? About ten o'clock?'

'Not early enough,' said Stevens. 'No, it arrives about eleven. And funnily enough I commented this morning that I thought it was arriving too late. The editor receives *his* an hour earlier – *at least*. So I'm not quite sure why I get *mine* so late because, I mean, it's coming off the presses at what, 9.30, 10, so there's no reason. On Sunday I get my *Sunday Express* at 8.15 on Saturday evening.'

'Which gives you time to check for mistakes.'

'Well I did stop the presses once – you'll want to hear this story – about two years ago. They had an article about tax on pension funds in the City column and it was complete nonsense. Complete nonsense from start to finish. So I phoned up – it was about 10 o'clock at night – I phoned up and got hold of the . . . who did I get? Someone on the back bench [night editors] anyway. And I said to the back bench that this was the chairman speaking and that this article was complete gobbledegook and would have to be rewritten. I said, "You can't possibly let the paper go out like this. *Stop the presses* and I'll hold on," you see. So he came back to me after a bit and said, "The presses have been stopped, Chairman." I said, "Thank you very much. But, purely as a matter of interest, how do you know that I *am* the Chairman?" ' Lord Stevens chuckled heartily at the memory of this exchange. 'Anyway, it was altered. Well I rewrote it. I dictated it to them and then asked them to read it back to me, which they did.'

'Was it a long article?'

'About 100 words.' A paragraph. 'Not difficult, if you know your business. If you know your business it is easy to dictate 500 to 1000 words, I can do it straight away without any notes on my subject. I mean, John Junor in his book – I haven't read his book – claimed that my House of Lords speech was ghost-written for me. I don't know why John Junor has to be so bitchy but I actually dictate my House of Lords speeches in about ten or 15 minutes straight off. Then I alter them a little bit and that's it. My view is if you can't speak on your own subject then you'd really better pack up. Now, the first House of Lords speech was *partly* written for me, and I altered it. So I suppose the answer is like lots of things: when you get a bit of confidence you do it yourself.'

I had been told that Lord Stevens, more than any other publisher apart from the late Maxwell, likes to make suggestions for articles. And when he makes them, he is impatient to read the article he suggested in his newspaper. At the fortnightly lunches he hosts for his editors, he makes his opinions known.

Lord Stevens likes: articles about medical transplants, women and babies, anti-litter campaigns.

Lord Stevens dislikes: hounding the Duchess of York, hounding the Royal Family generally ('we could destroy the social fabric'), ignorant disparagement of prominent City figures unless they genuinely merit it.

When pleased or displeased, he sends a note. 'Always a note. Otherwise you spend the whole day on the telephone. You can waste an awful lot of time on the telephone. I'm quite sparing with my notes – I don't do it that often because I think it reduces the role of it. I mean, if you get a note from the chairman periodically saying "well done" it has an effect, but if you get one every day it defeats the objective.'

'What merits a curt note from you?'

'Probably something silly like an out-of-date photograph, which is *inexcusable* because they ought to get an up-to-date one. Obviously I pick up mostly on the financial things. I mean, a total misquote, putting 100 billion instead of 100 million. It might average once a fortnight but you might get two in one day. And in terms of *likes* it's the same dimension. There's something I like today in the *Express* so I'm actually sending a note about that now.'

I asked Lord Stevens who would be receiving this herogram, and got the impression that he rather regretted mentioning it.

'I don't normally do this,' he said, 'but a friend of mine has organised an Italian art exhibition in London and she paid for it too which cost her £50,000. She's called Donatella Flick by the way; it's the Flick family of Germany [the Mercedes-Benz billionaires]. Anyway she phoned up on Sunday, very upset, and spoke to my wife and said this exhibition was starting on Monday and Princess Margaret was opening it, and that the people who had organised the pictures, which they'd borrowed from a foundation in America, had told her that although she had *paid* for it, it was *nothing to do with her*. She was not going to be in the receiving line and would she kindly stay out of the way. So my wife told me the story and I said that's extraordinary. If she'd *paid* for it, why shouldn't she meet Princess Margaret? So I said, 'This doesn't sound fair to me. Ask her *if* she'd like to be in an article in the *Daily Express*.' The answer came back yes, so I said to the *Daily Express* would they please do an article and give her the credit for the exhibition. Now you're going to say, "OK, Lord Stevens rigs the news" but my view is that firstly I don't see why she shouldn't get the credit and secondly since she didn't ask *me* to do it – she talked to my wife – so I didn't *mind* doing it. The note I'm sending is to the journalist who wrote it, thanking her.'

Occasionally Stevens will summon contributors to the *Daily Express* to his office, to put them right on topics of the day. Charles Moore [now editor of Conrad Black's *Sunday Telegraph*] was once called to Devonshire Square when he wrote a weekly *Express* column to be given the Stevens line on Hong Kong which was diametrically opposite to his own.

I asked Lord Stevens whether these proprietor-to-columnist briefings were routine practice.

'No, but I thought he got Hong Kong wrong. Charles Moore's an able man, but I think he's a trifle arrogant, let's put it that way. His views are a bit entrenched. And I thought he could do with the benefit of my advice on Hong Kong. On the other hand I respect him for sticking to his views. What I'm not keen on is when you talk to somebody and he says, "Oh yes Chairman, you're absolutely right Chairman, you're absolutely right, I got it all wrong" etc. I don't necessarily want people to do that.'

People tell you that Lord Stevens is rather shy. Their evidence for this theory is that at dinner parties he often appears self-absorbed, as though his mind has strayed, from boredom or bashfulness, away from light conversation and off into the more worthy realm of investment. And yet he has none of the self-effacement of Lord Thomson, and is self-deprecating only when talking about his golf.

He is capable, too, of impetuousness. There is, for instance, his own heroic story of how he obtained the last bedroom in an overbooked Paris airport hotel.

'I was on a business trip to Brazil with a small group of people – Walter Salomon of Rae Brothers – remarkable old character – Sir Leslie Bowes, Lord Dartmouth – Gerald Dartmouth – and one or two others, and we were booked into some hotel at Orly airport, whose name I've now forgotten, it's a fairly ugly-looking hotel. Anyway, we flew in and all went out to dinner and we got to the hotel at about 10.30 at night, which isn't actually that late by French standards and we'd reconfirmed our rooms, obviously, and we'd also reconfirmed them from the restaurant. When we got to the hotel there was a sort of milling crowd at the desk, and the receptionist said the hotel was completely full and there were no rooms available for any of us. There were arguments going on with everybody you see. Now, Walter Salomon was at that time a man of, what, 75. The rest were somewhat younger. That wasn't the point. But there were a huge number of keys in the rack, you could see them. So I was watching this and I said to Walter, "To hell with this. I'm not going to put up with it – we've reconfirmed our rooms from London, we've reconfirmed them from the restaurant. I'm going to take a key and go to bed." So I climbed over the desk, took a key – which happened to be the key to a huge suite – and went upstairs. Fortunately the room was empty. The receptionist, I think, was just being bolshie. But I paid the bill the next morning.'

David Stevens was born in London in 1935 in a nothing-special terraced house in Edgware. But when he was ten years old his father, Edwin, transformed the family fortunes by inventing in his back room the world's first wearable electronic hearing aid. He founded a company, Amplivox, which was sold to Racal in the early seventies and enabled him to become an energetic philanthropist: he built Stevens Close for example, (a hall of residence at Jesus College, Oxford). One theory about Lord Stevens, widely credited by *Express* managers, is that he took over the group partly to delight his father, a lifelong *Sunday Express* reader. The same theory explains Stevens's timidity in allowing the broadsheet to go tabloid to challenge Rothermere's more successful *Mail on Sunday* head on; David Stevens didn't want to unsettle the old man before his Sunday lunch in Woking, Surrey. 'By the time he hired Eve Pollard, and gave her the go-ahead, there'd been five more years of drift,' I was told by an *Express* executive.

'He's very, very shrewd and clever at examining piles of printouts and figures,' Sir Nicholas Lloyd told me, 'and picking on salient points. He notices everything: how much has been spent this week on overtime for machine minders, how much we spent buying serialisation on a book and whether it was worth it in terms of the circulation we put on. It's nit-picking in a way, but he keeps you on your toes. The culture can sometimes be a bit irksome but he's a man of great sanity. I don't actually know what his newspaper strategy is, if I may say so – he's a professional manager really. It's not perhaps quite so romantic to adhere to this budget-driven system as some other places – it's quite different to the way Murdoch operates – but I'm given enormous freedom and there's no unsolicited "help" from above.'

I asked Lloyd what Stevens's achievements are as a proprietor.

'It's not too hysterical to say that he's probably saved the *Daily Express* and *Sunday Express*.'

'Is he clever at picking editors?'

'His technique when he doesn't know you is to ask slightly mischievous questions. It's done without a smile. You can be asked something that sounds a bit naive and peculiar. He's a fisherman, he casts flies on the water. He enjoys floating a view that he doesn't hold himself, to see what the reaction is. He'll say, "Don't you think the *Daily Express* is far too slavish in supporting the Conservative government, and that we should take a more independent line?" If you're poodling your way into the job you might agree, and then you'd be off the list.'

Stevens was sent to Stowe, read economics at Sydney Sussex College, Cambridge, then had the eccentric idea of going into industry.

'I wanted to go into production, and when you left Cambridge in 1959 there were very few companies that would take graduates into that area, they didn't believe in it, which was an extraordinary reflection on this country, I think. I had an interview at Ford's in Dagenham and they offered me a job but said no way could I go on the shop floor, I would have to go into accountancy because that's all they would take graduates for, so I said no thank you. I then got a job with Elliot Automation, at that time probably the only electronic equipment manufacturer in the UK and one of the first people to manufacture computers here. I got a shop-floor job there as management trainee and stuck it for two years.'

He moved into the City and the emergent investment trust division of Hill Samuel, then switched to the Drayton Group to set up an investment division for them; when Drayton was taken over by the merchant bankers Samuel Montagu he surfaced as the chairman of their fund managers Montagu Investment Management. Montagu, as it happened, held a 10 per cent stake in United Newspapers (then purely a provincial newspaper group with a few magazines like *Pig Farming* and *Punch*) and Stevens joined their board as MIM's representative. Seven years later United's chairman, Lord Barnetson, died somewhat prematurely and Stevens, though only a part-time director, took charge.

'His approach was immediately quite different from Barnetson's,' says a colleague. 'David had always got on immensely well with Barnetson, who was of course an impressive old school newspaper man, but their mindset is absolutely different. David is an investment man through and through. He wants a return. He wants cashflow. He wants a good dividend for shareholders. He's not that interested in newspapers as institutions to be kept going out of charity. Once you've established that the return is of paramount importance – and he did this straight away – emphatically – then other decisions rather follow from that.'

Taking the view that the United's profits were too narrowly based – 90 per cent deriving from British newspapers – Stevens spent four years expanding United, taking the group into the United States where it bought the satellite based communications network, Newswire, and two specialist publishers in New York and San Francisco. He also launched United's chains of free newspapers across Britain and acquired the small- ads newspaper *Exchange & Mart*. Worth just over £20 million when Stevens took it over, United Newspapers was valued at £240 million by the time he set his sights on becoming a national press baron.

Hanging behind Lord Stevens's sofa in his Devonshire Square office is the framed cartoon that was originally published in the *Sunday Times* when he was battling for the *Express*. It shows Stevens dressed as Mr Punch in a cap with a bell, striding purposefully towards the outgoing Express chairman, Lord Matthews, and clonking him on the head with a heavy cosh. Victor Matthews, who is caricatured as the trademark Express Crusader in a suit of armour, has the flattened, bulbous nose of a pugilist and eyes that are regarding Stevens with something close to fear.

'Stevens won because he understood the institutional investors better than anyone – he *is* one,' is what people say now about the vindictive scrap for the Express. 'Victor Matthews claimed he knew more about newspapers, itself debatable, but he hadn't been lunching with fund managers in their boardrooms for the previous ten years. Stevens knew exactly what they wanted to hear and trotted it out.'

After he'd won, goes the legend, David Stevens rang Lord Matthews on his carphone. 'Don't take it too hard,' he said, 'You've already *got* your peerage out of the *Express*. Just enjoy it.'

David Stevens received his own Life Peerage in 1987, shortly after Margaret Thatcher's third election victory.

At some point during my interview I mentioned globalisation. Globalisation is a woolly concept in communications, but it was cropping up over and over again in other proprietors' conversations.

Murdoch talks up global publishing incessantly, so did Maxwell and so, to different degrees, do Ralph Ingersoll, Dean Singleton and Otis Chandler.

Lord Stevens finds this inexplicable.

'I've never believed in the globalisation of media. There's been a lot of chit-chat about it, but I don't see anything common about owning newspapers here and in America, like there is with say a motor car which is the same product internationally. There's no cross-fertilisation. OK, you can have the most efficient production methods but, I mean, a good manufacturer or consultant can give you that. I don't mean to run down the opposition, but personally I don't think Murdoch will survive. He's paid too high prices for certain businesses and I suppose he's the man one would immediately think of as a global player.'

'Do you know Murdoch?'

'I don't know anybody really. Not the other publishers. I mean there's no real reason why I should. Well, OK, you can say "Well maybe you *ought* to know all the publishers." Well the fact of the matter is I don't and there's no business, necessarily, for me to know them. You can spend an awful lot of time just chatting people up, not getting anywhere. If you asked me, "Do I know all the merchant bankers?" then yes, but that's because I've been in the business for 30 years. But as for the publishers, you spend your time running your business, not chatting people up. Well, anyway, that's my view of it.'

I thought that I detected, in this strange reply, both disappointment and defiance. If they don't want me in their club, he seemed to be saying, that's fine by me, because I don't want to be in it anyway. I've got my own gang to play with which is a much *better* gang – the merchant bankers.

'Other newspaper owners,' he said, 'are the only people in the world I can think of who run a major industry in this way. They're not motivated in the same way as a publicly quoted company [like United Newspapers Plc]. Cover prices, for instance, are depressed in the interests of circulation despite the fact they represent 70 per cent of the revenue in the middle market.' Lord Stevens seems to regard his rivals as men less exacting than himself, working to agendas in which the purity of profit is muddied by priorities of pride and prestige.

'Other considerations,' he said gravely, as though he were the one sane helmsman on the ship of fools, 'Yes, *other considerations* come into play.'

The Ménage of *Figaro*

The Secret World of Robert Hersant

There is a theory that just as a dog-owner will over many years come to resemble his pet, so a newspaper over the passage of time comes to resemble its proprietor. *Le Figaro*, like Robert Hersant, is a right-wing Parisian heavyweight – dry, literal, well-ordered and serious, neither given to surprises nor flights of imagination. The front page is as carefully portioned-out as a row of allotments: the stories contained in neat little boxes, each about three inches square. No headline runs higher than three-quarters of an inch, which makes the paper appear not just sober but downright furtive. An opinion column called 'Cacophonie' trails down the left side of the page, getting at the socialists, and this is complemented by a large unfunny cartoon with the same intention. A typical one depicts a socialist politician, dressed as a cowpoke in a stetson, riding wearily into the sunset and commenting 'AIE AME A POUR LONESOME COWMUNIST'. Inside there are more neatly hoed columns of political opinion, and some of the most technical weather charts I've ever seen, full of isobars, mistrals and perturbations.

As a daily newspaper *Le Figaro* is much duller than the British broadsheets, more biased than the American, less comprehensive than the Chinese and less quirky than the Indian; the journalism reminded me of raw steak that has been pulverised with a mallet, fed through a mincer, liquidised in a blender and kneaded into perfect, flavour-free patties. I could imagine its tissue-thin pages being perused on the Metro by petty officials in government service and by suburban doctors and dentists in Limoges. I could, in short, understand exactly why Robert Hersant's *Le Figaro* is the most successful national newspaper in modern France.

Robert Hersant is the most secretive press baron in Europe. In 30 years as France's foremost proprietor, controlling 23 newspapers and 38 per cent of the national newspaper market, he has never given a proper interview. The photographs that exist of him are either so old that the 72-year-old Hersant resembles the young Jean-Paul Belmondo, or so wooden and unprepossessing that he looks like the mayor of some two-bit town in the prefecture of Loiret. Conrad Black says he reminds him of 'Carroll O'Connor playing Archie Bunker in *All in the Family*'.

'When you first see this guy, he is so unassuming, you think, "My God, *who's he*?" ' a French countess who writes for Hersant's flagship told me. 'He has no chic. My God, I've only ever seen him wear a white shirt and dark tie.'

People tell you three things about Robert Joseph Emile Hersant: that he had a bad war and has never quite shaken off his apparent support for an anti-semitic youth league during the Nazi occupation; that his right-wing politics, relentlessly espoused through his papers from Normandy to Lyons, have made a decisive impact on the mindset of bourgeois France; and that the Groupe de Presse Robert Hersant is so obsessively private that it is startling it can bring itself to do anything so public as to publish newspapers.

For 25 years Hersant's headquarters has been a stucco mansion in the Rue de Presbourg, at the apex of the Champs Elysées and the Avenue de la Grande Armée. It is here around a triangular courtyard, with an external teak lift like an ascending coffin and a view from Hersant's desk through none-too-clean net curtains of the Arc de Triomphe, that he planned the acquisitions of *Le Figaro*, of Paris's evening paper *France-Soir* and his powerful roster of provincial press like *Paris-Normandie*, *Nord-Matin*, *Le Havre-Libre* and *Lyon-Matin*. It is said to have been a point of pride to Robert Hersant, with his equivocal opinion of journalists, that his strategic headquarters was wholly insulated from his newspapers.

In 1992, however, acting on what can only be explained as a whim, Hersant unveiled an enormous shiny new headquarters. With its grey marble cladding and curvy walls, ten storeys high, it looks like a beached silver whale, occupying an entire block of the Avenue de Général Mangin. I can only imagine the owner played no part in the decoration of the building, since the flamboyant post-modernist lobby with its aluminium pillars shaped like sugar shakers and metal chairs with their orange and pink antimacassars, are more Christian Lacroix than Robert Hersant. A grey signboard on the wall informs you that *Le Figaro*, *Le Figaro Economie*, *France-Soir* and the Publiprint Régions occupy this storey and that. The top three floors – seven, eight and nine – are left blank on the board. These floors are the preserve of the proprietor.

I had made numerous attempts to interview Robert Hersant. My letters, if they were acknowledged at all, met with short dismissive replies. Nor was he susceptible to peer competitiveness. My recital of the growing list of fellow proprietors whom I'd visited left Hersant unmoved. The longer became my letters, the shorter his replies. Proprietorship is anyway an emotive concept in the Fifth Republic. In a country where the law still, rather oddly, prevents one man from owning more than one newspaper, Robert Hersant's rapacious expansion has always incited criticism. In *Who's Who in France* he even avoids describing himself as a newspaper owner: '*Editeur, Homme politique, Parlementaire Européen*'.

I was anxious to see Hersant in the flesh, and had been told that every weekday he left the building at 25-minutes-to-one to be driven to lunch. A silver Mercedes would draw up at the front entrance of the beached silver whale, Monsieur Hersant descend in the lift, cross the gleaming lobby and climb into the back seat of the car. I decided one morning to station myself across the Avenue and spectate.

At 28-minutes-to-one the silver Mercedes arrived at the ramp leading down to the entrance. Two minutes later there was a flurry in the lobby, and the chauffeur walked round the car to open the passenger door. Just then two sinister security guards appeared alongside me on the pavement, intentionally blocking out my view across the street.

'You are searching for a taxi, *non?*' said one firmly grasping my arm, 'You will best find a taxi at the other end of the street.'

'No taxi will arrive here,' warned the second. 'This is a bad place to wait.'

By the time they moved away, the silver Mercedes was turning the corner of the Avenue de Général Mangin in the direction of the Seine.

Robert Hersant occupies a pivotal position in the galaxy of Continental European proprietors. He is practically the only individual whose power matches that of the great owners in America, Britain and the Far East. So many European newspapers are subject to tortuous cross-ownership, or are controlled by diversified entre-preneurs whose papers represent only a miniscule part of their huge portfolios, like Silvio Berlusconi with *Il Giornale*, Carlo de Benedetti with *La Repubblica* and Gianni Agnelli with *Corriere della Sera*. In Sweden the Bonnier family dominates its home market with *Dagens Nyheter* and *Expressen*, but they are remote from global combat and their ambitions seem not to extend beyond the fjords. In Greece too the tzatsiki press of Christos Lambrakis is xenophobic and self-absorbed. Hubert Burda, following his failed foray into newspapers (in partnership with Murdoch to launch the raunchy tabloid *Super! Zeitung* in eastern Germany) has retreated back to his magazine empire in Hamburg. Only Hersant meets the criteria of an engaged pro-prietor, rolling his presses north, east and west across the French frontiers. By the spring of 1993 Hersant had newspapers in Belgium (42 per cent of *Le Soir*), Hungary (49 per cent of the regional daily *Petoefi Nepe* and *Magyar Nemzet*), Poland (*Rzeczpospolita*), Czechoslovakia (48 per cent of *Mlada Fronta*) and a salad niçoise of sleepy papers in former French colonies like French Guyana, Guadeloupe, New Caledonia and Tahiti.

For a man whose ambitions are apparently so international, it is striking how many of his employees describe him as insular.

'Monsieur Hersant is "hexagonal",' I was told. 'I mean, his brain has six sides to it, like the map of France. Beyond France, he is not interested. His prejudices are all French. For Monsieur Hersant those other countries exist only to make money in, or maybe to glorify France a little bit more through his newspapers.'

'Look at *Le Figaro*,' I was advised. 'The policy is all handed down from Hersant, whatever people tell you otherwise. And you find very little international perspective in the paper. Sure there is some news from overseas. But everything that is written, it says I think that Paris is the most important city in Europe and the whole world.'

Hersant makes a point, however, of publicly admiring the United States; a foible some say he affects expressly to irritate his fellow countrymen, many of whom have an anti-American bias. He takes most of his holidays in America and has a son living in Los Angeles with his family. It delighted him when his twelfth grandson was born an American. Hersant has eight children – five daughters and three sons – born of his three marriages. The first two marriages ended in widowerhood and divorce; the third has lasted 35 years. His children – like the Maxwells before the fall – mostly work in the empire. And like Robert Maxwell he takes a perverse pride in proclaiming that he gives his children no money beyond their salaries.

Robert Hersant was born on 31 January 1920 at Vertou in the Loire-Inférieure, the son of Victor Hersant, a merchant navy captain, and Juliette Hugot. He was sent to the lycées at Rouen and Le Havre and emerged from his education as an enthused young socialist. By his twentieth birthday, however, he had defected to the Jeune Front, an ultra-nationalist youth organisation in Nazi-occupied Paris, and briefly volunteered to edit their magazine. He has spent the subsequent fifty years insisting this magazine wasn't actually pro-German but pro-French. Nevertheless, in the post-war turbulence of accusations and counter-accusations, Hersant was tried for his activities, imprisoned for a month and sentenced by a Liberation Court to ten years of 'national indignity', but was granted an amnesty five years later. He now refers to this period as 'the problem of my youth' and becomes infuriated by socialist opponents who still exhume the incident for their own ends.

He founded a car newspaper, *L'Auto Journal*, in the post-war French craze for motoring, and by 1957 had used the cashflow it produced to embark upon a series of provincial newspaper acquisitions in central France, which he called Centre Presse. His strategy, which he would repeat throughout the sixties and early seventies in Normandy and again in 1986 in Lyons, is to buy a cluster of medium-sized regionals, amalgamate their advertising departments and print facilities, impose new technology and drastically reduce staffing. Hersant's routines at Lyons (where he took over *Le Progrès* in great secrecy), Le Havre (*Le Havre-Libre*) and Nantes (the amusingly-named *L'Eclair*) have been classics of the Ralph Ingersoll or Dean Singleton school, with stringent cost-cutting and rationalisation. As soon as the programme of Hersantisation is completed at each newspaper group, he takes the acquisition trail to a fresh region. If you flag Hersant's empire on the map of France you see that he now dominates almost the entire north coast (his *Nord-Matin* and *Paris-Normandie* are the leading northern regionals) and the whole central vertebrae of the country from Le Havre to the Pyrenees (where he has the tiny *La Nouvelle République des Pyrénées*). By the end of the eighties more than a quarter of the French provinical press was controlled by Hersant.

In global terms most of Robert Hersant's proprietorial techniques are standard, and would pass unnoticed anywhere else but France. He does nothing that would shock or surprise Jim Cox Kennedy in Atlanta or Lord Thomson in Toronto. And yet, in Paris, Hersant's reputation is broadcast as though it was something unique. The explanation for this says less about Hersant than the French government's fierce and sanctimonious restraints on newspaper ownership.

'The difference between Rupert Murdoch and me,' Hersant has said, 'is that Murdoch lives in a country where information is free. I have neither the same hope nor possibilities. In France, information is supervised by the government and that's been increasing since [the socialist victory of] 1981. A press empire in France is a fragile thing.'

To keep hold of his papers, Hersant has been locked into almost unceasing political and legal wrangles. The 1944 post-Liberation rule of one-man, one-newspaper has been raised against him again and again, most dangerously in the mid-seventies when he bought *Le Figaro*, and the mid-eighties when a Socialist bill was devised specifically to limit Hersant's power. He survived on both occasions only after unprecedented lobbying, which itself drew accusations that Hersant had twenty members of parliament on the payroll of his newspapers, as columnists or special advisors. In October 1984 a new anti-trust law was passed against him, restricting ownership to 10 per cent of national daily sales. Initially it seemed that Hersant was obliged to divest half his empire until the Constitutional Council ruled that the law could not be applied retroactively. The socialists nevertheless confidently assumed that the new law would prevent any further expansion by the group. Barely a year later, however, he showed his complete contempt for it by announcing his purchase of eight newspapers in Lyons, thereby giving himself a virtual monopoly in the Lyons area, the second biggest metropolis after Paris.

The government protested that the takeover was illegal and that Hersant would be prosecuted. Hersant retorted in a front-page editorial in *Le Figaro* that the government was ready to hand over its mass media to foreigners – he referred to the licence for France's first private television channel being granted to a Franco-Italian group – while attempting to prevent natural-born Frenchmen from rescuing unprofitable newspapers.

'Sometimes, in order not to be behind in a war, it is necessary to be in advance of a law,' he proclaimed.

Impasse had been reached when, happily for Hersant, the government changed and the in-coming right-wing administration quashed the statute.

Another complaint you continually hear about Hersant is that he's tough on journalists.

'The best writers in Paris, after one year with Hersant many have moved elsewhere,' I was told by an editor on the rival Paris paper *Libération*. 'It is good for us sometimes, because these people write for us instead, but it is not good for Hersant.'

On the other hand, the newspapers he buys are generally grossly overstaffed. Because French law requires owners to pay high severence payments to journalists they wish to fire, it is the custom to kick burnt-out staff upstairs and invent some nebulous role for them, rather than fund their redundancy, with the result that staff costs often account for one-third of major French newspapers' budgets, against one-fifth or one-tenth of comparable American newspapers. Hersant takes the view that he would rather pay now, benefit later. French media owners must also grapple with the *clause de conscience* that permits journalists to leave a newspaper with full redundancy if they feel an in-coming owner will change their paper's political character. It is a consideration that proprietors elsewhere are spared, and makes a material difference to media values. Most owners, when they change a paper's politics, depend on the old guard resigning unless they choose to play Vicar of Bray. When Hersant was calculating how much to pay for the mildly leftist *Le Figaro* and the liberal Lyons *Progrès*, he had to factor in severence cheques for staff who didn't like the right-wing cut of his jib.

He has been tenacious, too, in implementing new technology. A surprising fact of French life is that few senior journalists can type. This has historically been a point of pride: columnists and reporters *dictate* their stories to secretaries. Hersant's moves to direct-input of copy strike not just at staff numbers but journalists' prestige. Former

Le Figaro contributors in Paris speak, with great affront, of 'Hersant's scheme that we all become secretary birds instead of writers.'

Hersant's political views are satirised as nationalistic, but are more complex than that. His newspapers have given more credibility to the National Front leader Jean-Marie le Pen than their rivals, but Hersant submits that he has simply reported le Pen's rise dispassionately, and it is the other, left-leaning papers that are guilty of bias by exclusion. *Le Figaro* has been at the forefront of a vigorous anti-immigration campaign, but Hersant can legitimately point to the widespread support the campaign received. He is staunchly pro-European and has twice been a member of the European Parliament in 1984 and 1989. He has twice been elected as mayor, of Ravenel and Liancourt, and twice become the member for l'Oise in the National Assembly. All these political offices leave him open to criticism for conflict of interest. Hersant responds, 'I'm no Citizen Kane or Randolph Hearst. I don't have mines, oil wells, factories. I'm only a man of the press. I'm obliged, condemned, to ensure its survival with no outside influence. [Mine is] a clean press.'

As in India, French newspaper owners are expected to endorse the winning side in elections or face the consequences later. Robert Hersant's proprietorship has seen him play kingmaker and public prosecutor to every administration since the sixties. His alliances and froideurs with successive presidents and prime ministers have been transparent to even the most casual reader of his newspapers. His squabble with Mitterrand extended throughout the latter's presidency, reaching its nadir during the socialist campaign to strip him of his empire, when Mitterrand appeared to have sanctioned the Ministry of Finance's harassment of the group over taxation. A striking example of the French government's interference with the press is that media owners have to ask permission to raise the cost of their newspapers. The Ministry of Finance refused Hersant's request, alone among proprietors in being denied permission, to put up the cover price of *Le Figaro* and *France-Soir*. No sooner was the order issued than Hersant announced his intention of defying it, and hiked both papers by ten centimes. The government threatened him with two years' imprisonment, but later backed off. Some saw, in this capitulation, the hand of Mitterrand since Hersant, strangely enough, had a special claim on the President's gratitude. In 1985 Mitterrand staged an extraordinary fake attempt on his own life, perhaps to gain political sympathy. When parliament voted to lift his parliamentary immunity so that Mitterrand could face charges of bearing false witness, Robert Hersant was one of the only five members who voted against this motion. This favour lay unspoken between them throughout their public battles.

On other occasions he has directly benefited from government largesse. His first foreign deal to set up the paper in Guadeloupe, *France-Antilles*, came from the then Gaullist regime, and Hersant still uses it as his training school for newspaper executives. President Georges Pompidou helped Hersant acquire *Paris-Normandie* when it had become politically irritating to his government. Jacques Chirac, then Prime Minister, gave Hersant crucial support when he presented himself as the controversial purchaser for the almost bankrupt *Le Figaro*. Aides of President Giscard d'Estaing are said to have played a decisive role in the group's 1978 purchase of *L'Aurore*, the small, influential, conservative newspaper. When Hersant subsequently fell out with Giscard d'Estaing, claiming he showed him insufficient respect and treated him 'like a dog', the support for his presidency evaporated across all titles.

A popular journalistic pastime in Paris is guessing what Robert Hersant might choose to buy next.

'He would buy papers in the South,' I was told. 'Nice. Marseilles. Around Cannes. Hersant owns nothing in the South. If something good became available, he would jump up at this chance.'

An adventure in French network television with Silvio Berlusconi and others – the La Cinq channel – developed into a fiasco, draining his newspaper profits to an alarming degree and culminating with blank screens when the partners turned off the cashflow. Newspaper analysts estimate that the La Cinq investment pushed the Hersant group into mild loss for three consecutive years in the late eighties, and that he is unlikely to risk another television foray. But he has money to spend; total Groupe Hersant media revenues for 1991 were estimated at $1.56 billion, and profits at $100 million.

Another Parisian guessing game is how on earth Robert Hersant spends this money. He drives two smart cars, a BMW and Mercedes-Benz, lives in an apartment in suburban Saint-Cloud, has a small estate in Normandy where he plays golf and listens to classical music. But he is not a bon viveur, neither drinks nor smokes, and spends much of the weekend rooting around in the small print of his newspapers' accounts.

'What's Robert Hersant like?' said Ralph Ingersoll who considered forming a joint partnership with him for a European venture. 'Three words: Serious. Puposeful. Dry.'

Born a Catholic, Hersant has become contemptuous in old age of what he sees as the French Catholic work ethic. 'The idea,' he says, 'is that the last will be the first in Heaven, and the rich will be punished. That's why France has always lagged behind the Protestant and Jewish capitalism of England, Germany and America.' He talks increasingly, too, of passing on the empire in some form to his children when he dies: to run it, if not to own it. 'You know,' he says, 'it's the ultimate, vanity of a man to believe that he is passing on the flame and that his children will perpetuate it; that his work will not be as fleeting as his life but will continue to the end of time. Usually there's nothing to it – nothing; but it's consoling.'

But by the spring of 1993, an alternative scenario was suggesting itself. Rumours swept Paris that Hersant, driven by old age and ill health, was considering selling his company instead. Three acquisitors in particular were widely mentioned: the luxury-goods conglomerate LVMH, the telecommunications company Alcatel Altsholm, and France's largest media group, Havas, the TV-into-publishing-into-tourism giant. At the same time, the incoming right-wing administration seemed to promise the possibility of wider – or rather narrower – ownership. The theory ran as follows. A radical conservative government, committed to privatisation and deregulation, could relax the restrictions on foreign ownership. The Groupe de Presse Robert Hersant might be broken up, with his Eastern European papers sold to Hubert Burda, and *Le Figaro* auctioned off to the usual suspects, led by Rupert Murdoch, Vere Rothermere and Conrad Black.

African Thoroughbreds

The Aga Khan's East African Stable

If you cut a swathe through the news kiosk area of Central Nairobi, down Kenyatta Avenue, up one block into Banda Street and then east along Moi Avenue in the direction of the railway station, you get not the slightest indication that you are passing through a great outpost of the world's media empires. Until the collapse of Robert Maxwell's caliphate, Nairobi was unique in having three daily newspapers owned by competing Western-based proprietors: Maxwell's *Kenya Times*, Tiny Rowland's *Standard* and, mightiest and most interesting, the Aga Khan's stable of newspapers which comprises a daily and Sunday in English, *The Nation*, and a daily and Sunday in Swahili, *Taifa*. The great set-piece engagements between media barons are fought out in great cities – New York, Lost Angeles, London, Jerusalem, Sydney – but the jousts and skirmishes take place on the frontiers of empire. Nairobi to media barons plays much the same role as Konya to the Seljuk Turks and Astrakhan to Timur and the Mongols: a secondary theatre of war, but strategically interesting, drawing in the usual suspects – the proprietors – each with his own agenda.

As a media battleground, Nairobi has parallels with Cairo or Geneva at the onset of the Second World War; the opposing sides all too aware of the presence of one another, but circumspect and disengaged, perhaps conscious that the greater conflict is taking place elsewhere. The media barons on their periodic tours of inspection of this farflung possession are in benevolent mood: Maxwell used to stride out from his hotel, the Inter-Continental, to inspect the *Times* in a lightweight turquoise suit and dark glasses; Tiny Rowland flies into Nairobi overnight on his corporate jet and is driven directly to the *Standard* en route to Lonrho's corporate headquarters; the Aga Khan will fly in on his biannual review to declare a new building open or set in motion a new printing press for *The Nation*.

That His Highness Karim Aga Khan, 49th Imam of the Shia Imami Ismaili Moslems and direct descendant of the Prophet Muhammad through his daughter Fatima, has a newspaper empire at all is very little known. And yet his four Kenyan papers have a combined circulation of 1.6 million copies a week. Strategically the group is extremely important as the largest selling free-press in black Africa. As neighbouring countries one by one eject the despots, it is the Aga Khan's empire, more than any other, that is best positioned to expand across the borders into Tanzania and Uganda, perhaps eventually even north into Somalia, Ethiopia and Eastern Equatoria. You cannot review his powerbase in Nairobi without being reminded of Sally Aw Sian and her Chinese newspaper rivals in Hong Kong, gazing across the New Territories towards mainland China and a thousand million new readers.

His newspaper expertise and enormous capital reserves make the Aga Khan a long-shot purchaser for just about any newspaper. He was seen as a convincing candidate for the London *Observer* pre-Tiny Rowland, for *The Times* pre-Murdoch, and has been floated with varying degrees of seriousness as the next proprietor of three daily newspapers in Pakistan, an Ethiopian weekly in Addis Ababa and, in the improbable event of the Jain family selling out, *The Times of India*. Before the arrival of Conrad Black, he was discussed as a contender for the *Daily Telegraph* since his stepfather, Lord Camrose, is [the former *Daily Telegraph* owner] Lord Hartwell's younger brother, and there were rumours that his mother, Princess Joan Aly Khan, wanted the Aga Khan to step in.

His headquarters, the Secretariat de Son Altesse l'Aga Khan, is an hour's drive outside Paris near Chantilly, at Aiglemont; the horse-racing centre of France, a trim suburb of studs and training stables and strings of thoroughbreds being led to the gallops. You feel that around every next bend in the road you will find a large, dank clump of rhododendrons. Only the occasional glimpse of a Viollet le Duc château between the trees reminds you that this isn't Ascot.

The visitor is driven at low speed to the outskirts of the village, waits outside a high gate bristling with surveillance equipment, hoots, seeks clearance and is eventually admitted to the Aga Khan's 200-acre enclave. This contains not only his home, a grey stone 17th-century château, but the modern, low-rise administrative building that is head office for his newspaper holdings and for a portfolio of cultural, educational and environmental programmes.

Inside the Secretariat, the white marble lobby with its sleek mahogany desks and fusiform ashtrays on steel plinths reminded me of the reception area of a luxurious city-centre hotel; not altogether fanciful, since one of the Aga Khan's investment groups controlled Ciga hotels (such as the Excelsior in Rome and the Gritti Palace in Venice). Displayed along the Secretariat walls are fragments of museum-quality Islamic architecture and ceramic tiles, interspersed with glossy brochures about his multifarious endeavours. They make odd bedfellows: the *Costa Smerelda* magazine puffing his hotels, tennis clubs and golf courses in Sardinia – the cover shows a par-boiled Milanese manufacturer gregariously monoskiing into a marina full of yachts – side by side with literature about the Aga Khan University Medical Centre in Karachi and development projects in Zanzibar.

Through a window into the garden I could see a black marble pool, so designed that the perfectly still surface remains unbroken as a film of water laps soundlessly and incessantly over its edges.

'It is good of you to make the journey to Aiglemont,' said the Aga Khan, as if my presence at his Secretariat was a courtesy on my part rather than an indulgence on his.

His accent contains so many contending strains that it is difficult to dissect: part-Italian, part-upper-class English, part-Arabic with a discernable pleaching of the Upper East Side in about every third sentence. It is the amorphous international accent of the Concorde speedwing lounge and the terrace restaurant of the Cipriani hotel; smooth, undulating and worldly. The once dashing youth who skied for Iran in the winter Olympics has evolved, in his late fifties, into a plump but polished figure with manicured fingernails. He wore an impeccable grey flannel suit, thick gold cufflinks and signet ring engraved with the arms of the Imamate, a shirt of brilliant whiteness and a jet-black tie embossed with shoals of little white tadpole-shaped serifs. In profile, his Asian heritage is more apparent than the European and there are vestiges, in the slope of his forehead and the deep lidding of his eyes, of India and Baluchistan.

There is an expression 'a confidential manner', which could have been forged personally for the Aga Khan. In conversation he leans forwards like a yacht tacking gently into the wind, and speaks in a peculiarly soft voice. He has developed the habit, recurrent among a certain kind of European mandarin, of responding to questions with a languorous tentativeness.

'For what reason did you start your newspapers in Kenya?'

'Oh, you know,' he replies, as if it were the most natural thing in the world to found a media empire in East Africa, 'it seemed to me important that there should be one or two media establishments in that part of the world which could report *hopefully* competently, *hopefully* responsibly, *hopefully* seriously on the constitutional moves, on the political structures, on the economic evolution, on the social evolution, on the objectives that were on the minds of African leaders at the time for their countries.'

It was in 1958, less than a year after the twenty-year-old Prince Karim Khan inherited the mantle of Aga Khan from his grandfather, and while he was still a student at Harvard, that he hit on the notion of owning African newspapers. His motivation, he says now, was that decolonisation was well advanced throughout East Africa, and that the immigrant communities – which included his Ismaili sect – were being asked to choose between Kenyan and British nationality. He and the Ismaili leaders were recommending to their followers that they choose Kenyan, and having done so, felt they should emphasise their confidence in a democratic Africa by establishing a free press.

The Aga Khan dispatched an old Fleet Street hand, Michael Curtis, to Nairobi with instructions to buy an existing paper. 'There was this very old settler paper,' says Curtis, 'called the *Sunday Post*, unbelievably right wing, which we thought might be open to offers. So I went along to see the board and told them that the new Aga Khan was interested in acquiring an interest with a view to maybe eventually buying it. There was a man called Rathbone, a Yorkshireman, very blunt and disdainful, who was chairman of the *Post*, who asked me to wait outside the room while they discussed my offer. When I was recalled Rathbone said in his broad Yorkshire accent, "Well, Mr Curtis, we've considered your proposal very carefully. But have come to the conclusion that *nothing on earth* would induce us to sell out to an *Asian*." '

Instead the Aga Khan bought a small Swahili paper called *Taifa* – 'The Nation' – along with the jobbing printer that produced it. *Taifa* at this stage was a pitiful publication, a sheaf of scrappy pages and blotchy ink, distributed mostly in the native bazaar. When Karim Khan, the new proprietor, first saw a copy of his paper, he was thoroughly underwhelmed, and resolved to install state-of-the-art printing equipment. Michael Curtis was sent on a world tour of printing plants, discovered photocomposition, and two years later Nairobi was the first newspaper capital in the world, outside the United States, to have the new technology. The Aga Khan remains second only to Vere Rothermere and Pinch Sulzberger in his proprietorial enthusiasm for smart presses. At Aiglemont, it is the printing of the *International Herald Tribune* and the new robotic presses of *The New York Times* that most fascinate him. When a newspaper arrives with his breakfast anywhere in the world, his first reaction is to rub his thumb across the front page to see if it smudges. His second reaction is to hold the paper close to his face, to study the density of micro-dots on the photographs. One of the few editorial topics on which he will intervene is poor photo-reproduction. When the French Prime Minister Edith Cresson appeared in *The Nation* as a spooky smear, he sent this message: 'Madame Cresson may not be the prettiest thing, but we sure haven't helped with our photograph of her on page six of today's edition.'

On the day the Americans landed on the moon, he was determined that *The Nation* should be the first newspaper in Africa to carry photographs. Unfortunately the promised picture, which was being wired from America, failed to turn up. The editor, all too aware that his proprietor was eagerly awaiting the first edition in Paris, was at a loss. As he sat eating supper, however, his eye settled upon a stack of Ryvita biscuits. He took a close-up photograph of one of them and rushed it to the printers who marked the picture with lunar craters and the route of the astronauts' moon-walk. When *The Nation* reached Aiglemont, the Aga Khan was delighted. 'Marvellous,' he exclaimed. 'Marvellous. No one else in Africa has this. Photo off-set printing: that's the way to go.'

Shortly before the launch of *The Nation* – the English-language *Taifa* – the Aga Khan brought in four international media groups to invest and advise.

'Because I wasn't a newspaper owner by education or tradition,' he says, 'and it wasn't necessarily something that was a mandate of mine in terms of the Imamate, I decided to do it with a consortium of know-how partners. I was able to put together a team which was Lord Thomson's *Sunday Times*, what was then the *Times of Ceylon*, the *Toronto Globe and Mail* and, if I remember correctly, *Svenska Dagbladet* in Sweden: they all had varying degrees of financial investment and were the partners on whom we were going to rely for editorial training and this sort of thing.'

Of the four, says the Aga Khan, Roy Thomson (who already owned a string of farflung papers including the *Bangkok Post*) was the only proprietor to become fully engaged, instructing his people to help *The Nation* hire appropriate columnists. 'They had to be empathetic with Africa because it was the sixties. The whole psychology and attitudes of the Western World towards the African continent and independence have changed a lot in the last 30 years,' he says. 'As the papers became established and self-sustaining, the outside groups moved out because we didn't need that sort of support any more.'

In order to understand the Aga Khan's early trials as a proprietor, it is necessary to place them in political context. Kenya in the years immediately following independence was an unstable, mercurial place with little genuine commitment to a free press. 'Anything could happen in those days,' he says. 'Anything and everything. When situations are tense in developing countries anything can make the situation worse, unfortunately. That's just the nature of those countries and they know it. In the sixties anything could happen and it would never even be reported. The world wouldn't know it.'

The Aga Khan's proprietorship remains contentious. What motive, ask Kenyan politicians, does a religious leader have in owning our national newspaper? And they are not slow to devise conspiracy theories. As recently as 1989, when *The Nation* briefly fell out with the government and its journalists were barred from reporting parliament, the Aga Khan was accused of training his staff to 'misreport deliberately, twist public opinion and cause confusion', and inculcating them with 'anti-establishment American attitudes'. This was a hysterical interpretation of the fact that some of his black reporters are sent on sabbaticals to the *St Petersburg Times* in Florida to learn about the American press. It was similarly claimed that 'half the cover price of *The Nation* finds its way to Geneva or France where the Aga Khan resides.' All these criticisms are oddly reminiscent of attacks on Rupert Murdoch by the Western liberal press.

In the mid-seventies it seemed that President Kenyatta's government might attempt to wrest control from the Aga Khan altogether. His media advisor, Gerard Wilkinson, remembers the circumstances. 'It was the official opening of the Nairobi Serena hotel, which the boss partly owns, and when the boss [the Aga Khan is always known by his courtiers as "the boss"] went into the cloakroom to spend a penny Kenyatta followed him inside. Two boys were with him, both from his own tribe, the Kikuyu, and one of them – his son-in-law – had recently been appointed chairman of the *Standard* [Tiny Rowland's paper] at Kenyatta's request. The President turned to the boss in the cloakroom and said, "I'd like to talk about this boy" – the other boy – "becoming chairman of *The Nation*." The Aga Khan replied that he found the idea surprising, since the boy had no knowledge of newspapers. "Think about it," said Kenyatta, menacingly.

'Wind of the move immediately leaked out,' says Wilkinson, 'and there followed a convoy of cars belonging to government officials imploring the boss not to agree to the imposition of this chairman. Many ministers, including the then Vice-President, Daniel Arap Moi, and the Finance Minister, Mwai Kibaki, advised him against allowing Kenyatta to concentrate control of the press in the hands of one segment of the Kikuyu tribe. The boss, having weighed up the potential cost of any refusal on the newspaper, flew back to Kenya, put this point directly to Kenyatta and to the unbounded relief of *The Nation* the proposal was never raised again.'

This showdown, says Wilkinson, was to have a more profound consequence for Kenya than the Aga Khan could have envisaged. 'Shortly before Kenyatta died, the same group that had attempted to assume control of *The Nation* tried to change the country's constitution to subvert the succession of Moi to the Presidency. They failed largely because of *The Nation*'s vigorous opposition to any tampering with the constitutional process. Had Kenya's newspaper already become a monopoly of that single group, and if the Aga Khan had not acted so decisively despite the implicit threats, the course of Kenya's history would probably have been very different.'

The Aga Khan's development of *The Nation* has consistently been politically adroit. At exactly the moment that an African editor became a psychological necessity, he appointed Hilary Ngweno as the first African editor-in-chief. In 1973, when Kenyans called for a dilution of foreign ownership, he floated 40 per cent of the company and a further 15 per cent in 1988, retaining the controlling but not majority shareholding. In circulation terms, all his papers have performed strongly against their competitors. *The Nation*'s daily edition has a 70 per cent market share (185,000) against Tiny Rowland's *Standard* with 17 per cent (48,000) and Robert Maxwell's old *Kenya Times* with 13 per cent (35,000). *Taifa Leo*, his daily Swahili paper, has 92 per cent domination of its market over the rival *Kenya Leo*. And Nation Newspapers Limited is profitable: K£3 million in 1990 with rising profits projected as new computerised systems come into use. In 1992, *The Nation* moved into an astonishing twin-towered post-modern building, designed by Henning Larson: the Canary Wharf of downtown Nairobi.

When the Aga Khan discusses the financial aspect of his newspapers, there is a perceptible change in his conversation. His language becomes infused with Harvard Business School jargon: 'corporate objectives', 'economic good health in balance sheet terms' and 'entrepreneurial validity'.

'The East African stockmarket has, maybe, ten or 15 bluechip companies,' he says. 'So if a media corporation is within those ten or 15, as we are, it automatically has an entrepreneurial validity which the economic environment of the country respects. And therefore people who work within that company know that there's an entrepreneurial horizon to it, and an entrepreneurial horizon is a condition of a good newspaper. And that means we get people who are, I think, responsible to the balance sheet, and not just responsible to the production profession.'

He paused impressively. 'That's a very maturing concern,' he said gravely, suddenly sounding uncannily like Tony O'Reilly in full flow. 'It's something which makes people realise that there *is* a corporate objective.'

Nothing in the Aga Khan's background prepared him to be a newspaper proprietor, although he says his grandfather, Sir Sultan

Mahomed Shah Aga Khan, 'read everything, *everything*. He certainly appeared to me to have taken speedreading courses because the amount of reading he was able to absorb was amazing.' When he toured the Ismaili communities in Karachi, Quetta, Kandahar or Dar-es-Salaam he somehow managed, before the rest of his household was even awake, to scour all the papers from front to back. But, despite a long friendship with Lord Beaverbrook, he never sought ownership.

As a family, the Aga Khans strike one as singularly improbable newspaper proprietors. Instinctively secretive, prepared to go to the utmost lengths to try and protect their own privacy, they make eccentric champions of a free, investigative press. Since 1841, when the first Aga Khan arrived in Afghanistan from southern Persia with a hundred tousle-haired tribesmen to assist the British, they have seldom been out of the newspapers. The Aga Khan III, Karim's grandfather, lived his life through a maelstrom of publicity: his celebrity as a racehorse owner; his villa parties in the South of France; his weighing against diamonds in Bombay upon his Golden Jubilee, when his ample frame was matched on the scales with precious stones; his four wives; his lengthy sojourns at the London Ritz; all of this excited newspaper coverage on a scale that would only be exceeded by his son, Aly. At the height of his reputation in the late forties, Aly Khan filled much the same role in the public imagination as the Kennedys would occupy two decades later. The collated column inches devoted to Prince Aly Khan could have filled *The Nation* for most of its 30 years: his episodic adventures as a heartbreaker; disregard for his personal safety which led him to rescue his family's racehorses at gunpoint from the Nazis; his second marriage to Rita Hayworth with a wedding reception centred around a swimming pool filled with 200 gallons of scent and decorated with floating flowers; his recklessness out foxhunting, shooting, nightclubbing; it seemed that there was no activity minor enough, no liaison so fleeting, that it wasn't writ large in scores of newspapers as the epitome of glamour or the object of reproach. That the secretive son of Prince Aly Khan should become a newspaper owner is in many respects as extra-ordinary as if a daughter of the Duchess of York, dogged since childhood by Fleet Street paparazzi, would choose to do such a thing.

Prince Karim Khan – the present Aga – was born in Geneva in 1936, the son of Aly and his English wife, Joan Yarde-Buller. At 19, Joan had married Thomas Loel Guinness, one of the Anglo-Irish merchant banking Guinnesses, whose job as a Tory MP often prevented him from accompanying his wife on summer holidays. Alone in Deauville, Mrs Loel Guinness was invited to a dinner party and found herself placed next to Aly Khan. Throughout the first course he addressed not a word to her until, during a general lull in the conversation, he turned to her and asked clearly and loudly, 'Darling, will you marry me?' Less than two years later, having obtained a decree nisi from Guinness, Joan married Aly in Paris in May 1936. At the end of that year Prince Karim was born.

Karim was brought up in Nairobi, then returned to Switzerland where he attended Le Rosey for nine years. A Le Rosey contemporary remembers him as being 'rather inclined to come into your study and say, "You will want to hear what so-and-so has being saying about you behind your back." ' On the other hand, gossip at Le Rosey, full as it was of the sons of deposed kings, princes and industrial tyros, was probably well worth paying attention to. According to legend, at exactly noon every Sunday during termtime, a chauffeur-driven Rolls Royce with blacked-out windows would loom through the college gates and circle the courtyard. As it drew to a stop, two boys would emerge from the front hall of the school and fall to their knees by the car door. One darkened window purred automatically open, and a large, be-ringed hand would emerge. First one boy, then the other, would bow his head and kiss the hand, which would retreat into the car and reappear with a shiny five franc piece for each of them. Then the window would be raised and car would proceed back up the drive in the direction of Lausanne. This was the weekly visit of the old Aga Khan to his grandsons, Prince Karim and his younger brother, Prince Amyn.

The old five-franc-dispensing Aga died in July 1957, shortly before his eightieth birthday, in his villa at Versoix, a suburb of Geneva. The following day his family gathered in the drawing room to hear his solicitor read the will. It is the tradition of the Aga Khans that each Aga chooses his own successor from among the male members of his family, and had bets been taken on this particular classic race, the shortest odds would have been on Prince Aly Khan followed by his brother Prince Sadruddin, who is now United Nations co-ordinator for humanitarian relief. Eventually the solicitor came to the crucial clause:

'In view of the fundamentally altered conditions in the world in very recent years . . . I am convinced that it is in the best interests of the Shia Moslem Ismailian Community that I be succeeded by a young man who has been brought up and developed during recent years in the midst of the new age and who will bring a new outlook on life to his office of Imam. For this reason . . . I appoint my grandson Karim, son of my son Aly Salomone Khan, to succeed to the title of Aga Khan and be the Imam and Pir of all my Shia Ismaili followers.'

Karim, who was now the leader of 12 to 15 million people and one of the richest men on earth, immediately became an *ex officio* object of fascination to the press, and did everything possible to shield himself against its intrusions. All the more remarkable then, that within less than a year of his ratification, he should be purchasing newspapers himself.

His role as Imam of an often conservative Muslim sect make his motives perpetually mixed. I knew he had been considering buying national newspapers in Pakistan, and wondered why he hadn't gone ahead.

'You know,' he replied, 'it's the same problem that we had in East Africa: what is the *reason* for the Aga Khan to own a newspaper? Is it in the interests of his community? Is it in the interests of the country? Is it risky? Is it not risky? That is what people ask themselves. And for us, where is the trade-off between risk and benefit? Every time we look at that question we find a different answer, depending on what the government is. And I must admit that having been asked several times – including by the government in Pakistan – to become involved [with a newspaper] I have *not* become involved. I've looked at it – we're still looking at it, that's not a secret – but it's a tough one. It really is a tough one, because I'm not in a political office. Therefore no matter what government is in power I must be able to work with them, so long as it's not a communist government.'

The job of Aga Khan is diffuse. His grandfather once said of it, 'My duties are wider than those of the Pope. The Pope is only concerned with the spiritual welfare of his flock; the Imam looks after his community's temporal and spiritual interests.' In fact, the Aga Khan is Pope, tax collector – his richer followers pay a tithe – and goverment of a dispersed Ismaili community in 25 countries, all at different stages of development and sophistication; some inhabiting mud and stone huts in Zanzibar and Afghanistan, some working in factories in China and the Muslim Soviet countries, others ranging right across the economic spectrum in Bangladesh, Pakistan and India, while still others – like the Asians displaced from Uganda by Idi Amin – are prospering in large numbers in Canada and the United States.

Since the eighth century when the sect broke away from the rest of the Shias, the Ismailis have had parallels with the Jews, a wandering, landless tribe, often rather cultured, that roamed from Persia to North Africa, reputedly founded Cairo, and only fully found a focus when the first Aga Khan became their Imam. The present Aga Khan perpetuates the rootless tradition of an Ismaili, shuttling in his Gulfstream III jet between New York and Porto Cervo, Nairobi and Geneva, Karachi and his southern Irish studs at Sheshoon and Ballymany. His official foreign tours usually have more than one purpose: in Pakistan, for instance, he will open a girl's school at Karimabad – the Aga Khan Academy – inspect irrigation canals sponsored by the Aga Khan Rural Support Programme, open a new luxury hotel run by the Aga Khan Fund for Economic Development, visit a clinic run by the Aga Khan Health Service and then – having landed by helicopter – address hillside gatherings of the Ismaili faithful. As his progress through the Chitral gathers pace, he is pressed with gifts by his followers: a white wool robe and matching cap, a gigantic head of cabbage, four yaks, one of which has a red banner stretched between its horns that says 'WELCOME'. It is not quite clear what becomes of these well-meant presents afterwards; the yaks, presumably, eat the cabbage, but the white wool cap can be worn only locally.

The non-newspaper activities of the Aga Khan are intricate, half of them emanating from the Imamat, the other half from private investments in tourism, airlines, insurance and thoroughbreds at stud. The usual estimate put on his financial worth is between two and three billion dollars, but frankly, since few of the details are published, no one outside has a clue; all that can be said with certainty is that he is well-advised and financially astute. His public programmes are almost all based in the developing world. Twelve separate arms – the Aga Khan Foundation for this, the Aga Khan Fund for that – are engaged in every conceivable project: teaching hospitals in Pakistan, wasteland development of saline coastland in Gujerat, retraining landless labourers outside Jaipur, fertiliser-loans for villagers in Gilgit. There is a cereal-based rehydration therapy project for Kenyan farmers. There is a jute bag factory on the Ivory Coast, a suitcase factory in Nairobi, a Bangladeshi venture capital company. In Mombasa, the Aga Khan enables local workers to manufacture ladies' hosiery; in Dar-es-Salaam they produce 'garments' and polyester suiting; in Zaire, an Aga Khan bursary has launched them into copper household goods.

There is an enormous Aga Khan University in Karachi. There is a project to conserve old wooden houses in Zanzibar, and another to save a fortress in the Hunza valley. And there are prizes for modern Islamic architecture – the Aga Khan Award – which the Imam personally supervises, and which are presented to glistening, mirror-cladded buildings that could easily blend into Houston or Atlanta until you notice the ingenuous integration of an Islamic *mihrab* or *mashrabiyya*.

His private ventures are a million miles away from the suitcase and jute bag factories of Africa. He owns, or is a substantial shareholder in, three Italian airlines – Alisarda, Avianova and Meridiana – had his decisive stake in Ciga hotels which he sold to Forte in October 1993. His most visible investment, however, has been the development of an immense barren spur of northern Sardinia, the Costa Smerelda, which he transformed into a super-luxurious province of hotels, yacht clubs and golf courses. He keeps a small private villa at Porto Cervo where he and his English wife, the Begum Salimah, born Sally Croker Poole, spend the summer with their three children. It is here too that he indulges his passion for high-tech powerboats. Like Punch Sulzberger of *The New York Times*, the Aga Khan has a fascination for high-tech gadgetry. His most recent jet-propelled boat *Shergar*, named like its predecessor after his missing horse, is one of the three fastest boats in the world; so modern that, once at sea, you simply dial your destination and the satellite-linked navigation system locks into autopilot. This enables the seven-man crew to concentrate on serving lunch.

To the world at large, it is as the owner of Shergar that the Aga Khan remains best known. 'Oi, Aga, what news of Shergar?' is the only question reporters yell at him in the paddock at racemeetings. Ever since the bay colt with its white blaze, winner of the Epsom and Irish Derbies, was kidnapped from the Ballymany stud by five masked men, its whereabouts has been a continuous focus of speculation. Rumoured sightings over the intervening ten years are legion; only a week before my visit to Aiglemont, Rupert Murdoch's *Sun* had sufficient misplaced confidence to headline on the front page 'Shergar Alive'. A couple of months later, Rupert Murdoch's *Sunday Times* claimed in another exclusive that Shergar had been shot and buried years earlier in the Ballinamore hills since the IRA kidnappers couldn't control the horse's panic. As good a reason as any for the Imam to buy a British paper would be to suppress the false alarms and exclusives in at least one place for good.

Notwithstanding his aversion to personal publicity, the activities of the Aga Khan actually equip him rather well to run newspapers. Apart from his financial muscle, one reason his name is regularly tipped to buy a major national in London, Paris or Bombay is that his five areas of expertise commend him as a convincing, hands-on proprietor: big business, horseracing, jet-set society, spirituality and concern for the Third World and the environment. One can imagine him ringing his editor shortly after the first edition comes up and pointing out a dozen errors in every section of the paper from the gossip column and City pages to health and sport. One can hear him saying in his confiding but faintly imperious way, 'This paragraph about Agnelli and the Rothschilds is quite incorrect. Gianni told me about the deal last week,' or, 'Your powerboat correspondent doesn't know what he's talking about here: the turbojets don't cut out until the revs reach a certain level.'

How charismatic is the Aga Khan? By newspaper barons' standard, not especially. He has none of the bravado of Rupert Murdoch, Conrad Black or the late Robert Maxwell. If he resembles any other media owner it is Vere Rothermere: a strategist, somewhat aloof from the day-to-day machinations of his empire, but capable of bursts of insight and charm.

There is a story he tells against himself involving a US hotel switchboard operator. He was trying to reach a friend who was out at that time, so asked to leave a message.

'Just tell him the Aga Khan called,' he said.

'The who? The who?' the operator replied.

'The Aga Khan.'

'The who? The who?' and so on until he gave up, exasperated.

'At least she didn't say "The what? The what?"' the Aga Khan remarks drolly.

On the wall of the Aga Khan's boardroom hangs a 17th-century Persian tapestry from Yazd. On the teak boardroom table in front of him lay a perspex folder of papers, fastidiously neat, full of faxes and briefings and a folded copy of the *International Herald Tribune*.

I could see no copies of the Aga Khan's own newspapers.

'I get them weekly. I get all of them actually, the competition too: the *Standard*, the *Times*, *The Nation*, *Taifa* – obviously I don't speak or read Swahili – but the English-language papers I review with whatever time I have. I don't have a lot of time, frankly. So the objective has been to build up competence, capacity, quality, professionalism out there in East Africa. But I do watch them.'

'And tell your editor if you think Tiny Rowland's *Standard* has beaten them to a scoop?'

'No.' The Aga Khan looked incredulous. 'I think in 30 years I've hardly more than maybe twice communicated to the editor directly. I would always go through the board. Because, to me, the answerability of the editor is to his board which represents all the shareholders in the company.'

'But in the last resort you surely are responsible. You started the papers. You are the major shareholder.'

'I think my role today,' he replied, equivocally, 'is more in the form of an underwriter of certain standards in terms of business management, in terms of quality of the publication, in terms of quality of reporting. That's a role which is in a sense *pre-emptive* because the editors have terms of reference. Their *employment contracts* tell them exactly what is their relationship to the company. The shareholders actually have been involved in confirming the editorial policy. The editorial policy was put to the shareholders in a formal meeting.'

(This is true. At a meeting perhaps unique of its kind, the papers' 10,000 shareholders, many of them owning only a handful of shares, travelled from upcountry to Nairobi clinging on to the roofs of trucks and buses to formally endorse the editorial policy of Nation Newspapers: 'Fair and impartial in comment . . . independent of vested interests or external influences . . . will not shrink from constructive and objective criticism etc.')

'And so in a sense,' went on the Aga Khan, 'my role is to sustain that sort of continuity, not to lead on an individual story on an individual day or that sort of thing.'

This detached, ethereal attitude was puzzling. What possible purpose can there be in owning a newspaper full of political comment and astringent editorials if you distance yourself from it so completely that your responses are those of any other reader? He watches his racehorses on the gallops, knows every detail of their training, but does he never interfere? And at his hotels, do the menus, the curtains, the colour of the soap take him by surprise each time he stays?

'But you have your own enthusiasms,' I said. 'Health, science, technology. Don't you instruct your editor to cover those subjects?'

'There are,' he conceded, 'areas of knowledge which come to me from my exposure to development concerns. In so far as a newspaper can articulate those issues, and try to bring them into focus and try to deal with them in terms of their social impact, in terms of their economic cost, then the newspaper has to do that.'

'And is there a reluctance among your editorial people to write about them?'

'I think it's just that unless a newspaper in a developing world sets out to find the people who can write on those subjects competently, it wouldn't naturally happen.'

I had repeatedly been told that the Aga Khan's presence in Africa had pushed up salary levels for journalists. Before *The Nation* came along you could earn more money doing just about anything: selling oranges, shining shoes, soaping car windscreens.

'It was absolutely necessary,' said the Aga Khan. 'If a journalist who is a foreign correspondent or a sub-editor receives less money than a trainee secretary, then that whole profession is disqualified. And it's liable to lose the best people because they will not commit their futures to something that cannot guarantee them something secure. We had to remunerate to a point where it was appealing.'

'Are yours the most highly paid newspaper people in Africa?'

'Certainly in terms of the neighbouring countries, Uganda and Tanzania. But I wouldn't know about Nigeria or Ghana.'

'So have your salary levels made Tiny Rowland pay more? And did it up-the-ante for Maxwell?'

'Very definitely so. And I'll accept the blame for the owners if they think it's blame, and the credit if the journalists think it deserves credit!'

I asked him whether there were times he regretted owning newspapers. *The Nation*'s relationship with the government has so often been strained that I doubted it was worth the Imam's investment of time and money.

'That,' he said, 'is the very, very central question. I'm always faced with this conflict between the short term and long term. Very often the short-term answer would be to back away. But the truth is that if I were to back away on a matter of importance, probably the long term would be impossible. So you have to pass through these crises because there is a purpose in having an independent, serious newspaper in the country, or otherwise you shouldn't be there at all. Interestingly enough, every time this sort of situation has arisen, it has been the staff of the company that come to me and say, "Please stand back. Please don't pull the rug." They're wonderful people. In those times their courage is great; and they're at risk.'

'Would it make the slightest difference to readers if you did pull the rug and sell the papers?'

'One thing I would say is that there is a tendency – or there has been a tendency – to underrate the sophistication of African readership. It is a very sophisticated readership.'

'Who's been doing the underestimating? Your editors?'

'Who knows?' He shrugs. 'Owners?' He laughs. 'Maybe editors. Maybe marketing Nicks. Accountants! Our history has been up-market, upmarket, upmarket, upmarket. It's interesting because the more you go upmarket in Africa, the more you grow in circulation. Vice versa, if you go downmarket in our part of Africa, your circulation collapses. It's a totally different situation from Western Europe or North America. International and economic news is very, very important to the African readership.'

I found this extraordinary. It goes against the experience of every other owner I'd met. Even though they don't use the word 'down-market' – they say *accessible, lively, reader-responsive* – it is implicit in every coloured logo, every graphic redesign, every shrinking digest of world news.

'Not really extraordinary,' he said. 'Not *really*. African and Western society are very different. Editors in the downmarket

Western media are every day looking for something that will titillate the curiosity of the readership. You cannot titillate African curiosity with the same things, they're not interested. Their tribes live differently; their families live differently; their dress habits are different; their get-togethers are different. So that form of journalism doesn't have any relationship to African society whatsoever. It's of no interest to them. Political garbage. One's beginning to see in Asia now – in India – it's not page-three trash, it's political trash, but it's the same mode of journalism.'

'Are you thinking of Goenka's *Indian Express*?'

'They're not the worst in the country, by far not the worst.'

Then he said, 'There are certain things I will fight for in the Western world, which are important in the developing world also. The right to privacy is an important issue which is going to become *more* important rather than less. Technology is so sophisticated now that, in effect, there is no privacy left – either voice privacy or identity privacy by day or by night. Technology enables you to do anything you want. If you don't do it from the ground you do it from space. Interestingly enough, that's much more sensitive in the developing world than the industrialised world. You will find there will be a lot of resistance to the invasion of the individual in the developing world, because society and tradition don't admit that. It's an issue that's got to be addressed.'

'Do you address it,' I asked him, 'when you see other newspaper owners like Rupert Murdoch? Have you discussed it ever with them?'

'No. I haven't. Simply because, interestingly enough, I don't see that much of them except at charity affairs, galas. I'm a newspaper owner by accident, really, aren't I?'

The Yellow Press

Hong Kong's media mandarins

The burgundy-coloured Rolls Royce – licence number 82 – pulled up at the front entrance of the high-rise Hong Kong Club building, and the Chinese driver hastened round to open the passenger door. It took a moment or two for the passengers to gather themselves, and then, with tiny, resolute steps they scuttled across the pavement into the lobby. Both were women, identically dressed in dark blue raincoats firmly belted over Chinese cheongsams. The younger of the two was small even by Chinese standards, stockily built with heavy jowls and raised shoulders that gave an impression of suppressed irritability. Her black hair was scraped severely back from her forehead, revealing bushy brown eyebrows as thick as a man's, and prominent above her lip was a small black mole. This was Sally Aw Sian, Chairman of Sing Tao newspapers and for 35 years the most influential Chinese proprietor in the world. The other woman was her 87-year-old widowed mother, Madame Aw Boon Haw, widow of the founder, who lives with her unmarried daughter and accompanies her everywhere, to the Sing Tao headquarters, abroad to the overseas offices and to board meetings where she waits outside in her dark blue raincoat, perched on a stool.

'To see Miss Aw and her mother together,' said a former American employee, 'is like a vision of old Shantou or Fuzhou. Two crafty old Chinese women, the mother in her wig, they should be squeezing melons and haggling over the price of cabbage.'

As it is, Sally Aw Sian has extended the newspaper group she inherited from her father into an empire that publishes in four continents. Her Chinese-language flagship paper *Sing Tao Jih Pao* is printed in eight different local daily editions – in Hong Kong, San

Francisco, New York, Vancouver, Toronto, Auckland, Sydney and London – with part of its contents transmitted by satellite from Hong Kong, and local news gathered and processed by autonomous overseas Sing Tao bureaux. It is Sally Aw's boast that she has succeeded where the Sulzbergers' *New York Times* failed, in successfully establishing editions beyond her traditional sphere of influence.

'Others have tried this,' she was keen to tell me. '*The New York Times* tried to publish its West Coast edition in Los Angeles, but could only sustain it for two years before the experiment was abandoned. In Japan, it is true, the three largest newspapers [the *Yomiuri Shimbun*, the *Asahi Shimbun* and the *Mainichi Shimbun*] are printed in five centres, but these are all *inside* Japan – not international. The *Wall Street Journal* the same. Only the *International Herald Tribune* comes close to our operation but the *Trib* has no individual local editorial teams. Same for *USA Today*. OK, they are printing in Singapore, Switzerland and here in Hong Kong, but *only we* are a genuine international newspaper. And, listen to me, each one of our foreign operations makes money.'

Whether or not it is a good experience to work for Sally Aw Sian is by no means clear.

'She's seen as a pretty tough old bird round here,' says Phillip Crawley, then editor of Murdoch's *South China Morning Post*, which competes with both *Sing Tao Jih Pao* and Sally Aw's English-language *Hong Kong Standard*. 'Not a particularly warm or friendly personality. She has the reputation of being hard on her staff. If you don't perform, the contents of your desk are pretty soon in a cardboard box outside the door.'

'A fairly typical Chinese boss in as much as she keeps all control to herself,' says a Hong Kong PR man who worked for her. 'She signed every cheque – still does so far as I know – down to the messengers' salary of a few thousand HK dollars a month. And she scrutinises expenses with a toothcomb, an abacus, whatever. God knows how she finds the time, with several thousand people working for her. If you take a taxi and not a tram from Central to Wanchai she wants to know why. It is the office joke that she takes every expenses claim home with her in the evening to that great gloomy ancestral mausoleum she lives in at Tiger Balm gardens, and she and her old mother pore over them all night.'

'She never, ever appears on the editorial floor,' says a Chinese news editor who has worked for *Sing Tao* for 30 years, 'and yet you are always aware of her. You feel that, even when you are not seeing her, she is watching you. In the old offices in Wanchai Street we used to see her one time a year, when there was a memorial service held in front of a shrine to her father, Aw Boon Haw. The shrine was in the entrance to Miss Aw's office, like a big cupboard with incense and joss sticks and photographs, and every reporter was required to attend the ceremony. She has great respect for her ancestors, for her father especially. He was very protective of her, like a good Chinese father, and shielded her from fortune hunters, so she never fell into their clutches. And now she is constantly venerating his memory.'

'She keeps her word, tolerates mistakes and even admits her own mistakes,' said Thomas Kwok, the Chinese lawyer who is a family friend. 'As a woman she is very un-Chinese. It is highly unusual for a Chinese woman to run a business empire as diverse as hers. She can be moody and quick tempered because she has never really had the right calibre of people working for her. Chinese family businesses often don't, they won't pay properly. So all the pressure is on Sally Aw. A lot of people are wealthier than her now in Hong Kong, but not many have her respect. She could walk into any bank round here and get a hundred million Hong Kong dollars without collateral just like that.'

In addition to the three newspapers – *Sing Tao Jih Pao*, *Sing Tao Wan Pao* and the *Hong Kong Standard* – Sally Aw is chairman of 77 subsidiary companies. Fourteen of them, with names like Wealthpop Limited, Jade Holdings and The Clever Company Limited, are property investment firms. Five, including Imperial Parking (California) Limited and Park-UR-Self Canada Limited, are international car park servicing companies. Sixteen are financial services operations. The rest are a stir-fry of bright ideas: movie production companies and dental consultancies, medical laboratories, Silver Planet records and firms that rent digital signs. You get the impression that anything at all that might generate additional dollars is of interest to Sally Aw Sian. One of her latest companies, incorporated and operating in Hong Kong, is Pointglobe Limited, an immigration – more accurately an emigration – consultancy for Hong Kong residents seeking advice on securing foreign passports before the Chinese takeover in 1997. She has negotiated to buy Australian radio and newspaper businesses from Fairfax, owned a newspaper group in Fiji until it was taken over by the government after a military coup, and was tipped as a possible bidder for the London *Times* (before Rupert Murdoch's acquisition) and for the London *Observer*.

'As far as editorial freedom is concerned, she gives a lot,' says Edward Hung, Group General Manager of her Chinese papers. 'Once you've got an assignment, you've got a free hand. And if you goof up and it's an honest mistake, it's normally no problem. She has a lot of concern over local issues, and if she thinks you've got a wrong opinion, then she'll voice out, and tell you the right opinion on that subject. I would say she's very approachable, anyone can see her from cleaner to top management. There's a sort of magic about her. And she has a very good memory. Sing Tao has 2900 staff around the world and I would say that she can recognise 50 per cent. There's a story that a few years back she was at the opening of a beach resort in Australia in which she had some investment. A waiter came up to her to take her order, and she immediately recognised him. He had been a member of staff 20 years earlier in the typesetting department. And she was so happy to see that man. Miss Aw never forgets loyal staff members.'

Sally Aw's publishing empire had its genesis in Singapore in 1929 where Aw Boon Haw, her podgy, mercurial, bow-tie-wearing father established a newspaper called the *Sing Zhou Daily*. In the previous three years Aw Boon Haw and his brother Aw Boon Paw had made a vast fortune in a very simple way. Both had been born in Burma, in Rangoon, the sons of a Chinese backstreet herbalist named Aw Chu Kim, and in 1925, when they were both already in their forties, they travelled down the Malay peninsula to Singapore and began selling a cure-everything lotion called Tiger Balm, an invention of their father. It was a remarkable success. Even today, if you walk into any pharmacy in the Far East, you see rows and rows of the small turquoise and green hexagonal jars with a tiger printed on the label. Inside is a transparent balm smelling strongly of eucalyptus, similar to the Western invention, Vicks. From the moment the Aws introduced it, the Chinese began prescribing it for everything from blisters to brain cancer.

Children daub the cold burning balm on cut knees, pregnant girls massage their bellies with it, old women recommend it as a cure for rheumatism and heart failure. The patent was extended to Bangkok, Penang, Jakarta, Hong Kong and China, and factories producing the secret Aw formula were established everywhere. By the time the Japanese overran South East Asia in 1941, the Aws were one of the three richest families in the Orient, and Sally Aw Sian is seldom prefixed in any other way than 'the Tiger Balm heiress'. This must be irritating for her, because whenever she starts a new property company – Milliongroup Development Limited, say – or a publishing initiative like her China Review Publications, her competitors are quick to undermine her achievement. 'It is easy for Sally Aw,' they say. 'Don't forget she is the Tiger Balm heiress.'

In fact the Tiger Balm business was sold in the sixties to the British tycoon Jim Slater, and the proceeds divided between Sally Aw, her mother Tan Kyi Kyi – Aw Boon Haw's second wife – a trust for Aw's remaining three wives and their offspring, and Aw Boon Paw's descendants in Singapore who had by now fallen out with their Hong Kong cousins. For the next 20 years there was constant discord over the ownership of the hideous Aw mansion in Tiger Balm gardens, and even today Asian magazines refer to the 'bitter Aw family feud'. Informed opinion concurs that while the Tiger Balm inheritance undoubtedly provided massive seed capital, Sally Aw's empire was largely founded on the profits of her newspapers and restless property speculation.

Aw Boon Haw had the style and appetite of a contemporary press baron. He was a Chinese Murdoch or Maxwell, and he could not visit a city without attempting to buy or set up a newspaper. He had consulted a fortune teller in Malaya who predicted that if ever he stopped building, he would die and lose his entire fortune. In the next 15 years he built 26 castles – more accurately ugly gothic houses – around Asia, and established newspapers over a massive territory: the *Sing Hua Daily* in Shantou in 1931, *Sing Guang Daily* in Xiamen and *Sing Zhong* in Singapore in 1935, and a third Singapore title the following year. *Sing Tao Jih Pao* was launched in Hong Kong in 1938, and then more newspapers for China became his obsession, with titles set up in Canton and Guangzhou. The official *Sing Tao* hagiography of Aw Boon Haw, in their Golden Jubilee souvenir, makes a great deal of his mission to carry the torch of Chinese culture and his commitment, beyond political bias, for social justice and well-being. This sounds like flim-flam to me, and his contemporaries – now immensely old – remember best his fondness for advertising revenue; an enthusiasm inherited by his daughter, along with a respect for the Malaysian fortune teller's advice. 'Sally Aw is Boon Haw's daughter all right,' said a retired news editor at *Sing Tao*. 'She will never stop building and making deals. For on that day the Tiger Balm fortune will come to an end. And she is faithful to her father's ambitions. For too many years the *Hong Kong Standard* lost money, but she would never close it, against the best advice, because it had been founded by Boon Haw. She would rather lose money than betray his legacy. And for that reason too she looks towards China for expansion. She would love to fulfil her father's desire for newspapers across China.'

All her actions, however, suggest that Sally Aw has no such burning, filial ambition for Chinese newspapers. Her media ambitions look towards Australia and Canada, far more than across the border. If Sally Aw has any prejudice about China and the East in general it is caution, engendered by the fate of her father's papers. The newspaper in Guangzhou was abandoned because of the Sino-Japanese war, and four years later in 1941 *Sing Tao* in Hong Kong and the three Singapore papers were closed by the Japanese, the presses smashed and the offices occupied. *Sing Tao* was restarted in 1945, and newspapers set up in Bangkok and Fuzhou. China once again became Aw Boon Haw's great ambition. He used to sit on the verandah of one of his ugly gothic castles on Kowloon side, overlooking the New Territories, and marvel at the almost limitless potential Chinese readership for his newspapers, and their display advertisements. Plans were advanced for daily newspapers in Shanghai and Canton when the communists seized power and press tycoons suddenly had no place in the scheme of things.

Aw Boon Haw had a son, Aw How, who had long been designated his heir. But in 1951 – the same year that Sing Tao newspapers became a limited company – Aw How was killed in an aeroplane crash. There is a slight element of mystery about this crash which, happening so long ago, would scarcely be of consequence if it wasn't for emphatically diverging stories.

According to the Aws, the heir died on a business trip to Singapore when the aeroplane fell into the sea. This version of events is stressed in the official company history, which goes out of its way to mention Singapore as Aw How's destination. On several occasions, however, when I was questioning Chinese media figures about Sally Aw, they made a point, amidst great secrecy, of informing me of the rumour that the plane crash actually took place in the Burmese jungle in the Golden Triangle. They would give no explanation as to why the Aws might wish to conceal Aw How's real destination. Later, when I interviewed Sally Aw, she made a point of saying, 'I took over the newspapers unexpectedly you know. It was not foreseen. My brother would have inherited them, but he died in a plane crash in Singapore.'

In any event, Aw Boon Haw died three years later in a clinic in Honolulu, by which time Sally Aw Sian had in everything but name assumed the chairmanship of Sing Tao. Her chairmanship, however, was to be made awkward for her. Partly because she was female, and partly because it is the prevailing Chinese custom, she found herself cocooned by advisors, old cronies of her father, who were not slow to impart their wisdom and experience. Her business life, people kept telling me, has been frustrated by the advice of these old men. Never quite summoning the necessary ruthlessness to dismiss them, Sally Aw Sian has endured – still endures – their opinions to a surprising degree. 'She took over as a teenager almost,' says the publisher Albert Cheng, 'and was dominated by the old hands for a considerable time. They tried to stop her doing sensible things. When she brought back the first computer for typesetting, they persuaded her to put it into a warehouse for two years before she insisted on introducing it. They are still too influential, those old hands, and Sally Aw has allowed her ears to take over her own eyes.'

The corporate offices of Sing Tao Limited are geographically almost as far removed from the newspapers themselves as it is possible to be in the colony; but it is still possible, if you peer across the harbour from Sally Aw's corner office – beyond the ferry stations and Ocean Terminal, across Tsim Sha Tsui towards Kai Tak airport – to catch a glimpse of the industrial estate on Kowloon Bay where the immense new newspaper and print plant have been sited. Later, when I visited some of her journalists at Kowloon Bay, they had a habit – whenever the name Sally Aw Sian came up – of looking over their shoulder towards Hong Kong island and her office, as though she might be scrutinising us from afar.

The Aw headquarters on the 13th floor of the Hong Kong Club tower overlook three of the colony's most interesting buildings – the Hong Kong and Shanghai Bank, the Bank of China and the Mandarin hotel; but when Sally Aw has visitors she chooses to receive them, not in her own office with its panoramic views, but in a tiny, grey, windowless closet, largely filled by a circular formica table. When I arrived to see her, Sally Aw was already sitting in this room, waiting for me, and a second chair had been placed opposite her own. Then the door was shut behind me and we were left alone together in this claustrophobic, airless space, Sally Aw with her arms folded firmly in front of her on the formica table top.

At close quarters you are struck by the extreme severity of her expression. Her mouth is set in an almost permanently fixed line of disapproval, and only twice during my visit did her face soften with laughter. Her feet, even from a low Chinese chair, did not quite reach the floor, and as we talked she rocked them gently to and fro beneath her, an oddly skittish trait in such a stern person. Aside from the gently swinging feet, there was nothing spontaneous about her at all. Most questions she answered monosyllabically, or with the phrase 'that is not for me to say', even when they addressed subjects on which only the proprietor could possibly express an opinion.

I asked her about her relationship with her father.

'I was close to him,' she replied in an accent with a discernable Australian inflection beneath the Chinese cadence. 'He was I suppose a typical Chinese dictatorial type, you know, he makes the money and everyone is sort of respectful and scared of him at the same time.'

'Was he confident when you took over Sing Tao?'

'No.'

'Why was that?'

'Because he never would have imagined I could run a newspaper. He was surprised he was proved wrong. Though he never lived long enough to see the fruit of it.'

'When your brother, Aw Hoe, died in the plane crash . . .'

'In Singapore,' interjected Sally Aw.

'. . . did you not have other brothers who could have taken over?'

'They were not around.'

'Why not? Where were they?'

'Dispersed,' she replied, and shut her mouth tight.

'Can you tell me how you control your editors?'

'I don't see them. Not at any set time anyway, not on a weekly consulting basis. But I keep in regular contact by telephone.'

'To tell them what?'

'Oh, just to keep in touch about the progress of certain situations.'

'Political advice you mean?'

'No, that is no place for the owner. I leave all that to the editors.' Then, after a moment's reflection, she added, 'On political matters I like to check their approach. My way of playing the stories might be different from their way.'

'And if they are?'

'I try to give them a chance to explain why they choose to run this particular story from a particular angle. And then I make suggestions. It should be up to them; they should know their job well.'

'Is it hard choosing the right editor?'

'I always give preference to those who have been working for us for a long time. Then they know the situations.'

'Are Chinese editors loyal to their companies?'

'They tend to stay you know. The *Hong Kong Standard* is different. The people there tend not to stay, five or six years the longest. Editors too. Now we have a new one, Alan Armsden, who applied straight from London, he was with Maxwell. He flew out and joined us and is working quite well.'

The sheer proximity of Sally Aw, our physical closeness in the hot little room, was uncomfortable. Her eyes have a mesmeric quality; they unblinkingly regarded my own throughout our meeting like rifle sights trained point-blank on bullseyes. This concentration and refusal to give much away made it easy to see how effective she must be in any negotiation. The irises of her eyes are without colour of any kind – the deepest oriental black – and suggest opaque shrewdness.

I asked her what guarantees she had, official or unofficial, from the Chinese government about the freedom of her papers after 1997.

'None, we haven't requested any. If we discuss it now, the policy might change, maybe even for the better.'

'Are you relying then on the Chinese making a special exception for

Hong Kong? On their having a strictly government-regulated press in China itself, but allowing a free press here?'

'So much depends on what happens in the next few years in China itself. It is hard to predict the future. Maybe it'll be like the Eastern Bloc, I don't think many people predicted that would fall apart. But we have so many other businesses outside of Hong Kong. If necessary the newspapers could be run independently from the rest of the company, be more or less contained. We could plan it in that way. My feeling is that we should not predict too much what will happen in advance. We should not expect a clampdown. When Murdoch bought the *South China Morning Post* he wasn't deterred by what might happen after 1997.'

'Do you see much of Rupert Murdoch and the other press barons?'

'I saw Murdoch recently at a meeting of the International Press Institute. We talked about Fiji. He has the *Fiji Times* and I used to have the *Fiji Sun* until Mr Rambuka shut it down. We talked about the climate in Fiji. It is hot there you know. One other proprietor I saw recently is Conrad Black. That was in Toronto and I was quite impressed by him, by his knowledge. He told me he was on the verge of buying the *Jerusalem Post* and that I should keep this information to myself.'

Sally Aw Sian was born in Burma in 1941, at the old family home in Rangoon, to which her parents had retreated as the Japanese army advanced across South East Asia. When the Japanese got close to Rangoon, the family fled north to Mandalay, part of the great migration of refugees. 'Each week we were moving on,' said Sally Aw. 'Then each day, as we fled from small village to small village, always going ahead, further north, the troops followed behind us. Eventually we couldn't get any further because we'd reached the Indian and Chinese borders, so we had no choice but to wait for the Japanese to come. My mother was very fearful, but we were not badly treated. After the war the family returned to Hong Kong and I went to a French convent, a Catholic school, near to our house. Somehow I'm not very good at my study. I'm still somehow yearning that I should have more educations; when I visit Cambridge and Oxford I wish I could have studied in such a beautiful environment.'

'Was it usual for a Buddhist to have been sent to a Catholic convent?'

'Although my father was a Buddhist, he donated money every year on his anniversary to all religions: Buddhism, Tao-ism, Catholic and Protestant. He gave to religious charities that look after old people, because we respect the aged.'

At this very moment, as though she had been waiting on cue, Sally Aw's much respected and aged mother, Tan Kyi Kyi, appeared at the door and stared blankly at her daughter. Then mother and daughter muttered a few sentences in Chinese before Madam Aw Boon Haw shuffled back to her own large office with its leather furniture and harbour view.

'Do you and your mother add to your father's collection of jade at Tiger Balm gardens?'

'Not add, only preserve. It is quite a task you know, there are so many pieces. My father collected at random. I can still remember in my youngest days, he started work at five o'clock in the morning, and dealers used to come to him with baskets full of jade and pink quartz and he'd pick out a few good pieces. We add nothing and sell nothing as a memorial to his achievements. My father you know was the person who started Tiger Balm.'

'Do you wish you owned it still?'

'When my father died, my cousins were running it, and it was they who sold it. I do wish we could have kept that, it was the family root, one of the best things ever invented, a golden goose, it lays golden eggs really. And now it belongs to a group of bankers in Singapore. And that happened because there was no proper heir to inherit.'

'Have you appointed your own heir yet? Your nephew in Australia, Fred Aw, has been mentioned.'

'I haven't appointed. I think there'll be a sort of committee. One has to retire one day, eventually, but I haven't found a satisfactory concept yet as how to do it.'

Hong Kong Inc's annual list of the top 110 richest people on the island puts Sally Aw at number 20 with an estimated HK$3.38 billion ($433 billion US dollars in 1993). This places her well behind Ka-shing Li of Hutchison Wampoa at HK$19.5 billion and the property tycoon Tak-seng Kwok at HK$10.36 billion, but significantly ahead of her rival Hong Kong press barons Ching-Kwan Ma of the *Oriental Daily News* and Louis Cha of *Ming Pao*, neither of whom clear the billion threshold with HK$910 million and HK$800 million respectively.

As is often the case with newspaper proprietors, her employees – with easy access to the details of her financial manoeuvrings – are unusually interested by Sally Aw's attitude to money, with all its confusion and inconsistency. She is personally parsimonious. Until the very late eighties, when she was setting up the Sing Tao international editions, she flew only economy class. 'Sally Aw, her mother and sometimes her sister-in-law, the three of them together, would fly all over the world at the back of the plane. They'd be dropped at Kai Tak in the Rolls Royce but nothing would induce her to pay more than the minimum fare for aeroplane tickets,' remembers a former *Sing Tao* manager. 'She is the same with clothes. Everything comes from the clothing market – cheap coats, cheap handbags.'

Her talent for downward negotiation has ensured the success of her spectacular property coups: she is reported to have made HK$200 million on one deal over the Ramada Renaissance building which she had bought shortly before in a well-publicised fanfare of renewed commitment to Hong Kong, and sold on to the Japanese property firm Sun's Enterprise; she bought and sold the Watsons industrial site on Causeway Bay in a revolving deal that captured the imagination of the Far East property world; she acquired the landmark Carlton hotel only to turn it a few months later in a deal with Chang Soh Lui; and sold her second home on Middle Gap Road for HK$30 million because she correctly anticipated a residential property dip. Her foreign property investments have been mostly astute. She is the largest Chinese landlord in Chinatown in Sydney, and has investment properties in the Chinatowns of San Francisco, Vancouver and Toronto and in London around Wardour Street and Shaftesbury Avenue. She has commercial property in New York, shopping centres and a Holiday Inn in Ontario, and a tower block in Sydney, the Sing Tao building by the harbour. At the same time her property decisions for the media empire have been at least as profitable as the newspapers themselves. The group offices in Boston, Philadelphia, Monterry Park, Honolulu and Calgary were all bought ahead of the market, and it is her policy to shift offices and printing plants as soon as a cheap area comes good. 'When the land price goes up,' she told me, explaining *Sing Tao*'s journalistically out-of-it new situation in Kowloon Bay, 'we move. Newspapers shouldn't operate on high land prices.'

'She'd have us over the border at Shenzhen [the enterprise zone in mainland China] if she could get a site,' said a New Zealand reporter on the *Hong Kong Standard*.

Not everybody in Hong Kong applauds Sally Aw's deals. 'It looks to me like she's made some pretty unwise investments around the Asia pacific basin,' says Phillip Crawley, then of the *South China Morning Post*. 'She's been involved in some pretty messy takeovers, and the reputation of her group is of short attention spans, a coming and going sort of place.'

Albert Cheng, the editor and publisher of the Capital Communications Corporation, is regarded as the most astute Chinese media analyst in Hong Kong. He presides behind a vast circular desk of tubular steel and vanilla-coloured wood, on the top of which sits a large pillar-box red toy Ferrari. As you enter his office through a hingeless revolving door, and see the view through the window of the roofs and air-conditioning ducts of a dozen skyscrapers, it is only with effort you remember this is Hong Kong and not Manhattan. Cheng has launched a string of metropolitan and business magazines since the late-eighties, as well as holding the local franchise for *Forbes*, but at an earlier stage of his life he worked for Sally Aw as Director of Marketing and Business Development for *Sing Tao*. 'I re-organised it,' he says, 'made it more aggressive in its ad-sell. Working with Sally Aw was interesting. She's energetic, she's curious, she enjoys new concepts and has vision to a certain point. She's very quick to make financial decisions, but is also quick to change them. Her newspapers made HK$70 million in the first half but if they were properly run they could make HK$200 million. She's very much alone, and doesn't always take professional advice. It doesn't help that she's got a weak board. She can be obstinate. When she's finally – finally – made up her mind on something, she'll stick to it, like sticking with the *Hong Kong Standard* even though she's lost a pot of money. But these irreversible decisions take a long time. Her chopping and changing of her mind over the *Sing Tao* registration was typical incidentally.'

This was the remarkably complex but just about explainable 1985 share shuffle that shifted control of the Sing Tao group from Hong Kong to Australia, which Aw partially reversed six months later when Sing Tao newspapers were relisted on the Hang Seng. Before the shuffle she had personally owned 78 per cent of Sing Tao and 75 per cent of an Australian company called Cereus which itself had a wholly owned Hong Kong subsidiary, Cereus HK. After this shuffle, Sally Aw became a 75 per cent shareholder in Cereus Australia Limited which wholly owned Cereus HK which in turn owned 100 per cent of Sing Tao. Cereus Australia was the listed shell of a former printing firm, Smith and Miles, which Aw had bought eight months earlier from the Chinese-Australian investor Eddie Long. The transfer arrangement called for Cereus HK to acquire all the issued capital of Sing Tao newspapers at a cost of US$24.9 million after a distribution of assets worth HK$34.75 million to Sing Tao shareholders in a newly formed subsidiary Cinclus. The next stage was for the Aw family to sell its entire 78 per cent holding in Cinclus to a subsidiary of a Brisbane-based listed company called Ariadne Australia, which in turn became the Impala Pacific Corporation.

As soon as Sally Aw announced her company's Australian control she came in for a degree of criticism that took her by surprise. Notwithstanding the fact that her own newspapers broke the story positively, in a pre-emptive strike intended to influence other media, she was widely rebuked for jumping ship and having insufficient confidence in Hong Kong's future less than a year after the signing of the Sino-British declaration. The irony of the *Hong Kong Standard*'s slogan 'The Independent Newspaper with confidence in Hong Kong' was widely enjoyed. Rumours that the ultimate owners of Sing Tao would be Murdoch's News Corporation or the (pre-fall) Fairfax group had to be denied, and Sally Aw was dismayed when comparisons were made between Sing Tao and Jardine Matheson who had recently transferred their domicile from Hong Kong to Bermuda, a move *Sing Tao* had condemned in its leading articles. Denying that she was selling out, Sally Aw explained, 'We feel that the company is more internationally orientated and so we picked Australia, which is much closer to Hong Kong, as a first step.'

The Hong Kong *Business News* pointed out that Hong Kong itself is 'much closer to Hong Kong' than Australia.

People who worked closely with Sally Aw through this period say she took the criticism personally. She was genuinely confused about whether she'd behaved honourably, and for the first time found that her fondness for financial ingenuity and for Aw Boon Haw's adopted home were in conflict. At board meetings and with friends she returned to the subject again and again, though there could be no real question of reversing the shuffle after it had been announced, and East Asia Warburgs were already advising Sing Tao minorities. Nevertheless it was only in January 1986, when Cereus Australia floated 25 per cent of its new subsidiary Sing Tao Newspapers (HK) Limited on the Hang Seng, that Sally Aw felt her relationship with the island had been restored. It was noted that, through the first six months of Sing Tao's Australian domicile, Sally Aw based herself almost entirely away from home in Sydney, Vancouver, Toronto or at her small London flat in St John's Wood, and that during her few stopovers in Hong Kong she was even more reclusive than usual. After the reflotation she began to be seen again at the only four public places at which she regularly eats: the World Trade Club, the Pacific Club, the Hong Kong Club and the Jockey Club.

One night in Hong Kong, on the eve of my second visit to Sally Aw Sian, a typhoon moved across the South China Sea from Zhongshan and whipped up the harbour; a force eight robust enough to clear the anchorages of junks and suspend the ferry. Immense bundles of newspapers, collected from printing plants all over Kowloon and the New Territories, were delivered as usual to the quays opposite the Mandarin hotel, but such was the force of the wind that they were ignored by the warehousemen. From the balcony of our room at the Mandarin, we watched the string around the bales slowly work itself loose, and the papers – at first singly, then in great sheaves as the typhoon intensified – billow along the road. Thousands of pages were sucked into the sky, blown this way and that, dashed like enormous injured seagulls against the portholes of the Jardine Matheson building. Scores of Chinese newspapers gusted before us; the *Oriental Daily News*, *Sing Pao Daily News*, *Ming Pao*, *Sing Tao Jih Pao*, *Wen Wei Po* and the *Tin Tin Daily News* in which Sally Aw has a stake, their sections jumbled together, their front pages vibrant with Cantonese calligraphy. A rather pompous criticism often levelled against Sally Aw runs along the lines that she doesn't understand the newspaper's function in society as an independent, unbiased source of news. Western journalists in Hong Kong are harsh on her, citing her papers' partial coverage of her non-media activities, and the way she appears to condone the roughing up of business rivals in her business sections.

What they don't take into account is that the Chinese press – the literally hundreds of Cantonese-language papers that were whipping against our balcony – emerged from a distinct journalistic tradition. Chinese newspapers, unlike the African and Indian press, were never edited by Western hired hands who imposed their own news values. Impartiality is neither encouraged nor admired by the Chinese. 'Long exposed to idealogical struggle, we have acquired a sixth sense for propaganda,' says Sally Aw. World news is simplistic and partisan. Gossip and rumour are published without substantiation. In a single edition of *Wen Wei Po*, one of the smaller Hong Kong dailies, there were corruption stories involving three respected Chinese business-men which, had they been true, would have provoked a major scandal. No mention was made of these revelations the following day, nor were they taken up by the other Chinese papers. In all likelihood the corruption stories were nothing more than cheerful innuendo, lightly written and lightly read.

Of Sally Aw's two major rival Chinese proprietors, the first, Ma Sik-chun, is living in exile in Taiwan where he escaped after being charged with masterminding a massive Golden Triangle heroin ring; the second, Louis Cha, the proprietor of *Ming Pao*, was a convenor of Hong Kong's Basic Law Drafting committee. There are two Ma brothers, Sik-chun and Sik-yu, both Chiu Chow-speaking Chinese who managed, in less than fifteen years, to elevate themselves from roadside fruit hawkers to multimillionaires with strings of racehorses, Chiu Chow restaurants and *fokis*, triad bodyguards. It was somehow inevitable that, having amassed their fortune from a *tse fa* gambling racket and importing heroin by a fleet of junks from Thailand into Hong Kong, the 'White Powder Mas' should purchase a newspaper. The younger brother, Ma Sik-chun, appointed himself publisher of the *Oriental Daily News*, which not long afterwards was to face the awkward editorial challenge of reporting its owner's arrest by the Hong Kong narcotics bureau. During the short period of his publishership, the *Oriental Daily News* enjoyed sharp circulation increases attributed to slick downmarket reporting of crime and low life. After the Ma brothers' escape to Taiwan, executives of the *Oriental Daily News* made regular trips to their proprietors-in-exile to report on the paper's progress. In due course Ma Ching-Kwan, a 39-year-old nephew of Ma Sik-chun, succeeded as publisher and the paper has since established itself as market leader with a circulation of 493,333, ten times higher than Sally Aw's domestic sale of 43,667 at *Sing Tao Jih Pao*. The Mas' advertising revenue from the *Oriental Daily News* for 1989 was HK$343,936,049 against Sally Aw's HK$95,952,631. As long ago as 1976 Ma Sik-chun seemed set to challenge Sally Aw for the overseas Chinese market when he entered into a joint venture with Taiwan's leading newspaper, the *United Daily*, and launched a Chinese-language newspaper in New York called *World Daily*, but the paper never achieved the authority or brand recognition of *Sing Tao*.

If you stand on the corner of Java Street and Healthy Road, just off the Quarry Bay expressway, you are able to inspect both the façade and side elevation of Louis Cha's Ming Pao Holdings Limited. It is in many respects a classic Chinese office block: the front entrance and bottom three storeys faced with imported grey and white marble, reeking of corporate swank. Around the side, however, and above the third storey, the building resembles nothing more than a Kowloon tenement, with heaps of rubbish festering over the lip of steel bins, cast-iron electricity vents and air-conditioning units, metal fire doors and precarious, droopy wiring.

The chairman of *Ming Pao*, Louis Cha, has his corporate offices on the seventh floor – the Chairman's Floor as it is identified on a painted sign in the lobby – but in order to reach it you must run the gamut of the building as the lift door opens at each of the six lower storeys. At every floor the lift jolts to a halt, and then tarries for ten seconds while the steel grey doors creep open. And each time they open they reveal another vast, bleak office in which scores of Chinese sub-editors are making their marks on raw copy, and galley proofs hang like noodles from overhead racks.

But, like the New York Times building, when they open on to the chairman's floor the contrast could not be greater, with avenues of ankle-deep brown carpet extending to distant horizons in every direction. The chairman's office itself is remarkable not only for its immense size, but for the fact that it is entirely windowless. His desk, shaped like a pulpit with a pine lectern, stands beneath a wall of red and gold panels decorated with writhing golden calligraphy, bugles, harps and bulls. The chairman's tapestry chairs have elaborate gilded frames, and his marble topped tables with their spindly legs, bear boxes of fat Alto cigars. Along one whole wall there is a mural depicting mythological scenes from the legend of Kwok Ching – Chinese swordsmen and archers and soaring eagles – and against a third wall is the chairman's executive bar fitted out with several dozen peppermint liqueurs, premium brandies and bottles of Chinese rice wine. Somewhat at odds with this remarkable bar is a statue of Christ, barefoot and destitute, a gold-tooled edition of the complete works of Mao, and a photograph of the lone student in Tiananmen Square halting the column of Chinese tanks.

Louis Cha and Sally Aw have for two decades competed for Hong Kong's middle market. The rivalry between *Ming Pao* and *Sing Tao* reminds you of that between Lord Rothermere's *Daily Mail* and Lord Stevens's *Daily Express* in Britain, or the *San Francisco Herald* and the *San Francisco Examiner*.

'But you must understand,' said Louis Cha smiling mischievously, 'that Sally Aw and I come from very different backgrounds. She of course inherited a great fortune, including her newspapers in Hong Kong, whereas I was a very poor boy when I came here from Shanghai.'

And there is a further difference between them too, of which Louis Cha is all too aware. Sally Aw commands a certain chilly respect in Hong Kong, but Cha is a hero. People kept telling me that he is a courageous man and that he uses the muscle of his paper to take political initiatives to determine the future of his country.

At 67, Louis Cha's outward appearance is not that of a political activist but of an immensely rich Chinese banker. In his grey wool and cashmere suit, tortoiseshell glasses and Chopard watch, he is indistinguishable from the scores of dealmakers you see eating Western food at the Mandarin Grill or milling about the mezzanine bar at the Peninsula. As a newspaper proprietor, however, he is an anomaly. His political influence has been direct, not circumspect, through his involvement with Hong Kong's law drafting in preparation for Chinese sovereignty, and he is a best-selling author, under the pseudonym Jin Yong, of novels about Chinese warriors. Fiercely anti-communist for the 30 years since he fled from Shanghai, he is passionate about two things: free market capitalism and the historical

Chinese chivalry that he propagates – some say invents – in his novels. He was born in Hangzhou in 1924, and studied international law at Suzhou University in Shanghai before working as a sub-editor and translator on a communist-owned literary and political supplement, *Ta Kung Pao*. Twelve years later, after his escape to Hong Kong in 1959, he founded *Ming Pao* – it means "light" or "bright" and Ming is also a Chinese character, literally half-sun, half-moon – which was initially conceived as a vehicle for publishing fiction. Louis Cha's own stories about Chinese knight-errants and kung-fu warriors somersaulting off horses surfaced first in the early *Ming Pao*s and played a decisive role in building circulation.

'At this point,' says Cha, 'we were still selling less than 10,000 copies a day, while *Sing Tao* had the biggest circulation in Hong Kong. It wasn't until the mid-seventies that we were able finally to overtake Sally Aw Sian in circulation.'

Cha used the book royalties to increase *Ming Pao*'s pagination and began contributing leader columns and editorials. Those that he didn't write himself he oversaw, in the manner of Robert Maxwell. Often he seemed to be consciously competing with *Sing Tao*'s leader writers for the role of official spokesman of the Right. Throughout the Cultural Revolution he was something of a national hero as both he and his newspaper were publicly and consistently hostile to Beijing. Which is perhaps why the recent apparent softening of his views has aroused such hostility. When Cha proposed at a Basic Law Drafting committee meeting that free elections should not be introduced for Hong Kong citizens for another fifteen years, he was accused both of sucking up to Beijing to secure immunity for *Ming Pao* after the communists moved in, and of canvassing for the job of Chief Executive of Hong Kong in a post-1997 administration. Copies of the *Ming Pao Daily News* were burnt by students outside the newspaper offices in Quarry Bay, and Cha was gleefully condemned in *Sing Tao* editorials. Cha responded in a series of prominent leader page articles in his newspaper that he had no ambition whatever to be Chief Executive. The suggestion that he was protecting the future of *Ming Pao*, in which he owns 80 per cent of the stock, persists however, and Louis Cha was widely accused of muzzling the opinions of his senior editorial staff because they disagreed with him. Cha refutes this, pointing out that he allowed Margaret Ng, the former publisher of *Ming Pao*, to write an article critical of his own position.

'Are there any other papers that allow their staff to speak against its boss?' he asked me. 'Anyway, it is always the boss that determines the editorial line of a newspaper in a capitalist society.'

Cha's belief in journalistic market forces is absolute. As we spoke, he sat straight-backed on one of the tapestry chairs and buckled and unbuckled his Chopard watch, the strap of which he wore one notch tighter than was comfortable, leaving a livid red weal on his wrist. 'Because we have many newspapers here,' he said soothingly, 'there is very keen competition. It is a very free market here, so everybody tries to steal key staff from other groups. We pretend we don't, because we wish to be seen to be civilised, but we do. There is no gentleman's agreement between the proprietors. If I feel we need someone very much, I will increase his salary three or four times to get him. Hong Kong newspapers are flexible in that way, very quick and also I hope . . .' he gave a small bow, '. . . very good.

'But we are also,' he went on, 'decisive about *not* keeping people. If, after calculation, the staff member we have brought in is not worth it, I say, "Let him go". I'm sorry, but we are very capitalistic here. Usually we don't have any contract between owners and staff, only if they earn more than one million Hong Kong dollars a year, so it is very flexible.'

Louis Cha's proprietorship closely matches that of Lord Northcliffe at an earlier period in the West: his passionate patriotism for Hong Kong and belief that he alone knows what's right for it, his political pragmatism, his flair for readable journalism, a certain buccaneering competitiveness, a refusal to name any definite successor from among his staff and an ability to play them off against one another. For several years there has been speculation that Cha is poised to appoint one of the four members of his editorial executive committee as acting chairman – most likely the *Ming Pao Daily News* editor-in-chief Tung Chiao or deputy general manager Paul Hui Hau-tung – and this speculation was heightened in 1989 when Louis Cha stood down as president of the company but retained the chairmanship. At the same time it was rumoured that he might be ready to sell *Ming Pao*. Albert Cheng of Capital Communications was said to have actually written out a cheque for HK$800 million, and was eager to deliver it, and Rupert Murdoch was reported to be interested as a means of gaining a foothold in Chinese-language publishing. ('Actually I wasn't that interested,' Murdoch told me in Los Angeles. 'It was *he* who was interested in selling his paper to *me*.') The dramatic events in Beijing of 4 June 1989, however, altered everything. The circulation of the *Ming Pao Daily News* shot up from 120,000 to 200,000 a day, Louis Cha's enthusiasm for his newspaper was rekindled, and the For Sale notice was taken down. Instead he floated 25 per cent of the company on the Hang Seng in February 1991, retaining a 55 per cent controlling shareholding and the executive chairmanship.

'What we all believe happened,' says a *Ming Pao* executive, 'is that Mr Cha suddenly realised, in the middle of all the exciting news coming out of China, that without his own newspaper he would have no reliable platform in which to publish his opinions. He would no longer be able to ring down to the editor and tell him to hold him a space on the main editorial page. He would have to explain his views in advance to have them accepted on their merits. And if *Ming Pao* wouldn't publish them where would he go? Ring up Sally Aw and ask her for space?'

Sally Aw Sian's *Sing Tao* offices on Wang Kwong Road, Kowloon Bay, look like a giant high-tech bottling plant. The existence of a popular Chinese beer called Tsing Tao – with an initial T in much the same broad typography – only heightens the confusion, and at night, when the orange neon Sing Tao logo stands out against the landing lights of the airport, you are more than anything struck by the sheer physical process of manufacturing Hong Kong newspapers. The computerised conveying and typesetting systems, and the printing presses with 100 per cent capacity for colour, are as modern and sinisterly silent as anything in North America, (except perhaps *The New York Times*'s Edison plant). The seven expansive editorial floors are oddly subdued by the burden of all this technology, and it is perhaps for this reason that Alan Armsden – with his great bull-like shoulders and neck like Robert Maxwell's – seems to be the one strong physical presence not only in the *Hong Kong Standard* but the entire building.

Alan Armsden is Sally Aw's latest strategy for reflating the *Hong Kong Standard*, but his role, as he is keen to make clear, is wider than that. When I visited him at his big corner office in Kowloon Bay he handed me not one but three business cards. These read:

ALAN L ARMSDEN
Editor-in-Chief
Group General Manager
The Hong Kong Standard
FORWARD WITH HONG KONG

and:

Alan L Armsden
Assistant to the Chairman
Miss Sally Aw Sian

and:

Alan L Armsden
Executive Director
Sing Tao Limited

He left me on my own for a few minutes, perhaps to ensure that I'd read my way through all three cards, then set about describing the experience of working for Sally Aw.

'Well let's say this,' he said, 'she's not a bully and she's not a sucking boss. She's not like Bob Maxwell who I worked for before coming here. Maxwell did bully people, he was very present, a big strong man and he got good things from people because of it. Sally Aw's different, though equally tough in her way. You end up being very, very careful with her money. You don't want her to be able to turn to you and say, "You've wasted my money." '

Many people believe that Alan L. Armsden is an Australian. He was described to me as 'That Aussie Sally Aw's got down there at her evening paper'. In fact he isn't Australian at all, but British. His strong Melbourne accent is a conscious or unconscious homage to Rupert Murdoch, whose toughness, decisiveness and journalistic nous Armsden admires.

'Sally Aw's the kind of boss who expects results,' went on Alan Armsden. 'It wasn't written down when I came here that I had to get it right, but it was still explicit. You couldn't miss the point. She's the type of person who just says "I've brought you out here to do a job, now get on with it." '

'On the other hand, she doesn't expect to be treated like royalty. There are no outward trappings. When Maxwell came into a room with his entourage, it really was like the arrival of royalty, with people clearing out of the way or pushing themselves forwards. I took Sally Aw to the media awards at some fancy hotel ballroom the other night and she was humble. She feels quite insecure at those functions. She said to me at the end, "I don't want to be escorted to my car or anything, I'll just slip home quietly." '

I asked Alan Armsden why he thought Sally Aw had kept the *Hong Kong Standard* going for so long when it lost so much money. He seemed displeased by this question, and replied irritably, 'I wish people would bloody shut up saying my paper loses money. It doesn't. It makes money. I've only had one month – one month, December 1987 – when I didn't make a profit. Only one month in brackets. And I told her about that then. I said, "Miss Aw" – I always call her that – "Miss Aw, this is never going to happen again." And it hasn't.

'You have to remember one thing about this paper and what it means to Sally Aw,' he said. 'And that one thing is face. She wants a product that gives her face in the expatriate community. It didn't before. Students on vacation would breeze in from Sri Lanka or Bali with a backpack and land a job here next day. Which didn't do a lot for the paper. It's important to Sally Aw that the paper stands up on its own two feet financially, but face is every bit as important.'

'And if you provide insufficient face?'

'I'll be out. Out quick. No warnings. No second chances. Chinese are non-confrontational. She'd probably send some Chinese manager down here to fire me for her.'

The Chinese manager she'd probably send would be Edward Hung. He would not have to travel far, since his office is situated directly above Armsden's in the Sing Tao building where he is group general manager of Sally Aw's Chinese-language papers.

What does it mean, I asked him, to be group general manager. Is this administrative or editorial?

'Both. In Hong Kong this basically means chief editor in charge of whole damn shooting match.'

As the only Chinese executive below the age of 40 with daily access to the chairman, Edward Hung is viewed within Sing Tao as the catalyst for progress. He may be so, but it will be the cautious, evolutionary progress of the bright corporate *apparatchik*. In his dark Armani suit, white button-down Italian shirt and dark tie, he looks as much like the group general manager of an international chain of casinos as the group general manager of a Chinese newspaper. His accent is two parts Chinese to three parts Canadian.

'I have a Canadian passport you know,' he said. 'I'm Canadian now. Miss Aw sent me, at my request, in '84 to look after her West Coast operations for her, from Mid-West to Honolulu. I am very grateful to Miss Aw for this assignment since it enabled me to become Canadian citizen.'

'Is she easy to work for, Sally Aw?'

'Oh yes. I have plenty of respect for Miss Aw from long time. After all, everyone in Hong Kong knows about the legend of Tiger Balm and the Aw family.'

This struck me as a somewhat equivocal reply.

'I meant as a boss. Is it a good experience to work for her? Is she inspiring, compassionate, interested in you personally?'

Edward Hung nodded keenly.

'Oh yes. The decisions Miss Aw is making are very fast and firm. I think she has a lot of highsight [overview] and has grown her satellite operation overseas into a very strong network. Every day we are doing three transmissions which are dispatched by cable from Kowloon Bay to Cable and Wireless and then to satellite dishes in Stanley.'

'On a more personal level though, is Miss Aw someone you like as a friend?'

Edward Hung nodded most vigorously.

'Let me give you a good example. Two or three months ago we at Sing Tao negotiated a special deal with Hong Kong government to run the Civil Service job vacancy public service display advertisements overseas. Now they are being published not only in Sing Tao Hong Kong edition, but in all overseas editions in Canada, United States, UK and Australia. This is for the purpose of reversing the brain drain of educated Chinese who have left Hong Kong. We are giving them an opportunity to return home to a good job here on Hong Kong island. And Miss Aw was very instrumental in this new idea. She was a prime mover.'

What motivates Sally Aw Sian? One theory that goes beyond money and family obligations is a weakness for awards, conferences and big wheel advisors. There is a species of proprietor who, finding the day-to-day business of producing newspapers humdrum, yearns to discuss larger, abstract questions about the future of the media and their place on the planet. For Sally Aw, happiness is a convention in an hotel ballroom in Manila or Kuala Lumpur debating journalistic training in the year 2000, or the environmental implications of electronic media. She was the first Asian woman to be elected chairman of the International Press Institute, and rarely can an appointment have been more fulsomely covered by the Sing Tao group. She is founder and chairman of the Chinese Language Press Institute and chairman of the Hong Kong National Committee of the International Press Institute, in which capacity she likes to pontificate on the differences between the English and Chinese-language press. 'The English papers,' she has said, 'are more objective in their reporting, whereas the Chinese give more colour, not sensationally but in great detail. In court reporting the Chinese reporter would put much more colour into the facts of the case than the English press. This helps to sell newspapers.'

What this actually means is: when the Triad pays a midnight grudge call to a Yau Tong tenement, machetes flailing, the *Hong Kong Standard* records the incident and adds a quote from the local police, but Sally Aw's yellow press gives you, quite literally, a blow by blow account. In her conversations with editors she often implies she'd like to see more of this low-life reporting in all her papers, but then her Establishment instincts intervene, and she prevaricates.

She is said to measure her success, to an extraordinary degree, by the applause of foreign institutions. When the Scripps School of journalism at Ohio University gave her the Carr Van Anda Award for her contribution to the Chinese press, the citation was fulsomely reproduced in all her newspapers, along with the fact that Walter Cronkite, Katharine Graham, A M Rosenthal and Ted Turner had been previous recipients. And her International Advisory Board – a raft of non-executive directors who lend tone and gravitas to the annual report – is third in distinction to Conrad Black's and Kay Graham's boards and includes Lord Shawcross, described as an Advisor on International Operations for the Morgan Guaranty Trust Company of New York; Joseph Pulitzer Jr, Editor and Publisher of the *St Louis Post-Dispatch*; Lee Huebner, formerly of the *International Herald Tribune*; Tadayoshi Yamada, president of the World Trade Centre of Japan and Allen H Neuharth, Chairman of the Gannett Corporation, America's mega newspaper chain which owns *USA Today*. When I questioned Sally Aw about their contribution and remunerations, she replied, 'They are giving me advice. There is no set pattern. If I need to know something, I will fax their office with my question, and later ring them for their response.'

'What kind of advice do they give?'

'On all matters.'

In Hong Kong her board includes the multimillionaire Chinese entrepreneur Sir Kenneth Ping-fan Fung and her nephew Fred Aw Toke Tone.

'If you want my opinion of the foreign editorial board,' says a former news reporter, 'I think that Sally Aw sits in that office of hers, lovingly reading their names and positions, and taking some kind of vicarious kick having all that distinction on her writing paper. Just having the words '*International Herald Tribune*' and '*St Louis Post-Dispatch*' makes her feel plugged into some kind of secret society of newspaper owners.'

How skilful is Sally Aw as a proprietor? In Hong Kong, even people who have watched her strategy for twenty years are equivocal about her performance.

The lawyer Thomas Kwok, who not only has one of the largest legal practices in the territory but possibly the largest collection of equestrian Hermès ties, regards her as shrewd and honourable. 'I must tell you,' he said in his office on the 16th floor of the Jardines building, 'that she has been a friend of my family for longtime, and that as a woman she is very unChinese. What she has achieved is highly remarkable. Don't forget that her father's business empire was knocked out first by the Japanese occupation of China, in Shanghai and Amoi, and then by the arrival of the Chinese army. A lot of people think Sally Aw has done nothing but inherit her empire, but I disagree. I think she has greatly increased her family assets. One of her buildings on the harbour in Sydney, the Sing Tao building, is 50 storeys high and the idea for this development was all her own. I tell you 280 million Australian dollars was offered to her for that building. And another thing about her is that she's not aiming to screw people, to use an American word. A lot of people do, you know, especially in newspapers, and especially in Hong Kong newspapers, but that's not Sally Aw's style.'

The editor of the *Far East Economic Review*, Philip Bowring, is less indulgent. '*Sing Tao* used to be – how to describe it – the *Daily Telegraph* of Hong Kong, a reliable rather boring Establishment newspaper, certainly the most reliable in Hong Kong with the biggest readership at a time when the competition was all rather small and unprofessional. But the trouble with *Sing Tao* over the years is that it hasn't changed as much as it should. It's got all this facsimile printing to make bits of itself available all over the world, but the product is fundamentally unchanged. And I think much of the trouble is that Sally Aw can't make up her mind about anything. She's forever shuffling her empire about, but she's been overtaken on three fronts. The *Oriental Daily News* has overtaken her in terms of being the largest circulation paper, through the Ma family's passion for scandal stories and also, I should add, passion for getting the news. And she's been overtaken by *Ming Pao* as the respectable Establishment paper. And on another level she's allowed herself to be overtaken by the *Hong Kong Economic Journal* which has cornered the reliable financial market. All this is really rather leaving *Sing Tao* standing and immobile. She hasn't *done* anything with it. There's been talk about her buying newspapers in Europe and America, and expanding into China which she could certainly afford to, but somehow I doubt that she will now. She's been around so much longer than anyone else in this business in Hong Kong, but like a lot of inherited companies there's been a tendency for drift.'

She is widely criticised for allowing Rupert Murdoch to buy the *South China Morning Post* from under her nose, when her access to all the Hong Kong-based vendors was so much easier than his.

A British financial PR man in Hong Kong, who's done work for the Sing Tao group, disagrees that Sally Aw has done nothing, while subscribing to Philip Bowring's dim view of her strategy.

'Do you know what her real trouble is? She's a sucker for a new idea. She's always on for one, a catchwater for other people's money. It would have been difficult for her to go wrong with what her father left her, and yet she's been such a sucker. Take that scheme of hers to start up a newspaper in Singapore. Nobody but Sally Aw would have plunged in without planning it properly first.'

(This isn't entirely fair. Sally Aw was not alone in being stung by Lee Kuan Yew's awkward relationship with foreign press owners. Sally

Aw later told me, 'I did clear it – the *Singapore Herald* – with Lee Kwan Yew's foreign minister of the time. But really the government didn't want this newspaper. There was inexplicable hostility. The Singapore government deliberately tried to suggest some associations between the *Herald* and the communist-supported newspaper the *Eastern Sun*. They did so by insinuation and innuendo. I offered every proof that my interest in the paper was purely commercial and without sinister motives, but it was to no avail. In the end Mr Lee achieved a return to a monopoly situation of the English-language press in Singapore which he could control.')

Other of her media investments have also been unsuccessful. She was a joint partner with the Swiss publishers Christoph and Michael Ringier in the disastrous launch of the magazine *Billion*. Sixty-two million dollars were invested in a global financial publication to compete with *The Economist, Fortune* and *Forbes*. It was positioned particularly to emphasise business with China, and so it was unfortunate that a mailing drive to nearly two million people in Europe and Asia coincided with the events at Tiananmen Square. By July 1990 Sally Aw's partners had sold their share of *Billion*'s assets to Sing Tao and written off $15.5 million debt in return for immunity from future liability.

If you drive up to Tiger Balm gardens after nine o'clock at night, the faint low-wattage light you can see shining above the ornamental rocks comes from Sally Aw's bedroom. Her mother will have switched off her own light an hour earlier, and then Sally Aw sits up alone, in her room lined with dusty glass cabinets of jade, scrutinising the weekly accounts and circulation figures.

Only filial sentimentality can possibly keep her at Tiger Balm gardens. With its steep concrete terraces and a pagoda, open to visitors, directly overlooking the house, privacy is impossible, and she has covered the windows with dark green frosted glass like a public lavatory. The gardens themselves are hideous: characters from Chinese legends, some garishly repainted, others left to moulder, line the terraces like a derelict Disneyland, mythological dragons in grubby concrete rampage next to cute Peking ducks and kitsch rabbits and there are damp grottoes stippled with translucent green slime. During the day there are guards who blow whistles at visitors who stray too close to the house; at night, with their looming, grotesque shapes, the gardens remind you of the deserted lot of a horror film.

Sally Aw's reclusive character was emphasised in a 1985 kidnap attempt, when three Chinese gangsters, who had intended holding her to ransom, discovered from their surveillance of Tiger Balm gardens that virtually every evening in Hong Kong she spends at home. Their van, parked outside every night eventually aroused suspicion and the kidnappers were intercepted, with their handguns and chloroform, before the plan got anywhere.

In her statement to the police, Sally Aw explained, 'I keep to the same routine every day unless something special comes up. I go straight home after work and seldom go out. Sometimes I make a short trip by chauffeur-driven car accompanied by my mother. But otherwise, most nights, I am working on my administration.'

Chop-Chop Journalism

Sensationalism and Censorship in Thailand

From what is comically called the airport Super Highway into Bangkok you can just about make out, between the semi-permanent traffic jams of Daewoo lorries and white stretch limousines, the security fence around Kamphol Vacharaphol's family compound. There is a 20-foot concrete wall with guards in fatigues at the gate and, beyond, a green glimpse of lawn dotted with wooden Thai guesthouses. The set-up reminded me of the kind of place James Bond might penetrate, at dead of night, by springing over the wall from the roof of a moving truck.

Kamphol Vacharaphol – always known simply as Kamphol, pronounced Kampon – is the most powerful newspaper proprietor in Thailand, probably the whole of South East Asia, but he is a virtually invisible man.

His lurid broadsheet, *Thai Rath*, sells almost a million copies a day, and yet his name appears in no newspaper cuttings libraries. He gives no interviews – indeed, he responds neither to letters nor faxes – and should you mention him to other newspaper owners, advertising executives or Thai hotel managers, they become shifty and evasive.

'There is no question that Kamphol is anything but the most influential and best-connected man in Bangkok,' said a Thai analyst at Morgan Stanley. 'The reason that you won't get to see him is because he very probably wishes not to see you, and what Kamphol wishes in Bangkok, happens.'

Kamphol is a suave but very burly man, who seldom appears at parties other than his own. Pansak Winyarat, the party-loving former Thai senator who was chief foreign policy advisor to Prime Minister Chatichai Choonhavan, told me, 'I'd say he has "Manila taste": big collar shirts and awful Gucci neckties, drinks Hennessey XO.'

Aside from the great wealth his newspaper generates, Kamphol's influence derives from his closeness to the Thai royal family, particularly the Crown Prince. Since nothing whatever has ever been printed about Kamphol's friendship with the girl-mad, fast-aeroplane-mad Prince Vajiralongkorn, Thais have developed massive conspiracy theories about their joint trips abroad from a private airstrip. For his loyalty to the royal family, Kamphol has been awarded the Order of the White Elephant, Thailand's senior decoration, which entitles him on state occasions to wear the red and green sash with narrow blue and yellow bands, and the great sixteen-point star engraved with an ivory elephant. It is observed in Bangkok that it is only at these state functions that Kamphol changes out of his regular uniform of a dark suit, dark glasses, topaz and diamond ring, white silk shirt, white silk tie and pointed white shoes. At the office, he wears a crocodile-skin belt with a personalised buckle, the letter K encrusted with diamonds.

The biography of Kamphol's life is so sketchy, even to those who work for him, that you are reminded of those oriental mandarins in novels by John Le Carré who disappear from Shanghai in the twenties only to re-emerge, 50 years later, in Manila at the head of a mysterious strategic trade delegation which may be a front for something else. A rival newspaper owner, Thanachai Theerapatvong, told me, 'He was in the navy as a young man, an ordinary seaman, not an officer. And it is often said that he left under something of a cloud, I cannot say what. He was a tough young man: raised on the streets, a gambler and womaniser. That Italian word *gigolo* seemed to suit him. And I feel it was the toughness of these early days that made him successful, because he started his newspaper from nothing, and knows every nook and cranny of the business, and every means by which people might cheat him or steal from him. He is known to be a very tough cookie, and I think it would be a brave man who ever tried to cross him.'

The few biographical details that do exist are these. He was born on 27 December 1919 in the Kratumban district of Samut Sakhon province, and began work as a ferry boat conductor when he was 14. Two years later he joined the Thai navy as an engineer and served in the engine room of a warship. At 21, he applied for a place at an officer training school, but seems not to have got in since, three years later, he was a non-commissioned officer in the Indo-China war serving on a larger warship called the Sichang. At this point in his career, he is fond of telling his subordinates, his salary was two baht a month (there are now 40 baht to the pound sterling) and he subsisted entirely on ball noodles. In 1946 he resigned from the navy and tried journalism.

Kamphol had more than one failure establishing his press empire before inventing the formula for *Thai Rath*. It is a vile newspaper, and if you read a copy of it outside Thailand you are shocked there is a demand for it at all. But no sooner are you immersed in Bangkok than you realise Kamphol's genius. His sleazy editorial recipe of massage parlour sex, physical deformity, tacky glamour, political proselytising, tendentious columnists, buffalo fights and violent murder brilliantly engages some part of the Thai psyche. His eldest daughter, Ying Lak, likes to compare *Thai Rath* to the *New York Post*.

'Kamphol invented, or rather popularised, the genre of the chop-chop murder,' the chairman of a Thai advertising agency told me at the Siam Intercontinental. 'One way or another there's a chop-chop murder in every issue, or anyway you get that impression.' These stories all follow similar patterns: a gang – always a gang, masked and therefore unidentified – draws up in unmarked cars outside a cinema/Thai boxing stadium/sex bar armed with machetes. Their motive is always revenge, and by the time they depart – moments before the arrival of the police and the *Thai Rath* photographers – the premises are littered with stray hands and feet. *Thai Rath* is a compulsive newspaper, read by a quarter of all Thais every day, transcending all barriers of background and education. Its market penetration is twice that of Rupert Murdoch's *Sun* in London. You see workmen in the roadside cafés off Sukhumvit Road reading *Thai Rath* with the same dumb absorption as sapphire and ruby salesmen in the Patpong gem centres and Thai businessmen in the coffee shops of the Royal Orchid and Shangri-La hotels. None of them look remotely disturbed by the daily inventory of severed limbs. And *Thai Rath*, in turn, is not the sort of newspaper to waste precious space on shrill editorials demanding that something be done about the carnage.

The more you study the paper, however, the more conscious you become of a spectre at the feast. No gossip about the royal family ever appears in *Thai Rath*, even obliquely. You get the impression that the Thai royals could do anything – even draw up in a marked car outside a boxing stadium wielding an axe – and the story would appear nowhere. About once every three months an exclusive interview with the King or the Crown Prince is published in *Thai Rath*, in question and answer form, accompanied by a portrait of the sovereign in full decorations, in which the obsequious questions are twice the length of the replies. Kamphol is said to devise the wording of the questions himself in his family compound.

The policy of *Thai Rath* is, in this respect only, no different from its competitors. Like Kamphol himself, the royal family is a non-subject in Thailand. Decree 42, the press Bill introduced after a military coup in 1976, which enables the government to shut down newspapers on any pretext whatever, only endorses the Thai press's self-preserving reluctance to report on the court. This is a country in which to discuss the Crown Prince rudely in your own home is an offence. Foreigners in Bangkok refer to him by the letters CP, and tell you the story of the expatriate dinner party raided by Thai police after guests had been shopped by a servant for making jokes about the King.

Once or twice a year Kamphol brings his family for dinner at a private suite at the Mandarin Oriental hotel, and he gives an annual birthday dinner for three or four hundred business associates in the banqueting hall at his home. The guests at this event are an uneasy mixture of politicians and newsagents. Kamphol prefers the company of the newsagents. His relationship with them has always been close, and the success of *Thai Rath* has made them rich. Even now, in his early seventies, he makes regular tours into the regions – north to Chang Rai or down as far south as Surat Thani – to visit the men who distribute his newspaper. On these occasions Kamphol never forgets to remind them how fortunate they are to be handling *Thai Rath*, and how unwise it would be if ever they offered their expertise to a competitor. On the same trips Kamphol visits the network of health clinics he has set up throughout Thailand, in 74 of the 75 provinces, which are his charitable bequest to the nation and secured him his Order of the White Elephant.

'Every year on his birthday,' said Pansak Winyarat, 'two Las Vegas casino owners are flown over specially for his party. I just love to see the Chinese Thai who tries to have good taste! Above his printing plant at *Thai Rath*, Kamphol has the entire sixth floor as a reception room. He's decorated it in a combination of art nouveau, French empire furniture and modern sculpture. Very, very expensive. Do you know why so expensive? Because on Rodeo Drive in Beverly Hills there are three or four of those boutiques that sell limited edition reproductions of contemporary sculpture by Mexican artists, and Kamphol's decorator bought many, many of these and had them flown out to Bangkok.

'When I was working for Chatichai,' Pansak went on, 'Kamphol's paper was nasty to us for two months so we [the government] raided his discotheque.' The Palace Club on the airport road, partly owned by Kamphol's daughter, is the largest discotheque in the world. 'The Police Department wouldn't do it, they refused because it was Kamphol. But eventually we found some policemen crazy enough to raid it. After that Kamphol made a deal with us and promised not to attack us so much in *Thai Rath*.'

Kamphol has three children, all of them except the youngest, Khun Inthira, involved in the newspapers. Saravuth, his son in his mid-thirties, plays an increasingly significant editorial role, and is credited with introducing the odd economic titbit to leaven the chop-chop stories. The eldest daughter, Ying Lak, who works on the financial side of the newspaper, lives in a heavily guarded villa on the Chaophya river near the Klong Bangkok Noi. Her husband arrives by speedboat at the Oriental hotel to collect take-away dinners. Late at night they like to pile a group of friends – some in their teens – into a Mercedes and head off to one of the nicer discotheques on Patpong.

The private enthusiasms of Kamphol are almost sketchier than his public ones. He plays takraw, the ferocious Thai national sport in which woven rattan balls are propelled by head and feet. He is an enthusiast for Japanese ten-pin bowling and chartered a private plane to Osaka to watch a tournament. He has a brilliant aptitude for figures which enables him to convert any currency into Thai baht faster than a computer, a skill he demonstrates by challenging employees armed with pocket calculators. An aide who accompanied him on a trip to Tokyo to buy a printing press says that he converted 33,000,000 Yen into American dollars and then into Thai baht in three seconds. When he gambles in Macao, he is capable of memorising hundreds of cards while assessing probability. He is a believer in the Chinese art of reading the face, and says he can judge a man's sincerity from a photograph. Like many Thai businessmen, he will make no deal without relating it to his lucky numbers. Kamphol's lucky number is 13.

The antique dealer and political lobbyist Joey Shawcross, who got to know Kamphol in the seventies when he acted for a West German printing company, is impressed by his benevolence. 'If you're drawn to self-made men, he is a very good example of some of their best qualities. He's a tough character, but very generous and loyal to his friends. He is larger than life and rather surrounds himself with larger than life figures. Two of his closest associates were murdered while I was in Bangkok; one was his public relations advisor I seem to remember. Their murders had nothing whatever to do with their relationship with Kamphol of course.

'The thing you have to remember about Kamphol is he's a man who enjoys life. I remember one evening we were all having dinner in a Chinese restaurant in somewhere like the Shangri-La, and afterwards we ended up at the Oriental in what is now the Chao restaurant. It was pretty late by this time, and everyone else had left, but because it was Kamphol they opened the whole place up and we all drank Hennessey XO. He's a very generous man who enjoys himself. He's the sort of man who, if you were in trouble, would seek to help you.

'They have tremendous influence,' said Shawcross, 'but when you first meet Kamphol or his daughter Ying Lak, you wouldn't realise just how powerful they are. Kamphol potters around the house in his Chinese pyjamas, or drives about the compound in a go-kart. As a family they are not pretentious, which is rare for rich Thais who are normally high falutin'. It is other people who make you realise how incredibly powerful they are. *Thai Rath* is *untouchable*. If Kamphol is on your side, other Thais raise their eyebrows in admiration.'

Once asked the secret of his business success, Kamphol replied in 11 alliterative Thai words: *Jhap, Jum, Jong, Jauh, Jhai, Jud, Jig, Jaek, Juang, Jaid* and *Jaew*. Some of these cannot be precisely translated, but they are interesting because they crystalise the divergent sides of his character. They have become known as *The Eleven Principles of Kamphol*.

Jhap In order to really succeed you must specialise in what you know best.

Jum When you get hurt, you must learn by your mistakes. Or, with a different nuance, take revenge.

Jong Adapt to changes around you.

Jauh   Dip into the heart of the market. Or, give people what they want [chop-chop stories].

Jhai   Be prepared to pay for quality.

Jud   Organise people properly.

Jig   Peck like a chick for grains of rice to ensure your survival.

Jaek   Do not think solely in terms of money, but never neglect your pecking like a chick for survival.

Juang   Reward your loyal followers.

Jaid   Captain your ship firmly so that it can withstand storms.

Jaew   Do not swallow diamonds [grasp golden opportunities].

Nobody who has dealings with Kamphol, however distantly, has ever accused him of insufficient *Jaew*. He does not swallow diamonds. The Thai advertising man Thor Santisiri, who used to work at Collett, Dickinson, Pearce in London before returning to Bangkok to establish his Next agency, says of Kamphol, 'He is more powerful than any media tycoon I've encountered in the West for one reason. He has no competitor, not on his scale, and this enables him to call the shots. He does business *his* way. For instance if you want to buy advertising space in *Thai Rath* you must pay for it in advance in cash. It is unheard of anywhere else in the world for an advertising agency to pay cash for whole page advertisements.'

What this entails is a parade of security guards delivering packages of cash – thousands upon thousands of baht – to the *Thai Rath* offices. Kamphol Vacharaphol understands, as well as any newspaper proprietor, that when you get it right you do indeed have a licence to print money. There is, however, one peculiar thing about *Thai Rath* that I encountered nowhere else. Every single day, I was told, the paper turns away $400,000 of advertising that it doesn't have space for in the 32-page broadsheet. To place an advertisement at all is regarded as a small triumph and an honour. This struck me as very odd. Why on earth didn't Kamphol simply make the paper fatter, add pages, add sections? In Thailand's boom economy he could rapidly own something as obese and prosperous as *The New York Times*.

'The answer to that,' I was told, 'is simply that he doesn't care to. He doesn't *choose* to make it fatter. They've made so much money, they really don't *want* any more.'

It struck me as little less than miraculous that a country capable of producing *Thai Rath* can also support a newspaper as morally and ethically alien as *The Nation*. The cultural contrast is much greater than that between the *Sun* and the *Independent* in Britain, though *Thai Rath*'s triumphant xenophobia and *The Nation*'s chaste global-ism reminds you of them both.

In appearance, too, *The Nation* resembles the *Independent* – the design is full of explicit homages – and in some uncanny way the joint proprietors, Thanachai Theerapatvong and Suthichai Yoon, conjure up Andreas Whittam Smith and his sober, informed, painstakingly reasonable cohorts in the City Road.

The Nation Publishing Group's headquarters, like everywhere of importance in Bangkok, is located in the eye of a traffic jam near the airport Super Highway. Goodness knows how their reporters venture across town to report on anything, since the exit from Soi Chan Road is blocked by a near-permanent convoy of stationary lorries. Perhaps this lack of mobility explains *The Nation*'s fondness for foreign stories: it would be easier to receive a faxed report from Phnom Penh or Haiphong than command a man to cross the street.

I visited Thanachai Theerapatvong and Suthichai Yoon in their boardroom; a long, low, teak-lined office dominated by a long, low, teak boardroom table and 22 chairs (five for the five directors, and 17 spares). On a sideboard at the end of the room stood three arrange-ments of talismans, variously indicative of modern Thailand. On the left, a china statue, two feet high, of the King of Thailand in his full dress uniform of an admiral of the fleet. In the centre, a gold Buddha beneath a glass cloche, surrounded by gold and silver lotus flowers, joss sticks and a tumbler of water for the deity to drink from. Before the meeting began an elderly retainer in a white mess jacket – the chairman's waiter – entered with a jug to freshen the Buddha's glass. Since none of the water had been drunk since the previous day, an inch or two was carefully tipped from the glass into a saucer, and fresh water poured in its place. On the right of the sideboard was an architect's model of a sleek 40-storey office block, the Nation II building, with a red helicopter landing pad on the roof. This building (which is strikingly similar to the Aga Khan's new headquarters for his flagship – also called *The Nation* – in Nairobi) will partly house new offices for the newspaper.

Thanachai Theerapatvong – Thanachai – is chairman of the group, and Suthichai Yoon – Suthichai pronounced Sudichai – is styled publisher, though more accurately editor-in-chief. As equal partners they own 35 per cent of the company each, with the remaining 30 per cent floated on the Securities Exchange of Thailand in 1988. At the age of 46, Thanachai looks like a template for the vigorous but mature Thai businessman in an airline advertisement: grey herringbone jacket, striped Ivy League tie and a chunky gold Rolex on his wrist. Suthichai – younger, balder and the editorial conscience of the group – was the original founder in 1971 when the paper was titled *The Voice of the Nation*. In 1976, following cash flow traumas, Thanachai came into the company as chairman and the newspaper became *The Nation Review*; in 1985 after further restructuring, it became *The Nation*.

'Yoon Suthichai and many, many investors, groups of friends mostly, were publishing *The Voice of the Nation* for almost five years before I joined them, and they were facing many big problems financially, heavy losses and everything in a very bad shape. I was asked by a mutual friend of ours to save the company, and fortunately today we are still in business.' Thanachai chuckled to himself in the approved international newspaper owner's manner: a veneer of worldly-wise modesty masking latent self-satisfaction.

'Before I joined *The Nation* I worked for JUSMAG – the joint US-Thai military corporation to support the war in Vietnam. The Americans hired a lot of local people to work on this, and after the war it continued in other strategic areas.'

So much in Thailand depends on an accident of geography. Many people reckon that, by the end of the century, Bangkok will be the communications capital of South East Asia, if only by default. Media analysts urge you to study the map: to the west, Burma and a press censored into submission: to the south, Malaysia, financially unstable; beyond that, Singapore and a 20-year tradition of government intervention on every aspect of press freedom, domestic and foreign. On the northern and eastern borders of Thailand lie Vietnam and Cambodia, neither country likely to inspire confidence as the head-quarters for a communications industry.

In April 1988 a photograph of Rupert Murdoch appeared in *The Nation*'s main rival, the *Bangkok Post*. It showed him having dinner, alone, at the Oriental hotel and being presented with a garland of purple orchids by a hotel waitress. The incident was nothing more than a set-up by the hotel's PR department, to grab some coverage on the back of a famous guest, but it made a sensational impact on Thai news barons.

Three years later they still refer to Murdoch's visit.

'He was putting out feelers,' says Thanachai. 'Making a reconnaissance because he would love a South East Asian powerbase.'

(In fact he was doing nothing of the kind: he was breaking his journey with a 12-hour stopover between Sydney and London.)

'Perhaps you know that Mr Rupert Murdoch was recently in Thailand,' – *recently*, how recent is four years? – 'seeking out media opportunities,' the editor of the *Bangkok Post*, Paisal Sricharatchanya, later told me indignantly.

'Not that the Thai government would ever allow in a Murdoch or a Maxwell,' said Suthichai. 'A great opportunity is coming for us. Bangkok's position, our closeness to China, and Hong Kong being anybody's guess after 1997, is an advantage we won't pass to a Rupert Murdoch. Our government has been very aggressive on this subject, and we are building up the facility for ourselves.'

If the Thais get it right, they see vast new markets opening up from Penang to Hanoi. 'Cambodia,' said Thanachai, 'should return to normal politically within a matter of years and then we'll go in with a big distribution. Already we have a news bureau in Phnom Penh. That is the first of many. And we've spoken already – not negotiated but spoken – to the Vietnamese. Next we'll take *The Nation* in there. And we are working on Korea, Taiwan, Japan and Indo-China.'

Behind these grand schemes lies one poignant hurdle: press freedom. 'It is coming – slowly, slowly,' said a Thai advertising man without much conviction. He pointed to Eastern Europe. Newspapers, he said, that three years earlier were to all intents edited by the Ministries of Information of Bucharest, Budapest, Prague and Warsaw, are now part-owned by Mr Murdoch. There is a theory put about by Western journalists based in Asia, that Asian countries will never achieve full press freedom, for the simple reason that they neither desire it nor fully comprehend its worth. 'Asian values' is Singapore's euphemism for authoritarian government, and part of their defence of press censorship (which includes regulation of foreign titles: the *Far Eastern Economic Review*, *Asiaweek* and the *Asian Wall*

Street Journal are restricted to selling 400 copies of each issue) is that the Asian mind is made anxious by too much freedom. It is unsettled by behind-the-scenes political discord. It wants its leaders to be unassailably strong, and for policy to be handed down, not as the result of debate and lobbying. When Lee Kuan Yew said, 'The idea of a loyal opposition does not come naturally in a mainly Chinese electorate,' he spoke not only for Singapore but for his neighbours too.

When the Singapore Minister of State for Communciations and Information – he would more accurately be titled the Minister of State for Non-communication and Disinformation – Mr Mah Bow Tan, said, 'It is a privilege, not a right, for foreign newspapers to circulate in Singapore,' his warning was directed as much at the press of Singapore's neighbours in Malaysia and Thailand as the Western-controlled liberal media. And the Thai press itself, though not actually censored by government agencies, still operates under the shadow of the censorship law, Decree 42. There are numerous examples, humorous, surreal or disturbing, of the decree being invoked. Mana Rattanakoses, a Thai Education Minister, sued *Krungthep 30* magazine for depicting on their cover a monk with a shaven head reading *Playboy*; the editor, publisher and even the model hired to impersonate the monk all underwent a criminal trial. Murdoch's *South China Morning Post* was banned by Police Chief General Pow Sarasin for running a speculative news report on a possible coup in Bangkok. The *Naew Na* newspaper was closed down for 'irresponsible' coverage of a murder of three Saudi embassy officials in Bangkok. Nobody disputed that the murder had taken place, only the newspaper's judgement in recording the fact. Often Thailand's reputation as a holiday destination lies behind these fierce clampdowns. When the *Far Eastern Economic Review* published an unhelpful piece about the Thai Tourist Authority, the magazine was suspended. When the *Asian Wall Street Journal* reported on the suspension, it too was suspended.

'In practical terms we are quite free,' says Thanachai. 'We are free for instance to raise questions against the government and the military; I stress to *raise questions*, not to mount a sustained campaign against these things, even if we should wish to. On two subjects only we are not free to comment: the monarchy and religion. Both are highly sensitive in Thailand and it is better not to talk of them at all.'

The absence of royal coverage is interesting, because it provides an insight into what a press-free society must have been like in the kingdoms of medieval Europe, or more recently in the final years before the fall of the Pahlavis in Iran. On one level, the King and Crown Prince are all too evident. Statues and framed photographs of them abound. The newspapers, by contrast, almost lead you to believe you're in a republic. And yet there is no shortage of gossip and conjecture about the royal family, once you are inside private houses. It is simply that none of it is relayed through the conduit of newspapers. Nothing has ever been printed about the Crown Prince's mistress, though there cannot be a taxi driver, or boatman in the floating market, who does not know every twist of this glamorous liaison.

'Recently,' said Thanachai, 'there has been a very intensive campaign to put pressure on the government to repeal Decree 42 – the Printing Bill as it's called – but I must make one important point about it. The campaign is happening now not because journalists don't have enough freedom, but precisely because there is more and more democracy. And we want to seize the opportunity to repeal the letter of a law that is already, in practice, enforced less vigorously than it was.'

'This is true. In relative terms we are free, in absolute terms, not so,' Paisal Sricharatchanya told me in the editor's office at the *Bangkok Post*. 'And there is another thing you must remember, which is that libel remains a criminal offence in Thailand. An editor who libels somebody of importance can be sentenced to several months in jail. Not a fine but a jail sentence.'

This is because the maximum fine for press libel has not been increased since 1940 when it was set at 2000 baht. By 1992 this was the equivalent of about £70. No court considers this sufficiently punitive to be worth imposing, so hands out a custodial sentence instead. Consequently the Thai press is the only press in the world that actively lobbies for steeper libel fines.

For Suthichai Yoon the single greatest challenge is the balance of editorial tone. It is a restraint faced by none of the great world newspaper proprietors, beyond the normal commercial judgements about a paper's tone reflecting its market. In Thailand there are nuances over what can and cannot be reported that must be instinctively understood throughout the whole newspaper in order for it to survive. The paper's strength, he believes, lies in its independence and Thai ownership.

'As a Thai-owned company we have the moral right to comment critically on our own country. The *Bangkok Post* is now 51 per cent Thai owned and 49 per cent foreign, but it still remains a *foreign* newspaper, the Thais involved are mainly nominees. The irony of this country is that we were never colonised, but still we had no intelligent Thai newspaper. That is why we founded *The Nation*. The fact that we are Thais empowers us to criticise – I hope constructively – from within. The editors of the *Bangkok Post* have no such right. Even when the paper was owned by Lord Thomson* they had no such right, because they needed always to look over their shoulder at the government who might revoke their licence. It hasn't changed. The working executives of the *Bangkok Post* cannot criticise. They are hired hands. The editor and managing director are foreigners on five-year contracts.'

Behind Suthichai's pervasive nationalism, however, lies a measure of disinformation. The majority is certainly Thai owned (Chirathiwat, the manufacturing and retail group that includes Bangkok's main department store and the Central Plaza hotel, has 20 per cent and significant shareholdings are held by the Bangkok Bank, Siam Commercial Bank and RCL Shipping Line). At the same time, *The Nation* is not wholly free of foreign investment. Three Hong Kong-based trust funds collectively own 20 per cent, registered as the Bermuda Trust. In addition the Dow Jones Company, owners of the *Wall Street Journal* and the *Far Eastern Economic Review*, have taken 4 per cent of *The Nation*. The Nation Group in return print the *Asian Wall Street Journal* using artwork transmitted to Bangkok by satellite.

Thanachai and Suthichai's position as proprietors in Thailand is full of inherent contradictions. They own a newspaper more Western in form and attitude than anything east of Calcutta or west of Hong Kong. At their daily editorial conferences they examine the previous day's *New York Times* and *Independent* for news leads, but little of the objectivity of those newspapers can be brought to bear on great areas of Thai society. They are ambitious to take *The Nation* into every adjacent country and beyond, but are paranoid about the territorial

* It is currently a semi-public company, with large stakes held by Thai department stores and shipping lines.

ambitions of foreign media barons. They explain this paranoia by pointing to the easy money available to foreign proprietors, and yet Thailand is experiencing massive growth – 12 per cent GNP in 1991 – and a property boom and access to low interest borrowing similar to that which propelled the Australian and American owners into global expansion. They see *The Nation* as an editorial bulwark against first world exploitation, and yet the group is increasingly divesting into Western-style high rise developments, condominiums in Hua Hin, sports complexes and a 27-hole championship golf course in partnership with the hardly Thai-sounding Majestic Creek Country Club Limited.

'Have you made money yet, out of *The Nation*, for yourselves?' I asked them.

Thanachai laughed decorously. 'I still live a very simple life,' he said. 'No big mansion yet. But this year we are enjoying another excellent growth, and with our diversification into real estate and the golf course almost ready to tee-off, who knows?'

The previous day, he said, he had returned from an historic trip to China, accompanying his 80-year-old mother who had left the country as a refugee at the age of nine. They had travelled together to Chantou, her birthplace, to try and find her old house.

'I left my mother in the hotel,' said Thanachai, 'because we might have been all day searching, and maybe never finding the house of our cousins. But after only a few enquiries we do find, and the family is reunited once again. For me it is an omen. I hope, I pray in my lifetime we will sell copies of *The Nation* in my mother's birthplace.'

19

The Gates Clang Shut

Part Two: The tycoon, the vultures and the fall of Asil Nadir

When Asil Nadir was detained at Heathrow airport on 15 December 1990, handcuffed and charged with 14 counts of theft from his company, there was consternation at the *Günaydin* offices on Alaykosku Cadessi. For several months his journalists had experienced difficulties drawing their pay and there had been other indications, too, of impending turmoil. The barrage of television advertising had abruptly stopped, which led to a tumble in the circulations of all his newspapers. Asil Nadir may have been inexperienced as a proprietor, but he knew enough to fire the editors, including Metin Munir, when the going got tough.

A former Turkish chief of police named Fahri Görgülü, hitherto Nadir's fixer and factotum in Istanbul, was appointed to run the national newspapers. His duties to date had involved the exporting of fruit and the arrangement of human shields on either side of Nadir in the back of cars, in case of an assassination attempt. Now he was given instructions to kick ass. The editorial, Nadir conceded, was too upmarket and it was taking longer than he had anticipated to turn the business around. Eighteen months earlier he had spoken of posting profits of TL100 billion (£19 million) a year from the newspapers by 1990, but now they were reckoned to be haemorrhaging at the rate of a million pounds a month.

The vultures circled. Robert Hersant, sitting behind the net curtains of his office opposite the Arc de Triomphe, instructed his executives at *Le Figaro* to prepare a bid. Hersant had recently acquired papers as far east as Warsaw, and Istanbul beckoned. Robert Maxwell – having let Nadir down once before over the purchase of *Hürriyet* – blithely suggested himself as a candidate to buy *Gunes* and *Günaydin*. Nadir, still entrenched in his rococo suite in Berkeley Square, rebuffed all overtures.

Instead he took the papers downmarket. In a move reminiscent of Rupert Murdoch and the *New York Post* in the late seventies, Istanbul rediscovered low-life and lotteries. Denied coach smash stories for almost two years, readers were once again reunited on their front pages with blood-spattered corpses, articles about Anatolian dwarfs, performing bears, Kurdish terrorists and more coach smashes. The tracts of newsprint previously devoted to the speeches of Turgut Ozal were given over to coupons, lottery tickets and lucky numbers. Readers were inveigled with prizes of motor scooters, cars and splashy concrete villas with solar-panelled roofs.

In London, Nadir appeared at Bow Street magistrates' court to hear the charges read out. It took less than fifteen minutes, and then he was released on bail of £3.5 million, the highest in British legal history. The accusations remained vague. In Istanbul, beyond the jurisdiction of British *sub judice* laws, it was widely assumed that Nadir had channelled Polly Peck assets into his newspapers, as Maxwell would shortly do during his final days with the *New York Daily News*, but there was no concrete evidence of this. In the financial world, it was the purchase rather than the operating of the papers that was blamed for his demise. Nadir had borrowed a total of about £80 million from a network of banks, including Barclays de Zoete Wedd, Merrill Lynch and Carr Kitcat Aitken, using his shares in Polly Peck as collateral. At the time he bought the *Gunes* and *Günaydin* groups, these were worth £450 million. As the share price faltered, and then collapsed as the companies were put under administration, Nadir's borrowings on the papers were unsecured.

In January 1991, the contents of Nadir's office in Berkeley Square were sold at auction on the instructions of the administrators, and raised £3 million. More upmarket than the sale of the contents of Maxwell's corporate apartment 13 months later, the lots included the George III mahogany easel, the fluffed-up tapestry of the Golden Horn, a pair of Turner watercolours, several onyx cigarette lighters and the fax machine that had disgorged so many blurred front pages for his approval.

Why did Nadir buy the newspapers in the first place? Commercially, he must have known they were a bad proposition. Although the circulation of *Günaydin* was 350,000 when he acquired it, making it the number-three paper, its prospects were not buoyant. Alone of the big Turkish dailies, *Günaydin* had no plans for a new printing plant and was hugely overmanned. Its predicament was similar in many respects to that of the *Sun* pre-Wapping, *The New York Times* pre-Edison and the *New York Daily News*. And what was curious was that, having bought the papers, Nadir (like Maxwell in Manhattan) did very little to address these problems. It was as though buying the papers was an end in itself.

There is a theory that Nadir regarded newspapers as a simple business tool, as essential to the tycoon as a good merchant bank and a good chauffeur. 'To build a castle,' he said, 'you need two towers: banks and newspapers.' In Cyprus he had always had them. The synergy was excellent. Ownership of both the local bank and the local paper meant an uninterrupted supply of capital and sycophancy. As he moved to become a major player in Turkey, the papers were intended to smooth his path.

There are other, less calculating theories that seem even more convincing. Nadir had an emotional attraction to newspaper owner-ship, partly tied up with prestige. As a child in Cyprus, he had sold bundles of newspapers from café to café on the streets of Famagusta, and the prospect of taking a large stake in the Turkish press – the motherland – held tremendous allure because it so conspicuously celebrated his passage from one state of life to another. The press barons of Babiali have in any case always given the impression that they are members of an exclusive, sybaritic club. Photographs of Erol and Haldun Simavi, and Dinc Bilgin who owns *Sabah*, the largest selling Turkish daily, rarely show them behind their desks or examining early editions from their presses. They are photographed on the decks of their yachts or eating in big, expensive restaurants overlooking the Bosphorus in the company of big, expensive blonde companions. In no other country is the Kudos of the press baron so unambiguously associated with pleasure and social cachet.

Moreover, like the Indian press, the Turkish media takes sides, promotes and forecloses the careers of politicians and industrialists. Asil Nadir understood this. In order to ensure favourable coverage, he had to seize the means of promotion.

It was his tragedy that, at precisely the moment he needed it the most, the newspaper empire he had so rapidly built, just as rapidly slipped away.

20

The Nerd has Flown

Part Two: The bitter end of the Fairfax fiasco

On 17 January 1990 – his final day as proprietor of the family newspapers – the 29-year-old Warwick Fairfax decided to make a farewell tour of his editors. It cannot have been a happy prospect, this leave-taking. For over four months Fairfax had barely been sighted in the building; he'd been holed up in his corner office on the 14th floor attempting, time and time again, to reschedule his debts. Finally the bankers had lost patience and told Fairfax to clear his desk and get out. Citibank, which was owed about $345 million, and the Australia & New Zealand Banking Group, which was owed about $421 million, said a receiver was about to be appointed. The coup had failed.

Fairfax took the lift down to the editorial floor where the *Sydney Morning Herald* and the *Australian Financial Review* had their offices. As he walked for the last time along the linoleum-covered corridors, with their sludge-coloured walls and fire hydrants, he saw his own picture everywhere. Facetious posters captioned 'Have you seen this man?' beneath a photograph of his awkward, nerdy face had been pasted up all over the building. And some of the journalists and secretaries who passed him in the passage were wearing Warwick Fairfax T-shirts showing him lying prostrate in his mother's arms like Jesus cut down from the cross.

When he reached the office of the *Sydney Morning Herald*'s editor, John Alexander, he was kept waiting 40 minutes. Alexander was in a meeting and couldn't be interrupted. So the young man, who until that morning had been the proprietor of Australia's most distinguished newspapers, sat down in the editor's secretary's office and waited, while scores of his ex-employees, hearing he was there, found pretexts to pass by and take a last curious look at him.

Eventually the editor finished his meeting and Fairfax went inside and sat down on the tan-coloured sofa. Alexander vividly remembers the parting: 'Warwick had his normally vacuous, normally nervous conversation. It was essentially a conversation about nothing. We never had much to say to each other, since he never seemed to read the paper. In fact I don't believe he read anything. He was almost subterranean in terms of his personality; he had no presence – corporate or editorial – of any kind.

'I remember saying to him: "Well, how are you going to support yourself now that you've lost two-and-a-half billion dollars?" And he replied: "Lots of 30-year-olds have no money, it's not a problem." '

Then, in a request that left Alexander speechless, Fairfax asked: 'I was wondering whether there might be a vacancy here for a junior news reporter? I think I could make a good reporter.'

Told that there was not going to be a reporter's job for him, he loped along the corridor to the editor of the *Australian Financial Review* to make the same request, and hear the same disappointing reply.

By now, a *Sydney Morning Herald* journalist had had the idea of conducting a valedictory interview with the erstwhile proprietor, and followed him to the lift.

'Have you anything you want to say before you go?' he called out to Fairfax.

'Only that I'm sorry,' he replied flatly as the metal lift doors closed behind him. Then he crossed the great art deco lobby of the Fairfax building for the last time, walked round to the corporate garage and drove away in the red Toyota Camry that had been his company car for the previous three years.

Sydney in February 1990 was a city still in shock from Warwick Fairfax's fatal act of hara-kiri. Among the financial and journalistic community, the talk was of nothing else. Until Robert Maxwell's media empire imploded 22 months later, it was the most extraordinary reversal of proprietorial fortune for three decades. It gave one an insight into how cataclysmic the fall of News Corporation would have been, if Rupert Murdoch hadn't managed to roll over his corporate debts that autumn, and the 26,000 employees of his newspapers, magazines, film studios and book publishing divisions had suddenly found themselves adrift. Conspiracy theories about Fairfax were proliferating so fast that, as I raced by taxi across town through the mid-summer heat, I felt new theories and suppositions were overtaking me on the highways and suspension bridges and establishing themselves as certain fact.

Fairfax's reclusiveness during his thousand-day proprietorship had made him a natural object for hypothesis. People were making expeditions out to Neutral Bay to view the outside of his modest house where he lived with Gale, and every fleeting conversation he'd ever had was reviewed for clues to his character.

Vic Carroll, a former editor of the *Sydney Morning Herald*, had become a particularly fertile conduit for fresh theories. 'He was never *comfortable* in Australia, you know,' he told me. 'He's much more comfortable in America, and was always rather contemptuous of Australian institutions – our politicians, our banks, our art galleries and newspapers. His father was always very pro-Australia and took young Warwick around when he first came back, to meet Bob Hawke and the politicians. But Warwick seemed to show no interest in these people. Why? God knows. Bad memories perhaps. Maybe his whole view of the country had been soured by his childhood. It can't have been easy living with his mother at Fairwater, with 60 of her closest friends coming for dinner most nights.'

One evening, Lady Fairfax invited me to one of these dinner parties on which her reputation as a hostess rests. Since her son's downfall, dinners at Fairwater have become less frequent because Mary Fairfax has chosen to spend much of her time in Manhattan where she owns the top two floors of the Pierre Hotel on Fifth Avenue, including a 110-foot-long ballroom. But nothing in the scale and scope of the hospitality at Fairwater suggested she had lost any of her appetite for entertaining. About 40 guests milled about at her spooky Edwardian mansion on Double Bay.

There is a swimming pool, somewhat in need of a scrub, and beyond five acres of lawn leading down to Seven Shillings Beach and, beyond that, across the harbour, the Sydney skyline. Three tables surrounded by spindly gold chairs were set upon the lawn, each covered by a profusion of spectacularly vulgar flowers and place settings: splays of precarious red carnations fought for table space with elaborate silver salt cellars shaped like carriages pulled by silver winged cupids.

'Have you got your dance card, darling?' Lady Fairfax enquired of each guest in her squeaky Australian accent as she scurried about from group to group. 'Filling out a dance card is a great tradition here in Sydney.' (It isn't. Only at Fairwater is this arcane practice perpetuated.)

In the corner of the verandah a perpetually smiling pianist in a white tuxedo kept up a seamless medley of 'Strangers in the Night' and 'New York, New York' on an electric keyboard, to which guests were expected to dance. But many of them – who seemed to be financial or property consultants – preferred to sit out the dances and hypothesise on Warwick, so that a gloomy, wake-like atmosphere hung over the party. Every time the name Warwick was mentioned, and a new post-mortem embarked upon, his mother bobbed up to the table in her bright orange Valentino suit. 'Don't talk, gentlemen,' she commanded her guests. '*Dance!* There's no point sitting back in life. Take the floor, darlings.'

You couldn't help but imagine her giving exactly the same advice to her son when he mooned about the garden planning his future.

'Tell the guests what you're going to do later on in life, darling,' a friend recalls Mary saying when seven-year-old Fairfax ran into the drawing room one day. 'I'm going to be the chairman of John Fairfax,' little Warwick is said to have replied. 'Yes you are, my treasure,' cooed his mother.

According to the company historian Gavin Souter, Lady Fairfax's Christmas cards from Fairwater followed Warwick's progress over the years through childhood and adolescence. They were the most flamboyant cards ever seen: a flourish of red ribbon surrounding photographs of the favoured son, accompanied by gushing eight-page commentaries on his general brilliance, and selections of her own poetry. At the age of seven Warwick could be seen seated astride the stone lions in St Mark's Square, Venice; at eight he was holding the silver cup for endeavour at St David's School, London; at 13, playing tennis at Cranbrook school, Sydney; at 19, briefcase in hand, starting his first job at J Walter Thompson before going up to Balliol; and at 21, lunching alfresco on vacation from his second job (personal assistant to the chairman of Gordon Berg and Co Inc, investment bankers in Boston) before returning for his final year at Oxford.

On 7 December 1987, 21 days after he had secured the dizzy loan facility that enabled him to take over the company, Warwick Fairfax had installed himself in the chairman's office. But he was very seldom seen; occasionally large bowls of fruit were spotted being carried in his direction, along with a pair of silver grape scissors. And crates of Coca-Cola were trundled up to the 14th floor on trolleys.

Three terms were repeatedly heard drifting along the corridors: 'refinance', 'reschedule' and 'junk bonds'. It was rare for the lift doors to open on any floor in the building without a banker, or more usually a group of bankers, standing inside. As the months went by, their faces, it was noticed, became longer and more despondent. By mid-December 1990, nobody was much surprised when the Supreme Court in Sydney approved the appointment of a receiver.

It is within the gift of few men in their twenties to unleash as much devastation as did Warwick Fairfax in just three-and-a-half years. Not only did his intervention trigger the break-up of Australia's largest newspaper group, with several good newspapers being closed and hundreds of people losing their jobs, but the level of disruption, wasted money, unnecessary debt and corporate angst, exceeds anything else of its kind.

In a way it was a fiasco that could only have been conceived and executed at the easy money fag end of the eighties. Many of the bankers who helped Fairfax set up the deal now look back on it and ask: 'Did we really lend two billion to a guy of 26, who knew very little about the business he was planning to take over, whose main experience of newspapers was a holiday job, and who appeared hardly capable of conducting a coherent conversation?' Well the answer is yes, they did, and paid themselves handsomely for it.

What have never been satisfactorily explained are Warwick's own motives. Marty Dougherty, Lady Fairfax and Jesus Christ have variously been accused of putting him up to it. But none were caught red-handed.

It was – still is – fashionable in Sydney and beyond to lay the blame at Mary Fairfax's door. 'When we're talking about the Fairfax debacle, we're talking about Mary; Warwick was just an agent,' reckons Ralph Ingersoll.

But with the passage of time, Warwick himself is emerging as the author of his own downfall. His gaucheness, his inability to get on with his contemporaries (and, later, his bankers), and his apparent belief that Jesus Christ was at his side advising him, all contributed to his evident obsession that he, and he alone, knew what was best for the company.

'There was a fatalistic side to his character, brought on by his insecurity,' says one of his former employees on the Melbourne *Age*, 'and also by his Low Church Christianity. You got the feeling all the time that if the crazy takeover went right, then Warwick would give the credit to God. And that if it went wrong, then that was God's will, too, and that God or Jesus or someone up there willed it that way.'

'He didn't have to lose it all, I reckon,' Rupert Murdoch told me. 'I think he could have got through it. I knew him as well as anybody, which is not very well at all. Nice man, misguided and a bit unlucky. It would have been very difficult but the way to get through it would have been to roll up your sleeves and say, "I'm the chief executive, I'm running this" and to have gone and seen the banks and said where the revenue was coming from and how he was going to pay the interest and so long as he paid interest he could have hung in there. Instead of that he wasn't there and he brought in an executive – nice man who was totally foreign in newspapers, previously ran a cardboard box factory or something, a sensible man – but it was hopeless.'

To me, the oddest fact was Warwick Fairfax's apparent lack of curiosity about the contents of his newspapers themselves. Weeks would pass and he'd scarcely open the Melbourne *Age*, the *Sydney Morning Herald* or the *Australian Financial Review*, not even to read the articles about himself. It seemed strange, to go to such lengths to acquire them, and then rarely open their pages, but to leave the bundles of new issues in a mounting pile in the corner of the office.

When he came to take leave of Graham Nounam at the *Australian Financial Review* – and to make his half-hearted bid for a reporter's job – Nounam asked Fairfax whether he felt either bitter or devastated about the disaster that had overtaken him. 'Fate's an odd but not very cruel thing,' he had replied. 'I have a wife who I love very much, and a strong faith.' He added: 'In a way I feel quite unburdened.'

Within a week, Warwick and Gale Fairfax had closed up their small suburban house, returned the Toyota to the office car-park and left Australia for Chicago. They had no plans for the future, beyond the birth of their first child later that month. Fairfax told friends in his Christian fellowship that he was considering joining a newspaper company on the management side. He said he wanted to join at the bottom and work his way up.

He had not left Australia for 48 hours before the predators took up their positions in the Regent hotel. In Pittsburgh, Tony O'Reilly had for several months secretly been working on the Fairfax numbers and was now poised to make his ambitions public. And in London, Conrad Black, having digested the *Telegraph*, was beginning to feel the first pangs of hunger and the need to hunt.

For a Few Dollars More

The cost-cutting charm of Tony O'Reilly

When you fly north from Coffs Harbour along the Australian Pacific Coast, zig-zagging across the Great Divide into Queensland over Lismore, Ipswich, Toowoomba, Rockhampton and Emerald and land at the state's north-eastern airstrip at Mackay, you have overflown the greater part of Tony O'Reilly's Australian newspaper empire. From the air you are struck by the immense, scorched tracts of land, treacle-gold fields and desolate properties, and then, every few hundred miles, by the parcels of grey roofs that herald a township, each with its own O'Reilly newspaper. Their titles are as quaint as anything belonging to Conrad Black in the Canadian outback: the Rockhampton *Bush Telegraph*, Bundaberg *Drum* and *Noosa News*. For some reason these 36 small papers reminded me, more than any other provincial chain, of a private newspaper estate; instead of herds of Aberdeen Angus or Dunbeath longhorn cattle, the passenger in a light aircraft may look down on Dr O'Reilly's herds of indigenous Australian newspapers.

He is unique among his peers in that his newspapers are a profitable hobby. Numerous media owners have non-media business too, but O'Reilly alone is retained by a public company as the chairman, president and Chief Executive Officer of the global food company H J Heinz, for which he earned $75 million in 1991 in salary, bonuses and stock options, making him the highest paid executive in North America. As a sideline, he has assembled an aggressive second league empire of 47 newspapers across two continents. In addition to the Queensland and New South Wales chain, he is controlling shareholder of Independent Newspapers in Dublin which owns 60 per cent of the Irish press, including the *Sunday Independent*, the *Evening Herald*, the *Sunday World* and (with Lord Stevens) an Irish edition of the *Daily*

Star, plus a string of weekly papers in East London as well as a controlling stake in South Africa's largest newspaper group, Argus.

He has also emerged as the world's number one proprietor-in-waiting. His frustration in not owning a world-class paper is highly evident. Through Independent Newspapers he has access to a reservoir of goodwill with the banks, and practically no big newspaper in the English speaking world comes up for sale without O'Reilly leafing through the prospectus. His tussle with Conrad Black for the Australian Fairfax newspapers was acrimonious, since success would have propelled O'Reilly on to the high table of proprietorship. As it is, he was left like the underbidder at an auction house, with a bad case of anti-climax and the money jangling unspent in his pocket. He is a director of the *Washington Post* which has further stimulated his hunger to own a famous, blue-chip newspaper. By the spring of 1992 O'Reilly had become a form of superior ambulance chaser, in hot pursuit of any paper – the *Daily Mirror* in London, the *Sunday Tribune* in Dublin – that might have need of the Doctor. In February 1994 he made a series of surprise dawn raids on the British *Independent* and *Independent on Sunday*, snapping up 29·9 per cent of the stock, days before the Mirror Group consortium (including the Spanish and Italian groups *El Pais* and *La Repubblica*, which between them own 36·8 per cent of the papers) took control. O'Reilly asked for board seats which in March 1994 were still being denied.

Ask anybody who works for him for an adjective for Dr O'Reilly and they all come up with the same one: charming. Rival media owners are less indulgent. Conrad Black's team in the Fairfax episode considered him a relentless adversary and ultimately a bad loser. When Black's consortium won the papers, O'Reilly sued on a technicality. Black dismissed the litigation as 'frivolous and vexatious'. The political lobbying, he said, had been 'the most tawdry of its kind. What has gone on has been like a fight among alley cats'. Several months after his victory I asked Conrad Black whether O'Reilly had yet forgiven him for winning. 'Has O'Reilly forgiven us?' he rumbled. 'Has *he* forgiven *us*? Horse manure. He defamed us. He's got all those Irish politician friends of his, reeking of peat and potatoes. But he never had a hope.'

O'Reilly is a broad-shouldered man with wide nostrils, pinkish grey hair, heavily freckled forehead and a semi-permanent suntan, possibly the result of unfiltered ultra-violet rays through jet windows. In

Ireland, where society is limited enough for such judgements to be made, he is regarded as the most famous living inhabitant. In fact he scarcely now qualifies as an inhabitant at all, spending only about 40 days a year there. His world tours for Heinz outstrip anything undertaken by the British Royal Family or His Holiness the Pope. In any six-month period the corporate Grumman Gulfstream taxis along runways in several dozen areas of operation from South America to Asia to Central Africa. Or else he is to be found shuttling between the Heinz headquarters in Pittsburgh, Washington and the Bahamas. Like Lord Hanson and Lord White, he manages to be taken seriously by both financial press and gossip columnists. He will appear in a *Fortune* magazine profile on 'the cost-cutting imperative' in the same week as a social item recording his attendance at a racemeeting at Goodwood with his second wife Chryss Goulandris, the Greek shipping heiress. He shares with the late Robert Maxwell a delight in the company of world statesmen; playing tennis with George Bush, gladhanding Nelson Mandela, Lady Thatcher, Yashuhiro Nagasone. In the course of 120 minutes of conversation he invoked, with equal enthusiasm, George Shultz, Mark Birley of the nightclub Annabel's, Seamus Heaney, Dr Henry Kissinger, Oscar Wilde and the financier and Reaganite advisor Walter Wriston.

'The legendary charm is all true,' says Brendan Keenan, former *Financial Times* man in Dublin who was headhunted by O'Reilly as financial editor of the *Irish Independent*. 'When you have a meeting with him he makes it seem like you are the only person he is seeing all day. He is not like other tycoons: he never appears as though he's itching to go, never looks fretful, never looks at his watch, is always calm and relaxed. The charm is authentic, and the reason he can achieve it is superb organisation. His diary is meticulously planned. People are given 20 minutes, 25 minutes, an hour, but they don't realise this because Dr O'Reilly handles his time so expertly. And he has the same people around him for ever: Olive who's been his personal secretary for 20 years, Arthur his driver.'

'The charm is his genuine nature,' says Independent Newspapers Chief Executive Liam Healy. 'At the same time I don't think anyone would feel that there isn't a genuine *toughness* there too. However in his dealings with people on the newspapers he is genuinely appreciative of their contribution, he remembers them, remembers what it is they do, rarely forgets a name, even out of context. If he's only met someone once before, and then runs into them at Shannon airport, he'll know exactly what they're called. People of course find great charm in that.'

'He has a marvellous trick,' says *Irish Independent* editor Vincent Doyle, 'of being introduced to 18 or 20 new people around a dining table and remembering every one of their names, even the fifth person to his left who is sitting too far away to speak to.'

'I've been with him on flights for 20 hours, the most arduous night flights, but I've never seen him drop his sense of humour,' says O'Reilly's vice president of corporate affairs, Ted Smith, who previously worked in the Irish Prime Minister's office. 'In fact I've never seen him speak sharply. He seems to be very disciplined in that respect.'

Tony O'Reilly's holiday house in County Cork, overlooking the tiny fishing port of Glandore, may have the best views in southern Ireland; from the long chairs by the swimming pool you can see the crenellations of a Victorian Gothic castle, hills sloping gently into the sea, and then the whole tranquil bay with its pair of grassy skerries at the headland called Adam and Eve. Until O'Reilly bought Shorecliffe House 15 years ago, it was a boarding house run by an elderly Danish gentlewoman, at which guests could lodge only by recommendation. When the landlady, reaching retirement age, wished to sell up, she offered the house first to her regular summer guest Dr O'Reilly; he accepted, but on condition that she continued living there as his housekeeper. This happy arrangement still prevails. The old landlady, now 83, presides at lunch like a Molly Keane heroine, and the decoration, unaltered since its boarding house days, is a pleasing mélange of faded chair covers, rugs and watercolours. It is about as great a contrast to O'Reilly's other homes (an expansive brick house in the Fox Chapel country club enclave of Pittsburgh, and Castlemartin, and his 750-acre estate in Kilcullen, formerly the family home of Sotheby's British chairman Lord Gowrie) as could possibly be conceived; and it is here that O'Reilly gravitates to escape the circuit of conferences, strategy beanfeasts and marketing jamborees that embellish his Heinz programme. The sole concession to corporate life is a cumbersome fax machine in the corner of the study which, even as I admired it, emitted sheaves of urgent documents addressed to Dr O'Reilly: the week's Heinz soup sales in Japan, Qatar, Bahrain and the United Arab Emirates, market share updates for Zesties (crispy seasoned french fried potatoes) and Amore (ocean whitefish and tuna dinner for cats) and then, just as the incoming post was seeming a little serious, the available dates for a beach house in Nassau at Lyford Cay.

To reach Glandore I had been driven for 30 miles along single track lanes skirted by foxgloves, past encampments of gypsies in horse-drawn caravans and across the great flat tidal harbour of Rosscarberry with its oyster beds. 'Complete seclusion,' said Tony O'Reilly, 'if you discount my near neighbours Patsy and David Puttnam [the film producer] and my next-door neighbour Peter Jay [the BBC economics editor and chief-of-staff to the late Robert Maxwell].'

His accent retains a strong Irish lilt, but you detect in his vowels a nasal Pittsburgh twang. He says *Peader* not *Poyter* Jay. When he talks he smiles a good deal.

Almost all the portrait photographs ever taken of O'Reilly show him wearing Prince of Wales check suits, American-style blue shirts with contrasting white collars, Irish green or purple silk ties and pocket handkerchiefs, and a flat-faced gold watch emerging just far enough from white cuffs to put over an appropriate degree of presidential prestige. Whether for *Forbes* or Heinz corporate litera-ture, O'Reilly is invariably pictured holding (as opposed to wearing) a pair of spectacles; an affectation no doubt intended to emphasise gravitas without detracting from his vigour. At Glandore, he wore an old pair of linen trousers, a checked shirt, rubber-soled holiday shoes.

It is at Glandore that he gets to grips with newspaper strategy and budgeting; balance sheets were spread out on the slatted wooden table in front of the poolhouse. Draped in a white towelling dressing gown, he chisels superfluous dollars from the overheads of the *Richmond River Express Examiner* in New South Wales, or expendable Irish pounds from the *Sunday World* of Dublin; then, in the faded boarding house study, conducts global conference calls that strain the local telephone exchange to its limits.

'Last night,' he said, 'about eight of us were on the phone, on a conference call for about two-and-a-half hours.'

'Where were the other participants?'

'Three were in Sydney, one in Dublin, one in Rockhampton in

Queensland – that was my son Cameron – one was in Melbourne, and I was here.'

'This was a Fairfax conference call presumably?' O'Reilly's Independent Newspapers were then still engaged in their losing battle to secure the Sydney and Melbourne crown jewels.

'Indeed. They're outstanding papers. And an outstanding business too I might add. Murdoch has thrown the 14th Panzer division [the *Australian*] against it and it's still there rock solid.'

'Will you win?'

'We certainly *deserve* to win. If you like I'll give you our presentation to the banks. It's *terrific*. I really am proud.'

'And the competitors?'

'Are pretty smart too. I suppose we must regard Chris Corrigan's Jamison Equity as the leading contender. And there's Jim Leslie, Chairman of Qantas, who's heading up a Melbourne consortium. And of course the 900 pound gorilla in the background is Kerry Packer sharing the branch with Conrad Black.'

'Is Black an authentic bidder here do you think?'

'I reckon he's a *tweaker* on this one. It certainly won't be very assuring for the Australian Labour Party to know that an alliance of Black and Decker – Black and Packer – could get together.'

'Would it be a workable consortium?'

'More like a particularly vicious polo match,' said O'Reilly, smiling bleakly. Then he said, 'I've always been fascinated by newspapers on all levels, provincial as well as national. They all have their own charm.

'I heard a lovely story recently,' he went on, watching a small, brightly painted fishing vessel chug into the estuary and head for the Glandore quay, 'I was at a dinner party of Drew Heinz's in New York and I saw [former Secretary of Defense] Caspar Weinberger and he said to me, "Tony, don't you happen to have some papers down in Australia?"

'I said, "Yes, we do, Caspar."

'And then Caspar asked, "You don't happen to own a paper down there in a place called Rockhampton do you?"

'And I said, "Yes, by chance I *am* the proud owner of the Rockhampton *Morning Bulletin*."

'Then Caspar said, "*What a goddamn provincial paper it is you own*! My God, during the war we did our basic training for D-Day on the beaches of Rockhampton. We spent almost six months there, we thought we were fully integrated in the community and then we went back to Europe prepared for the greatest assault since Hannibal crossed the Alps. We landed on the 6th of June on the beaches of Normandy and the Rockhampton *Morning Bulletin* managed to ignore this most important event in world history for four days. Eventually on page 6 there was a little item 'Where are they now?' It began, 'You may remember that a year ago' . . ."

'I thought to miss D-Day is a real achievement for any newspaper. My job as the present proprietor is to make sure our papers remain properly provincial but don't miss the next D-Day!'

Chryss Goulandris appeared at the poolside holding a copy of *The New York Times*.

'You've found a *New York Times* in *Glandore*?' exclaimed O'Reilly. 'Where in God's name did you come by that?'

'It isn't today's,' she laughed. She had accumulated it somewhere at an airport between Manhattan and Normandy (where she has a stud farm) and Ireland, but couldn't remember exactly where.

'*The New York Times*, that's a paper I'd love to own,' said O'Reilly. 'A smashing newspaper. "All the news that's fit to print" – that's a slogan anyone'd like to have.'

'You'd like to buy the *Independent* too, wouldn't you?' Goulandris asked her husband. (This was two years before his 1994 dawn raid when he took his 29·9 per cent stake.)

'The *Independent*? I own that one already, Chryss.'

She laughed. 'Not the *Irish* one, the *English Independent* that everybody knows about.'

'I certainly admire it,' he agreed. The folklore was that unless you had an awful lot of money you couldn't start a newspaper. Whittam Smith [the editor-in-chief and founder] has proved that – at least temporarily – to be incorrect. The *Independent* is in one respect like *The New York Times* – a *dissonant* voice. Newspapers are about dissonance. I'm suspicious of proprietors who want to push their personal prejudices, especially since most of the newspaper proprietors I've met are of limited education. Successful commercially, but *limited* educationally.'

'Who are you thinking of?'

'One must, by definition, think of Maxwell. He had a selective education, a narrow view of the world. You could almost say the same thing about Murdoch. And Rothermere. With Rothermere there's a class background that's limiting. Well that gives zest and zing, but it makes him rather less *plural*. And so I suppose I find a Punch Sulzberger very attractive in that context – I really do like Punch. What I'm looking for are people with *wide* experience in life who are unmarked by the selectivity of their own particular experiences. That may not be what the newspaper reader wants, but I'm just saying the ideal. Don Graham at the *Washington Post* is particularly attractive and comes close.'

'Is Don Graham the proprietor you most admire?'

'Well I admire Rupert [Murdoch] greatly. Very simply put, I think Rupert's one of the three most outstanding businessmen I have met in my life. Just in the general ranks of businessmen who have courage, you couldn't possibly meet anyone who has had the courage and vision to withstand the last five years in the way Rupert has. He has continued to innovate in the face of enormous pressure from the banking world. It's been an act of genius. But Don Graham is the most *knowledgeable* proprietor, technically, about the newspaper industry, certainly in America and possibly the world. He knows even more than Rupert about how a paper is put to bed; the whole process, the whole nature of cut-off, press, new plant, all the various technologies. He just went out of his way. He's an extraordinary fellow, a policeman for two years, a Vietnam veteran. One of the most estimable men I've met in American business. But it was his mother, Katharine Graham, whom I knew first, and I've had most to do with her. It was Kay who appointed me a director of the *Washington Post*.'

Can Tony O'Reilly parlay his way into the first division? That is the question his fellow newspaper owners ask about him.

'He's a marvellous asset on our board,' Katharine Graham told me. 'Tony's fun, and knows everybody, and has a real feeling for the newspaper business.'

'I'm rather an admirer of his in a way,' said Conrad Black, 'but frankly I don't believe he has what it takes from an economic standpoint to buy significant newspapers. He can schmooze his way with the bankers, but there's an element of horse feathers.'

In the battle for Fairfax, which O'Reilly had initially appeared to be winning, he was scooped at the final hour by Black's more heavily financed Tourang consortium.

'What actually happened at the end,' said O'Reilly, 'was that the terms under which the final offers were made were dealt with, in my view, in a partisan fashion by the parties who were accepting the bidding. In other words, we were encouraged to believe that an underwritten offer, which we had for 1.56 billion dollars Australian – underwritten by J. B. Weir & Co, the largest underwriters – would be an acceptable offer. And then we were told at the very end, "Sorry, but the deal is done with Tourang and you have to be good for your money on next Saturday week," which gave us the phrase "to be good for your money". This at a time when we had been led to believe that an underwritten public flotation was an acceptable route for the receiver and for the banks. So, quite simply put, we felt we were misled, led down a fool's path.

'We went at it [Fairfax] in a straightforward, honourable and honest way,' O'Reilly went on, 'and we feel we were not treated fairly and we have taken that feeling to the courts. We sued Tourang immediately, and we're in the high court in Australia as we speak.'

'Oh that's a joke,' said Conrad Black. 'He can't be serious. That was thrown out like a dead mouse in his opening gambit, and he's back now. It's a straight spoiling operation. O'Reilly's endeavour is just an undignified and unseemly act of sour grapes and he's making an ass of himself.'

The campaign to win Fairfax was not only the most drawn-out media beauty contest of the decade but, by virtue of its contestants, the most widely publicised. For eight months barely a single edition of any Australian paper was published without mug-shots of Black, O'Reilly and Kerry Packer leering out of the front page. The more protracted the contest became, the more gratifying for the victor and galling for the loser. Tony O'Reilly had developed what was almost an obsession with Fairfax, ever since he conceived the notion of buying it over dinner in a Sydney restaurant called Darcy's in Paddington, following a party given by Lady Mary Fairfax at Fairwater. 'I *want* Fairfax,' he is reported to have vowed as the main course was delivered. 'I *want* Fairfax.' And in the months that followed nobody devoted more effort to charming the bankers, editors and politicians of Sydney and Canberra than he did.

'As you know he's a very charming and persuasive man,' Conrad Black told me, 'and he'd gotten away with bloody murder in Australia. He'd got the whole press of the country believing: one, that he was an Australian, and two, he was a newspaper man. And I felt called upon to point out a few basic facts. I said that he did not develop that splendid brogue at the Billabong, that he was no more an Australian than I am and that he was a very talented man and a friend of mine. But he wasn't a newspaper man, his job is manufacturing Ketchup in Pittsburgh. But there's nothing wrong with that at all, it doesn't disqualify him as an owner of Fairfax, it just gives the lie to this mystique he was endeavouring to propagate as a lifelong, committed newspaper man. He was *swaddling* himself in the raiment of this non-interfering owner and bandying about the well-respected names of Kay Graham and Punch Sulzberger.'

The view of the majority of media brokers, however, is that O'Reilly will eventually secure a major paper, if not a Fleet Street one, (the *Independent* would have been ideal had he been able to pull it off) then a serious metropolitan daily in America or Canada. His February 1994 victory in South Africa which gained him, among others, the Johannesburg *Star* and the Cape Town *Argus* is indicative of the prizes he is now after.

Ideologically, he is more flexible than most proprietors. He would find no inherent contradiction between his life as a prominent American industrialist and ownership of a socialist newspaper. 'When I first went to work at Heinz in 1969 my predecessor, Anthony Beresford – a charming fellow – said, "Look, there are only two papers here that you need to read to keep you fully in touch with the United Kingdom. One is the *Financial Times* and the other is the *Daily Mirror*." There's a certain amount of truth in that. I'd have no problems [owning the *Daily Mirror*] because my image of it is very much a Cudlippian image – I was very friendly with Cecil King [legendary chairman of the Mirror Group] when he lived in Dublin at the end of his life, I used to see him a lot.

'The one fundamental benefit of the Fairfax competition for us,' said O'Reilly, 'was that the name of Australian Provincial Newspapers became very public as did the name Independent Newspapers. People know us now. We get offered more properties and get to see them earlier.'

O'Reilly was not yet the biggest enchilada at Heinz when he assumed his dual role as press baron. In 1973, through a complex and opportunistic deal, he secured control of Ireland's largest newspaper group, Independent Newspapers in Dublin. The Murphy family – who have certain social parallels with the Carrs who had sold the *News of the World* to Rupert Murdoch five years earlier – owned 100 per cent of the voting shares in Independent but only 4 per cent of the equity. O'Reilly bought their apparently ceremonial voting stock for $2.3 million, then immediately put up the ingenious proposal that all shares should have voting rights, provided that he received an enormous tranche of bonus shares which gave him a 28 per cent voting and controlling shareholding. By March 1991 he held ten million shares in Independent – about 30 per cent of the company – valued at £19 million. His proprietorship has been largely by remote-control, and yet much of the credit for the group's strategy is fairly attributed to him.

'He is not an intrusive owner by the standards of others,' says Brendan Keenan. 'He makes his editorial point through the board which is the proper way to go about things. But he has certainly had the effect of upgrading the standards and status of Dublin journalists, and upgrading their pay too I might add. When he got control of Independent Newspapers he did what was then a remarkable productivity deal with the unions, introducing more flexibility. It was an example of the O'Reilly flair if you like. Other men might have said, "This is too ambitious," but O'Reilly pushed it through. He might subsequently have regretted it sometimes, mind, it was generous, but it has produced enormous benefits. I would say in general he is liked and admired by his journalists. This is Ireland of course, so nobody who has made a great fortune like Dr O'Reilly has can altogether escape the usual badmouthing. But on his newspapers it is rare for people to have any particular gripe against O'Reilly; against his emissaries, yes sometimes, but O'Reilly is just a little too removed from the day-to-day scene for the average journalists to badmouth him.'

He is credited with four separate proprietorial initiatives: new technology for direct input (which he sanctioned years before Irish union agreements permitted their use, and which sat around on desks until they no longer caused offence); his purchase of the splashy tabloid *Sunday World* three years after its mislaunch, which has been revitalised; his circulation victories with his *Sunday Independent* which has edged ahead of its rival, Ralph Ingersoll's *Sunday Press*, and his *Evening Herald* which also has the edge on Ingersoll's *Evening Press* ('He has that willingness to spend a bit of money,' says Keenan, 'even when the circulation benefits could be dismissed as purely short term.'); and his diversification into the English suburbs with his string of local papers and freesheets.

'Two paid, five free. Damn good business,' O'Reilly told me with relish. 'Circulation 500,000 per week. All the commanding heights of the British economy: Barking, Dagenham, Waltham Forest – all down there – Greater London and Essex newspapers. Normally profitable. I have to say, lucky to break even this year.'

'O'Reilly diversified the company into other sectors of the media and out of Ireland,' Kyran McLaughlin, a director of J&E Davey, the Dublin brokerage house, told *The New York Times* Business section. 'He then went back and reformed the domestic newspaper business.'

I asked him how often he talked to his newspaper managers.

'I would say I talk to Liam Healy [Chief Executive] on the telephone every day. He's extremely crisp. And he knows detailed things about newspapers that I'll never know, about cut-off lengths and pagination and why we will or will not put colour on page six – all those things that make money. He's very bottom-line orientated, a 32-year veteran of the Irish newspaper wars. He's also a major stockholder.' (L P Healy has 131,975 ordinary shares to A J F O'Reilly's 10,066,767.)

'Dr O'Reilly is not a minute details man,' confirms Healy. 'He's more the type that likes to be fully informed in a general way. We talk a lot in this organisation which is how Dr O'Reilly likes it. He has this great business capacity for getting to the bottom of things through discussion. He doesn't like surprises. Not at any level. Everything has to be foreseen and discussed.'

'What about your editors,' I asked O'Reilly. 'Do they ring you, for instance, seeking your permission to run a particularly contentious story or are they left to work autonomously?'

'Totally autonomously. I don't think it would be fair on me and it certainly isn't fair on them to feel there's that level of expectation. Secondly it's not possible for me in the job I have, running a huge world corporation like Heinz, to give them the measured judgement they require. You'd become capricious, and there's enough of those around! I'd be more in the Thomson camp than the old Maxwell camp on this issue. I only really have contact with my Irish editors at our annual international conference which takes place for three days at Castlemartin. All the editors are there into the long reaches of the night, which is when I really talk to these guys. Of course, editorially in newspapers, history is the dictator. You can't take a *Daily Telegraph* and thrust it into the tabloid sector, or conversely turn socialist papers like the *Daily Mirror* into Tory papers, so most of the broad strategic directions are a product of history. The one other thing I do is pen the chairman's message in the annual report of the Independent – it's a kind of internal memo to all our editors: *this is what we stand for*. So they can read it and take what they want from it and reject what they didn't like. But at the end of the day if we find an editor constantly chafes at the sort of policy we've laid down then we obviously don't want him in the group.

'I have only once had a major disagreement with Tony and that was over our coverage of terrorism,' said Vincent Doyle, who has edited his *Irish Independent* for eleven years. 'There was an exceptionally violent spate of tit for tat murders in the North and I decided we would publish two lengthy interviews with the then known heads of the UVS and the IRA, stating their views and motives as they saw them. And we attracted quite a lot of criticism for what we'd done, because you know people are understandably concerned when a newspaper gives a platform to terrorists in this way. And when we next met O'Reilly was fairly concerned – in fact very concerned – about the effect it would have. I explained the position to him, how it looked to us in Dublin, and how I thought the articles had been in the public interest. I'm not sure I entirely convinced him though he saw the point of view. Normally O'Reilly and I are like-minded because we both detest the IRA. They have sent me a bullet through the post with my name scratched on the side with a nail: the IRA calling card. I don't know whether Tony has ever received one. Some things are not asked in Ireland.'

A perpetual awkwardness for O'Reilly's editors is how to report on their owner. His status in Ireland would normally guarantee him daily mentions in at least five sections of the papers: social, sport, business, politics and racing. His marriage to Chryss Goulandris, his youthful fame as an international rugby player, his attention-holding salary and involvement with Irish oil exploration and the Waterford glass company, his friendship with virtually every Irish Cabinet minister and love of racehorses could legitimately propel him on to every single page. He is like a reverse Robert Maxwell, in that he merits his column inches without having to demand *droit de seigneur*. It is a problem that his editors have never satisfactorily resolved. There was widespread carping in Dublin when he allowed his *Sunday Independent* to publish an eight-page colour supplement entirely devoted to its proprietor, including 17 photographs of him shaking hands with Henry Kissinger, Margaret Thatcher, Valery Giscard d'Estaing and Robert Mugabe, as well as pictures of him striding on to the tarmac from the Heinz corporate jet and posing with his first wife, Susan, and their six handsome children.

O'Reilly's not implausible explanation was that other celebrities are given similar treatment every week, so why should he censure a valid journalistic idea just because he is controlling shareholder?

'That's reverse nepotism,' he said. 'The editor said, "Tony, you're an interesting person. It doesn't matter that you have an interest in this paper. You are somewhat larger than life. Why are we going to be barred from writing about you?" '

And O'Reilly is more sanguine than most proprietors about having his non-media businesses criticised by his own newspapers. 'Sometimes we'll cringe when we see it,' says Liam Healy, 'but Dr O'Reilly stands by his non-interventionist policy.'

'There could be some awkwardness during the bitter strike at Waterford Crystal,' says Vincent Doyle. 'The unions and the management [O'Reilly is Deputy Chairman] were saying some pretty angry things about one another. But Tony didn't ring me up once, not once, to discuss our reporting.'

Since making his bid for Fairfax, O'Reilly has achieved much higher visibility in Australia, and this has presented similar problems to his editors there too. By chance he was embarked upon a pre-flotation inspection of his Australian papers during the August 1991 coup in the Soviet Union against Mikhail Gorbachev. Accompanied by a large retinue of executives, he kicked off the tour with a speech in Mackay, where he owns the little *Daily Mercury*. The next day his newspaper divided its front page horizontally. The top section showed a large photograph of O'Reilly, fist raised in a victory salute, making his after-dinner speech. Beneath the fold was a picture of the newly reinstated Gorbachev and the secondary headline 'Coup Fails'.

He bought his Australian empire from Rupert Murdoch.

'I know Rupert socially, I see him at dinner sometimes in New York,' said O'Reilly. 'So I was aware that he had a TPC [Trade Practices Commission] problem incurred through his acquisition of the *Herald and Weekly Times*, because he got Queensland Newspapers with it including 46 per cent of what were then called Provincial Newspapers of Queensland. He was clearly going to have to divest them. I talked to him about it at dinner and he agreed that he'd be happy to divest with me, so I bought 19.9 per cent off him, which was the maximum allowed, and then made a bid for the whole company. I can tell you it was well contested. At one stage it looked like that Chinese newspaper proprietor, Sally Aw from Hong Kong, was going to join the bidding. But unluckily for her she doesn't have six children with Australian passports* so that rather undermined her credibility with the Foreign Investment Review Board. I think we pitched it at a fine price. It looked at the time like a multiple of 13 times operating income, which seemed very high. Now it looks as if we got it relatively cheap because at $27-and-a-half million annual profit for a $150 million purchase it's a rather good deal.'

'Was Murdoch easy to negotiate with?'

'He has an extremely brief staccato style of negotiation, very rapidly makes up his mind and then sticks to it. His phrases are [broad Australian accent] "Great. Good as gold. Yeah right, that's OK". Then he normally has to catch a plane. His purchase of the *Herald and Weekly Times* was the biggest acquisition he ever made in Australia. It bought him the paper his father had managed, so in terms of family icons he had secured the high ground. Queensland Provincial Newspapers was a very low priority. Which is why we were able to do a deal with him. He was extremely helpful, I have to tell you, because I had thought that we could buy 50 per cent of it directly as Independent Newspapers and then we collided with these Foreign Investment Review Board rules and I had to come up with 85 per cent of the financing myself. And Rupert Murdoch left 23 million in the deal – in

---

* The six O'Reilly children have Australian passports through their mother, Susan, who is Australian.

other words he took a note from the new acquiring company *and* 14 per cent interest, so he wasn't falling over backwards for us, but it was helpful at the time. What I liked about Rupert Murdoch in this deal was that a) he got a good price, b) he facilitated in the financing of our acquisition and c) he kept his word absolutely to the letter. Rupert doesn't chisel.'

As soon as he took control, O'Reilly drastically restructured the management. 'Essentially we disestablished a large central overhead in Brisbane – there were about 47 people working there – for a series of essentially autonomous daily newspapers. Queensland being the size of France, it is a very large area; the distance between our southern-most and northernmost newspaper is 1270 miles, so you don't *need* a central overhead. If you happen to be the *Mackay Daily Mercury* you want everything in Mackay. This very large overhead was essentially the result of a coalition of three families, the Irvines, Dunns and Mannings, who had built the great newspapers of their region. These were very, very nice, gentlemanly, elegant people. I'm not critical of them but they did not march to the beat of the drum that the company currently marches to. So we did away with the Brisbane overhead altogether and installed John Reynolds as Chief Executive, who's an extremely tough, lantern-jawed Cantabrigian who's six foot nine, I think, at the last measurement. He and Stevens [Lord Stevens, chairman of United Newspapers, who is O'Reilly's partner in the Irish edition of the *Daily Star*, and frequently the butt of jokes because of his small stature] would average about six foot between them! Profits dramatically increased from $12 million to close on $30 million.'

Four years later in May 1992, O'Reilly floated 44 per cent of the company. 'The float price was a dollar and the shareprice went to a dollar 45 on opening day. They're 137 today. Essentially what it meant was we put 10 million into a highly geared bid in 1988 when I bought it from Rupert, and that 10 million is today worth 138 million. Absolutely outstanding. We took a big risk and we got an *unreasonable* reward.'

Something bemused me however about O'Reilly's Australian papers. I couldn't see where his satisfaction lay. In his keynote speeches at Heinz conferences, his priorities are defiantly global. He heralds the advent of the global consumer: an international brand-conscious shopper whose responses to pulp television, satellite quiz games and bottles of Ketchup are increasingly homogenised. It struck me that Tony O'Reilly would be the logical proprietor of a continent-wide paper like Gannett's *USA Today* or the Barclay brothers' *European* rather than a stable of township tabloids in 'Florida without the kitsch' as Ted Smith describes Queensland. His Australian papers are lively rather than excellent: wired stories from press services combined with neighbourhood chit-chat – an old lady who has achieved some great age, a redneck grocer who has run the local dry-goods store for 20 years, agricultural items about the drought or a proposed kangaroo fence. His ownership meets only one proprietorial criteria – making money. At dinner parties, the table doesn't fall silent when the owner of the Ipswich *Rural Times* broadcasts his views on the world trade deficit. But O'Reilly asserts that he enjoys owning such papers. 'A local provincial newspaper should be both highly provincial and investigative,' he says, 'without being destructive within the community. But also inform people that there is a world outside, to break down the barriers of provincialism. I enjoy that mission.'

'Do you have the Rockhampton *Morning Bulletin* and your other papers sent to Pittsburgh, to check them for xenophobia?'

'I get sent a range, just so I'm in the know. My favourite is the *Sunshine Coast Daily* because that's where the action is. The paper with the most potential is the *Queensland Times*. Make no mistake, Queensland is where the action is going to be in Australia; it's growing at two-and-a- half per cent population per annum – that's pretty dramatic stuff. The Rockhampton *Morning Bulletin* is an important paper too because it covers such an enormous area, and is central to a number of things that condition Australia's export performance. The biggest coal- and beef- exporting city in Australia.

'What changes have you ordered editorially in four years?'

'Great editorial emphasis rather than change. I like to emphasise that the product is all-important, despite the fact that we've 70 per cent circulation and penetration in all our markets. We can hardly sell any *more* copies but we can sell *better*. And one thing you can absolutely guarantee is that each year I'll go to the editors' conference and talk to them. It's an enjoyable commitment. Queensland offers a luxuriant *à la carte* menu for conferences. I mean we can hold it at Coffs Harbour or up on the Reef or at Cairns with that marvellous new hotel up there. Just stunning. It's a triumph of Japanese pension funds over sanity!

How could they have funded these things? They'll get their return in Heaven!'

O'Reilly's tender documents for the Fairfax businesses said as much about him as a newspaper proprietor and marketing expert as they did about Fairfax: two volumes of statistics, perfect-bound in clear perspex, containing several dozen bar charts, pie charts, Venn diagrams, rhomboid graphs, algorisms and miscellaneous runes. They were the kind of documents – so detailed and cocksure in their predictions about the future – that old-school newspaper men such as Lord Hartwell's board of directors at the *Daily Telegraph* would have found thoroughly impertinent.

There were assumptions about the state of the Australian economy until the end of the decade, assumptions about the volume of display advertising, demographic matrices contrasting the implications for Fairfax properties with Murdoch's News Corporation, bar charts comparing the classified advertising segments of the *Melbourne Age* with the *Melbourne Sun*, predictions of exchange rate movements through the next millennium and a three-phase management strategy – oddly reminiscent of an old Soviet five-year plan – for 'realising the full potential of the group'. Still more chilling were his cost-cutting blueprints – set out in computer graphics in the shape of giant arrows imposed on existing balance sheets – demonstrating how 'the editorial expense ratio of the *Australian Financial Review* is too high, despite the intrinsically high cost nature of staff involved' and how reductions in group editorial expenditure were both viable and desirable. Reading these meticulously dispassionate formulae, all constructed before O'Reilly had met more than a handful of the Fairfax journalists, made one realise why he is such an effective manager at Heinz; a company's balance sheet is seldom a history of how profit was achieved, it is an incitement to further profit.

'When Dr O'Reilly studies a set of accounts,' I was told by one of his Dublin executives, 'he is like a surgeon, having no knowledge of the personality of the patient, but who can nevertheless find a host of inert organs waiting to be tightened or extracted. He has a gift for operating on many apparently conflicting levels at once. For instance, I don't believe he has ever lost his sense of romance about newspapers and yet he can be a dispassionate businessman where they're concerned too. He is quite in love, you know, with the idea of the *Washington Post*.

Serving on their board of directors means a very great deal to Dr O'Reilly.'

I asked O'Reilly if he turned up to all their board meetings.

'They only have six a year and I don't miss them. Also I've introduced a wonderful group of what I call the Irish "Murphia" on to the board, much to Kay's amusement and dismay, because the board now has a fellow called Don Keough, who's the president of Coca-Cola; Jim Burke of Johnson & Johnson; Bill Ruane who's an investment man from New York and George Gillespie. All Irish Murphia. Five directors. And a lot of us are of suspiciously Republican sentiment for this great Democrat-run newspaper, so board meetings are a lot of fun. After the meeting we have a good lunch at which all the editors appear – Bob Kaiser, Len Downie, Meg Greenfield . . . And the night before we have a full dinner of the board at which *everything* is discussed. So the board meeting *per se* is mechanistic, the flanking opportunities.'

'Are you paid to be on the board of the *Washington Post*? Is there an honorarium?'

'I think it's 25,000 dollars.'

'How did Kay Graham come into your life?'

'Well Kay has a very close relationship with Warren Buffett – America's greatest investor – and I think Warren Buffett has been a supporter and investor in and admirer of the Heinz company, and in advising her about new directors he said, "You should consider Tony O'Reilly." I went on an Institute of Foreign Relations trip to Israel with her and we got a chance to meet socially. I liked her immensely and immediately. So, for my Heinz background, she asked me would I like to join.'

Anthony John Francis O'Reilly was born in Dublin in 1936, the only child of an Irish customs officer who didn't marry O'Reilly's mother until 1973, after his first wife had died. School was Belvedere, the Dublin boys' school run by Jesuits where one of the monks, Father O'hAoah, as chance would have it, would later teach the Marxist President Robert Mugabe at an African Jesuit school in Zimbabwe; a coincidence on which O'Reilly capitalised when he talked Mugabe into establishing Heinz's vast Zimbabwean baked beans and washing soda factories. It was at University College, Dublin, where he studied law, that he became an exceptional rugger player, who by the age of 25 had played for Ireland 29 times, for the British and Irish Lions team ten times (including the championship British Lions tour of South Africa in 1955) and established himself as a national sporting hero. The Dublin press nicknamed him Lover Boy. His rugger player's physique also earned him a screen test for the lead part in the film *Ben Hur*, the role which later went to Charlton Heston.

'Tony O'Reilly was a celebrity at the age of 22,' says a sports editor on Ralph Ingersoll's opposition *Sunday Press*, 'and he never lost his taste for recognition.'

After university he took a succession of courses and jobs that were not in fact particularly long on recognition: a PhD in agricultural marketing at Bradford University in England – which enables him to style himself Dr – followed by stints with industrial consultants and agricultural product suppliers. In 1966 he got the top job at the Irish Dairy Board where he transformed the image of Irish butter, wrapping it in gold foil and renaming it Kerrygold. He was headhunted by Heinz as managing director of the English company, and three years later relocated to Pittsburgh as senior vice president for North America and the Pacific. Caught in a relentless upwind at Heinz World Head-quarters, he was promoted to vice president and Chief Operating Officer, and only a year later, aged 37, his business cards and corporate writing paper were once again rendered redundant when he was named president. Within five years he had mopped up the last corporate role in the building not already his own, that of Chief Executive Officer, and saw Heinz's market capitalisation soar in his first decade of power from $908 million to $11 billion by the end of 1990.

One of the enigmas about Tony O'Reilly is how he choreographs his working life. Like Murdoch, his speed of movement gives an impression of being in several places simultaneously. Within any ten-day period he will address a Heinz convention of security analysts at an hotel in San Francisco; attend board meetings of the Washington Post Company in Washington DC, the New York Stock Exchange in Manhattan, Atlantic Resources, the company he set up to hunt for oil and gas off the Irish coast, and the Graduate School of Business Administration at Harvard, Massachusetts; chair further board meetings for Independent Newspapers in Dublin, for Wedgwood china and for the European Advisory Committee of Bankers' Trust; and pop up at a conference on the nutritional value of skipjack and yellowfin tuna ('less fat and more protein per calorie than prime turkey'). The fact that he holds the triptych of key executive posts at Heinz means no colleague can easily question his lightning absences from Pittsburgh, and he has developed the knack, by sending a stream of detailed faxes on Heinz business from hotel suites, of appearing to be in Pennsylvania even when altogether elsewhere.

'I don't divide my time in any strategic way, I respond to it,' he told me. 'You get to a certain level in a corporation where you've been around for such a long time that the rhythms of the company are pretty clear. Firstly it has a staccato quality to it: that is, if they need me that's my first responsibility. Secondly there are periods in the year of low intensity and high intensity. An American corporation like Heinz bases itself very much on business planning. The whole process of trying to lend a spurious illusion of precision to the future fascinates Americans and amazes Europeans, but I'm prepared to play the game. So we go through this planning cycle that takes about three months and during that period I'm incommunicado to all but the most extreme and urgent requests from Greece . . .'

O'Reilly shot a fond glance in the direction of Chryss Goulandris who was attempting to place a telephone call from Glandore to Athens, but having difficulty in obtaining the international dialling tone from the local exchange.

'Then I travel to all the affiliants,' he went on, lapsing into the business school jargon to which he is alarmingly prone when discussing corporate matters. 'We share time with their executives and try and understand the capital appetites of the future. That then gives way to a period in late May through August in which the basic structure and goals of our businesses, which are autonomous, are set. There's a sort of clinical absolutism about it that enables us to luxuriate in the notion that the individual executives of the company are working hard. From my point of view it means that I don't have to worry about China at the moment. I know there's a guy in China worrying about China a lot more than I am! We don't pay very much to come and work at Heinz but we pay an *enormous* amount for achievement. The goals are firmly set: if you get them you get the money, if you don't you don't.

'The theme is quite clear in all the businesses I'm involved in,' he went on. 'Everybody who works with me should be capable of setting up the Knight Trust when they leave, hopefully under less fractious terms than the founder of the Knight Trust!'

This was a sly reference to Andrew Knight's defection from Conrad Black's *Daily Telegraph* to Murdoch's News International, and Black's reported indignation that Knight should have assigned part of the £14 million he made from Telegraph share options into a charitable trust. O'Reilly claimed to take the opposite view: he would like his retired Ketchup and newspaper executives to be setting up charitable trusts all over the place.

His Heinz and newspaper strategies both combine stringent cost-cutting and delegation (he calls it 'empowering') with heroic marketing. Each year his managers are challenged to slim another cent from the unit cost of seafood cocktail or print contracts. 'We're in a tough, unyielding, low-margin, nickel-and-dime business, and I guess I bring a European pragmatism to the job,' he says. He is developing a sophisticated computer system at Heinz which will adjust production levels in every country based on factors like raw material costs, local taxes and the exchange rate ('Take our Ketchup production. We make it in Holland, England and Spain. The computer will tell us which country, economically, would be best for us to produce the most Ketchup in. If the Spaniards have a deteriorating exchange rate, we may use the plant there. If we see the Dutch guilder strengthening against the English pound, we might use the English plant. It gives us an extra 5 per cent operating profit'). O'Reilly once saved one-and-a-half million dollars by eliminating the back label from the tomato Ketchup bottle.

Colleagues say he will make light of any subject 'except marketing and brands'. Editors of his papers sometimes mistakenly tease their proprietor about his Heinz enterprises, implying there is something not quite respectable about devoting so much energy to Kozy Kitten dry cat food. O'Reilly's response is icily to compare the return on equity at Heinz with less efficient media brands. His sincerity about branding cannot be overestimated: to Tony O'Reilly the *Irish Independent* is a premium brand, the *Daily Star* is a brand, the Warwick *Bush Telegraph* is a brand exactly like spaghetti hoops and Skippy dog food.

Conversely he struck me as more open-minded about the content of his newspapers, and more committed to the certainty of editorial change, than any other European proprietor.

'It is rare,' said one of his Dublin editors, 'for Dr O'Reilly to say no to anything. He seems not to understand the meaning of the word, and certainly doesn't see it as a useful one in his vocabulary. By the same token he doesn't expect anyone who works for him to say no either. Occasionally in newspapers you need the no word too, saying no is part of the discipline of editorship. So it sometimes concerns me when he sees his newspaper editors and his brand managers at Heinz in the same light: people who lack the imagination to make the papers prosper without his own vision being sold to them on a regular basis. Having said that, when he summons you for a ride in the back of the Bentley, which generally means a meeting on the way to the airport because he's flying off somewhere, it never quite seems like that because he gathers you up in his charm.

'One of Dr O'Reilly's great skills – possibly his *greatest* skill,' he continued, 'is that despite all the dollar-crimping that goes on, his businesses retain a kudos and swank. You never feel, on the inside, that his enterprises are tacky. And a lot of this feeling stems from Dr O'Reilly himself. He's such a charismatic, *big* fellow, with so much personal style, that when he jets into wherever you happen to be, with a broad smile across his face and all the appearance of being so pleased to see you, you forget while he's there that he's made you sweat for the sake of those few extra dollars.'

First Degree Murdoch

The rapacious appetite of the unstoppable media machine

You report to the gatehouse, clear security and are collected by a cleancut youth in a battery-operated golf cart. He is dressed in ironed jeans, sneakers and a Fox Studios baseball cap and looks like a hired hand from Disneyworld.

'Hiyya,' he says. 'Climb in the buggy. My name is Clancy. And you're visiting with Mr Murdoch today, OK?'

We purr off together in the golf buggy, shielded from the Beverly Hills glare by a dinky linen canopy, and Clancy points out interesting sights as though I were on a full studio tour.

'These posters,' said Clancy, as we passed a thicket of billboards, 'are advertising the big shows right now, *Beverly Hills 90210* and the Simpsons, right. And see those buildings over there, Main Street and the old Western saloon? They're façades. They're still used for shooting.'

'Do you see much of Mr Murdoch around the studio?' I asked.

Clancy shrugged. 'Sharon Stone was here on the lot yesterday. And Jack Nicholson.'

We drew up outside a two-storey office block, cream-painted and, it emerged, not merely a façade.

'Mr Murdoch's still speaking on the telephone to Sydney,' said one of his three assistants. 'I think he's finishing now.' She checked the time on the wall of clocks, which showed that it was 4 p.m. in New York, 9 p.m. in London and 6 a.m. in Sydney. I wondered which of his Australian executives had been woken by Murdoch at such an early hour. In any global corporation the telephone can be the equivalent of a dawn raid by the Gestapo; call them when their blood sugar is at its lowest.

'Sorry to keep you waiting out there,' said Rupert Murdoch bowling through into his outer sanctum. 'It's good to see you again. Flight OK?' he asked, shepherding me through into his office. 'It's good to see you again.'

All this *again* treatment was startling. My two previous encounters with Murdoch had been fleeting and long ago, in a room full of his eldest daughter's friends. It seemed nothing short of miraculous that he had any memory of them at all. Some days later I learnt that Prue Murdoch had rung her father prior to my arrival 'to remind Dad that he'd met you before and to be nice to my friend and not to be grumpy with you.'

Rather like one's first sight of the Taj Mahal, there is a slight feeling of disappointment on first seeing Rupert Murdoch, that he isn't bigger. This is what he looks like in real life, the world's most famous newspaper owner. At 61, his height is just below average, his hair has recently completed its transition from black to grey, and the deep furrows across his brow are as pronounced and regular as the backbone of a large pike. His left eye narrows darkly when he concentrates, like a gunslinger in an early Fox Western, and he has a habit of clenching his teeth when prevaricating. He gives off a powerful aura of determination and strength, but not, as I had been warned by some parties, of profane menace.

Of all the newspaper empires on the planet, Rupert Murdoch's is the greatest, both in size and geographical spread. He operates in more continents (four: North America, Europe, the Far East and Australia) than any other owner. Although he owns fewer newspaper titles than Conrad Black and Lord Thomson, his total circulation of 60 million a week is far greater. He owns more world-class newspapers than the others (three: *The Times*, the *Sunday Times* and the *Australian*) and more big circulation populars (six: the *Sun*, the *News of the World* and *Today* in London, the *Boston Herald*, New York *Post*, the *Daily Telegraph Mirror* in Sydney). He owns papers in specialised places too: Tasmania, Fiji, Papua New Guinea, Hungary and Cairns on the Great Barrier Reef. For a man with media properties in every time zone around the globe (he is never, I worked out, much more than an hour's flight from an office where he pays the rent) he also looked strikingly fit and stress-free.

'Actually I'm *not*,' he said. 'I'm stressed out all the time.'

He laughed ruefully. 'Actually I don't think I call it stress. Normal day-to-day stress is excitement and I love it and handle it very well. If you can handle it it's *fun*, and most times I can absolutely. There's no stress like going to the races, backing a few horses, not that I've been to the races for 30 years, I'm just giving that as an analogy. But seriously, there *have* been times – perfectly normal times – when I get overtired and the stress is about a couple of problems or something that can get you down. And that's when I think it's dangerous – not in terms of breakdown but in terms of the physical. Stress can be very bad for you physically if you let it get to you.

'And jetlag,' he went on. 'I used to be jetlagged all the time, rushing about with an incredible schedule, one country to the next and all of which time you're jetlagged. It became a cumulative thing, so I really have tried very hard this year to cut down the amount of travel I do, I use the telephone instead. I still go to New York once or twice a month, and someplace else overseas at least once a month. I went to London the other day just for a day, from here and back, and I was really surprised at myself that I handled it well. I just think perhaps I'm older and wiser and drink less and all those other things that help you survive. If you're physically fit it helps handle all this. I live atop a big hill [in Beverly Hills] and I use my bicycle, other times I walk down the hill and up again like I did this morning at half-past-four. It's a pretty heavy 40-minute walk.'

'You went for a walk at half-past-four in the morning? It must have been pitch dark.'

'Yeah, that's right. I got back just as the sun was coming up, the light was coming up in the east.'

'And then what did you do?'

'Grabbed a bite of breakfast, came in here. I find I can get by pretty well on six hours' sleep. It's good to get in early. You think you're going to get your desk clear, and you can have longer conversations than you would otherwise to London or New York or the other direction to Hong Kong. Only problem is you then have other people coming in early too who want to see you at 8.30, so you don't get your desk clear the way you wanted to, but the only way to get out of that is to be in here at five and I'm not going to start doing that, that's Si Newhouse's game.'

Murdoch sat opposite me on a cream-upholstered armchair, his legs rather skittishly tucked underneath him on the seat. At the end of his long, oatmeal-coloured office a screen broadcast the Foxnet cable network via satellite. The volume was turned down and an episode of *Cops* unfolded, unwatched, over his right shoulder. On a bookshelf were biographies of Kissinger, de Gaulle and Donald Trump, and a terracotta statue of a Chinese horse. The paintings – rather beautiful abstracts of the Australian countryside by Fred Williams – have moved with Murdoch from office to office, and hung at different times in London, Sydney and Manhattan.

'How much time are you able to give to your newspapers now?'

'A couple of hours a day.'

'As much as that?'

'Oh at least. I guess half of that time is spent managing them and the other half reading them. But my reading the newspapers these days is more like copy tasting, I go in and out of them and look at them and read what interests me.'

'Is it difficult to tell from this distance whether they're performing well or badly editorially?'

'I don't think so. You can be wrong about specific stories, the importance and so on, but the real test is do you enjoy picking up the paper and reading it?'

'Does it frustrate you if you don't?'

'It kills you. I tell you, it's *terrible*. You know they're getting it wrong over there and then you find they're persistently getting it wrong. Then it's time to start shaking the bushes a bit.'

'Do you still ring up and say you think a headline is no good.'

'Yeah. Mmmm.'

'Or that the *Daily Mirror* beat the *Sun* to a story?'

'I never think that. That's no risk. Not with the *Mirror*. But I certainly call and speak to all the editors – the tabloid editors perhaps two or three times a week and the Sunday editors more likely once.'

'But that's about 400 telephone calls a week. You own fifteen Sunday papers and 109 dailies or bi-weeklies.'

Murdoch laughed – it sounded like a man clearing his throat – and said, 'Yeah, well to be honest with you I concentrate on the big city papers. The four big city ones from Australia, and all the papers from London of course – the competitors too – and Boston. The only drawback of living here is that they tend to be 24 hours late, sometimes 36 hours late. So by the time I read them and call anyone about them they've forgotten what the hell they published and it all seems a bit irrelevant.

'When I lived in New York,' he said, 'I could get the British papers the same day, the whole pile of them. I miss that, especially the Sunday ones. It's a bit disappointing on a Monday and it keeps me awake half Monday night. There's so much good stuff in the British Sundays. So much better than the American Sunday papers which, journalistically, are almost afterthoughts. They have more sections, more supplements, but the news pages are the worst of the week – lazy rubbish. In London and Australia you have a separate reporting staff to do research and keep their stories for Sunday. Sunday papers actually break news, a lot of news. They don't in America.'

'What about your own American Sunday papers?'

'Yeah, they break news. In San Antonio [Texas] we follow the British pattern and have, not a totally separate staff but some separate reporting and writing staff for Sunday. It has made a big difference. We were way behind in San Antonio. [Murdoch had the *Express-News*; his competitor was Hearst's *San Antonio Light*.] We reversed it. I would say that we are now in revenue terms taking at least two dollars for every one dollar they take and it used to be the other way around.'

'Do they put up a good fight, Hearst newspapers?'

'A pretty good fight. They fight particularly hard there, because San Antonio is Frank's home city [Frank Bennack, CEO of the Hearst Corporation]. I call them stickers, they hang in a situation and lose money for twenty years before they close a paper down. They did it here, they had the *Herald Examiner* here in LA and goodness knows what they were losing for years and years and years. Every now and again there'd be a new initiative or a new publisher or a new editor would come in and dress it up and it didn't work. But they must have lost 200 million dollars before they conceded the turf to the Chandlers.'

'Is it strategy that wins the day in circulation wars or simply money?'

'Money's important. You need promotion money. But the product matters more so I'd answer strategy. It was my basic strategy in San Antonio that did it here; it wasn't *all* right that we did, we drew a lot of criticism. [This was an unspoken reference to the sensationalism he imported to Texas, the violence and crime reporting and the headlines that have become journalistic classics: "Uncle Tortures Pet With Hot Fork", "Handless Body Found" and a completely fictitious front-page lead "Killer Bees Move North".] One thing that was obvious,' he said, 'is that all the advertising money is on Sunday, we must pull ahead on Sunday. So we added sections and we promoted on television and put in competitions and things and generally pushed it very hard for three years before we got ahead. The key was the product: getting the paper right. San Antonio was a pretty transient kind of place when we bought the paper – still is – and spreading fast. We studied the TV programmes to see what people were watching. The leading station by a mile put out two hours of local news every afternoon, just following the cops around with hand-held cameras. It could be quite violent. And so we turned our paper pretty sharply, with lots of crime reporting and the courts. It's a violent city, San Antonio, and that's what people wanted to read. We're ahead in circulation 50,000 a day now, maybe 45,000. I think it's 70,000 on Sunday and 45,000 daily, it's to that order, enough to certainly dominate. And we dominate in the right part of town: where the money and middle class is.'

I said I'd heard a rumour that he was nevertheless searching for a buyer for the *Express-News*; that it was one of the items at the top of his selling list.

'I've not heard that rumour,' Murdoch replied. 'I'm always being told I'll sell this, I'll sell that. But I've not heard it about San Antonio.'

Three weeks later the sale of the *Express-News* to the Hearst Corporation was announced. The price was $185 million. A condition of the agreement was that Murdoch's paper wouldn't be closed, and that the Hearsts' own *Light* would be put up for sale and, in the event of not finding a buyer, shut down. Murdoch had conceded the patch, but done so on his own terms.

One of the most extraordinary things about Rupert Murdoch is how he manages to keep track of his 125 papers when the newspapers themselves form only one-third of his media empire. (In 1992 his revenues by industry segment were newspapers 37 per cent, magazines 24 per cent, films 8 per cent, books 13 per cent, television 16 per cent and strange miscellaneous operations like electronic computerised road map data 2 per cent.) I had visited proprietors who owned only a handful of papers who assured me that it was impossible for them even to slip away on holiday for a fortnight, for fear that the whole thing would collapse in their absence: that their editors would fill up the papers with libels and their management embark on harebrained schemes of their own. With Murdoch, the scale of operations is impossibly large. Every week – in some cases every day – the circulation figures of 125 newspapers hit his desk at Twentieth Century-Fox, along with the numbers for all his papers' competitors.

'They're faxed,' he said. 'Because of the time differential they generally come through during the night. When I arrive here at about six I look through some, but usually I take a handful home to read.'

It struck me that Murdoch's existence in a distant time zone, poring over the circulation results while the editors who achieved them are asleep in their beds, only added to his potential for terrorisation. Like a schoolmaster presiding over a huge class of 125 boys, there must be editors he has singled out for substandard work that he's keeping an eye on, new boys, trusted seniors left to get on with it until they eventually get above themselves, boys sitting miles away at the back of the class, almost out of range of the blackboard rubber, like the editors of his *Sunday Tasmanian* or the *Post Courier* in Papua New Guinea. But exactly like the schoolmaster he will sometimes appear without warning behind an editor's shoulder, to check his prep and, if necessary, boot him out into the corridor.

It struck me, too, that the potential for drift in a corporation as large as News must be enormous. There must be newspapers that, however good Murdoch's intentions, never get a minute of his personal attention from one year to the next. What time could he possibly earmark for his *Pyramid News* or *Northern Beachcomber*, both in Queensland, or for his daily *Mai Nap* in Hungary?

I questioned him on his peripheral titles to test how informed he really is.

'How's *Mai Nap* doing?'

'Really very well. Holding steady in circulation, about 14 or 15 per cent up in advertising. Not much is happening in Hungary right now, except we get offered more and more newspapers. There must be a hundred newspapers for sale there!'

'What about *Super!Zeitung* in eastern Germany?'

Murdoch grimaced. 'By the time your book is published we'll have either sold it or closed it,' he replied. He wasn't kidding. He closed the paper before I'd even arrived back in London fifteen hours later. When I took off from Los Angeles he owned it, when I landed it had already gone.

I said, 'Are you sorry about closing it?' The launch had been attended by a good deal of razzmatazz – the first Western publishing venture in former East Germany after the Berlin Wall came down. Murdoch had formed an equal partnership with Hubert Burda, the German media tyro, and it had been conceived as a kind of East German *Sun* for sex-starved and disorientated old communists, full of bare-breasted women, flashy cars they couldn't afford and advice on how to adapt to Western ways. It had developed instead into a newspaper for readers who already regretted unification, despised the West and had a deep interest in hard porn.

'Circulation's been extremely good from the start,' he said. 'We reached 450,000, but it's turned into an awful, prolonged argument with Hubert Burda so we've said "call it quits". It got politically – after a while – crazy, in taste, everything. Anti-West in an extreme way. It's one thing to stand up for the rights of the East and tell them how to convert and how to become Westerners and what to do and be on their side; it's another thing to really cause deep divisions. And in terms of taste its entertainment and sexual stories went way beyond my limits. Although I admit it's a different culture in Germany – who knows what you're meant to do over there? I mean you couldn't run the London *Sun* in America, you couldn't run *Super!Zietung* anywhere else for sure – not in an English-language country.'

'Doesn't it anyway take away some of the fun of owning a paper if you can't read the language?'

'It takes away *all* the fun. Someone reads it for me every day and translates it and draws it to my attention, but it's pretty futile unless you're sure of what's going in.'

'You must have the same problem with *Nai Lalakai*.'

Murdoch looked blank. 'Which paper's that? Not one of ours.'

'It's your Fijian-language newspaper. In Fiji.'

'It's in English, the paper I have. The *Fiji Times*.'

'In fact,' I pointed out, as though jogging the memory of some elderly marchioness that she has a small Vermeer that she's overlooked among her greater treasures, 'In fact you also have two small foreign-language papers in Fiji, one in Fijian, the other in Hindi.' Both are clearly listed in the 1991 report and accounts.

'I haven't seen those,' replied Murdoch sceptically. 'The one I'm sent is in English.'

In the previous four years I had bumped into News Corporation journalists peddling an identical complaint. It didn't seem to matter where I was – Boston, Sydney and then in Bangkok – it was the same grievance. And it was always phrased in such similar terms that it is clearly part of the corporate subculture. What the three journos – they were all Australians – bellyached about, was the way they believed their work is syndicated by Murdoch around the world. You write an article for the *Australian*, they said, or for one of his other rags, and the minute it's left your terminal – virtually before it's been read by your own editor – *whoosh*, it's gone halfway round the globe and been slapped into some other Murdoch paper too. No extra payment for you either, mate, they don't even tell you most of the time. Think about it, they said, all that free material, no wonder he's loaded.

Rupert Murdoch's own perspective, as a media owner, is more elevated. He speaks in terms of global publishing, the media village, the New World Order, the digital electronic network by which tens of thousands of words of copy can ricochet around the planet from one newspaper to another along optical-fibre wires. In newspapers, big can sometimes be better as well as blander.

'How much of your papers' journalism gets printed simultaneously in several countries?'

'Well, *The Times* and particularly the *Sunday Times* is enormously useful to the papers in Australia, Boston and Hong Kong. And photographs from all papers go around pretty fast. It's a sort of loose network. All the editors know each other, they've all worked together at some time and they help each other enormously. A huge story that someone gets eaten by a shark in Perth, you can bet the editor of the Perth *Sunday Times* is going to ring the editor of the *Sun* in London and the editors of the papers in Sydney. It gets around in such a way that we probably beat the opposition.'

'How exactly do you juggle all these territories simultaneously?'

'Day to day I trust the executives on the spot to get on with it. They should solve the problems themselves. If they're very big they'll certainly consult or call about it, but the executive on the spot really is boss; they don't refer to me as the boss – I hope. I'd like to go [to each area of operations] for about ten days every three months: you get a feel, there's real quality time, you get involved and you can withdraw and not leave a great vacuum. If you go in and out every two weeks people wait for you to come, you make decisions, you go away and there's a vacuum and it's really bad. It's bad for management. You've *got* to let your people manage and let your people edit too. If you go and spend two weeks every three months – or every four months – you really get a deep understanding and your telephone calls that follow for the next three months are a lot more intelligent. But the fact of the matter is I usually can't do this. I fly into a crisis that's blown up, or a crisis that I've more or less precipitated myself.'

Murdoch laughed again, this time in a series of raucous gurgles as though he was gargling in a bathroom. When he wants to use it, his charm is overwhelming and you can understand how the crocodile of ex-editors, who ever afterwards shake their heads in wonder that they didn't know better, were so easily seduced into working for him. He can give out a strong impression of being instantly likeable and informal, that he's taking you into his confidence, that he's sharing private insights because he holds you in special esteem. And there is an attractive modesty, a playfulness, in the way he describes his schedule of work. It is a powerful weapon.

'It is quite a balance you need to strike,' he said, 'between giving your editors elbow room and playing your full part yourself, taking responsibility. Take an outfit like Fairfax. That place has had no boss for – I'll shock you when I say this – for at least twenty years. I'm not sure it's not thirty years, it can't be. James Fairfax, the chairman before Warwick, absolutely *abdicated*. He played little role, he was only there for a couple of hours in the morning, not running the business. I think in fairness James would say he took it as his role to be a non-executive chairman, to encourage the editors and so on but he certainly didn't influence them. He would say that was a proper role; I would say myself that it was an abdication, he had the greatest opportunity of his life. And so then came the big kerfuffle of the takeover and the fight, and Warwick took over except *he* didn't really take over either. Warwick had never seen anyone in his family go to work on a regular basis and run the thing. I said to him, "You ought to be there," and he said, "No, I'd just like to be known as the owner." And so the banks came and took it away from him.'

I said that I thought the pressure on Warwick Fairfax during his brief tenure after hijacking the company must have been immense, the constant profiles and carping in rival media including his own.

Murdoch shrugged. 'Yeah well we all get that. Look at what some of the media all over the world have called me: "arrogant Aussie" – that was the title of a book about me for Christ's sake – "a sinister force", "a shark in the guise of a snake". It's tough but you get used to it. I've been around too long and developed a pretty thick skin. I don't read books about me, I don't read most of the attacks on me, it's basically water off a duck's back as far as I'm concerned. When someone says something and you think there's a greater truth in it, that worries you a bit – I don't want to suggest that one's oblivious to criticism. I can remember once or twice I've been stung by something. You only get stung when they're right. You have to try and distinguish between the genuine criticism and the blind bleating.'

'And you can at least get your own back through your papers. People keep telling me that you only keep the *Boston Herald* going to annoy Teddy Kennedy because he forced you to divest the *New York Post*, and because Boston's his city.'

'No, no, that's not true.' Murdoch chuckled. 'It makes a little money and we're proud of it. We have fun with it too. It's a little outpost up there amongst all those Harvard Marxists or Socialists or whatever they are.'

'On the subject of Marxists, every article about you recently says you've turned to religion. Is that true?'

'No. They say I'm a born again Christian and a Catholic convert and so on. I'm certainly a practising Christian, I go to church quite a bit but not every Sunday and I tend to go to Catholic church – because my wife is Catholic, I have not formally converted. And I get increasingly disenchanted with the C of E or Episcopalians as they call themselves here. But no, I'm not intensely religious as I'm sometimes described.'

Just then Rupert Murdoch's studious-looking youngest son, Lachlan, appeared at the door escorting a Chinese businessman. He needed his father to say goodbye to him before his flight back to Peking. The businessman, it emerged, had played some decisive role in News Corporation's contract to print the new Chinese telephone directory.

After they left the room, Rupert Murdoch said, 'The son you just met is out of Princeton, and I've got another boy – James – just out of

Harvard. My daughter Elisabeth's working in television, works as long hours as I do, in the programming department in downtown LA. She's only 24 but she's eager. And there's my daughter Prue, her husband's the circulation manager at *The Times* in London and doing very well at it. He's very modest, works hard though.

'They'll all have the opportunity to prove themselves at least,' he said. 'And my wife's an outside director of the company now. I find Anna's the most critical of all our directors at board meetings. I say to her afterwards, "Why didn't you say that at home if that's what you think?" She'll speak up, you bet she does. She's got least to fear! She's there because I just want the assurance, should anything happen to me, that there'll be someone keeping the door open for the children to come along.'

To write about Rupert Murdoch is to invite criticsm. Long before I visited him in Beverly Hills, people I scarcely knew began to contact me with their own impressions and experiences. They were concerned that I might fundamentally misread his character; that I might *like* Rupert Murdoch.

The network of his detractors circles the globe. Its membership of sacked editors, sacked managers, embittered competitors, aggrieved journalists and sullen former colleagues crosses ideological and cultural frontiers. They reminded me of a victims' support scheme; a freemasonry of malcontents with a story to tell, emphatic that their own reading of Murdoch is the orthodox one.

As a pressure group, they were emotive. They said, 'I trust Murdoch's going to come out of your book very badly.' And, 'As a journalist yourself, you can see better than most people what a terrible effect he's had on newspapers.' The specific accusations varied from place to place. In Britain, his critics charged him with republicanism and downmarketing his papers (in discussion of Rupert Murdoch, the verb 'to downmarket' is often so employed) and, by the political left, of right-wing manipulation. In America, they restricted their criticism of the quality of the journalism. In Hong Kong, two Chinese journalists on the Murdoch payroll expressed their fears that the *South China Morning Post* would inevitably become less objective with time, though they accepted there was no sign of it so far. They asked, as a society only now emerging from half a century of communism, were they not merely exchanging one species of ideological totalitarianism for another? And in Australia, where Murdoch phobia is strongest, his critics tended to denigrate the entire culture of News Limited. In Sydney, a well-educated former reporter on the *Australian* had this to say about life on Murdoch papers.

'I don't think News Limited tolerates integrity. I think it's afraid of integrity. The editors are all cut from the same cloth, they're terrorists in suits. They all subscribe to the old school that the more fear you instil into the people who work for you, the better the product. They are men who in my view show all the signs of being anti-intellectual and homophobic. Journalists on Murdoch's papers aren't given the freedom to operate as journalists should operate. There are subjects you just can't write about. You don't write about aboriginal land sites, giving the aboriginal side of the story. You don't include union misgivings in any labour dispute. During the Gulf War you were very hard pushed to get a story into the paper about anyone in the whole of Australia *opposed* to the war. Take the AIDS issue: the greatest public health issue of our time. Because it's transmitted primarily by homosexuals, the dissemination of news about AIDS is derelict in Murdoch's papers out here. Murdoch doesn't have to spell it out. He doesn't send memos, to my knowledge, on the attitude his editors should take. The people who become Murdoch editors just know instinctively what is acceptable, what is not.

'That is why,' he said, 'there has always been a three-lane highway from News Limited to Fairfax, but only a footbridge from Fairfax to Murdoch.'

I include this long spiel because it is representative of countless others I heard elsewhere; the unvarying line of the disgruntled left-leaning journalist.

But the critics of Keith Rupert Murdoch are not restricted to the left. Perhaps it is fitting, in a global communications company engaged in every stratum of media, that he should attract every stratum of critic, from the British intellectual right (and the non-intellectual right: what Murdoch disparagingly calls 'the Establishment') to the American liberal consensus ('those Harvard Marxists'). And the roster of Murdoch's detractors has accelerated with his empire; each acquisition, each change of editor and policy has added another. Harold

Evans, once of *The Times*; Clay Felker, once of *New York* magazine; Eric Beecher, once of the *Melbourne Herald*; Barry Diller, once of Twentieth Century-Fox; Stephen Chao, once of Fox Television, the clamour of articulate carping becomes ever louder. Rupert Murdoch after forty years a media owner reminded me of Margaret Thatcher after eleven years as Prime Minister, encircled by deposed Cabinet ministers each with his own chronicle of disillusionment. When News Corporation ran into its debt crisis in 1990, there were almost as many former Murdoch henchmen around the world revelling in his discomfiture as there were bankers rescheduling the borrowings to save the empire.

People said he can be querulous and cynical about his employees and their motives. 'He is genuinely of the opinion that money can change everything. He uses money both as a panacea and a weapon,' a former News Corp manager told me. 'When he wants you at News, he'll pay you what it takes (that's if he *really* wants you, News aren't the best payers). When your face no longer fits, he pays you off, or gets someone else to; Rupert's quite a coward when it comes to firing colleagues. You generally get the message your time is up because he begins to pick on you in public, in meetings. Nothing you say or do is right. It is unpleasant to watch it happen to somebody else, worse when it happens to you.'

A senior editor at the *Sunday Times* told me. 'He is charming one-to-one, nobody is more charming. In large set-piece executive meetings he can be difficult and impatient. He will often single out a fall-guy, a victim, maybe *pour encourager les autres*. And he never forgets anything, which can be another means of intimidation. There was a meeting with some of the machine managers, a routine production meeting, and Rupert was furious about a press that was continuing to break down after it had been expensively repaired. "You told me that when I'd spent this money it would never give us trouble again," he kept shouting at this poor guy. "Did you or did you not say that? You did say that! Well, are you telling me now that you didn't mean it, or are you telling me that you don't know your job? Which is it?" '

It would be misleading, however, to infer that Rupert Murdoch at 61 is a proprietor without supporters. The pro-Murdoch lobby is less loquacious but at least as strong as his detractors. His principal lieutenants are not so much loyal as bedazzled. There is more genuine admiration for Rupert Murdoch inside News than for any other proprietor in their own companies. Other media owners, asked which proprietor they most rate, almost all replied Murdoch. Katharine Graham, Conrad Black, Tony O'Reilly, Sally Aw Sian, Ralph Ingersoll all nominated him as the most impressive of their peers. 'Charming', 'direct', and 'unstoppable' were the three, not always compatible adjectives they used to describe him.

'I have a problem about Rupert,' says Elizabeth Rees-Jones who ran his British magazine company. 'I'm the person in the world who says Rupert Murdoch is the best-mannered, most courteous person I've ever met. When I say this to other people, even people who know him well, they ask, "Are we talking about the same person here?" I think the explanation is that Rupert's intuitive about people. The way he deals with you is the way you are; if you're a hooligan, he deals with you like a hooligan. If you're courteous, he deals with you in an immensely courteous way in return. I never once went into his office when he didn't stand up from his desk and come round his desk and shake your hand. And this was someone who *works* for him, not a visitor. He shows the same good manners on the telephone. Because most of our telephone conversations were transatlantic, he tended to ring me at home in the evenings. Every call would start, "I'm sorry, is this a good time to call you, otherwise we can talk another time." And at the end of every conversation he'd say, "Liz, I can't thank you enough for everything you do for us." It makes you feel like a star. You end up thinking, "I'd walk the gangplank for that man." John Evans says you end up as a junkie working for him: you need your daily fix of Mr Murdoch.'

John Evans, who has worked for Murdoch for 17 years and currently heads up his News Electronic Data division in New Jersey, says, 'When you have a meeting with him he makes you feel that you're the only person in his cogniscence, he takes no calls, gives you his complete attention. It's kind of cat-like, the narrow focus he gives to things. His mind moves from one narrow focus to another. Either he's absolutely riveted by something, or he's not interested. After 17 years working for him, I have really two observations about the culture. The first is that Rupert's never failed to deliver anything he says he'll deliver, and I've never been asked to lie. This is the only company I've ever worked at where I've *never* had to tell a lie. The environment is a very easy one once you understand it. He rewards loyalty above any other attribute. If you do something good, you don't get an immediate reward. In fact he gets quite grumpy if you're too successful; you get chided a bit like a precocious boy to keep you honest. But if you run into a problem and come to him and say, "Rupert, contrary to what I told you before, I don't think this is going to work," he's immediately in the trenches alongside you, helping you solve it. So in that way it's easier to get along with Rupert when you're unsuccessful than when you're too successful.'

People kept assuring me that he's a 'hands-on' owner, that he is aware of every detail of what's happening at all his papers. He rings his editors from a distant time zone, minutes before their front page is due to be printed, and makes suggestions over the telephone to improve it. He never stops changing things, changing people, never rests. His principal secretary, Dorothy Wyndoe, who accompanies him to meetings from country to country, keeps a dossier of public holidays around the world, to ensure he avoids them and never unwittingly loses a day of work.

'Mr Murdoch, where is your base of operations?' he was once asked.

'Wherever the action is,' he replied.

His homes are in Beverly Hills, Aspen, St James's Place in London and Cavan, his property not far from Canberra, but he travels with a series of lap-top computers that give him continuously revised circulation figures, advertising revenue and profit and loss statements of all 531 of his subsidiary companies listed in his consolidated report and accounts. These include 126 separate companies in Australia, 152 in the United Kingdom, 131 in the United States, 14 in the Cayman Islands, four in the Netherlands Antilles and sundry lonesome subsidiaries in Bermuda, Panama, Peru, Jersey, Guernsey and Cuba.

The empire is so spread out, I found it inconceivable that he could possibly know as much of the detail as he is credited with.

A former financial assistant to Murdoch told me, 'He mugs up on the different operations in the aeroplane on his way there. You've got to remember he's been doing this a long time. Ten minutes with the accounts and he can find four points to throw questions out about. And he'll read a stack of his newspapers – a fortnight's worth at a time – and pick out half a dozen articles he liked or disliked. If there's a spare half hour at either end of the day, he'll pick up three papers at random, skim through them, and dictate three faxes to three editors in three different countries, passing some comment on the content. It gives the illusion he's always watching.

'And he asks a lot of questions in cabs,' he said. 'He'll always ask the cab driver or the limo driver "What newspaper do you read? Why, why?" He loves to get opinions. He asks everyone everything, cab drivers, secretaries, anyone he meets. "Should I buy this newspaper? Should I be buying companies in the recession?" He never stops asking these questions.'

'Rupert descends on his people for a few days,' Conrad Black told me, 'rushes about like a blue-arse fly, drives them all crazy, then flies on someplace else and things go pretty much back to normal.'

'He is coming less frequently to London but for longer,' says Andrew Knight who runs Murdoch's British operation. 'Previously he'd blow in and be a whirlwind and then he'd go out and come in again and be another whirlwind. It was highly effective. I think what he's doing now is even more effective because it means that he comes in two or three times a year and when he comes he comes for a worthwhile amount of time which means that a lot of people get to see him – somebody of his energy – and he can really make a difference.'

When you question Murdoch men about KRM's character, the same five observations are made again and again, as though they were the only five things that could possibly be said about him; his energy, memory and egalitarianism, the closeness of his family and his carefulness with money. They tell you that he works harder and more singlemindedly than any other proprietor; that he still finds England as complacent and class-ridden as it was when he first arrived in the early sixties; that when he's in London it pleases him to eat in the News canteen at Wapping surrounded by journalists and printers (until 1992 there had deliberately been no executive dining room for directors at all); that his (second) marriage to Anna is strong and that his family are tight-knit and well brought up.

'There are moments on trips when I've seen him lie down on the corporate plane and close his eyes, but I've never seen him stay in that position for longer than three mintues,' says John Evans. 'He's a very, very tough man to keep up with. And it's not *simply* energy; the energy is the useful fuel, but his memory is the phenomenal thing. He can remember *everything* you tell him. Everything. You have to beware telling him anything you don't want to have quoted back at you three years later. I remember when I was publishing the *Village Voice* for Rupert, he'd come straight off Concorde, and he could remember details of circulation and profit – both sets of numbers – that we hadn't discussed for three years. And with people it's even more frightening than that. He never forgets anyone's name – or their wife's name. He'll meet one of his people, who he maybe hasn't met with for a couple of years, and ask, "And how is Sheila? How is Alice?" He's phenomenally good at it and of course it's very flattering when the head of a multi-national corporation can do that.'

'He never really let up, whatever time of day or night it was,' says Roger Woods who edited Murdoch's *New York Post*. 'If there was time for another edition or to redo page one, he'd be right in there. Even when the final realistic deadline has passed, if an excuse to replate in the early hours of the morning came up, he'd take it. When we were producing the Sunday *Post* during the newspaper strike, he used to come to the office midday on Saturday, be there all evening suggesting headlines and drawing up pages, and then when the final edition had gone he'd ask a couple of pressmen to join him and play a hand of poker until the presses had finished rolling, just in case some excuse arose at three o'clock in the morning to replate. He always gets on very well with pressmen. That strikes some people as ironic, in the light of the battle with the printers at Wapping. But he's a very open guy. Always ate in the cafeteria at the *Post*. Anyone could join him at his table, pressmen, the post room guys, he doesn't care who.'

'He's very family orientated,' says a News director. 'His children are very conservatively brought up, in the French sense of *bien élevé* – extremely well-mannered and bright. I don't mean well-mannered in the sense that they're just sitting there. When he's with his family he's very close to them and they dominate him, I would say. In other words they know what all the television programmes are, what the latest books are, this or that, and he absorbs a lot. They have a lot of time for each other. I have known him be in London when, so far as I know, maybe only me and one other knew he was in London and he was going to visit his grandson.'

And people kept emphasising, strange as it may seem, how unmotivated he is by money; that he is less impressed by rich men's toys and extravagance than any comparable tycoon.

494

'He doesn't go out to grand restaurants very much,' said another member of his London board. 'Very seldom goes to the Savoy Grill these days. He's much more comfortable in just an ordinary, reasonably well-run Italian restaurant or whatever. He's not living a huge grand lifestyle, he hasn't got a large collection of cars or paintings, he's not at all interested in that kind of thing, though he certainly doesn't have any false modesty of sort of going round in a Morris Minor. He has got a very, very lovely house in Beverly Hills which I certainly couldn't afford, but he's not out to be a multimillionaire in the vulgar sense.'

A former Murdoch aide remembers that his executives quickly learn to dissemble over extravagances he would disapprove of.

'One of his top people had returned to Manhattan after a short business trip to London. "Trip go well?" asked Murdoch. "Where did you stay?"

' "Claridges," replied the executive.

' "Claridges? Isn't that a very pricey place?"

' "Normally, Rupert, but there's a special deal on."

' "Oh, that's OK then."

'Only Rupert Murdoch,' says the aide, 'would believe for one moment that Claridges of all hotels would offer discount deals.'

Nor is Murdoch's puritanism restricted to corporate spending.

'There were four of us travelling down together in the elevator at the New York office,' says the same aide. 'Three of us from corporate and Rupert. As we were standing there, we became aware that he kept looking from one of us to the next, staring at our ties. We all three happened that day to be wearing those Hermès ties with animals on them, elephants and giraffes. After a while he said: "Those ties are pretty pricey ties you're all wearing aren't they?" He continued to regard them suspiciously. "Are they *designer* ties?" All three of us vehemently denied it – though where on earth you find a tie that *isn't* a designer one I've no idea. We said we'd bought them duty free at an airport. "Oh, that's OK then I suppose," Murdoch said doubtfully.'

It is almost axiomatic that a paper purchased by Rupert Murdoch will move downmarket. It is a fact so frequently and emphatically stated, that it has become a journalistic cliché, an *idée fixe* of modern newspapering. His critics are virulent and articulate. 'No self-respecting dead fish would want to be wrapped in a Murdoch paper,' wrote the Chicago columnist Miko Royko when his paper, the *Sun-Times*, was bought by News Corporation from Marshall Field V, the department store heir. When Murdoch became hot candidate to buy the London *Observer* (ahead of the American oil company Atlantic Richfield and the Aga Khan), Clive James, the paper's TV critic, protested that Rupert Murdoch was one of the principal reasons he had left Australia to come to Britain, adding, 'Giving the *Observer* to Rupert Murdoch is like giving your beautiful daughter to a gorilla.' Tom Winship, an editor of the *Boston Globe* which competes with Murdoch's *Herald* has described Murdoch journalism as 'circus journalism'. Alexander Cockburn, in a now famous piece in the *Wall Street Journal*, said that for Rupert Murdoch to sell the *New York Post* 'would be like Dracula selling his coffin'. A M Rosenthal, when he was executive editor of *The New York Times*, took the view that Murdoch was 'a bad element, practising mean, ugly, violent journalism'. Kay Graham, Otis Chandler and Punch Sulzberger all told me that they'd feel uncomfortable owning most of his papers, because of their downmarket drift.

And yet the more I reflected on the Murdoch empire the less certain I became that the cliché holds true. The culture of his newspapers, particularly the tabloids, may indeed be brutal and chauvinistic and downmarket, but that is not quite the same thing as invariably *moving* the paper downmarket.

One can assess the Murdoch effect by comparing his impact across 14 of his papers over ten or so years of ownership, gauging their 'downmarket' quotient in news values, scandal and lay-out. There are two additional, and even more subjective, scales of assessment: professionalism (a lively middle-market paper being preferable to a ponderous and neglected one, however lofty its intentions) and circulation (the only quantifiable measure of a paper's heartbeat).

1. An assessment of his Australian flagship is immediately distorted by the fact that the *Australian* is a 1964 Murdoch launch and thus has no pre-Murdoch era to compare it to. Certainly nothing about the *Australian*, the country's first national paper, available just about everywhere from Canberra to Brisbane to Darwin, can be

described as downmarket. It is what the English describe as a 'proper' newspaper, what Murdoch calls an 'unpopular' (as opposed to a 'popular', ie a tabloid), a serious broadsheet, somewhat grey in appearance, with many sober columns of parliamentary affairs, state politics, international news, sport and the economy. To my eyes there is something slightly po-faced and dreary about the *Australian*; it doesn't quite hold your attention as you expect it to on the short air hop between Sydney and Melbourne. But it is in every sense a genuine and coherent newspaper; when the Third World War breaks out, this item of news will unquestionably be posted across the front page and will not be leapfrogged by the tale of some headless toddler or killer mosquito. The *Australian* struck me as exactly the kind of newspaper, in fact, that if Rupert Murdoch didn't already happen to own it, and put in a bid, numerous do-gooders would throw up their hands in horror and demand government intervention to block him.

2. The Perth *Sunday Times*, however, which is often cited as a coarse Murdoch creation, needs to be seen in context. The pre-Murdoch *Sunday Times* was also coarse, and drab to boot. When he acquired it in 1956, he sharpened the paper's persona from a longbar soak muttering profanities into a vulgar and prurient jack-the-lad. The page lay-outs are slicker, the graphics bolder and more arresting. It was in Perth that Rupert Murdoch honed his talent for sensational newspapering: the peerless headline 'Leper Rapes Virgin, Gives Birth To Monster Baby' was conceived here. To say that he's taken the paper downmarket isn't strictly accurate. He's reinterpreted downmarket for another generation in a greatly enlarged Perth.

3. Murdoch's Sydney-based *Daily Telegraph Mirror* is a curious hybrid of the old Fairfax tabloid *Mirror*, which Murdoch bought in 1960, and Kerry Packer's *Daily Telegraph* that he acquired fourteen years later. Nobody disputes that when the Murdoch *Mirror* was a stand-alone operation, embroiled in a fierce circulation war against the rival *Sun*, it redefined the possibilities of downmarket, with Murdoch himself, shirtsleeves rolled up, rewriting headlines and snarling at scrupulous sub-editors who missed the point. There are, of course, two classes of downmarket: unwittingly downmarket, when the people who put it together don't know any better, and

strategically – cynically – downmarket when the owner decides it will do better that way. Everything about the *Daily* and *Sunday Mirror* was strategically downmarket: the headline type as big as roadsigns, the titillation, the competitions that beckoned new readers with bigger and bigger prizes – swimming pools, cars, real estate – and above anything the headlines themselves 'Gang Rapes Girl 10', 'Prowler Strips Woman Naked' – the three most over-employed words in sixties *Mirror* headlines were, in fact, 'Prowler', 'Strips' and 'Rapes'. In its combined form with the *Daily Telegraph*, however, it cannot really any longer be fairly described as salacious. In appearance, the amalgamated paper has a certain kinship with Conrad Black's London *Daily Telegraph* which also manages, in its grave way, to register the rapes, the strips and the prowlers. On present performance, the *Daily Telegraph Mirror* is neither upmarket nor downmarket of its precursors.

4. The *San Antonio Express-News* in Texas (like the Perth *Sunday Times*) was acquired in a classic Murdoch manoeuvre: buy the number two metropolitan paper (in an airport lounge from the Harte-Hands corporation in 1973) in a competitive, fast-growing city with an anti-intellectual frontier-town atmosphere. The number one paper, Hearst's *San Antonio Light*, was already pretty lurid. He faced the choice of positioning his own paper above the *Light* or beneath it; he chose the downmarket position, or rather – as he'd put it – to meet them head-on, vigorously competing for the same readers by doing much the same thing, only better, with more verve and crackle. Headlines increased in size and licence ('Armies of Insects March on SA'), stories received more 'spin'. After twenty years of Murdoch, (he sold out to Hearst in October 1992) the *Express-News* has unquestionably moved downmarket, but when it is slipped under your hotel room door at the Hilton Palacio del Rio you are amused.

5. The *Boston Herald* is particularly interesting as a case study since Murdoch invested a lot of time and thought in the *Herald*, as well as money, and indeed chose to hold on to it when faced with divesting either his Boston newspaper or control of his more lucrative Boston television station. When he acquired it from Hearst in 1982 (which described Murdoch, somewhat defensively, as 'the buyer of last resort') the paper was reckoned to be losing $10 million a year. His

new editorial formula imposed shorter stories, enormous type – the front page often comprises only a triple-decker headline – sport, sex, competitions and a shift away from liberalism. Circulation rallied and the rival *Globe*, recognising that parts of the Murdoch coverage were sharper than its own, expanded its local beat. 'The *Herald*'s got its nose in front from a business point of view and if we poured more resources into it we could overtake the *Globe* I'm sure,' Murdoch told me. 'The papers here are so different from Britain though. In America you have to service one community geographically, you have to reach everybody. You've got to go broad here and be very acceptable to everybody. And you've got to look at the retail advertising, you've got to look at department stores. And that in turn leads to a sort of blandness. American papers don't have the edge to them that the London *Sunday Times* or the *Sun*, even the *Daily Mail* have – they've all got an edge to them.' The theory goes that a thoroughly lurid tabloid simply wouldn't work in America. 'If you introduced, say, a London *Sunday Mirror* in Boston and you got pro rata circulation of what it gets in London you might sell 100,000 whereas in London it sells 2.7 million. And you'd simply be out of business, there'd be no advertising. You just simply couldn't make it pay.'

6. Murdoch's proprietorship of the Chicago *Sun-Times* has elements of his effect on the *Boston Herald* except that this time Murdoch ultimately chose to keep the television station instead. When he outbid Katharine Graham and the Washington Post Company in 1984, the level of hysteria and conviction that he would ruin the *Sun-Times*, turn it into a *National Enquirer*, was unprecedented. He shipped in News executives who understood the Murdoch credo from four of his other papers – *The Times* in London, the *San Antonio Express-News*, the *Boston Herald* and the *New York Post* – and this only fanned suspicion of his intentions. Stories were once again shortened, photographs and headlines enlarged, crime coverage increased. But there were upmarket innovations too: coverage of world affairs also increased. By the time Murdoch got rid of it, few Chicagoans noticed much difference in their paper and his tenure, in financial and circulation terms, was inconclusive. 'I never lived in Chicago,' Rupert Murdoch told me. 'I wish I had in some ways for a while, I would have driven it harder. But it was a

nightmare financially, perhaps we didn't have the resources to put into it – we were too busy with *The Times* in London – but if we had we would have at least walked away prouder of our record.'

7. Of all his ventures the *New York Post*, along with the London *Sun*, has been most responsible for the downmarket monster-Murdoch myth. This is largely a consequence of location. Were the *New York Post* the metropolitan paper of San Antonio it would pass more or less unnoticed. But it competes in the most public arena of all, against the Sulzbergers, the Chandlers and Mort Zuckermann and its overnight transformation from the self-effacing liberal paper that Murdoch acquired from the elderly heiress Dorothy Schiff, into a racy entertainment sheet for blue- collars, took place under the wrinkled noses of his peers. As at the Sydney *Mirror*, Murdoch took personal charge: flying in seasoned 'Murdoch men' from London and Sydney to assist him, assigning reporters, making up pages on the stone and slashing copy to make it fit the shrunken news slots. One reason that both New York tabloids, the *Post* and *Daily News*, look so vehemently downmarket is their tawdry grey newsprint – it has the pallor of dead man's skin – which disposes the page make-up to become outsized and boastful to divert attention from the paper quality. But the content too became increasingly downmarket and violent, and Murdoch's critics detected in the histrionic coverage of heatwave riots and murders, a journalism that had moved beyond simple reporting. In its twisting and slanting of the news, it became a journalism of incitement. Rival proprietors felt that he had crucially misjudged and underestimated the taste of the American reader. 'We are waiting to see how long it's going to take him to fail in this country,' said Otis Chandler. Murdoch himself concedes that he failed to anticipate the fundamental difference between working-class America and Britain. 'New York is a middle-class city,' he told me. 'If you drop below that level you're left with a sort of ghetto where advertising doesn't matter much to the big stores – not that there are many big stores left. And there's a question as to whether those people can even read, let alone afford a newspaper.' None the less when Teddy Kennedy won his campaign to make him divest the *Post* under the cross-ownership rule, and he was obliged to agree a forced sale to the real estate developer Peter Kalikow, Murdoch was distraught.

He felt that the curtain had been brought down on him halfway through the show, well before the final denouement when his strategy would have had time to come good. In March 1993 Kalikow bowed out to Abe Hirshfeld, a parking-garage magnate, and the staff mutinied. By April, Murdoch had seized back the *Post*.

8. The *South China Morning Post* – 'The Times of South East Asia' as Murdoch dubbed it shortly after he outbid Pearson, the publishers of the *Financial Times*, for it in 1986 – on balance moved upmarket, not down, during his seven-year stint. For a century pre-Murdoch it had been a reliable and comprehensive paper – part of that great crescent of post-colonial broadsheets that begins with the *Straits Times* in Singapore and ends in Australia with the *Sydney Morning Herald* – but there was a certain flatness in its reporting and a tendency to publish agency stories off the wires rather than cover the local beat. Murdoch strengthened the news and cleaned up the graphics while doing nothing to erode its franchise as the cash-cow of the Pacific Rim. He later floated the paper on the Hang Seng, retaining 49.9 per cent. In September 1993 he sold out to the pro-Chinese Malaysian billionaire Robert Kuok.

9. *Mai Nap*, the raunchy Budapest daily of which Murdoch owns a half share with Hungarian partners, has also moved up rather than downmarket. His influence has largely been technological, cleaning up the printing, but the lay-out has gained clarity too, and he has decreased the number of nudes that initially paraded across pages 3, 5, 7 and 9 in the aftermath of communism.

10. No newspaper in the empire has been so remorselessly scrutinised as *The Times* since he bought it in 1981 from the Thomsons, and the odd juxtaposition of successive editors – William Rees-Mogg, Harold Evans, Charles Douglas-Home, Charles Wilson, Simon Jenkins, Peter Stothard – has left the impression that the paper has been stuck on a two-way escalator, heading alternately up and downmarket. Whether Rupert Murdoch has ever had a master plan for *The Times* is questionable. He says he told Harold Evans, as their relationship deteriorated, 'Please be consistent. You must have some underlying philosophical direction and follow it. Consistency is what we need.' Murdoch told me that, 'With *The Times* it's all about circulation. You look at *The Times* and you ask

how many homes can broadly be described as middle to upper-middle class and professional and academic and so on. So you say the potential there is 1,500,000, perhaps 2,000,000. So you say how do we get our share of that because we've got three or four strong competitors, and we want to be the biggest input, the best input. Or can you slice the salami a bit differently so you just get the top half million? Once you do that, you can define what you want to go for and then you've got to get leadership in that area, I think, and consistency.' It didn't strike me that he greatly minds whether *The Times* salami is sliced in a refined way by a Charles Douglas-Home or a Simon Jenkins, or in thick populist wedges by a robust Charles Wilson, so long as the man behind the charcuterie counter knows what the customer likes. When Simon Jenkins informed Murdoch, on being interviewed for the job of editor, that he wished to make *The Times* politer and less Thatcherite, and that the stories should be longer at the expense of big headlines, he was told to do what he thought fit. Eleven years into the Murdoch era there is little prima-facie evidence of downmarketing. *The Times* has become a modern two-section paper with on-the-run colour, but its purpose and quality remain fundamentally unaltered.

11. This isn't true, however, of the *Sunday Times* which under the editorship of Andrew Neil – the paper's first editor who could accurately be described as a 'Murdoch man' – seems consciously to have been repositioned into an Americanised, multi-sectioned and pugnacious newspaper, managing to be simultaneously both aspirational and republican in tone and thus rather brilliantly mirroring the Jeckyll and Hyde-ish tenor of modern Britain. If you ask any mini-cab driver what he reads on Sunday, he will invariably reply the *Sunday Times*. It is a long way from the campaigning, liberal *Sunday Times* of Harold Evans, with its lofty commitment to public service journalism (the anti-thalidomide campaigns and not-much-read articles about the underdeveloped world). On the other hand the big, brash Murdoch *Sunday Times*, like a skyscraper in the middle of a mews of Georgian cottages, or a drunk on a bus, cannot be ignored; and its position as Britain's highest-selling Sunday broadsheet has strengthened during the Murdoch era. That the *Sunday Times* has moved downmarket is accepted as fact by the vast majority of both Britain's liberal and

traditional Tory educated elite. It is not, however, unequivocally true. Vast tracts of the paper have not gone downmarket; others are simply written by journalists whose outlook would not, in earlier regimes, have been considered. The *Sunday Times* reminds one of a mixed ability comprehensive school, the product of a recent merger between a historic grammar and a delinquent secondary modern.

12. Rupert Murdoch's 1987 purchase of *Today* – the middle-market tabloid born of Eddie Shah (a distant relation to the Aga Khan and catalyst for the defeat of the British printworkers' unions), briefly sold to Tiny Rowland, the chief executive of Lonrho, and then swiped from under the nose of Robert Maxwell a couple of hours before he was due to sign a contract for it – was intended to complete News International's presence in every sector of the British market, and enable it to gain ground against Lord Stevens's *Daily Express* and Lord Rothermere's *Daily Mail*. This has proved a tougher challenge than Murdoch envisaged. His *Today* has not, however, taken the same route as the *Boston Herald* or the *New York Post*, and the paper today is if anything a shade upmarket of Eddie Shah's *Today*.

13. The London *Sun* had the same sort of parentage as the *Boston Herald*: an editorially flailing, exhausted, left-leaning paper, conceived by Hugh Cudlipp to service the new notionally better-educated working-class, and acquired by Murdoch for £50,000 from an IPC desperate to offload it. Every trick of promotion and editorial learnt at the Sydney *Mirror* was thrown at the *Sun* – the hoodlum headlines, sex surveys and television hype – plus new ones like Sunbirds, the topless page three girl who made her early appearances in bra and knickers. The Murdoch *Sun*, and particularly under its second editor Kelvin MacKenzie, is a British institution – raucous, xenophobic, impertinent, leering, often incredibly witty – posting profits of anywhere between £80 million and £100 million a year and, at 3.6 million, the biggest daily circulation of any tabloid in Europe and North America.

14. It is widely held by the same chattering classes that accuse Murdoch of downmarketing the *Sunday Times* that he did the same thing to Britain's highest-selling, most salacious Sunday tabloid, the *News of the World*. In fact the pre-Murdoch *News of*

the Screws (as it was known long before he acquired it from the Carr family under the nose of Robert Maxwell in 1968) was already a pretty sleazy operation, specialising in stories about dirty vicars and kinky personal services that the journalist was by tradition offered and then evaded with the line 'I made my excuses and left'. Post-Murdoch it specialises instead in stories about dirty vicars and kinky television personalities.

If there is a pattern to all this it is not exactly that Rupert Murdoch downmarkets newspapers, rather that his responses are invariably market-driven which leads him to take whatever steps are required to sell more copies, but he finds no difficulty in operating at both ends of the scale simultaneously. It occurred to me too that had he acquired his papers in a different order – if *The Times*, the *South China Morning Post* and the *Australian* had come first – and he'd only then moved on to buy the tabloids, the world's perception of him would be substantially different. His bids for the Chicago *Sun-Times* and the Melbourne *Herald* would then have been applauded; he would have been welcomed as a white knight when he rolled into Boston and New York. But that is an idle scenario, since in the Murdoch empire it has always been the profits of the tabloids that have funded the loftier acquisitions.

Three or four months before he died, I asked Robert Maxwell which newspaper he would buy next. I asked it mischievously, because there was only one feasible reply: 'Nothing'. It was apparent even then that he was massively overextended – editorially as well as financially. The *European* and the *New York Daily News* were faltering, and everything I heard about his papers in Israel, Kenya and Eastern Europe made one wonder why he held on to them.

'Buy next?' he boomed, looming over me like a great black Alaskan bear. 'You know that I may not tell you that. There are things you cannot know. But I can tell you this much. I will be buying a British newspaper from a *very prominent publisher* who cannot pay his debts. I want you to accept my word on this.'

He regarded me darkly. 'A *very prominent publisher*,' he repeated. It was clear that I was expected to supply suggestions.

'Rupert Murdoch?'

'You know I may not confirm that.' But he looked pleased. 'Nor may I name the daily newspaper in question. But I will tell you this. It does not compete with any of *my* papers.'

This left *The Times*. I took a punt on it.

'You must not press me on that,' he replied. 'You cannot press me.' He beamed, and actually winked at me conspiratorially.

Six months later, I asked Murdoch whether he'd known that Maxwell had been stalking *The Times*.

Murdoch gave a ghoulish laugh. 'You see I always knew he was a total buffoon really. But once he got the *Mirror*, part of his buffoonery was, "This is a massive battle worldwide, Murdoch and Maxwell, Maxwell and Murdoch." He kept saying this and whenever he went on television he'd be asked about me in interviews. I never spoke about him, but he couldn't stop talking about me. Whatever we did, he wanted to do it too.'

Murdoch said he had always found these comparisons exasperating. Because they both owned racy tabloid newspapers and have surnames that begin with the letter M, they were lumped together – either as the two foreign marauders come to pillage the British press or two high rolling gamblers trying to build world-class media empires in a hurry. But the similarities stopped there. Rupert Murdoch is a sophisticated newspaper technician, who understands every stage of the production process from sub-editing to page make-up. Robert Maxwell was almost defiantly ignorant on these subjects. It is a privilege of proprietorship that, if you so choose, you can know nothing whatever and still own newspapers.

With hindsight, one can see too that their respective debt crises were of a different nature: Murdoch's fuelled by over-rapid investment in new media properties which eventually came good, Maxwell's by media dodos for which his strategy was unequal to the challenge. And despite Maxwell's constant attempts to lumber on to the world stage, his newspaper operations were never more than a fifth of the size of Murdoch's.

'I recall asking Conrad [Black] about Maxwell,' said Murdoch. 'It was the first time I'd met him. He'd come to see me in New York about our print contract in Manchester or something. We were with [Sir] Frank Rogers and Conrad said, "Maxwell's a thief, a crook, a buffoon and probably a KGB man" and he's been proved right on at least three.

And I was so shocked I actually wrote it down. This was two years before he died.'

I asked Murdoch, 'Did you never consider exposing him if you knew so much?'

Murdoch made a wish-we-could-have kind of face. 'It would have been difficult,' he said. 'If we had ever set the dogs on his business, which we knew all about, everyone would have said that's just being competitive. He would have got some court to side with him and say this was unfair. He was quite clever the way he did that. But as I've said I never took Bob seriously as a competitor. It's a totally different culture at the *Mirror*. And now of course they're all trying to clear their names, trying to abuse Maxwell, overlooking the fact they were brown-nosing around him for five years – I shouldn't have said that, it makes me sound very crude.'

Robert Maxwell was eight years Murdoch's senior, which only fuelled Maxwell's competitiveness. He felt that time was not on his side. 'All that big talk about building a global communciations company that would overtake ours in three years, that was bullshit,' said Murdoch. 'I heard him say it on television several times. You'd switch on the TV in some hotel bedroom and there'd be Maxwell in his bow tie and dark suit, telling you about his global communications company.' Murdoch shrugged.

They none the less chased some of the same rabbits for 24 years, first crossing swords during the 1967 episode when Maxwell attempted to sell Murdoch 50 per cent of Pergamon, his scientific publishing business, in Australia. The deal was all but sealed but Murdoch got cold feet when the audited figures he kept being promised failed to materialise, and pulled out. This was the inauspicious prelude to two and a half decades of skirmishing.

It is possible, when you tally the score of their many media duels, to feel almost sorry for Robert Maxwell: Played 9. Lost 8. Drew 1. Whenever Rupert Murdoch bid for a newspaper in England, the rival candidate was Maxwell. Invariably the prospect of Maxwell helped Murdoch. Given a choice between the devil and Maxwell's deep blue suit, people hastened to endorse the devil. The arrival of Captain Robert Maxwell MC on the scene to buy the *News of the World* so horrified its proprietor Sir William Carr that over dinner at the Mirabelle he embraced Murdoch as a knight in shining armour, a judgement he would subsequently have cause to regret since the knight duly toppled the king. When Murdoch bid for the *Sun*, it was once again Robert Maxwell who provided the competition. This time the unions made it clear that Maxwell was unacceptable to them as an owner, a judgement they would subsequently have cause to regret when Murdoch moved the *Sun* to Wapping and smashed them completely. When Lord Thomson declared that he'd had enough of the stoppages and union disputes at *The Times* and the *Sunday Times*, and that he was putting the titles up for sale, Robert Maxwell was the first to announce he was interested in buying them. Within three weeks he had also filed a detailed proposal promising among other things, a comically small payment of £5 million in cash and, more comically still, complete editorial independence. When Murdoch ultimately scooped the prize, Maxwell, sounding increasingly like a three-times jilted lover, complained that Murdoch had won only because of his special relationship with the government.

Rupert Murdoch's supposed cosiness with Downing Street was an obsession of Maxwell's, used to explain every triumph of his rival over himself. Whenever Robert Maxwell heard that Murdoch had attended some government dinner or reception, he would leap upon it as evidence of 'Mr Murdoch's pact with the Establishment'. It is perfectly true that Murdoch has always massaged his relationship with the party of government – every government in every country – more assiduously than Maxwell (who preferred communist dictators), but this does not alone explain Murdoch's greater success. When Tiny Rowland decided to sell *Today* after his short tenure of ownership, Maxwell wanted the paper badly (some said to punish Lord Rothermere by competing with his *Daily Mail*, in retaliation for Vere Rothermere's recent and galling victory with the *Evening Standard* over Maxwell's *London Daily News*) and it seemed likely that he would get it. Rowland was prejudiced against Murdoch because of derogatory articles published about Lonrho in his *Sunday Times*, and Maxwell was so confident of success that he cockily rang Murdoch in Los Angeles to tell him the deal was clinched. Murdoch, however, was sceptical, and his scepticism was justified. The deal would not be signed until after the weekend, 72 hours away. There was certainly a mixture of motives propelling Murdoch into action, but the opportunity to snatch the prize from under Maxwell's nose at the eleventh hour was certainly one of them. Tiny Rowland was tracked down to his yacht in the Adriatic while Murdoch flew to his home in Aspen to direct operations. A rival offer was put to Lonrho, a cash bid four times higher than Maxwell's, and new contracts prepared, to be signed two-and-a-half hours before the historic signing-session that Maxwell was anticipating. Murdoch flew the Atlantic overnight and, even as Robert Maxwell made his way across London to Lonrho's offices in Cheapside with a bevy of photographers to record the transaction, the *Today* newspaper had been lost to News.

With each reverse, Maxwell's obsession with Rupert Murdoch grew. He conceived an extraordinary fascination for the minutiae of how his rival ran his life and controlled his empire, and by extension for anyone who worked for Murdoch. At meetings he would gleefully declare, 'Let us see Mr Murdoch's face when he hears this,' though the subject under discussion – a new newspaper promotion or competition – would generally have left Rupert Murdoch underwhelmed, if he ever heard about it at all. The one exception to this was Maxwell's introduction of colour printing at the *Daily Mirror*. Murdoch has never championed colour in newspapers, but was forced to concede that colour did boost the *Mirror*'s circulation at the expense of the *Sun*, and soon installed colour himself. Maxwell regarded his leadership in the coloured tabloid episode as a considerable personal triumph.

Often Maxwell's competitiveness was foolhardy. He tried to buy the *Melbourne Herald* from the Fairfaxes in Australia to challenge Murdoch on his home turf. When Murdoch bought newspapers in Hungary, Maxwell felt piqued, protesting that he, not Mr Murdoch, had a special relationship with Eastern Europe. In retaliation he bought a Hungarian paper too, the *Magyar Hirlap*. Unfortunately, such was the speed with which he moved, he chose badly and landed himself with a paper that had been so compromised by the old communist regime that its prospects were completely unsound. Similarly Maxwell's purchase of the *New York Daily News* was at least partially engendered by his belief that it would annoy Murdoch. 'Mr Murdoch,' he loved to claim, 'failed in New York,' a reference to his enforced sale of the *Post* under cross-ownership laws. 'Let us see Mr Murdoch's face when I become the publisher of the *New York Daily News*.'

There is a story that expresses better than anything the childishness of Robert Maxwell's obsession with Murdoch. The two proprietors were by chance both lunching on the same day at the Savoy Grill, sitting at separate booths along the back wall. After lunch, on his way out, Maxwell lumbered over to Murdoch's table to exchange bumptious pleasantries. In the course of their short conversation, Murdoch mentioned that he was catching the 5 p.m. Concorde flight back to New York and that he had a business dinner in a restaurant that evening in Manhattan.

While Robert Maxwell was being driven back to his office in Holborn, he decided on a whim that he would turn up in the same restaurant himself. Since Murdoch would know that Maxwell hadn't been on the Concorde flight, he would realise that he had flown the Atlantic by private jet. Maxwell had recently bought a Gulfstream G-4, of which he was inordinately proud, and this would be a brilliant means of impressing his superiority over Murdoch, who flew only by public transport.

Maxwell's secretaries were always adept at discovering where other tycoons were going to eat (Maxwell originally forced an introduction to the financier Saul Steinberg by reserving the adjacent table at a breakfast meeting) and it was duly reported that Rupert Murdoch would be dining that night at the Four Seasons Grill Room on East 52nd and Park. Beaming with delight at his crafty plan, Maxwell was shuttled by helicopter from his private helipad on the roof to the airfield and by Gulfstream to New York and his strategically placed table for one. He waited and he waited. At every moment he expected to astonish Rupert Murdoch. But he waited in vain. Exhausted by his long day, Murdoch had altered his plans. His dinner guest had been invited for a drink at his apartment on Park Avenue instead.

Andrew Knight, chairman of News International Plc, is Rupert Murdoch's number one gun in London. Along with Chief Executive Gus Fischer, he is a contender, should the proprietor keel over on one of his pre-dawn jogs, to run News Corporation. But he conforms to none of the clichés of News management. By tradition Murdoch selects men who are overtly tough, extrovert, Australian or Scottish. Andrew Knight is intellectually tough, cerebral and an Anglo-New Zealander.

It so happened that the appointment Andrew Knight made for my visit to Wapping fell in the midst of one of Rupert Murdoch's quarterly visits to London. Through Knight's office door you could hear Murdoch's voice as he pounded to and fro along the executive corridor. It occurred to me that very few executives would have chosen to talk about their boss (even when they had cleared the interview, as Knight had with Murdoch) on the very day he was in town. And I noted too that Knight had chosen to wear a grey pullover in the office over his stripy yellow shirt and dark blue tie. In every other newspaper company, it is the owner who pulls on the casual cardigan and the henchmen who wear suits. I wondered whether Andrew Knight was sending surreptitious signals about the quality of his rapport with Murdoch.

His office is capacious and white, reclaimed out of Rupert Murdoch's former dining room and bathroom. From the window, beyond the executive car-park and perimeter security fence, you catch a glimpse of the Thames between Victorian warehouses; the only office in Wapping, Knight said, with a decent view. Suspended from the ceiling is a bank of eight television sets broadcasting eight SKY channels. As in Rupert Murdoch's office in Beverly Hills, the volume is turned permanently down. Fluency in lip-reading is mandatory at News.

I asked, 'When did you first meet him?'

'Rupert Murdoch?' Who else? You could hear him exchanging gregarious greetings right outside: 'Catch ya later, Gus,' he was saying.

'I first met him in the early eighties,' said Knight, 'but I really got to know him when I was at the *Telegraph*.' Before he defected to News, Knight had been Conrad Black's right-hand man and their parting had not been without acrimony.

'I arranged to go and see Murdoch in Australia because we needed to find a partner for our printing plant in Manchester and he was very short of print capacity, particularly once he'd started expanding his papers after the Wapping revolution. I saw him in his office in Sydney and in 25 minutes – literally 25 minutes – we'd agreed the principle of a deal. He makes up his mind very quickly, and when he's made up his mind he does it.'

Knight smiled. He was reclining full length on a wicker rocking chair, tilting back and forth.

'You can imagine,' he said, 'that our plant was completely covered in leases and banking arrangements – the Telegraph was in terrible trouble and needed to borrow a lot of money – and the legal documents would have filled half this room just over the conveyancing of the half share to Rupert Murdoch. And yet, despite the negotiating points that came up over and over and over again, he stuck completely to his word. Never varied. My dealings with him were always very straight and very honest and very immediate.

'Prior to that,' Knight said, 'I had spent a very long time negotiating with Robert Maxwell – he wanted to buy our Manchester plant, a wonderful plant, beautifully built, I mean Michael Hartwell's two plants were great printing plants and beautifully designed and very efficient potentially. The tragedy of what Michael Hartwell did was that he not only invested more than he could finance, he over-invested grossly. And Maxwell buggered us about. Every day I used to walk back from the Mirror's office to the Telegraph – about a seven-minute walk – and I used to say, "Do you think there'll be a call by the time we get back to undo what we've just shaken hands on, or will it be tomorrow?" As often as not by the time we got back there was a call from Mr Maxwell to call him. He was pathologically unable to agree anything because he always thought he could do better. I coined a phrase which is that when you shake hands with Maxwell it's the *beginning* of the negotiation; when you shake hands with Murdoch it's the *end* of the negotiation.

'I can remember the day Rupert hired me,' said Knight. 'December 1989. He rang me up out of the blue – I'd actually got 'flu, just recovering from it, not particularly looking forward to going out – but he rang up and said "Come over, I want to show you SKY" [Murdoch's new satellite television company] so I went over. I hadn't seen him for a long time, so I got out of bed and went to see him, and he took me round SKY and it was all terribly interesting and fascinating and I was terrified by it. Then we sat down, and it turned out he must have had another thought in his mind because he said, "Would you like to come?" And I said, "That's very interesting," and we talked about it for a little bit and I said, "But you do realise that what I've just seen here is something which I suspect I would constantly be questioning inside the company." I could not see how SKY could possibly succeed. And he said, "I want you to be involved and you can argue against it as much as you like but you'll be proved wrong." It seemed to me absolutely unbelievable that it could work, but it has worked.'

'Did Murdoch ever have his own doubts?'

'Never heard him waver for a second, never. Everybody around him wavered in those early days except him and Gary Davey. Everybody. Initially there wasn't anybody that I can remember who had the complete conviction and determination that he had to see it through. You asked me what his strengths are, and I'd reply risk-taking, but risk-taking in a very particular way; namely taking on what is established every time and seeing what is possible. And the other thing is just a phenomenal intellectual energy. I don't mean a phenomenal intellect only – he has that as well, he's very, very clever – but intellectual *energy* which is quite different. Not so much the tireless-ness – a lot of us are tireless, have stamina – but he has that extraordinary ability to go into a meeting where he is less well-briefed than anybody else (because everybody is there to brief him) and have the energy to pick that meeting up and just simply cut through it. You could imagine many a good intellect going out of a meeting like that and thinking about it and saying, "that's very interesting and what we should do is this," but his energy is such that he is always looking for a way to make that particular gathering *count*, rather than it just being a meeting where everybody goes out and says, "Let's have another one." It's the energy of the mind. A lot of people he talks to, editors he talks to, production, advertising, business people, financiers, politi-cians are constantly surprised by this amazing grasp he has. He was brought up the old-fashioned way in newspapers where he worked on printing presses, on the sub-editing benches and so forth. So that intellectual energy is applied to an industry which he knows better than most of the managers here. I think the distinction between the entrepreneurs of this day and age is between those who have *done it* and those who haven't. Neither Maxwell nor David Stevens had ever done it. Whereas Murdoch and Hartwell have.

'The other quality I would say about Rupert Murdoch is that he's completely unfrightened of competition. One of the biggest ironies I live with is the constant way his adversaries, political or otherwise, keep on talking about "Murdoch, is he unhealthily dominant?" or whatever. Lord Thomson forecast that there would be only three or four national newspapers left in this country by the end of the 1990s.

We have eleven and you have to reckon that but for Wapping two or three major ones would have gone under. So also in television. Murdoch breeds new competitors. Obviously you can see I'm an admirer.

'He is not out there, as is sometimes said, tilting at institutions which need to be reformed. He's not a reformer. He just simply, extremely, optimistically believes that if there's something that he knows about, and interests him, then there is a better way of doing it and by doing that you can make it a huge success.'

Outside in the passage you could hear Murdoch padding past again. He was saying, 'Dorothy will take care of that. Just make sure she has all the details, will you please.' Andrew Knight, supremely unruffled, became reflective.

'I think Rupert and I have an affinity, but a difference too,' he said. 'We're both outsiders and we like challenging what is going on. I did at the *Telegraph* – cheerfully made enemies to get a total change in attitude. Whenever anyone brings something to me which needs sorting out, I have a tremendous desire to go in and sort it. But in my case there's a sort of annoyance of the outsider that the English Establishment is so cosy. I don't think Rupert has that sense of annoyance, he just enjoys it so much. It's just a wonderfully cheerful impatience with the way things are done.'

Not very long after Andrew Knight took up his job at Wapping, he spent a skiing holiday with Rupert and Anna Murdoch at their house in Aspen. One afternoon on the piste, Knight had a near-fatal skiing accident. Murdoch rushed him to hospital and scarcely left his bedside for 36 hours, while Knight was internally haemorrhaging, until he was out of danger.

'I wouldn't really like that to be carried, because it'll sound a bit sentimental and gooey. But he was very attentive indeed and there are countless stories in the company of how he's done that. But you get that with a lot of great names – you used to get that with Mrs Thatcher. I think that enthusiasm comes not because he cares in a *sentimental* way, it's just sheer enthusiasm for anyone who happens to be part of his team. And it's reciprocated.

'I think a lot of us got to know Rupert much better during the whole debt crisis the company went through. He physically aged, as a lot of people mentioned in their articles, but all I can tell you is that everybody else looked grey and was really worried and he never ever sounded downcast. He was always thinking, "How can we get to tomorrow by doing this, this and this?" Always thinking of the next step and the next thing to do. I would talk to him on the telephone every day virtually, and what Rupert was really doing was making sure that the rest of the business was still being run and that we were actually producing a profitable result, instead of getting distracted by it [the debt crisis]. And I can remember telephone calls when I knew for a fact he'd been up all night squaring some particular circle, because he had these 146 banks, and he'd hardly had any sleep. But the extraordinary thing about those telephone conversations was that *I* would be the one wanting to talk about the banks and what was going on, and what he wanted to talk about – [to give examples] if it was today – was "What's happened to sterling?", "Do you think Lamont's going to change his line?", "Did the *Daily Mirror* scoop us on the David Mellor affair?" John Evans calls him a news junkie and I know what he means. That's what Rupert's really interested in: "What's going on and have we got the best stories?" So he was amazingly cheerful. The company never went on to autopilot in that period because he was off doing something else.'

I asked, 'What's your response to people who say that Rupert Murdoch has taken his London newspapers downmarket?'

'Well the *Sun* isn't downmarket of anything. The *Sun* is the *Sun*. Let's come to *The Times* and the *Sunday Times*. I don't know how to answer it other than to say that Harry Evans, Charlie Douglas-Home, Simon Jenkins and Peter Stothard were all his ideas and appointments personally. And so was Charlie Wilson. And most of the accusations at *The Times* were levelled during Charlie Wilson's editorship; I think unfairly. Andrew Neil, whatever else, you can't accuse him of being interested in frivolous things. He's tremendously serious. I think that making newspapers interesting is very easily misrepresented by using convenient labels such as upmarket and downmarket.'

I said that nevertheless he was aware that a body of people – especially journalists of the Harold Evans generation – are adamant that the Murdoch *Sunday Times* is less serious in intention than previously; less interested in international news, in the Third World, in investigative journalism. They are always insisting that the conscience of the paper had been replaced by party gossip.

'Well let's take a look at last week's,' said Andrew Knight, springing out of his rocking chair and covering his coffee table with a fan of sections.

'Take this one,' he said. ' "Books". This is the most comprehensive thing on books around. And this section – "News Review" – is Andrew Neil's pride and joy. Just simply did not exist in Harry Evans's time. Here we have one, two, three, four, five, six pages of columns by columnists, all of them rather serious blokes. All this on male rape, David Hughes on politics, Gavin Laird, Barbara Amiel – gee, Barbara Amiel is a wonderful columnist. Nobody can accuse Barbara Amiel [Mrs Conrad Black] of being light or frivolous in what she does.

'The "Business Section",' he went on, paging through the tower of newsprint, 'speaks for itself and I wouldn't have thought that the standards have fallen. I don't know but I certainly wouldn't have thought so. "Style and Travel". "Style", I suppose you could say "Style" is downmarket but I don't think it's downmarket myself. The "News" – I don't know what's going on in the underdeveloped world this week. Let's see. We've got the Italian plane knocked down in Yugoslavia, and – what do we have – we have Pakistan, India – Brussels is not underdeveloped – here we have Brussels, but here we have Pakistan, India, Winnie Mandela, Soweto, Hong Kong and China, Islam in Bosnia, Clinton and the election, Mitterrand, Nazis in Germany – this complete spread is European.

'The magazine: Ivan Fallon's cover story this week is a deeply serious piece and actually *very unfashionably serious* in that it's all about, when you really get into it, the predicament of the inner cities and the trapped, isn't it. Front page of the paper itself is very British this week, but it isn't always – it is actually completely British this week, I hadn't noticed that: BBC, big business losers, GCSE, the lost Beatles songs, Maastricht is sort of British.'

Andrew Knight rocked back into his chair. His educational tour of the *Sunday Times* had taken seven minutes.

'You won't have room for all this stuff, I imagine,' he said, 'but what I'm trying to say is that I think there's a *tremendous amount of cliché-mongering* about anything to do with Rupert Murdoch and his appointees and himself. And I think that cliché-mongering comes from these totally accepted conventional beliefs about somebody, whether it is that he's a republican or whether it is that he's downmarket. It comes from the fact that Murdoch does constantly challenge the Establishment, he constantly shakes trees and makes people feel uncomfortable. He's constantly saying that what's interesting may be things that you never thought were interesting before and appealing to people and getting them to read because he has this great belief that you can get them to read frivolous things *and* important things. This isn't always readily understood in this country. We live in a culture where I think people *do* resent success in a strange way. They keep dragging down our heroes.'

People were always telling me that Rupert Murdoch has fallen out of love with his newspapers. Even people who worked for his newspaper division said this, and it made them sound like long-suffering wives complaining that their husband was happiest these days at the office. And they were suspicious, too, of his mistresses: satellite television, movies, the Fox network. Their attitude was 'After all we've done for him'.

But Rupert Murdoch emphatically denied any boredom on his part with newspapers.

'They're still number one in terms of interest and affection and psychic return, if you like, or whatever one might call it,' he said. 'I love newspapers. I enjoy my involvements with them, after forty years I feel I understand them pretty well. I was trained in newspapers and the company's founded in newspapers but that used to be the *only* form of medium.' Then he said, 'Now there's other media and I would maintain that one needn't look at one media form so differently from another – there are different techniques but they're still the same editing functions and very largely the same skills.'

He stressed that News Corporation is still investing in new newspapers, still expanding 'despite the temporary restraints we're operating under following the events of the autumn of 1990 [the complex refinancing, involving nearly 150 banks, of its debts of more than $7.6 billion], a sufficiently unpleasant experience to make you swear you're not going to go through all that again. But we're doing things with newspapers,' he said, 'sure we are.'

I asked him what else he'd like to get his hands on.

'No question,' he said. '*New York Times, Washington Post, LA Times*, I think you'd put it in that order. But as a business, of those three I'd choose the *Washington Post*.'

I said I was surprised he'd mentioned the *Los Angeles Times*. I could see that its scale was tempting – the vast circulation and advertising revenues – but wasn't it exactly the kind of woolly, rambling newspaper he disliked? I could imagine him, on his first day as the new proprietor, ordering all the articles to be shortened by a third.

He laughed. 'It's certainly very hard work. There's good stuff in it but you've got to know your way through it, otherwise you're lost. My problem coming here is that, having had 17 years or whatever of having *The New York Times* delivered every morning – ahead of the *LA Times* – I still tend to pick it up first precisely because I *do* know my way around that one. And really what I've got to do – to be part of this community – is to wean myself on to the *LA Times*. At home I should have the *LA Times* and *nothing else* and spend half an hour at breakfast with it *and nothing else*.' He looked rather unhappy at the prospect of the *LA Times* welcoming him home after his pre-dawn jog. 'It'll be hard work,' he said.

I said, 'I notice you didn't mention the *Daily Mail* in London as something you'd like to own.'

'That's because even if Vere Rothermere sold it – and there's not one hundredth of a per cent chance – I wouldn't be allowed it [under monopoly rules] unless I sold a paper. Probably wouldn't be allowed it anyway. That being said, I admire the *Daily Mail* a lot, you have to admire it because it has a lot of good writing, a lot of ideas. I think it will get better with Dacre. [Paul Dacre, recently appointed successor to Sir David English, after Murdoch tried to poach him to edit *The Times*.] For one thing Dacre will be there every day – English was often away on holiday or whatever – and for another it won't have David's schizophrenia. Under David it would on the one hand be going upmarket but very learned – theatrical reviews – and on the other he would be giving it a feminine *Daily Express* populist touch of twenty years ago and both would be done brilliantly. But it left publishers and journalists looking at it and saying isn't this clever, but failing to make it. The circulation today is the same as when David English became head of it. The market has shrunk and he's made a pretty good achievement to hold on. What has happened is that the *Daily Express* has undertaken it, it's just slipped out behind it.'

'Do you see much of the other proprietors?'

'I run into Vere Rothermere in a restaurant maybe once or twice a year or at an annual Reuters luncheon or something. I'd run into Conrad a couple of times a year, same as Vere, or I'd meet him at a big dinner in Washington or something. I enjoy Conrad very much. And I used to see quite a lot of Donald Newhouse in New York, he's a good friend. Kay [Graham] socially with her daughter.'

'Which are the ones around the world you admire?'

'Oh, Conrad Black and Vere Rothermere. Vere is like his father, he's very deceptive, you don't see much of him or hear much of his activities, but he understands you've got to play for the long term and he's got the courage to do that. Here it's different, I mean they're all sitting on basic monopolies. Some of them are very great publishers like Kay Graham, but they don't need to compete. When you have a monopoly it changes the whole culture of the company.'

'What is the culture of News?'

'Oh, we do have a particularly strong corporate loyalty and strength. Obviously in our newspapers if someone comes and offers them double the money they're gone, but there is stability and I think loyalty – the idea of the company and everything. And we try to run a fairly paternalistic company. We make great demands on people's energy and effort and brains but I hope we pay back in more than just financial terms.'

'Which means what exactly?'

'You get a sense of achievement, a sense of being recognised, a sense of pride.'

Rupert Murdoch gestured out of the window. Somewhere outside on the Fox lot Sean Connery was starring in Murdoch's new thriller *The Rising Sun*, set against a background of total Japanese economic domination of the United States. But Murdoch was still expounding on the sense of achievement, recognition and pride of being a News Corporation man.

'It's very hard to transfer that and inspire that here [in LA],' he said, 'but we're getting there. One of the reasons I came out here personally was to do it. But the culture of the movie industry and the television industry, on the creative side, is to go from job to job in the companies, hoping one day you'll strike it rich. And so there's no particular loyalty. There's pride in what you do but no one thinks I'm going to be here in ten years' time doing this job or doing the job of the guy next door.

'Oh, you asked me a question earlier on,' he said, 'about newspapers it might be fun to have. I'd have to add the *New York Daily News*. I couldn't legally. But if they changed the law would I be tempted? Yes I'd be tempted. They'd probably stop me doing it and that would be a good thing. It may be mission impossible.'

'Do you know what you'd do with it?'

'I haven't thought about it but yes, I think I know. Take it back 30 years, keep absolutely involved in the city.'

Rupert Murdoch became suddenly animated. He could perhaps already see himself drawing up at the News building, sprinting across the *Daily Planet* lobby with its vast globe – scene of a dozen Robert Maxwell press-conferences – and grabbing the paper by the scruff of its neck and shaking it and shaking it and shaking it.

'Common sense,' he said, 'tells you not to touch the *Daily News*. But it's got a franchise and it would be terrific fun to have.

'Ah well,' he said, 'Mort Zuckerman will probably get it a month from now. It would be a shame if it disappeared. Good luck to him. He may make a success of it and a fool of me, so we'll see.'

It was precisely four weeks after this prophetic threat that Rupert Murdoch first announced his prodigal return to the New York *Post*.

23

The *Mirror* Cracked from Side to Side

Robert Maxwell: the shredding of a paper tiger

Rupert Murdoch was shaving in the bathroom of his house in Beverly Hills when he first heard Robert Maxwell was missing at sea. 'There was a telephone call from London at about 6 a.m. local time, and it was Kelvin MacKenzie [editor of the *Sun*] and he said, "Guess what? Bob Maxwell's gone over the side." I immediately assumed suicide and remain pretty sure of that judgement. It may have been out of character, but he certainly had the incentive.'

The death of Maxwell has become, for his fellow proprietors, an episode frozen in time, like the assassination of Kennedy and the first landing on the moon.

Punch Sulzberger was travelling back to New York from a conference of museum executives in Toledo, Ohio, when the drama caught up with him at the airport: 'I thought it must be an accident – a heart attack – but I've since come to the conclusion that Bob committed suicide. Frankly I'm dumbfounded that when he made up his mind to do this, he didn't try to get his house more in order and keep his sons out of the loop.' Tony O'Reilly, who was at a Heinz board meeting in Pittsburgh, believes it was 'suicide from despair'; Jim Kennedy heard the news on his car radio as he drove himself across midtown Atlanta, broadcast by his family radio station WSB, and has since concluded 'natural causes'; Otis Chandler was driving to his motor museum at Oxnard – 'Since nothing has been reported in the responsible press other than that it was an accident, I don't subscribe to any other theory'; Dean Singleton was chairing a meeting at the Chippendale boardroom table in Houston when the news flash was passed to him with a sheaf of telephone messages – 'suicide'; Lord Stevens, the proprietor who was closest to Maxwell, was in Tokyo –

'misadventure'; Samir Jain, returning to Delhi from a *Times of India* seminar in Bombay, read the news in the afternoon paper that had been purchased for him by his driver and was waiting on the back seat of his car at the airport – 'suicide'; Sally Aw Sian read the story in her *Hong Kong Standard* – 'misadventure'; Aveek Sarkar was at home in Calcutta when his *Telegraph* broke the story – 'Somehow it never occurred to me that he might just have slipped. I rang the office which was full of conspiracy theories. Had he been drowned by Mossad frogmen? Had he done a John Stonehouse and assumed a new identity in some far away land?'; Vere Rothermere was in Paris 'when I first heard he had jumped, or fallen, or was pushed. I heard in Montreal the following week that he had desperately tried to sell his Canadian investments a fortnight earlier, failed and had gone straight from Montreal to his yacht and a date with fate.' Conrad Black was at a Toronto board meeting for his magazine *Saturday Night* – 'This bulletin came in from Max [Hastings] in London. It was sort of ricocheted through to me and we were quite flabbergasted by it. I went out and rang Max who at that point still thought it might be some publicity stunt of Bob's and that he might pop up somewhere. I admonished Max not to write as negative a comment as he would be tempted to do, and said that, whatever Maxwell's frailties, we should be respectful of the recent dead. And Max wrote a lovely piece, something to the effect that the distance Bob had travelled from the place and circumstances of his birth commanded the respect of all of us who've had to travel much less far to rise much less high – that's pretty much a verbatim quote. It was elegantly done. Needless to say, as the passing weeks sped by I was held up to considerable ridicule by my editor who said, "If you'd just let me write what I wanted to we'd have been thought prophetic"! When you see how close Bob Maxwell was to the revelation of the enormities that apparently went on, I assume he did away with himself.'

There are so many conflicting theories and accounts of the final days of Robert Maxwell, each differing in some vital respect over the unfolding of events, that one quickly encounters the same problems as a theologian struggling to rationalise the Passion Week in the Synoptic Gospels. Incidents appear, or attain significance, in one account but not in another: the Mossad frogmen, the two white motor cruisers that could have been shadowing the *Lady Ghislaine*, the KGB hit squad, the Bulgarian secret police, the empty safe in the tycoon's cabin, the unusual absence on board of his faithful butler Joseph Caetano Pereira ('the only man who knew his master well'), the maudlin leavetaking with George Wheeler, the Savoy Hotel barber who had dyed Maxwell's hair and eyebrows every two weeks for the past 25 years ('Maxwell's only friend'), the East German Stasi, the mood swings, the ceremonial flypast of his Gulfstream-4 over the yacht, the last outing to the Ta-Madeira casino at Funchal, the eschatalogical instructions given and rescinded, the locked stateroom doors, his nakedness, the stowaway in the wetsuit, the remorseless faxes found by his bedside from Shearson Lehman, Goldman Sachs and the Swiss Bank Corporation which, sheet by sheet, sealed every avenue of his escape from bankruptcy.

The standard version of events has Maxwell ringing the skipper of the *Lady Ghislaine*, Captain Gus Rankin, on the evening of 30 October from the tenth-floor apartment in Holborn announcing that he would be arriving on board the next day. He explained he had a cold that he couldn't shake off, and hoped a short cruise would cure him. The call was untimely, since the *Lady Ghislaine* was undergoing maintenance in Gibraltar in preparation for a voyage across the Atlantic, where it would first rendezvous with Maxwell in Bermuda for his traditional Caribbean Christmas cruise and later sail on to the Water Club on the East River in Manhattan, to act as base for meetings at the *New York Daily News*. Rankin explained that the yacht was ill-prepared to receive visitors, but Maxwell replied it was of no consequence, since he was coming alone. Rankin added that there would be no time to lay on the stores of special food that usually awaited him – the wild strawberries, two-kilo tins of caviar, chicken soup ('Jewish penicillin', as Maxwell always insisted on calling it) and pickled gherkins – but was again told not to worry, he would eat whatever the galley could produce. Because Maxwell never travelled with fewer than a dozen briefcases, these and the rest of his luggage were driven to the airport in his Rolls Royce by his cockney chauffeur, John Featley, while Maxwell himself set off later by helicopter. Featley, like Wheeler the barber, seems to have enjoyed the role of court jester to Maxwell, and was permitted to make remarks that would have cost other employees their jobs. That morning, as he collected the baggage, Featley told *The Times* that he'd 'said to the guv'nor that the share price was going down the tubes, what was occurring?' Maxwell apparently chuckled and started talking about football. Featley said later, 'I thought, "Here we go again, the boss is going to pull another giant white rabbit out of the hat at the eleventh hour".'

Maxwell arrived in Gibraltar and was delivered by limousine to the *Lady Ghislaine*, where its eleven crew were lined up to greet him. The proprietor of the *Daily Mirror, Sunday Mirror*, the *People*, the Scottish *Daily Record* and *Sunday Mail*, the *New York Daily News*, the *European, Magyar Hirlap* in Hungary, *Maariv Vremia* in Israel, the *Kenya Times* and sundry no-hope weeklies in Bulgaria, Argentina and Mongolia gave his instructions to Rankin: the yacht should set sail for Madeira, a 600-mile journey that would take almost 36 hours, where he would be met by his plane and fly home again at the weekend. Maxwell sat out on deck, surrounded by the wall of briefcases which always made him resemble an obese bellhop, and worked through his papers. Later it would be argued that he was suffering from a softening of the brain, which enabled him to suspend reality for days on end, but it was a condition that came and went: sometimes objectivity could still take hold, and at these moments the truth must have weighed heavily upon him. Faxes and telephone calls brought only more bad news: Goldman Sachs were selling Maxwell Communication Corporation shares, as they'd threatened to do if the price collapsed further; the previous day, as Maxwell flew to Gibraltar, they'd sold 2.2 million, and if they were planning to jettison the 24 million they still held then the price might crash to zero. It was becoming obvious to Maxwell that almost no City institution was recommending his stock at any price. As he rummaged through the briefcases, he was rung from Holborn and informed that MCC was likely to be officially removed from the Stock Market's top 100 companies, which would in turn lead to a defection of index-linked funds, almost the last big holders of shares. By the time the mighty Maxwell Communication Corporation was put into administration a month later, almost the only three remaining shareholders seem to have been Robert Maxwell, Goldman Sachs and the present author, who held 197,102,080 shares, 24 million shares and fifteen shares respectively.

After breakfast on Saturday morning the yacht docked in Madeira at Funchal. Maxwell went ashore to go shopping, bought newspapers (single copies to read, not on this occasion newspaper companies) and searched unsuccessfully for a guide book to the island. It has been suggested that this eagerness to learn more about the history of Madeira proves that Maxwell had no premeditated plan to kill himself – otherwise why bother to mug up on new facts – but personally I don't buy this argument; he had a restless energy and curiosity whatever the circumstances. Later, accompanied by the yacht's second mate, he took a taxi to Reid's hotel, famous for its genteel British clientele, and paced crossly about the lobby for ten minutes before going for a beer in a bar by the port. After lunch, he instructed the captain to set sail for an uninhabited island called La Desertas, where he spent a couple of hours watching a colony of seals and swimming in the sea. It should be emphasised that Robert Maxwell was not a strong swimmer, and seldom ventured further than ten yards from the side of the boat. There is a theory that his vast girth would have prevented him from drowning, keeping him buoyant for hours on end, but this is not quite correct; his 21-stone bulk would indeed have prevented him from sinking, but not from rolling forwards or tipping upside down. That he was enormous in a bathing suit I can vouch from personal experience. One Sunday afternoon, about three months before he died, I was invited for lunch and to swim at the Maxwells' Oxford mansion, Headington Hill Hall. Arriving without bathing trunks, I was invited to borrow a pair from the changing hut. This is a low concrete edifice, very ugly, like an air-raid bunker, incorporating a sauna bath (with telephone: pre-programmed lines to Ian Maxwell's bedroom, Kevin Maxwell's bedroom, Pergamon boardroom) and a chest of drawers stocked with spare swimsuits. The drawers were labelled 'Average-sized Ladies', 'Children', 'Stout Men' and, finally, 'PRIVATE – FAMILY SWIMMING COSTUMES'. Unable to find serviceable trunks in the public drawers, I eventually explored the family one. Inside were several dozen pairs – there could have been as many as sixty – of Robert Maxwell's bathing costumes – boxer shorts and Y-fronts, each with a circumference as wide as a redwood, in bright oranges, purples and cherry reds. I could easily have slipped my whole body through one leg.

The *Lady Ghislaine* returned to Funchal at 7 p.m. and Maxwell ate his dinner alone on board. Later he decided to go ashore for another drink in a bar, noticed the Ta-Madeira casino, returned to the yacht for his passport and $3000 from the safe in his cabin and spent half an hour alone at the roulette and blackjack tables. History does not reveal how lucky he was that night, but certainly he did not recoup the $2 billion shortfall in his publishing empire. Before going to bed he informed Rankin that he intended to return to London the following day.

By the time he woke up he'd changed his mind. He asked to be dropped off somewhere midway across the Atlantic, but on being told this was not feasible, decided to sail 250 miles south to the Canary Islands instead. As they prepared to draw anchor, he instructed the pilot of his G-4 to collect his sons, Ian and Kevin, from London and fly them to the yacht, but then almost immediately rescinded the order. Instead he directed the jet to fly to Tenerife, from whence he would return to England the next day, and to make a ceremonial flypast over the yacht en route. Captain Rankin subsequently told *The Times*, 'He seemed in very good spirits watching the aircraft circle the boat.'

They approached the Canary Islands, Maxwell taking telephone calls on his private patch of deck. Ian Maxwell rang to remind him of a commitment to speak the following evening at the Anglo-Israeli Association dinner at the Grosvenor House hotel. His friend Samuel Pisar, the youngest survivor of Auschwitz, rang to talk about Gorbachev and Eastern Europe and Maxwell's impending nomination for the *Légion d'Honneur* for services to science, and as Man of the Year by the Jewish Scientific and Cultural Institute at the Plaza hotel in New York. Reaching Tenerife he took another swim, then resolved to have dinner alone at the only five-star restaurant on the island, the Hotel Mencey in Santa Cruz, where he chose salad followed by hake with clams in a parsley and mushroom sauce. Introspective and self-absorbed, only his trademark baseball cap and the fact that he seemed frustrated at not being able to make calls on his pocket telephone singled him out from the other diners. On arriving back at the yacht he instructed Captain Rankin to put out to sea and cruise all night. Like a fretful small baby which only drops off to sleep in a moving car, so Robert Maxwell found it difficult to sleep properly without the vibration of the yacht's engines. The *Lady Ghislaine*, her great turbines churning, set off down the eastern coast of Gran Canaria while the proprietor studied the faxed front page of the next day's *Daily Mirror*: the last front page for many weeks, as it happened, that wouldn't have his own face prominently upon it. Later he made an unannounced appearance in the pantry, not to scrounge food as was so often his custom an hour or so after dinner, but to complain about exhaust fumes from the engine in his cabin. The two stewardesses among the crew tried to clear the air with a hand-held fan, but Maxwell remained petulant. At midnight he was still taking satellite calls: from Ian, who had stood in for him at the Anglo-Israeli dinner, and from a Russian rabbi in Moscow who was soliciting Maxwell's help in his campaign to rescue Jewish archives. Depressing faxes from New York – six hours behind Tenerife – continued to arrive and were slipped underneath the stateroom door, where their detrimental effect on his insomnia outweighed the benefits of the yacht's engines. At the changing of the watch at 4 a.m., a crew member saw Maxwell leaning over the stern rail towards the flickering lights of Gran Canaria. Robert Maxwell called up to the bridge, 'It's hot', the air conditioning was switched on, but half an hour later he rang to demand it be turned off again.

Biologically he was cold blooded, and craved heat. His offices were customarily kept at 95 degrees. In New York, he found the executive floor of the *New York Daily News* so chilly that he decamped first to the presidential suite at the Waldorf Towers, until he found that too intolerably cold, then to the Helmsley Palace where he lay draped with blankets on a sofa. The call to the bridge was the last occasion Robert Maxwell was known to be alive. At about the same time he ate his last meal, a whole bunch of bananas, which was subsequently discovered in his stomach by amazed pathologists.

Telephone messages began to arrive the next morning at 9.30 a.m. local time. A caller from the New York offices of Rothschild's was told that Maxwell had not yet appeared on deck and was presumed asleep. An hour later a senior vice president of Maxwell Macmillan rang with an urgent message and demanded to be put through. The call was unanswered which activated a search. All doors to the stateroom were locked and, after much knocking, had to be opened with a pass-key. Maxwell's nightshirt was discovered on the floor, but of the proprietor himself there was no trace. Within ten minutes a mayday call had been raised. Rescue helicopters rushed to the scene and overflew the course of the yacht and by late afternoon the body of Maxwell was spotted floating, naked, on his back. A special wicker basket was lowered down from a helicopter to collect the body, but this proved to be inadequate, and eventually six men were obliged to use a nylon harness, normally employed to rescue cattle and horses from flood zones, to winch the dead proprietor's macroscopic carcass from the sea.

An investigation by the local authorities, led by Dr Luisa Garcia Cohen, swung into action, as it would have done for any ordinary tourist found drowned in Spanish waters. The post-mortem concluded death by natural causes, probably as a result of cardio-respiratory failure, and his family were told that he accidentally toppled over the rails into the sea after suffering a minor heart attack. This is the verdict that Maxwell's widow, Betty, chooses publicly to believe. Because of Robert Maxwell's extraordinary life, however, alternative theories clustered around his death like steel filings to a magnet. Within a fortnight, over four million words had been devoted by newspapers and magazines to speculation on the real cause. Pathologists, toxicologists, psychiatrists, neurologists, clairvoyants, underwater espionage experts, all were invoked to lend credence to ever more complex conspiracy theories. The ten principal theories, in escalating unlikeliness, are these

1. *Simple suicide*. Maxwell accepted that nothing could redeem him from his financial predicament. The banks were dumping stock which would shortly precipitate a stampede by other sellers. His auditors Coopers & Lybrand Deloitte were scheduled to do their next audit of the Mirror Group pension funds in six weeks' time and would discover that most of them were missing. His dream of building a world-class media empire like Time Warner and Murdoch's News Corporation was over; the future, if there was a future, would consist only of dismantling everything he'd built up. There would be a fire sale of the newspapers, the yacht, the Gulfstream, the apartment, at the end of it all nothing left to him but ignominy and the prospect of a jail sentence. For five days he brooded alone. The stream of faxes convinced him nothing could save the empire. He ordered the yacht to cruise all night, reducing the likelihood of being heard as he landed in the water, and rescued. Then he swayed to the rail, having satisfied himself that he wasn't being watched from the bridge, and jumped.

   The main objections to this theory are Maxwell's character, religion and nakedness. According to Dr Thomas Stuttaford, suicides who choose to take their lives by drowning very seldom do so naked; typically they remove their jackets and coats, which they leave neatly folded on rocks, but elect to be discovered in their clothes. A dead swimmer found naked, or wearing a bathing suit, is statistically an accident. On the other hand Robert Maxwell felt no shame in wandering about stark naked. Visitors to his apartment often found him undressed, fixing a drink at the bar in the sitting room, and at Headington Hill Hall he regularly swam in the buff, unbothered by the presence of friends, children or servants. He may well have considered it a macabre joke that the air-sea rescue team, or fisherman, or whoever first chanced upon his corpse, should have to deal with a twenty-stone nudist. More importantly, there are those who argue that Maxwell was a fighter and would never for a moment have submitted to suicide. He had been in tight corners all his life, and had an unshakeable belief in his ability to get out of them. His self-confidence certainly appeared to be all-encompassing; he believed he was cleverer than every competitor, auditor and banker and survival was merely a question of reshuffling his pack of assets, as he'd done so often before. Thirdly, there is a religious objection: 'Suicide,' the New York rabbi Arthur Schneier told *Vanity Fair*, 'is the last thing a traditional Jew would do. People who commit suicide are considered outcasts. Mourning is not permitted for them. They must not be buried in that part of a Jewish cemetery that consists of hallowed ground.' Maxwell had already secured his burial plot on the Mount of Olives: a difficult, expensive honour to secure that he would be unwilling to jeopardise by killing himself.

None of these objections, when weighted against bankruptcy and public derision, sound conclusive.

2. *Food poisoning*. The clams at the Hotel Mencey in Santa Cruz could have been unsound. At 5 a.m., nine hours after eating them, Maxwell was racked with intense stomach pains. According to this theory, he did not ring for a stewardess (most unlikely: he regularly rang on the slightest pretext) but remained doubled up in bed. The *Lady Ghislaine* rolled, the sliding doors between his cabin and the deck slid open, Maxwell toppled to the floor, rolled out on to the deck, and as the yacht lurched backwards, he fell

over the side. A drawback of this theory is that no other clam-eating guests at the hotel that evening made any complaint about the molluscs.

3. *The wet deck.* Maxwell took a stroll at about 5.15 a.m., the cabin having again become unbearably stuffy. He was naked; he had already thrown off his nightshirt to keep cool. The swell of the sea, which became rougher as dawn approached, meant the deck was slippery. Already dizzy from seasickness tablets and sleeping pills, Maxwell simply lost his balance and skidded overboard. As he fell, he managed to grasp the rail for a few minutes before losing his grip, which explains the torn ligaments in his left shoulder, recorded by the pathologist.

4. *Accidental death while defecating.* A limitation of almost all yachts, even yachts the size of the *Lady Ghislaine*, is that the bathrooms are cramped. The lavatory leading off Robert Maxwell's stateroom was barely adequate for a human of normal proportions, but for Maxwell every visit was a precision manoeuvre. He found it almost impossible to lever his enormous frame on to the seat and close the door behind him. This was a problem that he encountered not only on the *Lady Ghislaine*. In his Maxwell House office in Holborn he had a glass door installed in the adjoining bathroom, and he would continue to dictate letters while sitting upon the wooden seat, his legs stretched out before him into his secretary's sanctum. In his apartment upstairs, the lavatory was concealed behind a wall of dummy books in the sitting room, which he would kick open while sitting there, to the surprise of visitors awaiting an audience. One theory has Maxwell, in order to avoid using the yacht's coffin-sized latrine, deciding to defecate over the side. Removing his nightshirt and stepping through the gap in the rails, he could have positioned himself, backside aft, holding the rails with outstretched arms. A sudden roll, or even a minor heart tremor that momentarily relaxed his grip, would have caused him to plunge into the sea below.

5. *Poison.* Considerable attention was given in the days immediately following his death to the possibility that some deadly substance had been slipped into Maxwell's food, either by a member of the crew or by a third party who had somehow slipped aboard and

infiltrated the pantry. The theory gained credence when neither the Forensic Institute of Las Palmas nor the Toxicology Institute in Madrid would categorically reject the possibility that a hard-to-detect drug had been administered. 'There is always the possibility of a substance in the body that wasn't found,' announced Dr Maria José Meilan Remos. The unimpeachable reputation of the crew, however, and the fact that Maxwell ordered his choice of meals on the spur of the moment, does not lend much credence to it at all. The widely reported fact that he had an abrasion the size of a pinprick behind the ear that smelt of alcohol was later refuted as 'pure fiction' by the local doctors.

6. *Foreign agents board ship.* The problem with this theory – that a midget submarine manned by agents of the KGB, Mossad or the Bulgarian or East German security services approached the *Lady Ghislaine* by stealth, boarded ship, threw the tycoon overboard and made good their escape – is principally one of motive. Maxwell was a prime champion of Israeli causes and of all newspaper tycoons remained on good terms with all three Eastern Bloc governments. There is a theory that Maxwell at some stage in his career accepted funding from the Soviets, which he might subsequently have refused to reimburse, or that he was involved in a laundering scam for President Honecker and had absconded with the funds. But the fact that he had recently signed a deal to produce a publication for the KGB, to burnish their image in the West, makes it less than probable that they'd want him out of the way.

7. *A stowaway.* Was it feasible that, even before the yacht left Gibraltar, an extraneous passenger had slunk aboard and was concealed in a lifeboat or within one of the many suede-covered bars that stood in the corner of every stateroom? Robert Maxwell had for some months been convinced that a cartel of right-wing politicians, both British and American, were out to get him; to destroy him financially, defame him and quite possibly have him killed. There is a parallel theory that a New York family of the Mafia, which may have controlled the printing and distribution of the *New York Daily News* at the time he bought the paper and sacked staff, had a contract out on his life, since he declined to pay for protection either at the *News* or for the impending American

edition of the *European*. One of his managers was warned that he and Maxwell would 'end up in the East River with your throats slit'. Maxwell had consulted private investigation firms that specialised in all-round cover for tycoons. One of these, Kroll Associates of New York, had been summoned to a meeting at the Helmsley Palace hotel only a fortnight before his death, a meeting held on Maxwell's private terrace to frustrate electronic bugging, and he had recently insisted on using only telephones with advanced scrambler technology. The stowaway theory has a hired hood in a wetsuit awaiting the optimum moment, then breaking into Maxwell's cabin, beating him up (which explains the bruises found on the corpse, otherwise accounted for by his fall from the yacht) and propelling his concussed body into the sea (which explains the absence of sea water in the lungs, since he would have been unconscious before hitting the waves). The weakness of the theory is that the man in the wetsuit would scarcely have waited five days before carrying out his deadly mission, particularly since Maxwell kept extending his cruise without warning. Anyone with a contract out on Maxwell would have struck on the first night, and made his escape over the side before the yacht was too far from Gibraltar.

8. *A rival newspaper baron*. Five days after Maxwell's death, an American media analyst passing through London said to me: 'Look at it this way. Who had most to gain by his removal from the scene? Think about it,' he added darkly. 'Make a schedule of the newspaper owners who compete with him in his markets, and who might stand to gain something. Bob Maxwell was very competitive. He competed fiercely. He didn't make friends. And watch who makes their bids now to buy his papers.'

I had once asked Maxwell, in the aftermath of an AGM at the Mirror Building, what distinguished him as an owner from his competitors. He replied instantly, 'Because I am a *hands-on* publisher. I am a publisher who *publishes*. I control the chequebook. You cannot hire a pussycat in a Maxwell newspaper unless I say she can have food.'

'But most of your rivals run tight organisations, even if they don't sign the cheques themselves.'

'You are right to remind me of my rivals. There are many

upstarts. I have many detractors. I am a socialist and a royalist. Mr Murdoch and many of my other rivals are republican and anti-royalist.'

'Will they last?'

Maxwell shook his head magisterially. 'They have borrowings they are incapable of supporting. History will prove me right on this. *They all want my businesses* but it is their own communications companies that will have to be scaled down. They will peel away like a Gentile's foreskin in a Jewish sauna bath.'

Maxwell may have had enemies but the unlikely theory that a rival tycoon arranged for him to disappear breaks down completely once you start analysing the quality of the properties he left behind. With the exception of the Mirror Group and *Maariv* in Israel (which was bought by Yaacov Nimrodi, the arms dealer, after he fought off a bid from Conrad Black), none were sought after. When David and Frederick Barclay (the mysterious identical twins, distinguishable only because they part their hair on different sides) bought the *European* and property developer Mortimer Zuckerman took over the *New York Daily News*, they were viewed as philanthropists. And his papers in Bulgaria, Kenya, Argentina and Mongolia, far from supplying a motive for murder, were liabilities.

9. *Accidental death while swimming away*. Was Maxwell trying to make a clean break? This would account for the open safe with all its contents missing. Realising that nothing could now save his empire while he remained at its helm, he arranged to disappear, leaving his sons to shift as best they could. He had arranged for another motor yacht to shadow the *Lady Ghislaine*, and at a pre-arranged time jumped into the sea, unhampered by clothes, intending to be rescued within a few minutes and spirited away. Instead he drowned in the rougher-than-expected swell before he was picked up. No trace of the missing cash or documents (which would presumably have been in a waterproof bag) has been found.

10. *The decoy corpse*. This is the most elaborate conspiracy theory of all, initially floated in London in the *Guardian*, thereafter adopted by the kind of mythomaniac who believes that Martin Boorman, Adolf Hitler, John Lennon and Jimi Hendrix are all alive and

living in shacks in the Paraguayan jungle. The *Lady Ghislaine* made a detour from her cruise to the thinly inhabited east coast of Tenerife and Maxwell jumped ship on to a smaller white yacht. More than one of these were spotted in the vicinity of Maxwell's yacht, anchored off a part of the island normally rarely visited by luxury craft. Local tuna fishermen noticed one in particular, which bore no name or flags, moored off the village of El Palm-Mar, that struck them as acting suspiciously. The hypothesis continues that a decoy body, bearing a close resemblance to Robert Maxwell and of similar weight and build, was then tipped into the sea to be discovered thirteen hours later. Fingerprints couldn't be checked since the only extant set dated from his wartime military service and were too blurred to count; permission to consult his dental records was refused by the family, and waived on humanitarian grounds since they were anxious to fly the body to Israel before sundown on Friday, the start of the Jewish Sabbath. Much is made, in this conspiracy theory, of the fact that Maxwell's corpse wasn't burnt from the sun after what would have been thirteen hours floating in the sea, nor was it as wrinkled as might have been expected. The Civil Grand described the cadaver as that of a 'white male, with athletic build and prominent belly, chestnut hair – probably dyed – with a slight widow's peak, 1 metre 90 centimetres tall and weighing 130–140 kilos'. Maxwell's hair was, of course, dyed jet black, and the official version has it that long exposure to salt water turned it light brown; some authorities on autopsy point out, however, that while dyed hair is lightened by sea water, it does not change its colour.

When you ask advocates of the theory where precisely they believe Maxwell to be, they airily mention South America and visualise him living quietly and contentedly on the proceeds of an undetected Liechtenstein trust. To me, the most preposterous Achilles' heel is not the difficulty of acquiring a substitute corpse but the notion of Robert Maxwell living anywhere quietly and contentedly; he was fulfilled only at the centre of a maelstrom of activity. In the improbable event of his still being alive, he will have undergone advanced cosmetic surgery and be busy raising the capital to buy a chain of daily papers in Guadalajara.

24

The Proprietor Through the Looking-Glass

Epilogue

'It doesn't really matter much in the end who actually owns the various newspapers,' Lord Rothermere told me with majestic self-deprecation. 'When one proprietor gives up, or runs out of money or whatever, another one pretty soon comes along to take his place. The newspapers carry on more or less the same. I rather doubt the general reader has much idea when one owner hands over to the next fellow.'

But, as Lord Rothermere well knew, Lord Rothermere was simply being polite. The more I pondered the role of owners in determining their newspapers' future, the more pivotal it seemed. Much more than his editors or general managers who might at any moment be dismissed and replaced, the proprietor sets not just the agenda but the whole mood and context and level of expectation. The proof of this lay in imagining how greatly newspapers would change if chance gave them different owners; if, as at some proprietorial wife-swapping party where newspapers rather than car-keys are drawn from a hat, every owner slunk off with someone else's broadsheet or tabloid.

On the fifth anniversary of the swap, the proprietors and their new partners have a reunion to compare notes. Rupert Murdoch, arriving with *Le Figaro* on his arm, can scarcely recognise his old flame the *Sun*. For a start, she has traded in her novelty garter belt for an executive two-piece suit buttoned up to the neck. She clings rather nervously to the elbow of Donald Graham, refuses a drink and cigarettes, and when she finally speaks instead of her old cackle of prejudices and goodtime expletives, makes some politically correct observation about the slit up the side of *Le Figaro*'s skirt.

Otis Chandler blinks twice before he registers his old flame the *Los Angeles Times* across the room. She's got so thin, she must be bulimic. Dean Singleton is plumper though, as he escorts her into dinner. Lord Rothermere steps out of his limousine with the *Washington Post*, who everyone agrees looks very skittish and dizzy and much more of a party girl than they remember her before. Punch Sulzberger, catching a glimpse of *The New York Times*, is astonished to find her dressed up as a Chinese courtesan, and excitedly discussing chop-chop murders with a sinister-looking old gentleman in a white suit and dark glasses.

Acknowledgements

Several hundred people across five continents helped, advised and entertained me while I was researching this book. Many of them for obvious reasons elect to remain anonymous, others I am able to thank publicly: John Alexander, Nicholas Allan, Alan Armsden, Larry Ashmead, David Bar-Illan, David Barchard, Pilar de la Béraudière, Philip Bowring, David Burgin, V J Carroll, E Graydon Carter, Albert Cheng, Bruce Clark, Daniel Colson, Charles Cooper, Phillip Crawley, Karon Cullen, Michael Curtis, Tessa Dahl, Willie Dalrymple, Nigel Dempster, Jessica Douglas-Home, Vincent Doyle, David Elliott, Sir David English, John Evans, Leslie Evans, James Fairfax, Lady (Mary) Fairfax, Clay Felker, Max Frankel, John Fraser, Ursula Gill, Sydney Gruson, Michelle Han, Max Hastings, Liam Healy, Rob Hersov, head of Media at Morgan Stanley IBD in London, John and Lea Hoerner, Edward Hung, Bert Irvine, Brendan Keenan, Andrew Knight, S B Kolpe, Thomas Kwok, David Laventhol, Dominic Lawson, Valerie Lawson, Joseph Lelyveld, David Leser, Sir Nicholas Lloyd, June McCallum, Prue MacLeod, Jackie Mari, Ghislaine Maxwell, Vinod Mehta, Rosemary Millar, Charles Moore, S Mulgaokar, Hylton Murray-Philipson of Pall Mall Capital, Graham Nounam, Geraldine Ogilvy, Bruce Palling, R V Pandit, Camellia Panjabi, Naveen Patnaik, George Plimpton, Elizabeth Rees-Jones, Pat Robinson, the late Lady Rothermere, Vir and Malavika Sanghvi, Leo Schofield, John Scott, Joey Shawcross, Sonia Sinclair, Lynda Stewart, Ted Smith, Ted Thomas, Barbara Tims, Tony Turner, Gerard Wilkinson, Simon and Catherine Winchester, Roger Woods, Dorothy Wyndoe, Ada Yee.

I would particularly like to thank my father-in-law, George Metcalfe, who suggested the title *Paper Tigers*; Anthony Gardner who kindly devised the chapter headings; my publisher Helen Fraser, my agent Leslie Gardner, and Emma Rhind-Tutt who edited the manuscript. Above all I owe a great debt to Julia Elliott and to my wife, Georgia, both of whom assisted me with the project from its inception, and without whom it might never have seen the light of day.

Photographic Credits

Every effort has been made to trace copyright on photographs used in this book, but in certain cases this has proved impossible. The publishers would like to thank the following for their permission to reproduce pictures. 1,2, Ron Galella; 3,4,5,9, Fairchild Publications; 6, Pam Francis Photography; 7, *St Louis Post-Dispatch*; 8, Cox Enterprises Inc; 10,28, John Fairfax Group Pty Ltd; 11,13, *Ananda Bazar Patrika*; 12, Raghu Rai; 15,31, Dafydd Jones; 20, *International Herald Tribune*; 22,24, *South China Morning Post*; 23, Sing Tao Ltd.

Appendix

The World's Greatest Private Newspaper Empires

The inventory includes newspapers part-owned by the proprietor

THE AGA KHAN

Flagships
The Daily Nation (Nairobi)
The Sunday Nation

Swahili Newspaper
Taifa Leo

GIANNI AGNELLI

Flagships
Corriere della Sera (Milan)
La Stampa (Turin)

SALLY AW SIAN

Flagship
Sing Tao Daily
(Hong Kong, Toronto, Vancouver, New York, San Francisco, Los Angeles, London, Sydney, Auckland)

Chinese newspapers
The Hong Kong Standard

Sing Tao Evening
Tin Tin Daily News

CARLO DE BENEDETTI

Flagship
La Repubblica

SILVIO BERLUSCONI

Flagship
II Giornale

CONRAD BLACK

Flagships
Le Soleil (Quebec City)
The Daily Telegraph (London)
The Sunday Telegraph (London)
The Jerusalem Post
The Australian Financial Review
The Melbourne Age
The Sydney Morning Herald
The Chicago Sun-Times

Caribbean newspaper
The Caymanian Compass

Canadian newspapers
Brantford Expositor
Calgary Herald
Cranbrook Townsman
Dawson Creek Peace River Block News
Edmonton Journal
Fort St John Alaska Highway News
Hamilton Spectator
Kamloops News
Kimberley Bulletin
Kingston Whig-Standard
Kitcherner Waterloo Record

Le Droit (Ottowa)
Le Quotidien du Saguenay Lac St-Jean (Chicoutimi)
Medicine Hat News
Montreal Gazette
Nelson Daily News
North Bay Nugget
Ottowa Citizen
Owen Sound Sun Times
Port Alberni Valley Times
Prince George Citizen
Prince Rupert News
Sault Ste Marie Star
Summerside Journal-Pioneer
Trail Times
Vancouver Province Sun
Windsor Star

American Newspapers
Atlantic News-Telegraph
Benton Evening News
Blackfoot Morning News
Boonville News Advertiser
Bradford Era
Camdenton Reveille
Canton Daily Ledger
Carmi Times
Charles City Press
Cheboygan Daily Tribune
Chillicothe Constitution-Tribune
Clay County Advocate
Columbia City Post & Mail
Corry Journal
Crookston Times
Decatur Daily Democrat
Du Quoin Evening Call
El Dorado Times
Eldorado Daily Journal
Fort Morgan Times
Greensburg Daily News
Harrisburg Daily Register
Hartford City News-Times
Hornell Evening Tribune
Jamestown Sun
Kane Republican
Lamar Daily News

Macon Chronicle Herald
Marion Daily Republican
McPherson Sentinel
Monmouth Review Atlas
Naugatuck Daily News
Neosho Daily News
Newport Independent
Olney Mail
Punxsutawny Spirit
Ridgway Record
Rolla Daily News
Rushville Republican
Salamanca Republican
Sault Ste Marie Evening News
Sayre Evening Times
St Mary's Daily Press
St Mary's Evening Leader
Sterling Journal Advocate
Stillwater Gazette
Titusville Herald
Wapakoneta Daily News
Waynesboro Record Herald
Waynesville Fort Gateway Guide
Wellsville Reporter
West Frankfort Daily American
Woodward News

LOUIS CHA

Flagship
Ming Pao Daily News

OTIS CHANDLER

Flagships
Long Island Newsday
The Los Angeles Times
New York Newsday

American newspapers
Allentown Morning Call
Baltimore Sun
Greenwich Time
Hartford Courant
The Stamford Advocate

COX NEWSPAPERS

Flagships
The Atlanta Constitution
The Atlanta Journal

American newspapers
Arizona Pennysaver
Austin American-Statesman
Bilbert Tribune
Chandler Arizonan
Dayton Daily News
Dayton Down Towner
Daytona Beach News-Journal
Florida Pennysaver
Gilbert Tribune
Grand Junction Daily Sentinel
Longview News-Journal
Lufkin Daily News
Mesa Tribune
Nacogdoches Daily Sentinel
The Orange Leader
Palm Beach Daily News
Palm Beach Post
Post Arthur News
Springfield News-Sun
Tempe Daily News Tribune
The Valley Foothills News
Waco Tribune-Herald
Yuma Bajo El Sol
Yuma Daily Sun

WARWICK FAIRFAX

Newspapers pre-1991

Flagships
The Australian Financial Review
The Melbourne Age
The Sydney Morning Herald

Australian newspapers
Illawarra Mercury
The Newcastle Herald
The Sun-Herald
Warrnambool Standard

THE GOENKAS

Flagship
The Indian Express
(Bombay, Ahmedabad, Bangalore, Chandigarh, Cochin, Hyderabad,
Madras, Madurai, New Delhi, Pune, Vijayawada, Vizianagram)

Indian newspapers
The Financial Express
Lokasatta (Marathi)
Samakaleen (Gujarati)

THE GRAHAMS

Flagships
The International Herald Tribune
The Washington Post

American newspaper
The Everett Herald

THE HEARSTS

Flagships
San Francisco Examiner & Chronicle
Houston Chronicle

American newspapers
Albany Times-Union
Bad Axe Huron Daily Tribune
Beaumont Enterprise
Edwardian Intelligencer
Laredo Morning Times
Midland Daily News
Midland Reporter-Telegram
Plainview Daily Herald
San Antonio Express-News
Seattle Post-Intelligencer

ROBERT HERSANT

Flagships
Le Figaro
France-Soir

French newspapers
Le Havre-Libre
Journal du Dimanche
Journal Rhône-Alpes
L'Aurore
L'Espoir
L'Indépendent
L'Union
La Tribune
Le Courier de Soame-en-Loire
Le Dauphine Libéré
Le Havre Presse
Le Progrès
Le Sport
Les Dépèches
Liberté du Morbihan
Loire Matin
Lyon Figaro
Lyon Matin

Midi Libre
Nord Eclair
Nord Matin
Paris Normandie
Paris Turf
Presse Océan
Vaucluse Matin

Other European newspapers
Le Soir (Belgium)
Magyar Nemzet (Hungary)
Mlada Fronta (Czechoslovakia)
Petoefi Nepe (Hungary)
Rzeczpospolita (Poland)

Newspapers in former French colonies
France Antilles
France Guyane
La Dépêche de Tahiti
Les Nouvelles Caledoniennes

RALPH INGERSOLL

Some Ingersoll newspapers at the zenith of his empire

American newspapers
Alton Telegraph
Anderson Daily Bulletin
Anderson Herald
Asheboro Courier-Tribune
Claremont/Springfield Eagle-Times
Coatesville Record
Dover-New Philadelphia Times-Reporter
Fall River Herald-News
Festus/Crystal City News-Democrat
Ionia Sentinel-Standard
Lorain Journal
Mansfield News-Journal
New Haven Journal-Courier
New Haven Register
Niles Daily Times
North Adams Transcript
North Tonawanda News

Pawtucket-Central Evening Times
Phoenixville Evening Phoenix
The St Louis Sun
Sheboygan Press
South-Haven Daily Tribune
Terre Haute Tribune-Star
Trenton Trentonian
Troy Times Record
Warren Tribune Chronicle
West Chester Daily Local
Willoughby-Mentor Lake County News-Herald
Woonsocket Call

British newspapers
The Coventry Evening Telegraph
The Birmingham Post and Mail

Irish newspapers
Evening Press (Dublin)
Sunday Press (Dublin)

SAMIR JAIN

Flagship
The Times of India
(Delhi, Bombay, Bangalore, Jaipur, Patna, Lucknow, Ahmedabad,
Gujarat)

Indian newspapers
The Dinaman Times
The Economic Times
The Independent
The Maharashtra Times
The Navbharat Times
The Sandhya Times

KAMPHOL VACHARAPHOL

Flagship
Thai Rath (Bangkok)

ROBERTO MARINHO

Flagship
O Globo (Rio de Janeiro)

THE MAS

Flagship
The Oriental Daily News

ROBERT MAXWELL

Newspapers pre-November 1991

Flagships
The Daily Mirror
The European
The New York Daily News
The Sunday Mirror

British newspapers
The Daily Record (Scotland)
The London Daily News (1988)
The People
The Sporting Life
The Sunday Mail (Scotland)

Miscellaneous world newspapers
The Kenya Times (Nairobi)
Maariv (Tel-Aviv)
Magyar Hirlip (Hungary)

RUPERT MURDOCH

Flagships
The Australian
The News of the World (London)
The Sun (London)
The Sunday Times (London)
The Times (London)

Appendix

European newspapers
Mai Nap (Budapest)
Reform (Budapest)
Today (London)

American newspaper
The Boston Herald
The New York Post

Australian and Pacific newspapers
The Advertiser
The Cairns Post
Cairns Sunday
Centralian Advocate
The Courier-Mail
The Daily Telegraph Mirror
Derwent Valley Gazette
Douglas Times
The Fiji Times
Gold Coast Sun
Gold Coast Bulletin
Herald-Sun
Hinterland Sun
The Mercury
Nai Lalakai (Fiji)
Northern Beachcomber
Northern Territory News
The Perth Sunday Times
Post Courier (Papua New Guinea)
Pyramid News
Shanti Dut (Fiji)
The Sporting Globe
Sportsman
Sunday Herald-Sun
The Sunday Mail
Sunday Mail
Sunday Morning Post (Hong Kong)
The Sunday Tasmanian
The Sunday Telegraph
Sunday Territorian
Tablelands Advertiser
Tasmanian Country
Townsville Bulletin
Treasure Islander
The Weekly Times

ASIL NADIR

Flagships owned until 1991
Gunes
(Adana, Ankara, Istanbul, Izmir)
Günaydin
(Adana, Ankara, Istanbul, Izmir)

Turkish newspapers
Aktuel
Ekonomik Bulten
Ekspres
Fotospor
Kocaeli
Meram
Sakarya
Tan
Ulus

Cypriot newspapers
The Cyprus Times
Kibris

British newspapers
Bristol North Mercury
North Avon Mercury
Stroud and Cirencester Mercury

THE NEWHOUSES

Flagships
The Birmingham News/Post Herald
New Orleans Times-Picayne
The Newark Star-Ledger

American newspapers
Ann Arbor News
Bay City Times
Cleveland Plain Dealer
Flint Times
Grand Rapids Press
Harrisburg News
Harrisburg Patriot

Harrisburg Patriot-News
Huntsville News
Huntsville Times
Jackson Citizen Patriot
Jersey City Journal
Kalamazoo Gazette
Mobile Press
Mobile Press-Register
Mobile Register
Muskegon Chronicle
Pascagoula Mississippi Press
Pascagoula Mississippi Press-Register
Portland Oregonian
Saginaw News
Springfield Republican
Springfield Union-News
Staten Island Advance
Syracuse Herald-American
Syracuse Herald-Journal
Syracuse Post-Standard
Trenton Times

TONY O'REILLY

Flagships

The Irish Independent (Dublin)   The Independent (Britain – 29·9%)
The Sunday Independent (Dublin) The Independent on Sunday (Britain –
29·9%)

Irish and British newspapers

Barking and Dagenham Express   The Irish Star (Dublin)
Barking and Dagenham Post   Islington Chronicle
Docklands Express   Islington Gazette
The Evening Herald (Dublin)   Romford and Havering Post
East London Advertiser   Stratford and Newham Express
Hackney Echo   The Sunday World (Dublin)
Hackney Gazette   Waltham Forest Express
Ilford and Redbridge Post

South African newspapers

The Cape Town Argus   The Kimberley Diamond Fields
The Durban Daily News   Advertiser
The Durban Sunday Tribune   The Pretoria

Australian newspapers
Biloela Central Telegraph
Bribie Weekly
Bundaberg Drum
Bundaberg News-Mail
Bush Telegraph
Chinchilla News
Coffs Harbour Advocate
Dalby Herald
Emerald Central Queensland News
Express Examiner
Gladstone Observer
Gold Coaster
Grafton Examiner
Ipswich Freeway Press
Lismore Happening
Lismore Northern Star
Mackay Daily Mercury
Mackay Midweek
Maryborough Chronicle
Maryborough Hervey Bay Observer
Miners Midweek
Near North Coast News
Noosa News
North Coast Advocate
Northern Farmer
Queensland Times
Richmond River
Rockhampton Country Bulletin
Rockhampton Morning Bulletin
Rural Times
Sarina Midweek
Satellite/Weekly Times
Sunshine Coast Daily
Sunshine Coast Weekly
Super Southsider
Toowoomba Chronicle
Toowoomba Chronicle Country
Toowoomba Downs Star
Tweed Daily News
Warwick Bush Telegraph
Warwick Daily News
Whitsunday Times

LORD ROTHERMERE

Flagships
The Daily Mail (London)
The Evening Standard (London)
The Mail on Sunday (London)

British newspapers
Ashby & Coalville Mail
Axholme Herald
Belper Express
Beverley Advertiser
Billericay & Wickford Gazette
Boston Target
Brentwood Gazette
Carmarthen Journal
Carmarthen Citizen
Cheltenham News
Cornish Guardian
The Cornishman
Crambourne, Redruth Leader
Derby Evening Telegraph
Derby Express
East Grinstead Courier
East Hull Target
Essex Chronicle
Exeter Express & Echo
Exeter/Exmouth Leader
Falmouth/Penrhyn Leader
Gainsborough Target
Gloucester Citizen
Gloucester Echo
Gloucester News
Grimsby Evening Telegraph
Grimsby Target
Halternprice Target
Helston/Lizard Leader
Holderness Target
Horncastle, Collingsby and Woodhall Spa Target
Hull Daily Mail
Hull Target Series
Ilkeston Express
The Kent & Sussex Courier
Leicester Mail
Leicester Mercury

Lincoln Target
Lincolnshire Echo
Llanelli Star
Loughborough Mail
Louth Target
North Devon Journal
North Staffs Advertiser
Oadby & Wigston Mail
Penzance Hayle Leader
Plymouth Extra
Retford Times
Ripley & Heanor Express
Romford Observer
Scunthorpe Evening Telegraph
Scunthorpe Target
Sevenoaks Chronicle
Sevenoaks News In Focus
Sleaford Target
South Lincs Target Group
South Wales Evening Post
Spilsby & Skegness Target
Stoke Evening Sentinel
Swansea Herald of Wales
Tiverton Gazette Series
Torbay Weekender
Torquay Herald Express
Truro Leader
Tunbridge Wells News In Focus
Wellington Weekly News
West Briton
West Hull Target
Western Evening Herald
Western Morning News

Hungarian newspaper
Kisalfold (Gyor-Sopron)

AVEEK SARKAR

Flagships
The Calcutta Telegraph
Ananda Bazar Patrika
The Financial Times (Indian edition, with Pearson)

Indian newspapers
Business Standard
The Hindustan Standard
Ravivar
The Sunday Telegraph

DEAN SINGLETON

Flagships
The Denver Post
The Houston Post

American newspapers
Alameda Times-Star
Arcadia Tribune
Bristol Press
The Elizabeth Daily Journal
Fairbanks News-Miner
Farmington Valley Herald
The Fremont Argus
The Gloucester County Times
The Graham Leader
Green Sheet East
Green Sheet West
The Hayward Enterprise
The Hayward Herald Sampler
Independent Press
The Jack County Herald
The Jacksboro Gazette
The Johnstown Tribune-Democrat
Jordon Valley Sentinel
Las Cruces Sun-News
Monrovia News-Post
The Murray Eagle
North Jersey Herald & News
The Oakland Tribune
The Park City Park Record
The Pasadena Duratean
Pasadena Star News
The Passaic Fairlawn Shopper
Passaic Suburban News/Town News
The Pleasanton Tri-Valley Herald
The Potomac News
The Quantico Sentry

The Review
The Rigewood Newspapers
The Salem Today's Sunbeam
Sandy Sentinel
Sentinel West
South Bergenite
The Stafford Sun
Suburban News
Suburbanite
Temple City Times
The Thomaston Express
Today Newspapers
West Valley View
The Winber Era
The Winber Shopper
The Woodbury Advertiser
The Woodbury Record
Yakima Herald Republic
Ypsilanti Press
Ypsilanti Shopper Showcase

LORD STEVENS OF LUDGATE

Flagships
The Daily Express (London)
The Sunday Express (London)
The Yorkshire Post

British newspapers
Ashton-under-Lyne Reporter
Barnet Advertiser
Barnoldswick & Earby Times
Barrow Reporter
Batley News
Birstall News
Blackpool Extra
Blackwood & Risca News
Brighouse Weekly News
Burnley Express & Burnley News
Campaign Blackwood
Campaign Caerphilly & Rhymney Valley
Campaign Ebbw Vale & North Gwent
Campaign Merthyr Tydfil & Cynon Valley

Campaign Pontypridd & Llantrisant
Campaign Rhondda Valley
Cardiff Independent
Champion Shopper
Chepstow & Caldicot News
Chorley Guardian
Cleckheaton Reporter
Clitheroe Advertiser & Times
Colne Times
Cwmbran & Pontypool News
The Daily Star (London)
The Dales Champion Shopper
Denton Reporter
Dewsbury Reporter
Droylsden Reporter
Ealing, Southall & Acton Informer
East Cambs Town Crier
East Manchester Reporter
Edgware Advertiser
Enfield Advertiser
Epsom Informer
Evening Gazette
Farmers Guardian
Finchley Advertiser
The Garstang Courier
Garstang Guardian
Glossop Chronicle
Hampstead Advertiser
Haringey Advertiser
Harrogate Advertiser
The Harrogate Herald
Harrow Informer
Heckmondwike Reporter
Hendon Advertiser
Hertford & Ware Advertiser
High Peak Reporter
Hoddesdon & Cheshunt Advertiser
Hounslow & Chiswick Informer
Kingston Informer
Knaresborough Post
Lakeland Echo
Lancashire Evening Post
Lancaster Guardian
Leeds Weekly News
Leigh Reporter

The Longridge News
Lytham St Annes Express
Maghull & Aintree Advertiser
Mirfield Reporter
Monmouth & Abergavenny News
Morecombe Guardian
The Morecambe Visitor
Morley Observer
Mossley & Saddleworth Reporter
Nelson Leader
Newport News
North Cheshire Herald
North Yorkshire News
Northallerton, Thirsk & Bedale Times
Northampton Chronicle & Echo
Northampton Mercury & Herald
Ormskirk Advertiser
Pateley Bridge & Nidderdale Herald
Prescot Reporter
The Preston & South Ribble Weekly Mail
Pudsey Times
Richmond & Twickenham Informer
Ripon Gazette & Boroughbridge Herald
Sheffield Star
Sheffield Telegraph
The Sheffield Weekly Gazette
Skelmersdale Advertiser
South Cambs Town Crier
South Ribble Guardian
South Wales Argus
Spen & Calder Weekly News
St Helens Reporter & Leader
Staines Informer
Stalybridge & Dunkinfield Reporter
Uxbridge Informer
Walton & Weybridge Informer
Wembley & Greenford Informer
West Cambs Town Crier
Wetherby, Boston Spa & Tadcaster News
Wharfe Valley Times
Wharfedale Champion Shopper
Wigan Leader
Wigan Observer
Wigan Reporter
Wimbledon & Merton Informer

Woking Informer
Yorkshire Evening Post

Spanish newspapers
Claxon Castellon
Claxon Costa Duarada
Claxon Ebra
Claxon El Espolon
Claxon Girona
Claxon Lleida
Claxon Manresa
Claxon Mataro
Claxon Navarra
Claxon Sabadell

THE SULZBERGERS

Flagships
The International Herald Tribune
The New York Times

American newspapers
Boston Globe
The Daily Corinthian
The Dyersburg State Gazette
Florence Times Daily
Gadsden Times
Gainesville Sun
Hendersonville Times-News
Houma Daily Courier
Lake City Reporter
Lakeland Ledger
Leesburg Commercial
Lenoir News-Topic
The Lexington Dispatch
Madisonville Messenger
Ocala Star-Banner
Opelousas Daily World
Palatka Daily News
Santa Barbara News-Press
Santa Rosa Press Democrat
Sarasota Herald-Tribune
Silmington Morning Star
Spartanburg Herald-Journal

Thibadaux Daily Comet
Tuscaloosa News

THANACHAI THEERAPATVONG, SUTHICHAI YOON

Flagship
The Nation (Bangkok)

KENNETH THOMSON

Flagships
The Newcastle Evening Chronicle (UK)
The Repository (Ohio, USA)
Scotland on Sunday (UK)
The Scotsman (UK)
The Toronto Globe and Mail

Canadian newspapers
Barrie Examiner
Belleville Intelligencer
Brandon Sun
Cambridge Reporter
The Charlottetown Evening Patriot
Charlottetown Guardian
Chatham Daily News
Corner Brook Western Star
Cornwall Standard-Freeholder
The Guelph Daily Mercury
Kelowna Daily Courier
Kirkland Lake Northern Daily News
Lethbridge Herald
Lindsay Post
Moose Jaw Times-Herald
Nanaimo Daily Free Press
New Glasgow Evening News
Niagara Falls Review
The Orillia Packet & Times
Oshawa Times
Pembroke Observer
Penticton Herald
Peterborough Examiner
Prince Albert Daily Herald
Sarnia Observer

Simcoe Reformer
St John's Evening Telegram
St Thomas Times-Journal
Sudbury Star
Sydney Cape Breton Post
Thunder Bay Chronicle-Journal
Thunder Bay Times-News
Timmins Daily Press
The Truro Daily News
Vernon Daily News
Victoria Times-Colonist
The Welland Tribune
Winnipeg Free Press
Woodstock Daily Sentinel-Review

American newspapers
Ada Evening News
Adrian Daily Telegram
Albert Lea Evening Tribune
Altoona Mirror
Americus Times-Reporter
Anderson Herald-Bulletin
Ansonia Evening Sentinel
Appleton Post Crescent
Ashtabula Star-Beacon
Atchison Daily Globe
Austin Daily Herald
Barstow Desert Dispatch
Beckley Register/Herald
Benton Harbor-St Joseph Herald-Palladium
Big Spring Herald
Bluefield Daily Telegraph
Bridgeport Post
Canton Repository
Carthage Press
Chardon Geauga Times Leader
Charleston Daily Mail
Charleston Sunday Gazette Mail
Conneaut News Herald
Connellsville Daily Courier
Corbin Times-Tribune
Cordele Dispatch
Coshocton Tribune
Council Bluffs Nonpareil
Cumberland News

Dalton Daily-Citizen-News
Del Rio News Herald
Dickinson Press
Dothan Eagle
East Liverpool Evening Review
Easton Express
The Elizabeth City Daily Advance
Enid News & Eagle
Enterprise Ledger
Escanaba Daily Press
Eureka Times-Standard
Fairmont Times-West Virginian
Fergus Fall Daily Journal
Fitchburg-Leominster Daily Sentinel & Enterprise
Florence Morning News
Fond du Lac Reporter
Greenville Daily Advocate
Greenville Record-Argus
Griffin Daily News
Hamilton Journal News
Hanover Evening Sun
Herkimer Evening Telegram
Houghton Mining Journal
Huntsville Item
Iron Mountain Daily News
Jackson County Floridan
Jacksonville Journal-Courier
Kerrville Daily Times
Key West Citizen
Kittanning Leader-Times
Kokomo Tribune
Lafayette Daily Advertiser
Lancaster Eagle-Gazette
Laurel Leader-Call
Leavenworth Times
Lebanon News Pennsylvanian
Lock Haven Express
Manitowoc Herald-Times-Reporter
Mansfield News-Journal
Marion Star
Marquette Mining Journal
Marshall News Messenger
Meadville Tribune
Mexico Ledger
Middletown Journal

Mitchell Republic
Monnessen Valley Independent
Monroe Enquirer Journal
Mt Vernon Register-News
New Albany Ledger & Tribune
New Albany Tribune
New Castle News
Newark Advocate
Newburg Evening News
Northwest Arkansas Times
Oelwein Daily Register
Olean Times-Herald
Opelika News
Orange Park Clay Today
Oswego Pallidium-Times
Oxnard Press-Courier
Pasadena Star-News
Petersburg Progress-Index
Piqua Daily Call
Portsmouth Herald
Portsmouth Times
Rensselaer Republican
Richmond Register
Rocky Mount Evening Telegram
Salem News
Salisbury Daily Times
San Gabriel Valley Daily Tribune
Sedalia Democrat
Shamokin Mt Carmel News Item
Sheboygan Press
Shelby Star
Sikeston Daily Standard
St George Spectrum
Sterling-Rock Falls Gazette
Steubenville Herald-Star
Taunton Daily Gazette
Terre Haute Tribune-Star
Thomasville Times-Enterprise
Tifton Gazette
Valdosta Daily Times
Valparaiso Vidette-Messenger
Warren Tribune
Warren Tribune Chronicle
Waukesha Freeman
Weirton Daily Times

West Bend News
Whittier Daily News
Wisconsin Rapids Daily Tribune
Worthington Daily Globe
Yreka Siskiyou Daily News
Zanesville Times Recorder
Zenia Daily Gazette

British newspapers
Aberdeen Evening Express
Aberdeen Press & Journal
Bedford Herald & Post
Belfast Sunday Life
Belfast Telegraph
Bishops Stortford Herald & Post
Brackley and Towcester Herald & Post
Bracknell/Wokingham Herald & Post
Burton Herald & Post
Cambridge Times
Cardiff Western Mail
Chester Chronicle
Corby Herald & Post
Daventry Herald & Post
Derby Herald & Post
Derbyshire Herald & Post
Edinburgh Evening News
Ely Standard
Gateshead Post
Harlow Herald & Post
Hemel Hempstead Herald & Post
Hinckley & Bosworth Herald & Post
Hoddesdon Herald & Post
Hunts Herald & Post
Ilkeston & Ripley Herald & Post
Kettering Herald & Post
Leicester Herald & Post
Leighton Buzzard Herald & Post
Long Eaton Herald & Post
Loughborough Herald & Post
Luton & Dunstable Herald & Post
Mid-Beds Herald & Post
Middlesborough Evening Gazette
Milton Keynes Herald & Post
Newcastle Evening Chronicle
The Newcastle Journal

Newcastle Sunday Sun
Northants Herald & Post
Nottingham Herald & Post
Nuneaton & Bedworth Herald & Post
Peterborough Herald & Post
Reading Evening Post
Reading Herald & Post
South Wales Echo
St Albans & Harpenden Herald & Post
Stamford Herald & Post
Stevenage, Hitchin & Letchworth Herald & Post
Wales on Sunday
Wellingborough, Rushden Herald & Post
Welyn & Hatfield Herald & Post
Wisbech Standard
Wokingham Times

MORTIMER ZUCKERMAN

Flagship
The New York Daily News

Bibliography and Sources

Chapter 1

Bagdikian, Ben, *The Media Monopoly*, Beacon, 1983

Braddon, Russell, *Roy Thomson of Fleet Street*, Collins, 1965

Bray, Howard, *The Pillars of the Post – the making of a news empire in Washington*, Norton, 1980

Brendon, Piers, *The life and death of the Press Barons*, Secker & Warburg, 1982

Cornwell, Rupert, 'Gorbachev in the role of press baron', *Independent*, 22 November 1989

Cudlipp, Hugh, *Walking on the Water*, Bodley Head, 1976

Dawson, Charles, 'Giants battle for Eastern Europe' *The Campaign Report*, 8 June 1990

Friedman, Alan, *Agnelli and the network of Italian power*, Harrap, 1988

Goldenberg, Susan, *The Thomson Empire*, Methuen, 1984

Jacobs, Eric, *Stop Press – the inside story of the Times dispute*, André Deutsch, 1980

Pound, Reginald and Geoffrey Harmsworth, *Northcliffe*, Cassell, 1959

Randall, Jeff (with Fiona Walsh and Ivan Fallon), 'A bid too far' *Sunday Times*, 7 October 1990

Robinson, Jeffrey, *The Risk Takers – Portraits of Money, Ego & Power*, George Allen & Unwin, 1985

Talese, Gay, *The Kingdom and the Power*, World Publishing, 1966

Taylor, A J P, *Beaverbrook*, Hamish Hamilton, 1972

Tifft, Susan E and Alex S Jones. *The Patriarch: the rise and fall of the Bingham Dynasty*, Summit, 1991

Wintour, Charles, *The Rise and Fall of Fleet Street*, Hutchinson, 1989

Chapter 2

Archer, Miles (with Huntley Haverstock, J J Hunsecker), 'Naked City: The Times', *Spy*, February 1987 – April 1990

Barnes, Fred, 'The Post vs The Times: Which is Better?' *The Washingtonian*, May 1987

Barrett, Wayne, 'No Shame at the Times', *Voice*, 19 September 1989

Close, Ellis, *The Press – Inside America's most powerful newspaper empires*, Morrow, 1989

Diamond, Edwin, 'The Times of Frankel', *New York Magazine*, 10 August 1987

Diamond, Edwin, 'Old Times, New Times' *New York Magazine*, 30 September 1991

Goodwin, Michael, 'The Rising Power at the New York Times', *On the Avenue*, 4 November 1989

Goulden, Joseph C, *Fit to Print – A M Rosenthal and his Times*, Lyle Stuart, 1988

Halberstam, David, *The Powers that Be*, Knopf, 1975

Hellman, Geoffrey T, 'Viewer from the 14th Floor' *New Yorker*, 18 January 1969

Kappstatter, Bob, 'Sulzberger Jr has the Times on his hands', *New York Daily News*, 17 January 1992

Klein, Edward, 'Prince Pinch' *Manhattan inc*, August 1988

Marchese, John, 'The Max Factor' *7 Days*, 13 December 1989

Moses, Paul, 'Times Publisher Punches Out', *New York Newsday*, 17 January 1992

Moss, Linda, 'A gray outlook at the Times' *Crain's New York Business*, 11 March 1991

Nadler, Eric, *Sex and the New York Times*, Forum, 1990

Sulzberger, Arthur Ochs, Keynote Address, ANPA 103rd annual convention, Chicago, 24 April 1989

Walls, Jeannette, ' "Styles" Victims', *New York Magazine*, 16 November 1992

Chapter 3

Adelman, Ken, 'So Long, Sweetheart', *The Washingtonian*, September 1991

Coleman, Terry, 'The Fourth Estate's First Lady', *Guardian*, 29 March 1974

Felsenthal, Carol, *Power, Privilege and the Post: The Katharine Graham Story*, Putnam, 1993

Gordon, Meryl, 'Oh Kay!' *Mirabella*, June 1991

Graham, Katharine, 'The Press and the President' *Observer*, 31 March 1974

Graham, Katharine, 'The right to manage' *Time*, 29 December 1975

Griffith, Thomas, 'Kay Graham and the Haldeman Snafu' *Time*, 20 March 1978

Heren, Louis, 'The Lady who took on the President of the United States and won', *The Times*, 21 August 1978

Mandrake, 'Mrs Katharine Graham, the Post's mistress', *Sunday Telegraph*, 8 December 1985

Mortimer, John, 'The reluctant Joan of Arc', *Sunday Times*, 14 July 1985

Rawsthorn, Alice, 'Graham: the grande dame of the US media scene', *Campaign*, 13 December 1985

Reilly, Patrick M, 'Katharine Graham to Quit as Chief', *Wall Street Journal*, 15 March 1991

Robinson, Derek, 'The Press and the White House', *The Listener*, 29 May 1980

Van Dyne, Larry, 'The Bottom Line on Katharine Graham', *The Washingtonian*, December 1985

Zec, Donald, 'The woman who rocked the White House', *Daily Mirror*, 11 June 1973

Chapter 4

Atlas, Rita, 'Ingersoll Community Newspapers faces probable restructuring', *Investment Dealers' Digest inc*, 26 February 1990

Berman, Phyllis, 'A quixotic father's acquisitive son', *Forbes*, 20 October 1986

Cheeseright, Paul, 'In an age of ink and innocence', *Financial Times*, 3 January 1992

Downs, Peter, 'Junk Swaps Ingersoll', *Hartford Business Journal*, 23 July 1990

Gabor, Andrea, 'A media baron's strategy – Ralph Ingersoll II aims to launch first successful city daily in years', *US News & World Report*, 24 April 1989

Geary, Martin, 'Ingersoll meets provincial grit', *Independent*, 31 August 1990

Goozner, Merrill, 'Ingersoll sheds US papers – Warburg Pincus buys out debt-laden empire', *Chicago Tribune*, 3 July 1990

Hammer, Joshua (with Bruce Shenitz), 'Fall of the marionettes', *Newsweek*, 23 July 1990

Jones, Alex S, 'Ingersoll in swap sheds his US papers', *The New York Times*, 3 July 1990

Picht, Randolph, 'Ingersoll making new start', *Chicago Tribune*, 15 July 1990

Reilly Patrick M, 'Ingersoll closes down St Louis Sun', *Wall Street Journal*, 26 April 1990

Thapar, Neil '100 m pounds Ingersoll deal', *Independent*, 31 August 1991

Chapter 5

Adler, William M, 'The Man Who Would Be Hearst', *Business Month*, February 1988

Anderson, John (with Valerie Wright), 'Close, but no cigar: richest people in Texas', *Texas Monthly*, August 1989

Balfour, Victoria, 'Dean Singlton, Media King in the Making', *People*, 5 October 1987

Benenson, Lisa, 'Rocky Mountain Low', *News inc*, May 1990

Calkins, Laurel Brubaker, 'Daily Newspapers Tighten Belts', *Houston Business Journal*, 27 May 1991

Collingwood, Harris, 'Singleton sells his flagship', *Business Week*, 20 June 1988

Consol, Mike, 'Star-News anchor for Houston magnate's network', *Los Angeles Business Journal*, 12 February 1990

Fitzgerald, Mark, 'The media entrepreneurs speak', *Editor & Publisher*, 4 November 1989

France, David (with Michael Skory), 'Swinging New Deal Still Tops on Dean's List', *News inc*, March 1991

Garneau, George, 'Houston Post sheds debt', *Editor & Publisher*, 10 November 1990

Greene, A C, 'Old Times – Before Dean Singleton Came Along', *Texas Monthly*, November 1989

Hudson, Berkley, 'Pasadena Star-News sold', *Los Angeles Times*, 22 August 1990

Jubera, Drew, 'Paper Boy – Now Comes the Hard Part', *Texas Monthly*, November 1987

Paikowski, Lisa, "Media News" William Dean Singleton', *Adweek*, 26 April 1988

Perry, Nancy J, 'Beneath the mogul', *Fortune*, 12 October 1987

Schumuckler, Eric, 'Dean dodges a bullet', *Forbes*, 11 June 1990

Stein, M L, 'Singleton-Thomson deal', *Editor & Publisher*, 15 July 1989

Zuckerman, Laurence, 'William Dean Singleton keeps collecting papers', *Time*, 28 September 1987

Chapter 6

Barry, David, 'Muscle Car Magnate', *Autoweek*, 17 July 1989

Sharkey, Betsy, 'The Quiet Newspaper Warrior', *Manhattan inc*, February 1990

Star, Jack 'LA's Mighty Chandlers', *Life*, 29 September 1962

Weymouth, Lally, 'The Word from Mamma Buff', *Esquire*, November 1985

Chapter 7

Allison, David, 'Cox trusts shrinking', *Atlanta Business Chronicle*, 16 July 1990

Boyer, Peter J, 'Atlanta Burns', *Vanity Fair*, February 1989

Fisher, Christy, 'How top circulation gainers pulled it off', *Advertising Age*, 12 August 1991

Gersh, Debra, 'Cox antitrust suit', *Editor & Publisher*, 16 March 1991

Grove, Lloyd, 'The First Lady of Atlanta', *Vanity Fair*, August 1988

Mieher, Stuart, 'The Heir becomes apparent at Cox' *Georgia Trend*, September 1987

Schonbak, Judith, 'Acquisition Fever', *Business Atlanta*, October 1990

Chapter 8

Basu, Kajal, 'Newsprint policy makes bad news', *Sunday Observer*, 15 February 1989

Belle, Nithin, 'The Changing Times', *Gentleman*, October 1988

Chakravarti, Sudeep (with Olga Tellis), 'The taxman cometh', *Sunday*, 19 March 1989

Gangadhar, V, 'Oh, Calcutta', *Sunday*, 15 July 1990

Gangadhar, V, 'Value-based editing', *Sunday*, 12 August 1990

Gangadhar, V, 'Khaki chaddi investigators', *Sunday*, 10 March 1991

Gangadhar, V, 'Rajiv-baiters', *Sunday*, 9 June 1991

Kamath, M V, 'Mediawatch – The wheels within', *Telegraph*, 6 April 1989

Kapoor, Coomi, 'Girilal Jain: "The publisher must become the editor" ', *Indian Post*, 7 January 1989

Kolpe, S B, 'V P Singh, A Hope Turned Disaster', *Clarity Press*, July 1989

Kolpe, S B, 'A Fraud on Indian Press, Politics and People', *Clarity Press*, 1989

Kumar, Kuldeep, 'Press to pay', *Sunday*, 1 January 1990

Kumar, Kuldeep (with Olga Tellis), 'Who's the boss?' *Sunday*, 4 March 1990

Mehta, Harish (with Sulie Chatterjee), 'The Newspaper of the Future', *Gentleman*, 27 November 1986

Nanporia, N J, 'My years in The Times of India', *Indian Post*, 4 December 1988

Profile, 'Citizen Goenka', *Sunday*, 16 December 1990

Raghavan, A, 'Right-Left-Right', *Blitz*, 23 February 1963

Raghavan, A, 'V P's in Goenka's pocket', *Blitz*, 13 January 1990

Ramaswami, T R, *Goenka Unmasked*, Shanmurgavel Press, 1989

Ramaswami, T R, 'The Goenka story retold', *News Today*, 21 June 1989

Rao, Joga (with Pradyot Lal), 'Freedom of Press or Potatoes', *Blitz*, 18 March 1989

Rao, Joga, 'Express "Guru" in tax dodge', *Blitz*, 30 May 1989

Sanghvi, Vir, 'Conversations with Goenka', *Sunday*, 13 October 1991

Sidhva, Shiraz, 'Untruth involves us all', *Sunday*, 2 September 1990

Singh, R Bhagwan, 'For God's sake – Ramnath Goenka invokes religious help', *Sunday*, 19 November 1989

Vakil, Dina, 'Between two giants', *Indian Post*, 13 April 1989

Chapters 9 & 20

Brown, Kevin, 'Battle for Fairfax enters last round', *Financial Times*, 15 October 1991

Carroll, V J, *The Man Who Couldn't Wait*, Heinemann, 1990

Carroll, V J, 'Warwick's wonderland', *Independent Monthly*, November 1990

Colacello, Bob, 'Publish and perish: was the outrageous Lady Fairfax behind the dynastic crash?', *Vanity Fair*, April 1991

Dunn, Ross, 'Fairfax loses control of publishing empire', *Guardian*, 11 December 1990

Dwyer, Michael, 'How a media dynasty came to an end', *Financial Review*, 11 December 1990

Gidley, Isobelle, 'Fool of the House of Fairfax', *Today*, 11 December 1990

Hoffman, John, 'Young Warwick crowns himself king', *Press Journal*, November 1987

Holberton, Simon, 'Like father, like son', *Financial Times*, 31 December 1990

Huxley, John, 'Australia's Dynasty show', *Sunday Times*, 23 October 1988

Lawson, Valerie (with John Lyons), 'Mummy Dearest: the family union that ripped apart Fairfax', *Sydney Morning Herald*, 15 December 1990

Leser, David, 'That Fairfax woman', HQ, February 1991

Masefield, Bruce, 'Torrid summer in Australia's media war', *Sunday Times*, 25 January 1987

Miller, Russell, 'Warwick the Terminator', *Sunday Times*, 20 November 1988

Milliken, Robert, 'Predators covet Australian jewels', *Independent*, 22 February 1988

Shulman, Nicola, 'Devilled Sydney', *Harpers & Queen*, February 1989

Souter, Gavin, *Heralds and Angels: The House of Fairfax*, Melbourne University Press, 1991

Vincent, Lindsay, 'The incredible Fairfax affair', *Observer*, 10 July 1988

Warneminde, Martin, 'Dougherty versus Lady Fairfax', *Bulletin*, 22 January 1991

Chapters 10 & 19

Barchard, David, *Asil Nadir and the rise and fall of Polly Peck*, Gollancz, 1992

Gillard, Michael, 'Waiting for Asil Nadir', *Observer*, 1 May 1983

Grove, Valerie, 'Giving as good as he gets', *Sunday Times*, 5 November 1989

Helm, Toby, 'Where the man from Polly Peck is King', *Sunday Telegraph*, 7 October 1990

Hindle, Tim, *The Sultan of Berkeley Square*, Macmillan, 1991

Levi, Jim, 'Mr Nadir and his magic touch', *Evening Standard*, 19 December 1983

Mackay, Angela (with Colin Narbrough), 'Nadir plans buyout of Polly Peck', *The Times*, 13 August 1990

Paice, Catherine, 'The transformation of Baggrave Hall Estate', *Farmers Weekly*, 11 August 1989

Searjeant, Graham, 'Nadir scales new heights', *The Times*, 15 January 1988

Chapters 11 & 23

Bagli, Charles V, 'If Maxwell's House falls, will Daily News go, too?', *New York Observer*, 28 October 1991

Ball, Ian, 'Bamble tickling Maxwell's fancy', *Daily Telegraph*, 13 March 1991

Boggan, Steve (with Jason Nissé and David Hellier), 'Lost Maxwell millions found', *Independent*, 7 December 1991

Bower, Tom, *Maxwell the Outsider*, Aurum, 1988

Boyer, Peter B, 'Maxwell's Silver Hammer', *Vanity Fair*, June 1991

Bruce, Peter, 'Maxwell tissues tested for poison', *Financial Times*, 11 November 1991

Carpenter, Rosemary, 'The cruel lies they spread about Bob: Elizabeth Maxwell's anguish', *Daily Express*, 3 December 1991

Caseby, Richard, 'Off the leash', *Sunday Times*, 15 December 1991

Cassidy, John (with Ivan Fallon), 'The Plunderer', *Sunday Times*, 8 December 1991

Cassidy, John, 'Maxwell: the net closes', *Sunday Times*, 15 December 1991

Chester, Lewis, 'Maxwell: Man of the Year', *Independent*, 28 December 1991

Confino, Jonathan, 'Maxwell close to Daily News deal', *Daily Telegraph*, 13 March 1991

Crovitz, L Gordon, ' "Getcha Daily News" ', *Baron*'s, 18 February 1991

Davidson, Andrew, 'Power Games', *Marketing*, 26 July 1990

Diamond, Edwin, 'To the Max', *New York Magazine*, 25 March 1991

Dovkants, Keith, 'New tests on Maxwell's fingernails', *Evening Standard*, 8 November 1991

Dovkants, Keith, 'The woman who really loved Robert Maxwell', *Evening Standard*, 11 December 1991

Elliott, Christopher (with Robert Tyerman), 'Maxwell facts fight fantasy', *Sunday Telegraph*, 17 November 1991

Fallon, Ivan, 'The Boys Take Charge', *Sunday Times*, 10 November 1991

Fallon, Ivan, 'Boys on the Burning Deck', *Sunday Times*, 24 November 1991

Fishlock, Trevor, 'Maxwell: Mystery of the Lost Tycoon', *Sunday Telegraph*, 10 November 1991

Freeman, Simon (with Martin Tomkinson), 'The Great Pretender', *Independent on Sunday*, 8 December 1991

Gillard, Michael (with John McGhie and John Hooper), 'Maxwell's last £100 m gamble', *Observer*, 8 December 1991

Gillard, Michael, 'Banks press Maxwell heirs for fire sale', *Observer*, 10 November 1991

Gillie, Oliver, 'Caught up in father's web', *Independent*, 16 December 1991

Graham, Mike, 'Maxwell holds front page in US paper fight', *Sunday Times*, 10 March 1992

Greenslade, Roy, *Maxwell's Fall*, Simon & Schuster, 1992

Haines, Joe, *Maxwell*, Macdonald, 1988

Harris, Paul, 'Maxwell: It gets more mysterious', *Daily Mail*, 8 November 1991

Hinsey, Carolyn, 'The boss as tyrant', *Independent on Sunday*, 9 February 1992

Hinsey, Carolyn, 'Eight months before the Masthead', *New York Magazine*, 10 February 1992

Hooper, John, 'Random pieces fail to fit death puzzle', *Guardian*, 15 November 1991

Hooper, John, 'Muddied waters of Maxwell's death', *Guardian*, 5 November 1992

Jenkins, Lin, 'Foreign office to study Maxwell "Soviet link"', *The Times*, 14 November 1991

Kampfer, John (with Marcus Warren), 'Talks on publishing a KGB propaganda journal in Britain', *Daily Telegraph*, 12 November 1991

Kane, Frank, 'Maxwell's bobbing float', *Sunday Telegraph*, 20 October 1991

Klein, Edward, 'The Sinking of Captain Bob', *Vanity Fair*, March 1992

Knox, Patricia, 'Swift Mac millions for Maxwell!', *Evening Standard*, 13 November 1992

Koenig, Peter, 'The Final Act', *Independent on Sunday*, 10 November 1991

Kreitman, Mody, 'Maxwell latest: the grave-digger is still waiting to be paid', *Mail on Sunday*, 5 January 1992

Langton, James, 'When the stealing had to stop', *Sunday Telegraph*, 8 December 1991

Langton, James, 'The week that really bugged Kevin Maxwell', *Sunday Telegraph*, 15 December 1991

Levin, Bernard, 'A life stranger than fiction', *The Times*, 1 January 1992

Mackay, Angela, 'Liquidator sues Kevin Maxwell for £450 million', *The Times*, December 1992

Maddox, Bronwen, 'Devil take the hindmost', *Financial Times*, 17 June 1992

Maddox, Bronwen (with Andrew Jack), 'Private empire consumed £1.7 bn', *Financial Times*, 5 November 1992

Marckus, Melvyn, 'Revealed: Maxwell's video nasty', *Observer*, 26 January 1992

Maremont, Mark (with Mark Landler), 'Can Robert Maxwell afford his new "pet"?', *Business Week*, 25 March 1991

Merritt, John, 'Maxwell: How did he die?', *Observer*, 10 November 1991

Muir, Kate, 'He was childish, like a choirboy', *The Times*, 15 November 1991

Nkwocha, Kizzi, 'Murdered! Man Who Knew Too Much', *Daily Sport*, 6 November 1991

Page, Bruce, 'Press failure that helped a serial swindler', *Independent on Sunday*, 8 December 1991

Parker-Jervis, George, 'Maxwell's legacy', *Observer*, 10 November 1991

Parker-Jervis, George (with Peter Watson), 'Banks close in on Maxwell', *Observer*, 24 November 1991

Parker-Jervis, George, 'Maxwell's shady "support" for MCC', *Observer*, 15 December 1991

Pringle, Peter, 'Maxwell cash from Moscow', *Independent*, 9 November 1991

Purnell, Sonia, 'The ledger of horrors', *Daily Telegraph*, 12 December 1991

Randall, Jeff, 'Bears on the prowl', *Sunday Times*, 14 October 1990

Reilly, Patrick M (with Meg Cox and Richard L Hudson), 'Media Mogul Maxwell Revealed in Growth', *Wall Street Journal*, 13 September 1991

Sheff, David, 'Playboy Interview: Robert Maxwell', *Playboy*, June 1991

Shrimsley, Robert, 'Inside Maxwell's penthouse flat', *Daily Telegraph*, 21 January 1992

Skeel, Shirley, 'Maxwell Ogles the Globe', *Management Today*, March 1990

Snoddy, Raymond, 'Barclay Brothers buy the European', *Financial Times*, 7 January 1992

Stuttaford, Dr Thomas, 'Evidence fit for an inquest', *The Times*, 14 November 1991

Taylor, John, 'Mad Max', *New York Magazine*, 10 February 1992

Tyerman, Robert, 'Maxwell's links with Stevens', *Sunday Telegraph*, 15 December 1991

Walton, Ashley, 'Maxwell's Last Journey', *Daily Express*, 8 November 1991

Watson, Sandy, 'The secretary's tale', *Evening Standard magazine*, November 1992

Willcock, John, 'Receivers on standby for Maxwell collapse', *Guardian*, 21 November 1991

Willcock, John (with Rebecca Smithers), 'High court sets Monday deadline for Maxwell', *Guardian*, 14 December 1991

Willcock, John, 'Banks fury at US move', *Guardian*, 18 December 1991

Williams, David (with Paul Harris), 'Maxwell's last secret', *Daily Mail*, 6 November 1991

Wintour, Charles, 'Maxwell's European campaign', *The Times*, 2 May 1990

Young, Hugo, 'Maxwell the megaphone', *Guardian*, 5 March 1990

Chapter 12

Alderson, Andrew, 'At the court of King David', *Sunday Times*, 12 July 1992

Amaya, Mario, 'Bubbles – there she blows', *Tatler*, May 1986

Brown, Maggie, 'The family firm', *Independent*, 15 February 1989

Hall, Anthea, 'Press Baron reveals why he is marrying his lover', *Sunday Telegraph*, 17 October 1993

Mackwood, Neil, 'Larger than Life – Lady Rothermere, ultimate party girl', *Sunday Times*, 16 August 1992

Obituary, 'Stylish hostess with a zest for life', *Daily Mail*, 13 August 1992

Olins, Rufus, 'The Last Tycoon', *Sunday Times*, 19 July 1992

Snoddy, Raymond, 'Last of the old breed of Fleet Street press barons', *Sunday Times*, 10 June 1988

Tytler, David, 'It's a funny old chess game', *Guardian*, 13 July 1992

Vincent, Lindsay, 'Newspaper war lord', *Observer*, 1 March 1987

Whitley, Edward, 'A Very Private Person', *Spectator*, 26 October 1991

Chapter 13

Beatson, Jim, 'Black takes Fairfax with £600 m offer', *Guardian*, 17 December 1991

Bell, Emily, 'Bidders await Daily News deadline', *Observer*, 16 August 1992

Bevan, Judi, 'Black prince of the prints', *The Times*, 18 December 1991

Black, Deborah, 'The thoughts of Conrad Black', *Business*, March 1986

Black, Larry, 'Black would invest $275 m in New York Daily News', *Independent*, 19 June 1992

Boulding, Chris, 'Black power', *Marketing Week*, 31 July 1992

Buchanan, Brian, 'Black wins Fairfax group race', *The Times*, 17 December 1991

Clark, Michael, 'Black sells United Newspapers stake', *The Times*, 2 April 1992

Ellis, Eric, 'Black lashes out: "sleazy, venal and despicable" ', *Sydney Morning Herald*, 12 December 1991

Field, David, 'Media mogul on the future of newspapers', *Washington Times*, 13 September 1990

Frith, Bryan, 'Does Conrad Black have a death wish?' The *Australian*, 12 December 1991

Graham, Mike, 'Black moves nearer to Daily News deal', *Sunday Times*, 31 May 1992

Hargreaves, Ian (with Bernard Simon), 'Black magic at work around the world', *Financial Times*, 21 October 1992

Hart-Davis, Duff, *The House the Berrys Built*, Hodder & Stoughton, 1990

Hart-Davis, Duff, 'Will he become the wizard of Oz?', *Independent*, 18 December 1991

Hurst, John, 'Black accuses O'Reilly of "snake oil" tactics', *Australian Financial Review*, 2 December 1991

Jones, Mark, 'Newspaper Man of Destiny', *Media Week*, 12 June 1992

Klein, Edward, 'Black Mischief', *Vanity Fair*, November 1992

Lynch, Paul, 'Baron Black begins "nice guy" campaign', The *Australian*, 18 December 1991

McKay, Peter, 'Life and Death on the Isle of Dogs', *Tatler*, December 1989

Nevin, Charles, 'The Baron in Black', *Harpers & Queen*, January 1990

Newman, Peter C, *The Establishment Man: A Portrait of Power*, McClelland and Stewart, 1982

Paterson, Peter, 'The rise of Citizen Black', *Daily Mail*, 12 December 1985

Quinn, Eamon, 'Black magic stops the rot', *Campaign*, 22 April 1988

Riley, Mark, 'Black vows; There'll be no vengeance', *Sydney Morning Herald*, 18 December 1991

Ross, Alexander, 'Black ink', *Canadian Business*, November 1991

Ruddock, Alan, 'I'm no Maxwell, says the Telegraph's Black', *Sunday Times*, 28 June 1992

Ryan, Colleen (with Glenn Burge), *Corporate Cannibals – The taking of Fairfax*, William Heinemann, 1992

Sachar, Laura, 'His Three Passions', *Financial World*, 22 August 1989

Simper, Errol, 'Fairfax victors claim their prize', *Weekend Australian*, 11 January 1992

Snoddy, Raymond, 'Back to the Black', *Financial Times*, 17 August 1987

Snoddy, Raymond, 'A remarkable transformation', *Financial Times*, 18 November 1989

Snoddy, Raymond, 'Out of the red and into the Black', *Financial Times*, 22 February 1992

Stannard, Bruce, 'How I would run Fairfax', *Bulletin*, 23 July 1991

Stephens, Tony, 'No cloven feet, no horns, just Black humour', *Sydney Morning Herald*, 18 December 1991

Thorpe, Helen, 'Press lord eyes the News, but a Post merger is denied', *New York Observer*, 15 June 1992

Wintour, Charles, 'Newspaper Napoleon of the Isle of Dogs', *The Times*, 15 November 1989

Yallop, Richard, 'Fireworks over Fairfax', *Observer*, 20 October 1991

Zagor, Karen, 'Black wins more time in Daily News talks', *Financial Times*, 18 August 1992

Chapter 14

Atkinson, Dan (with John Willcock, Rebecca Smithers), 'Lord Stevens to quit investment empire', *Guardian*, 29 July 1992

Barber, Lionel, 'Banker who holds the front page', *Sunday Times*, 24 April 1983

Brown, Maggie, 'A shift in the middle-market', *Independent*, 8 March 1989

Brown, Malcolm (with Julia Bright), 'Even Stevens', *Sunday Times*, 10 October 1985

Cassidy, John, 'Stevens lashes "biased" Telegraph', *Sunday Times*, 2 August 1992

Cornelius, Andrew, 'Boom time for the boss of the bonking Star', *Guardian*, 10 October 1987

Maddox, Bronwen, 'Bumpy transition for a lord of the City', *Financial Times*, 8 August 1992

Pitcher, George, 'United's supporter – Lord Stevens', *Observer*, 15 July 1990

Profile, 'How to pack a quiet punch', *Sunday Times*, 20 October 1985

Randall, Jeff (with Kirstie Hamilton), 'Fatal Attraction', *Sunday Times*, 2 August 1992

Shulman, Alexandra, 'Paper Mate', *Tatler*, June 1986

Snoddy, Raymond, 'Newspaper magnate in the making', *Financial Times*, 8 April 1989

Chapter 15

Fitchett, Joseph, 'Paris papers from Right to the Left', *International Herald Tribune*, 27 January 1979

Geddes, Diana, 'Man in the French news', *The Times*, 9 January 1986

Housego, David, 'Press takeover defies Mitterrand', *Financial Times*, 6 January 1986

Kranse, Axel, 'France Moving against Press Chains', *International Herald Tribune*, 23 November 1983

Roy, Frederic, 'Robert Hersant part à la conquête de la Tchécoslovaquie', *Tribune*, 23 May 1990

Roy, Frederic, 'Hersant s'offre trois nouveaux quotidiens regionaux', *Tribune*, 11 March 1992

Shore, Joan Z, 'France's embattled press lord', *International Herald Tribune*, 14 May 1984

Webster, Paul, 'Press boss eyes the Presidency', *Observer*, 12 January 1986

White, Sam, 'Why a press baron is fighting an old friend', *Evening Standard*, 29 July 1983

White, Sam, 'The happiest marriage of Figaro', *Evening Standard*, 16 May 1986

Young, Jacob (with Michael Lerner), 'Mitterrand vs the Press Lord', *Newsweek*, 12 December 1983

Chapter 16

Aga Khan, His Highness Karim, Address to the 30th General Assembly of the IPA, Nairobi, 2 March 1981

Dawkins, William (with Edward Mortimer), 'Prince of development programmes', *Financial Times*, 12 August 1991

Elliott, John, 'Sowing seeds on thin soil', *Financial Times*, 7 January 1986

Gupte, Pranay, 'A Time for Pragmatism, *Newsweek*, 24 November 1986

Howell, Georgina, 'The Story of K', *Vanity Fair*, June 1988

Jordo, Philip, 'Ten Questions to the Imam', *Connaissance des Arts*, September 1990

Knevitt, Charles, 'Building up a modern prince', *The Times*, 21 October 1989

Morgan, Jean, 'Milestone for the Aga Khan's paper', *UK Press Gazette*, 25 March 1985

Revzin, Philip, 'Prophet Ability: He's no stern Ayatollah, he enjoys horses, yachts, skiing and the Super-Rich', *Wall Street Journal*, 29 January 1988

Chapter 17

Chan, Cynthia, '$130 m ready for Wong's Jademan bid, court told', *Business News*, 2 June 1990

Chang, Harold, 'Last nail in drug king's coffin', *South China Morning Post*, 26 August 1977

Chang, Harold, 'Ma Sik-Yu under watch in Taipei', *South China Morning Post*, 27 August 1977

Chang, Harold, 'Heroin – a family business', *South China Morning Post*, 1 June 1986

Chi-Keung, Chan, 'Concert Party claim by Jademan', *Business News*, 2 August 1990

Chuan, Ong Hock, 'Hong Kong cannot afford Communist involvement', *Hong Kong Standard*, 20 December 1988

Davies, Valerie, 'Gentle, unmilitant feminist', *South China Morning Post*, 3 February 1970

Ellis, Eric, 'Sing Tao returns for local listing', *Business News*, 7 January 1985

England, Vandine, 'The Aws: Remnants of an empire', *Asia Magazine*, 28 July 1985

Green, Shane, 'Cha's Chinese puzzle', *South China Morning Post*, 27 May 1989

Hill, Penelope, 'Experts predict profit showdown for Sing Tao', *Sunday Money*, 2 July 1989

MacDonald, Hamish, 'Judge in, Aw, out', *Far Eastern Economic Review*, 6 June 1985

Mollison, Avril, 'The satisfactions of a press baroness', *Independent*, 19 April 1989

Mulcahy, John, 'Sing Tao's assets set to go down under', *Business News*, 23 May 1985

Nip, Joyce (with Ann Quon), 'Rocky Times for Ming Pao', *South China Morning Post*, 18 March 1990

See, Lai, 'Comic capers in world of Chinese', *Business News*, 4 January 1990

Volgenau, Gerald, 'Hong Kong's "Yacht people"', *South China Morning Post*, 23 July 1987

Wai, S Y, 'Sing Tao Chairman applauds the community for 50 years of support', *Hong Kong Standard*, 2 December 1988

WuDunn, Sheryl, 'Chivalry and Kung-fu: Chinese clamor for Cha', *International Herald Tribune*, 7 January 1989

Yeung, Chris, 'Cha denies move for personal gain', *South China Morning Post*, 9 December 1988

Yeung, Chris, 'Cha states his case', *South China Morning Post*, 23 December 1988

Yu, Lulu (with Kent Chen), 'Louis Cha; drafter in the firing line', *Sunday*, 11 December 1988

Chapter 18

Boyd, Alan, 'Bangkok clamps down on media', *South China Morning Post*, 17 November 1989

Boyd, Alan, 'Brief Thai ban likely of Journal', *South China Morning Post*, 18 November 1989

Tasker, Rodney, 'Decree deterrent', *Far Eastern Economic Review*, 27 May 1990

White, Helen, 'Thai Journalists Fight Press-Control Law', *Asian Wall Street Journal*, 9 May 1990

Chapter 21

Blackhurst, Chris, 'O'Reilly may go solo on MGN', *Independent on Sunday*, 6 September 1992

Carnegy, Hugh, 'Never a foot in touch', *Financial Times*, 13 April 1987

Fay, Stephen, 'The life of O'Reilly', *Business*, June 1986

Henkoff, Ronald, 'Cutting Costs: How to do it right', *Fortune*, 9 April 1990

Jay, John, 'Irish eyes on the Mirror', *Sunday Telegraph*, 23 August 1992

Loane, Sally, 'Full of beans, that's Anthony Joseph O'Reilly', *Melbourne Age*, 28 November 1991

Lohr, Steve, 'O'Reilly, Publisher and Prospector', *The New York Times*, 8 May 1988

MacGregor, Ian, 'Beanz meanz buck$', *Daily Express*, 12 May 1992

McGeough, Paul, 'Irish eyes on Fairfax', *Sydney Morning Herald*, 11 May 1991

Miles, Greg, 'Hunger for Growth', *Best of Business Quarterly*, Summer 1989

Mullin, John, 'O'Reilly on the ball at Heinz', *Independent*, 8 May 1989

Robinson, Philip, 'Heinz meanz dollars for O'Reilly', *The Times*, 2 February 1992

Rouvalis, Cristina, 'Heinz shareholders "handcuff" O'Reilly', *Pittsburgh Post-Gazette*, 12 September 1990

Tascarella, Patty, 'Man of Infinite Variety', *Pittsburgh Executive*, August 1988

Tyler, Christian, 'The player who fell on his feet', *Financial Times*, 6 July 1991

Westfield, Mark, 'No black day for the Irish', *Sydney Morning Herald*, 12 December 1991

Chapter 22

Chippindale, Peter (with Chris Horrie), *Stick it up your punter! – The rise and fall of the Sun*, Heinemann, 1990

Davenport-Hines, Richard, 'Getting away with Murdoch', *Tatler*, July 1992

Evans, Harold, *Good Times, Bad Times*, Weidenfeld & Nicolson, 1983

Fidler, Stephen, 'Operation Dolphin rescues Murdoch', *Financial Times*, 4 April 1991

Jones, Alex S, 'Maxwell fights Murdoch on a new front', *The New York Times*, 10 June 1991

Koenig, Peter, 'That's Infotainment!' *Independent on Sunday*, 29 July 1990

Lamb, Larry, *Sunrise – the remarkable rise and rise of the best-selling soaraway Sun*, Macmillan, 1989

Lawson, Valerie, 'The Trouble with Rupert', *Good Weekend*, 2 July 1991

Leapman, Michael, *Barefaced Cheek*, Hodder & Stoughton, 1983

Light, Deborah (with John Lyons), 'Mere Mortal: Murdoch feels the strain', *Sydney Morning Herald*, 2 February 1991

Nissé, Jason, 'Debt restructure costs push News Corp into red', *Independent*, 23 August 1991

Profile, 'Who is Rupert Murdoch?' *M*, February 1991

Shawcross, William, *Rupert Murdoch*, Chatto & Windus, 1992

Snoddy, Raymond, 'Rupert Murdoch: Down and up in Beverly Hills', *Financial Times*, 27 August 1992

Tuccille, Jerome, *Murdoch: A biography*, Piatkus, 1989

Weever, Patrick, 'Murdoch's sky turning blue', *Sunday Telegraph*, 27 October 1991

Index

95–100; personality 99, 100; praised by
rivals 94, 129–30, 193; and other
proprietors 56, 61–2

Graham, Katharine 'Kay' (*Washington Post*)
7, 8, 23, 37, 318, 345; appearance 77;
background 80, 81, 89; editorial interest
18, 19, 76, 78–9; interview with author
76–85; and journalists 83; personality 9,
76, 77, 81–2, 91–2, 92–3; as new
proprietor 17, 75, 80–1, 90–1, 98; and
other proprietors 169, 465, 518

Graham, Philip 7, 76, 86–8; suicide 75, 88

Green, Canon Michael 246

Greenfield, Meg (*Washington Post*) 75, 99,
472

Greenslade, Roy (*Daily Mirror*) 262

Greenwich *Time* 170

Gregg, Gail, Mrs 'Pinch' Sulzberger 58–9

Gruson, Sydney (*New York Times*) 45, 46–8

Guardian story of Maxwell's survival 532–3

Guggenheim, Harry, sale of *Newsday* 172

Gulf War 127

Günaydin 252, 253, 254, 364, 444, 445–6

Gunes 252–3, 254, 364, 444

Gurumurthy, S. 234

Gwinnett Daily News 70–1, 193

Haines, Joe, and Maxwell 264

Hambro, Rupert 334, 335, 345

Hammer, Dr Armand 297

Handelsblatt 130

Hanson, James, Lord 334, 345–6

Harte-Hanks chain, sale to Singleton 146

Hartford Courant, sale to Chandler 170

Hartwell, Michael Berry, Lord (*Daily
Telegraph*) 333–4, 336, 346, 511

Haslam, Nicholas 298

Hastings, Max (*Daily Telegraph*) 338; on
Conrad Black 314–15, 315–17, 354; on
Maxwell 521

Healy, Liam (Independent Newspapers) 465,
468; on O'Reilly 456–7

Heaney, Seamus 456

Hearst, William Randolph 2, 20, 66

Hearst Newspapers 85, 133, 481, 482, 498;
list of newspapers 545

Hersant, Robert 2, 5, 155, 373–82;
acquisitions 377–8, 381; background 377;
editorial control 376; Eastern bloc interest
26, 27, 376; family 376–7; *Le Figaro*,
acquisition 378; possible future 381–2; and
government 378–9; headquarters 374–5;
interest in Istanbul newspapers 444; and
journalists 379; newspaper empire 374,
376; list of newspapers 545–6; personality
24, 373, 374, 376; and politics 8, 374, 380;

and presidents of France 380–1; and other
proprietors 109–10; technological interest
379; television channel La Cinq 381

Heston, Charlton 473

Hickie, David (*Sun Herald*), on Warwick
Fairfax 245

Hilton, Conrad 75

Hirshfield, Abe, 501

Hitchens, Christopher 319, 342

Hobby, Mrs 135

Hobby, Oveta Culp (*Houston Post*) 90

von Hoffman, Nicholas 315

Hoge, James (*New York Daily News*) 260

Hollinger Mines Ltd (Conrad Black) 309,
310, 318, 322, 330, 335; board 344–5

Holmes à Court, Robert 241, 248, 347

Hong Kong Economic Journal 427

Hong Kong Standard 402, 406, 409, 421, 422

Hong Chronicle (Hearst) 133, 152

Houston Post 133, 134–5, 152; purchase by
Singleton 137, 153

Hudson, Rock, story 287

Huebuer, Lee 425

Hung, Edward 423–4; on Sally Aw Sian 404,
424

Hürriyet 251, 253

Hussey, Marmaduke 363

Impala Pacific Corporation 414

Independent 16, 460

Independent Newspapers (O'Reilly) 454–5,
464

India, press 200–40; journalists in 210–11

Indian Express (Goenka) 215, 232–3, 234–5,
239, 400

Ingersoll, Ian 113

Ingersoll, Ralph 3, 4, 5, 6, 15, 18; background
113–19; and Conrad Black 318, 328–9, 333,
335, 353, 355; cost- cutting 118; editorial
action after purchase 108–9; interest in
Eastern block press 26, 27, 28; and the
Fairfaxes 110–12, 244; on the future of
newspapers 181; interview with author
106–32 *passim*; journalism 114–15, 116; on
monopolies 108; newspaper empire 20, 21–
2, 105, 106–7; dismantlement of empire
125–8; list of newspapers 546–7; personality
24, 104, 113, 128–9; and other newspaper
proprietors 104, 106, 109, 110–12, 129–30,
137–8, 382; other proprietors on 136–7; *St
Louis Sun* 16, 113, 119–25; and Dean
Singleton 106, 137–8; and Chet Spooner
115–17; and Thomson 126, 328–9; wife
Ushi 128

Ingersoll, Ralph McAllister I 113, 114, 115,
116, 117, 118–19

International Herald Tribune 31, 102, 171